# THE
# HARPER
# HANDBOOK
## OF
## COLLEGE
## COMPOSITION

FOURTH
EDITION

# THE HARPER HANDBOOK

## OF COLLEGE COMPOSITION

### GEORGE S. WYKOFF
*Professor Emeritus of English,*
*Purdue University*

### HARRY SHAW
*Formerly Director, Workshops in Composition,*
*New York University*

**HARPER & ROW, PUBLISHERS**
*New York      Evanston      London*

# CONTENTS

# FOREWORD

**O**UR belief is that the needs of most beginning college students, perhaps all, are best served by genuinely solid work, under supervision, in thinking, writing, and rewriting. This, the Fourth Edition of *The Harper Handbook of College Composition,* has, like its predecessors, these major aims: (1) *to help students to think and write correctly, clearly, effectively, and appropriately,* and (2) *to assist instructors in achieving these aims for their students.* Such objectives, we hold, are important and significant. Learning to think clearly and learning to write correctly, clearly, effectively, appropriately are worthwhile intellectual processes valuable not only in composition classes but in all other outreachings of the mind. Furthermore, writing that is routine, correct, and clear is not enough; any correct, clear, competent writing can also be effective, interesting, and even artistic.

In this textbook, we have relied on various recent dictionaries which through their prefatory articles and their consulting editors have the backing and approval of the foremost linguistic authorities in the United States. To reputable dictionaries English instructors constantly refer their students. We have tried to avoid the minor embarrassments that occur or might occur when what the instructor or *Handbook* says disagrees with what the student's reputable dictionary says.

In the three preceding editions and the present edition we have tried to follow the advice given by Alexander Pope:

> Be not the first by whom the new are tried,
> Nor yet the last to lay the old aside.
> —*Essay on Criticism,* II, 135, 136

Our attempts to follow this advice lead us to make the same comment that W. Cabell Greet made about following a middle course for pronunciation in *The American College Dictionary:* "This middle course may grieve young radicals and old conservatives, but it is hoped that it will please the judicious" (p. xx).

In following a middle and common-sense course, we have used much of the vocabulary of traditional grammar and usage, mainly for five reasons: (1) it is the vocabulary used by current reputable dictionaries in the identification and discussion of grammatical terms; (2) it is the vocabulary that, we believe, is most easily understood by the first-year college student; (3) it provides a foundation on which English majors can later build as they study structural or transformational grammar (for brief introductions to both, see Appendix C); (4) the vocabulary of traditional grammar is still widely applicable to *written* English; the vocabulary of structural and transformational grammar applies particularly to spoken English; and (5) some evidence shows that students of traditional grammar (middle-course adaptations) perform just as competently, or incompetently, in writing as do students of structural linguistics.

Our attitude toward language and usage is that stated in the conventional definition of good English: written and spoken English used correctly, clearly, effectively, appropriately in carrying on the business, professional, and social affairs of our country. In applying this definition to various parts of this *Handbook,* we have been influenced by the dictionaries to which we refer students: for example, we apply widely the attitude toward pronunciation expressed by one dictionary, that correctness is a flexible term, that a word or expression is correct and standard when it is in actual use by a sufficient number of cultivated people or when it "prevails among the educated and cultured people to whom the language is vernacular."

*The Harper Handbook of College Composition* is filled with specific recommendations and definite suggestions; such may be the needs of students seeking positive answers. Agreeing that much about language and grammar is descriptive, we believe that the application of this information is prescriptive, that much that is prescriptive is necessary in giving directions to students about writing. Our belief, further, is that improvement in thinking and writing involves replacing bad habits with good, that learning composition—or any intellectual or social activity—is necessarily negative in part.

Experience suggests no ideal plan of organization or order of assignments in freshman English. Any instructor will naturally follow the order of assignments which he or his department has found most satisfactory and will vary this order from year to year according to the needs of his or her students. Since many students are weak in more than one division of writing, we recommend early assignment of "The Theme—Preliminary Survey" (pp. 2–9). The six major divisions of the text ("The Theme," "The Paragraph," "The Sentence," "The Word," "Grammar," and "Punctuation and Mechanics") may be taken up in any order. The authors have each started at various times with every one of the six divisions save punctuation.

As a textbook of teaching and learning, *The Harper Handbook of College Composition* has three purposes: (1) to serve as a text for profitable use in the classroom, with an adequate supply of theme subjects and exercises; (2) to serve as a text for independent use and reference on the student's desk; and (3) to serve as a text useful to the instructor in marking themes and to the student in making corrections. The second purpose explains partly the predominating use of the imperative mood (for variety, at the risk of being considered inconsistent, we have occasionally been impersonal or used the passive voice). The last purpose explains some of the detail in certain sections, on the comma, for example, Section **88**; our own experience has been that a student learns more from a specific reference than he does from searching for an answer in several pages of print. We have therefore tried to be thorough in treating all varieties of student errors; we naturally do not expect any student to memorize detail of this kind or any instructor to assign it for memorization. Instead, we believe that such thoroughness allows the instructor to pinpoint a specific mistake rather than marking an error with some symbol that explains the trouble only in part.

In conclusion, we have done everything we (and our colleagues and consultants) could do to make the book as easy to use, as sensibly comprehensive, as flexible, and as attractive as possible. If our efforts are successful, we owe much to those who have shared their experiences: to former instructors and to students, from whom we have learned much. Many of these students have permitted us to use both their good and their bad writing; some have been unconscious victims. Most of the illustrations and exercises in this *Handbook* are based upon or have been adapted from a careful perusal of some 15,000 freshman themes, thanks to colleagues who have lent us many of their already carefully marked and graded papers. Experience has shown us that exercises from such themes, and not synthetic ones, are usually best for student use. This plan can have specific adaptation by any instructor, who can find, in any set of freshman themes, numerous exercise materials, impressive to students because the vices and virtues are their own; by the various duplicating methods available these exercise materials can easily be placed in the hands of each student.

Particularly do we extend our hearty thanks to the gifted and experienced teachers—many present or former users—whose suggestions and advice have immeasurably improved this book. Names of 49 of these were recorded in the Forewords to the first, second, and third editions. For this new edition we have received suggestions from other eminently successful teachers who have used the book in their classrooms. We can give only this record, inadequate as it is, of our indebtedness to the following: Bernard R. Campbell, John Carroll University; Frank Case, Eastern Michigan University; George Crane, California State College at Long Beach; Edward E. Dixon, Southeast Junior College, Chicago; Richard L. Greene, Wesleyan University; John W. Nichol, University of Southern California; H. J. Sachs, Louisiana Polytechnic Institute; the late Cecil B. Williams, Texas Christian University; and Eric M. Zale, University of Michigan.

Incidentally, the observant reader will note that some of our precepts are not always followed in this book. Thus paragraphs are not indented when they begin new sections, important words within certain headings are not capitalized, and periods are omitted after certain statements of basic principles. As we have said a number of times, rules may be broken when there are good reasons. The good reason in this case is artistic—the designer of the book decided these variations would make it look better.

Finally, we can never adequately express our appreciation to a most efficient helper, Brenta H. Wykoff.

GEORGE S. WYKOFF

HARRY SHAW

# THE
# HARPER
# HANDBOOK
## OF
### COLLEGE
### COMPOSITION

# THE THEME
## (SECTIONS 1-20)

To the man with an ear for verbal delicacies—the man who searches painfully for the perfect word and puts the way of saying a thing above the thing said—there is in writing the constant joy of sudden discovery, of happy accident.

—H. L. MENCKEN, *A Book of Prefaces*

# THE
# THEME

HE *aim* of freshman English is to give you regular practice and supervised training in correct, clear, effective, and appropriate written expression[1] of your own ideas, reactions, emotions, and thoughts. The prescribed *method* of accomplishing this aim is theme-writing.

The word *theme* has, in one of its various uses, a unique and peculiar meaning. In this meaning it is the word applied to written work done in English classes during the freshman year in college and sometimes to written work done in English classes in high school. In this meaning dictionaries include various brief definitions: "a short, informal essay, especially a school composition"; "a brief composition, especially one written as an exercise as part of a course of instruction"; "a written exercise"; "a short essay, especially one written as an assignment in a school course."[2] (Note the use of *especially* in three of the foregoing statements.) As a type of writing, the word *theme* has no other use.

In length a theme may vary from short to moderately short to moderately long to long—like a research theme or *paper* (a word sometimes used as a synonym for *theme*). It may deal with any subject and may be one of the four main kinds of writing: narration, description, exposition, argument (see Section **17**).

Regularly through your freshman year and in later college assignments you will be expected to write papers of varying length. The primary purpose of these assignments, especially of first-year

[1] These four characterizing words—*correct, clear, effective,* and *appropriate*—are the key words in this *Handbook* for writing improvement. They can be summarized, the last three especially, in the old but recently repopularized words, *rhetoric* and *rhetorical*. (For the meaning of *correct* as used in this *Handbook,* see note 3, p. 5.)

[2] From, respectively, *The American College Dictionary, Standard College Dictionary, Webster's Seventh New Collegiate Dictionary, Webster's New World Dictionary.*

themes, is to help you recognize and establish writing standards desirable in one with your degree of education. You will learn to write by writing and by later rewriting in accordance with your instructor's constructive criticism and his markings of errors you make in planning, phrasing, and thinking.

As and when you profit by such critical evaluation of your themes, your writing will begin to conform to acceptable standards of "good English"—written and spoken English used effectively in carrying on the business, professional, and social affairs of our country, and, increasingly, of the entire world.

Worth serious study is the chart on p. 4. It explains in some detail the characteristics of superior, average, and unacceptable papers.

## PRELIMINARY SURVEY

As a general introduction to theme-writing, these suggestions for improvement and competency in writing and for ease in planning and writing a theme are worthy of consideration.

### CONCENTRATE ON METHODS FOR
### *IMPROVEMENT* IN WRITING

For rapid improvement in writing, concentrate on 10 important topics. (The following list provides an overview of many aspects of theme-writing as well as a convenient guide to follow in checking all work in composition.)

⟶    1. *Subject.* Is the subject of the theme properly chosen and limited so that, in the number of words assigned, the reader is given a clear and reasonably complete account? See Sections **2** and **3**.

⟶    2. *Planning.* Does the theme have an orderly plan? Is it clearly based on a written or mental outline, with its parts clearly ordered? See Section **6**.

⟶    3. *Paragraphing.* Does each paragraph of the theme constitute an adequate treatment of one division of the subject? Is each paragraph unified? Does each paragraph contain a topic sentence, expressed or implied? Is each paragraph effective in its order, proportion, use of transitional aids, and comparative length? See Sections **23–30**.

⟶    4. *Sentence fragments.* Does the theme contain any unjustifiable sentence fragments? See Section **31**.

# GRADING STANDARDS IN FRESHMAN COMPOSITION

| | Content | Organization: *Rhetorical and logical development* | Organization: *Sentence structure* | *Diction* | *Grammar, punctuation, spelling* |
|---|---|---|---|---|---|
| Superior (A–B) | A significant central idea clearly defined, and supported with concrete, substantial, and consistently relevant detail | Theme planned so that it progresses by clearly ordered and necessary stages, and developed with originality and consistent attention to proportion and emphasis; paragraphs coherent, unified, and effectively developed; transitions between paragraphs explicit and effective | Sentences skillfully constructed (unified, coherent, forceful, effectively varied) | Distinctive: fresh, precise, economical, and idiomatic | Clarity and effectiveness of expression promoted by consistent use of standard grammar, punctuation, and spelling |
| Average (C) | Central idea apparent but trivial, or trite, or too general; supported with concrete detail, but detail that is occasionally repetitious, irrelevant, or sketchy | Plan and method of theme apparent but not consistently fulfilled; developed with only occasional disproportion or inappropriate emphasis; paragraphs unified, coherent, usually effective in their development; transitions between paragraphs clear but abrupt, mechanical, or monotonous | Sentences correctly constructed but lacking distinction | Appropriate: clear and idiomatic | Clarity and effectiveness of expression weakened by occasional deviations from standard grammar, punctuation, and spelling |
| Unacceptable (D–F) | Central idea lacking, or confused, or unsupported with concrete and relevant detail | Plan and purpose of theme not apparent; undeveloped or developed with irrelevance, redundancy, or inconsistency; paragraphs incoherent, not unified, or undeveloped; transitions between paragraphs unclear or ineffective | Sentences not unified, incoherent, fused, incomplete, monotonous, or childish | Inappropriate: vague, unidiomatic, or substandard | Communication obscured by frequent deviations from standard grammar, punctuation, and spelling |

SOURCE: *Joint Statement on Freshman English in College, and High School Preparation* by the Departments of English of Ball State University, Indiana State University, Indiana University, and Purdue University. Used by permission.

⟶ 5. *Fused sentences.* Are any separate sentences carelessly combined with no punctuation between them? See Section **33**.

⟶ 6. *Punctuation.* Is all punctuation in the theme designed to reveal the intended relationships of words in sentences and does any punctuation occur which distorts meaning or is unnecessary? Guard especially against comma splices (Section **32**) and semicolon misuse (Section **89d**) . See also Sections **86–95, 100**.

⟶ 7. *Grammar.* Are all grammatical relationships clear and correct (subject and predicate, verb form, case, etc.)? See Sections **71–85**.

⟶ 8. *Diction.* Is word choice in the theme correct, clear, and effective? See Sections **53–70**.

⟶ 9. *Spelling.* Is each word in the theme correctly spelled? Has the theme been proofread for misspellings? See Section **52**.

⟶ 10. *Sentence construction.* Is each sentence constructed or built so that it is clear, effective, and appropriate? See Sections **34–50**.

Only after a theme has been carefully planned, written, rewritten, and proofread for all kinds of errors and slips will it approach correctness in its diction, grammar, punctuation, mechanics, spelling, and sentence and paragraph structure. Careful attention to your instructor's marks and comments on returned themes, as well as systematic study of *Handbook* sections dealing with your particular weaknesses inevitably will cause rapid improvement in your theme-writing.

## CONCENTRATE ON METHODS FOR
### *COMPETENCY* IN WRITING

Having checked your writing in the foregoing 10 areas, you should do still more. Thus far, you have largely been ensuring *correctness*,[3] an important but somewhat negative quality in writ-

---

[3] *Correct, correctly, correctness* are used through this book not in an absolute sense but in the meaning permitted by every standard dictionary: "in accordance with an acknowledged or accepted standard; according to recognized usage."

ing. What you and your instructor are seeking for your writing style is *competency,* a quality far more desirable than mere correctness. At first your instructor will be satisfied with proper handling of the preceding checklist, but, as you progress, he will wish you both to expand and compress the list so that of every theme you write you will ask these questions:

1. Does my theme have a *central purpose?*
2. Have I carefully *analyzed* the subject?
3. Does the theme have *ample* content?
4. Is the theme *arranged* logically and effectively?
5. Is the theme *unified?*
6. Is the theme *clear* to my reader?
7. Have I used adequate *transition* between sentences and between paragraphs?
8. Does my theme have *interest?* Is my content presented effectively so that it makes a *definite* appeal to the reader?
9. Have I *adapted* my material to my reader and made it *appropriate?* Have I kept my reader constantly in mind?
10. Is my theme *correct* in all details of grammar, punctuation, spelling, diction, sentence structure? See Items 4–10, pp. 3, 5.

If you can truthfully answer "yes" to these 10 questions, your task is completed. Otherwise, you need the guidance and constructive criticism that both your instructor and your textbook give. None of these requirements is beyond the ability of any serious student who will work intelligently, industriously, and faithfully. This *Handbook* is designed to help you give "yes" answers to the foregoing questions. Although each of its sections is separate, for those who need specific instruction, all the sections are interrelated; they form the basis, framework, and finished structure of *competent* writing.

Remember, also: "The easiest reading comes from hard writing" and "It takes hard work to make easy reading. It takes courage to write well."[4]

## USE THE WORK-SHEET PLAN FOR
## IMPROVEMENT IN WRITING

To write competently, even painlessly, many students have found effective the following process, pursued step by step:

[4] Ellis Gladwin, *Letter Logic,* October and August, 1966.

Prepare a number of work sheets, 5½ by 8½ inches (half-size standard stationery), a desirable size, since each work sheet can contain all necessary step-by-step information.

*Work Sheet 1.* On this sheet put preliminary miscellaneous information: number of the theme; date due; number of words required; reader or readers aimed at; general title; specific title or titles, if given (otherwise, several specific titles suggested by the general title); general tone of paper (see Section 4f); *theme* sentence, the sentence summarizing the content of the theme you plan to write.

*Work Sheet 2.* Here put your preliminary analysis for possible content (see Section 4d). List 15 to 25 items you might include, each of which might serve as topic or subject for a paragraph.

*Work Sheet 3.* From the 15 to 25 items on Work Sheet 2 make a tentative outline (see Section 6). Your outline can be changed later, if necessary, as you develop it in writing.

*Work Sheet 4.* On this work sheet write topic sentences, one for each paragraph that you plan for your theme. The number will depend upon the major divisions of your outline. Preferably, make each topic sentence a simple sentence (see Section 23). If, however, your tentative outline on Work Sheet 3 is a "sentence outline" (Section 6c) and each sentence of a major division is written as a topic sentence for the paragraph, then Work Sheet 4 can be omitted.

*Work Sheet 4* or *5,* and *6, 7, 8, 9,* etc., depending upon the number of paragraphs, using one work sheet for each paragraph. On each work sheet copy a topic sentence from Work Sheet 3 or 4. Expand this into an adequate paragraph (see Section 24).

When you have expanded the last topic sentence into its paragraph, you have written your theme. Do your revising and correcting on these work sheets. Add necessary transitions between paragraphs. When you are satisfied with your revisions and corrections, copy your material on regular theme paper. Give your theme a final rereading before you turn it in. Your instructor may ask for a final draft of your outline, to be turned in with your theme. He may also wish to see all your work sheets.

In the light of the Grading Standards on p. 4, study the theme, "Give That Man a Hand": its content and the instructor's methods of marking and commenting. (Not all instructors use

## GIVE THAT MAN A HAND

It is better to accept some things as they are instead of questioning them. Take for example the simple handshake. I often wonder what good it does. Does it have a purpose? Why did we ever stray from the Indian's custom of greeting friends with a raised

*Tense* hand? If we [*had*] retained this custom, we would have fewer broken fin- [*Abrupt transition from the purpose of handshakes to the annoyance of firm handshakes.*]
[*One word*] gers at least. My self, I hate handshakes! Ever since some guy with a dozen or more degrees wrote that handshakes reveal character, everyone seems to want to analyze his friends. According to this theory, unless you grab someone's hand in a vise-like grip and try to pull his arm from its connections, your character isn't worth two cents. This is all very unfair to us weaker persons who find it difficult and [*Sp.*] partically impossible to turn on the supposedly neces- sary pressure. Everytime a man holds out his hand to me with that

[*You work pretty hard for a joke here.*] "Let me analyze your character" look in his eye, I feel like putting my fist somewhere besides in his hand. As he holds my hand I can almost hear him mentally saying "hmm," and then he turns away with a satisfied and self-pleased look on his face. All this is very up- setting and embarrassing to my sensitive nature.

These "amat[*Sp.*]uer analyzers" are making the world handshake con- [*Hyphen*] scious and me self-conscious. Of course, if [*Ref?*] this continues the [*Punct.*] world will be a sorry place to live in. I pity the fellow who is [*You have been talking about firm hand- shakes; now you abruptly introduce the idea of warm handshakes. Perhaps ¶ 3 should precede this ¶ ?*] struggling for success but can't get ahead because (Horrors! Even his best friend won't tell him) his handshake is clammy and lifeless. Instead of capable, intelligent, business-minded men at the head of [*Repetitious*] business, the jobs will be open to none but the members of the grunt- and-gr[*Sp.*]oon profession (wrestling, to anyone who didn't know!).

[*Not necessary and not funny.*]
I have heard it said that a handshake should be warm and friend- ly. Are those poor unfortunates whose hands are usually clammy and cold doomed to be social outcasts because they can't give their hand- clasps the required touch of congeniality?

*From* **Joint Statement on Freshman English in College, and High School Preparation** *by the Departments of English of Ball State University, Indiana State University, Indiana University, and Purdue University; used by permission*

I have come to the conclusion--though I may never be able to convince another person--that handshakes should be abolished. The rapid shaking of a man's favorite possession, his right arm, is as useless as the French custom of planting a kiss on both cheeks of a friend. Many times I have vowed that I would not budge my hands from my pockets for anyone. But I continue to offer my hand with an *Now you* obliging smile and a prayer that not all of the bones will be crushed. *return to the idea of* I guess that I am doomed to spend the rest of my life shaking *firm handshakes.* hands, and the only thing I can do about it is not to think about it.

this system of indicating errors, nor do they all comment so elaborately.) The theme received a grade of C—.

Comments on the good and bad points of the theme and the reason for the C— grade were as follows:

This theme discusses a clear central idea of some interest, supports it with freshly observed and usually relevant detail, and develops it, for the most part, fully and emphatically. Its paragraphs are unified and coherent, and its sentence structure is effectively varied (consider the placement of modifying phrases and clauses in paragraph 2, for example) . Its colloquial diction is fresh, appropriate, and usually accurate; except for a few deviations, its grammar, punctuation, and spelling are conventional. Despite these strengths, however, the theme fails to be as good as it could have been because the writer does not wholly fulfill his plan and purpose. In his first seven sentences he suggests that he may either discuss the need of conforming to convention or investigate the purpose of the convention of handshaking. In sentence 8 he begins to discuss his annoyance at firm handshakes, but then in the second and third paragraphs he considers the necessity of warm and friendly handshakes, and in the fourth and fifth paragraphs he returns to the ideas of conforming to convention and the annoyance of firm handshakes. If the point of the theme is the futility of questioning convention, that point needs to be clearly developed and supported by establishing relevance between the various aspects of his topic.

# 1  *Manuscript form*

### 1a  *Conform to specific standards in preparing manuscript*

If in your English composition or other classes you are given directions for the preparation of manuscript, follow those directions. Otherwise, use the following as a guide for your final draft:

*1. Paper.* Use a good quality, preferably white bond, standard-sized stationery, 8½ by 11 inches. Ruled paper is convenient for longhand, but most standard paper is unruled.

*2. Title.* Center the title on the first line of ruled paper or about two inches from the top of unruled paper. Capitalize the first word and all other important words in the title (see Section **97a**). Do not use a period after the title, but use a question mark or exclamation point if necessary for interrogative or exclamatory titles. Do not underscore the title or enclose it in quotation marks unless it is itself a quotation or unless you quote it *in* the theme (see Section **9k**).

*3. Beginning.* On ruled paper, leave one line blank between title and theme beginning; then write on each line. On unruled paper, begin the theme about one inch below the title and leave about one-half inch between the lines.

*4. Margins.* Leave a margin of at least one inch on the left side of each page. Standard theme paper may have a margin of one inch ruled off; leave a similar blank space on paper not having this vertical line. Leave a margin of about a half-inch, or even better, one inch, at the right. Make the margins even and fairly uniform down the page. At the bottom, leave a margin of at least one inch.

*5. Indentations.* Indent the first line of every paragraph about one inch. Use indentations of equal length for all paragraphs in the same paper. Make no exception if you have occasion to use *numbered* paragraphs. On the second and following pages, indent the first line *only* if it is the beginning of a paragraph.

Indicate a paragraph division not shown by indentation by placing the sign ¶ before the word beginning the paragraph. Cancel a paragraph division by writing *no* ¶ in the margin. But, in general, avoid the use of this paragraph symbol. Preferably, recopy the entire page, correcting the indention.

6. *Insertions and closures.* Use ∧ (named caret) when inserting an omitted word or expression (see Section **95f**). Use ◡ to join letters accidentally separated.

7. *Cancellations.* Draw a straight line through material you wish to cancel. Do not use parentheses or brackets to cancel words.

8. *Order.* Number your pages with Arabic numerals in the upper right-hand corner of each page. Arrange the pages in proper order: 1, 2, 3, etc.

9. *Endorsement.* With pages in proper order, page 1 on top, fold the theme lengthwise through the middle. On the right-hand side of the back of the last page write your name, course, instructor's name, date, and number of the paper. Write these items in the order desired by your department or your instructor.

NOTE: For other "basic mechanics" in the preparation of manuscript, see "The Hyphen" (Section **92**), "Capitals" (Section **97**), "Abbreviations" (Section **98**), "Italics" (Section **96**), and "Numbers" (Section **99**).

### 1b  *Make your handwriting legible*

Illegible writing taxes the patience of a reader and causes him to give so much attention to the words themselves that his thought is turned away from the important ideas that should engage his interest. Make your handwriting easily readable by observing the following:

1. *Do not crowd your writing.* Do not run words together; do not run consecutive lines too closely together; do not crowd writing at the bottom of a page.

2. *Do not leave gaps in words.* The consecutive letters in a word should be joined.

3. *Do form your letters carefully and correctly.* Dot every small-letter *i* and *j*. Cross every *t*. Make small letters *m* and *n* and *u* distinct, and small letters *a* and *o*. Do not carelessly write small letters as capitals, or capitals as small letters (see Section **97g**).

4. *Do write with a good pen, using black or blue-black ink,* and *do write legibly.* Avoid the reader's possible comment on your theme: "This *looks* interesting, but I can't *read* it!"

*1c   Preferably, type your themes and other written work*

Not only is typescript more legible than handwriting, but errors are also more easily detected in typescript than in handwriting. Observe the following conventions in typing:

1. Do not use onionskin paper for your reader's copy; use onionskin only for the carbon copy you keep.

2. Indent paragraph beginnings either 5 or 10 spaces.

3. Leave margins at both the left and right: an inch or an inch and a half at the left, about an inch at the right.

4. Leave a blank space of an inch at the bottom of each page.

5. Double-space all lines (single-space only in business letters, which have double-spacing only between paragraphs; see pp. 652–653).

6. To form a dash, use two hyphens (--), with no space preceding or following. To form an exclamation point, use period (.) or apostrophe (') and then backspace and use, respectively, apostrophe (') or period (.). (Late models of typewriters have a separate exclamation point.)

7. After terminating marks of punctuation (period, question mark, exclamation point), space twice or thrice; after internal punctuation marks, including the period after abbreviations and initials, space once. Before and after the dash (—) use no spaces.

8. For numbers, use small letter l for Arabic one, capital I for Roman one, and, if your typewriter has no zero, capital O for zero. (Some typewriters have a separate numeral one.)

The endorsement on a typewritten manuscript is usually placed in the upper left-hand corner of the first page. If the paper is folded, it is endorsed like a handwritten theme (see "Endorsement," 1a).

*1d   Avoid numerous and unsightly erasures and corrections*

*1. Recopying.* Everyone is likely to make errors even in preparing a final draft. If such errors are numerous, it is far better to recopy an entire page than to leave it filled with blots, blurs, and canceled and inserted words. If only one or two corrections must be made on a page, see "Indentations," "Insertions and closures," and "Cancellations" above (1a).

*2. Proofreading.* Every manuscript should be reread carefully for errors of all kinds, especially for careless errors. ("Oh, I knew better than that" is slim excuse for the writer.) Though typescript makes detection of errors easier, typed papers often contain more errors than papers written in longhand because of the insidious way in which letters seem to change places and because of careless proofreading. For a guide to proofreading, see Section 16.

3. *Final draft.* Always reread the final draft of a manuscript before passing it on to a reader.

# 2 *Theme topics*

Every writer has had the experience of writing something with great care, something which pleased him and seemed correct and clear, only to find that others derived no pleasure or profit from reading it. Although everything has interest for somebody, some subjects are more interesting than others and can be presented more effectively.

## 2a *Choose a topic that interests you*

To write effectively, you must be interested in your material. Vagueness, aimlessness, dullness, and sketchiness are evidence of uninterested writing; force and vigor are present when you are wrapped up in your subject and let yourself go. You can write more vigorously and interestingly about people and activities that you have been associated with, either pleasantly or unpleasantly, than you can about people and activities that you have known about only through the experience of others.

For example, you may not have been interested in labor unions, but if members of your family or intimate friends are favorably or unfavorably affected by unions, you are likely to discover that labor unions are an interesting topic.

Do not neglect, either, possible subjects suggested by your reading or by your conversations with others.

You necessarily will write several themes on topics in which you are not greatly interested, an experience not uncommon for any speaker or writer. Usually, however, even when a theme topic is assigned by your instructor, you can choose a limited part of the subject that comes closest to your interests.

### 2b  Choose a topic that will interest your readers

Except on rare occasions, like keeping a diary or taking notes, all writing is done primarily for a reader or a group of readers, with the purpose of giving information or entertainment, or both. Far more important than yourself as writer are your readers, who may be your classmates, friends, relatives, readers of campus publications, or instructor. Your theme may be specifically required as a class exercise, but you can indicate for what type of reader you intend it. Your instructor then becomes a "reader over your shoulder," who visualizes himself as one of your designated readers and judges whether your writing is appropriate.

A writer, like a salesman, has to appeal to his readers. He will profitably spend time in analyzing the likes and dislikes of his readers, their backgrounds, their general range of information on the chosen subject. He will plan ways to interest them in his material or to present in new or different ways material in which they are already interested.

In general, among many others and with some natural overlapping, the following subjects and suggested limitations of these subjects have genuine appeal for most people:

*1. Amusements, hobbies, recreation:* radio, television, movies, recordings; growth of, development of, interest in, pleasure in, and profit from hobbies; spectator and participation sports, games, directions for playing games, exciting or dramatic episodes in sports.

*2. Animals:* wild or tame, usual or unusual (several of Walt Disney's movies had for leading living characters, respectively, a deer, a cougar, an eagle, a dog, a cat!) .

*3. The college or university world:* living conditions, study conditions, academic life, social life, cultural life, recreation, sports.

*4. Life, property, and welfare:* important matters which involve the life and property of others and which have a relation to the reader's own welfare—ideas, perhaps, concerning "life, liberty, and the pursuit of happiness."

*5. Local, national, and world affairs* (much limitation needed) ; examples: local recreation facilities, slum areas, teen-age problems; national: government aid to education, higher taxes, Selective Service; international: UN, UNESCO, brother-hood in a world of conflict.

6. *Nature:* in all its animate and inanimate appearances—animals, plants, flowers, trees, metals, atoms, geology, astronomy, etc.

7. *Occupations:* what they are, how they came into being, what they involve, what they mean in terms of money and happiness.

8. *People:* unique, prominent, well-known, unforgettable; also conflicts between people, between man and nature, between man and space, and conflicts within the individual.

9. *Personal and autobiographical:* various episodes, tragic, comic, appealing, and interesting in your past, present, or planned future, or those of your relatives; personal reminiscences, reactions, and reflections.

10. *Places:* historical, unusual, scenic, off-the-beaten-path, even uncommon features of common places and unfamiliar features of familiar places.

11. *Pure and applied science:* accounts of past, present, and planned achievements, as in the pure sciences of astronomy and mathematics, or in the applied sciences, like engineering, or in both, like chemistry and medicine. A broad subdivision of applied science—manufacturing: factory visits, machines, mechanisms, processes, directions, recipes.

12. *Religion:* reasons for one's beliefs, a personal creed, attitudes toward the soul and immortality, a code of ethics.

13. *Timely topics:* recent events, new ideas, or late facts or the development of some old idea through contact with recent developments.

14. *Travel:* both places themselves and actual experiences and people encountered in getting from place to place—on foot, by auto, by train, by boat, by plane.

15. *The universe:* natural planets and satellites, man-made satellites, radiation, interspace exploration, men and animals in space.

NOTE: You may be aided in choosing topics by keeping in mind four general purposes of writing: to tell a story (narrative) ; to give a picture in words (description) ; to explain (exposition) ; or to convince (argument) . See Section 17.

## 2c   Choose a topic you know something about

Just as you cannot expect to handle a tool, instrument, or machine efficiently and expertly without some previous experience or some firsthand acquaintance, so you cannot expect to write effectively without some experience and firsthand acquaintance with the topic of the composition. Most current magazine articles and nonfiction books—and fiction, too—are based on many months or years of direct observation, study, and personal familiarity with the materials treated. Every writer goes to his own experience—to those things he knows or has thought about or seen or heard. You, likewise, can do so profitably and effectively.

## 2d   Choose a topic you can treat adequately

You should have in mind, in choosing a topic, approximately the length of the paper you plan to write. A short paper requires a limited subject; a longer paper naturally permits a broader subject, a more extended treatment, a wider point of view, the inclusion of more details.

The word *theme* implies a single, well-defined *phase* of a subject. You cannot write an effective 500-word theme on a subject that requires 5000 words. If you choose a broad subject and fail to limit it, you are likely to write sketchily and superficially. "College Fraternities," "Professional Football," "Chicago," and "Aviation" are examples of such topics. A small composition on a large subject is necessarily a fragmentary, disconnected, ineffective treatment.

General topics or broad subjects must therefore be narrowed. "Should College Fraternities Be Abolished?" or "How Professional Football Players Are Recruited" or "When in Chicago, See the Planetarium" are examples of such limitation. "Aviation" is a hopelessly broad subject; limited to "Aviation in America," it is still too large, even for a book; "The Careers of the Wright Brothers" might be developed in a very long paper; "Orville Wright's First Flight" would be more suitable for ordinary-length theme treatment.

## 2e   Choose a topic that is concrete and specific

Even though you have a topic that can be adequately treated in the number of words allotted, it may be one of the many that are uninteresting because they are general, vague, or abstract. If any of these words describe your selection, restudy it to make it concrete and specific.

Consider these successive narrowings of a broad general subject, in the light of a student's interest, observation, and experience, and aimed at readers also interested in college activities. An asterisk (*) indicates the broader subject that is narrowed in the next group of topics.

| | |
|---|---|
| *Very general* | College Activities |
| *General* | Fraternities and Sororities |
| | Physical Activities |
| | Intellectual Activities |
| | Social Activities |
| | Studies in College |
| | *Student Organizations |
| *Less general* | Our Intramural Sports |
| | College Dramatics |
| | Weekends on the Campus |
| | Departmental Clubs (Science, Chemistry, French, Debating, etc.) |
| | Interest Clubs (Camera, Model Railroads, Painting, Ceramics, etc.) |
| | *Musical Organizations |
| *Fairly specific* | Our Student Chorus |
| | Our All-Campus Musical Show |
| | Student Dance Bands |
| | Impromptu Music |
| | Broadcasting Music to the Dormitories |
| | *Our Glee Club |
| *Limited* | How I Joined the Glee Club |
| | Why I Joined the Glee Club |
| | How to Become a Member of the Glee Club |
| | What Our Glee Club Does |
| | How Our Glee Club Helps Our College |
| | Join Our Glee Club and See Our State! |
| | Let's Sing! |

## 2f  *Be prepared to write on assigned topics*

Many composition subjects in your classes will be assigned. They may need some adaptation or limitation; they may need none. Writing on assigned subjects is excellent experience and practical training for post-college work, since most routine writing (and speaking) is done on assignment. Answers to letters, research reports in business and industry, papers read before specific groups, newspaper reporting, feature articles, and many nonfiction articles in general and trade magazines are examples of assigned materials.

## EXERCISES

NOTE: In addition to the theme subjects just below, many additional topics are suggested in the exercises at the ends of some sections, especially Section 17, pp. 104–107.

A. For each of the 15 classes of subjects on pp. 14–15, make a list of five to 10 limited topics, each suitable for a 350-word to 500-word theme.

B. Using the following for general subjects (or substituting others of more immediate interest to you), for each write three to five limited topics which you think will interest specific readers whom you designate: Childhood, Contests, Favorites, Food, Friends, Heroes, History, Jobs, Memories, Money, Sorrow, Transportation, Superstition, Vacations, Weather.

C. Using the following official or unofficial American holidays as general subjects, for each write three to five limited topics which you think will interest specific readers whom you designate: New Year's Eve, New Year's Day, Lincoln's Birthday, Washington's Birthday, St. Patrick's Day, Good Friday, Easter, April Fool's Day, May Day, Memorial Day, Fourth of July, August Vacation Days, Labor Day, Columbus Day, Homecoming, Halloween, Armistice Day (Veterans' Day), Thanksgiving, Christmas Eve, Christmas Day.

D. List 10 incidents in your life which, expanded, would be interesting to your readers, your instructor, and the members of your class.

E. Apply the five tests (Section 2a,b,c,d,e) for topics to the following suggestions for themes and suggest what readers you have in mind:

1. The history, including a description, of a building on your campus.
2. A commentary on a popular TV or radio program.
3. An account of the conversation among a group of friends after some college activity (dance, show, game, etc.).
4. Favorite magazines and newspapers.
5. Personalities of high school and college teachers.
6. What you want to be, and to be doing, 10 years from now.

7. A list of five books, with reasons for their selection, which you would choose for a summer's reading.
8. A commentary on the "easiest" and the "most difficult" courses and professors in the college.
9. Desirable qualities you want your friends or roommate or future wife or husband to have.
10. The ideal preparation for college.

# 3  *The title*

A well-chosen title helps you stick to your subject throughout a theme, reminding you that all material included should bear upon the subject. It is also an effective means of gaining the reader's attention. Most of us are led to read a certain book, magazine article, or story because of its attractive title. Give your theme a good title and you have taken an important step in making the whole composition effective.

## 3a  *Avoid confusion of title and subject*

The term *subject* is usually broader and more inclusive than the word *title*. If your instructor asks for a composition on "Reading Habits," he has assigned a *subject,* not a *title,* and you should sharpen this subject to a more specific title. Conversely, if the actual title is assigned, you must discover precisely what subject it covers. Do not assume that the title of a specific paper is the same as a general subject which has been assigned. The best titles indicate not a general subject but the actual *theme* of the composition.

## 3b  *Use clear and effective phrasing in the title*

Your title, of course, cannot mention everything a theme contains, but it should indicate, or give a hint of, the contents. Do not announce a title and then develop ideas with no relation to it. And do not use a title, no matter how catchy, which is deliberately misleading.

1. *Avoid long titles.* As a title, "Browsing Among Current Magazines" is certainly more effective than "How to While Away an Afternoon Among the Magazines in the Periodical Room of the Belvedere Library." Lovers of William Wordsworth's poetry refer to a well-loved poem as "Tintern Abbey" rather than by the title the poet gave it: "Lines Composed a Few Miles Above Tintern Abbey, on Revisiting the Banks of the Wye During a Tour, July 13, 1798."

2. *Rephrase vague and commonplace titles.* Titles like "College Football Is Overemphasized," "A Camping Trip," "Contemporary Etiquette," and "The Importance of Using Short Words" can be rephrased for greater concreteness and uniqueness: "Dollar Marks on the Gridiron," "Alone in a Civilized Wilderness," "Best Foot Forward," and "Little Words, but Mighty."

At the other extreme, however, titles which puzzle or mislead are questionable. To be clear, a title should be short, informative, definite. In addition, to be effective, it must be fresh and provocative. A survey of many titles shows three frequently used kinds:

*Informative titles,* which tell exactly and concretely the content:

The Method of Scientific Investigation
Learned Words and Popular Words
What Should Colleges Teach Women?
The American Student as I See Him
Why an Airplane Flies

*Suggestive titles,* which become clear as the reader uses a little imagination:

Lo, the Old College Spirit (a contrast of past and present "college spirit")
That Burrowing Bean (an article about peanuts)
Snapshot of America (a brief survey of American culture)
Ten-Gallon Hero (an article on the American cowboy)
300,000,000 Americans Would Be Wrong (an argument against overpopulation in the U.S.)

*Intriguing titles,* which neither tell nor suggest but which later become clear:

The Monster (a profile of the great musician, Richard Wagner)

Farewell, My Lovely! (an article expressing regret at the passing of a once nationally popular automobile model)

A Game of Wild Indians (an investigation of an outbreak of typhoid fever in New York City)

No Tears, No Good (a reminiscence of judging a motion picture by the tears the spectators shed)

Look Out, Here I Come! (a study of the reasons for our increasing number of automobile fatalities)

**3c   Place and punctuate the title correctly on the page** (see Section 1a2)

**3d   Avoid vague, indirect reference to the title in the first sentence of the theme** (see Section 8a)

## EXERCISES

A. Buy, or consult in your library, current copies of three or four magazines like *The Saturday Evening Post, Esquire, The American Scholar, The Atlantic Monthly, Harper's Magazine*. Look at the titles of some 10 to 20 articles; then skim through the content of the articles: (1) are the titles commonplace and/or appropriate? (2) classify the titles into the three kinds discussed in Section **3b.** Put in parentheses after each title the general subject of the article.

B. Apply the directions in the last two sentences of Exercise A to some 10 to 20 articles in your book of readings.

# 4   *Analysis of subject*

The first step in preparing a theme, after you have chosen or been assigned a subject and have limited it, is a careful analysis of the subject. You should understand what the subject involves by asking and satisfactorily answering certain questions. Your answers can well be your *controlling purpose* in planning and writing. You need an objective other than completion of a required assignment, since good purposeless writing does not exist. Consider carefully answers for these important questions:

⟶ 1. How long is my paper to be?

⟶ 2. For what reader or readers am I to write? (The instructor is a "reader over your shoulder," an adviser, a kind of editor.)

⟶ 3. What is my specific purpose in writing this paper, the purpose which controls and centralizes my writing? Can I express the content of my planned paper in a single summarizing sentence, a thesis sentence, a theme-topic sentence?

⟶ 4. What do I already know about the subject? Where can I find additional material, and what kind of material do I need?

⟶ 5. What type of writing will best suit my subject: narrative, descriptive, expository, argumentative? (See Section **17**.)

If you use the work-sheet method, put such information on Work Sheet 1 (see p. 7) .

## 4a   Begin your analysis on the basis of the number of words you are to write

Themes vary in length. Some are 250 or 300 words—or even shorter, others are 500 words or 1000 words, and long research papers may extend to 5000 or 8000 words. Choice of subject, narrowing of a fairly broad subject, choice of details, and plan of organization to be followed—all these are directly affected by the number of words you are to write.

## 4b   Make your analysis according to your prospective reader

Nearly every piece of writing is a project for communicating to someone a series of thoughts and emotions. That "someone" may be a specially chosen individual, like the recipient of a business or friendly letter, or he may be one of a group. However, a group should not be too large, too broad. Such labels as "the average reader," "anyone interested," "city people," "college students," "high school graduates," "average driver," "a job hunter," "a stranger," "a person who intends to take a vacation" include people of such varied interests and backgrounds that a composition aimed at them can at best be general. Narrow "the reader" or "the group" for whom you are writing. Make sure, too, that your choice of reader is appropriate. It is inappropriate to choose a reader whom you talk to a dozen times a day, such as your room-mate, or, if you live at home, a member of your family.

Writing aimed at an appropriate person or group is likely to be clear, concise, and effective. Your English instructor tries to judge how appropriately and effectively you have written for the reader or readers you have designated. For example, a theme on "My Background in English" may be written for your present English instructor to indicate the strong and weak points of your training. It may be written for your high school principal, sug-gesting changes in the course for students going to college. It may be written for your former high school English teachers and may give critical evaluation of their courses in the light of your present course.

### 4c   Determine the central purpose of the theme

Before you begin to write, state in a single sentence (which may or may not be included in the theme later) your central purpose, your controlling idea. To play on words, what is the *theme* of your theme? Write a *thesis* statement, a *topic sentence* for the paper, a sentence, either general or specific, that summarizes your entire material. Until you have done this, you have not fully or clearly defined your purpose. (For examples of thesis statements, see below and p. 33.)

On the general subject, "A Camping Trip," you might clarify your purpose and procedure by jotting down for your own guidance:

| | |
|---|---|
| *Limited subject* | "Advice to a Young Camp Leader" |
| *Possible title* | "Let's Take the Boys Camping" |
| *Reader* | A camp leader who is starting his first sum-mer of service |
| *Length* | 1,000 words |
| *Thesis sentence (general)* | Boys between 12 and 15 enjoy most those group activities—especially outdoors—which call for vigorous exertion. |

*Thesis sentence (specific)*    Kinds of recreational activities that appeal to boys between 12 and 15 are (1) athletic and competitive (softball, tennis, swimming, horseshoes) ; (2) athletic and social (rowing, canoeing, hiking, woodcraft) ; (3) handicrafts; (4) mental (reading appropriate books, group discussions) .

This material, also, might go on Work Sheet 1. The specific thesis sentence aids in making an outline; see pp. 39–40 for the outline developed from the specific thesis sentence above.

### 4d   *In determining your central purpose, list 15 to 25 details that you might possibly use*

Make an inventory of what you know of the subject or make specific plans to find out more. (See Section 5.)

Put your inventory into words. Make a list of, say, 15 to 25 items that *might* be included and that *might* serve as the topic for a paragraph each. The items at first listing may come in no special order, for you will prepare a revised list from them.

For example, in a theme on "When in Chicago, Visit the Planetarium," your list might include:

1. What a planetarium is
2. History of the Planetarium
3. Location
4. Cost
5. Description of building (exterior)
6. Description of building (interior)
7. Special exhibits
8. Special lectures
9. Maintenance of Planetarium
10. Personnel
11. Comparison of Chicago's Planetarium with New York's
12. Value of planetariums
13. Mechanics of the projecting machine
14. Famous astronomers who have lectured there
15. Best days to go ("free" days or "fee" days)
16. Necessity of making two or three visits
17. My outstanding experiences there
18. My personal recommendations to the visitor

Or, on a simpler subject, like "Meet My High School," "The High School I Attended," or "Important Facts About My High School," your list might include, as they come to mind:

| | |
|---|---|
| 1. Size | 11. Commercial courses |
| 2. Building | 12. Vocational courses |
| 3. Location | 13. Athletic program |
| 4. History and name | 14. Basketball championships |
| 5. Number of students | 15. Publications |
| 6. Kinds of students | 16. Social activities |
| 7. Number of teachers | 17. Class trips |
| 8. Kinds of teachers | 18. Dramatic presentations |
| 9. Courses of study | 19. Musical activities |
| 10. College prep courses | 20. English courses |

Naturally, you would not include all such details in your theme, nor would you use this first-draft order. But such a listing gives you an overview and suggests details to include or exclude. Your central purpose, after a study of the Planetarium list, might be limited to giving directions for reaching the Planetarium and to calling attention to special exhibits and lectures. From the list about your high school, your central purpose might be an evaluation of extracurricular activities or a discussion of how well your high school studies and activities prepared you for college.

Using the work-sheet plan, you would put this material on Work Sheet 2. (See p. 7.)

### 4e  Choose a consistent method of development

Even when you have sharply limited your subject to fit the number of allotted words, when you have chosen a specific reader or readers, and when you have made a list of possible items to include, you must do still more in your analysis. You must choose some method of development and treatment which will most clearly and effectively accomplish your purpose.

You may wish to narrate (anecdote, history, biography, etc.) ; to describe (details of persons or places) ; to explain (give directions, define, classify, tell how a mechanism works or a process develops, etc.) ; or to argue (give reasons for and against, state advantages and disadvantages, show the need for or value of, etc.) . Or one type of development may be aided by another: in an expository paper, the use of specific narrative incidents, descriptive details, or comparisons and contrasts. (See Section 17.)

### 4f  Maintain a consistent tone or style

Find a word or two (an adjective or noun or two adjectives) which describe your purpose and planned treatment. Keep the characterizing term constantly in mind as you write; let your own choice of words be guided accordingly. When you have finished writing, check your written material for *consistency* with the specific descriptive word or phrase. Among such, the following are examples: *serious, dignified, solemn, formal, elevated, critical, humorous, flippant, facetious, light, light-hearted, cheerful, conversational, chatty, familiar, breezy, racy, witty, whimsical, tranquil, peaceful, sad, mournful, eerie, persuasive, contentious, ironical, satirical, savage, vitriolic, cantankerous.* In the following examples, notice the differences in tone:

A *solemn* and *reflective* tone was used by Joseph Addison in *The Spectator* (No. 26, 1711), after he had visited the tombs of the great and near-great in Westminster Abbey, London:

When I am in a serious humour, I very often walk by myself in Westminster Abbey, where the gloominess of the place, and the use to which it is applied, with the solemnity of the building, and the condition of the people who lie in it, are apt to fill the mind with a kind of melancholy, or rather thoughtfulness, that is not disagreeable. I yesterday passed a whole afternoon in the churchyard, the cloisters, and the church, amusing myself with the tombstones and inscriptions that I met with in those several regions of the dead. Most of them recorded nothing else of the buried person, but that he was born upon one day and died upon another: the whole history of his life being comprehended in those two circumstances that are common to all mankind. I could not but look upon these registers of existence, whether of brass or marble, as a kind of satire upon the departed persons, who had left no other memorial of them, but that they were born and that they died. They put me in mind of several persons mentioned in the battles of heroic poems who have sounding names given them, for no other reason but that they may be killed, and are celebrated for nothing but being knocked on the head. The life of these men is finely described in Holy Writ by *the path of an arrow,* which is immediately closed up and lost. . . .

I know that entertainments of this nature are apt to raise dark and dismal thoughts in timorous minds, and gloomy imaginations; but for my own part, though I am always serious, I do not know what it is to be melancholy, and can therefore take a view of nature in her deep and solemn scenes with the same pleasure as in her most gay and delightful ones. By this means I can improve myself with those objects, which others consider with terror. When I look upon the tombs of the great, every emotion of envy dies in me; when I read the epitaphs of the beautiful, every inordinate desire goes out; when I meet with the grief of parents upon a tombstone, my heart melts with compassion; when I see the tomb of the parents themselves, I consider the vanity of grieving for those whom we must quickly follow. When I see kings lying by those who deposed them, when I consider rival wits placed side by side, or the holy men that divided the world with their contests and disputes, I reflect with sorrow and astonishment on the little competitions, factions, and debates of mankind. When I read the several dates of the tombs, of some that died yesterday, and some six hundred years ago, I consider that great day when we shall all of us be contemporaries, and make our appearance together.

By contrast, in a tone of *vitriolic satire,* abundantly illustrated throughout his masterpiece, *Gulliver's Travels* (1726), Jonathan Swift[5] wrote about the human race. His hero, Gulliver, a captive among people 70 feet tall, has just boasted about his country's government, religion, elections, courts of justice, army, and history; to this boasting, the Brobdingnagian king replies (Part II, chapter vi) :

. . . you have made a most admirable panegyric upon your country; you have clearly proved that ignorance, idleness, and vice are the proper ingredients for qualifying a legislator; that laws are best explained, interpreted, and applied by those whose interest and abilities lie in perverting, confounding, and eluding them. I observe among you some lines of an institution, which in its original might have been tolerable, but these half erased, and the rest wholly blurred and blotted by corruptions. It doth not appear from all you have said, how any one virtue is required towards the procurement of any one station among you; much less that men are ennobled on account of their virtue, that priests are advanced for their piety or learning, soldiers for their conduct or valour, judges for their integrity, senators for the love of their country, or counsellors for their wisdom. As for yourself (continued the King) , who have spent the greatest part of your life in traveling, I am well disposed to hope you may hitherto have escaped many vices of your country. But by what I have gathered from your own relation, and the

5 For comment on Jonathan Swift as a writer, see p. 366.

answers I have with much pains wringed and extorted from you, I cannot but conclude the bulk of your natives to be the most pernicious race of little odious vermin that nature ever suffered to crawl upon the surface of the earth.

## EXERCISES

A. Make a list of five theme subjects suitable for treatment in 250–500 words; five for treatment in 1,000–1,500 words; and five for treatment in 4,000–6,000 words (see pp. 16, 22).

B. Choose one subject from each of the three length groups in Exercise A and write a sentence or two for each, stating your central purpose (see Sections 4c and **6g**).

C. For each subject chosen in Exercise B, list 15 to 25 details that you might consider using in developing the theme (see Section **4d**).

D. For each subject chosen in Exercise B, indicate your probable method of development (see Section 4e).

E. Choose five of the *tones* listed in Section 4f, and for each list three theme subjects which might be developed illustrating the particular tone chosen.

# 5 Content

A successful theme depends on effort to collect material *before* you begin to write. In gathering this material, keep in mind the necessity of giving specific details to bolster the theme idea. A lamentable weakness in the content of some student themes is the tendency to make general statements with little use of concrete material or evidence to support the central idea or position. (See Section **24b,d.**)

## 5a   Gather content from your own observation, experience, and reflection

Many students believe that their own ideas and experiences are not significant or interesting. Actually, just as you are interested in what others say to you, others are interested in what you say to them. Significant and interesting materials are available from your own *experience, observation, curiosity, imagination, reflec-*

*tion,* and *thinking.* Indeed, every writer necessarily puts something of himself into everything he writes—his own ideas, reactions, and observations. An excellent source of content, therefore, is one's self.

## 5b  Gather content from the thought and experience of others

Although you necessarily gather content from yourself, you should not neglect the material you may derive from others.

An easy and pleasant way of getting material for themes from other people is *discussion.* This may take the form of an *interview,* in which the ideas of the interviewed person constitute almost the whole of the theme. Or it may be a *conversation* with a member of your family, an acquaintance, or an instructor: an interchange of ideas, a give-and-take resulting in clarified and expanded thought. Classroom discussions are often an excellent source of material for compositions.

Another important way of getting content is *reading.* Magazines, newspapers, and books are almost inexhaustible sources of material. Ideas of your own may be intensified and expanded by reading. Entirely new phases of thought may be suggested, which, when reflected upon, can legitimately be used as your own. A fruitful source of material, a combination of conversation and reading, is discussing with your classmates and instructor the ideas, and their significance, in book-of-readings assignments.

Still other important sources of content are the audio-visual media: *radio* and *television programs, films, phonograph records,* and *works of art in color and form* (i.e., *painting* and *sculpture*). Although usually listened to or seen, not read, they constitute the experiences and thoughts of other people and are fertile sources of content.

For special information, a *letter of inquiry* to a company or to a recognized authority provides valuable content, a method useful for a longer research paper.

Using these various sources, especially discussion and reading, you can write why you agree or disagree or what your own opinions and beliefs are. But in drawing upon the experiences and reflections of others, be careful to make them your own by assimilating ideas and expressing them in your own words, unless you quote directly.

When you make use of an idea new to you, either in your own or in quoted words, acknowledge your indebtedness. Sometimes a phrase is sufficient: "As Woodrow Wilson points out in his definition of 'liberty' in *The New Freedom,* . . ." or "These novelists, Joseph Warren Beach says in *American Fiction, 1920–1940,* were profoundly affected by the social conditions. . . ." Sometimes—in a research paper, for example—fuller acknowledgment is necessary; for the proper method and forms of documentation in research papers, see Section **20g.** You must avoid the charge of plagiarism—that is, taking the ideas and words of another and passing them off as your own.

## EXERCISES

A. For each of the following groups make a list of five limited subjects which can be developed using your own thought, experience, and observation:

1. Past and Present Physical (Social) Activities
2. My Environment (home, community, college)
3. Vocational Experiences (full-time; part-time)
4. Financial Responsibilities
5. Philosophy of Life

B. Mention some experience or an incident that could be used in developing a theme based on one of the following topics:

1. Activities and Studies Do Not Mix
2. The Value of a Time Budget
3. Earning and Saving Money
4. A "Never Again" Experience
5. Safe Automobile Driving

# 6  Outlines and outlining

After analyzing your subject and gathering ample content, you must consider the problem of arranging your material and of treating it according to the principle of proportion.

The most frequently used method for clear ordering of parts in a theme is an outline: a framework for the builder-writer of the theme or, in one sense, a recipe containing the names of ingredients and the order in which they are to be used. An outline need not be overly detailed: for a very short paper, only the main heads or the main heads with the first division of subheads; for a longer paper, from a half-page to a page or a page and a half. An outline is only a guide to the writer, to be consulted as he writes, to be varied when other important ideas are suggested in the actual writing. In fact, as you write, you may find certain changes in plan effective and necessary.

Why have outlines? Many instructors require them for submitted themes because they know that a theme must be clearly ordered and proportioned to be effective, and because an outline aids the advisory reader as well as the writer in grasping organization. Certainly, no one can write an orderly composition without using *some kind* of outline, mental or written, actual or implied.

An outline existing only in the student's mind is of no help for an instructor who would like to make constructive suggestions about ordering and subdivision of ideas. Even a brief outline might well be written, and written *before* you write the theme. Only apparently logical is any student's statement that he cannot make an outline until he finishes his theme and knows what he has said.

## 6a Follow a consistent plan in arranging your outline

The order of the more common divisions of a subject or major division is frequently one of the following:

⟶ 1. Chronological or time order  (narrative, usually—see first example in Section **6b**)

⟶ 2. Space order  (description, usually)

⟶ 3. Order of logic  (exposition and argument, usually)

⟶ 4. Order of easy understanding  (exposition and argument, usually)

⟶ 5. Order of climax  (exposition and argument, usually—see second example in Section **6b**)

⟶ 6. Order of choice or psychological interest  (if other orders do not apply; see second and third examples in Section **6c**)

NOTE: Since these six methods are also frequently used in arranging sentences in a paragraph, they are discussed in slightly more detail in Section **26b,c.** Also, for narrative order, see Section **17a;**

descriptive order, Section **17b**; exposition order, Section **17c**; argument order, Section **17d**.

In form, three types of outlines are *topic outline, sentence outline,* and *paragraph outline;* each serves its own special purpose (see Sections **6b,c,d**) .

Preliminary to these three types of outlines is the "scratch" (or impromptu) outline, which is useful when time is short or the writer under pressure, as in planning a short class theme or preparing good answers for an essay-type examination. Five minutes can be profitably spent in making such an outline: listing a number of points, major and minor, directly or indirectly related, and then quickly, with lines or numbers or both, indicating the relative and logical order of these points. With more time, the writer can develop the "scratch" outline into a topic or sentence outline.

### 6b   Use a topic outline to make clear to yourself the arrangement of your ideas

The topic outline consists of parallel words, phrases, or dependent clauses, not sentences. It has meaning to the writer for immediate use; perhaps six weeks later he will not know what the topics mean. Such an outline may be very simple:

*My Most Memorable Day*
  I. The evening before
 II. The day itself
    A. Morning
    B. Afternoon
    C. Evening
III. The day after

*Why "Go On" with Latin?*[6]
  I. The popular reason why people go on with any subject (136 words)
 II. The practical reason why people go on with any subject (75 words)
III. The attractive reason why people go on with any subject (148 words)
IV. The effective reason why people go on with any subject (134 words)

   [6] For a 995-word article from this outline, see Warren E. Black, "Why 'Go On' with Latin?" *School and Society,* LXIX (May 7, 1949) , 334–335.

V. Application of "the effective reason" to Latin  (199 words)
  A. An enlightened perspective  (97 words)
  B. An accompanying sense of intellectual mastery  (102 words)

NOTE: The figures in parentheses indicate how proportion and proper length (see Section **7b**) can be achieved. In addition, in the article written from this outline, an introductory paragraph had 44 words and a concluding paragraph had 59 words.

The topic outline may for clearness be more elaborate, more detailed. For proper symbols and indentation, see Sections **6b,e.**

### 6c  *Use a sentence outline to make clear to yourself and to a reader the arrangement of your ideas*

The *sentence outline* consists of grammatically complete sentences. Such an outline should be clear, now and later, to the writer; it should be equally clear to any reader who would make constructive suggestions. For this latter reason many instructors insist on sentence outlines. The outline may be simple:

*My Most Memorable Day*
  I. I spent the previous evening putting my soap-box racer into perfect condition.
  II. The day itself was memorable.
    A. In the morning I won all my preliminary heats.
    B. In the early afternoon I won my semifinal heat and in the late afternoon I won the final race.
    C. That evening, at a banquet honoring all contestants, I was given a beautiful trophy and a four-year scholarship to college.
  III. The day after, I was greeted with a parade in my home town and given various kinds of civic honors.

The outline may also be more elaborate, more detailed:

*University Days*[7]
*Thesis sentence*    I never could pass botany, but I passed all the other courses that I took at the university: economics, physical education, and military drill.

  I. I never could pass botany.
    A. I was unable to see through a microscope.
    B. I repeated the course.

  [7] For this well-known and widely reprinted essay, see James Thurber, *My Life and Hard Times* (New York, 1933).

      1. The professor vowed that he would make me see.

      2. I did see, but it was only the reflection of my own eye.

II. I did not like economics, but I managed to pass it.

  A. I had my own troubles with the course.

  B. They were nothing to the troubles of a football tackle, Bolenciecwcz.

III. I had more anguish in gymnasium work than I had in botany and economics.

  A. I could not see to do the exercises or play the games.

  B. I could not pass the swimming requirement.

  C. I disliked the physical examination.

IV. I did not have the trouble with journalism that a certain agricultural student had.

V. I had trouble passing the military drill requirement.

  A. We drilled with outmoded rifles and studied Civil War tactics.

  B. I spent four years on military drill.

  C. I had one moment of military glory in the presence of General Littlefield.

  D. I had an interesting interview with General Littlefield the next day.

NOTE 1: Use declarative sentences in the sentence outline for clearness. Interrogative sentences are usually uninformative; exclamatory sentences are somewhat unusual and inappropriate (imperative sentences, though only when appropriate, are clear).

NOTE 2: Unless carefully phrased, even declarative sentences may not be clear; such sentences should outline content, not procedure.

*Auto Accidents*

Not clear    I. The major causes of accidents will be discussed.

          II. Methods of preventing accidents will be presented.

          III. Suggestions for making the methods effective will be given.

Clear       I. Auto accidents are caused by both mechanical and human failures.

          II. Accidents can be reduced by careful check of cars and greater responsibility by drivers.

          III. City officials, police, school authorities, and clergymen can lead in a campaign to make effective the suggestions for fewer accidents.

**6d   Use a paragraph outline primarily as a
first step in outlining the work of others**

The paragraph outline consists of groups of sentences—perhaps, but not necessarily, topic sentences (see Section **23**), indicating the contents of whole paragraphs.

Such an outline is valuable only when the theme is to consist of two, three, four, or five paragraphs. The outline is in the form of topic sentences or summarizing sentences, usually designated by Arabic numbers.

The paragraph outline is especially useful as a first step in outlining someone else's work, such as a magazine article or book chapter. Topic sentences are chosen, or summary sentences are written, to present the thought of successive paragraphs in a selection being studied. From these sentences a topic outline or sentence outline can be built that reveals major and minor divisions.

Here, as an example, is a paragraph outline of James Thurber's "University Days"; from this outline the sentence outline on pp. 33–34 was prepared:

1. I could not pass botany because I could not see through a microscope.
2. I tried again a year later.
3. The professor was sure that he could teach me to use the microscope.
4. We tried every adjustment known to man, but we did not succeed.
5. I did not like economics, but I managed to pass the course with less trouble than Bolenciecwcz, the tackle on the football team.
6. 7, 8, 9, 10, 11, 12, 13 (dialogue). With encouragement from the professor, Bolenciecwcz answered one question correctly.
14. Gymnasium work was worse for me, for I could not see without glasses and I disliked swimming and the physical examination; I finally passed, anyway.
15. Haskins, a student from a farm, was not a success in journalism.
16. Ohio State required two years of military drill, with outmoded equipment and Civil War tactics.
17. I failed military drill at the end of each year and was still taking it as a senior.
18. By executing one command correctly, I became a corporal.
19. General Littlefield summoned me to his office the next day, but the interview did not lead anywhere.

## 6e  Make your outlines correct in form

Since the purpose of an outline is to show the structure or plan or arrangement, mechanical correctness, so-called, is important only as it serves this purpose. Actually, the usual outline form is neither correct nor incorrect; writers in the past, however, have followed certain conventions, and it is these conventions that are described in this and the next section.

The outline, whether topic, sentence, or paragraph, is based on division of material into parts. Analysis of your subject shows major divisions and the order in which you can best discuss them. You make these divisions the foundations of your outline and examine them to determine what subtopics will complete the discussion.

The examples of outlines in Section **6b,c,d** show the conventional use of symbols, indentation, and punctuation.

In making the *topic outline,* follow these directions:

1. Indicate the major divisions by using Roman numerals, I, II, III, IV, etc. Begin flush at the left margin.

2. Indicate the first series of subdivisions under each main division by using capital letters, A, B, C, D, etc., indented equally.

3. Indicate the next series of subdivisions (if needed) by Arabic numbers, 1, 2, 3, 4, etc., also equally indented; and if still further subdivisions are needed, use small letters, a, b, c, d, etc., equally indented. But do not divide too minutely; avoid excessive detail; keep the number of main headings and major subdivisions to a minimum, consistent with clearness, order, and meaning.

4. Use a period after each symbol. Periods at the ends of topics are optional, but be consistent in their use or omission.

In making the *sentence outline,* follow the directions given just above for the topic outline. The only difference is the use of some terminating mark of punctuation—period, question mark, exclamation point—at the end of each division and subdivision.

In making the *paragraph outline,* use Arabic numbers. Roman numerals would serve, but for some 30 to 50 paragraphs the numbering would become complicated (see Section **99e**). A period follows the symbol; a period or a question mark comes at the end of the sentence. The beginning of each sentence may be indented, or it may begin flush at the left margin, with run-over lines indented.

## 6f Make your outlines consistent in their divisions and their wording

A few words and phrases jotted down at random are not an outline. A usable outline requires thought. You must give it a consistent organization (see Section **6a**) if the theme you will write from it is to be well arranged and clear. Therefore, you must critically examine your first draft of the outline and carefully revise it. Remove repetitions and overlappings; add specific details where necessary; remove illogical relationships; rearrange parts for more effective organization.

To attain these aims in outlining, follow these suggestions:

1. Be sure that the first or any main heading *does not repeat the title*.

*Advice to a High School Student*

Wrong      I. Advice to a high school student
           II. Types of courses to take in high school

*How To Be a Good Friend*

           I. Friend—a definition
           II. Types of friends
              A. Fair-weather friends
              B. True friends
Wrong     III. How to be a good friend
              A. Be loyal
              B. Be sincere
              C. Be helpful
           IV. Rewards in being a good friend

2. Use *parallel phrasing* (see Section **44**) to make your outline divisions clear and effective: use words or the same kind of phrases or clauses or sentences for all main divisions and subdivisions. Do not use a word for one topic and a phrase or dependent clause for another, and do not mix the two kinds of outlines, topic and sentence.

*Who I Am*

| Wrong | Improved | Improved |
|---|---|---|
| I. About my name | I. My name | I. What my name is |
| II. About my home | II. My home town | II. Where I come from |
| III. Occupation | III. My occupation | III. What I am doing |

3. Do not put in a subhead any matter that should be in a larger division, and do not put in a main heading any matter that should be in a subdivision.

*Meet My Roommate*

Wrong
I. Physical appearance
  A. His name
  B. His outstanding character trait
  C. His worst fault

Wrong
I. Physical appearance
II. Height, weight, age, complexion

4. Remember that outlining is division, that subdivision means *division into at least two parts.* If a single minor topic must be mentioned, express it in, or as part of, its major heading, or add another coordinate minor topic.

*Why Accidents Happen*

Wrong
  I. Major reason for accidents
    A. Drivers at fault
  II. Minor reason for accidents
    A. Roads and highways at fault
  III. Proposed solution
    A. Better driver training

Do not artificially seek a subdivision B or a subdivision 2 to correspond to a possible A or 1. Carry a single subdivision in your mind or make it part of the larger division. Some instructors accept and advise a single subdivision when it is to serve as one example or one illustration, since an outline can be a plan of additions as well as of divisions; however, such an example or illustration can usually be incorporated as part of a larger division.

Advisable
  I. Major reason for accidents: drivers at fault
  II. Minor reason for accidents: roads and highways at fault
  III. Proposed solution: better driver training

*Kinds of Restaurants*

Advisable
  I. Those specializing in American food
  II. Those specializing in foreign foods

A. Italian (Antonelli's in Pittsburgh for spaghetti)
B. Chinese (Fu Yung in St. Louis for chop suey)
C. Swedish (Swenson's in Detroit for smörgåsbord)

5. *Avoid meaningless headings* such as *Introduction, Body, Conclusion.* If you know what these parts are to contain, put your ideas into words and use them as headings. Avoid even such headings as *Reasons, Causes, Results, Effects,* unless you accompany them with explanatory material or subheads.

6. If your theme is to contain short introductory and concluding paragraphs, you need not indicate such paragraphs by outline topics. For example, the article written from the outline "Why 'Go On' with Latin?" on pp. 32–33 has a brief introductory paragraph of 44 words and a brief concluding paragraph of 59 words.

**6g   *Use a* thesis sentence *in the preparation or development of your outline***

Many writers like to use a *thesis sentence,* one sentence providing the gist of the whole paper or a kind of topic sentence (see Section 23) not for one paragraph but for all. The thesis sentence may summarize a writer's thinking before he begins making his outline or it may serve to tie together his various thoughts after the outline has been written. Your instructor may ask you to prepare a thesis sentence and to place it between title and outline. An example of a thesis sentence is given preceding the outline for "University Days" on p. 33.

You may, of course, write your thesis sentence from a tentative or final outline. If you thoughtfully prepare your thesis sentence first, it may make your preparation of an outline easy. Study the closeness of the thesis sentence and the outline of "University Days," p. 33. Note also there and in the example below that the main-heading topics or sentences add up to the thesis sentence.

The specific thesis sentence for "Let's Take the Boys Camping," pp. 23–24, develops into the following outline:

I. Participation in competitive athletics
   A. Softball (team effort)
   B. Swimming (two or many competitors)

      C. Tennis and horseshoes (two or four contestants)
  II. Sharing of noncompetitive athletic activities
      A. Rowing and canoeing
      B. Hiking and woodcraft
 III. Instruction in handicrafts (woodcarving, carpentry, ceramics, cooking)
 IV. Guidance in mental activities
      A. Reading appropriate books
      B. Participating in group discussions

### 6h   Write your theme from your outline, using the method most efficient for you

Now you are ready to begin writing, unless you wish to consider in advance the principle of proportion (see Sections **7a** and **b**).

Like professional writers, students differ in their abilities: some write easily and rapidly; others write slowly and painstakingly, revising as they go. Even a professional writer cannot plan, write, and proofread all at one time. Perhaps the best plan to follow is this: First, gather material for your theme and then plan and arrange it. Next, write the theme with all the vigor and interest you can. If you are a slow, methodical writer, you may wish to compose carefully each phrase, clause, and sentence, checking for spelling, grammar, punctuation, and word use as you go. Or if you want to get something down on paper, as many writers do, and not break your train of thought, proceed as rapidly as you can without paying special attention to grammatical, stylistic, or mechanical details until your first draft is finished.

Simply follow the plan that best assures your writing a good theme. After that, and preferably some time later, revise your theme carefully before you make the final copy. (See Section **16**.)

### EXERCISES

A. Make correct topic outlines for the three themes indicated by the topics you chose in Exercise B on p. 28.

B. Make correct sentence outlines for the five themes that you could write on the topics chosen in Exercise A on p. 28.

C. Make a paragraph outline of one of the articles (not too short, not too long) in your book of readings or a current magazine.

D. Change the paragraph outline (Exercise C) into a sentence outline.

E. Change the sentence outline (Exercise D) into a topic outline.

# 7 *Proportion*

The principle of proportion is that of giving any part of a theme the space and attention appropriate to reader and to subject.

## 7a Develop divisions of a theme in proportion to their importance

Proportion concerns the amount of space, or details of treatment, for the various parts of a composition. It requires that the development given each division of a theme—each paragraph or each group of paragraphs—be in accord with the relative importance of the division. Note the word *relative*; importance is not absolute. In determining which parts of a theme should be developed at length and which less fully, you must be guided by the *purpose* of the theme and the *readers* for whom it is written. Ordinarily, do not give disproportionate space to less closely related or minor sections of your theme or to material which your reader already knows. Ordinarily, also, give greater space to sections which may be difficult to understand otherwise or which are to be emphasized.

If, for example, your purpose in writing on "TV Advertising" is to show that such advertising is overdone, your theme will be badly proportioned if you devote more than half the space to a discussion of the origin and growth of general advertising—and you will violate unity as well (Section 9). Similarly, if you are writing a theme on "Campus Customs" for your classmates, you can appropriately give less space to many important details well known to them than if you are writing on the same subject for high school students. Even for your classmates, if you argue for the abandoning of certain customs and the retaining of others, the ones you wish to change will get more space than the ones with which you have no quarrel.

## 7b   *Use an outline to give your theme proportion*

A good outline enables you to achieve proper order, proportion, and appropriate length—an adequate number of words for each major division and subdivision for purposes of clearness and effectiveness.

Careful planning helps you to write a well-balanced paper, neither too long nor too short. If you do not follow some guide to proportion, you may write a narrative of five pages, of which four deal with relatively unimportant details and only one with the really important part of the story. Or in an expository theme, you may write 400 words of introductory material and then realize that you have only 100 left, into which you may attempt to compress important ideas that needed most of the 400-word space.

As a practical suggestion for proportion, place in parentheses after each part of your outline the number of words you plan to write on that division or subdivision. The sum of the subdivision words should equal the major division; the sum of the major divisions should equal the total number of words required. This allocation is, of course, only tentative; you may find expansion or contraction necessary. (For an example of such an allocation, see the outline of "Why 'Go On' with Latin?" on pp. 32–33.)

## EXERCISES

A. On the topic outline you have prepared in Exercise E, on p. 41, write after each of your main divisions and subdivisions the approximate number of words used by the author. Study this word-numbered outline with the article from the point of view of proper or inadequate proportion.

B. Count the number of words in each paragraph of three of your recent themes. Put the numbers after the appropriate divisions in the outlines for these themes. Comment in a paragraph or two on your use of proportion, giving consideration to both subject and reader.

# 8 Beginning and ending the theme

After gathering, outlining, and proportioning content, you must *begin* the composition and, later, *end* it.

A theme *does* have a beginning, a middle, and an end. Avoid the mistake of thinking that the body of a theme is its only important element and that beginnings and endings may be tacked on as appendages. Just as prefixes and suffixes are real parts of words, the introduction and conclusion of a theme are genuinely important to the theme as a whole. Indeed, because of their position, they receive more than usual attention and are remembered—somewhat as are first and last impressions of people we meet.

Do not, however, write a *formal* introduction or conclusion unless your theme actually requires one or the other, or both. Usually, only long papers—such as a report on research or a lengthy critical essay—require an elaborate beginning involving general statements, an explanation of terms and details, or comments on the history and significance of the subject. Similarly, a short composition normally requires no ceremonial conclusion. Except in argumentative writing (which is rare in most freshman composition classes), little excuse exists for concluding remarks like "thus we see" and "in conclusion, let me state." When you have said all you intended to say, all that needs saying, *stop*. Reflect on the guest who lingered at the door, mumbling, "There was something else I wanted to say," to which the hostess aptly responded, "Perhaps it was 'good-by.'"

If a theme does require a formal beginning or ending, remember that neither should be wordy, vague, and rambling or, conversely, abrupt and confusing. The beginning and ending of a well-written theme often are interchangeable because both are direct, forceful, and clear statements or illustrations of ideas to be expressed or of those which have been developed. Further, each should be an actual part of the theme, an organic element of the whole composition, not an unnecessary exercise in warming up or cooling off.

## 8a Avoid a beginning referring indirectly and vaguely to the title

Since the title is independent of the composition, the opening sentences should be fully self-explanatory. The reader should not have to refer to the title for the reference of pronouns like "this," "that," "such," or for the meaning of openings like "This subject . . .," "On that trip . . .," "Such a happening . . .," "These evils . . . ." Here are four fully understandable opening sentences preferable to the foregoing beginnings:

Collecting old silver coins is a fascinating hobby.
Our trip to Montreal was both exciting and frustrating.
The head-on collision of rioters and police could have been avoided.
The evils of TV advertising are numerous and obvious.

## 8b   *Begin themes directly and clearly*

The beginning of a theme should have only one purpose: orientation of the reader. At the end of the first paragraph you have written, ask yourself: "Does my reader have his bearings?" "Have I made it clear where he is in this discussion and in what direction he is moving?" If not, your opening is neither clear nor direct and you should scrap what you have written and start over.

Direct and clear beginnings that avoid false starts and loose generalities are of many kinds, and the opening sentence, when appropriate and effective, may be a declarative, imperative, interrogative, or exclamatory one. Here are 15 suggestions for consideration—types of openings which can be applied to different kinds of themes and which can be adapted or modified to suit the particular purpose of a given composition.

### 1. *Repetition of the title in the opening sentence*

The method of scientific investigation is nothing but the expression of the necessary mode of working of the human mind. . . .
—THOMAS HENRY HUXLEY, "The Method of Scientific Investigation"

Does history repeat itself? In our western world in the eighteenth and nineteenth centuries, this question used to be debated as an academic exercise. . . .
—ARNOLD J. TOYNBEE, "Does History Repeat Itself?"

### 2. *Rephrasing or paraphrasing the title in the opening sentence*

The White Star liner *Titanic,* largest ship the world had ever known, sailed from Southampton on her maiden voyage to New York on April 10, 1912. . . .   —HANSON W. BALDWIN, "R. M. S. *Titanic*"

The difficulty in approaching the question of the relations between Religion and Science is, that its elucidation requires that we have in our minds some clear idea of what we mean by either of the terms, "religion" and "science." . . .

—ALFRED NORTH WHITEHEAD, "Religion and Science"

## 3. A setting or framework within which the subject will develop

At this moment of time, when humanity stands upon the threshold of space and has already launched its first vehicles beyond the atmosphere, there is a centuries-old question which presses more and more urgently for an answer. In almost any astronomy book you will find a chapter devoted to the subject: "Is there life on other worlds?"—the answer given depending upon the optimism of the author and the period in which he is writing (for there are fashions in astronomy as in everything else) .    —ARTHUR C. CLARKE, "Where's Everybody?"

To most people, I fancy, the stars are beautiful; but if you ask why, they would be at a loss to reply, until they remembered what they had heard about astronomy, and the great size and distance and possible habitation of those orbs. The vague and illusive ideas thus aroused fall in so well with the dumb emotion we were already feeling, that we attribute this emotion to those ideas, and persuade ourselves that the power of the starry heavens lies in the suggestion of astronomical facts.    —GEORGE SANTAYANA, "The Stars"

## 4. A summary or outline paragraph enumerating the main divisions to be discussed

Two things become increasingly evident as the sickness of our American democracy approaches its inevitable crisis: one is the surpassing genius of the founders of this Republic; the other is the transience of even the greatest of political resolutions. . . .

—ARCHIBALD MAC LEISH, "Loyalty and Freedom"

Having finished one semester at Atwood University, I believe that the three most important things I have learned are the following: how to study properly, how to work together with other people, and how to assume responsibilities.

—Student theme, "A Review of My First Semester in College"

## 5. First person (I, we)

The day I was graduated from college I believed—modestly, and yet with a nice warm glow of conviction—that I was an educated young

woman. I had salted away an impressive supply of miscellaneous information. My mind, after constant limbering up with fancy mental gymnastics, was as supple as a ballerina. I was all set to deal with Life.
—MARION WALKER ALCARO, "Colleges Don't Make Sense"

We do not think enough about thinking, and much of our confusion is the result of current illusions in regard to it. Let us forget for the moment any impressions we may have derived from the philosophers, and see what seems to happen in ourselves. . . .
—JAMES HARVEY ROBINSON, "On Various Kinds of Thinking"

## 6. Second person (you)

It finally happened. After months, maybe years, of watching the other fellow squirm on a platform, you've been called upon to make a speech. . . .                          —Anonymous, "Our Speaker Is . . ."

Suppose that some morning you should awaken in a place you have never been before; everything is new to you. Around you is a strange field, with unfamiliar creatures moving in it. You see objects which you do not recognize, and hear sounds which you cannot interpret. What would you do? . . .
—JULIAN ROSS, "Philosophy and Literature"

NOTE: Use the *you* beginning carefully and appropriately, not as an impertinent or buttonholing device to involve your reader by mechanical means. Make sure that the *you* is a genuine and appropriate address to your reader, that the *you* and the problem stated really concern him.

Ineffective and inappropriate for most readers
    Have you ever built a bird house?
    Have you ever climbed a mountain peak in the Himalaya Mountains?
    Did you know that the air we breathe is often called ozone?

Appropriate
    Your local, state, and national taxes are high and may go higher. What are you going to do about them? (Group of tax-paying citizens)
    Are you observing the necessary precautions for safety in your school laboratory? (Laboratory students)
    Your eyes are your most precious possession. Learn about them and their proper care. (College students)

7. *A significant or startling statement;* such a statement should not be used for attention and interest alone; it should have some connection with what is to follow.

Does a college education unfit women for their role as wives and mothers? A good many people seem to think so. . . .

—MIRRA KOMAROVSKY, "What Should Colleges Teach Women?"

Washington is the last person you would ever suspect of having been a young man with all the bright hopes and black despairs to which youth is subject. In American folklore he is known only as a child or a general or an old, old man: priggish hero of the cherry-tree episode, commander-in-chief, or the Father of his Country, writing a farewell address. . . .

—SAMUEL ELIOT MORISON, "The Young Man Washington"

8. *Timely news events or seasonal occurrences*

The two greatest nations in the world are now preparing to land men on the Moon within the next decade. This will be one of the central facts of political life in the years to come; indeed, it may soon dominate human affairs. . . .

—ARTHUR C. CLARKE, "The Uses of the Moon" [1961]

Every fall on every college campus you can see them—the hordes of incoming freshmen. In the excitement, the welter of new experiences and sensations, they are not aware that they are beginning the four most traumatic years of their lives.

—JAMES FEIBLEMAN, "What Happens in College"

9. *Reference to a historical event*

Andrew Jackson has long been the symbol of fighting democracy in American political life. On the lips of Democratic spellbinders his name is a call-to-arms: Jefferson, the sage of Monticello, is the serene philosopher of democracy, but Jackson is the militant champion, rude, brawling, and irresistible. . . .

—ARTHUR M. SCHLESINGER, JR., "The Legacy of Andrew Jackson"

More than three centuries ago a handful of pioneers crossed the ocean to Jamestown and Plymouth in search of freedoms they were unable to find in their own countries, the freedoms we still cherish today: freedom from want, freedom from fear, freedom of speech, freedom of religion. . . .     —SEYMOUR ST. JOHN, "The Fifth Freedom"

## 10. An illustrative incident or anecdote, personal or impersonal

Some time ago guards at Independence Hall in Philadelphia noticed that a graying, shabby little woman came in frequently to visit this national shrine. Then they discovered that on occasion she would leave a dollar bill beside the Liberty Bell. Questioned, the refugee from an Iron Curtain country explained in halting English, "Now I know what freedom mean to me. I give something back."
—PAUL FRIGGENS, "Sacred Hall of Independence"

## 11. A combination of narrative and descriptive details

Late last autumn, when the first snow flurries dusted across the northern half of the United States, an estimated three million pairs of knees began to twitch. This mass flexing was the first symptom of a seasonal phenomenon that has progressed in twenty years from the status of a foreign foolishness to that of a national mania. Although still in early stages of development, this phenomenon has reversed migratory instincts, cut scars in the faces of ancient mountains, created an economic revolution in rural areas, upped the income of the medical profession, and released several million inmates of modern society into flights of ecstatic freedom.    —ERIC SWENSON, "Let Fly Downhill"

## 12. References to people—contemporary or historical, prominent or unknown

When I was in St. Augustine, Florida, in the winter of 1932, Helen Keller appeared at the Cathedral Lyceum, and I went to see and hear her there, drawn by curiosity, such as one feels for any world-famous person.    —VAN WYCK BROOKS, "Helen Keller"

Some years ago, in one of his wittier columns, James Reston pointed out that the American language is suffering from inflation. He deployed our tendency to elevate the janitor to the post of Custodial Engineer and the file clerk to the position of Records Supervisor.
—ROBERT CLUETT, "Language Inflation"

## 13. Directly or indirectly quoted material of some kind or the report of a conversation or interview

When a Frenchman wants to explain his country, he speaks simply of *"la belle France."* The Britisher says, "There'll always be an England." These and other nations of the earth can tell a lot about themselves just by the use of the proper names. But the citizen of the U.S. has a different problem. . . .

—The Editors of *Fortune*, "The American Way of Life"

"Nobody warned me about a thing before I went to a near-slum district in Brooklyn," the young schoolteacher said. "I was full of ideals, and after six months I was certain I just couldn't stand another day of it. I made myself stick—I told myself that my ideals wouldn't be worth much if I didn't fight for them, and I stayed on for four years before I gave up. . . ." —*Time* Magazine, "Boys and Girls Together"

NOTE: Much overused is the beginning using a quotation from a dictionary. Avoid such beginnings as "According to the dictionary . . .," "*Webster's Seventh New Collegiate Dictionary* says that . . .," etc.

## 14. *Creation of suspense*

In Moulmein, in Lower Burma, I was hated by large numbers of people—the only time in my life that I have been important enough for this to happen to me.     —GEORGE ORWELL, "Shooting an Elephant"

Have you ever wondered what would have happened if the people who are in charge of television today were passing on the draft of the Declaration of Independence?

—ART BUCHWALD, "Let's See Who Salutes"

## 15. *Posing a Problem*

I wish to argue an unpopular cause: the cause of the old, free elective system in the academic world, or the untrammeled right of the undergraduate to make his own mistakes. . . .

—HOWARD MUMFORD JONES, "Undergraduates on Apron Strings"

I believe in art for art's sake. It is an unfashionable belief, and some of my statements should be of the nature of an apology. . . .

—E. M. FORSTER, "Art for Art's Sake"

## 8c   *End themes effectively*

Remember that formal endings in ordinary themes are rarely necessary but that every composition does come to a conclusion, one which should not be overly abrupt, incomplete, or excessively wordy. The final paragraph of a theme should provide an effect of completion, of having rounded off a topic and reached a goal. Perhaps the most effective ending is one that brings the reader back to some phase of the main thought or leaves him with an idea that is a direct contribution to the subject being discussed. Possibly the most ineffective endings are those that are wordily unnecessary or that introduce some totally new subject or unrelated idea.

Ten specific methods for ending themes effectively are illustrated in the following closing sentences. Alone or in combination, they may be adapted to suit the particular purposes of a given composition.

## 1. Use of the appropriate kind of sentence

. . . Remember, then, that the more you study and learn in high school, the less trouble you will have when you come to college. [Imperative sentence]
—Student theme, "Advice to a High School Freshman"

The "mass mind" is a delusion. How many dictators have been amazed when their rule, which seemed so strong, has collapsed in a few hours, without a friend? [Interrogative sentence]
—JOYCE CARY, "The Mass Mind: A Piece of Modern Nonsense"

## 2. Use of the appropriate personal pronoun

The public as a whole—that is, the public barring the Intellectual Snobs—shows its sensible preference for having its artists in sufficient possession of their faculties to put us all, and immediately, in possession of their meaning. The artist who does not know his own intentions is a pretender. If he does know them and cannot express them, he is merely incompetent.

I hope I have made myself plain.
—IVOR BROWN, "The Case for Greater Clarity in Writing"

And, reader and writer, we can wish each other well. Don't we after all want the same thing? A story of beauty and passion and truth?
—EUDORA WELTY, "The Reading and Writing of Short Stories"

What the reader should strive for, then, is a more *active* kind of listening. Whether you listen to Mozart or Duke Ellington, you can deepen your understanding of music not only by being a more conscious and aware listener—not someone who is just listening, but someone who is listening *for* something.

—AARON COPLAND, "How We Listen"

## 3. *Reference to or restatement of title or central idea*

. . . Only the free can be educated, but only the truly educated will find the spiritual spark of genius and morality necessary to remain free.

—SIDNEY J. FRENCH, "Only the Educated Shall Remain Free"

## 4. *A summarizing or clinching of the theme of the article*

There is still much to deplore about my education. I shall never read Latin verse in the original or have a taste for the Brontës, and these are crippling lacks. But all handicaps have compensations and I have learned to accept both cheerfully. To have first met Dickens, Austen, and Mark Twain when I was capable of giving them the full court curtsey is beatitude enough for any reader. Blessed are the illiterate, for they shall inherit the word.

—PHYLLIS MC GINLEY, "The Consolations of Illiteracy"

## 5. *An outline sentence or paragraph enumerating the main divisions that have been discussed*

Friendliness and enthusiasm are twin horses for your chariot in reaching your listeners' minds and hearts. Look and act as if you're pleased to face this group. To add it all up: (1) have something important to say; (2) prepare carefully; (3) deliver your talk convincingly, sincerely. —Anonymous, "Our Speaker Is . . ."

## 6. *A direct or indirect quotation*

. . . Language communicates most effectively to those who love it, just as food more easily nourishes a man who is hungry. And, as Mr. Orson Welles was asking recently, "If a man cannot communicate, can he be expected to control his destiny?"

—JOHN WAIN, "An Instrument of Communication"

## 7. *A generalized statement or logical conclusion growing out of the material presented*

One is forced to the conclusion that the American woman—according to the advertisements—has a wonderful life until she's twenty-five. After that she'd better be dead.

—AGNES ROGERS ALLEN, "Is It Anyone We Know?"

. . . His country could and almost did fail Washington; but Washington could not fail his country, or disappoint the expectations of his kind. A simple gentleman of Virginia with no extraordinary talents had so disciplined himself that he could lead an insubordinate and divided people into ordered liberty and enduring union.

—SAMUEL ELIOT MORISON, "The Young Man Washington"

## 8. *A statement of significance, some new or practical application, or a linking of the subject with some matter of current interest*

One thing is certain: men are no longer taking grass for granted, and we have only begun to discover what may be done with the commonest and potentially the most valuable of all our plants.

—MILO PERKINS, "Grass Made to Your Order"

You can't escape reading fifteen minutes a day, and that means you will read half a book a week, two books a month, twenty a year, and 1,000 or more in a reading lifetime. It's an easy way to become well read.     —LOUIS SHORES, "How To Find Time To Read"

## 9. *Offering a warning*

Most important of all, the contest for technical pre-eminence must not lead us into the trap of encouraging that type of technician who has been called the "skilled barbarian"—the specialist tightly fitted into his own slot and serenely indifferent to the "unscientific" turmoil in which the rest of us live. Such a luxury we can ill afford.

—GEORGE S. ODIORNE, "The Trouble with Engineers"

. . . There is hope that law, rather than private force, may come to govern the relations of nations within the present century. If this hope is not realized, we face utter disaster; if it is realized, the world will be far better than at any previous period in the history of man.

—BERTRAND RUSSELL, "The Future of Man"

## 10. *Suggesting a course of action or giving advice*

. . . Educators now find that what was once the recreation of students in school has been transformed into a responsibility of the educational system to supply the public with entertainment. It is essential that educators carry through a fundamental revision of concepts of athletic management appropriate to this transformation.

—HAROLD W. STOKE, "College Athletics: Education or Show Business"

## EXERCISES

A. Choose five articles from your book of readings or from current magazines (like *The Atlantic Monthly, Harper's Magazine, The Saturday Evening Post, Holiday, The National Geographic Magazine*) . Study their beginnings. (1) What methods or combination of methods do they use to begin directly and clearly? (2) Have you found other methods in addition to those listed and illustrated in Section **8b?**

B. Examine the endings of the articles that you chose in Exercise A. (1) What methods or combination of methods are used to achieve effective endings? (2) Are there other methods in addition to those listed and illustrated in Section **8c?**

C. From articles in magazines or in your book of readings find five examples of beginnings and five examples of endings using personal pronouns. Label the kinds of pronouns.

D. Which of the following theme beginnings are direct and clear and which are not? Give your reasons.

1. Have you ever thought what life was like on the earth ten million years ago?
2. Three important steps toward effective studying are selecting a definite place to study, planning ahead, and concentrating.
3. Naturally, the answer to the above question is no. (Theme title: a question)
4. I think this is one of the most important questions a high school graduate can ask himself. (Theme title: "Am I Ready for College?")
5. I have known my roommate for only three weeks, but I wish I had never met him at all.

E. Which of the following theme endings are effective and which are not? Give your reasons.

1. Experiments in teaching tricks to animals are most enjoyable to me. Why don't you try them? You might enjoy them, too.

2. Then the band began to play the recessional, and the line of graduates began to move. I smiled, and we walked forward to meet tomorrow. (Theme title: "Graduation Day")
3. In the two adjoining towns, which are only five or six miles away from my home, several churches can be found.
4. After this brief introduction, I hope you know a little more about the Philadelphia of the past and of the present.
5. I have almost completed my first semester in college, and seven more await me. However, I have learned three important things in one short semester: how to study, how to manage money, and how to enjoy college.

# 9  *Unity* (*oneness*)

Unity means *oneness, singleness of purpose,* or, as the *New World Dictionary* defines it, "an arrangement of parts or material that will produce a single, harmonious design or effect in an artistic or literary production." Unity applies to the theme, to the paragraph (Section 25), and to the sentence (Section 34).

A *theme* (a short paper, a composition in words) contains and treats a *theme* (subject of a discussion, meditation, composition). Keep in mind constantly "the *theme* within the *theme*" so that you will treat a *single* phase of one subject. A composition should clearly and fully develop this one phase, should stick to the oneness of its central idea, should be guided by its controlling purpose. If it does, it has unity.

## 9a  *Discuss in your theme only one phase of a subject*

A writer is not likely to violate unity so grossly as to discuss completely unrelated subjects, such as a game of professional football in a composition whose theme is the horrors of nuclear warfare. The danger is that he may thoughtlessly slip from one phase of his subject into another phase which is remotely related but which has no bearing upon the central theme. Nothing is more confusing or irritating to a reader than the insertion of irrelevant detail whose connection with the main theme is not clear.

Unity in a longer piece of writing is violated in three ways:

1. An irrelevant introduction or a useless conclusion is tacked on to meet a word quota (see Sections 8b, 8c).

2. Material that has little to do with the subject is included merely for its own sake or for padding. When a student has a scarcity of ideas and a great need for words, he may fill a paragraph or two with material that deals with a phase of the subject other than the one being treated. As an illustration, many student-written book reviews give too much space to facts about the author and too little space to the book. A student writing on the subject "The Ingenuity of Robinson Crusoe on the Desert Island" began his theme: "Before giving a discussion of Robinson Crusoe's ingenuity on the deserted island, I think it well to give the main facts of Daniel Defoe's life." Over half the paper was devoted to Defoe's biography.

3. Material is included which bears on the general subject but which has little bearing on the particular topic discussed. The writer, forgetting or ignoring his outline, may be misled by his train of ideas and may include a paragraph or paragraphs of material not necessary and not related. For example, the title of a theme is "My High School," and the particular phase of the subject is the *instruction* in the school. The purpose of the theme is to show that the school the student attended gave him instruction that enables him to do his college work successfully. Discussion of courses, of teachers, of educational facilities like the library is needed, but if the student includes paragraphs describing the school plant, its playgrounds, and the like, he has shifted the purpose, the central idea, of the theme.

Unity, then, as applied to the theme, means the use of paragraphs properly developing the subject. Violations of unity within the paragraph and within the sentence are discussed in Sections 25 and 34.

### 9b  *Give your theme unity of purpose and tone*

In addition to treating a single phase of one subject, you should seek to achieve also a threefold general purpose:

1. If you wish to inform, amuse, interest, satirize, persuade, convince, or arouse to action, be consistent in this aim of your writing.

2. Decide on the basic form of writing that you will use (see Section 17). If you plan to write narration, do not overburden your writing with description. If you plan to explain, do not become involved in detailed arguments. If you plan to argue, do not

introduce anecdotes which have little or no bearing on the evidence.

3. Make your theme consistent in its *tone* or *mood* (see Section 14e). Do not unnecessarily mix tragedy and comedy, pathos and satire, humor and stateliness, reverence and irreverence, dignity and absurdity, or any two similar extremes. For examples: a serious paper on Abraham Lincoln's last day should not introduce the humorous anecdotes Lincoln was fond of, nor should a fair-minded discussion of international relations on the campus include comical or satirical stories about any particular race or nation.

## EXERCISES

A. Show how a theme may lack unity even if all its component sentences and paragraphs are themselves unified.

B. Considering unity, discuss the place or use of the following paragraph—it was the third paragraph—in a theme on "City Life Is the Life for Me":

I have always enjoyed meeting people and having many friends. I believe that one may always benefit from one's acquaintances in one manner or another. Every acquaintance a person may make teaches that person something. The acquaintance may be a professor who will educate one from books or a man whose pleasing personality may teach one to make his life pleasant for other people or maybe a self-centered egotist whose unpleasantness may teach one tolerance.

C. Why does the following theme lack unity (Section 9) and proportion (Section 7)?

*The Inventor of the Automobile*
  I. The inventor of the automobile
 II. Menace to humanity
III. Increasing popularity

Credit is usually given to a group of men who were said to have invented the automobile. These 15 or 20 inventors each contributed something toward the invention of the automobile. The period of years for the contributions of these inventors fell between the years of 1880 and 1903. These inventors gained significance by the invention of a horseless carriage or a motor-driven vehicle. However, the latest facts prove that a man named Siegfried Marcus should receive full credit for the invention. In 1861 the first automobile chugged down the street in a small town in Germany. This information has been presented quite recently, and has startled many automobile fans.

In the first years of automobiles, people were decidedly against them. Automobiles were declared a menace to humanity. Farmers were constantly suing drivers for scaring their chickens and horses. A few states tried to obtain laws against automobiles, but did not succeed.

As time went by, the public gradually realized that automobiles were becoming more useful. Roads and other conditions were now in favor of the automobile instead of against it.

# 10  Coherence

Coherence, meaning "holding together," is an essential quality of a good theme because without coherence no clear communication of thought passes from writer to reader. The thoughtful writer remembers that he is attempting to *transfer* ideas to a reader. In a coherent theme each paragraph must grow out of the preceding one, and each group of paragraphs dealing with one division of the theme must be clearly connected with other paragraph groups, just as within each paragraph each sentence is logically and coherently related to the sentences that precede and follow. A composition is coherent, therefore, when its parts have been so carefully woven together that the reader is never confused about the relationships of ideas.

## 10a  Check your theme and your outline for orderly arrangement

Steps unrelated or arranged in a puzzling order confuse your reader. Test each part of your outline, the arrangement of paragraphs, the arrangement of sentences within each paragraph. Does each element lead logically and clearly to the element that follows? Make sure not only that you have *order* in the theme but that you *reveal* this order.

## 10b  Do not leave any missing links in thought

In writing a composition, remember that your reader cannot read your mind. The omission of ideas that are clear to you will leave him confused; you must include these ideas.

Sometimes connection between paragraphs, or between sentences in the same paragraph, is faulty because the writer fails to give all pertinent details of relation. For example, one paragraph may discuss the value of superhighways, and the next may discuss them as a menace to life and property. The reader naturally asks "Why?" A link has been left out in the thought and must be filled in with, perhaps, a statement that superhighways, because they are a temptation to speed and reckless driving, are a menace as well as an asset. Or a student, writing on "Rules for Safe Driving," may jump from a paragraph dealing with the running of red lights and stop signs to a paragraph discussing ice and snow. The relation of the two paragraphs should be made clear in some such manner as this: "In addition to observance of traffic lights and signs, certain precautions are necessary also because of road conditions."

# 11  Transition

Since good writing is characterized by skill in the revelation of thought relationships, transitional aids are indispensable to the writer who wishes clearly, smoothly, and effectively to *communicate* his thoughts, and the exact shadings of his thoughts, to his reader. In other words, transition is closely related to coherence (Section **10**) : between paragraphs, between sentences, and within sentences it is an important aid to attaining coherence.

*Trans* literally means *over, across, beyond, on,* or *to the other side of. Transition,* in general, means passage or change from one position, part, place, state, stage, or type to another.

Applied to writing, transition means showing evidence of the links or bridges between related units. This evidence—a word, phrase, clause, sentence, or group of sentences—may link parts of sentences or two sentences; it may link paragraphs. When we say that a theme should be coherent, we mean in part that the paragraphs should be properly tied together. If the order of the sentences within the paragraph is clear and fully logical, then the secret of coherence lies in the uses of transitional devices between the paragraphs. The progress of thought must actually be *marked* so that the reader will immediately know when one point has been finished and another is taken up. Transition within or between sentences is discussed in Section **42**; the following sections deal with transitions between paragraphs.

**11a** *Make the relationship between paragraphs*
*clear by using transitional words, phrases,*
*clauses, sentences, and short paragraphs*

Shifts in thought are always puzzling to a reader unless he is prepared in advance for them. Transitions are similar in function to signs on highways, such as "CURVE, 100 YARDS" or "SLOW: DOUBLE LANE ENDS." By definition, a paragraph is a sentence or a series of sentences dealing with one part of a larger topic. When the discussion of this part has been finished, the careful writer so informs his reader and prepares him for the next part of the discussion. Sometimes he finds it necessary to sum up what has been said. More often he uses the beginning of the new paragraph to point out the road to be followed: a continuation in the same direction, a pause to give examples, a reversing to show contrast, a paralleling to make a comparison. Such direction-pointing to the reader is a major aid to clearness and effectiveness.

Important as transitions are, they should be relatively brief and inconspicuous. Virtually a mechanical feature of style designed to make the machinery run smoothly and easily, they should not protrude so awkwardly that they distract the reader's attention from ideas. Since transition reveals relationships, transitional devices are inherent in the material, should grow out of the nature of the material, and need only be put into adequate words to show the already existing relationships.

Devices to accomplish bridging between paragraphs are the following:

*1. Transitional words and phrases.* Most transitional words are conjunctions—pure, correlative, conjunctive adverb, subordinating—and most transitional phrases serve the purposes of conjunctions. For a fairly complete list of transitional words arranged according to their relationship-uses, see Section **84**.

The following classification is merely suggestive and lists some of the more common transitional phrases, not single words.

Addition or in the same or similar or parallel direction: *and then, another reason, equally important, in addition, in like manner, in the second place, in the next place, of course.*

Comparison or example: *as an illustration, for instance, for example, by way of comparison.*

Contrast: *on the other hand, on the contrary, in contrast, by contrast.*

Reason, result, purpose, cause, summary: *as a result, from what has been said, in brief, in conclusion, in short, most of all, to sum up, to summarize.*

NOTE: Additional transitional relationships are: alternation, affirmative or negative; concession; condition; manner, place, time (see Section **84a,b,c,e**).

Employed at the beginning of a paragraph, although not necessarily as the opening words, such connectives serve to link what is to follow with the thought in the preceding paragraph.

2. *Transitional sentences.* Such a sentence, frequently containing transitional words, comes usually at the beginning, rarely at the end, of a paragraph. In a complex sentence, the dependent clause may be merely parenthetic (*as I said* or *as was indicated*), but it is usually more important in that it looks to the preceding paragraph, while the independent clause looks forward.

*Since it has been proved that Brookwood University needs new dormitories,* let us now discuss means of financing them. . . .

*If college activities are important on the intercollegiate level,* they are no less important on the intramural level. . . .

Or the first independent clause may look backward, the second forward:

*The greatness of a college depends not only upon its buildings and equipment; it depends also upon its faculty and students.*

*We have seen how words, phrases, and sentences can be used as transitional aids; let us now consider the transitional paragraph.* For clear and effective writing, . . .

3. *Transitional paragraphs.* Sometimes the shift in thought between two paragraphs, or two groups of paragraphs, is so

marked that a word or phrase, or even a sentence, is not sufficient fully to indicate transition. In this situation a short transitional paragraph of one or two sentences may be used to look back to the preceding paragraph, to give a summary of what has been said, or to point forward to the next paragraph and to suggest what is to follow. The second example under "Transitional sentences," just above, could have served as a transitional paragraph. The writer, considering effectiveness and appropriateness, must decide whether to paragraph such sentences separately or include them at the ending or, preferably, beginning of other paragraphs. In the following example, the italicized sentences are a transitional paragraph:

Four characteristics have been defined and discussed as marking the good theme: correctness, clearness, effectiveness, and appropriateness. If a theme lacks any one of these elements, it is not a good theme; if it lacks more than one, or lacks any one to an unusual degree, it is a very poor theme.

*These elements are essential. It now remains for us to apply each of these terms to such matters as diction, punctuation, and sentence structure.*

A good theme must be correct in its diction. Correct diction implies . . .

## 11b    Make the relationship between
##         paragraphs clear by repetition

Often transition may be shown by repetition of key words, especially key nouns, at the close of one paragraph and the beginning of the next—a method especially effective if the key word is also the subject of the composition. Pronouns are rarely effective for paragraph transitions. In fact, a fairly safe negative principle is this: Never begin a paragraph with a personal or demonstrative pronoun; the antecedent in the preceding paragraph is too far removed for the pronoun to be clear. Instead, an effective paragraph usually begins with a strong word or words, such as the topic of the paragraph and its relation to the topic of the theme. In the following examples, the repeated material is italicized:

*Three key safety elements* involved in curbing or preventing automobile accidents are important in promoting *highway safety: the car, the road, and the driver.*

The *first,* though perhaps least important, of these *safety elements* is *the car*—the detecting and repairing of mechanical defects. . . .

A *second* and more important element in *highway safety* is *the road* and its condition. . . .

But of the *three safety elements* involved—*the car, the road, and the driver*—safety authorities generally agree that *the driver himself* is the major cause of accidents. . . .

From the examples given, you will note that a combination of methods of paragraph transition (Section 11a,b) is not only possible but also coherent, clear, and effective.

## EXERCISE

In your book of readings or in the nonfiction articles of a current magazine, look for examples of the kinds of transitional devices described in Section 11a,b. Limit your search to transitional devices between paragraphs. Prepare for class a brief discussion of your findings.

# 12 Clearness

Correctness, clearness, effectiveness, and appropriateness are essentials of all good writing, but clearness is perhaps the most important. As British novelist Anthony Hope said, "Unless one is a genius, it is best to aim at being intelligible." If an idea, even if incorrectly and ineffectively expressed, is understood by others, communication, the purpose of all writing, has been achieved.

On the other hand, a theme may be substantially correct in its writing and not be clear to the reader. It is theoretically impossible for writing to be effective without being clear; yet many a reader has read and reread material obviously correct and seemingly emphatic without being able to understand its central meaning.

Thus, because clearness is essential, nearly every section of this book deals with it. In addition, two specific suggestions (Section **12a,b**) for attaining clearness deserve particular attention, and four suggestions (Section **13a,b,c,d**) give in some detail directions for clear *logical thinking.*

## 12a Restate in simple, direct language the meaning of any passage not clear

A sentence or series of sentences may be clear to you but not to your reader. Put yourself in his place and read through his eyes. Perhaps your instructor as "reader over your shoulder" may be implying, "This is almost or quite opaque," but what he will probably say is: "Now just tell me in your own words what you had in mind here." Such a secret thought and such a voiced comment concern the sentence or paragraph that is grammatically acceptable and seems to have a kind of meaning playing over its surface but which is still far from communicating anything definite. Use simple, direct language to make your meaning clear.

## 12b Define all terms that are not completely clear

A writer aiming at clearness never takes too much for granted; it is his responsibility to make sure that the reader understands.

Certain terms familiar to you may be foreign to your reader. Since thinking begins with terms (ideas, concepts, names), the reader cannot understand your thought unless he understands the terms used. Strange or unusual words puzzle him; even in context he may be unable to guess their meaning. An attentive reader should, of course, look up words if he expects to grow in wisdom and word power, but the writer should not assume that readers will take this trouble. Appropriateness of words for the occasion and to the reader is a fair test; you as writer should use words that you can reasonably expect the reader to understand.

If it is necessary to use technical words (terms peculiar to and generally understood only by members of a certain sect, class, or occupation), define them clearly. The following are not everyday words: *cassock, quinazoline, gravamen, counterpoint, idiopathy,* and *syncope.* If you use such words, define. Explain also common words used in a specialized way. But before defining, consider the reader or class of readers for whom you are writing; for example, if you are writing a paper for musicians, you need not explain words like *counterpoint.*

Even many common words that are seemingly clear can cause confusion. What do you mean precisely and what will your reader understand by *average person, typical college student, sincere, beauty, truth, justice, honor, patriotic, un-American*? (For clearness in word use, see Sections **61, 62, 63, 64, 65.**)

# 13  *Logical thinking*

"The man who can think clearly can talk and write clearly," says a present-day writer of wise sayings. Clear, orderly thinking must underlie effective writing and speaking. Its presence in the writing and speaking of others should similarly be evident as you read and listen.

## 13a  *Test your statements for evidence of clear, logical thinking*

In narrative (storytelling), description (word painting), and some forms of exposition (explanation), your material follows a clear, orderly plan—each part leading logically to the part that follows (see Section 6).

In other forms of exposition (such as fact-finding and accounts of experiments, in both of which a chain of reasoning is necessary to lead to a definite conclusion) and in argumentative writing or speaking (designed to convince or persuade of the truth or falsity of a proposal or statement), the process of clear thinking becomes more complicated than mere planning and arrangement.

Errors in thinking often occur in fact-finding and experiment-describing exposition and in argument, especially when the writer or speaker is concerned with establishing his "case" and yields to the temptation to ignore, twist, or even falsify the evidence. Some are errors in logic; others simply violate, purposely or unconsciously, plain common sense. For clear and straight thinking, therefore, guard against the errors briefly discussed below when you write or speak.[8] Train yourself also to look for *observance* or *violation* of straight thinking in the writings and speeches of others: fruitful sources to use are political speeches, letters to newspapers and magazines, and advertisements.

### 13b Understand what is meant by induction and deduction and by the applications of each

Two common methods of clear thinking, used and violated every day, are *induction* and *deduction*.

*Induction* seeks to establish a general truth, an all-embracing conclusion. The inductive process begins by using observation of a number of specific facts; it classifies these facts, looks for similarities among them, and from a sufficient number of these facts or particulars draws a conclusion or "leads into" a principle. Once the principle is stated, other particulars or examples are sought to support or verify it. The movement is always *from the particular to the general*.

*Deduction,* on the other hand, seeks to establish a specific conclusion by showing that it conforms to or "leads down from" a general truth or principle. The movement, implied or expressed, is always *from the general to the particular*.

Consider some examples of these processes. Very early in the history of the human race men became convinced from their ob-

---

[8] Those who do much writing and speaking of the kinds mentioned (exposition and argument) will find in the following books excellent extended treatments of methods for attaining clear thinking:

Altick, Richard D. "Patterns of Clear Thinking," chap. 3 of *Preface to Critical Reading,* 4th ed. (New York, 1960) .

Beardsley, Monroe C. *Thinking Straight: Principles of Reasoning for Readers and Writers,* 3rd ed. (Englewood Cliffs, N.J., 1966) .

Bilsky, Manuel. *Logic and Effective Argument* (New York, 1956) .

Black, Max. *Critical Thinking,* 2nd ed. (Englewood Cliffs, N.J., 1952) .

Boatright, Mody C. *Accuracy in Thinking* (New York, 1938) .

Chase, Stuart. *Guides to Straight Thinking, with 13 Common Fallacies* (New York, 1956) .

Emmet, E. R. *Thinking Clearly* (New York, 1959) .

Sherwood, John C. *Discourse of Reason: A Brief Handbook of Semantics and Logic* (New York, 1964) .

Thouless, Robert H. *How To Think Straight* (New York, 1939) .

Weinland, James D. *How To Think Straight* (Paterson, N.J., 1963) .

servation of many particular instances that no man lives forever, that sooner or later all men die. Through *inductive* thinking, then, mankind arrived at a general conclusion about itself, a conclusion that the Greek philosophers phrased: "All men are mortal." A generalization so well established that it no longer needs to be re-examined and tested to be widely believed is sometimes called a major premise, and is used as the starting point in a piece of *deductive* thinking. Thus in the light of the general truth that all men are mortal, we examine the particular truth that John Johnson is a man, and we conclude that John Johnson is mortal, that he will die sooner or later. This deductive process is as follows:

| | |
|---|---|
| *Major premise* | All men are mortal. |
| *Minor premise* | John Johnson is a man. |
| *Conclusion* | Therefore, John Johnson is mortal. |

Through *inductive* reasoning the "laws" (here meaning "principles" or "descriptive, generalized statements") of any science, such as medicine, biology, chemistry, or physics, have been arrived at; and through *deductive* reasoning they are being applied every day in particular situations—the development of a vaccine, the manufacture of a complex computer, the preparation and launching of space rockets. Such reasoning can be virtually foolproof in pure and applied science; loopholes often occur in the social sciences (language, history, politics, economics, psychology), where human beings and human behavior are concerned. But even there, many reasonable conclusions can be reached.

For example, consider the "laws" or "rules" (i.e., principles) of language: pronunciation, grammar, word use, punctuation. Even with the perversity and variations among human beings, which account for exceptions, there are enough examples to make possible some generalizations. If you examine carefully words like *cat, catty, stem, stemmed, dim, dimmer, hot, hottest, cut, cutting, infer, inferred, admit, admitting, admittance,* etc., noting likenesses and differences before and after certain endings are added you will reach the spelling conclusion or rule stated in Section 52e3.

So, too, with punctuation. Most students do not develop their own punctuation rules by *induction,* although they could if they wanted to spend the time and effort required. If you were to read several hundred pages of prose and note how the commas were used, you would doubtless reach as one conclusion the principle that a comma is usually placed after an introductory adverbial clause, a *when* or *if* or *although* or *because* clause at the beginning of a sentence. This process is also *descriptive.* You could then apply the principle *deductively* to your writing, a process which is also *prescriptive.* Ordinarily, however, you will be content to accept the generalization from your instructor or from a handbook, doing your inductive thinking in fields where principles have not been so thoroughly investigated and established.

### 13c  Train yourself to watch for inductive and deductive errors in writing and speaking

Trouble in clear thinking occurs with both induction and deduction.

1. The major error in induction is *hasty generalization*: observing only a few instances and then jumping to a dogmatic conclusion. What is the inductive evidence for labeling certain groups "absent-minded professors," "dumb blondes," "irresponsible women drivers," "teen-age gangsters"? Have enough specific examples been examined to justify such generalizations? What is the inductive evidence for "Every schoolboy knows . . ." or "All Americans realize . . ."?

Many proverbs and other general statements, as well as many popular superstitions, are often hasty-generalization errors, such as "Oh, well, you know how women are!" or "Isn't that just like a man?" or "Fools rush in where angels fear to tread" versus "Nothing ventured, nothing gained" or "Friday the 13th is always unlucky." A true proverb, warning also against all hasty generalizations, is this: "Let's remember that *one* swallow or *one* robin does not make a summer."

So, too, with *statistics* and *samplings.* When "statistics show . . .," what statistics? Who gathered them? Under what conditions? If 100 students chosen at random (out of 12,000) are interviewed and a majority favor a certain policy, is this policy the favored policy of the entire student body?

Also, if the generalization in the major premise of a syllogism is not true, any conclusion based upon it is unsound:

*Invalid*     All students who attend classes faithfully will receive high grades.
Henry attends classes faithfully.
Therefore, Henry will receive high grades.

2. The major error in deductive thinking is the *it-does-not-follow error (non sequitur)*, which in precise language is limited to deduction and which should not be used loosely as a label for any error in clear thinking. *Non sequitur* is an inference or conclusion that does not follow from the materials or premises upon which it is apparently based. It usually occurs because one of the premises is not stated but implied, or assumed to be true. Thus, in "John Johnson is mortal because he is a man," the major premise, that all men are mortal, has been irrefutably established. But in the statement "Joe Brown is a poor student because he is an athlete," has the statement "All athletes are poor students" been proved true? A deductive conclusion, then, based on a false major premise is one example of the *non sequitur* error. Also, when the minor premise is only apparently related to the major premise, the *non sequitur* error occurs. For example, many great men have been wretched penmen, but is anyone justified in inferring from his own bad penmanship that he, too, is destined to greatness? Such errors often arise when in the expressed or implied syllogism the words *all, some,* and *only* are used or understood:

*Valid*       All members of X Club are snobbish.
Mary is a member of X Club.
Therefore, Mary is snobbish.

*Invalid*     All members of X Club are snobbish.
Sue is not a member of X Club.
Therefore, Sue is not snobbish.

*Invalid*     Some members of X Club are snobbish.
Mary is a member of X Club.
Therefore, Mary is snobbish.

*Invalid*     Only members of X Club are snobbish.
Sue is not a member of X Club.
Therefore, Sue is not snobbish.

*Invalid*    Only students who attend classes faithfully receive high
             grades.
             Henry received a high grade.
             Therefore, he attended classes faithfully.

Other specific types of errors which may or may not relate to
induction and deduction but which violate principles of clear
thinking are the following:

3. A variation of the hasty-generalization error is the error
of *post hoc, ergo propter hoc* (Latin for "after this, therefore on
account of this"), a mistake in thinking which holds that a happening that precedes another must naturally be its cause, or that
when one happening follows another, the latter is the direct result of the first.

Many popular superstitions began or continue in this way:
"No wonder I had bad luck today; yesterday I walked under a
ladder [or saw a black cat cross my path, or drew the number 13,
or broke a mirror, etc.]." If you have a cold today, you must have
got your feet wet yesterday. Day follows night, or night follows
day—is one the cause of the other? The great ancient Roman Empire fell after the ascendancy of Christianity; would anyone argue
that Christianity was the cause? Some hurricanes, floods, and tornadoes followed a series of American atomic-explosion tests? Were
these tests the cause? Scientists competent in the field said no.

4. *Biased or suppressed evidence* should be guarded against
in any attempt to think clearly. Evidence consists of facts which
furnish ground for belief and which help to prove an assumption
or proposition. The use of biased evidence results in unwarranted
conclusions; it means that evidence for only one side of a problem is considered and that any evidence on the other side is suppressed or ignored. Suppression of evidence, in favor of another
view or casting some doubt on our own presentation, is completely dishonest, as in any changing or falsifying of evidence,
even slightly, to serve our own purpose.

Furthermore, *figures* or *statistics* themselves can lie if evidence is biased or suppressed.[9] Much of the so-called truth about
advertising or national income or the value of sports—or any writ-

9 Darrell Huff's "How To Lie with Statistics," *Harper's Magazine,*
August, 1950, gives an entertaining and revealing account of nine tricks by
which statistical presentations can be made misleading. (The article was
expanded into a book of the same name; New York, 1954.)

ing intended to sway the public—comes from biased sources, from paid propagandists and directly interested apologists. The testimony of enthusiastic fraternity members is insufficient in itself to support a contention that fraternities promote high scholarship; the evidence of girls who are not sorority members may be biased and insufficient to prove that sororities are socially undesirable.

Another excellent example of biased and suppressed evidence is the use of *a statement out of context,* ignoring any qualifying phrases. An advertisement might describe a book as "at last, the great American novel," thus distorting the complete statement: "This might have been, at last, the great American novel if the author had paid more careful attention to the development of his characters and the accurate portrayal of American life." Or an American statesman might be condemned for saying, "The United States will be a fifth-rate power in five years," unless we know that he also said in the same sentence, "if we do not keep in the forefront of scientific achievement and military preparedness."

5. *Not distinguishing fact from opinion* is an error appearing in much thinking. A *fact* is based on actuality and can be positively proved or verified. If it is a statistical fact—such as the population of a city, the number of students in a college or university, or the cost-of-living index for January in a specified year—it is the result of systematic enumeration and mathematical calculation. If it is a biographical or historical fact—the birth or death of George Washington, the outbreak of the Civil War, the stock market crash on October 29, 1929, the Normandy invasion in June, 1944, etc.—it is attested by a record of some sort: statements of witnesses or participants, a newspaper account, an entry in a private journal or letter, a government document, or, if we go back far enough in time, a tapestry, rock carving, or fossil. A generalization such as the one that all men are mortal is considered a fact only when the evidence in support of it is so overwhelming that its acceptance is virtually unanimous.

*Opinion,* on the other hand, is a personal inference or preference mingled in with a fact. That is, it is a belief, the value of which is determined by the validity of the facts that support it and the judgment of the person holding or expressing it. That Ernest Hemingway was "an American novelist" is a fact; that he was "the greatest novelist America has ever had" or that his *A*

*Farewell to Arms* is "the greatest American novel of the twentieth century" are only opinions of those who hold them. Similarly, "a United States citizen," "the Rocky Mountains," "the Swiss Alps" can be proved to exist as facts, but the following statement is opinion: "A United States citizen who prefers the Swiss Alps to the Rocky Mountains is unpatriotic." A favorite trick of propagandists is to mingle opinions with facts and thus obscure the difference between them.

6. *Begging the question* consists in taking a conclusion for granted before it is proved or assuming in the premises what is to be proved in the conclusion. Common forms are *name calling, slanting,* and *shifting the meaning of a word.*

*Name calling* appeals to prejudice and emotion, not to intellect; its technical name is *argumentum ad populum* ("appeal to the people," i.e., to their passions), using bad words to reject and condemn, good words to approve and accept. Our minds are so quick to accept epithets that we fail to look behind the propaganda. Frequently, name calling appears as sarcasm and invective. Examples: "wolf in sheep's clothing," "rabble-rouser," "second-rate college," "bloated bondholder," "radical," "plutocrat," "sexagenarian."

*Slanting,* similarly, uses colored, unfairly suggestive words to create an emotional attitude for or against a proposal or movement or person; it is also *argumentum ad populum.* Examples: "saintly," "wise and experienced," "infallible," "progressive," "bigoted," "superstitious," "progress-obstructing," "undemocratic fraternities and snobbish sororities," "unworkable and makeshift substitute," "dangerous proposal," "nauseatingly sentimental."

*Shifting the meaning of a word* consists in using the same ambiguous word several times with a shift in meaning that, it is hoped, will escape the reader or listener. College *unions* are one thing, labor *unions* are another. So, too, are *sport* and *sports.* *Literature* as *belles lettres* is not *literature* as the written record of the entire life and thought of a people, nor is *literature* in *journalistic literature* the same as *literature* in *A History of American Literature.* Should every citizen of the United States vote the *Republican* ticket because this is a great *republic,* or should he vote the *Democratic* ticket because this is a great *democracy?*

7. *Evading the issue* occurs most frequently in heated personal arguments but is common everywhere. It consists in ignor-

ing the point under discussion and making a statement that has no bearing on the argument. If you tell your roommate that his study habits need improvement, and he retorts that you do not handle your finances properly, he has ignored the question; he may be quite right, but he has not won the argument. He has merely employed what logicians call *ad hominem* argument (argument against the person). Dealing with personalities rather than principles, *argumentum ad hominem* seeks to discredit proposals by emphasizing alleged undesirable characteristics of men or groups who favor or are associated with those proposals. *Slanting* and *name calling* are also used for this purpose. Such argument is especially common in political campaigns when issues are not met squarely; a candidate or his supporters may attack the past record, character, and even family of his opponent without once confronting the issues themselves. Intelligent listeners or readers watch for such illogical thinking.

8. *Argument from testimonials and authority,* citing statements from historical people or well-known contemporaries, is not necessarily straight thinking. Hasty generalization, again, occurs in statements such as "Doctors say . . . ," "Science proves . . . ," and "Laboratory test show. . . ." Or, specifically, George Washington or Abraham Lincoln may not be good authorities for solving economic, scientific, or even political problems of this atomic era. Is a well-known TV star's statement on automobiles better than the opinion of an unknown but experienced garage mechanic? Is an authority in one field an oracle of wisdom about any subject on which he speaks or writes or only on his specialty? Would an eminent surgeon, for example, necessarily be a good witness for or against an important university policy change, such as an increase in tuition?

9. *Faulty analogy* occurs when we infer that because two objects or ideas are similar in one or more respects they must be similar in some further way. Analogy can be accurate and effective; otherwise, we could never make use of two rhetorical devices based upon it: simile and metaphor. When we use figurative-language analogy, however, we are not trying to prove something; we are trying to make something clear. When William Shakespeare wrote

That time of year thou mayst in me behold
When yellow leaves, or none, or few, do hang

Upon those boughs which shake against the cold,
Bare ruin'd choirs where late the sweet birds sang . . . ,

he was not attempting to prove a point; he was seeking to give a vivid and moving picture of old age, and he succeeded memorably.

In an argument about Social Security, someone might say, "Look here. We don't do anything to help or protect or comfort trees when they lose their leaves and the autumn winds shake them. Why, then, should we provide assistance to old men and women?" If anyone were to argue thus, he would be so clearly committing false analogy as to make himself ridiculous. Sometimes even literal analogies are faulty because the stated points of similarity are not essential; they are either superficial or less important than the differences. Colleges are large and small; some have all men students, some have all women students, some are coeducational. Will what has been effective in one kind of college necessarily be effective in another kind? Although a certain type of student government, say, the honor system, has worked well in a small college, it does not necessarily follow that it will work equally well in a state or city university of 20,000 or 30,000 students. Analogy, therefore, is more effective in other forms of discourse than in closely reasoned or argumentative writing. In all writing and speaking it is effective only as illustration; in most analogies differences outweigh similarities.

Errors in clear thinking (technically, fallacies in logic) not only are common but frequently overlap. You should try to find and analyze evidence; you should not permit emotional bias and prejudice to take the role of sound reason in your thinking, speaking, and writing; and you should not let unsound reason corroborate your prejudices. In short, you should attempt to acquire honest habits of thought and to express this honesty in speaking and writing.

### 13d   *Revise or rewrite your material to show evidence of clear thinking*

Although you may have checked your statements according to the directions given in Section 13a,b,c, your material may need further improvement. Your instructor may refer you to one of the following to guide you in revising or rewriting parts of your paper.

⟶ 1. The statement needs qualification; it is too sweeping or dogmatic. This assertion is *not* altogether false or irresponsible but simply covers too much ground too positively and needs to be qualified with a limiting phrase or clause (specifying the degree of certainty warranted, taking account of possible exceptions, or confining the generalization to what you are reasonably sure of).

⟶ 2. The facts cited are not such as are likely to be accepted on your bare assertion. You should supply informally in the current of your development some authority, occupational experience, or other reason why you should be believed.

⟶ 3. Your argument is good so far as it goes, but it is unconvincing because you have failed to dispose of some obvious and overriding argument that can be made on the other side. Your case is strengthened when you evaluate your own argument and show that you have disposed of possible alternatives.

⟶ 4. The evidence supplied is pertinent but falls far short of proof. One good reason does not build a case.

⟶ 5. There is such a thing as being too specific, if you do not make clear what generalization is supported by the instances given. A well-developed train of thought works back and forth between the general and the specific, showing the connections and applications intended at each point.

⟶ 6. Your treatment here is obviously marked by particular bias and prior emotional commitment. This does not necessarily make your conclusions false, but it does make them all suspect.

⟶ 7. Your approach here is essentially moralistic and directive, rather than analytical. No law exists against preaching, but distinguish preaching from investigation, analysis, and reasoning.

⟶ 8. Here you are exploring religious or philosophical questions that have been examined for thousands of years by serious thinkers without being brought to an issue. You, of course, have a right to try your hand at them, but don't expect an easy success, and remember that no certain conclusions are possible when the assumptions with which you start out are untestable.[10]

## EXERCISES

A. Look through advertisements, letters to newspapers and magazines, and, if it is election time, some recorded or reported campaign speeches. Find 10 errors in logical thinking, label each, and tell why it is an error.

B. Without paying too much attention to the exact, logical names, explain any errors in logical thinking in the following sentences:

1. A student who is a scholar and nothing more will never get ahead in the world.
2. Two years of military training are included in the freshman year.
3. In my part of Arizona we have 365 days of sunshine every year, and that is a very conservative estimate.
4. A wife explained to her husband at breakfast that it was not her fault that the grocery was out of three-minute eggs.
5. (Three meanings) Headline on the garden page of the Detroit *News*: "Rose Fans Invited to Hear Insect Talk."—*Reader's Digest,* August, 1967.
6. Jack became a great golfer because he was the son of an Ohio druggist.
7. Two women were in a restaurant: one, disliking smearcase, ordered cottage cheese instead; the other turned down horse mackerel salad in favor of tuna salad. How were these women fooled?
8. Can a man be a complete failure (success) because he never went to college except to accept honorary degrees?
9. To keep from hitting your thumb when driving a nail, you are advised to hold the hammer with both hands.
10. Did figures lie in the following? A college applicant was denied admission because he was not in the upper third of his class; he was only in the upper fourth.
11. A real estate agent recently sold a large quarter-acre wooded lot for $4000.
12. Since our grade schools and high school are located in a college town, we have the highest caliber of local education.

[10] For these suggestions the individual largely responsible is Professor Macklin Thomas of Chicago State College.

13. I have seen cars from almost every state in the Union, including Alaska and Canada, during a busy summer.

14. In national political campaigns, one party may send a "truth squad" to make speeches in cities where candidates of the other party have spoken. What definitions of *truth* are suggested by "truth squads"?

15. (True occurrence, names changed.) Henry Smith, 61 years old, a candidate for an important public office, was defeated by his rival, John Jones, aged 59. Throughout the campaign, Jones stressed in conversation and public speeches that Smith was a sexagenarian. Jones won easily. (In a 350-word paper, show why.)

C. With logical thinking as your guide, write a theme agreeing or disagreeing with the ideas expressed in the revised theme on pp. 203–205, "I Didn't Pledge a Fraternity."

# 14   *Consistency*

To write clearly and effectively, a writer must be *consistent* in his approach to his material and in its development.

Consistency concerns *mood, style,* and *point of view,* this last a phrase here meaning (1) from what point, place, or position a view is obtained; (2) through whose eyes something is seen or through whose mind something is considered—one person's, another person's, or the eyes or minds of many persons.

## 14a   *Be consistent in a personal point of view*

In discussing a subject, you may use one of four personal points of view. Your choice depends upon appropriateness to the reader or readers and appropriateness to the subject.

1. *The first person* (*I, my, mine, me, we, our, ours, us*), i.e., the person or persons writing or speaking. First person, singular or plural, is usually used in telling firsthand experiences, thoughts, decisions.

2. *The second person* (*you, your, yours*), the person or persons written or spoken to. The *you* should not be vague but should refer directly to your reader or readers (listener or listeners), in giving information, asking direct questions, making requests, giving invitations.

3. *The third person* (*he, his, him, she, her, hers, they, their, theirs, them*). Third person is used when you are writing (or speaking) about someone, male or female, or about some group.

4. *The impersonal,* from which point of view personal pronouns (1, 2, and 3, above) are replaced by indefinite pronouns (*one, everybody, anyone,* etc.—see Section **71d**), or nouns like *a person, a student,* or the passive voice (see Section **81**). The impersonal point of view is frequently used in descriptive, expository, and argumentative writing.

For the use of various points of view in writing narrative, see Section **17a**; for the use of personal pronouns in effective beginnings and endings, see Section **8b5,6** and **8c2**.

NOTE: Do not carelessly shift the point of view in any discussion from *I* to *we* or *you* or *one,* or from any one of these to another. When a shift is necessary or effective, as it sometimes is, give your reader warning of what you are doing (see Section **45e**).

## 14b  Be consistent in a subjective or objective approach

When you are *subjective,* you let your own feelings, emotions, prejudices control your attitude. You are personal: everything is seen through your eyes or through your mind as a thinking *subject.*

When you are *objective,* you refuse, or try to refuse, to let your own feelings, emotions, prejudices control your attitude. You are impersonal: everything is seen or considered outwardly, as it is related to the *object* of thought. An "objective test," for example, is a test on which the grader's own feelings or beliefs count for nothing; no matter who grades the test—even a machine may grade it—the result is the same.

One kind of writing may demand a subjective approach and attitude. When it does, guard against being too objective. Another kind of writing may demand an objective approach and attitude. When it does, guard against letting any subjective or slanting words or phrases creep in.

## 14c  Be consistent in the use of a physical point of view

A physical point of view concerns a point in *space* or a point in *time.* For certain kinds of writing you choose a point in *space* (inside or outside a building, an elevation, a point of the compass, etc.) or *time* (hour, season, weather, year) from which the subject is considered. The selection of a definite point of view is particularly important in descriptive and narrative writing. After you have chosen your position and time, do not needlessly shift them; and, when it is necessary, make such a shift clear to your reader by adequate transitional phrases.

If you are describing a building, for example, do not shift carelessly and without warning from the back to the front of it, or from the inside to the outside, or from one floor to another. The reader will be confused if he thinks you are looking at the outside of the house and suddenly you begin to describe striking features of the interior.

A confusion in *time* is just as mystifying to the reader. Do not carelessly jump from one year to another or go suddenly from night to the afternoon of the next day. If the time is midwinter, do not without warning interject details about summer activities. (For consistency in the use of tense, see Section **80d**.)

Both space and time were ignored in the following; over a thousand miles disappeared between the two sentences:

Not long after dawn the four survivors were picked up by a French naval ship some thousand miles offshore. To their surprise, they were immediately seized by the authorities in port and clapped in jail to await trial.

## 14d   *Be consistent in the use of a mental point of view*

For certain writing, especially expository and argumentative, you choose a mental point of view, a position or "point in the mind," as it were. You have heard about a doctor's point of view, a teacher's, a clergyman's, a lawyer's, a college student's, a high school student's, a child's. When you attribute views to such a person, make them consistent and appropriate. You would not expect a four-year-old child to say: "Honored and revered parent, will we all eventually reside in an eleemosynary institution?"

Furthermore, after you have chosen a mental point of view from which to consider a subject, keep this point of view constantly before you. If you are discussing intercollegiate athletic competition, you may properly present arguments for and against it, but you must make perfectly clear any shift from one side to the other. Similarly, if you are arguing that intramural sports are preferable to intercollegiate athletics, do not present arguments in favor of the latter unless you use them to further your central point. And do not subtly shift to a different phase of the subject, such as women's part in intramural sports, without indicating the shift. Never cause confusion in the mind of your reader about the mental point of view.

### 14e   Make your writing consistent in mood or mental impression

Occasionally you will wish to establish a certain *mood* for your reader, to create a certain *impression* in his mind. To succeed, choose words and phrases which best express that mood.

A few of the many moods from which you can choose are *peacefulness, cheerfulness, lightheartedness, optimism, sarcasm, bitterness, anger, carelessness, sadness, hopelessness, pessimism, weirdness, gloom.* You can add many more. (See also Section 4f.)

Notice how the italicized words in the following build the mood or atmosphere or impression of gloom and fear and how inconsistent would be a statement about birds chattering gaily in the trees:

> During the whole of a *dull, dark,* and *soundless* day in the *autumn* of the year, when the clouds hung *oppressively low* in the heavens, I had been passing *alone,* on horseback, through a *singularly dreary* tract of country, and at length found myself, as the *shades of the evening* drew on, within view of the *melancholy* House of Usher. I know not how it was—but, with the first glimpse of the building, a sense of *insufferable gloom* pervaded my spirit. I say *insufferable*; for the feeling was *unrelieved* by any of that half-pleasurable, because poetic, sentiment with which the mind usually receives even the *sternest* natural images of the *desolate* or *terrible.* I looked upon the scene before me—upon the *mere* house, and the simple landscape features of the domain—upon the *bleak* walls—upon the *vacant* eye-like windows—upon a few *rank* sedges —and upon a few white trunks of *decayed* trees—with an utter *depression* of soul which I can compare to no earthly sensation more properly than to the after-dream of the reveller upon opium—the *bitter lapse* into everyday life—the *hideous dropping off of the veil.* There was an *iciness,* a *sinking,* a *sickening of the heart*—an *unredeemed dreariness* of thought which no *goading* of the imagination could *torture* into aught of the sublime. What was it—I paused to think—what was it that so *unnerved* me in the contemplation of the House of Usher?
>
> —EDGAR ALLAN POE, "The Fall of the House of Usher"

## 14f   *Make your writing consistent in* physical impression

In addition to creating a mental impression, you will occasionally wish to create for your reader a *physical impression.* You appeal to one or more of the senses: sight, sound, smell, taste, touch. The impression you wish to create may be favorable, positive, pleasant, or it may be unfavorable, negative, unpleasant. (See Section **64.**)

To create physical impression, use vivid, effective, sensation-appealing words (see Sections **64, 65**) : adjectives, nouns, verbs, adverbs. Notice in magazine advertising the words used to sell appetizing foods, fragrant perfumes, melodious music. Notice, also, in Section **15d,** Charles Dickens' use of words to give the physical impression of *stagnant* and *extreme heat.*

In the following, the dominant physical impression is one of *smell*; notice how the italicized words help make the appeal to that sense:

Of all hours of the day there is none like the early morning for *downright good odours*—the morning before eating. Fresh from sleep and unclogged with food a man's senses cut like knives. The whole world comes in upon him. A still morning is best, for the *mists* and the *moisture* seem to retain the *odours* which they have *distilled* through the night. Upon a *breezy* morning one is likely to get a *single predominant odour* as of *clover* when the wind blows across *a hay field* or of *apple blossoms* when the wind comes through the orchard, but upon a perfectly still morning, it is wonderful how the *odours* arrange themselves in upright strata, so that one walking passes through them as from room to room in a *marvellous temple of fragrance.* (I should have said, I think, if I had not been on my way to dig a ditch, that it was like turning the leaves of some *delicate* volume of lyrics!)

So it was this morning. As I walked along the margin of my field I was conscious at first, coming within the shadows of the wood, of the *cool, heavy aroma* which one associates with the night: as of *moist woods* and *earth mould.* The *penetrating scent* of the night remains long after the sights and sounds of it have disappeared. In *sunny spots* I had the *fragrance* of the *open cornfield,* the *aromatic breath* of the *brown earth,* giving curiously the sense of fecundity—a *warm, generous odour* of *daylight and sunshine.* Down the field, toward the corner, cutting in sharply, as though a door opened (or a page turned to another lyric) , came the *cloying, sweet fragrance* of *wild crab-apple blossoms,* almost *tropical* in their *richness,* and below that, as I came to my work, the *thin acrid smell* of the *marsh,* the place of the *rushes* and *the flags* and *the frogs.* —DAVID GRAYSON, "The Marsh Ditch"[11]

### 14g  Make your writing consistent in style

Think of *mood* and *impression* as the mental or physical atmosphere that a writer creates to surround his reader and wants the reader to receive. Think of *style,* which occasionally may include mood and impression, as mainly the manner in which a writer expresses himself. In that expression, variety of phrase, clause, and sentence patterns is not only consistent but desirable; consistency in style is also a matter of word choice. What kind of style are you aiming at? Formal? Dignified? Conversational? Simple? Archaic? Quaint? Whimsical? Flippant? Humorous? Breezy? Breathless? Concise? Whatever it is, be consistent in choosing and arranging words.

Notice how consistent is the concise, pithy, parallel-characterized style in this paragraph from Francis Bacon's essay "Of Studies":

Some books are to be tasted, others to be swallowed, and some few to be chewed and digested; that is, some books are to be read only in parts; others to be read, but not curiously; and some few to be read wholly, and with diligence and attention. Some books also may be read by deputy, and extracts made of them by others; but that would be only in the less important arguments, and the meaner sort of books; else distilled books are like common distilled waters, flashy things. Reading maketh a full man; conference a ready man; and writing an exact man. And therefore, if a man write little, he had need have a great memory; if he confer little, he had need have a present wit; and if he read little, he had need have much cunning, to seem to know that he doth not.

Inconsistency in mood and style is illustrated by the following, suggested by H. L. Mencken's writing of "The Declaration of Independence in American" (in *A Mencken Chrestomathy*) : the first paragraph is straightforward, matter-of-fact; the second a kind of speechless anger without proper words for the expression:

11 David Grayson, *Adventures in Contentment.* Copyright 1925 by Doubleday, Doran & Company, Inc.

Gentlemen: One hundred years ago my great-grandparents were peasants in eastern Europe. They were intelligent and hard-working. Inspired by their love for freedom and democracy, they emigrated to this great country of opportunity, and instilled their loves and ideals in their children. One of them, my grandfather, was so impressed that he was willing to die for America. In fact, he did, giving his life for his country in the Battle of Belleau Wood in France in 1918. I have never forgotten the examples Great-grandfather and Grandfather set for their descendants.

Now, times have changed. The idealism held by Great-grandfather and Grandfather has been loused up. When I think about it, I get hot under the collar. I want to blow my top. Too many lousy cowards are taking advantage of dear old Uncle Sam. I think he should kick the living daylights out of every such dirty bum. If the skunks don't like it here, let them scram back to where they came from.

## EXERCISES

A. What is the *personal* point of view in several essays and short stories that you have read recently, either in your book of readings or elsewhere?

B. What is the *physical* point of view (in *space*) of some piece of description that you have read? Does this point of view shift? If so, explain.

C. What is the *physical* point of view (in *time*) of some narrative that you have read? Does this point of view shift?

D. What is the *mood* or *mental impression* created in one or more of several essays that you have studied recently? List some of the effective words and phrases used.

E. What is the *physical impression* created in one or more pieces of description that you have read? List some of the effective words and phrases used.

F. Write a paragraph creating a *mood* or *mental impression* described by one of the suggestions in Section 14e.

G. Write a paragraph creating a *physical impression*, pleasant or unpleasant, suggested in Section 14f; name the sense or senses you are appealing to.

# 15 Effectiveness and style

With the aid of textbooks and instructors, you can learn to write correctly and clearly, but correctness and clearness cannot assure effectiveness. Effective writing is not only clear and competent but also interesting, attractive, and artistic; it has a style marked by simplicity, by being conversational, individual, and concrete. In order to communicate ideas effectively, you must *interest* your readers by expressing ideas so as to gain and hold their attention.

The title of a well-known opera, *Aïda,* is a memory device which can apply to writing: *A*—Attention; *I*—Interest; *D*—Desire; *A*—Action. That is, a theme should command the *attention* of the reader, then attract his *interest* so that he will *desire* to read it, perhaps agree or disagree with what is said, and then take *action* suggested by the theme.

*15a Achieve effectiveness by conveying an actual sense of fact*

Many papers are not effective because of abstractness, indefiniteness. Good writing is definite, concrete: it contains specific details which arouse interest, it contains facts or conveys a sense of fact, and it tells what the facts are for.

A composition on taxation will hardly be effective so long as you abstractly discuss the theory of taxation. When you show that every one of us pays taxes in large or small amounts, even on small everyday items including food, and when you show also the concrete ways in which tax money is spent for education and other local, state, and national services, your paper conveys an actual sense of fact and suggests what the facts are for.

Specific answers to the questions Who?, What?, Where?, When?, How?, Why? are effective: they furnish realistic touches. To help answer such questions and thus convey an actual sense of fact:

⟶ 1. Enumerate specific details.
⟶ 2. Narrate specific and dramatic incidents and anecdotes.
⟶ 3. Use specific people and human relationships whenever possible.
⟶ 4. Use comparison and contrast.
⟶ 5. Show definite relationships of causes and effects.

⟶ 6. Make occasional use of dialogue or humor or satire.
⟶ 7. When they are appropriate, use a series of questions or exclamations or a single question or a single exclamation.
⟶ 8. Be definite and concrete as much and as frequently as possible.

## 15b   *Achieve effectiveness by variety of sentences and paragraphs*

Variety makes writing effective. Try using a variety of sentences: (1) those which vary in grammatical form: simple, compound, complex, compound-complex (Section 74a); (2) those which vary in meaning and purpose: declarative, interrogative, imperative, exclamatory (Section 74b); (3) those which vary in the use of suspense: loose and periodic (Section 74c); (4) those which vary in length: long, short (Section 48c); (5) those which vary their beginnings: some starting with the subject, others with one of numerous kinds of phrases, and others with dependent clauses (Section 48b).

So, too, with paragraphs: observing the principles of good paragraphing, vary the length of your paragraphs. Just as a reader tires of pages with no paragraph breaks at all, he loses interest in a group of paragraphs monotonously alike in length or in the kind of sentences they contain (Sections **28, 29**).

## 15c   *Achieve effectiveness by the use of parallel structure*

Parallel structure means that two or more ideas, two or more parts of a sentence, are expressed in the same grammatical form: prepositional phrases, participial phrases, predicate phrases, dependent clauses, independent clauses, and the like. A simple example of parallelism is the often-quoted line: "To err is human; to forgive, divine," in which the subjects (two infinitives) and the two adjectives are balanced:

| | | |
|---|---|---|
| To err | is | human |
| To forgive | (is) | divine |

(For more detailed discussion of parallelism within the sentence, see Section 44.)

Sometimes separate sentences and even paragraphs are made parallel. In the following, each sentence and the structure of each sentence in the first paragraph are parallel with each corresponding sentence and the structure of each sentence in the second paragraph.

Verse is patterned language. That is, verse is composition in which words are arranged according to a pattern, a form which is metrical, rhythmical. Verse may be mere doggerel, such as

Here lies the body of Samuel Blank;
He dropped a match in a gasoline tank.

These lines are verse because they consist of words arranged according to a pattern.

Poetry is patterned language, plus. That is, poetry is composition arranged in a pattern. But poetry is more than verse. It signifies high thought, imagination, or emotion.

Heard melodies are sweet, but those unheard
Are sweeter; therefore, ye soft pipes, play on.

These lines are poetry because they are patterned language which contains genuine thought and imagination. All poetry is verse, but not all verse can be called poetry.

## 15d   Achieve effectiveness by the skillful repetition of words

Skillful use of repetition helps achieve effectiveness; faulty, useless repetition of words and phrases prevents it (Section **67**). Reread the illustration of parallelism in Section **15c** and note the effectiveness achieved by repetition of words like *verse, patterned language, poetry.*

Notice how the repetition of the words *stare, stared, staring* adds to the physical impression of stagnant and extreme heat in the following description of Marseilles, the French port, in August:

Thirty years ago Marseilles lay burning in the sun, one day.
A blazing sun upon a fierce August day was no greater rarity . . . then than at any other time, before or since. Everything in Marseilles and about Marseilles, had *stared* at the fervid sky, and been *stared* at in return, until a *staring* habit had become universal there. Strangers were *stared* out of countenance by *staring* white houses, *staring* white walls, *staring* tracts of arid road, *staring* hills from which verdure was burnt away. The only things to be seen not fixedly *staring* and glaring were

the vines drooping under their load of grapes. These did occasionally wink a little, as the hot air barely moved their faint leaves.

There was no wind to make a ripple on the foul water within the harbor, or on the beautiful sea without. The lines of demarcation between the two colors, black and blue, showed the point which the pure sea would not pass; but it lay as quiet as the abominable pool, with which it never mixed. Boats without awnings were too hot to touch; ships blistered at their moorings; the stones of the quays had not cooled, night or day, for months. Hindoos, Russians, Chinese, Spaniards, Portuguese, Englishmen, Frenchmen, Genoese, Neapolitans, Venetians, Greeks, Turks, descendants from all the builders of Babel, come to trade at Marseilles, sought the shade alike—taking refuge in any hiding-place from a sea too intensely blue to be looked at, and a sky of purple, set with one great flaming jewel of fire.

The universal *stare* made the eyes ache. Towards the distant line of Italian coast, indeed, it was a little relieved by light clouds of mist, slowly rising from the evaporation of the sea; but it softened nowhere else. Far away the *staring* roads, deep in dust, *stared* from the hillside, *stared* from the hollow, *stared* from the interminable plain. Far away the dusty vines overhanging wayside cottages, and the monotonous wayside avenues of parched trees without shade, drooped beneath the *stare* of earth and sky. So did the horses with drowsy bells, in long files of carts, creeping slowly toward the interior; so did their recumbent drivers when they were awake, which rarely happened; so did the exhausted laborers in the fields. Everything that lived or grew, was oppressed by the glare, except the lizard passing swiftly over rough stone walls, and the cicala, chirping his dry, hot chirp, like a rattle. The very dust was scorched brown, and something quivered in the atmosphere as if the air itself were panting.          —CHARLES DICKENS, *Little Dorrit*

**15e   Achieve effectiveness through effective diction** (see Sections **63–69**)

**15f   Achieve effectiveness by using the active voice instead of the passive voice** (see Section **81e**)

**15g   Achieve effectiveness by striving for a style suited to the subject, to the reader, and to you, the writer, and your individuality and personality**

"Style" in writing and speaking has various meanings: "proper words in proper places" (Jonathan Swift) ; a "mode of expressing thought in language; esp.: a manner of expression characteristic of an individual, period, school, or nation" (a brief dictionary definition from *Webster's Seventh New Collegiate Dictionary*); or, applied to you, the way you express yourself: the kind of words, the kind of sentences, the tone you use. Often, following convention is the best practice, but frequently a unique way, in whole or in part, of expressing yourself, your personality, and your individuality, is valuable and effective.

To a college student, style should mean more than the negative aspects of writing and speaking—mere avoidance of mistakes in usage and mechanics. "Improving" one's style admittedly involves correctness and appropriateness, but it embraces far more than just this. To be truly effective, writing must be more than "adequate" in word choice and sentence structure. It must achieve its dominant purpose of communicating ideas from writer to reader, and so anything and everything that blocks or slows down communication must be removed, such as faulty diction, illogical sentence structure, nonstandard usage. Effective writing also employs whatever devices of style will smooth and speed communication from writer to reader.

Four devices for attaining an effective style are the following:

*1. Simplicity.* Simplicity is achieved by the use of organization, logical thinking, appropriate sentences, and word choices that appeal to and are understood by the persons (according to their age, education, knowledge of subject, etc.) for whom you are writing. (For aid in these areas, review Sections **6** and **7** on outlining and proportion; Sections **10, 11,** and **12** on coherence, transition, and clearness; Section **13** on logical thinking; Section **49** on sentence appropriateness; and Sections **53, 59, 62, 63, 66,** and **68,** on word choice: respectively, appropriateness, contemporary diction, idiomatic English, exact and precise diction, freshness of diction, gobbledygook and jargon.

*2. Conversational quality.* Good conversational style in writing is a happy compromise. On one side of it is formality: with the virtues of being dignified, elevated, didactic, even pontifical (like Samuel Johnson's speaking and writing), perhaps technical, perhaps humorless; and with the vices of being constrained, condescending, pedantic, perhaps stiff, wooden, "too high and mighty," and "talking down." On the other or extreme side of conversational style are talking and writing as if one had taken off coat and tie and rolled up his shirt sleeves: it is "locker-room" or "bull session" conversation—the style when "out with the boys" or "one of the girls."

The happy compromise—good conversational style—is characterized by these descriptive phrases: ease of expression, more relaxed, less didactic, an "author thinking with the reader," a human, friendly, man-to-man quality or a kind of face-to-face writing and talking (as in much of the writing of Charles Lamb, Robert Louis Stevenson, and John R. Tunis). (Also, for discussion of informal diction and idiom, see Sections 53 and 62.)

Illustrations of the two extremes and the happy compromise are seen in the advice given its correspondents by a large life insurance company:

Polite, stiff, formal, not the easy, natural language of conversation:
    We are most grateful for the promptness shown in forwarding to this office the information requested on the new policy forms. It will do much to expedite our operations here.

Too familiar, too casual:
    Thanks loads for the info on the new policy form. It'll sure come in handy in helping us get the ball rolling on this end.

Simple, natural, good conversational:
    Thank you for sending the information on the new policy forms so promptly. It will be very helpful to us.[12]

*3. Individuality.* Again, good individual style is a happy compromise. At one extreme, individuality in language may be too cold, too formal, too objective, even with the occasional use of "I" (as in the essays of Francis Bacon). At the other extreme, individuality in language may be excessively subjective: being too self- or inward-centered, with overuse of one's own experiences, opinions, standards, judgments, thoughts, needs, aspirations, and neglect of the needs, appeals, and interests of reader or listener (as in some autobiographical writing). As a happy compromise, good individual style lessens the extremes discussed; it makes moderate use of personal anecdotes and eye-witness accounts, moderate use of the author's opinions, reflections,

---

[12] *Effective Letters Bulletin,* Fall, 1967. Copyright 1967 by the New York Life Insurance Company.

comments, judgments, conclusions. (Excellent examples of individuality in writing are Charles Lamb's essays, especially the well-known "Dream Children.")

In much writing and speaking—as in many other situations in life—you must inescapably be conventional and follow routine patterns. But frequently, perhaps often, you can be yourself and choose expressions that will reveal your own personality, your own style, your own individuality. If what you write, or say, bears at least to some slight degree the imprint of your personality, your particular and inescapable individuality, then it will have "never been said before" in quite the same way. Bearing the marks of individuality, it will possess a genuinely important stylistic quality without which it might be dull and spiritless.

*4. Concreteness.* Applied to writing, concreteness is the use of expressions (words, phrases, clauses, sentences) that illustrate one or more of these easily understood synonyms: clear-cut, definite, exact, meaningful, particular, picturesque, precise, specific, special, vivid. When writing is concrete, it has eliminated general and vague ideas and abstract expressions (though these are useful in some areas like philosophy and the social sciences, but even then they are often immediately explained by specific, concrete expressions, examples, definitions, analogies). Concreteness is therefore another admirable and usually essential quality of an effective style. As someone said, "Nine-tenths of all good writing consists of being concrete and specific. Perhaps the other tenth doesn't really matter." (For *concrete* suggestions for concrete writing, see Sections **15a, 63, 64, 65,** and **66.**)

## EXERCISES

A. Choose an article from a current magazine or your book of readings. Prepare for discussion an analysis of the devices used for effectiveness in several of the paragraphs.

B. Read carefully another article, looking for the qualities of style discussed in Section **15g.** Write a paragraph or two summarizing your findings.

C. Write four fairly long paragraphs, in each of which you illustrate and apply one of the qualities of style discussed in Section **15g.**

# 16  *Revision*

"Good writing is good only because of good *rewriting*." Some
students do not accept this statement; they maintain that when
they really get started, they turn out first drafts that are superior
to anything they have laboriously revised or they recall having
heard of successful writers who rarely rewrote. The truth is that
most successful writers revise and rewrite, not once but many
times.[13]

As indicated in Section **6h,** some writers compose easily and
rapidly, postponing details of correct composition until later;
others write carefully, slowly, and painstakingly from beginning
to end. Whichever plan you have followed, your writing needs
revision.

## 16a  *Revise your theme for organization,*
##       *unity, coherence, emphasis*

Read your theme once to make sure that it is well organized,
unified, coherent, and effective as a whole. Delete any extraneous
material; recheck to assure that everything in the theme is relevant to the subject and in its proper place; rephrase all vague or
rambling thoughts; substitute specific details for broad generalities. Consider the content and organization of your paragraphs.
(Sections **6, 9, 10, 11, 15, 25, 30, 34.**)

## 16b  *Revise your theme for better sentences*

Read again the preliminary draft to improve the sentences in
phrasing and structure. Make certain that all sentences are unified
and complete (Sections **31, 34**) ; that all ideas are properly coordinated or subordinated (Sections **36, 37**) ; that no unjustifiable
"sentence fragments," unjustifiable "comma splices," or "fused

---

13 "Thomas Jefferson spent 18 days writing and rewriting the Declaration of Independence; Victor Hugo made 11 revisions of one novel; Voltaire
was known to spend a whole night toiling over one sentence. . . . In short,
most successes in writing can be explained by diligent work, seasoned by
lively imagination and warmed by sincerity."—*Royal Bank of Canada
Monthly Letter,* May, 1963.

scntences" remain (Sections **31, 32, 33**) ; that the sentences are clearly and effectively phrased; that the sentences are varied in structure (Section **48**) .

### 16c  *Proofread your theme for accuracy and correctness*

In composing a first draft, you may frequently make careless slips or you may neglect to check compositional matters you are not sure about. After you have written your first draft, reread it for accuracy of content and for correctness in writing.

1. Go through the theme once for the sole purpose of making sure that all the words are *spelled correctly* (see Section **52**) .

2. Read the theme through again to insure *grammatical correctness.*

3. Read the theme again to insure *correct punctuation.*

4. Read the theme again to insure *correct, clear, effective,* and *appropriate diction.*

### 16d  *Revise after an interval of time*

Allow time to elapse between writing a paper and final revision. With sufficient time between the two steps, actual composition and rereadings, you notice errors that were not apparent when you had just completed writing. You also approach your theme more objectively. Most of us can detect errors in another's work more easily than in our own. After a lapse of time, you see your writing almost as objectively as if it were the work of someone else.

Another helpful suggestion: proofread aloud, if possible. Since your voice slows down your eyes, you see errors you have already missed, you catch harsh or awkward-sounding word combinations, and you detect involved sentences that need simplification and clarification.

### 16e  *Proofread your final draft*

If you have carried out your revision thoroughly, flaws in the final draft are only those that result from slips of the pen or from errors in typing. Because such slips do occur, you need to proofread the final draft with care. Do this with pen or pencil in hand, pointing to every word and punctuation mark as you check its correctness. Read aloud this final draft also.

*16f    Revise your graded and returned theme
        according to a specific plan*

As in many other activities, one does not improve merely by
having his attention called to errors. He must correct those errors
under supervision. So, too, with theme writing.

When your theme has been graded and returned to you,
follow a careful plan of revision, as directed by your instructor.
This plan may include the following:

1. Utilize fully any comment your instructor makes on your
theme. Note carefully the errors he marks and the reference numbers indicating sections of this *Handbook*. Through his aid you
will find where your weaknesses lie, and you can make the necessary revisions so as to avoid making the same errors in later
themes.

2. Keep a record of the number and kind of your most common errors in writing. For your own guidance, use the Theme
Record on the third page from the back cover. Consult it each
time you have any writing to do. Your instructor may ask you to
make a copy of the Theme Record on a separate sheet, so that he
can check it from time to time.

3. Master the directions concerning the elimination of the
error or errors that you are making. A worthy ideal is to try never
to make the same mistake twice, or even the same kind of mistake.

4. If errors occur in organization or in various types of sentence structure, you may be asked to revise, rewrite, and resubmit
the theme, as illustrated in Section **30**. If errors are in spelling,
grammar, punctuation, or diction, you may be asked to make
corrections (1) on the theme itself, above or between lines, (2)
on the back of the theme, or (3) on a separate sheet, labeled
"Corrections for Theme No. ———." Your instructor will indicate
by some method, such as underlining the symbols, which errors
are to be corrected, and he may further indicate by some mechani-
cal device such as brackets [. . .] or double parallel lines ||. . .||
how much material is to be included on the correction sheet.

If you make out a correction sheet, follow the sample form
given on p. 94. In the left margin put symbol and *Handbook*
section number. In the left column copy the material from the
theme exactly as it is; in the right column copy the same material

but make sufficient change to correct the error. Do not, however, change wording or phrasing so much that no apparent relation is evident between error and correction. Be sure to include enough in both columns so that both error and correction are immediately understandable, even weeks afterward, without further reference to the theme.

Correction sheets can be valuable guides in future writing. Save them and study them, both before you do additional writing and before you make final revisions of succeeding themes. As the number of your correction sheets increases, you will have a per-

---

### CORRECTIONS FOR THEME NO. XX

| | *Incorrect* | *Correct* |
|---|---|---|
| sp 52e | admited | admitted |
| p 93a | a students first task | a student's first task |
| sp 52b | to many activities | too many activities |
| CS 32 | Many a freshman becomes a reporter for the student newspaper, this activity aids him in his writing. | Many a freshman becomes a reporter for the student newspaper; this activity aids him in his writing. |
| SF 31 | Another activity that everyone needs involves physical exertion. If he wants to keep in good physical condition. | Another activity that everyone needs involves physical exertion, if he wants to keep in good physical condition. |
| gr 76b | The major activity of many students are in the field of athletics. | The major activity of many students is in the field of athletics. |
| gr 75d | An individual activity appeals to my roommate and I. | An individual activity appeals to my roommate and me. |
| FS 33 | Such in brief are our extra-curricular activities every student should choose one of them and take an active part. | Such in brief are our extra-curricular activities; every student should choose one of them and take an active part. |

---

sonal guide to both the kinds of errors that you habitually make and the methods by which these errors can be corrected.

### 16g   Follow conventional practice in proofreading printed materials

NOTE: To those desiring guidance in preparing materials for printing and in proofreading printed matter, one or more of the dictionaries listed in Section 51a will give the needed information.

## EXERCISES

A. Make an honest analysis of the time spent on three of your themes written outside class. Estimate the amount of time spent in *preparation* for writing, the actual time spent in *writing*, and the time spent in *revising*.

B. Write a short paper discussing the meaning and application of the following statement: "Errors in writing hinder communication as much as stammering does in conversation."

C. Below are two short themes. The number under the title indicates when in the term they were written; "class" or "outside" means an impromptu theme in class or a theme written outside the classroom. Proofread each theme carefully, marking all the errors you see and giving each theme a grade. Write for each theme a paragraph of comment that should aid the writer in future themes; comment also on whether the outline is correct and whether an outline would have helped the writer who did not make one.

*Three Serious Errors in English*

(NO. 5—CLASS)

There were three reasons why I didn't get through English 101 the first time. One of them being the sentence fragment. Time and time again I made this error. I did just about everything I could to prevent this error, but it seem to be a hopeless case. I could recognize the mistake when it was pointed out to me, but in proff reading I couldn't find them.

The sentence fragment gave me quite alot of trouble and kept my grades low; but another error, which put my grades down even lower, was spelling. In most cases it was'nt not knowing how to spell a paticular word, it was carelessness more then anything else. I would misspell "there" and "their" all of the time. I knew the differences between the two; I was just careless in writeing them.

The last and biggest of my problems was the run-on-sentence. This I think was my biggest and worst mistake; if none of the other errors were on my themes you could be sure that the run-on-sentence was there to take care of the grade.

*Meet Chicago*
(NO. 6—OUTSIDE)
  I. Introduction to Chicago
 II. Description of city
     A. Its layout
     B. Its parks
III. Sketch of city
 IV. Detriments
  V. Conclusion

I'd like you to meet my home town, Chicago. To really introduce you to the city would take days and days, therefore it's nearly impossible to do anything now but give you a brief sketch of my favorite home.

Of course, you know the city has a "North Side", a "West Side", the "Loop", and last but not the least a "South Side" with Lake Michigan acting as a boundary line on the east of the city. Although Chicago has it's fill of parks we (the Southsiders) agree that our parks are the best. And who can dispute with us, for there is nothing as beautiful as the Loop at night seen from the vantage point of a lonely deserted beach.

Naturally the darkness of night hids some of the "Windy City's" dirt, but since the weather is so unpredictable the rain or snow will soon wash or cover this detriment. When people ask me how I can stand that filthy place, I can never find an answer. Maybe I'm crazy like the rest of the Chicagoans, or maybe I love the way the city reacts. I love the small town atmosphere of carolers at Christmas time; the bustling frantic shopping for last minute items in a bustling frantic department store as the whole town seems to be ready to burst with some of that lost Christmas spirit; the suppressed murmurings of children gazing in awe at some modern or ancient device in the Museum of Science and Industry; the sailors and their girls walking quietly in the park filled with blooming cherry trees; Buckingham fountain conceitedly showing it's splendid colors to a multitude of it's freinds; the people, young and old, lining up to drop their hard earned money into a box so that a child may someday walk without crutchs. All this I love and so much more that I'm afraid if I tell it you really might begin to think I'm quite conceited and that I'm hiding some of the facts, the true facts, about Chicago.

Yes, we have slums, horrible dirty places where ten humans exsist where two people could comfortably call home, but we are doing something about it and today you can see block after block of undefined rubble being cleared away and clear modern housing units going up in it's place.

Chicago has gansters and law breakers for which it is notorius, but I won't go into that as I can honestly say that I've never been afraid to walk home at night alone. If there are violators of law, I've never seen them. Now I'm not saying I haven't heard about them but . . . oh, lets drop this subject.

I can't write a conclusion for there isn't any. Chicago isn't concluded and never will be. We have just gotten started and if Texas doesn't watch out we may call her our suburb in another year or two.

# 17  *The basic forms of writing*

All writing can be classified as narration, description, exposition, or argument. These are what are known, once again, as the four main divisions of rhetorical writing. *Narration* (or *narrative*) tells a story; *description* gives a picture in words or a sense impression; *exposition* explains; *argument* seeks to convince or persuade. No one form exists alone, pure and unmixed; for example, descriptive details may be used in narration or in exposition; narration helps to clarify in exposition or argument; and argument may be used in exposition. Predominating tone, purpose, and style (Section 4c,f) determine the classification.

Cutting across boundaries and classifiable by content are such varieties of writing as the précis (Section 18a–f), the paraphrase (Section 18g–l), the research paper (Section 20), and letters (pp. 649–665).

Deceptively simple when so labeled, these basic forms of writing and their subdivisions are numerous and vary in difficulty. The following discussion is brief; you can receive further help from examples in your book of readings, from class discussions and lectures, and from books, magazines, and articles on specific basic forms. For a guide to finding these in your library, see Section 19.

## 17a   *Use narration to tell a story, true or imagined*
Narration answers the questions: What happened? How? When? Why? Where? With or by whom? It varies in length from ex-

tremely long to extremely short: novels, novelettes, dramas, biographies, autobiographies, histories, news stories, short stories, incidents, and anecdotes. Longer types of narrative are beyond the scope of freshman writing; some of the shorter ones, such as one-act plays, news writing, and short stories, require specialized study.

The plan or order in simple narrative is chronological: relating various events as they occurred in time. The narrative is told from a certain *point of view,* the phrase here meaning: Through whose eyes and thoughts do we get the story? Do we get it from a major character, from a minor character, or from an omniscient or all-knowing person such as the author, who knows all that his characters think, feel, and do, and who tells events and thoughts that could not possibly be known by *all* the other participants or characters? A story can be told in the first person (*I* or *we*), in the third person singular (*he* or *she*), or with multiple persons (*he, she,* and *they*). In writing narrative, the author must be consistent in point of view.

Shorter or shortened forms of narrative and narrative-exposition which you may choose or be assigned are the anecdote, incident, autobiography, interview, and profile.

1. The *anecdote* is a narrative bit told or written to illustrate a point. Its chief characteristic is that it presents individuals in an action that illustrates some definite idea, illuminates some aspects of personality or character. Dialogue, setting, characters are subordinate to the main point. The anecdote rarely stands alone but is a powerful method of making understandable a possibly difficult idea.

2. An *incident* is a short narrative told for its own sake. It deals with a single, simple situation. Its primary emphasis is on the character of the narrator or some person involved in the action or on the action itself. The incident may involve character, setting, action, and dialogue, but it is simple in structure, brief, and without undue emphasis on dramatic conflict. Good examples, from 75 to 200 or 300 words, are in each month's *Reader's Digest* (in the sections "Life in These United States," "Humor in Uniform," "Campus Comedy," "Laughter, the Best Medicine," and as miscellaneous filler). Sometimes these are so vividly written that an artist can easily draw an appropriate illustration.

A young college graduate got a job at a large timber complex in the Northwest. He was an eastern city boy and knew nothing about logging, but said he wanted to learn from the ground up. His foreman planned an initiation calculated to endure in the young man's memory. His first job was to take an inventory of all the logs floating in the large holding pond.

The usual procedure was to walk the logs, counting them as you went. The old-timers had a good laugh just thinking about the cold wet spills he'd take. But the young greenhorn fooled them all. He hired a small plane to fly him over the pond, took a picture, and counted the logs from the photograph.

Since that time this has been the yearly procedure at tax inventory time. The photograph is enclosed with the tax statement, and there have been no questions from the assessor.[14] [153 words; other examples may run to 300 words]

3. In *autobiography* you give a rounded and understandable picture of yourself, just as in biography you give such a picture of another person. In analyzing your subject (*you*) and gathering material, give consideration to the following: a brief account of your heredity and environment—ancestry, birthplace, places of residence; a series of descriptions of people, places, and events, including education, which have genuinely influenced you; your social beliefs; your religious beliefs; your political beliefs; your moral beliefs; your interests, hobbies, likes, dislikes; your ambitions; your qualities of character; your future plans; your ideas of happiness. An autobiographical theme composed of these and similar important matters, arranged in what you consider a clear and effective order, should be genuinely significant and revealing.

4. The *interview* is a narrative account of some person's opinions, beliefs, and attitudes about another person, politics, religion, education, science, and the like, or late developments in some field. The content consists of dialogue, direct quotation, and interspersed comment of the interviewer. The person interviewed need not be a "VIP" ("very important person") ; almost anyone who has an interesting occupation or hobby is a good subject. Before the interview find out as much as you can about the person. Plan in advance questions to ask and topics which you would like discussed. According to circumstances, modify these as neces-

[14] Troy Utley, "Life in These United States," *The Reader's Digest,* July, 1967. Copyright 1967 by The Reader's Digest Association, Inc.

sary during the interview. Be inconspicuous in the use of a notebook or in taking notes; try to rely on your memory in the subject's presence. In writing the interview, avoid exclusive use of a "question and answer" style. Give something of the background of the person. Build your interview around some high point or central thesis of the conversation. Finally, be careful to insure the mechanical accuracy of your interview, such as the use of punctuation marks and the paragraphing of conversation.

5. The *profile* combines biographical material with character interpretation. The profile differs from biographical writing in that it contains more anecdotes, human-interest stories, and humorous or ironic comment. As its name indicates, it is not a full-length portrait; it merely seizes on highlights, bearing somewhat the relation to a full-length biography that a short story does to a novel. Anyone, no matter who, is a potential subject for a profile.

Include in your profile more than merely "who's who" detail, which ordinarily constitutes a minor part of the whole. Be thorough in getting information: from the subject himself, his friends and acquaintances, members of his family, his roommate, his enemies, his teachers or students. Do not make your profile didactic: you are not writing a moral lecture or a piece of propaganda. Build the major portion of the profile around some dominant characteristic of the subject. Account for his attitudes toward various topics. Use incidents, anecdotes, description of appearance and actions, direct quotations.

Follow some clear plan of organization. A good and typical profile may be written as follows: First, describe your subject's physical appearance and follow up with a few flashes of him in action—teaching a class, serving a customer, treating a patient, etc. After that, give a rapid story of his life, stressing details of heredity and environment that have an important bearing. Then come back to him as of the present, showing why he is important, interesting, amusing, bitter, frustrated, happy, or whatnot. Here develop his guiding philosophy of life, his primary motives, his aims and hopes, the worth of his actual achievements. Such an outline is merely a suggestion.

### 17b Use description to give a picture or an impression

Description tells how something looks, tastes, smells, sounds, feels, or acts. It deals with objects, people, places, scenes, animals, moods, or impressions. It may supplement narrative, exposition, or even argumentative writing. Its primary purpose is to indicate a mood, portray a sense impression, or give a picture in words.

1. Maintain a consistent point of view to make description clear and effective. As in narrative, choose through whose eyes and mind the subject is presented, and be consistent. Furthermore, are the materials described outside the person: concrete physical things that help the reader to *see,* or *hear,* or *smell,* or *taste,* or *touch?* Or are the materials within the mind; are you using a *mental* outlook, by which you create for the reader a specific mood or tone (Section 4f) ?

2. Use "space order," ordinarily, in writing description. That is, choose some point in space or geography, from which point your description moves: from north to south or east to west; from left to right or right to left; from near to remote or remote to near; or, in personal description, from head to foot. Sometimes you can begin with prominent characteristics and move to less prominent ones.

3. For effective description, use words that appeal to one of the senses, pleasantly or unpleasantly, or that portray a mood: words of shape, size, color (*rectangular, bulbous, bluish*) ; sound words (*tinkling, harsh, melodious*) ; smell words (*pungent, acrid, rose-scented*) ; taste words (*sweet, sour, tangy, bitter*); touch words (*hot, soft, icy, velvety*) ; mood words (*sad, brooding, mournful, melancholy*) . (See Section 64.) Descriptive writing should have a single effect, provide a unified dominant impression.

4. A common form of descriptive writing is the *sketch,* a study of character or setting or mood. It contains little action or plot but places emphasis on descriptive details. Unlike the anecdote, it is not concerned with making a point or illustrating a thesis; unlike the incident, it emphasizes characterization—person, setting, mood—to the virtual exclusion of action.

## 17c  *Use exposition to explain or clarify or interpret*

Exposition includes a great part of what is written and read: textbooks; magazine articles; some newspaper editorials; and criticisms of books, motion pictures, radio and television programs, and musical compositions and performances. Some of these you may be called upon to write.

1. Follow a logical plan or order in writing exposition. Choose one of the following:

a. *Known to unknown.* Begin with what your reader knows and proceed to unknown material about which you give information.

b. *Simple to complex.* Begin with easily understood matters; proceed logically to the more difficult.

c. *Classification.* Divide your subject into its various parts according to a consistent, logical plan and discuss each part in order.

d. *Time.* Develop your subject according to the way its parts develop in time, as, for example, giving instructions on how to paint furniture or how to reach a certain place.

e. *Space.* Follow the order that the parts of your subject occupy in space, such as the points of the compass (see Section 17b2), but emphasize explanation rather than description.

f. *Deductive.* Begin with a general statement or truth and show how it applies to specific or particular instances or examples.

g. *Inductive.* Discuss particular instances or examples from which you draw a general conclusion or make a generalized statement.

h. *Cause and effect.* Start with cause or causes and lead to results or start with the effect or effects and explain by giving causes.

i. *Comparison or analogy and contrast.* Explain your subject, or some part of it, by using materials that show its similarity to some familiar object or by using contrast, which emphasizes differences.

2. Choose the form of exposition which most appropriately and effectively develops your subject:

a. *Expanded definition.* Other than giving a simpler synonym to define a term, most definition assigns a term, especially a noun, to a general class (*genus*) and then shows how it differs (*differentia*) from other members of this class. In such definitions, use simple words; exclude everything from the definition that does not belong in it; include everything that does belong; and avoid using any derivative of the term being defined. Expanded definition gives further details or examples; uses comparison or contrast; shows cause or effect; or divides the term into its component parts. A method of paragraph development, that by *definition*, is discussed in Section **24b.**

   b. *Narrative exposition.* Telling a story, usually following a time order, is commonly used in the explanation of a process. Subjects using the words *how, the method, the principle,* and the like, are developed by narrative exposition—for example, "How Petroleum Is Refined" or "Methods of Obtaining Oil from Coal."

   c. *Giving directions.* An important subdivision of narrative exposition is giving directions. Subjects may be impersonal, "How To Water-Ski," or personal, "How I Learned To Water-Ski." In either, directions should be so clear that your reader will have no trouble in following them.

   d. *Descriptive exposition.* Explaining by describing and, ordinarily, using space order is commonly used to make clear the working of either simple or complicated mechanical objects like a spark plug, a fishing reel, a ball-point pen, a microscope, an electronic microscope, a jet engine, or a nuclear-power plant. Frequently, descriptive exposition and narrative exposition are used together: examples appear in any issue of a semitechnical or popular scientific magazine.

   e. *Criticism.* Criticism is an estimation of worth or value, whether of a book, a magazine article, a movie, a radio or television program, or a musical composition. Ordinarily, as critic, you answer four questions: What was the author's purpose? What methods did he use in accomplishing his purpose: scope, characters, setting, kind of plot, dialogue, point of view, style, etc.? Was the purpose successfully accomplished? Was it worth accomplishing?

   Always give some indication of content. Select a controlling idea and mold your review around it. Make some use of quotations or examples. Be specific; avoid vague terms. Do not hesitate to inject your ideas into the review. Make necessary qualifications, but avoid contradictions and afterthoughts which destroy the unity of purpose and tone of your review.

   f. *Informal and formal essays.* The informal or personal essay is usually a friendly and conversational explanation of the writer's attitudes, opinions, or moods toward a specific subject, using some dominant tone such as whimsy, satire, irony, humor.

   The formal essay or article, commonly labeled "magazine

article," is a dignified and usually impersonal treatment of a serious subject; it may be descriptive or argumentative, but it is usually expository.

Examples of both informal and formal essays can be found in contemporary magazines: the former are infrequent now; the latter, an important part of the contents of almost all modern magazines, are mainly specialized types of exposition. However, by following directions given for writing themes (choosing and limiting and analyzing subjects, Sections 2, 4; getting material, Section 5, and organizing, Section 6) and by adapting directions for writing the research paper (see Section 20), you can approach successful writing of the formal essay or article. Bear in mind only that it is now usually written in an appropriately popular style and, though based on fact, is not accompanied by the paraphernalia of documentation (footnotes and bibliography).

## 17d   Use argument to persuade or convince

Formal argument, a complicated subject, includes four special steps: establishing the proposition, analyzing the proposition, formulating the argument, and preparing the brief (a form of outline).

Less formal argument—usually used in themes, magazine articles, and many newspaper editorials—is built around subjects containing the words "advantages," "disadvantages," "value," or "why": "The Advantages of Participating in Campus Dramatics," "The Value of Intramural Athletics," "Why Our College Should Abolish Final Examinations."

The plan in informal argument is classification: listing of reasons for or against, sometimes in order of climax, i.e., progressing to the most important, and sometimes in more or less arbitrary order. Under each reason discuss facts or materials, known as evidence, which support and establish that particular part of the argument. Guard against any weakness or errors that would destroy the effectiveness of the chain of reasoning or logical thinking (see Section 13c).

Make argumentative content lead to an inevitable conclusion. But sometimes you may give both sides and leave the reader to make his own decisions about the conclusion: "The Advantages and Disadvantages of Final Examinations."

## EXERCISES

In writing on any of the following subjects, remember that you should have in mind, and indicate, a specific reader or limited group of readers (see Section 4b, pp. 22–23) .

A. Prepare a list of 10 limited theme topics designed to be developed by telling a story (narrative) ; 10 to be developed by giving a picture in words (description) ; 10 to be developed by explaining (exposition) ; 10 to be developed by convincing (argument) .

B. Write a 400-word narrative, preferably but not necessarily from personal experience, which exemplifies an old proverb. Do not explain the expository idea of the proverb; simply state at the end the proverb which the narrative exemplifies. Suggestions:

1. Better late than never.
2. He who hesitates is lost.
3. Procrastination is the thief of time.
4. A rolling stone gathers no moss.
5. It's a long lane that has no turning.
6. He who laughs last laughs best.
7. Two heads are better than one.
8. Half a loaf is better than no bread.
9. A friend in need is a friend indeed.
10. You can't have your cake and eat it, too.

C. Write an anecdote to prove or disprove any of the following statements:

1. Men are better automobile drivers than women.
2. The most reckless drivers in the country are the group aged —— to —— years.
3. Chivalry among youth is nonexistent.
4. Few people have the courage of their convictions.
5. A loyal voter should always vote the straight party ticket.
6. Students should be allowed to choose all the courses they take.
7. Our campus does not know the meaning of "campus politics."
8. Athletes receive special consideration from their instructors.
9. Students should be allowed to cut as many classes as they please.
10. American traffic policemen are noted for their courtesy.

D. Read the departments "Life in These United States," "Humor in Uniform," and "Campus Comedy" in several issues of *The Reader's*

*Digest.* From your own experience write several similar incidents (limit: 300 words each).

E. Write a brief autobiographical theme (about 500 words) introducing yourself to your instructor.

F. If you do not write a fairly complete autobiography, you may be assigned (or wish to write) sections or divisions of your autobiography: Ancestry; Early Childhood; Environment; Early Education; College; Summer Activities; People, Places, and Events That Have Had Influence; Friends; Religion; Politics; Travel; Ambitions; Interests and Hobbies; Personal Characteristics; Ideals.

G. Choose someone on or near the campus who has a responsible position or who is known for some achievement or activity. Plan, carry out, and write an interview with this person. Suggestions: My College Adviser; A Receptionist or the Man (or Woman) at an Information Desk; An Interesting Teacher; A Coach; A Student Pastor; The Manager or Owner of a Cafeteria or Restaurant; A Bookstore Owner or Manager; The Librarian; The President of —— Class (or Organization); The Manager of —— (a student activity); A Campus Band Leader; A Campus Policeman; A Janitor; A Night Watchman; A Bus or Taxicab Driver; etc.

H. Write a *profile* of one of the people mentioned in Exercise G or in Exercise L.

I. Copy from a guidebook a formal description of some place you have visited. Then write a brief description in which you try to convey to the reader some idea of the *impression* the place made on you. Use your five senses liberally.

J. Make each of the following specific; then write a brief, literal description of any two: A Drug Store or Department Store Lunch Counter; A Chemistry Laboratory; A Student Room; A Dentist's Office; A Bus Station; The College Cafeteria; A Professor's Office; A Chain Grocery Store; A Skyscraper; A Filling Station; Backstage at a Theater; A Projection Booth; A Student's Notebook; An Airport; A Stadium; A Golf Course; A City Park; A Bridge; A Modernized Farm; A Mountain.

K. Assume that a friend of yours in a distant city has agreed to meet at the station someone he or she has never seen. Write for that friend an adequate description of a relative, your roommate, a classmate, or a close friend.

L. Make individual and write a character sketch of one of the following: A College Dean; A Typical Clubwoman; A Member of My Family; My Best Friend; The Cashier at a Motion Picture Theater; A Camp Counselor; A Fraternity Brother; A Coed; An Actress as She Appears in the Part of —— (a specific character); Our Family Physician;

A Good Teacher; My High School Principal; A Campus Leader; An Unforgettable Character; Campus Man (or Woman) of the Year.

M. Write an informal or expanded definition (300 to 500 words) of one or more of the following: Dictatorship; A Roommate; An English Composition Class; A Theme; Hydroponics; A State Fair; A Sorority Tea; Fraternity Rush; A Good Sport; The Ideal Wife (or Husband) ; Television; Student Government; 4-H Club; Campus Politics; Code of Honor; Rewriting; Radar; Cutthroat Competition; Scholars and Students; any limited term in sport (Lateral Pass; Offside; Strike; Let Ball; Three-Bagger; Technical Foul; Knockout; Hole in One; etc.) .

N. Write a narrative exposition explaining one of the following processes—fill in the appropriate words in your title:

1. How a —— Works
2. The Manufacture of ——
3. The Production of ——
4. The Principle of ——
5. The Method of ——

O. Write a "giving directions" theme. Suggestions:

1. How To Lead a Boy Scout (Girl Scout) Troop
2. How To Study Successfully
3. How To Prepare for an Examination
4. Rules for Driving in City Traffic
5. A Guide to (or Through) a Building, Factory, Park, Campus, Historical Site, etc. (make definite)
6. Directions for Getting to (name some place)
7. How I Learned To (some physical activity)
8. How I Budget My Time
9. How I Earn My Spending Money
10. How I Developed the Hobby of ——

P. Write a descriptive exposition of some fairly simple object in your room or home (suggestions: electric fan, alarm clock, ball-point pen, desk calendar, camera, etc.) .

Q. Choose from each of the following groups one that you liked (or like) best and one that you liked (or like) least. Write a criticism of each: book (fiction) , book (nonfiction) , magazine, newspaper, movie, radio program, television program, musical composition, recording, dramatic production, short story.

R. Write a theme (argument) for a named person on one of the following subjects. Begin each title with the words "This Is a . . ."

Town You Should Visit; Program (or Recording) You Should Hear; Meal You Would Enjoy; Girl (Boy) Whom You Should Know; Professor Whom You Should Have; Activity You Should Enter; Book You Should Read; Profession You Should Enter; Hobby You Should Have; TV Show (or Movie) You Should Not Miss.

S. Complete each of the following theme subjects to be developed as argument:

1. The Advantages (Disadvantages) of ——
2. The Value of ——
3. Why I Am in Favor of (Opposed to) ——
4. You Will Like (Will Not Like) ——
5. Three Reasons for (or Against) ——

# 18 *The précis and the paraphrase*

Many questions asked in conversation and on examinations require summarizing answers, an indispensable form of communication in modern college life. Each day we are called upon to give, in written or oral form, condensed versions of events, ideas, or impressions.

In fact, the method of summary is generally prevalent. A popular magazine, *The Reader's Digest,* is largely composed of summaries of more detailed articles in other periodicals, and the editorial technique involved (preserving so far as possible the exact wording of a full-length article but dropping out substantial portions of it) has been employed by other "digest" magazines. Certain periodicals publish digests of entire books. Radio and TV news commentators furnish what are essentially summaries of the latest news developments. Magazines like *Time* and *Newsweek* contain short articles which are, in one sense, condensations of events. Business and industrial executives frequently ask employees to submit brief reports concerning developments in their departments or trends in business or research or to write brief introductory summaries of longer reports. Illustrations need not be continued; every student could mention other examples of the use of summaries.

A summary, as a condensed version of a longer passage or a more extended account, has several names: *abstract, abridgment, condensation, digest, epitome, précis, résumé, synopsis,* even *outline,* and others. Distinctions between any two are of no great importance.

## THE PRÉCIS

A *précis* (form both singular and plural, pronounced "pray-see") is a brief summary of the essential thought of a longer composition. It provides a miniature of the original selection, reproducing the same proportions on smaller scale, the same ideas, and the same mood and tone, so far as possible. The maker of a précis cannot interpret or comment; his sole function is to give a reduction of the author's exact and essential meaning. Nor can he omit important details.

Précis are effective in developing your capacities for *careful reading, constructive thinking,* and *exact writing.* The composition of a good précis is difficult and requires time and effort.

### 18a   Select carefully the material to be condensed

Some selections can be reduced satisfactorily: novels, short stories, plays, speeches, magazine articles; but other materials are so short or so tightly knit that condensation is virtually impossible, such as Francis Bacon's essays, the style of which is especially compact and epigrammatic.

### 18b   Read the selection carefully

In order to group the central ideas, read carefully, analytically, and reflectively. In doing such reading, follow two steps:

1. Give the material a through and thorough reading once, to get a clear understanding of the whole.

2. Reread paragraph by paragraph, to get each paragraph topic and to note how it has been developed by various methods.

Look up the meanings of all words and phrases about which you are in doubt. Look for important or key expressions that must be used in your précis if it is to preserve the essential meaning and flavor of the original selection. Before starting to write, you must, to use Francis Bacon's phrase, "chew and digest" the selection, not merely "taste" it or "swallow" it whole in a single gulp. See how the material has been organized, what devices the writer has used, what kinds of illustrations support the main thought. You may want to question critically some of the writer's statements, but if your purpose is to write a précis, you must report faithfully and without comment what he has said.

### 18c  Use your own words

As you read, restate the main idea of each paragraph clearly and concisely. Quoting sentences, perhaps topic sentences, from each paragraph results in a sentence outline, not a précis. You must use your own words for the most part, although a little quotation is permissible; ordinarily, however, the phrasing of the original will not be suitable for your purposes. Once you have mastered the thought of the material, your problem is one of original composition: your own analysis and statement of the major thought.

### 18d  Set limits to the number of words you use

The length of a condensation cannot arbitrarily be determined, but for purposes of summary most prose can be reduced by two-thirds to three-fourths. A précis, therefore, should usually be about one-third to one-fourth as long as the original. Omit nothing of real importance, but remember that the central aim of a précis is condensation.

### 18e  Follow the plan of the original

Follow the logical order of the original so that the condensation will be accurate. Thoughts and facts should not be rearranged; if they are, the essence of the original may be distorted. Give attention to proportion. Try to preserve the mood and tone of the original.

### 18f  Write the précis in effective English

The condensation should be a model of exact and emphatic diction and clear, effective sentence construction, because it must be intelligible to a reader who has not seen the original. Bring together with logic and with transitions your various summarizing statements. Transition from sentence to sentence must be smooth and unobtrusive, emphasizing the unity and coherence of the summarization. As you proceed, you may need to contract certain parts. Although the précis is not likely to be so well written as the original, it should read smoothly and possess compositional merit of its own.

NOTE: If you use a précis as part of a theme or research paper, document it in a footnote by giving details of your source (see Section **20g**) .

The following example of a précis was written by a student. Criticize it in the light of suggestions given above.

*Original*

A third kind of thinking is stimulated when anyone questions our beliefs and opinions. We sometimes find ourselves changing our minds without any resistance or heavy emotion, but if we are told that we are wrong we resent the imputation and harden our hearts. We are incredibly heedless in the formation of our beliefs, but find ourselves filled with an illicit passion for them when anyone proposes to rob us of their companionship. It is obviously not the ideas themselves that are dear to us, but our self-esteem, which is threatened. We are by nature stubbornly pledged to defend our own from attack, whether it be our person, our family, our property, or our opinion. A United States Senator once remarked to a friend of mine that God Almighty could not make him change his mind on our Latin-America policy. We may surrender, but rarely confess ourselves vanquished. In the intellectual world at least, peace is without victory.

Few of us take the pains to study the origin of our cherished convictions; indeed, we have a natural repugnance to so doing. We like to continue to believe what we have been accustomed to accept as true, and the resentment aroused when doubt is cast upon any of our assumptions leads us to seek every manner of excuse for clinging to them. *The result is that most of our so-called reasoning consists in finding arguments for going on believing as we already do.*[15] [242 words]

—JAMES HARVEY ROBINSON, "On Various Kinds of Thinking"

*Précis*

A third kind of thinking occurs when we are told that our beliefs and opinions are wrong. We may have been heedless in their formation, but our self-esteem will not permit us to change. We may have to give up, but we are not convinced. We do not study the origin of our beliefs; we believe as we have been accustomed to believe, and we seek arguments for continuing to believe as we already do. [75 words]

---

[15] James Harvey Robinson, *The Mind in the Making.* Copyright 1921 by Harper & Brothers. Used by permission.

## THE PARAPHRASE

The *paraphrase* is another type of report on reading required frequently in college work. Whereas a précis is a digest of the essential meaning of an original passage, a paraphrase is a full-length statement of that meaning: a free rendering of the sense of a passage, fully and proportionately, but in different words; or, as *Webster's Third New International Dictionary* says: "A restatement of a text, passage, or work, giving the meaning in another form, usually for clearer and fuller exposition: a free rendering." A paraphrase does not include translation from one language to another, the technical name for which is *metaphrase*.

The paraphrase is frequently used to make clear any material that is vague, obscure, or difficult, a process usually consisting of both simplification and modernization. You may have read a difficult poem or an abstruse discussion which you could not make sense of until you put it in your own words. After you did so, its meaning was clear, and you felt that you had actually translated the passage into your own thought. Much of the discussion in English and social science classrooms begins with paraphrasing ideas expressed in assignments from textbooks. In other words, as a student you have almost daily need for reshaping source material to suit your own discussional purposes.

Three common uses of paraphrase, therefore, are the following: (1) paraphrasing technical, semitechnical, or otherwise difficult materials into understandable nontechnical English; (2) paraphrasing poems into clear prose; (3) paraphrasing poetry or prose of a bygone era into understandable present-day prose.

If the material to be paraphrased is poetry, remember: (1) A line of poetry is a *poetic* unit, not a *sense* unit; it need not be and very likely is not a sentence. As a first step, copy the poem as if it were prose; then reread it with special attention to the punctuation marks and the purposes they serve. (2) Poetry, for poetic reasons, often uses inverted, suspended, or transposed word order. Rearrange these words in normal, straightforward English word order: subject and modifiers, predicate and modifiers, object and modifiers.

In making a paraphrase, follow these additional suggestions.

### 18g   *Study the original passage*

"Study" here means that you should read the original passage as often as necessary in order to approach understanding its full and exact meaning. It is impossible to paraphrase a passage until you are familiar with its purposes, organization, development, and essential content. Some phrases and sentences you will probably have to reread several times, carefully and reflectively, before their meaning becomes clear. If the passage contains obscure words and allusions, consult a dictionary or other reference book to determine their meanings.

### 18h   *Use your own words*

Find understandable equivalents for words and phrases which are obscure, but do not strain for synonyms. Feel free to use words from the original material if their meaning is unmistakably clear, but do not hesitate to use your own words and phrases where simplification, clarity, or modernization requires them.

### 18i   *Leave out nothing of importance*

A paraphrase is a restatement and, as such, should contain the thought of the original in its entirety. Omitting significant detail is a violation of the original and results in distortion.

### 18j   *Add nothing that is not in the original*

A paraphrase is not designed to be a *full* interpretation, in which the paraphraser adds his own comments. Interpretation and explanation should be confined to making clear what the original author had in mind. Whether you like or dislike what the writer has said, whether you agree or disagree with him, whether you think his logic is sound or faulty—these considerations do not enter into the making of the paraphrase. Your making of a paraphrase does not mean that you, as a writer, cease to think; it means that your thinking produces a full-length statement of another's meaning.

### 18k   *Retain the tone of the original*

As closely as clearness permits, follow the tone, mood, and atmosphere of the material being paraphrased. Changing the purpose, mood, treatment, or tone of the original may distort, parody, or give a wrong meaning. Obviously, as paraphraser, you can hardly hope to achieve the same mood and tone quality as the author of, say, a great poem, but try to preserve as much of these existing qualities as possible.

## 18l   Use effective English

Any paraphrase of a good poem or prose passage is worth less than the original, but the better the paraphrase, the less the difference between it and the original. The making of a good paraphrase, just as of an effective précis, requires exact writing: correct, clear diction, effective sentence structure, and adequate transitions.

NOTE: If you use a paraphrase as part of a theme or research paper, document it in a footnote by giving details of your source (see Section **20g**) .

The following is a paraphrase (128 words) of a famous sonnet (117 words) . Study it in terms of the suggestions given above.

THE WORLD IS TOO MUCH WITH US

The world is too much with us, late and soon,
Getting and spending, we lay waste our powers:
Little we see in Nature that is ours;
We have given our hearts away, a sordid boon!
The sea that bares her bosom to the moon;
The winds that will be howling at all hours,
And are up-gathered now like sleeping flowers,
For this, for everything, we are out of tune;
It moves us not.—Great God! I'd rather be
A Pagan suckled in a creed outworn;
So might I, standing on this pleasant lea,
Have glimpses that would make me less forlorn;
Have sight of Proteus rising from the sea;
Or hear old Triton blow his wreathèd horn.
                              —WILLIAM WORDSWORTH

*Paraphrase*

We are surrounded by many earthly activities—both early and late and both in giving out and taking in—and we exhaust our energies, seeing little of Nature's beauty. In so exhausting our energies, we have made a sorry exchange. Moonlight on the ocean, the winds that may blow night and day, but at present are quiet like sleeping flowers—for these, for all such beautiful scenes, we are out of tune; we remain unmoved. Dear Lord, I'd rather be a pagan, believing in paganism's outworn creed. For then, standing in this pleasant meadow, I would see things to comfort and console me. I would see one great sea god, Proteus, rising from the waves, and I would hear another great sea god, Triton, blowing his curved horn.

**EXERCISES**

A. Write several précis of materials from your book of readings or from current magazines, selecting short articles or two or three paragraphs from a longer selection. Include one narrative and one expository selection. Perhaps your instructor will prefer to make uniform assignments for all class members.

B. Select several articles in a recent or the current issue of *The Reader's Digest*. In your library obtain the magazines referred to. Write a comment on the shortened versions compared with the original versions.

C. Choose an article in a current magazine or in your book of readings and condense it as *The Reader's Digest* would.

D. Choose five short poems which are your favorites (from your book of readings, collections of poetry, selected poems from one author). Write a paraphrase of each poem according to the directions given in Section 18g–1. Your instructor may also ask you to write a précis of each paraphrase.

# 19 Using the library

A library is virtually a laboratory where deposits of the written word and the graphic portrayal of thought preserved in manuscript, print, and picture are available to the reader, the investigator, and the creative worker. A knowledge of these resources and an understanding of their organization are prerequisites for your effective use and enjoyment of this library-laboratory.

As a first step, use a free hour for a trip to the library. Get its physical setup clearly in mind: number of rooms and their use (main reading room, study alcoves, and reserved-book room); labels on different offices of library personnel indicating activities that make a library effective; different sections for reference books, new acquisitions, fiction, bound magazines, current magazines and newspapers, and the like. Stroll along the reference shelves and note the kind and location of books.

Libraries differ in actual content and physical arrangement, but the basic principles which determine the organization of library resources have been sufficiently standardized to enable the student familiar with them to proceed with an investigation in any library. Also, regulations for users by a particular library appear in various forms. Before losing time by a trial-and-error method of learning to use your library, and especially before beginning research on any subject or for any paper or article, find out whether your library has a guide, handbook, or pamphlet which explains or interprets its organization.

Whether familiar or not with library organization, you should examine one or more of the following guides:

Winchell, Constance M. *Guide to Reference Books,* 8th ed. Chicago: American Library Association, 1967. (NOTE: This book, probably kept at the library reference desk, is comprehensive and invaluable. Its major divisions, each with many subdivisions, are as follows: General Reference Works, The Humanities, Social Sciences, History and Area Studies, Pure and Applied Sciences.)

Aldrich, Ella V. *Using Books and Libraries,* 5th ed. Englewood Cliffs, N.J.: Prentice-Hall, 1967.

Barton, Mary N., and M. V. Bell. *Reference Books: A Brief Guide for Students and Other Users of the Library,* 6th ed. Baltimore, Md.: Enoch Pratt Free Library, 1966.

Cook, Margaret G. *The New Library Key,* 2nd ed. New York: H. W. Wilson Company, 1963.

Downs, Robert B. *How To Do Library Research.* Urbana and London: University of Illinois Press, 1966.

Gohdes, Clarence. *Bibliographical Guide to the Study of the Literature of the U.S.A.,* 2nd ed. Durham, N.C.: Duke University Press, 1963.

Murphey, Robert W. *How and Where To Look It Up.* New York: McGraw-Hill, 1958.

Shove, Raymond, and others. *The Use of Books and Libraries,* 10th ed. Minneapolis: University of Minnesota Press, 1963.

Look up in these guidebooks some or many of the titles below for the rich information given, such as full bibliographic details and helpful critical discussions of materials on various subjects.

In every library a student has at his disposal three important kinds of material: reference works, periodicals, and the general collection of books.

## *19a   Become familiar with the reference works in your library*

Unless you already know what books and magazine articles are suited to your research needs, you should start with condensed, authoritative articles in reference books. Any book may be used for reference purposes, but reference books "are usually comprehensive in scope, condensed in treatment, and arranged on some special plan to facilitate the ready and accurate finding of information."[16] Such works are usually located on shelves open to the student in the main reading room or in a nearby reference room.

The following lists contain titles of works which are likely to be most valuable to the undergraduate student. Several titles may deal with the same general or specific subjects, and your library is virtually certain to have one or more of these books. Remember, however, that the preparation of a reference book is expensive in time and money. It cannot be revised and reprinted very often. Sometimes, too, supplements are added, and sometimes revisions and new editions may be in progress but may take several years for completion. Always a good starting point, reference books may become dated, and you should supplement any dated material by consulting annual publications, current indexes, and revised or new editions. (See Section **19b.**)

I. BOOKS OF GENERAL INFORMATION

A. GENERAL ENCYCLOPEDIAS

*Collier's Encyclopedia* (20 vols.; kept up to date with an annual volume, *Collier's Year Book Covering National and International Events*) .

*Columbia Encyclopedia,* 3rd ed.

*Columbia-Viking Desk Encyclopedia,* 3rd ed.

---

16 Isadore G. Mudge, "Reference Work and Reference Books," in Constance M. Winchell, *Guide to Reference Books,* 8th ed., p. xiv. Mudge's brief introduction, pp. xiii–xv, gives valuable suggestions for consulting and studying reference books.

*Encyclopaedia Britannica* (24 vols.; kept up to date with an annual volume, *Britannica Book of the Year, a Record of the March of Events*).

*Encyclopedia Americana* (30 vols.; kept up to date with an annual volume, *The Americana Annual, an Encyclopedia of Current Events*).

*Lincoln Library of Essential Information.*

*New International Encyclopaedia* (25 vols.; kept up to date with an annual volume, *New International Year Book, a Compendium of the World's Progress*).

Seligman, Edwin R. A., and Alvin Johnson, eds. *Encyclopaedia of the Social Sciences* (15 vols.; commonly known as E.S.S.; less comprehensive than the volumes listed above, it deals with many subjects directly and indirectly related to the social sciences; E.S.S. could just as well have been listed in Section II, "Books of and Guides to Special Subject Information").

Sills, David L., ed. *International Encyclopedia of the Social Sciences* (17 vols.).

B. GENERAL DICTIONARIES (see pp. 307–308)

C. YEARBOOKS, in addition to the annual yearbooks of the various encyclopedias (see A, above):

*Annual Register: World Events.*

*Europa Year Book* (2 vols.; Vol. I: International Organizations, Europe; Vol. II: Africa, The Americas, Asia, Australasia).

*Information Please Almanac* (miscellaneous information).

*International Yearbook and Statesmen's Who's Who.*

*Statesman's Year-book: Statistical and Historical Annual of the States of the World* (over 100 annual volumes have been published).

*Statistical Abstract of the United States.*

*United Nations Yearbook.*

*World Almanac and Book of Facts* (miscellaneous information).

Some of these books have been published annually for many years; some are comparatively recent. Like most of the books listed in this entire section (**19a**), the general nature of each is evident from its title or subtitle. Outstanding events, changes, statistics, and progress in the fields of industry, government, literature, and education should be sought in these yearbooks for the period. The *Statesman's Year-book,* for example, gives data regarding the government, area, population, education, religion, and industries of every nation and state in the world, including the United States.

## II. BOOKS OF AND GUIDES TO
## SPECIAL SUBJECT INFORMATION

Six subject lists follow, containing titles of encyclopedias, dictionaries, and handbooks, as well as indexes to specialized magazines. The six groups of subjects, likely to be among those most often considered in writing a term or research paper (Section 20), are Biography, Drama and Theater, History, Language, Literature, and Science. For those interested in other areas (such as Business and Economics, Education, Music and the Dance, Painting and Architecture, Philosophy and Psychology, Religion, and special sciences), the library guides on p. 115 provide necessary information.

In the indexes to magazines, both in these lists and in Section 19b, the words *cumulative* and *cumulation* mean "increasing by successive additions"; that is, lists of authors, titles, and subjects are arranged alphabetically and published in several issues of the index; then periodically—for example, quarterly, semiannually, annually, or over a two- or three-year period—all the lists are combined in one alphabet, and earlier separate issues are discarded.

The subject encyclopedias are especially useful for supplying a brief history of a special subject, together with a selected bibliography, i.e., a list of books, booklets, and articles about a certain subject or subjects or about a person or persons. In general, therefore, you should prefer the special encyclopedias for subjects within their scope rather than the general encyclopedias. The "best" encyclopedia to use for a given topic often depends on the phase of a subject being investigated.

In addition to the titles listed below, your library has many other handbooks, dictionaries, or encyclopedias. A random sampling reveals handbooks on the following: air conditioning, automotive engineering, aviation, electrical engineering, geography, heating and ventilating, history of science, industrial relations, mechanical engineering, nuclear science and technology, plastics, portraits, radio electronics, rare metals, refrigeration engineering, sociology, songs, and wool.

Among innumerable special bibliographies, i.e., lists of books and magazine articles, a random sampling shows bibliographies on these subjects: American mammals and birds, American natural history, ceramics, costume, detective short story, fairy tales, foreign affairs, handicrafts, labor, meteorites, North American folklore and folk song, papermaking, printing, stainless steel, swimming.

A. BIOGRAPHY

Barnhart, C. L., ed. *New Century Cyclopedia of Names* (3 vols.) .

*Biography Index,* 1947– (a cumulative index to biographical material in books and magazines) .

*Current Biography: Who's News and Why,* 1940– (11 monthly issues, cumulated in one alphabet annually, of "personalities prominent on the international scene, in the arts, sciences, industry, politics, education, and entertainment") .

Dargan, Marion. *Guide to American Biography, 1607–1933* (suggests original and secondary sources) .

Ethridge, James M., ed. *Contemporary Authors: A Bio-Bibliographical Guide to Current Authors and Their Works.*

Johnson, Allen, and Dumas Malone, eds. *Dictionary of American Biography* (21 vols.; commonly known as D.A.B. or DAB; it includes outstanding Americans who are no longer living) .

Kunitz, Stanley J., and Howard Haycraft, eds. *American Authors, 1600– 1900* (includes 1300 biographies and 400 portraits) .

Kunitz, Stanley J., and Howard Haycraft, eds. *British Authors Before 1800* (includes 650 biographies and 220 portraits) .

Kunitz, Stanley J., and Howard Haycraft, eds. *British Authors of the Nineteenth Century* (includes 1000 biographies and 350 portraits) .

Kunitz, Stanley J., and Howard Haycraft, eds. *Twentieth Century Authors* and *First Supplement* (includes over 1850 biographies and 1700 portraits) .

Magill, Frank N. *Cyclopedia of World Authors* (biographies of 753 world-famous authors, from Homer to James Gould Cozzens) .

*National Cyclopedia of American Biography* (47 vols.; in progress) .

Preston, Wheeler. *American Biographies* (excludes living people) .

Stephen, Leslie, and Sidney Lee, eds. *Dictionary of National Biography* (63 vols. originally, reissued in 22 vols., several supplements; commonly known as D.N.B. or DNB; it includes outstanding Englishmen who are no longer living) .

*Webster's Biographical Dictionary.*

*Who's Who* (principally British; includes only living people; for those who have recently died, see earlier volumes or volumes entitled *Who Was Who*) .

*Who's Who in America* (includes only living people; for those who have recently died, see earlier volumes or volumes entitled *Who Was Who in America*) .

Specialized books giving biographies of contemporary people in various fields and in foreign countries include *American Men of Science*; *Directory of American Scholars*; *Leaders in Education*; *Who's Who in American Art*; *Who's Who in Engineering*; *Who's Who in the Theatre*; *Who's Who of American Women*; and "Who's Who" in the East, Midwest, West, South and South-West, Canada, France, Latin America, the United Nations.

Your library also has special bibliographies of biographical and critical materials about earlier authors. A random sampling shows special bibliographies on the following: Miguel de Cervantes, Geoffrey Chaucer, James Fenimore Cooper, Stephen Crane, Charles Dickens, Robert Frost, Thomas Hardy, Oliver Wendell Holmes, John Keats, Abraham Lincoln, Edgar Allan Poe, James Whitcomb Riley, Walter Scott, William Shakespeare, Booth Tarkington, Mark Twain, Walt Whitman.

B. DRAMA AND THEATER

Baker, Blanch M., comp. *Theatre and Allied Arts.*

*Dramatic Index,* 1909–1949 (until discontinued, an annual index to articles and illustrations concerning the stage and players in American and British periodicals) .

Firkins, Ina Ten Eyck. *Index to Plays,* 1800–1926, with *Supplement* to 1934 (the two volumes index 11,156 plays by 3538 authors) .

Hartnoll, Phyllis, ed. *The Oxford Companion to the Theatre.*

Ottemiller, John H. *Index to Plays in Collections . . . 1900–1962,* 4th ed. (an index to 6993 copies of 2536 different plays by 1300 different authors in 814 collections—from ancient times to the present) .

Shipley, J. T., *Guide to Great Plays.*

Sobel, Bernard. *The New Theatre Handbook and Digest of Plays.*

West, Dorothy H., and Dorothy M. Peake. *Play Index, 1949–1952* (an index to 2616 plays in 1138 volumes) .

C. HISTORY

Adams, James Truslow, ed. *Dictionary of American History* (6 vols.) .

Bury, J. B., and others, eds. *Cambridge Ancient History* (12 vols.) .

Damon, Charles R., comp. *American Dictionary of Dates, 458–1920* (3 vols.) .

Douglas, George W. *The American Book of Days.*

Dutcher, G. M., and others, eds. *Guide to Historical Literature.*

*Guide to the Study of the United States of America.*

Gwatkin, H. M., J. P. Whitney, and others, eds. *Cambridge Medieval History* (8 vols.) .

Handlin, Oscar, and others. *Harvard Guide to American History.*

*Harper's Encyclopaedia of United States History from 458* A.D. *to 1912* (10 vols.) .

Hockett, Homer C. *The Critical Method in Historical Research and Writing.*

Langer, William L. *An Encyclopedia of World History.*

Keller, Helen Rex. *Dictionary of Dates* (2 vols.) .

Morris, Richard B., ed. *Encyclopedia of American History,* rev. ed.

Schlesinger, Arthur M., and D. R. Fox, eds. *A History of American Life* (12 vols.) .

*Social Sciences and Humanities Index,* 1965–   (cumulative author and subject index to over 200 magazines; supplements *Readers' Guide* and succeeds *International Index to Periodicals,* p. 126) .

Ward, A. W., and others, eds. *Cambridge Modern History* (13 vols.; *New Cambridge Modern History* in progress) .

*Webster's Geographical Dictionary.*

*Writings on American History,* 1906–1940, 1948–  (an annual index, arranged by author, title, and subject, to materials in books and periodicals dealing with United States history) .

D. LANGUAGE

Baugh, Albert C. *A History of the English Language.*

Berrey, Lester V., and Melvin Van den Bark. *American Thesaurus of Slang: A Complete Reference Book of Colloquial Speech.*

*Crabb's English Synonyms.*

Craigie, Sir William A., and James R. Hulbert, eds. *A Dictionary of American English on Historical Principles* (4 vols.) .

Evans, Bergen, and Cornelia Evans. *A Dictionary of Contemporary American Usage.*

Fowler, Henry W. *A Dictionary of Modern English Usage.*

Kennedy, Arthur G. *A Bibliography of Writings on the English Language from the Beginning of Printing to the End of 1922.*

Mathews, Mitford M., ed. *A Dictionary of Americanisms on Historical Principles* (2 vols.) .

Nicholson, Margaret. *Dictionary of American-English Usage.*

Partridge, Eric. *A Dictionary of Slang and Unconventional English,* 4th ed.

Partridge, Eric. *Slang Today and Yesterday.*

*Roget's International Thesaurus of English Words and Phrases* (revised constantly and title may vary slightly) .

*Webster's Dictionary of Synonyms.*

Wentworth, Harold. *American Dialect Dictionary.*

Wentworth, Harold, and Stuart B. Flexner. *Dictionary of American Slang.*

E. LITERATURE

*A.L.A. Index . . . to General Literature* (with *Supplement,* a guide down to 1910; a subject index, still useful for older books) .

Avery, Catherine B. *The New Century Classical Handbook.*

Barnhart, C. L., ed. *The New Century Handbook of English Literature.*

Bartlett, John. *Familiar Quotations* (first published in 1855, the book has been constantly revised by succeeding editors) .

Bateson, F. W., ed. *Cambridge Bibliography of English Literature* (4 vols.; Vol. 5, *Supplement,* ed. by George Watson, also the editor of a condensed 1-vol. version, *The Concise Bibliography of English Literature, 600–1950*) .

Blanck, Jacob, comp. *Bibliography of American Literature* (begun and continuing; 8 or 9 vols.) .

*Book Review Digest,* 1905– (an index to reviews of some 4000 general books appearing in some 75 American and British periodicals; it is published 11 times a year, but it is cumulative semiannually and annually) .

Burke, William J., and W. D. Howe, eds. *American Authors and Books, 1640–1940.*

Cary, M., and others, eds. *Oxford Classical Dictionary.*

Crimal, P. Larousse. *World Mythology.*

*Cumulative Book Index: A World List of Books in the English Language,* 1929– (author, title, and subject entries are in one alphabet; published monthly, except August, and cumulated frequently during the year, annually, and in four- or five-year cumulations; information given includes publisher, price, and date of publication; for books in print before the *Cumulative Book Index* started, see *United States Catalog,* 1st, 2nd, 3rd, and 4th editions) .

*Essay and General Literature Index,* 1900– (an index to essays and articles in volumes of collections of essays and miscellaneous works; supplements the *A.L.A. Index,* above; published semiannually) .

*Funk and Wagnalls Standard Dictionary of Folklore, Mythology and Legend* (2 vols.) .

Hart, James D. *Oxford Companion to American Literature.*

Harvey, Paul. *Oxford Companion to Classical Literature.*

Harvey, Paul. *Oxford Companion to English Literature.*

Hornstein, Lillian H., ed. *The Reader's Companion to World Literature.*

Jones, Howard Mumford, and Richard M. Ludwig. *Guide to American Literature and Its Backgrounds Since 1890.*

Kennedy, Arthur G., and Donald B. Sands. *A Concise Bibliography for Students of English.*

Leary, Lewis G. *Articles on American Literature,* 1900–1950.

Magill, Frank N., ed. *Quotations in Context* (2020 quotations from world literature revealing who said what under what circumstances).

Magnus, Laurie, ed. *A Dictionary of European Literature Designed as a Companion to English Studies.*

Mencken, H. L., ed. *A New Dictionary of Quotations on Historical Principles from Ancient and Modern Sources.*

Millett, Fred B. *Contemporary American Authors.*

Modern Humanities Research Association. *Annual Bibliography of the English Language and Literature,* 1920– .

*Oxford Dictionary of Quotations.*

*Publications of the Modern Language Association of America* (each year an early issue of this quarterly contains an extensive bibliography of the previous year's writings on language and literature: American, English, modern European).

Sanders, Chauncey. *An Introduction to Research in English Literary History.*

Sandys, John E. *Companion to Latin Studies.*

Shipley, Joseph T., ed. *Dictionary of World Literature: Criticism—Forms—Technique* (also published under the title *Dictionary of World Literary Terms*).

Smith, Horatio, ed. *Columbia Dictionary of Modern European Literature* (contains 1167 articles by 239 specialists, dealing with later nineteenth- and twentieth-century authors; 31 literatures are represented).

*Social Sciences and Humanities Index,* 1965– (cumulative author and subject index to over 200 magazines; supplements *Readers' Guide* and succeeds *International Index to Periodicals,* p. 126).

Spiller, Robert E., and others, eds. *Literary History of the United States* (3 vols.; *Bibliography Supplement,* ed. by Richard M. Ludwig).

Steinberg, S. H., ed. *Cassell's Encyclopaedia of Literature* (2 vols.).

Stevenson, Burton E. *The Home Book of Quotations, Classical and Modern.*

Thrall, William F., and Addison Hibbard. *A Handbook to Literature.*

Trent, William P., and others, eds. *Cambridge History of American Literature* (4 vols.).

Ward, A. W., and A. R. Waller, eds. *Cambridge History of English Literature* (15 vols.).

Whibley, Leonard. *Companion to Greek Studies.*

Wilson, Frank P., and Bonamy Dobrée, eds. *Oxford History of English Literature* (in progress).

Zesmer, David M. *Guide to English Literature.*

F. SCIENCE

*Agricultural Index,* 1916–1964 (a cumulative subject index to a selected but extensive list of agricultural magazines, books, and bulletins; succeeded by *Biological and Agricultural Index,* below) .

*Applied Science and Technology Index,* 1958– (a cumulative subject index to about 200 periodicals dealing with applied science and technology subjects; formerly *Industrial Arts Index,* below) .

*Biological and Agricultural Index,* 1964– (a cumulative subject index to periodicals in the fields of biology, agriculture, and related sciences; continues *Agricultural Index*) .

Crane, Evan J., and others, eds. *A Guide to the Literature of Chemistry.*

*Engineering Index,* 1884– (with changes over the years, this index has been since 1928 a selective subject-author index to periodicals in all engineering fields; it is published annually, but technical libraries receive weekly cards containing the information eventually published in the annual volumes) .

Gentle, Ernest J., and others. *Aviation and Space Dictionary.*

Henderson, Isabella Ferguson, and W. D. Henderson. *Dictionary of Scientific Terms,* 6th ed. (pronunciation, derivation, and definition of terms in biology, botany, zoology, anatomy, cytology, genetics, embryology, physiology) .

*Industrial Arts Index,* 1913–1958 (a cumulative subject index to a selected but extensive list of business, finance, applied science, and technology periodicals, books, and pamphlets; continued by *Applied Science and Technology Index,* above) .

Jones, Franklin, and Paul B. Schubert, eds. *Engineering Encyclopedia* (treats 4500 important engineering subjects) .

*McGraw-Hill Encyclopedia of Science and Technology* (15 vols.; an international reference work, kept up to date by the *McGraw-Hill Yearbook of Science and Technology*) .

Newman, James R., ed. *Harper Encyclopedia of Science* (4 vols.) .

O'Rourke, Charles E., ed. *General Engineering Handbook.*

Parke, Nathan G. *Guide to the Literature of Mathematics and Physics.*

Sarton, George. *Introduction to the History of Science.*

*Space Encyclopedia: A Guide to Astronomy and Space Research.*

*Technical Book Review Index.* 1935– (a cumulative guide to reviews of scientific and technical books in scientific, technical, and trade journals) .

*Van Nostrand's Scientific Encyclopedia.*

Whitford, R. E. *Physics Literature: A Reference Manual.*

## 19b   Become familiar with indexes to periodicals

If you are doing research on a subject of contemporary or revived interest or of recent occurrence, you need to consult magazine files and, perhaps, bound volumes of newspapers. Libraries usually display current issues of the best general magazines and some of special interest—some libraries even have special periodical rooms for such magazines—but older issues are bound in book form and can be obtained most easily after you have consulted index books which are a guide to the contents of the magazines.

In each of these indexes, look for directions to the reader, ordinarily given in the preface, so that you can interpret the entries and find your material without loss of time. The front of each index volume usually tells you which magazines are indexed and gives full instructions for use. For example, here are two entries from *Readers' Guide to Periodical Literature* and their meaning:

Author entry:
> **LINDBERGH, Charles Augustus, 1902-**
> Our best chance to survive. por Sat Eve Post
> **227:25 Jl 17 '54**
> Thoughts of a combat pilot. pors Sat Eve
> Post 227:20-1 + O 2 '54

*Meaning:* during the time covered, Charles A. Lindbergh published two articles, with portraits: "Our Best Chance to Survive" and "Thoughts of a Combat Pilot," both in *The Saturday Evening Post,* the former July 17, 1954, Volume No. 227, p. 25, the latter October 2, 1954, Volume No. 227, beginning on p. 20. (For unbound magazines, the date of issue is your guide; when the magazines are bound into book form, the volume number is your guide, with the date of issue important only when each issue is paged separately.)

Subject entry:
> **COLLEGE students**
> Americans as students. P. Emmanuel. Atlan
> **194:59-62 Ag '54; Discussion. 194:77-9 O; 19**
> N '54

*Meaning:* An article, "Americans as Students," written by P. Emmanuel, was published in the *Atlantic Monthly,* August, 1954, pp. 59 to 62; the volume number, when the magazine is bound, is Volume 194. Discussion of the article appeared October,

1954, pp. 77 to 79, and November, 1954, p. 19—both issues part of Volume 194.

In addition to the periodical indexes included in the lists of special subject information in Section **19a,** the most helpful of the other periodical indexes are those given below. To keep readers entirely up to date, with little loss of time for the reader, most of them are *cumulative* (see definition on p. 118) .

1. *Bulletin of the Public Affairs Information Service,* 1915– (cumulative subject index to current books, pamphlets, periodicals, government documents, and other library material in economics and public affairs) .
2. *Facts on File,* 1940– (a weekly news digest with cumulative index, including world, national, and foreign affairs, finance and economics, art and science, education and religion, sports, obituaries, and other miscellany) .
3. *International Index to Periodicals,* 1907–1965 (cumulative author and subject index to domestic and foreign periodicals dealing with literature, history, social science, religion, drama, and pure science; really a supplement to *Readers' Guide,* below, and succeeded by *Social Sciences and Humanities Index*—see History and Literature, pp. 121 and 123, respectively) .
4. *The New York Times Index,* 1913– (cumulative guide to events of national importance by reference to day, page, and column of *The New York Times;* material is entered by subjects, persons, and organizations; the only index to an American newspaper, it is an indirect guide to events in other newspapers) .
5. *Nineteenth Century Readers' Guide to Periodical Literature,* 1890–1899, with supplementary indexing, 1900–1922 (2 vols.) .
6. *Poole's Index to Periodical Literature* (7 vols.; subject index of articles in American and British periodicals from 1802 to 1906) .
7. *Readers' Guide to Periodical Literature,* 1900– (a cumulative index, most useful to the general reader, to over 100 popular and semipopular magazines; entries are according to author, subject, and fiction title) .

## 19c   Become familiar with the general collection of books in your library

The most important part of a library is the main collection of books. To obtain any book, you need to consult the card catalog, which is the index of the whole library. It consists of 3-by-5-inch

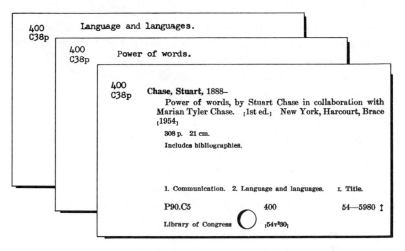

*Sample cards, library card catalog*

cards filed alphabetically in long trays or drawers in a series of filing cabinets; on the front of each drawer is a label (for example, A–ABN) giving the alphabetical limits of the cards there.

Book information is filed in the card catalog in three ways, by (1) author, (2) title, and (3) subject. Each book in the library is therefore represented in the card catalog by several cards, printed and supplied by the Library of Congress and thus uniform in all libraries. These cards are usually identical, except that certain lines may be typed across the top, giving the title, joint author, or subject headings, i.e., entries for the subject with which the book deals and which are obtained from the Library of Congress card.

Illustrated first is an example of one of the simpler cards in the card catalog. The typed numbers at the left are the call number of the book, according to the Dewey Decimal Classification (see pp. 129–130) . The typed words on the duplicate cards show that one is indexed by title, one by subject (this book also has one other subject entry) ; the top card is filed according to author. The first line gives the author's last name, given name, and date of birth. On the second, third, and fourth lines are the title, author's name again, collaborating author, edition, place of publication, publisher, and year of copyright (no brackets around the date would indicate that the date is printed on the title page) .

Line 5 gives number of pages and size (height) of the book in centimeters. Line 6 indicates that the book has bibliographies. Line 7 means that, in addition to the author card, the card catalog should have three additional cards, one under the subject "Communication," one under the subject "Language and languages," and one under title. In line 8, "P90.C5" is the call number of this book in libraries using the Library of Congress system; the middle number, "400," is the initial number for libraries using the Dewey Decimal Classification. The other figures have a specialized meaning intelligible only to librarians; for example, "54–5980" is the number of this card, when copies of it are ordered from the Library of Congress, which prepares and prints it. (The round hole is for the insertion of a rod in the filing drawer, so that if the drawer is accidentally dropped, some hundreds of cards are not hopelessly mixed up.)

A library card with more complicated information (can you explain it?) is illustrated on this page.[17] If you think that the information on any library card is important and you do not understand how to interpret it, ask a member of your library staff.

When you want a book, and you know the author or the title, you can easily get needed information from the author or title card. If you know neither author nor title, turn to the cards

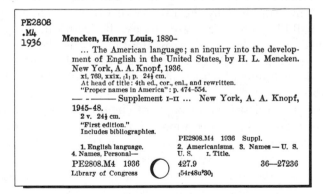

*Specimen card, library card catalog*

[17] H. L. Mencken died in 1956, but the Library of Congress does not print new cards when an author dies. Any new edition of a deceased author's book requiring a new card or a card for a posthumously published book contains the author's death year. Sometimes a particular library has a policy of typing in the death year on cards not having that information.

that list books dealing with the subject upon which you are working and make your choices from the collection there. If the author is not given, as may be true of many bulletins or pamphlets, or if there is no author, as is true of bound volumes of magazines, look for the title or the organization responsible for the publication.

In addition to revealing the resources of the library, the card catalog gives the call number by means of which each book is located on the shelves. This number appears in the upper left-hand corner (see illustrations) and corresponds exactly to the number placed on the cover and also inside the front cover of the book. Some libraries are so arranged that all or part of the books are placed on open shelves accessible to students. In other libraries the main collection is shelved in enclosed stacks. To obtain a book then, you fill out a "call slip" furnished by the library and present it at the Circulation or Loan Desk. On this call slip write the call number of the book, author, title, and your own name and address; the library attendant will then obtain the book for you from the stacks.

If you have access to the book collection, you will discover that the books are arranged acording to a definite system, the key to which is the first part of the call number. The two classification systems commonly used are the Dewey Decimal Classification and the Library of Congress Classification. Books classified by either system are arranged according to subjects treated.

In the Dewey Decimal Classification, the field of knowledge is arranged in 10 groups, including one group for reference books. Each major class as well as each subclass is represented by a three-digit number; further subdivisions are indicated by the use of numbers after a decimal point. The 10 main classes and the subclasses of the Pure Sciences and Literature are illustrated in the following:

000 General works
100 Philosophy and related disciplines
200 Religion
300 Social sciences
400 Language
500 Pure sciences
   510 Mathematics
520 Astronomy and allied sciences
530 Physics
540 Chemistry and allied sciences
550 Earth sciences
560 Paleontology
570 The anthropological and

biological sciences
580 Botanical sciences
590 Zoological sciences
600 Technology (applied sciences)
700 The Arts
800 Literature (belles-lettres) and rhetoric
    810 American literature
       811 Poetry
       812 Drama
       813 Fiction
       814 Essays
       815 Speeches
       816 Letters
       817 Satire and humor
       818 Miscellany
       819 [open]

820 English and Anglo-Saxon literature
830 Germanic languages literature
840 French, etc., literature
850 Italian, etc., literature
860 Spanish and Portuguese literature
870 Italic languages literature (Latin, etc.)
880 Classical and modern Greek literature
890 Literatures of other languages
900 General geography and history and related disciplines

Examples of further subclassification: American Literature is numbered 810–819; an edition of Henry Wadsworth Longfellow's *Evangeline* is numbered 811/L86e. British Literature bears the numbers 820–829; British Drama is 822; Elizabethan Drama is 822.3; an edition of Shakespeare's *Julius Caesar* is numbered 822.3/S5jA, in which the last letter, A, stands for Arden Edition.

The Library of Congress Classification uses letters of the alphabet followed by additional letters or by Arabic numerals. The main classes are these:

A  General works, polygraphy
B  Philosophy, religion
C  History, auxiliary sciences
D  History and topography (except America)
E, F  American history
G  Geography, anthropology
H  Social sciences, economics, sociology
J  Political science
K  Law
L  Education

M  Music
N  Fine arts
P  Language and literature
Q  Science
R  Medicine
S  Agriculture, plant and animal industry
T  Technology
U  Military science
V  Naval science
Z  Bibliography and library science

The letters I, O, W, X, and Y have not yet been used and will allow for expansion by five additional classes. Each general class has subclasses: **PB–PH** classifies Modern European Languages; **PN, PR, PS,** and **PZ** classify, respectively, General Literary History, British Literature, American Literature, and Fiction and Juvenile Literature.

Under **PS,** for example, PS 303–324 is American poetry; PS 700 on, individual authors; PS 2250–2298, Henry Wadsworth Longfellow; PS 2263, Longfellow's *Evangeline.*

In filing cards in the card catalog, libraries in general observe the following rules:

All libraries file by entry, i.e., according to what appears first on the card, whether author, subject, or title. The articles *the, a, an* appearing as the first word of a title are ignored. Most libraries file letter-by-letter to the end of the word. This means that the title card, *The American Way,* is filed in front of the subject card AMERICANISMS, just as all cards beginning "New York" are filed in front of cards with "Newark" as the entry word. Libraries which file in strictly alphabetical order, of course, place *-isms* before *way* and *-ark* before *York.* Incidentally, encyclopedias, as well as library catalogs, differ in their entry systems.

Books *about* an author—when his name is a subject entry, it may be typed in black capitals or in red—are usually filed after all books *by* that author.

Cards for authors having the same last name as the entry word are filed according to the given name; always make a note of the first name, or at least the initials, of an author and of the exact title of the book you want.

Abbreviations and numerals are filed just as they would be if the words they represent were spelled out.

When the entry word is the same, all authors by that nameword precede all subjects, and all subjects precede all titles. For example, Washington, George (books by), WASHINGTON, GEORGE (books about), *Washington merry-go-round* (title) are entered in that order.

## EXERCISES

A. Make a floor plan of the main reading room of your college or university library, showing the location of the more general kinds of reference books such as encyclopedias, dictionaries, biographical books, magazine indexes.

B. Where in your library are kept bound magazines, current magazines, bound newspapers, current newspapers, novels, reserved books, the card catalog?

C. Go to the library and fill out call slips or cards for five nonfiction books you would like to read. Get one of the books and bring it and the other four call slips to class.

D. Copy the following, leaving enough space where the dashes occur to fill in needed material. Find the information in your library, after you have filled in the blanks or have had them filled in for you by your instructor. Write after each of the 10 items the exact source of your information.

1. Give the birthplace, university attended, and date of death of ——.
2. —— was the discoverer (or inventor) of ——.
3. —— was first published the year ——, in the city of ——.
4. —— University was founded in ——.
5. —— was elected Vice-President of the United States in ——. He was a candidate of the —— party.
6. The scenes of action in Shakespeare's play —— are ——.
7. Two books about —— are by, respectively, —— and ——. For each, give the nationality of author and year and place of publication.
8. —— is the manufacturing center in —— of (the product) ——.
9. —— of —— University received his undergraduate college or university training at —— and did his graduate study at ——. He holds the degrees of —— from ——.
10. At one time or another —— has been a part of, or has belonged to, three different countries: ——, ——, and ——.

E. After you have become familiar with your college or university library, choose two or three or four of the following sentences, or write similar ones. Use each as the first sentence, the topic sentence, in a paragraph. Expand each sentence into a fair-sized paragraph, a half-page or three-fourths of a page long.

1. I have made my first visit to our library.
2. I have made a thorough tour of our library.
3. Several things impressed me about our library.
4. A library has many uses.
5. The —— room in the library is an interesting place.
6. The library has a newspaper room.
7. The library has a periodical room.
8. The library has a study room.

9. The library has a main reading room.
10. The library has a reserved-book room.
11. The card catalog is very helpful.
12. Here are directions for borrowing books from the library.
13. Fiction books are kept in a special place.
14. *The New York Times* is both bound and kept on microfilm.
15. Our library has encyclopedias and other reference books.
16. Here are directions for finding material in bound magazines (or newspapers) .
17. It is fun to browse through the bound magazines in the library.
18. You can even have dates in the library!
19. My high school (home town) has a satisfactory (unsatisfactory) library.
20. I have (hope to have) a private library.

## 20  *The research paper*

As an introduction to research and to writing the results of research, Cecil B. Williams begins a chapter, "The Nature and Uses of Research," as follows:

Your first research paper will not be your introduction to research. This you have already had, for the essentials of research procedure are almost as natural as breathing or walking. Probably on your own initiative you have gone to one store after another to locate the necktie which would best match your new suit—or to find a necklace to go with your new dress. In grade school and high school and home there are many situations calling for careful, thorough investigation to determine right decisions or procedures.

*Research* is a term which came into English from the Old French root word *cerchier,* meaning to search or seek, and the prefix *re,* meaning again. Research is reflective seeking or intensive search with a view to becoming certain. Many words develop specialized meanings; so you may have thought of *research* as the process whereby scientists in field or laboratory discover new principles or laws about the behavior of atoms and planets, of mice and men. This specialized meaning is important, and in modern society becomes increasingly so, as is testified to by the numerous heavily endowed research institutes and foundations and the results they achieve; but research as you are concerned with it now is closer to the etymological, general meaning.[18]

The *research paper*—also called *investigative theme* or *term report* or *term paper*—is a long theme, usually from 1500 to 6000 words, assigned in most college courses requiring outside reading. More than a routine report, its purpose is to make a careful investigation of some subject and to present and interpret the source material in the light of the researcher's findings. As James Harvey Robinson once wrote: "Research is but diligent search which enjoys the high flavor of primitive hunting." It is, therefore, not merely a reading report based on several books or articles read more or less haphazardly, nor is it a jumbled series of quotations and paraphrases. In fact, you should learn how to put ideas of others into your own words and give proper credit, without overuse of short or extended direct quotations.

At present the research paper consists of two types: the *controlled research paper* and the *library research paper*.

*The Controlled Research Paper.* The controlled research paper serves, among others, two purposes: it relieves pressure on libraries when several hundred to 7000 or 8000 freshmen may be milling around doing what is after all only one freshman uniform or varied class assignment; it also gives a reading and writing research experience and is an introduction to library research which will be more valuable in the student's later college and postgraduate years.

For the controlled research paper, usually only one special book is required. Several publishers now have numerous such books available, dealing with broad or limited subjects in literature, criticism, history, biography, and sociology. These books have various descriptive labels, such as critical editions, research anthologies or series, casebooks, and source materials. They usually contain an authentic text or texts (like a novel or several short stories) and, in addition, backgrounds, sources, theories, essays of criticism, and a fairly comprehensive bibliography. The student's task is to choose from the book a subject, limit it, assemble his notes and sources from the book, outline his material,

18 *A Research Manual for College Studies and Papers*, 3rd ed., pp. 1–2. Copyright © 1963 by Cecil B. Williams and Allan H. Stevenson. Reprinted by permission of Harper & Row.

write his paper, and document it. Some of the books have "guides" to research writing which are sufficiently complete that the student needs no help from other sources.

*The Library Research Paper.* In the library research paper, the student starts from scratch, on his own; he must do for himself what the author or editor of the source book has done for him. Because it demands more extensive knowledge, use of, and experience with the library, in many ways the library research paper is a more valuable, more rewarding experience, especially for students planning to major in one of the arts or one of the social sciences.

The pages that follow deal primarily with the library research paper, and the suggestions should be adequate for even a moderately long paper.[19] Such a good research paper is a care-

---

[19] Some English courses use more extended treatments in the form of books or booklets. Among these are:

Barzun, Jacques, and Henry F. Graff. *The Modern Researcher.* New York: Harcourt, Brace & World, 1957.

Cordasco, Francisco G. M., and S. M. Gatner. *Research and Report Writing,* 7th ed. New York: Barnes & Noble, 1963.

Grewe, Eugene F., and John F. Sullivan. *The College Research Paper,* 4th ed. Dubuque, Iowa: Wm. C. Brown Company, 1950.

Hook, Lucyle, and Mary Virginia Gaver. *The Research Paper,* 3rd ed. Englewood Cliffs, N.J.: Prentice-Hall, 1962.

Lester, James D. *Writing Themes and Research Papers: A Complete Guide.* Chicago: Scott, Foresman, 1967.

Lyerly, Ralph H. *Essential Requirements of the College Research Paper.* Cleveland: World Publishing Company, 1966.

Markman, Roberta M., and Marie F. Waddell. *10 Steps in Writing the Research Paper.* Woodbury, N.Y.: Barron's Educational Series, 1965.

Miles, Leland, and Frank Baker. *A Brief Guide to Writing Term Papers,* rev. ed. Dubuque, Iowa: Wm. C. Brown Company, 1959.

Pugh, Griffith T. *Guide to Research Writing,* 3rd ed. Boston: Houghton Mifflin, 1968.

Roth, Audrey J. *The Research Paper: Form and Content.* Belmont, Calif.: Wadsworth Publishing Company, 1966.

Schmitz, Robert M. *Preparing the Research Paper,* 4th ed. New York: Holt, Rinehart & Winston, 1957.

Sears, Donald. *Harbrace Guide to the Library and the Research Paper,* 2nd ed. New York: Harcourt, Brace & World, 1960.

Turabian, Kate L. *A Manual for Writers of Term Papers, Theses, and Dissertations,* 3rd ed. Chicago: University of Chicago Press, 1967.

Williams, Cecil B. *A Research Manual for College Studies and Papers,* 3rd ed. New York: Harper & Row, 1963.

fully controlled study, which sets out with a definite purpose and accomplishes that purpose. Its preparation and writing depend on four major steps: (1) choosing and analyzing the subject; (2) making a thorough investigation of the subject; (3) preparing an outline; and (4) writing and revising. As a preliminary to these four steps, review "The Theme," Sections 1 through 17, pp. 10–103.

### 20a   Choose and analyze your subject carefully

1. Choose a subject in which you are already interested or in which you can become interested. Furthermore, do not select so abstruse or technical a subject that your readers cannot be interested.

2. Do not select too large or too small a subject. Some subjects can be treated adequately in 1000 words; developing such a subject in a 5000-word paper results in padding, repetition, dullness. But do not choose a subject which cannot be handled in the assigned space.

3. Choose a topic upon which enough has been written to obtain adequate information. Keep in mind the resources of the library where you do your investigating; for example, avoid a subject that depends heavily on back copies of magazines your library does not have. Also, base your paper on material from *several* sources: reference books, periodicals, books, perhaps newspapers, and personal interviews.

4. Select a central purpose, a controlling idea, and state it in a thesis topic or theme sentence. Any assembling of material presupposes the support of some proposition, some general statement or idea, and all the facts you gather should lead toward your conclusions, the important part of any research paper. You may change your attitude toward and treatment of your subject when you have assembled and digested your materials, for you should never start out with a rigid, preconceived idea to be established in spite of all contrary facts and evidence. A research paper, like any theme, must develop one phase of a broad subject, fairly and convincingly, in order to achieve one central purpose.

5. Select, but modify if necessary, the basic type of writing for your research paper. Your report may be *descriptive exposi-*

*tion*: it may describe and explain the processes involved in the manufacture of some product. It may be *narrative*: a report of exactly what took place at a certain time or on a certain occasion in history. It may be *argumentative*: setting forth facts in favor of or opposed to some plan, movement, proposal, such as reasons for or against making 18 years the legal voting age in a particular state. Or it may be *analytical*: the component parts and significance of a somewhat abstract subject or a limited comparison-contrast treating the likenesses and differences of two systems. But whatever type of writing you use, your research paper must accomplish a clear, unmistakable *purpose*.

Since choice of topic depends upon your interests and those of your prospective reader or readers, literally hundreds of topics are available, many suggested by these broad fields:

| | |
|---|---|
| applied science | language |
| biography | literature |
| economics | manufacturing |
| education | politics |
| fine arts (music, painting, | psychology |
| sculpture, ceramics, ar- | pure science |
| chitecture, etc.) | religion |
| history | space exploration |
| land, sea, air | warfare |

Other hundreds of subjects are possible from somewhat more limited but still general topics, as, for example:

An outstanding or memorable episode or day or month or year in a well-known person's life

An account of the relatives of a famous person

A man, or men, in public office: president, vice-president, senator, governor, etc.

The friendship of two well-known people, or some phase of that friendship

The love affair of a famous couple

The reception, influence, effect of some book, some invention, some process, or the reputation of such about 10, 25, 50, 100 years later

The reputation of an author after 25, 50, or 100 years

The major achievement (s) of a major (or minor) biologist, chemist, discoverer, explorer, soldier, inventor, manufacturer, speaker, traveler, writer, etc.

Famous scientific discoveries or inventions

Interspace research and exploration: planets, satellites, rockets, animal-carrying rockets, man-carrying rockets, etc.

The next 5 (10) years in space exploration, or the last 5 (10) years in space exploration

Famous historical events, trials, sporting events, etc.

Famous or well-known battles or phases of battles (land, sea, air)

Famous or memorable shipwrecks, storms, fires, floods, cyclones, tornadoes

Famous peacetime sea tragedies or famous wartime sea tragedies

A famous structure, completed or proposed: harbor, canal, bridge, building, ship, tower, cathedral, pyramid, dam, tunnel, train, automobile, airplane, etc.

Famous places: summer resorts, winter resorts, health resorts, world capitals, cities, rivers, lakes, canyons, parks, etc.

Foods: nutritive value of foods, home freezing of fruits and vegetables, recent methods of food preservation, etc.

Language: British and American (Briticisms and Americanisms) ; Latin and Greek prefixes, suffixes, roots in English; slang; neologisms; localisms; dialect; logic and language; place names; long words vs. short words; spelling reform; making a dictionary, etc.

As suitable limitations of some of the foregoing, consider as examples:

The Presidential Campaign of 1960 (or 1964 or 1968)

(A President's) First Day as President

Lincoln's Son

Robert Browning's Courtship of Elizabeth Barrett

Noah Webster's First Dictionary

Thomas A. Edison's Minor Inventions

Abraham Lincoln and His Secretary of State, William H. Seward

Early Results of the Discovery of Anesthesia

Mark Twain's *Huckleberry Finn*—Its First Ten Years

April 19, 1775 (or July 4, 1776, or April 6, 1917, or November 11, 1918, or December 7, 1941, etc.)

The First Kentucky Derby

The Final Day of the Battle of Gettysburg

The Sinking of the *Andrea Doria*

The Straits of Mackinac Bridge

Saratoga Springs a Century Ago
A Tunnel Under the English Channel
The Development of the First American Satellite
Survival Under Atomic Attack

## 20b    *Make a thorough investigation of the subject*

The conscientious researcher ferrets out all information he can about a subject. A student may not ascertain *all* the facts, but he should make as thorough a search as possible for pertinent detail by utilizing information from reference books, periodicals, the general collection of books in the library, and newspapers. It is an illusion that using an encyclopedia and writing a term paper are the same thing. A term paper has no real value unless it does more than merely dip into a subject.

In order to make a competent investigation of a subject:

Learn how to use the resources of your library: reference works, periodical indexes, card catalog, and general collection of books (see Section **19a,b,c**). From these resources, notably the first three, prepare a preliminary bibliography on 3-by-5-inch cards, that is, a list of books and magazine or newspaper articles that are *likely* to contribute material, with one title to a card. You save time if you give complete information on this prelimi-

---

> Bittner, William
> *Poe: A Biography*
> Boston: Little, Brown and
> Company, 1962
>
> 928.1
> P 752 bi

*Preliminary bibliography card*

nary bibliography card, since it will serve as your information for your final bibliography. See page 139 for sample.

Note that the material is arranged in the order in which it would or does appear in a final bibliography (Section **20h**), except that the publisher's name might not appear there. Note also that the card contains the library call number—a timesaver if you have to return (and you usually will have to) to the book for further checking. Put this library call number on each preliminary bibliography card as soon as you begin your library search for specific materials.

## 20c   *Take careful notes from your reading*

Taking careful notes from your reading is a necessity in preparing a research paper. But since note-taking has other uses, a somewhat broader discussion of note-taking is given here.

As a college student you will spend much time taking notes in your room, in the library, and in the classroom. Both now and later you will be faced with the problem of taking notes on books and articles for research or other subjects about which you may write or for use in reviewing for examinations. You will need, too, to take usable notes on lectures and other speeches. Much of your success depends on your ability to take notes that are really helpful.

Note-taking should be a process of systematic thinking. Too frequently it is a hurried setting down of carelessly selected ideas on scraps of paper or miscellaneous jottings in a notebook. If you wish to get maximum benefit from reading, with intelligent labor-saving, you should organize both materials and methods of note-taking, in order to preserve notes for possible use at any future time—for example, until a long paper is written or an examination is over.

### MATERIALS

1. Many instructors and students believe that the most efficient note-taking is done on *cards* or *slips of paper* (3 by 5 or 4 by 6 inches or larger), *one note to a card*. All notes are placed on similar cards, a heading is put on each card, and the cards are filed for later reference. The advantage of this system is that all notes on the same subject, even taken at widely separated intervals, can be kept together. The use of the card system—both bibli-

ographical cards (p. 139) and content cards (p. 142) —is especially valuable in taking notes for the research paper.

2. Some students prefer to take notes on full-size or half-size sheets of paper, or *loose-leaf notebook* paper. (Bound notebooks are usually unsatisfactory.) If you use such materials, keep notes on a particular book or article together and organize your notes on the various phases of the subject as you proceed.

## METHODS

More important than the materials are the methods employed. To save time and trouble later and to avoid a hodgepodge of quotations and undigested raw material, follow this technique:

1. Before taking notes on a book, study its preface and table of contents. From these you learn the scope and purpose of the book. If you are going to read only one chapter from a book or a magazine article, skim through it first, and then begin to read carefully and take notes. The book probably has an index (almost all nonfiction books do) ; save time by examining it for your particular subject or for related materials.

2. Record accurately and fully the details about the source of information: author, book, title, article or chapter titles, magazine title, date, volume and page numbers, and the like.

3. Record accurately and fully the information itself. If you write a précis (p. 108) or a paraphrase (p. 111), check it on the spot with the original. If quoting directly, to use the material later either for direct quotation or summarizing, make a word-by-word check at once. Be careful to copy *exactly* all direct quotations, preserving original spelling and punctuation; mark clearly any variations from standard style in your *first* notes, and do not forget to use quotation marks.

Your notes must be clear and full, or you will have to make trip after trip to the library to supply missing information. Get all the information *the first time.* Make your notes *clear,* so that you can read and understand them later; *full,* so that you can supply adequate information about sources in both footnotes and bibliography; *exact,* so that you can quote or paraphrase accurately; *organized,* so that you can make ready use of what you have assembled.

4. Condense your notes, which should be as full as needed but not so full that main ideas are obscured in a mass of detail.

Make frequent use of topic sentences (Section **23**) and summaries (pp. 108–114).

   5. Rearrange and regroup your notes as your work proceeds. Keep your notes on a single subject together, not mixed with others even on the same general subject. This segregation is especially important whenever numerous books or articles are consulted.

   When you are writing a research paper, you will of course be analyzing your subject and making, through your analysis and through the arrangement and grouping of your notes, a preliminary outline of your paper. Thus you will keep on the main track of the investigation and not be surprised at the end of your note-taking by the way your investigation has run away with you. You will also be more thoroughly prepared for the next major step in the preparation of your paper.

---

*Contemporary Opinion*    (Poe as poet)
    As poet, "Poe was not held in very high esteem by his contemporaries"; "all but ignored until after the publication of 'The Raven' in 1845."
    "... his early reputation abroad... rested almost solely on his work as poet and romancer."
    p.37
    Killis Campbell, *The Mind of Poe and Other Studies*. New York : Russell & Russell, Inc., 1962

---

*Sample note card*

   6. Be careful to distinguish fact and opinion in your reading and in the notes themselves. In weighing opinions, consider the facts on which the opinions are based, the expert knowledge and

possible bias of the author, and the date of publication of the material.

The specimen card on p. 142 illustrates use of the methods suggested. The upper right corner gives the general subject, the upper left the specific subject; then come a direct quotation, summary or paraphrase, and full bibliographical details. If a number of note cards come from the same source, work out an abbreviated system whereby your bibliographical references will be explained by your preliminary or final bibliography cards.

Not all cards will be notes of material directly quoted. Some will be *précis,* summarizing in your own words the ideas of the source (see pp. 108–110). Some will be *paraphrases* giving a full-length statement of the source material (see pp. 110–114). All cards should be so complete that you need not return to the source to discover how much of the material is direct quotation, how much is paraphrase, or what the bibliographical facts are.

### 20d   *Prepare an adequate outline for your research paper*

When you have read and taken notes on available material, you can outline your research paper. It is helpful, however, to have in mind early some general plan, one you can adapt, change, and rearrange as you assemble material and become familiar with it. In fact, some instructors and some students find it useful to make an actual outline, even a tentative one, first, before beginning the research reading and note-taking. Whichever method you use, when you have worked long enough to reach definite conclusions and to see the framework of the whole structure, you can rearrange notes in final form under appropriate headings and from them prepare a topic or sentence outline (see Section 6b,c). The actual writing of the paper begins *only* after you have prepared such an outline and revised it carefully.

In making an outline for your paper, bear in mind that the object of your investigation is to find out the facts, arrange and interpret them, and present conclusions based upon them. You are not necessarily a propagandist—rather, a discoverer of fact— but you must assimilate and absorb what seems to you the truth so that you can present it to a reader who will see what definite purpose you had in mind.

A tentative but general outline, adaptable for many but not all subjects, might include the following:

I. Purpose of investigation
II. Importance or significance of the subject
III. Background or history of the subject
IV. Nature of the investigation (description of apparatus, procedure, results, chronological development, etc.)
V. Conclusions (generalized statements based on the investigation and rounding out of the paper)

## 20e   *Write your research paper correctly, clearly, and forcefully*

After you have investigated the field thoroughly, organized your notes, and prepared an outline, you are ready to write. If you have taken careful notes and arranged them properly, your work is more than half done. To give the results of your study correct, clear, and effective expression, write the body of your paper as clearly and forcefully as you can; take great care with footnotes and bibliography; and revise your paper to insure correctness and accuracy.

A term report need not be dull and lifeless. If you have chosen an attractive subject and investigated it fully, you should have little difficulty in making your paper effective. An occasional bit of humor, vigorous diction, and neatly turned phrases add effectiveness to the thoroughness and accuracy which the paper must have. Careful investigation, forceful writing, and pleasant, easy reading need not be exclusive of one another.

## 20f   *Revise your research paper carefully*

Your last task is the preparation of your final draft. When you are satisfied with your next-to-last draft, put your paper aside and forget it for a time. After this "cooling" process, you will be able to come back to it with more impartiality than was possible just after you had finished it. Your errors will be more apparent, and you can give your paper its final polishing. Also give it the readings suggested in Section 16, and add another for the sole purpose of making certain that footnotes are accurately and uniformly listed and that the bibliography is correctly and consistently arranged. Then make your final draft and proofread it carefully.

In addition to being correct, clear, effective, and appropriate, every investigative theme must be carefully documented. The following suggestions enable you to provide your paper with adequate and accurately listed footnotes and bibliography, *provided your notes on reading were carefully taken.*

### 20g   Use footnotes to document your research paper adequately and properly

The purpose of a footnote is to acknowledge the authority for some fact stated or some material quoted or to develop some point more or less incidentally referred to in the body of the paper.

Generally known facts do not require substantiation in footnotes, nor do well-known quotations, usually. With other materials you must avoid charges of plagiarism, and unless ideas and phrasing are completely your own, you should refer the reader to some source for your statement. To be entirely honest, you will acknowledge every source of indebtedness, even when no direct quotation is used.

Occasionally you may wish to develop, interpret, or refute some idea but do not wish an extended comment to interfere with the unity of your paper. Use a footnote, but, since footnotes for such purposes become distracting to the reader, do not use too many of them.

How many footnotes should appear in a research paper? Only as many as are necessary, in the light of the discussion above. One investigation may call for twice as many as another. Some pages may require a half-dozen or more footnotes; others may need none or only one or two. A good guiding principle is the following: Use footnotes to acknowledge credit where it is due and to supply discussion-explanations only when necessary for understanding.

**1. Adopt a standard form of footnote and be consistent in its use.**

Methods of footnoting are numerous, but whatever system you employ should be consistent throughout your paper and immediately clear to any intelligent reader. The Modern Language Association of America *Style Sheet* favors the forms for books and periodicals illustrated on pp. 146–147: five kinds of books (one author, two authors, an editor, a translator, two volumes) and four sources of articles (magazine, collection, newspaper, encyclopedia) .

*Books*

A. BOOK BY ONE AUTHOR:

    [1] John R. Tunis, *The American Way in Sport* (New York, 1958), p. 4.

or

    [1] John R. Tunis, *The American Way in Sport* (New York: Duell, Sloan and Pearce, 1958), p. 4.

NOTE: If the author's full name has been given in the text, the footnote reads:

    [1] *The American Way in Sport* (New York, 1958), p. 4.

and if both the author's full name and the title of the book have been given in the text, the footnote reads:

    [1] (New York, 1958), p. 4.

B. BOOKS BY TWO OR MORE AUTHORS:

    [1] John Tasker Howard and Arthur Mendel, *Our American Composers* (New York, 1941), p. 82.

C. BOOK PREPARED BY AN EDITOR:

    [1] Charles Mills Gayley, ed., *Representative English Comedies* (New York, 1916), I, xxiii.

    [2] *Great French Romances,* ed. Richard Aldington (New York, 1946), p. 17.

D. A TRANSLATION:

    [1] Homer, *The Odyssey,* trans. George Herbert Palmer (Boston, 1891), p. 46.

E. BOOK OF TWO OR MORE VOLUMES:

    [1] Douglas S. Freeman, *George Washington* (New York, 1948), II, 142.

*Articles (essays, stories)*

A. FROM A MAGAZINE:

    [1] Dwight D. Eisenhower, "Boyhood of a President," *The Saturday Evening Post,* CCXL (April 8, 1967), 32.

or

    [1] Dwight D. Eisenhower, "Boyhood of a President," *The Saturday Evening Post,* April 8, 1967, p. 32.

    [2] Russell Baker, "Wayward Washington," *Holiday,* XLI (February, 1967), 64.

or

    [2] Russell Baker, "Wayward Washington," *Holiday,* February, 1967, p. 64.

³ John Lear, "Exploration Race: Moon or Sea?," *Saturday Review,* L (March 4, 1967) , 51.

or

³ John Lear, "Exploration Race: Moon or Sea?" in *Saturday Review,* March 4, 1967, p. 51.

(Note the alternate expression after the question mark, just above.)

B. FROM A COLLECTION:

¹ Katherine Mansfield, "Bliss," *A Study of the Short Story,* ed. Henry S. Canby and Alfred Dashiell (New York, 1935) , p. 303.

² Burges Johnson, "Campus Versus Classroom," *Readings for Opinion,* ed. Earl Davis and William C. Hummel, 2nd ed. (Englewood Cliffs, N.J., 1960) , pp. 282–293.

C. FROM A NEWSPAPER:

¹ "Television for Adults," *The New York Times,* November 4, 1967, p. 32.

² Bernard J. Malahan, "Covered Bridges Making a Comeback," *The New York Times,* November 19, 1967, Section 10, p. 13.

NOTE: The first reference above is to the daily edition, the second to the Sunday edition.

D. FROM AN ENCYCLOPEDIA:

¹ "Edgar Allan Poe," *Encyclopaedia Britannica* (Chicago, 1967) , XVIII, 87–88.

## 2. Use the following standard footnote abbreviations.

In footnotes in research papers, abbreviations are permissible and desirable. If the need for abbreviations occurs, employ these forms:

1. anon.   anonymous
2. ante   before
3. art., arts.   article (s)
4. bk., bks.   book (s)
5. c., ca.   about, approximate date
6. cf.   compare   Never use "cf." in the meaning of "see."
7. ch., chs.   chapter (s)
8. comp.   compiler, compiled
9. ed., eds.   editor (s) , edition (s) ; ed. also means edited by
10. e.g.   for example
11. f., ff.   following line (s) , following page (s)
12. fig., figs.   figure (s)

13. ibid.  in the same place  If a footnote refers to the same source as the one referred to in the footnote *immediately* preceding, the abbreviation ibid. (from the Latin *ibidem,* "in the same place") may be used. If the volume, page, title, and author are the same, use ibid. alone. If the volume and page differ, use, for example, ibid., III, 206. Ibid. usually comes at the beginning of a footnote and is capitalized for that reason only.

14. i.e.  that is

15. l., ll.  line (s)

16. loc. cit.  in the place cited  If the reference is to the *exact* passage covered by an earlier reference not immediately preceding, use *loc. cit.* (from the Latin *loco citato,* "in the place cited") . Never follow loc. cit. with a page number. But see Note 2 at the end of this list.

17. MS, MSS  manuscript (s)

18. n., nn.  note (s)

19. N.B.  *nota bene*—take notice, mark well

20. op. cit.  in the work cited  After the first full reference to a given work, provided no other work by the same author is mentioned in the paper, succeeding references may be indicated by the author's surname, followed by op. cit. (from the Latin *opere citato,* "in the work cited") and the volume and page. But see Note 2 at the end of this list.

21. p., pp.  page (s)

22. par., pars.  paragraph (s)

23. passim  To be employed when no specific page reference can be given; it means "everywhere," "throughout," "here and there."

24. pseud.  pseudonym

25. pt., pts.  part (s)

26. q.v.  which see

27. sec., secs.  section (s)

28. sic  thus, so  Used between brackets in a quotation to show that the material preceding has been followed exactly, even if there is an obvious factual error or an error in spelling, grammar, punctuation, or word use.

29. v., vv.  verse (s)

30. vol., vols.  volume (s)

NOTE 1: The abbreviations *ibid., loc. cit.,* and *op. cit.* and the words *passim* and *sic* are so common now in footnotes that they are no longer italicized (underlined) .

NOTE 2: Many instructors and editors believe that *loc. cit.* and *op. cit.* are the most abused and overused of all abbreviations in research writing; they advocate, instead, the author's name alone with a short title for footnote references after the first. The following examples illustrate:

First entry:

  ¹ Sir Arthur Quiller-Couch, *On the Art of Writing* (New York, 1930) , p. 84.

*Subsequent entry for the same book:*

Allowed:

  ⁵ Quiller-Couch, op. cit., p. 92.

Preferred:

  ⁵ Quiller-Couch, *Art of Writing,* p. 92.

First entry:

  ¹ Clifton Fadiman, "Herman Melville," *The Atlantic Monthly,* CLXXII (October 1943) , 88.

*Subsequent entry for the same article:*

Allowed:

  ⁴ Fadiman, op. cit., p. 90.

Preferred:

  ⁴ Fadiman, "Melville," p. 90.

### 3. Place the footnote numeral and the footnote properly.

Unless otherwise instructed, you should apply the following:

1. In the text refer to a footnote by an Arabic numeral placed above and to the right of the word to be commented on. If the reference is to a statement or quotation, place the numeral at the end of the passage, and always after the punctuation.

2. Place footnotes at the bottom of each page, rather than all together at the end of the paper.

3. Before a footnote, repeat the number used in the text. Place this number also above the line. Do not use asterisks or other symbols in place of Arabic numerals.

4. Number the footnotes anew for each page, not consecutively throughout the paper.

5. Separate the first footnote on a page by leaving three typed spaces, or their equivalent, between the text material and the footnote.

6. If you type, use single spacing within each footnote and double spacing between footnotes.

### 20h   Use a bibliography ̗ document your research paper adequately and properly

A *bibliography* is a list of books or magazine or newspaper articles relating to a given subject and, in the research paper, placed at the end of the manuscript. It is usually a list, in one alphabet, or classified, containing the names of all the works actually quoted from or used generally in the paper and its preparation. Thus a bibliography may contain more references than the sum of all the footnote references. Every formally prepared research paper should contain a bibliography.

Arrange bibliographical items correctly and consistently. Usage in the arrangement of bibliographical items varies, but subject to adaptation by your instructor, follow the examples on pp. 150–151; these were prepared from the recommendations of *The MLA Style Sheet* for the writing of masters' and doctors' theses. Note carefully in those illustrations: alphabetical arrangement of items; order of material within each item; capitalization; punctuation; use of italics, Arabic numbers, Roman numbers, and abbreviations. Note, also, that the publishers' names are omitted; some instructors and research manuals prefer that they be included.

If the items in a bibliography are numerous, you may classify them in groups: books, magazine articles, public documents, reports, and newspaper accounts. The preferred method is to have *all* bibliographical items in one alphabetical arrangement.

A sentence or phrase under each item is sometimes helpful and desirable. Such statements, indicating the scope or content of the book or article, make the bibliography an *annotative* or *annotated* bibliography.

Place the bibliography at the end of the research paper, and begin it on a separate page, not on the last page of the text. Give it a title that fits it precisely, such as "List of Works Consulted," "List of Works Cited," "A Selected Bibliography," "A Brief Annotated Bibliography," or, sometimes, merely "Bibliography." It should include all your first references in footnotes. If the paper is typewritten, spacing is single or double, according to desire or instructions, but double spacing is preferable, and any run-over lines of a single item are indented. If the spacing is single, use double spacing between the items.

The following, an example of a short bibliography, follows the preferred method of including all materials in one alphabetical arrangement:

Allen, Hervey. *Israfel: The Life and Times of Edgar Allan Poe.* New York, 1934.

Boyd, Ernest. *Literary Blasphemies* (pp. 163–185). New York, 1927.

Campbell, Killis. *The Mind of Poe and Other Studies.* Cambridge, Mass., 1933.

Cooke, A. L. "Edgar Allan Poe—Critic," *Cornhill Magazine,* LXXII (November, 1934), 588–597.

"Edgar Allan Poe," *Encyclopaedia Britannica,* XVIII, 87–88. Chicago, 1967.

Gerber, Gerald E. "Additional Sources for 'The Masque of the Red Death,'" *American Literature,* XXXVII (March, 1965), 52–54.

Hough, Robert L., ed. *Literary Criticism of Edgar Allan Poe.* Lincoln, Neb., 1965.

Macpherson, Harriet Dorothea. "Dumas and Poe Again," *Saturday Review of Literature,* VI (February 22, 1930), 760.

Ober, Warren U., Paul S. Burtness, and William R. Seat, Jr., eds. *The Enigma of Poe.* Boston, 1960.

Ostrom, John Ward, ed. *The Letters of Edgar Allan Poe.* 2 vols. Cambridge, Mass., 1948.

Robertson, John W. *Edgar A. Poe: A Psychopathic Study.* New York, 1922.

—————. *Bibliography of the Writings of Edgar A. Poe.* 2 vols. San Francisco, 1934.

Stovall, Floyd. "The Conscious Art of Edgar Allan Poe," *College English,* XXIV (March, 1963), 417–421.

Woodberry, George Edward. *Life of Edgar Allan Poe, Personal and Literary, with His Chief Correspondence with Men of Letters.* 2 vols. Boston, 1909.

Following are four sample pages from a research paper entitled "Tennessee Williams: A Study in Anguish." They illustrate typing, footnotes, and bibliography. The paper itself, by Paxton Moore, consists of a title page; a two-page preface which is personal and gives the author's reasons for writing the paper; a table of contents; 18 typed pages of content (three shown); and two pages of bibliography (one shown).

to turn to the written work in order to pour out the black despair
that torments his soul.

"The bleak, melancholy story of Williams' life"[1] began on
March 26, 1911,[2] in Columbus, Mississippi, where he was born the
child of Cornelius Coffin Williams and Edwina Dakin Williams and
christened Thomas Lanier, his middle name having been bestowed in
honor of a paternal ancestor, Sidney Lanier. His father was a
traveling salesman for a shoe company when Tom was born, and, as
his work required him to be on the road constantly, Mrs. Williams
made her home with her parents. Williams' grandfather was an
Episcopalian minister, and it was in his house and his way of life
that the young boy spent his early years. Being nurtured in this
aura of genteel Southern aristocracy did not prepare him to accept
the periodic visits of his convivial, energetic, and bawdy father,
who would live with his family only as his traveling job permitted.

During the time that his grandfather had a church in Clarks-
dale, Mississippi, Tom contracted diphtheria in a form so serious
that it was doubtful for a while if the child would live. The
illness was to have a permanent effect, for it naturally kept him
even closer to his mother, his grandmother, and his gentle nurses,
and it gave him a constant and favorite companion, his sister Rose.

---

[1] Lincoln K. Barnett, Writing on Life: Sixteen Close-Ups (New
York, 1951), p. 245.

[2] Nancy M. Tischler, Tennessee Williams (New York, 1961),
p. 16. All other sources give the date as 1914, but Mrs. Tischler says
(pp. 66-67) that in a moment of truthfulness, Williams admitted his
real birth date, the three years having been dropped when he was
28 years old and wanted to enter a playwriting contest for authors
25 years and under.

*Specimen page (this and the following three pages from* **A Research Manual
for College Studies and Papers,** *3rd ed.; copyright © 1963 by* **Cecil B. Williams**
*and* **Allan H. Stevenson;** *reproduced by permission of Harper & Row)*

## 3

When the boy was eight years old and already incapable of adjusting to the world of his more earthy playmates, his father was transferred to St. Louis. The shock of the removal from the protected and semi-pastoral home of his grandfather, where the family had been a prominent part of the community, to the urban concrete of the Midwest, where they suddenly became nothing in the community, was something from which he never recovered. To this day, "Most of the ugliness Williams has seen in life he associates with St. Louis."[1]

In school he was bullied and teased and found no comfort in the bosom of his family, where he was referred to as "Miss Nancy" by his father. His inability to cope with the world outside threw him closer to his sister and they would spend hours playing with her collection of glass animals. Eventually, Rose, who like Tom was an extremely sensitive child, began to withdraw from the world, a withdrawal that ultimately ended in schizophrenia.[2]

It was during the early St. Louis years that Tom first turned to writing, for in his writing he could ignore the real world that passed threateningly and darkly in front of him. By the time he had finished high school, he had won several local poetry contests and had had one story published in Weird Tales and another in Smart Set. When he entered the University of Missouri in 1929, he continued to write, but his real world began to change for him. He found himself no longer the butt of classroom jokes. Instead, he was invited to join a fraternity, where he learned that alcohol could help him overcome his shyness, and he had fallen in

[1] Ibid., p. 25.

[2] Ibid., p. 29.

*Specimen page*

love, but the young lady eventually married another man. This girl has apparently been his one love.[1]

After his junior year of college, his father, infuriated by the excesses of Tom's fraternity life and his low grades, withdrew him from school and put him to work in the shoe factory. The boy had to endure this hated existence for three years, three years that would give us The Glass Menagerie, until his nervous system rebelled finally and he had a breakdown. He was sent to live once again with his beloved grandparents, who were at that time residing in Memphis. Away from St. Louis and the home he hated so much, he began to recover quickly.

In Memphis, he met "the theatre" for the first time. A girl who lived hear his home was able to interest him in a "little theatre" group and suggested that the two of them collaborate on a play. With Williams doing most of the writing, the result was a play called Cairo! Shanghai! Bombay!, which dealt with two sailors on leave who met two girls. This play was performed and the performance was the beginning of a new vision for the playwright: " 'That was when I first realized that this was a medium that was most attractive. I discovered the thrill of people reacting to my work in front of my eyes.' "[2]

When he returned to St. Louis and entered Washington University, he continued to write. This period saw the production of his second dramatic effort, The Magic Tower, by a little theatre group outside of St. Louis. More important than this, however,

---

[1] Kenneth Tynan, Curtains (New York, 1961), p. 268.

[2] Tischler, Tennessee Williams, p. 42.

*Specimen page*

# BIBLIOGRAPHY

Barnett, Lincoln K. "Tennessee Williams." Writing on Life:
    Sixteen Close-Ups. New York: William Sloane Associates,
    1951.

Funke, Lewis, and John E. Booth. "Williams on Williams."
    Theatre Arts, XLVI (January, 1962), 16-19; 72-73.

Gassner, John. The Theatre in Our Times. New York:  Crown,
    1954.

Kalem, Ted. "An Angel of the Odd." Time, LXXIX (March 9,
    1962), 53-60.

Kerr, Walter. "Playwrights." Pieces at Eight.  New York:
    Simon and Schuster, 1957, pp. 125-134.

Lumley, Frederick. "Broadway Cortege: Tennessee Williams
    and Arthur Miller." Trends in 20th Century Drama.
    London: Barrie and Rockliff, 1960.

New York Theatre Critics' Review, 1961. New York:  Critics'
    Theatre Reviews, 1961.

Tischler, Nancy M. Tennessee Williams: Rebellious Puritan.
    New York: The Citadel Press, 1961.

Tynan, Kenneth. Curtains. New York: Atheneum, 1961.

Williams, Tennessee. American Blues. New York: Dramatists
    Play Service, 1948.

_____. Camino Real. Norfolk, Connecticut:  New Direc-
    tions, 1953.

_____. Cat on a Hot Tin Roof.   Norfolk, Connecticut:
    New Directions, 1955.

_____. Garden District. London: Secker and Warburg, 1959.

_____. The Glass Menagerie. New York: Random House,
    1945.

_____. Intro. to Carson McCullers, Reflections in a Golden
    Eye. New York: New Directions, 1950.

_____. The Night of the Iguana. Esquire, LVII (February,
    1962), 47-62; 115-130.

19

*Specimen page*

# THE PARAGRAPH
## (SECTIONS 21-30)

Good—that is, clear, effective, entirely adequate—speaking and writing will ease and smooth the passage of general thought and the conveyance of a particular thought or impression in statement or question or command. Bad speaking and writing do just the opposite and, worse, set up doubt and ambiguity.

—ERIC PARTRIDGE, "Degraded Language,"
*The New York Times Book Review,*
September 18, 1966

# THE
# PARAGRAPH

Writing is a process of building. Letters of the alphabet are combined into words; words are linked to form phrases, clauses, and sentences; and sentences are combined to form paragraphs. Good themes or compositions are thus built with good paragraphs, which are fundamental to all good writing and which are predicated on clear thinking.

Anyone can create good paragraphs who has ideas, will think clearly about them, will develop them, will relate them to one another, and will write and rewrite thoughtfully. You speak in words and sentences, but you usually think and write in larger units.

To achieve good paragraphs, therefore, you should understand the meaning, purposes, and characteristics of paragraphs and paragraphing.

## 21  *Definition and characteristics*

### 21a  *Understand clearly the meaning and purpose of paragraphing*

A paragraph is usually a group of sentences developing either one single topic or a specific part of a larger topic. Sometimes, in serving an appropriate purpose, a paragraph may consist of only one sentence.

The purpose of a paragraph is to aid in communicating ideas by setting off the single topic which is developed or by providing clear distinctions between the separate parts of a longer composition. A complete theme or short paper may consist of one paragraph only (see section **29d**) or it may have two or three or as many paragraphs as the writer decides are necessary to give his subject adequate treatment.

### 21b   Make your paragraphs correct, clear, effective, and appropriate

A well-constructed paragraph is *correct* in its mechanics; it also is *clear, effective,* and *appropriate,* characteristics dependent on careful thinking.

Good paragraphing is essential for clearness. Properly separated groups of sentences enable the writer to plot his course and see the progress he is making. To the reader they make the structure and development of ideas easily apparent by serving as signposts or road markers to guide him along the paths of thought which the writer is developing. The reader, following the signs laid out to help him, obtains a grasp of the parts—how separated and how related—and of the whole which they constitute.

Good paragraphing is essential also for effectiveness, partly because readers easily tire unless a page of writing is broken into smaller units. The sign of the paragraph, *indentation,* helps, for the reader knows that he has completed a unified section of writing and can go on to another unit. Such smaller units with indentation give the reader inviting pages to read, make easy reading for his eyes, and help him in his ability to concentrate.

For convenience, preview, and ready reference, seven desirable paragraph characteristics are listed below; except for No. 7, each is discussed in later sections. These characteristics refer to the normal paragraph, that is, the paragraph as a group of related sentences. They do not apply to paragraphs *appropriate* for special purposes (see Section **29**) .

⟶ 1. A good paragraph is *mechanically* correct. (Section **22.**)

⟶ 2. A good paragraph contains a *topic statement,* expressed or implied. (Section **23.**)

⟶ 3. A good paragraph depends upon proper *analysis* of its topic; it contains a *body of thought,* not a mere fragment; it contains ample *content.* (Section **24.**)

⟶ 4. A good paragraph is *unified.* (Section **25.**)

⟶ 5. A good paragraph has its ideas arranged in proper *order.* Sentences in it are so worded and arranged that each sentence flows naturally out of the one that precedes it and leads naturally into the one that follows. (Section **26.**)

⟶ 6. A good paragraph is well *proportioned* and has appropriate length. (Sections **27** and **28.**)

⟶ 7. A good paragraph contains *transitional aids:* words, phrases, clauses, or sentences serving as links or bridges. The thoughts within paragraphs make orderly, clear progress, and one paragraph leads to another clearly, logically, and smoothly. (Sections **11** and **42.**)

# 22  *Mechanics*

The conventions of mechanical correctness in paragraphs are few and easily learned.

## 22a  *Indent the first line of every paragraph*

Indentation, although mechanical, is important. Indent the first line of every paragraph about an inch (or, if you type, five or 10 spaces). Exception: business letters using block form usually do not indent paragraph beginnings (see pp. 655, 659, 661).

The break of distinct paragraph indentation is a clear, effective aid to writer and reader in recognizing divisions of thought within the whole theme. It also aids in reading; the break serves as a signal that a clear distinction between separate parts of the composition is about to be made.

Use indentations of equal length for all the paragraphs in the same theme. Make no exception for *numbered* paragraphs (see such use in Section **23c** and elsewhere)

Avoid, in general, the use of the marks ¶ and *no* ¶, meaning, respectively, "a new paragraph intended" and "no new paragraph." Preferably, recopy the entire page.

Do not indent the first line of the second page or succeeding pages unless the indentation is the beginning of a new paragraph.

### 22b Do not leave part of a line blank within a paragraph

Unless a new paragraph begins on the next line, do not leave part of a line blank within a paragraph. Blanks in lines which are not last lines of paragraphs mislead your reader, who expects such a break to finish the discussion of one phase of a subject. Margins at the left of the page should always be uniform, not meander toward the right.

(For the conventional and appropriate use of very short paragraphs—convenience, conversation, short introductory and concluding paragraphs, transitional paragraphs, business letters, directions, summaries, conclusions, and recommendations—see Section **29**.)

## 23 The topic sentence or statement

A topic sentence or statement gives the subject of the paragraph; it contains the heart of the idea which is to be, is being, or has been, developed. It contributes to unity, clearness, and effectiveness of the paragraph by expressing the central thought with which the group of sentences is concerned. It contains, however, only the main point or points of the paragraph, not every idea mentioned.

### 23a Use a topic sentence or topic statement to aid in gaining paragraph unity

The topic sentence, although so called, may not be a "sentence" at all. It is the statement containing the subject or topic, which may be expressed in various forms: (1) as one of the clauses in a compound sentence; (2) as the main clause of a complex sentence; (3) as a phrase within the sentence; (4) even as a single word; or (5) as a short, simple sentence—usually the most effective kind of topic sentence.

The reason for such flexibility is that a writer may use part of the sentence containing the topic to serve as transition or to indicate either the manner in which the topic is to be developed or the direction in which the discussion is to go. Whatever its grammatical form, the topic sentence, or statement, is or contains the subject of the paragraph.

Not every well-constructed paragraph contains an expressed topic sentence, but every good paragraph is so well knit that it at least *implies* one. The reader, reflecting, can sum up the central thought of the paragraph in his own "topic sentence." Perhaps, however, a study of a number of paragraphs would show that the clearest and most effective paragraphs are those in which the topic is expressed, the least effective those in which it is implied. Consideration for the reader is certainly an argument in favor of an expressed topic.

A topic sentence or statement or word, therefore, is a guide to both writer and reader. For the writer, it is the guide by which he keeps on the subject and avoids introducing irrelevant material. It perhaps should be a simple sentence, at least in its first draft. Simple sentences are easier to phrase than other kinds, and a writer can write all the topic sentences or statements for a theme, or even a long paper, before he begins the more difficult task of developing them.

A well-planned topic outline, in which you have already decided the divisions to be expanded into paragraphs, provides the key words for topic statements; a sentence outline presents topic sentences ready-made. The paragraph outline, usually made of others' writing, shows how other authors composed their topic sentences. (See Section **6b,c,d.**)

As a check on the presence or absence of a paragraph topic and its effective phrasing, reread carefully each paragraph you write. Put in the margin the one or two words that are the subject of the paragraph. Or apply the methods of some textbooks which print the paragraph topic in boldface type at the beginning of the paragraph. (If you follow any of these suggestions, be sure to eliminate from your final draft all such mechanical indications of the topic.)

### 23b   *Vary the kind of sentences containing the topic*

Although simple sentences are clear and effective as topic sentences, you can include topics in the phrases or clauses of compound, complex, and compound-complex sentences. Use mainly declarative sentences, but for variety, and when they are appropriate, use interrogative, exclamatory, or even imperative sentences. Any of these kinds of sentences can make a topic sentence that generalizes or summarizes or particularizes.

## 23c  *Vary the position of topic sentences within the paragraph*

Ordinarily, since the purpose of writing is clearness of communication, the first sentence of the paragraph, especially in expository and argumentative writing, should be or contain the topic. Your reader should be told immediately what he is to read about. Since a series of paragraphs beginning with topic sentences may become monotonous, you can experiment with placing a paragraph topic in the second, third, or fourth sentence, letting the earlier sentence or sentences lead up to it. Occasionally, your last sentence may be or may contain the topic. Occasionally, too, you may repeat the thought of the topic sentence in other sentences in the paragraph.

Study the following examples. Note the unifying, clarifying effect of the topic sentences; note also their position and form. To emphasize their position, they are here italicized.

1. The topic sentence is the first sentence, a simple sentence, an interrogative sentence; its development tells why the question cannot be accurately answered.

*How many fish are there in the sea?* This is a question on which opinions differ widely. The trouble is that there is no quantitative method of sampling the fish of the open ocean. Many fish avoid the sunlit surface layer where they can be caught by hook and line. Nets have been towed at mid-depths but probably scare many of the fish away. Only in the last few years since the Japanese have been fishing in the tropical Atlantic has it begun to be realized that there may be as many tuna in the Atlantic as in the Pacific.[1]

2. The topic statement is the noun clause used as subject of the first sentence. It is repeated in the same words in the third sentence and in slightly different words in the sixth sentence.

*What makes an airplane fly* is not its engine nor its propeller. Nor is it, as many people think, some mysterious knack of the pilot, nor

[1] C. O'D. Iselin, "Our Water Planet," *The Saturday Review,* July 5, 1958.

some ingenious gadget inside. *What makes an airplane fly* is simply its shape. This may sound absurd, but gliders do fly without engines and model airplanes do fly without pilots. As for the insides of an airplane, they are disappointing, for they are mostly hollow. No, *what keeps an airplane up* is its shape—the impact of the air upon its shape. Whittle that shape out of wood, or cast it out of iron, or fashion it, for that matter, out of chocolate and throw the thing into the air. It will behave like an airplane. It will *be* an airplane.[2]

3. The topic sentence is the fourth sentence, a long simple sentence, a declarative sentence; the sentences before and after it illustrate and expand the idea expressed.

Suppose, however, that we had called that same animal a "mongrel." The matter is more complicated. We have used a word which objectively means the same as "dog of mixed breed," but which also arouses in our hearers an emotional attitude of disapproval toward that particular dog. *A word, therefore, can not only indicate an object, but can also suggest an emotional attitude toward it.* Such suggestion of an emotional attitude does go beyond exact and scientific discussion because our approvals and disapprovals are individual—they belong to ourselves and not to the objects we approve or disapprove of. An animal which to the mind of its master is a faithful and noble dog of mixed ancestry may be a "mongrel" to his neighbor whose chickens are chased by it.[3]

These illustrations indicate various positions for the topic sentence and a few of the ways in which it is expressed. Important to remember is this: One criterion of the good paragraph is that it must be so unified that its content is summarized in a topic sentence or clause or *can be* when a topic is not expressed. Thus a writer can be certain that he has kept to the subject and that his reader can follow clearly the development of the paragraph thought.

## EXERCISES

A. Underline the topic sentence or topic statement of each one of a number of paragraphs in (1) one of your textbooks; (2) an article in

2 Wolfgang Langewiesche, "Why an Airplane Flies," *Life*, May 17, 1943. Copyright Time, Inc.

3 Robert H. Thouless, "Emotional Meanings," *How To Think Straight*. Copyright 1939 by Simon and Schuster, Inc.

a current magazine; (3) an article in your book of readings. Discuss the position in the paragraph of each of these topic sentences and the kind of sentence it is.

B. From your reading, select a seemingly well-constructed paragraph which has no topic sentence or topic statement. Give the implied topic.

C. By means of the author's topic sentences, make a paragraph outline of some essay in your book of readings. (See Section **6d**.)

D. For each of five of the following theme subjects, write five or more simple sentences which could be used for topics of paragraphs developing the theme.

1. Why I Am Attending —— College
2. The Honor System on Our Campus
3. The Best Way To Buy a Second-Hand Car
4. The Most Remarkable Character in Our Town
5. How To Improve in Writing
6. Let's Ignore the Saturday Football Games
7. Reading as a Substitute for Travel
8. Why Golf Makes Walking Interesting
9. See Your Dentist Twice a Year, but Your Doctor Only Once
10. Are You Here To Study or To Have a Great Time?

E. Write 20 simple sentences to be used as topic sentences: five for narrative, five for description, five for exposition, and five for argument.

F. Using the following simple sentences as topic sentences, expand one or more into paragraphs of 150 to 300 words.

1. I favor (am opposed to) early morning classes.
2. The new wonder drugs help save lives daily.
3. Some teachers can easily be influenced.
4. I am looking forward to a trip to ——.
5. The fastest way to travel is by air.
6. Teachers change their personality outside the classroom.
7. I well remember my most embarrassing moment.
8. First impressions of people are often proved wrong.
9. A pet is an important part of a family.
10. I enjoy life in a dormitory (fraternity, sorority).
11. I have learned how to judge a used car.
12. Water-skiing (or ——) is a good summer sport.
13. A "blind date" can be an ordeal.
14. Some superstitions have an interesting history.
15. It is sometimes difficult to keep awake during a lecture.

# 24  Content

After you have determined the thought to be developed in the paragraph and put it in a topic sentence, expressed or implied, your problem is developing the thought. Topic sentences are only the beginning, the foundation, the summary of the thought to be presented.

Clear and effective paragraphs are completely developed and contain an abundance of pertinent detail. Ineffective paragraphs are weak not because the central ideas are necessarily weak but because their content is thin, dull, and meaningless. In other words, fully developed paragraphs require genuine mental activity. An effective, clear theme is the sum total of a series of paragraphs rounded with ample content.

### 24a  Gather content from your own thought and experience and from the thought and experience of others

After phrasing the topic sentence, draw upon your own experience and the experience of others as revealed in newspapers, magazines, books, radio, TV, and conversation. Make use of your own experience, observation, curiosity, imagination, and reflection. Since a single paragraph may be either a complete short theme or one of a series of paragraphs making up a theme, the suggestions concerning content for the theme (Section 5) apply equally to the paragraph.

To this content apply also the analysis suggested for theme topics in Section 4. Your paragraph topic is simply a more limited subject: What are its component parts? What, from your various materials, will you jot down concerning it?

For example, for a long theme, "Important Facts About My High School," designed to inform his freshman English instructor of his precollege background, a student chose for one paragraph subject, "Courses of Study Offered." As a start and in no special order, his jottings consisted of the following:

1. Two main courses
2. Academic course
3. Commercial course
4. General course for a few weaker students

5. Time of choosing courses
6. Content of academic course (composition, literature, history, science, mathematics, etc.)
7. Content of commercial course (typing, shorthand, bookkeeping, business English, etc.)
8. Purpose of academic course
9. Purpose of commercial course

The following outline for the paragraph resulted from these jottings:

   I. General information about courses
     A. Kinds
     B. Purpose
     C. Time of choosing
  II. The academic course
     A. Subjects included
     B. Subjects not included
III. The commercial course
     A. Subjects included
     B. Subjects not included

The paragraph written from this outline, with the topic sentence first, follows:

*Two main courses of study are offered at Valley View High School.* One is the academic course and the other is the commercial course. The high school freshman is required to choose the course he plans to follow during the next four years. The academic course consists of the subjects required for college entrance, such as written composition, English and American literature, mathematics, history, and some science. This course does not include typing, shorthand, or bookkeeping, although a student may elect one or more of these. The commercial course is designed for girls and boys preparing to become stenographers and secretaries. It does not include English literature or any of the sciences or higher mathematics courses. It is concerned mainly with the commercial courses, like shorthand, typing, bookkeeping, business English, and office etiquette.

**24b** *Follow a consistent method or methods in developing the idea contained in the topic sentence*

By various methods you can expand a topic into an effective paragraph. Your method may vary with the four kinds of writing—

narration, description, exposition, argument. Your topic sentence, if well chosen and phrased, will often indicate the most desirable method; sometimes it will suggest several methods, from which you choose the one that will most clearly, effectively, and appropriately accomplish your purpose. The choice of any one method does not exclude other methods of paragraph development; also, a short illustration—a sentence or two at the most— may always be inserted into the course of development by any method without destroying the unity of the paragraph or the directness of the thought.

Frequently used to develop a paragraph topic are the following: (1) particulars and details, (2) illustration or example, (3) comparison or contrast, (4) division, (5) causes or effects, (6) reasons or inferences, and (7) definition.

1. Development by *particulars and details* means expanding the idea contained in the topic by a series of specific details or concrete particulars, arranged in some logical order. Since any topic is broader or more general than its supporting material, every paragraph in a sense is developed by particulars and details. Apart from other methods, however, this method uses ideas related to or suggested by preceding ideas, and all taken together amplify, make vivid, make definite the topic. Notice how particulars and details support the topic, italicized, in the following paragraphs:

### MISCELLANEOUS *DETAILS*

*In an elevator,* ascending with strangers to familiar heights, the breath congeals, the body stiffens, the spirit marks time. These brief vertical journeys that we make in a common lift, from street level to office level, past the missing thirteenth floor—they afford moments of suspended animation, unique and probably beneficial. Passengers in an elevator, whether wedged tight or scattered with room to spare, achieve in their perpendicular passage a trancelike state: each person adhering to the unwritten code, a man descending at five in the afternoon with his nose buried in a strange woman's back hair, reducing his breath to an absolute minimum necessary to sustain life, willing to suffocate rather than allow a suggestion of his physical presence to impinge; a man coming home at one A.M., ascending with only one other occupant of the car, carefully avoiding any slight recognition of joint occupancy. What is there about elevator travel that induces this painstaking catalepsy? A sudden solemnity, perhaps, which seizes people when they feel gravity being tampered with—they hope successfully. Sometimes it seems to us as though everyone in the car were in silent prayer.[4]

## NARRATIVE *DETAILS*

*The bare, indisputable facts in the life of Mary Todd Lincoln* are few and simple. She was born of a good Kentucky family, in 1818, ten years after her husband. In 1839 she came to live with her sister, Mrs. Edwards, in Springfield. After a stormy courtship Lincoln married her in 1842. Her life then led her through Illinois law and politics to the White House, and the war, and the culminations of triumphant peace. All the triumph and hope were blasted by the assassination of her husband, and her remaining years, in spite of a brief sojourn to Europe, were darkened by sorrow and misfortune till a temperament, always impulsive and intense, was unbalanced to a point of oddity approaching and at times reaching actual derangement. She died in 1882.[5]

## DESCRIPTIVE *DETAILS*

For *sounds in winter nights, and often in winter days,* I heard the forlorn but melodious notes of a hooting owl indefinitely far; such a sound as the frozen earth would yield if struck with a suitable plectrum, the very *lingua vernacula* of Walden Wood, and quite familiar to me at last, though I never saw the bird while it was making it. I seldom opened my door in a winter evening without hearing it; *Hoo hoo hoo, hoorer hoo,* sounded sonorously, and the first three syllables accented somewhat like *how der do*; or sometimes *hoo hoo* only. One night in the beginning of winter, before the pond froze over, about nine o'clock, I was startled by the loud honking of a goose, and, stepping to the door, heard the sound of their wings like a tempest in the woods as they flew low over my house. They passed over the pond toward Fair-Haven, seemingly deterred from settling by my light, their commodore honking all the while with a regular beat. Suddenly an unmistakable cat-owl from very near me, with the most harsh and tremendous voice I ever heard from any inhabitant of the woods, responded at regular intervals to the goose, as if determined to expose and disgrace this intruder from Hudson's Bay by exhibiting a greater compass and volume of voice in a native, and *boohoo* him out of Concord horizon. What do you mean by alarming the citadel at this time of night consecrated to me? Do you think I am ever caught napping at such an hour, and that I have not got lungs and a larynx as well as yourself? *Boo-hoo, boo-hoo, boo-hoo!* It was one of the most thrilling discords I ever heard. And yet, if you

[4] E. B. White, *The Second Tree from the Corner,* Harper & Brothers. Copyright 1954 by E. B. White.
[5] Gamaliel Bradford, *Wives.* Copyright 1925 by Harper & Brothers.

had a discriminating ear, there were in it the elements of a concord such as these plains never saw nor heard.[6]

**EXPOSITORY *DETAILS***

We all appear to ourselves to be thinking all the time during our waking hours, and most of us are aware that we go on thinking while we are asleep, even more foolishly than when awake. When uninterrupted by some practical issue *we are engaged in what is now known as a reverie.* This is our spontaneous and favorite kind of thinking. We allow our ideas to take their own course and this course is determined by our hopes and fears, our spontaneous desires, their fulfillment or frustration; by our likes and dislikes, our loves and hates and resentments. There is nothing else anything like so interesting to ourselves as ourselves. All thought that is not more or less laboriously controlled and directed will inevitably circle about the beloved Ego. It is amusing and pathetic to observe this tendency in ourselves and in others. We learn politely and generously to overlook this truth, but if we dare to think of it, it blazes forth like the noontide sun.[7]

2. Development by *illustration* or *example* uses a series of sentences which furnish an instance representative of the more general statement in the topic sentence. The instance may be semispecific, like "Consider a man who is overly ambitious"; or, for greater effectiveness, it may be specific and concrete, like "Consider Shakespeare's Macbeth, who was overly ambitious." An example familiar to the reader carries its own explanation and thus aids clearness. Either a longer single example or several shorter instances serve to drive home to the reader the idea expressed in the topic sentence.

Following are two consecutive paragraphs developed by illustration or example. With topic sentences italicized, the first uses numerous illustrations, the second uses three examples:

The story of the Arizona rancher who made out a $500 check on a six-by-three-foot cowhide recalls the *many curious surfaces on which checks have legally been written through the years*: in lipstick on handkerchiefs, on cigarette paper, on calling cards, fragile valentines, on

[6] Henry David Thoreau, "Winter Animals," *Walden, or Life in the Woods.*

[7] James Harvey Robinson, *The Mind in the Making.* Copyright 1921 by Harper & Brothers.

whisky labels, Christmas cards, envelopes, newspaper, cigar-box tops, paper bags, laundry bills. A check written on a hard-boiled egg was cashed without trouble at the Victoria branch of the Canadian Bank of Commerce. A Midwestern lumberman made out so many checks on his own brand of shingle that his bank had to construct a special type of file cabinet for them. A contractor in Memphis once settled his weekly payroll by drawing on the bank with slabs of wood. A businessman eager to pay for a newly arrived television set recently pried off the side of the packing case and wrote his check on it.

*The odd ways in which checks have been written are a reflection of the foibles of those who make them out.* This was symbolized a few years ago when a check for $1,000, painted on the side of a 134-pound watermelon, was drawn against the account of the Parker County (Texas) Melon Growers Association to pay a contestant on a television show with the appropriate title, "People Are Funny." Then there was the sailor stationed at San Diego who was plagued with requests for money from home. In desperation he engraved a check on a piece of battleship plate with a blow torch and sent it home, confident that the annoying requests would now stop. At the end of the month, though, the steel check came back with his other canceled checks, with a proper endorsement on the back—also made with a blow torch. And recently a Connecticut perfume company drenched its checkbooks with samples of its product, printed the word "scent" instead of "cent," and the words "pay to the odor of" the customer.[8]

In the following, the long topic sentence is developed by a number of illustrations or examples:

*In many circles the notion of death seems to be more tolerable to the human consciousness if the verb "to die" is not spoken in reference to this most unpleasant and most unaesthetic of all the phenomena of life.* Miss [Louise] Pound has collected an impressive list of substitutions in her "American Euphemisms for Dying, Death, and Burial," published in *American Speech* for October, 1936, among them such fine growths as "laid down his burden," "the golden cord is severed," "breathed his last," "called to his reward," "gathered to his fathers," "the Angel of Death claimed him," "her frail tabernacle drifted away," "called to Jesus," "he has left a vacant chair," "his clock has run down," "slipped into the great democracy of the dead," "safe in the arms of Jesus,"

8 "Topics," *The New York Times*, September 20, 1960. Copyright © 1960 by The New York Times Company.

"passed within the pearly gates," "gone to the Great Adventure," "the bell rang and he went," and "at five o'clock in the morning she plumed the wings of her soul and took her flight to glory." Miss Pound concludes that "one of mankind's gravest problems is to avoid a straightforward mention of dying or burial."[9]

In the following, one expanded example is the major means of developing the topic:

The dividing line between name-calling and the smear or mudslinging technique is almost invisible, and in common usage the terms are virtually interchangeable. But *the mudslinger makes personal attacks on his opponent,* not merely by hurling a few choice epithets, but (often) by presenting an array of supposedly damaging evidence against his opponent's motives, character, and private life. Thus the audience's attention is diverted from the argument itself to a subject which is more likely to stir up prejudices. If, for example, in denouncing his opponent's position on the reduction of the national debt, a candidate refers to Mr. X's connection with certain well-known gamblers, he ceases to argue his case on its merits and casts doubt upon his opponent's personal character. His object is not primarily to hurt Mr. X's feelings, but to arouse bias against Mr. X in his hearer's mind. Every critical reader or listener must train himself to detect and reject these irrelevant aspersions. It may be, indeed, that Mr. X has shady connections with the underworld. But that has nothing to do with the abstract rights or wrongs of his position on a national issue. Although, as the history of American politics shows, it is a hard thing to do, issues should be discussed apart from character and motives. The latter are also important, since obviously they bear upon a candidate's fitness for public office, but they call for a separate discussion.[10]

3. A topic may be made clear and effective by the use of *comparison* or *contrast*. Comparison shows the likeness between the topic and some idea or object familiar to the reader; contrast shows differences. Not infrequently both comparison and contrast are used within the same paragraph.

[9] Thomas Pyles, *Words and Ways of American English*. Copyright 1952 by Random House, Inc.

[10] Richard D. Altick, *Preface to Critical Reading*, 4th ed. Copyright 1960 by Holt, Rinehart and Winston, Inc.

## COMPARISON

*The emotion of a mob is like a flooding river.* The river is at first quiet and still, but as the rain continues to fall day by day, and the waters rise higher, it begins to build up tremendous pressure. The river is no longer quiet. There is a murmur that grows in volume, grows louder and louder until finally the river breaks loose and surges over its banks, gathering momentum as it goes, rolling over everything in its path, wrecking homes, killing people. When the rampage is over, the river is once more quiet and still, showing no signs of its late turmoil, unmindful of the damage it has caused. So it is with the mob. It is one of the most destructive instruments on earth when aroused. It loses all power of reason and can only follow its leaders, roaring, destroying everything in its path, until the individuality of its members reasserts itself. Then the mob begins to break up, to disperse itself. Each member, going his own way, hardly remembers what the common bond was that had held them together. Even the memory of what has happened finally disappears.[11]

## CONTRAST

*It is a misfortune* of the English language in modern times *that the word "disinterested" is commonly confused with the word "uninterested."* The modern lexicographers who work on the principle that whatever is the usage of people is acceptable are beginning to accept the confusion, and perhaps they are very wise in their principle, but in this instance the usage of people—or at least of some people—has deprived us of our only word for a very important virtue. Up until recently the meanings of the two words were kept distinct, and it was a mark of ignorance to confuse them. "Disinterested" meant that one had nothing to gain from the matter at hand, that one was objective in one's judgment, that one had no selfish motive but was impartial and unbiased. "Uninterested" meant that one was bored with the matter at hand, that it did not engage one's attention. The distinction is still in force among almost all careful writers and speakers; they blame, say, a labor arbitrator who is *uninterested* in the case he is hearing, but they praise him for being *disinterested* in the way he decides it.[12]

---

[11] "Mob," an expanded simile in a one-paragraph theme by Phyllis Hahn, when a DePauw University student. *Indiana English Leaflet*, February, 1955.

[12] Lionel Trilling, prefatory note to Matthew Arnold's "The Function of Criticism at the Present Time," *Major British Writers*. Copyright 1954 by Harcourt, Brace and Company.

4. Developing a topic by *division* means that the writer calls attention to two or more parts of the topic and discusses each one briefly within the same paragraph. Of course, if each part is expanded in some detail, separate paragraphs are preferable. The following paragraph is developed by division:

*There are roughly three New Yorks.* There is, first, the New York of the man or woman who was born here, who takes the city for granted and accepts its size and its turbulence as natural and inevitable. Second, there is the New York of the commuter—the city that is devoured by locusts each day and spat out each night. Third, there is the New York of the person who was born somewhere else and came to New York in quest of something. Of these three trembling cities the greatest is the last—the city of final destination, the city that is a goal. It is this third city that accounts for New York's high-strung disposition, its poetical deportment, its dedication to the arts, and its incomparable achievements. Commuters give the city its tidal restlessness; natives give it solidity and continuity; but the settlers give it passion. And whether it is a farmer arriving from Italy to set up a small grocery store in a slum, or a young girl arriving fom a small town in Mississippi to escape the indignity of being observed by her neighbors, or a boy arriving from the Corn Belt with a manuscript in his suitcase and a pain in his heart, it makes no difference: each embraces New York with the intense excitement of first love, each absorbs New York with the fresh eyes of an adventurer, each generates heat and light to dwarf the Consolidated Edison Company.[13]

5. Development by *cause* (*causes*) or *effect* (*effects*) is ordinarily used for topic statements regarded as facts and hence is common in much expository writing. The topic sentence gives the generalized statement or conclusion drawn from the data; these data make up the supporting material of the paragraph, the causes or reasons. Or the supporting material tells what the various results or effects are of the general statement in the topic.

CAUSE

*The birth of a volcanic island is an event marked by prolonged and violent travail: the forces of the earth striving to create, and all the forces of the sea opposing.* The sea floor, where an island begins, is

13 E. B. White, *Here Is New York,* Harper & Brothers. Copyright 1949 by E. B. White and The Curtis Publishing Company.

probably nowhere more than fifty miles thick—a thin covering over the vast bulk of the earth. In it are deep cracks and fissures, the results of unequal cooling and shrinkage in past ages. Along such lines of weakness the molten lava from the earth's interior presses up and finally bursts forth into the sea. But a submarine volcano is different from a terrestrial eruption, where the lava, molten rocks, gases, and other ejecta are hurled into the air through an open crater. Here on the bottom of the ocean the volcano has resisting it all the weight of the ocean water above it. Despite the immense pressure of, it may be, two or three miles of sea water, the new volcanic cone builds upward toward the surface, in flow after flow of lava. Once within reach of the waves, its soft ash and tuff are violently attacked, and for a long period the potential island may remain a shoal, unable to emerge. But, eventually, in new eruptions, the cone is pushed up into the air and a rampart against the attacks of the waves is built of hardened lava.[14]

**EFFECT**

To most participating nations, *a modern war brings complex economic results.* Science and industry are occasionally advanced by researches derived from the stimulus and energy of war. Life and property are destroyed; vast sums are consumed in armament; impossible debts accumulate. Repudiation in some form becomes inevitable; currencies are depreciated or annulled, inflation relieves debtor governments and individuals, savings and investments are wiped out, and men patiently begin to save and lend again. Over-expansion in war is followed by a major depression in peace. International trade is disrupted by intensified nationalism, exalted tariffs, and the desire to develop at home all industries requisite in war. The vanquished are enslaved—physically, as in antiquity, financially, and by due process of law today. The victorious masses gain little except in self-conceit; the ruling minority among the victors may gain much in conquered lands, markets, spheres of influence, supplies, and taxable population.[15]

6. Development by *reasons* or *inferences* is a method usually used for topic statements regarded as opinions and hence is common in exposition of ideas and argumentative writing. Supporting material gives the reasons used in establishing the opinion or

14 Rachel L. Carson, *The Sea Around Us.* Copyright 1950, 1951 by Oxford University Press, Inc.
15 Will Durant, "Why Men Fight," *The Saturday Evening Post,* July 10, 1937.

it gives the data from which the statement of the topic sentence was inferred.

> A man on Mars would see *the planet Earth as a water planet*. Even the continents we live on would look to him like islands in the midst of salt seas. Land fills only one of the four quarters of the planet's surface. Yet we think of the Earth as land. Our lives are governed largely by what we know about the land. Science and popular thinking alike have yet to accept the truth that roughly three-quarters of the globe is covered by seawater three miles deep, containing all the chemical foods that have washed off the land since time began. We also ignore the probability that life originated within the sea.[16]

7. Development of a topic by *definition* (see Section 17c2a) involves the use of content that answers the implied question of the reader, "What do you mean by this?" To be clear and effective, the paragraph developed by this method also uses some of the foregoing methods: details and particulars, illustration and example, comparison or contrast. A definition using contrast is the following:

> *Novelette* [is] a form of fiction intermediate between the short story and the novel. (The cumbersome term "long short story" is sometimes used as a synonym.) No exact limits can be set as to length, but the novelette differs from the short story in that it is not only longer but is more elaborate and has greater scope. It is not only shorter and less elaborate than the novel but is designed to be read at a single sitting and to produce a single, concentrated effect. Practically speaking, the novelette can be defined as a piece of prose fiction between 50 and 150 ordinary pages long.[17]

### 24c   *Combine various methods of developing the topic sentence when they are necessary and appropriate*

You can write clear and effective paragraphs by developing topics according to one of the methods described above. On the other hand, frequently not only is it impossible to eliminate the overlapping of some of the methods, but doing so would be illogical

---

16 C. O'D. Iselin, "Our Water Planet," *The Saturday Review,* July 5, 1958.
17 Lillian H. Hornstein, ed., *The Reader's Companion to World Literature.* Copyright 1956 by The Dryden Press.

and undesirable. As seen in some of the illustrations, the use of several methods is effective; in fact, a few of the methods virtually require the use of others. An analysis of many well-written paragraphs, therefore, shows that the method of development cannot be rigidly exclusive; the important point is not to be limited to any particular method but to achieve adequate development of the topic.

The following student-written paragraph has elements of contrast, descriptive details, and example:

*Nature is a true artist.* To have the skill of an artist is surely worthy of esteem, but in my opinion no person will ever be the artist that Nature is. Nature has the advantage of possessing skill and originality, whereas people can do nothing but copy the works of Nature. The four seasons of the year provide a variety of subjects for the artist to work with: the fresh, bright greens of the grass, buds, and leaves in spring, the lavish multi-varied colors of the flowers in summer, the gorgeous red, yellow, and brown leaves of the autumn season, and the delicate lacework etchings of Jack Frost on the window panes in winter. These are all among the subject-models which Nature gives the human artist to choose from. When such an artist attempts to duplicate the colors and designs of Nature's subjects, he finds it impossible to duplicate them exactly. True, he may come close, but it seems that some slight or even major difference is always evident between the original works of Nature and the copies made by the human hand.

A single topic may be developed also in a series of paragraphs. To establish a certain statement, several expanded illustrations are given, each in a separate paragraph. Similarly, a series of paragraphs may support the truth of a major division or topic: one gives the causes; another gives the effects. Such a series results from the writer's desire to make materials convenient to the reader, as opposed to one long, complicated paragraph, and to attain clearness and effectiveness.

After practice you will find it easy to choose and use the various methods of paragraph development. Since the purpose in writing paragraphs is to let the reader see exactly and fully the developed ideas in expressed or implied topic sentences, the names of development methods are of little importance. The test of the content of a good paragraph is clear and effective communication.

## 24d   Avoid developing paragraphs with hazy generalizations

Adequate content consists of definite, concrete ideas, impressions, reflections, and observations. Generalizations are frequently trite, vague, and ineffective, and such paragraphs are sketchy and incomplete. Note the lack of worthwhile content in this student-written paragraph:

> Cheating never pays. After all, "honesty is the best policy"; also when one gets something for nothing he does not appreciate it. I think that every student should be on his own, even if his "own" is not good enough for him to pass his course. One should be honest, no matter what the cost. The student who thinks cheating is a sin only when it is detected is fooling nobody but himself. Sooner or later, his sins will find him out, and he will have nobody but himself to blame.

After revision the paragraph attained greater effectiveness through the use of specific illustration:

> Cheating does not pay. A friend of mine, whose identity I shall conceal by merely calling him J., thought that it did. He frequently said to me in high school: "Why should I study when it is so easy to get the desired results without work? The only sin in cheating is being caught." And so J. was dishonest all through his four years at school. But when he took the college board examinations, he could not cheat because of the nature of the questions and the efficiency of the proctors. He failed, and was bitterly disappointed, since he wanted very badly to enter —— University. As he read his letter of failure, he was convinced that cheating does not pay, that it is not a substitute for honest hard work.

## 24e   Avoid meaningless, ineffective repetition of the topic sentence

Repeating the topic sentence in different words is a device auxiliary to other methods of paragraph development, but no matter how varied the words, it is rarely used as the major method. Repetition that adds nothing new is merely thought going round in circles. Note the inadequacy of this repetitious paragraph:

> Some people pay too much attention to their diet. They spend hours every day wondering if they should eat this or that. They are too concerned about their digestive processes. One would think their great-

est concern was low-calorie food, and their talk shows that it is. Diet is not nearly so important as these people think it is; it's the amount they eat. Paying so much attention to diet does not warrant so much concern. They just pay too much attention to it.

Repetition, to be effective, should add clearness and should expand and develop the idea by specific details or other methods. Note, in the following, in the development of "the speaker's square forefinger emphasized his observations," the effective use of repetition among other methods like descriptive details and parallelism:

The scene was a plain, bare, monotonous vault of a schoolroom, and the speaker's square forefinger emphasized his observations by underscoring every sentence with a line on the schoolmaster's sleeve. *The emphasis was helped* by the speaker's square wall of a forehead, which had his eyebrows for its base, while his eyes found commodious cellarage in two dark caves, overshadowed by the wall. *The emphasis was helped* by the speaker's mouth, which was wide, thin, and hard set. *The emphasis was helped* by the speaker's voice, which was inflexible, dry, and dictatorial. *The emphasis was helped* by the speaker's hair, which bristled on the skirts of his bald head, a plantation of firs to keep the wind from its shining surface, all covered with knobs like the crust of a plum pie, as if the head had scarcely warehouse-room for the hard facts stored inside. The speaker's obstinate carriage, square coat, square legs, square shoulders,—nay, his very neckcloth, trained to take him by the throat with an unaccommodating grasp, like a stubborn fact as it was,—all *helped the emphasis.*[18]

## EXERCISES

A. For each of the methods of paragraph development discussed in Section **24b** (particulars and details, illustration or example, comparison or contrast, division, causes or effects, reasons or inferences, definition) write two topic sentences that you would like to develop into paragraphs.

B. Choose seven of the topic sentences (Exercise A) and write seven paragraphs, one illustrating each of the methods listed.

C. From your reading, select two paragraphs which illustrate each of the methods of development discussed in Section **24b**.

[18] Charles Dickens, *Hard Times.*

D. Develop each of the following topic sentences, each paragraph to illustrate a method of development listed in Exercise A:

1. Driving on icy roads is dangerous.
2. I have had an embarrassing encounter with the police.
3. Is courtesy to women a custom of the past?
4. What is a good student?
5. My grandfather (or someone else) is a "character."
6. A large college has more advantages (disadvantages) than a small college.
7. The greatest need of my home town is ——.
8. "A practical joke" and "a mean trick" are different.
9. I offer three solutions to the problem of the increase in traffic fatalities.
10. Getting involved in campus activities (politics) brings complex results.

E. Study the following paragraphs. Choose the topic sentence or topic statement of each or phrase the topic if it is merely implied. Identify the dominant method of paragraph development. What other methods are used in addition to the main method? Is a combination of methods used, with no one method outstanding?

1. In this by-place of nature, there abode, in a remote period of American history, that is to say, some thirty years since, a worthy wight of the name of Ichabod Crane; who sojourned, or, as he expressed it, "tarried," in Sleepy Hollow, for the purpose of instructing the children of the vicinity. He was a native of Connecticut, a state which supplies the Union with pioneers for the mind as well as for the forest, and sends forth yearly its legions of frontier woodsmen and country schoolmasters. The cognomen of Crane was not inapplicable to his person. He was tall, but exceedingly lank, with narrow shoulders, long arms and legs, hands that dangled a mile out of his sleeves, feet that might have served for shovels, and his whole frame most loosely hung together. His head was small, and flat at the top, with huge ears, large green glassy eyes, and a long snipe nose, so that it looked like a weathercock perched upon his spindle neck to tell which way the wind blew. To see him striding along the profile of a hill on a windy day, with his clothes bagging and fluttering about him, one might have mistaken him for the genius of Famine descending upon the earth or some scarecrow eloped from a cornfield.[19]

[19] Washington Irving, "The Legend of Sleepy Hollow."

2. The intricate architecture of a dictionary rests on the basic blueprint of the entries that are defined, illustrated, explained, and clarified. The selection of the words, names, places for inclusion in a dictionary must consider how and why a person goes to the dictionary. He goes to find the meaning of words such as *aorist,* or the preferred spelling of words such as *enclose,* or the pronunciation of words such as *stupefacient.* He also goes to find the location of places such as *Pohai* or the significance of names such as *Marie Antoinette.* Such a list of possible uses of the dictionary may, of course, be extended and amplified.[20]

3. Many of the natural wonders of the earth owe their existence to the fact that once the sea crept over the land, laid down its deposits of sediments, and then withdrew. There is Mammoth Cave in Kentucky, for example, where one may wander through miles of underground passages and enter rooms with ceilings 250 feet overhead. Caves and passageways have been dissolved by ground water out of an immense thickness of limestone, deposited by a Paleozoic sea. In the same way, the story of Niagara Falls goes back to Silurian time, when a vast embayment of the Arctic Sea crept southward over the continent. Its waters were clear, for the borderlands were low and little sediment or silt was carried into the inland sea. It deposited large beds of the hard rock called dolomite, and in time they formed a long escarpment near the present border between Canada and the United States. Millions of years later, floods of water released from melting glaciers poured over this cliff, cutting away the soft shales that underlay the dolomite, and causing mass after mass of the undercut rock to break away. In this fashion Niagara Falls and its gorge were created.[21]

4. For two years your liberal arts college introduces you to a mature experience in the four big areas of human knowledge and communication. Then you begin to specialize. A few of you may choose studies making you ready to go on toward higher degrees, beyond the B.A. to the M.A. and Ph.D. and a goal in advanced research or in college and university teaching. But most of you will choose studies from which, at the end of your senior term, you can apply for immediate salaried employment. You may aim for a post in laboratory research or

[20] Irving Lorge, "Selections of Entries and Definitions," *The American College Dictionary.* Copyright 1947–1966 by Random House, Inc.

[21] Rachel L. Carson, *The Sea Around Us.* Copyright 1950, 1951 by Oxford University Press, Inc.

in radio, in radar perhaps or in physiotherapy, in welfare work, in private or public school teaching, in nursing, perhaps. Possibly you may aim for an advertising job or a career in efficiency engineering and personnel. You may prepare yourself for government service, at home or abroad. You may aim for a bachelor's degree which has increased your skill toward a professional goal in music, theater, writing, painting or dance. Or, in your last two years, you may specialize in child care and home economics. Or you can have completed basic training for entrance into medical school or law school.[22]

5. Another aspect of the new age is the great increase in the number of married students. Before World War II most colleges had standing rules against marriage: get hitched and get fired. But since 1945 the rules have bowed before the reality, first, of the influx of veterans, and now of the lower marriage age and better economic resources of the average American. Married students have in turn contributed their bit to the demise of the Old College Spirit. Who feels like screaming oneself silly over a football game when back in the apartment is a baby who will soon be screaming for his bottle?[23]

# 25   *Unity* (*oneness*)

Unity, defined in Section **9**, applies to the theme (Section **9**), the paragraph, and the sentence (Section **34**). A paragraph, consisting of a series of related sentences, should develop consistently the larger idea, the topic, binding these sentences together. If a paragraph contains substance, no matter how excellent, which is irrelevant to the central thought, it is not unified. Two standard tests for unity, whether the writing be a theme, a paragraph, or a sentence: (1) *omit* all material which is not an essential, logical part; (2) *include* all material which is an essential, logical part.

[22] Jeremy Ingalls, "Catching Up with the Human Race," *The American Association of University Professors Bulletin,* Summer, 1951.
[23] G. Gaddis Smith, "Lo, the Old College Spirit," *A Collection of Readings for Writers.* Copyright 1967 by Harry Shaw.

### 25a  Omit material not related to the main thought of the paragraph

Material unrelated to the topic which is the subject of the paragraph should be omitted or placed in another paragraph where it does belong. In planning and writing, you will find that frequently unrelated ideas will occur to you, or you may inadvertently shift to related materials which may be interesting and necessary but which should be placed in a separate paragraph. Test each idea by asking: Does this material refer to the thought contained in the expressed or implied topic sentence? If it does not, exclude the material from your paragraph; its inclusion will both confuse and irritate your reader in his attempt to see what the relationship is. Let each paragraph develop and convey one idea, its own idea—and no other, and let it contain the words that belong with it, not with the preceding or following paragraph.

The following paragraph illustrates an inadvertent violation of paragraph unity. The first two sentences deal with the patent examiners; the last four sentences deal with patent office models. Suggested improvement: the two paragraph topics might have been expanded, each in its own paragraph, with suitable transition between the two paragraphs.

One thousand examiners, trained both in science and in law, examine some 80,000 patent applications in Washington each year. This work is done in an atmosphere of academic calm behind the tall white columns at the north end of the U.S. Department of Commerce, of which the Patent Office is a part. The Office no longer has its great tourist attraction, the collection of models. Since 1870, models have not generally been required to accompany applications. However, there are 200,000 of the models in a museum at Plymouth, New Hampshire, and others in the Smithsonian. The Patent Office itself displays only a handful, such as a keyboard violin, an earlier air conditioner with miniature blocks of ice, and a burglar alarm shaped like a watchdog.[24]

### 25b  Include all material necessary for adequate development of the topic sentence

Lacking adequate thought and careful consideration, a paragraph may be brief and underdeveloped (see "Revision," Section 30).

[24] "Patents and Progress," *The Lamp,* Summer, 1961. Copyright 1961 by Standard Oil Company (New Jersey).

Two or three sentences, at the most, supposedly give full development to the topic. Obviously, such paragraphs lack unity; being too short and underdeveloped, they omit a number of important ideas and details necessary to clear, adequate treatment of the topic of the paragraph (Section 24b) .

The following paragraph is representative of this kind. The writer omitted material with which, presumably, he wanted to prove the statement in the second sentence:

> When you do your own freezing at home and grow your own fruits and vegetables, the cost is very little as compared to the frozen food in the stores. It's no wonder that the 4-H clubs in Ohio are the largest in the United States.

The paragraph might have been revised and expanded:

> When you grow your own fruits and vegetables and do your own freezing at home, the cost is very little compared to the cost of frozen food in the stores. More and more Ohio families have learned the truth of this statement, and not only on farms but in many small towns and on vacant lots in cities, people are setting out vegetable gardens and fruit trees. The younger generation is in large part responsible; they are learning through 4-H clubs how to grow fruits and vegetables and how to freeze them. And this is only one of many 4-H activities. It's no wonder that the 4-H clubs in Ohio are the largest in the United States.

## 25c   *Include only enough related materials to develop and unify the paragraph*

In contrast to the underdeveloped paragraph is the overdeveloped one. Frequently you may be tempted to expand a single paragraph to greater length than you should by including too much material, even though pertinent, suggested by the method or methods of development that you are using. Skillful use of one method or of a combination of two or more methods can guide you in including, expanding, or excluding material so as to produce a well-rounded, unified paragraph. Check carefully to see that you have included *all* essential information, have left no unanswered questions to puzzle your reader, and have included *only* material that makes complete the discussion of your topic sentence. If you have too much additional pertinent material, consider including it in a separate paragraph.

## EXERCISE

Show why the following paragraphs lack unity:

1. My father tried to tell me when I bought the car that I would have trouble with the engine, but I did not listen. I had so much trouble with the engine that I decided to sell my car.

2. Greater New York City contains several main divisions. Originally, the city was confined to Manhattan Island, but it has enlarged through consolidation of other divisions. The city consists of five boroughs, Manhattan, Brooklyn, Queens, Richmond, and the Bronx. Manhattan is the heart of New York and contains its great commercial, financial, and mercantile institutions, and also its famous museums, libraries, cathedrals, railway stations, and imposing apartment houses. Brooklyn is a residential district with a large number of industrial establishments. Staten Island is mainly residential, while Queens, containing more than a third of the total area of Greater New York, is the "home" borough. Running through some of these divisions are many famous thoroughfares. The most well-known is Broadway, which is lined with fashionable shops, beautiful churches, elegant clubs, and immense hotels. Most of the great trans-Atlantic lines have their piers in the Hudson River.

3. The island of Malta lies almost in the middle of the Mediterranean Sea—55 miles from Sicily and about 150 miles from Africa. Its area is less than 100 square miles. The island was originally all rock, no soil whatever. Legend has it that all the soil was shipped in from Sicily years ago. The island was under the control of the British for many years. The highest point on the island is the small town of Rabat, 700 feet above sea level. Malta's strategic location made possible raids on Italian and German shipping to Africa, when General Rommel's German forces were in Egypt and Tunisia. This was during World War II. The population is mainly Italian. They remained loyal to the British during the war. The poet Samuel Taylor Coleridge was for a time the Secretary to the Governor of Malta. He wrote the famous poem, "The Rime of the Ancient Mariner," about how a sailor was accursed because he killed an albatross. Coleridge planned to come to America and establish a happy colony on the banks of the Susquehanna River. He died in 1834.

# 26  *Order*

With full, interesting, unified material, an important problem is *arrangement,* since excellent content will lose effectiveness if sentences are incorrectly and illogically arranged.

### 26a   *Arrange sentences in a paragraph in clear sequence*

Hasty and inaccurate thinking causes a lack of paragraph unity and may also result in a disorderly arrangement of sentences. Because your mind does not always work logically, you may write ideas as they occur to you, as they flow or drift into your stream of consciousness; you may illogically place ideas ahead of the place where they belong or forget them and add them later in the paragraph. Anyone who has attempted to tell a long story or who has heard one told ("Oh, I should have said" or "I forgot to say") knows how easy it is to get ideas arranged in the wrong order. Give each idea and each sentence a definite position in the arrangement; make each sentence lead clearly to the one that follows. Keep related parts together; finish one part of the thought before you begin another.

### 26b   *Use a definite plan in the arrangement of sentences*
### *to show clear progress or clear forward movement*

Arrangement of sentences requires progress. The thought must go from some place to some other place. For such forward movement, sentences may be arranged according to certain kinds of order.

1. *Chronological* (time) *order,* as in much narrative writing, expository processes, and some descriptions—all of which progress as the writer changes his temporal point of view. That is, one sentence follows another in the order that the events discussed followed one another in time. (See Section 17a.)

2. *Space order,* as in some descriptions, in which details are arranged according to the position they have in space: from near to remote or remote to near; from outside to inside or from inside to outside; from left to right or from right to left. (See Section 17b.)

3. *Order of logic,* as in some exposition and argument, in which the writer makes a general statement and then supplies

details to support it; or he presents a series of details for particular statements, all of which lead up to a generalized statement at the end of the paragraph (inductive method) ; or he makes a general statement or conclusion and then applies it in the succeeding sentences to a particular instance or example (deductive method) ; or he states a cause and shows what its result or effects are; or he states an effect or result and shows what its causes or origins are. For examples, see Section 24b5.

4. *Order of easy understanding,* as in some exposition—especially giving directions—and argument, in which the writer begins with simple materials and proceeds logically, through and to more complicated ones, or from materials known through a series of related understandable ones to those unknown. (See Section 17c,d.)

### 26c   *Arrange sentences in a paragraph in effective order*

Order in the paragraph involves not only clearness but effectiveness. Among others, three effective methods of arranging sentences within the paragraph are the following:

1. *Beginning and ending as effective positions.* Ordinarily, sentences developing the most important idea of the paragraph should be placed at the beginning or the end. The most trenchant statement should not be embedded somewhere in the middle. First and last impressions of paragraphs, as of sentences and of people, are genuinely important.

2. *Order of climax.* When various ideas are arranged in an ascending order of importance or strength, with the most important thought placed at the end, the arrangement is called order of climax. The reader reads on, lured by the prospect of a concluding climactic statement.

Study the following example for its use of climax. It contains three ideas or "adjustments," moving from the least important to the most important.

My first week on the campus I had three adjustments to make. The first and most minor was being away from home. Previously I had never been away from home for any period longer than a week. Not having any brothers and sisters, I was always very close to Mother and Father, and here I had to overcome any fear of homesickness. My second adjustment was learning to be on my own. In the past Mother and

Father had always helped me with all my decisions. Now that I was 200 miles away from home, I had no way of asking them about every little problem that came up; I had to solve each for myself. The third and greatest adjustment I had to make was living with someone else. After meeting my roommate, I discovered that we were nothing alike. Our sleeping, eating, and studying habits were completely different. By consideration and cooperation, we have solved this problem reasonably well, but it has been the hardest of the three adjustments for me to make.                                                    —Student theme

If you fail to keep something in reserve, if you fully inform your reader in advance what your statement implies, appropriate as that method is for certain kinds of writing, you lose the effectiveness that climactic arrangement affords.

3. *Order of choice.* When several ideas, related and coordinate, are presented in one paragraph and when neither of the preceding methods applies, choose the order of arrangement which you believe your designated reader will find interesting and attractive. For example, on subjects like "three ways to study," or "three places to eat," or "three reasons for joining x organization"—whether developed in one paragraph or in three paragraphs—the ideas, if of equal importance, can be presented in an order which you believe is best. Such order could be called the order of psychological interest; that is, material is so arranged that it is effective and has interest appeal both for you as writer and for your reader or readers.

A clear order is usually an effective order. Any distinction is arbitrary, made here for the purposes of discussion. Most well-developed paragraphs show both clear and effective order.

## EXERCISES

A. Write four topic sentences for which the development will emphasize clearness according to the respective methods mentioned in Section **26b.** Write the paragraphs.

B. Write three topic sentences, one each for development emphasizing effectiveness according to the respective methods mentioned in Section **26c.** Write the paragraphs.

C. Show why the order of sentences in the following paragraph is neither clear nor effective:

Since this is a theme on dictionaries, I have looked up some material on dictionaries and their background. The first dictionary aiming to give a complete collection of English words was published in 1721 by Nathan Bailey, and was called *The Universal Etymological English Dictionary.* This book was also the first in English to trace the derivation of words and to mark the accents as an aid to pronunciation. The greatest American lexicographer was Noah Webster. His dictionary was published in 1828 and has been repeatedly revised. It provided features such as illustrations, synonyms, abbreviations, and other helpful additions. The earliest Greek and Latin dictionaries did not contain all of the words of the language, but instead contained the more difficult words and phrases. Samuel Johnson published a dictionary in London in 1755; he had married a woman some twenty years older than he was. A pronouncing dictionary was prepared by Thomas Sheridan; he was the father of Richard Brinsley Sheridan, who wrote a number of plays and gave some speeches in Parliament. The earliest dictionary was written in the seventh century B.C. and was printed on clay tablets. The dates and specific information about these dictionaries were taken from a reference book I have.

# 27 *Proportion*

Paragraphs having adequate content, unity, and correct order of sentences need right proportion also. One paragraph should not, through its writer's carelessness or thoughtlessness, be made unduly long, another unduly short. Proportion means that the ideas in a paragraph are developed according to their importance and that all paragraphs are planned and written carefully and thoughtfully in relation to one another and to the whole theme.

## 27a  *Make sure that paragraphs are properly proportioned*

In writing a theme of 500 words, a student may compose a long introductory paragraph, follow with a transitional paragraph, and have left only 100 words or so for the final paragraph containing the actual *theme,* the central idea, the purpose for which the paper was written. Such writing, obviously, is badly proportioned.

If a paragraph contains discussion of a proportionately important idea, its length is greater than that of a paragraph which develops a comparatively minor topic. Occasionally, the inclusion of many or important details may need greater space, but readers are likely to attribute importance to ideas according to the length of the paragraphs in which they are discussed.

In general, therefore, do not expand ideas relatively subordinate or treat sketchily ideas of fundamental importance. Between these two extremes of overexpansion and underdevelopment is a golden mean: paragraphs which adequately deal with their topics and which, added together, give a unified, well-proportioned discussion of the subject.

### 27b  *Achieve proportion through careful planning*

Correct proportion demands careful planning. If you dwell at length on some part of the theme because you are interested in that part or know it thoroughly, you may not be taking into account its importance in relation to the reader. To achieve correct paragraph proportion, consider the relation of the paragraph to the whole subject, and also your reader's reaction. Study the following suggestions:

1. Consider the subject as a whole before writing an individual paragraph.

2. Think of the reader; determine the central purpose each paragraph is to have in communicating ideas to him.

3. Assign tentatively the number of words you believe will adequately develop each paragraph (see Section 7b). As you write, you need not be rigidly bound by your allotment; it is only a planning guide.

4. Shorten paragraphs if they are out of proportion in relation to the subject and the reader, even though they contain favorite ideas and their revision will sacrifice proudly written, precious words.

5. Lengthen paragraphs if they contain ideas that need amplification, illustration, or repetition, so that their significance may be seen by the reader.

### EXERCISES

A. Study one of the articles in your book of readings or a current magazine. Comment on it as an illustration of paragraph proportion.

B. Choose three to five topics for 500-word themes and estimate the proportionate importance of the several developing paragraphs.

C. Indicate the number of words proportionately correct for each paragraph of a 500-word theme based on a theme subject, "Learning To ——." Follow or adapt this plan:

*Learning To Swim*
1. Correct mental attitude for the beginner
2. Correct body position
3. How to handle the arms
4. How to handle the feet
5. How to breathe
6. Errors to be avoided
7. Summary

# 28  *Length*

Paragraph length, like proportion, is determined by the purpose of the writer and by the relative importance of the thought unit that the paragraph embraces. In present-day writing, paragraphs tend to be short, perhaps because of the influence of advertising materials, news stories, business letters, and the desire to have the reader obtain ideas by a swift eye-sweep of one sentence to three or four sentences. No specific rule, therefore, for paragraph length can be laid down, save the principle of importance and the principle of appropriateness (see Section 29) .

Many writers, it is true, apparently paragraph arbitrarily or by feeling. John O'Hara, for example, opens one short story with a 500-word paragraph, followed by two more almost as long; he begins another with a paragraph of 50 words.[25] Isolated paragraphs (see Section 29d) in "The Talk of the Town" section of *The New Yorker* magazine may be 450 words long or 40 words short. *The National Geographic Magazine* uses numerous one-sentence paragraphs, many two- and three-sentence paragraphs, very few of four sentences; most of the sentences are short, also.

[25] See *The Saturday Evening Post,* February 25, 1957, and December 17, 1966.

## 28a   *Avoid a short, underdeveloped paragraph*

At times short paragraphs are necessary, effective, and appropriate. Aside from such purposes, however, a short paragraph is usually an underdeveloped paragraph—much to the confusion and dissatisfaction of the reader. Too often some students take neither time nor trouble to study the topic and means of development and to expand the paragraph sufficiently. Instead, they are unwisely content to let two or three short sentences serve for what they consider adequate treatment. Each of the following, telling little about the key word or paragraph topic, italicized, is an example of such a short, underdeveloped paragraph:

The *curriculum* in the School of Home Economics is largely basic, for students follow the same plan of study for the first two years. At the beginning of the third year, you have the opportunity to choose the option in which you are most interested.

We met *several interesting people* as we walked up and down the Miami beach. Often we would meet someone from home. Once we met the daughter of the mayor of Caracas.

## 28b   *Avoid a series of short, choppy paragraphs*

A series of short, choppy paragraphs is usually a sign that a writer has not thought carefully about analyzing his topic sentence, has not developed fully and clearly the central idea of each paragraph, or has failed to see the relationship of ideas and has divided into several paragraphs what should have been united into one of greater length.

Note the choppy, disconcerting effect of these short paragraphs:

As we drove north after spending Christmas vacation in Florida, the whole country seemed to take on a different atmosphere.

While the ground farther south was green, the ground near Belleville was covered with a soft blanket of snow.

The trees and bushes glittered in the sun like a jeweler's window. The telephone wires drooped with their heavy weight of ice.

The sun, as it shone on our car windows, struck the ice on the windows and seemed to send rays of light in every direction.

The blue sky seemed to take on a silvery cast from the reflection below. Also in the sky was a huge cloud, probably of snow, which appeared to be a mountain ridge.

The scene reminded us of a desert in that the cloud looked very near and we would soon be where it was, but we never came any nearer to it.

As we drove into the city of Belleville, we saw more signs of Jack Frost's presence.

Boys and girls were sliding on the already slick hills. Some children were making jolly fat snowmen while others were having snowball fights.

And as we came to the campus, the prettiest and perhaps the most welcome sight of all came before our eyes—the Belleville University Union.

The Union Building reminded us of a huge cathedral in some foreign land. Its huge structure seemed to rise out of a king-sized snow drift and extend upwards into nothingness.

Through the windows of the Union came rays of light which seemed to welcome us back to Belleville University and to a new year of happiness, prosperity, and achievement.

To correct such short paragraphs, a writer should: (1) review and apply the methods of analysis and expansion discussed in Section 24; (2) write a topic sentence that can be developed by using the material in several short paragraphs; or (3) examine his paragraphs which precede or follow; perhaps with minor revisions these can be combined into a paragraph of adequate length.

## 28c   Avoid a group of long, uninteresting-looking paragraphs

A series of very long paragraphs, sometimes running to a page or more, is likely to strain your reader's attention. Why not furnish him with an occasional paragraph break which will afford opportunity to catch his breath and summarize the thought? Moreover, very long paragraphs may contain material not properly belonging in them; they thus violate the principle of unity (Section 25). Usually it is difficult to write an effectively unified paragraph of over 250 or 300 words.

When paragraphs are unduly long, it is often possible to break each one, at logical dividing places, into two or more shorter paragraphs without violation of unity, provided that appropriate transitional words or phrases are used.

### 28d   Choose long or short paragraphs in accordance with your central purpose

Do not avoid either long or short paragraphs, but use them according to the proportionate value of the thought units they express. It is only a *series* of either that may prove ineffective. As indicated at the beginning of this section, many writers today deliberately use shorter paragraphs, but in scholarly or technical papers paragraphs still run to considerable length. In popular magazines and newspapers the average length may be from 25 to 75 words. The use of long or short paragraphs, or a compromise between the two, is often a matter of convention and appropriateness. (See Section **29.**)

You might well give consideration, therefore, to this advice from the Modern Language Association *Style Sheet*: "For the sake of both appearance and emphasis, avoid writing many very short or very long paragraphs, especially in sequence. Remember that brief paragraphs on your typed page will usually look even briefer in print." Also, brief paragraphs in longhand look even shorter when typewritten.

### EXERCISES

A. Compare the average length of paragraphs in an article in *The Atlantic Monthly* or *Harper's Magazine* with the average length of those in an article in *The Saturday Evening Post*.

B. Read some of the articles in an issue of *The National Geographic Magazine*. Count or estimate the average number of words in the paragraphs. Can you account for the appropriateness of paragraphs of such brevity?

C. In your book of readings or in a magazine or two magazines, choose two articles: one using very short paragraphs and one using paragraphs averaging at least four or five sentences. Prepare a paper comparing the clearness, effectiveness, and appropriateness of the paragraphing in the two articles.

D. Count the number of words in five consecutive paragraphs of some article in your book of readings. How many words in the longest paragraph? In the shortest? What is the average? Repeat this exercise for another article by a different writer. Make a comparison of the two.

E. Compare the number of words in the opening three or four paragraphs of several articles in your book of readings.

F. Compare the number of words in the closing three or four paragraphs of several articles in your book of readings.

G. Ascertain the average length of the paragraphs in a newspaper news story. What effects are achieved by the brief paragraphs? Repeat this exercise with another newspaper and make a comparison.

# 29 *Appropriateness: special kinds of paragraphs*

The normal paragraph or series of paragraphs develops the various divisions of a subject, and each is unified by being built around a specific topic, especially in most description, exposition, and argumentation. Sometimes such paragraphs are deliberately short: properly used for emphasis, they often aid in achieving a vigorous, effective style, and in description or nondialogue narration may be called paragraphs of *convenience*. But, as a general guide, this kind of short paragraph should be written only for definite purposes and effects.

Other paragraphs—either long or short, consisting of loosely related or even single statements—perform special functions. The following suggestions concern specifically the appropriateness and propriety of the commonly used short paragraphs.

## 29a Use short paragraphs in writing dialogue or recording conversations

In the *writing of dialogue* or *recording of conversations,* conventional American practice has been pretty well established. It includes the following:

⟶ Each speaker's speech, even if one word only, is paragraphed separately. When several separate speeches are included in one paragraph, the result is usually reader confusion.

⟶ The same paragraph includes the "he said" or its equivalent; the "he said" may be in any position, introductory, concluding, or interpolated—usually in the first sentence.

⟶ Other brief introductory or explanatory words, i.e., description and narration, may also be included in the same paragraph.

⟶ Often, with only two speakers, the "he said" is omitted, once the speakers are identified, or perhaps repeated occasionally to remind the reader of their identity.

⟶ Narrative and descriptive materials, if longer than a word, phrase, or clause, are usually, not always, paragraphed separately.

⟶ Naturally, in recording conversation, most of the paragraphs are short, some very short.

Most of the foregoing conventions are illustrated in the following, a dialogue between a girl and a policeman:

"Oh, I'm not a bad driver, really. I do like to go fast, but I'm careful. In Buffalo, where we lived before, the policemen all knew I was careful and they generally let me go as fast as I wanted to."

"This ain't Buffalo. And this ain't no speedway. If you want to go fast, stay off Fifth Avenue."

The girl looked him right in the eye. "Would you like that?"

"No," said Ben.

She smiled at him again. "What time are you through?"

"Four o'clock," said Ben.

"Well," said the girl, "some afternoon I may be going home about then—"

"I told you I wasn't ready to die."

"I'd be extra careful."

Ben suddenly realized that they were playing to a large staring audience and that, for once, he was not the star.

"Drive on!" he said in his gruffest tone. "I'm letting you go because you're a stranger, but you won't get off so easy next time."

"I'm very, very grateful," said the girl. "Just the same I don't like being a stranger and I hope you won't excuse me on that ground again."[26]

### 29b   Use short paragraphs for introductory, concluding, and transitional paragraphs

For long or fairly long papers or long sections, a brief *introductory* paragraph is sometimes desirable, especially of the outline-

---

[26] Ring Lardner, "There Are Smiles," *Roundup.* Copyright 1929 by Charles Scribner's Sons.

beginning kind (Section 8b4) . The following is an introductory paragraph listing the topics to be expanded in subsequent paragraphs:

The causes of war are psychological, biological, economic, and political—that is, they lie in the impulses of men, the competition of groups, the material needs of societies, and fluctuations of national power.[27]

Similarly, for long or fairly long papers, a brief *concluding* paragraph is sometimes desirable. For the material introduced by the example above and discussed in detail in the article, the following serves as a summary and conclusion:

These, then, are the causes of war. How natural it seems now, in the perspective of science and history; how ancient its sources and how inscrutable its destiny.[28]

For a discussion of transitional paragraphs, see Section 11.

### 29c   Use short paragraphs in business letters

Paragraphs in *business letters* vary from one or two to six lines. Longer paragraphs are seldom used; short paragraphs permit the reader to get the message at a single glance, a major purpose of most business letter paragraphs. (For examples, see pp. 659, 661. On 8½-by-11 business stationery, the paragraphs of the sample letters would take even fewer lines.)

### 29d   Use a single, complete-in-itself paragraph to develop a simple subject or a single topic

In treating briefly *a single isolated topic* or *a simple subject,* use only one paragraph. Such a paragraph is independent and complete—a short theme or a theme in miniature. Many newspaper editorial writers, columnists, advertising writers, magazine editors, and textbook editors, among others, make use of independent paragraphs. Examples are common in the editorial columns of newspapers; news items in newspapers; editorial or commentary paragraphs in magazines, especially the news weeklies; brief in-

[27] Will Durant, "Why Men Fight," *The Saturday Evening Post,* July 10, 1937.
[28] Ibid.

troductory notes or biographical sketches in books of readings; brief articles in encyclopedias; and narrative or expository material in semitechnical or popular science magazines.

At the beginning of the term, especially, freshman English students are often required to write independent paragraphs. Later they are required to write on larger topics, and their paragraphs become units of longer compositions. Following is an example of the independent paragraph; it develops its topic, "free verse," by definition:

> *Free verse* is a type of poetry in which the line is based on the natural cadence of the voice, following the phrasing of the language, rather than a repeating metrical pattern. The rhythm of a free-verse line is marked by the grammatical and rhetorical patterns of normal speech and by the "sequence of musical phrase" (Ezra Pound). A single line of free verse will normally contain varied types of feet, and a single poem will contain lines with varying numbers of feet. Hence the poem is unconfined, "free" of the traditional repeated metrical patterns of foot and line. Free verse is never so free as prose, never really free in the sense of being formless or unrhythmical. Rather its rhythms follow a pattern more varied than that of traditional verse, moving away from and returning to certain rhythmical norms and regularities. Although most people associate free verse with modern poetry, the type is found throughout literature [beginning with] Hebrew poetry (Psalms and Song of Songs).[29]

Other examples are among the quoted paragraphs in Section 24.

**29e   Use a paragraph of not too closely related sentences for a summary, conclusions, recommendations, or directions**

Many longer papers require for their rounding out and for effective endings a paragraph giving a *summary, conclusions,* or *recommendations.* Such a paragraph consists of sentences that are not too closely related; that is, as the paragraph develops, the last sentence is somewhat or even far removed from the thought of the first sentence. The same kind of paragraph is used in writing that gives certain kinds of *directions*—for example, short "how

29 Lillian H. Hornstein, ed., *The Reader's Companion to World Literature.* Copyright 1956 by The Dryden Press.

to" articles. The unifying topic of such paragraphs, usually implied, is one of the foregoing italicized words.

The following is the concluding paragraph of a student theme in which advantages and disadvantages were discussed:

> Let me now summarize both sides of the problem. Phonograph records show us how poetry should be read; they help us in our comprehension of poetry; and they make class meetings more interesting. The chief disadvantage is that use of even one long-playing record allows little time for a lecture or class discussion. My conclusion is that using records in our English literature class is more beneficial and advantageous than detrimental and disadvantageous; in other words, the advantages outweigh the disadvantages.

An example of the summary of an entire book follows:

> Robert Gunning, the author of *The Technique of Clear Writing*, accomplishes what he sets out to preach. This whole book is one of the best examples of clear writing written about the subject. The opening chapters tell what has been learned about the habits and preferences of readers. The closing chapters review causes of and cures for foggy writing in business, journalism, law, and the technical fields. The main body of the book consists of Ten Principles of Clear Writing: (1) Keep sentences short; (2) Prefer the simple to the complex; (3) Prefer the familiar words; (4) Avoid unnecessary words; (5) Put action in your verbs; (6) Write as you talk; (7) Use terms your reader can picture; (8) Tie in with your reader's experience; (9) Make full use of variety; (10) Write to express, not impress.[30]

The following is an example of a paragraph *giving directions*. The general subject was "preparing reports"; paragraphs of advice concerned selecting a topic, building a bibliography, keeping an idea page, outlining the paper in detail, and then this on the actual writing:

> Write the paper; dash it off from the outline and polish it later. It is difficult to keep many things in mind as you write. Devote your initial writing efforts to getting your ideas stated; this initial draft can be gone over later in order to correct English mistakes and to put in

[30] "Reading About Writing," *Effective Letters Bulletin*, New York Life Insurance Company.

headings, references, and footnotes. Dashing this first version off helps a writer keep his attention on his theme rather than getting lost in details, and the sentence ideas tend to flow into each other much better. Usually all needed corrections can be inserted in this first draft, but, if necessary, parts can be cut out and pasted in order.[31]

### 29f   Use paragraphs of isolated statements to emphasize summaries, conclusions, recommendations, directions, or important statements

For effectiveness in writing *summaries, conclusions, recommendations,* certain kinds of *directions,* or *important statements,* use paragraphs of isolated statements: paragraphs consisting of single sentences or parts of sentences. Such paragraphs may be numbered. Their position in a theme or an article may vary: summaries may come at the beginning or end, conclusions and recommendations at the end, directions and important statements anywhere in the paper where they are most effective. Here is an example of *conclusions*:

As a result of this investigation, our conclusions are as follows:

1. Weather conditions that morning were not too favorable for flying.

2. The wings and steering apparatus of the glider did not receive their usual careful inspection and testing by the pilot.

3. Both the pilot and the driver of the tow-car, although they had passed their examinations, were young and inexperienced.

4. The pilot, especially, was comparatively inexperienced in flying under unfavorable weather conditions.

5. The University Glider Club and the University Airport should be absolved of responsibility for the accident.

Paragraphs of isolated statements sometimes come within the body of a paper or article. For example, these *recommendations* for new students during Freshman Week:

They are breezed through a very pleasant week—dizzying, perhaps, but new and different. They don't even have time to get homesick. That comes about two weeks later. Now, during this week, deans and advisers say many things which freshmen may, to their sorrow, ignore:

[31] Francis P. Robinson, *Effective Study,* Harper & Brothers. Copyright 1941, 1946.

Start studying at once.

Get to know the library immediately.

Set up a schedule for yourself—revise it later, if necessary—to include both social and academic activities.

Join one or two extracurricular activities, but not every one in sight.

Get enough sleep.

Don't forget chapel.

Don't cut classes.

You're on your own; make the most of your independence. But, if you get into trouble, see your adviser right away.[32]

## EXERCISES

A. From a magazine or your book of readings choose a short story and examine the paragraphing of dialogue. Note how much, if any, explanatory material is included in the paragraphs giving quoted speeches.

B. Write a short paper to illustrate paragraphing and use of quotation marks (see Section 94) on the subject, "A Dialogue Between —— and ——."

C. In an article in a magazine or in your book of readings mark all the short paragraphs (two to six lines). Determine what purpose they serve: introductory, concluding, transitional, etc.

D. Look through such magazines as *The New Yorker, Time, Newsweek, U. S. News & World Report,* or *The Reader's Digest* for one-paragraph articles or discussions. Estimate their length. Find the topic sentence or statement and discuss the method or methods of paragraph development used (Sections 23 and 24).

E. Look for one-paragraph editorials in several newspapers. Estimate their length. Find the topic sentence or statement and discuss the method or methods of paragraph development used.

F. Comment on the length and purpose of the paragraphs in several business letters written to you or to relatives and friends.

[32] Robert U. Jameson, "How To Stay in College," *The Saturday Evening Post,* October 2, 1954.

# 30   Revision

## 30   Give time and thought to careful revision of every paragraph

Although the preceding sections have discussed the paragraph as something separate from a theme or a longer paper, the distinction is artificial. A paragraph may be a theme, or a theme may consist of one paragraph or two paragraphs or many paragraphs.

The clearness and effectiveness of a theme depend upon the clearness and effectiveness of its paragraphs. Using the work-sheet method suggested on pages 6, 7 and also in Section 24a, anyone can put on paper the words and sentences that constitute a paragraph. The real work then begins, *revision*. Every paragraph should be carefully considered in the light of the preceding sections: characteristics, mechanics, topic statements, analysis, content, unity, order, proportion, length, and appropriateness. In addition, every sentence, even every word, should be checked with the *Handbook* advice given about sentences, diction, grammar, and punctuation.

*Revision is important.* Perhaps the most common faults of many unsatisfactory paragraphs are that they are too short, too underdeveloped; they lack additional supporting details for the topic sentence or they use vague and general details; and they lack clear and effective transition between paragraphs.

Your own writing of paragraphs can be improved through study of the following illustration of revision. It consists of two versions of the same theme, revised paragraph by paragraph by the student himself in the light of constructive criticisms given by the instructor in conference with the student.[33] The two versions show how much improvement is possible when careful attention is given to paragraph detail, organization, and transitions.

As you study these revisions, keep in mind the instructor's constructive comments concerning the unrevised paper:

1. On any controversial subject, it is good psychology to take into account, or at least show an awareness of, what an opponent would claim for the subject.

[33] For permission to use this material, the authors gratefully acknowledge their indebtedness to the student-author, Ronald Van Putte, his instructor, Professor William Stafford of Purdue University, and the *Indiana English Leaflet* (February, 1955), where this material first appeared in print.

2. Use of detail is inconsistent. Although the three main arguments are concretely illustrated, opportunities to be more convincing are lost because of vague generalities instead of facts, as in paragraphs one and three.

3. The original and most compelling of the arguments should be chosen and pointed up with the most effective composition devices possible.

4. Each paragraph should be examined and revised in the light of the foregoing and with the thought in mind that while a paragraph has a beginning, a middle, and an end, much as a theme has, each paragraph here is also a part of a larger whole.

## I DIDN'T PLEDGE A FRATERNITY
*Original*

I have learned from various sources about fraternities and I don't think that I should join one.

*Revised*

I have talked to many fraternity men and independents about fraternities. I listened to what they had to say and decided that I shouldn't join a fraternity. It is true that fraternity life has some benefits, such as living in a close-knit group, getting a feeling of responsibility, and learning the social graces. Since the disadvantages offset the advantages, however, I don't think that I should join one.

*Original*

Fraternity life takes up too much time. Everyone, especially the freshmen, has special jobs to do. These jobs may range from serving dinner to cutting the lawn. All of these jobs take time away from studying. The bad part about Hell-Week and initiation is that they take up the time a student should be using to build a firm foundation of studies. Although it is not supposed to, initiation takes preference over studies during Hell-Week. The members of a fraternity are required to go to the various social events whether or not they desire to.

*Revised*

One of the disadvantages of living in a fraternity is that the extracurricular activities take up too much time. Everyone, especially the freshmen, has special jobs to do. These jobs may vary from serving dinner to cutting the lawn. All of these jobs take time away from studying. Another time-consumer is the various social functions that a member must attend, many of them whether he wants to or not. Hell-Week and initiation also take valuable time—and from that crucial part of the semester when the new student should be acquiring good study habits. Little free time, then, is available to the fraternity member when he is pledging.

*Original*

   Another one of the sore spots of fraternity life is the money problem. The cost of a fraternity is usually above that of a university-sponsored dormitory. The cost usually doesn't include the price of parties, picnics, dances, trade functions, or displays for the fraternity lawn. Fraternity life is fine for the person who has a lot of money to throw away, but a student with a limited amount of money has a tough time. He will usually break his budget and the back of his bank account.

*Revised*

   Another one of the sore spots of fraternity life is the money problem. According to the Inter-Fraternity Council, the average cost per year at a Purdue fraternity is $675. The cost of living at a university-sponsored dormitory is $630. Although $45 is not much money, it does become a major factor when the cost of parties, picnics, dances, trade functions, and lawn displays is added to it. Fraternity life is fine for the student who has a great deal of money to spend, but a student with a limited amount of money has a difficult time. He will usually break his budget and the back of his bank account if he joins a fraternity.

*Original*

   Living in a clique may lead to prejudiced thinking. The fraternity may not allow foreign students, colored students, or students having a certain religion to pledge the fraternity. The fraternity member will not get a chance to meet these students and may get the wrong ideas about them. These rejected students will tend to cling together and worsen the problem by getting false ideas.

*Revised*

   The most important disadvantage of living in a fraternity, however, is the effect that it may have on a person's mind. Living in a clique may lead to prejudiced thinking. The fraternity may not allow foreign students, colored students, or students having a certain religion to pledge the fraternity. The member will not get a chance to be in close contact with these people and may misinterpret their ideas and beliefs. The rejection of some students may lead to rejection of others of the same race, nationality, or religion and thus instill in the student an intolerant attitude for the rest of his life.

*Original*

In general, I can't see that a fraternity can do a person much good, but I can see where it is possible to do him harm. The fraternity may provide a person with the social graces, but if his thinking is prejudiced and narrow-minded, what good can they possibly do?

*Revised*

In general, I can't see that a fraternity can do a person much good, but I can see how it is possible to do him harm. The fraternity may provide a person with the social graces, but if his studies suffer from lack of time, if his money is wasted, and if his thinking is prejudiced and narrow-minded, what good can fraternity life possibly do?

# THE SENTENCE
## (SECTIONS 31-50)

As everybody knows, meaning does not come from
single words but from words put together in
groups—phrases, clauses, sentences. A mysterious
bond links these groups of words with our ideas,
and this relation leads in turn to the miracle by
which ideas pass from one mind to another.

—JACQUES BARZUN AND HENRY F. GRAFF,
*The Modern Researcher*

# THE
# SENTENCE

Good themes, good articles, good papers are built with good paragraphs, which, in turn, are built from good sentences. Clearly, good themes are not made from faulty paragraphs, nor good paragraphs from awkward, incomplete, rambling, or choppy sentences. The paragraph is only as good as its component parts, its sentences, i.e., units of complete expression. To be a successful writer, therefore, you must achieve unity, clearness, effectiveness, and appropriateness in your sentences.

Obtaining such characteristics in sentence structure requires a solid foundation, a substantial framework. You must first know what a sentence is; you must understand grammatical structures and functions and upon that foundation and framework construct sentences that are correct, clear, effective, and appropriate.

A brief constructive definition of a *written* sentence is as follows: "a word or group of words expressing a complete thought, that is, conveying understandable meaning from writer to reader." For additional details, see Section 74. That section discusses primarily the grammatical completeness of the sentence. But in a broader sense you do not have a complete thought until you have read or written a whole *series* of sentences, perhaps an entire paragraph or theme. For instance, a pronoun in one sentence may take its meaning from an antecedent in another. Also, such words as *thus, these, another,* and *again* and such phrases as *for example* and *on the other hand* frequently show that the thought presented in a new sentence is intimately related to the thought in a preceding sentence or paragraph.

When we say, then, that a sentence conveys a sense of complete meaning to the reader, we do not mean that we can dispense with its context—its relation to other sentences. We mean only that we have a group of words so ordered as to be *gram-*

*matically* self-sufficient. For example, the statement, "He entered that profession when he was only 23 years old," is grammatically complete. It has a subject, the pronoun *he,* and it has a main predicate verb, *entered;* moreover, the dependent clause, *when he was only 23 years old,* is properly integrated into the sentence by the subordinating conjunction *when.* In this sense the entire statement is complete; it thus begins with a capital letter and is followed by a period. But so far as total meaning is concerned, we need other sentences to tell us that *he* refers to a specific man, Henry Brown, and that *that profession* refers to the profession of law.

Because punctuation and capitalization are governed in part by grammatical rather than logical completeness, understanding the grammar of the sentence is basic for clear and effective writing. Sentence clearness and effectiveness, however, are more than matters of punctuation and capitalization; they depend also upon forms and patterns of sentences, discussion of which is given in Section **74.** A review of this material may be helpful before you study the following sections, which deal with errors frequently made in writing the sentence and which suggest definite ways of avoiding them.

As with themes, paragraphs, and words, the results to be aimed for in writing sentences may be classed under four main heads: *correctness, clearness, effectiveness,* and *appropriateness.* Sections **31–49** deal with these four divisions as follows:

**CORRECTNESS**

Sentence fragment and incompleteness of meaning—Section **31**
Comma splice—Section **32**
Fused sentences—Section **33**

**CLEARNESS**

Unity (oneness) —Section **34**
Mixed and illogical constructions—Section **35**
Faulty coordination—Section **36**
Faulty subordination—Section **37**
Illogical dependent clauses—Section **38**
Misplaced modifiers—Section **39**
Dangling modifiers—Section **40**
Split constructions—Section **41**
Transition—Section **42**

**EFFECTIVENESS**
Conciseness—Section 43
Parallelism—Section 44
Consistency—Section 45
Choppy sentences and clauses—Section 46
Position and arrangement—Section 47
Variety—Section 48

**APPROPRIATENESS—Section 49**
Such a listing may help you keep in mind the four qualities of good writing. Note, however, that these topics are not mutually exclusive. Correctness and clearness depend on sentences complete in grammar, structure, and meaning; effective sentences result from correctness and clearness; sentence unity is probably as much a problem of correctness as of clearness and could have been placed under either heading. Or, for another illustration, both proper coordination and proper subordination are necessary for clearness and effectiveness. As you study the following sections, focus your attention on the larger problem: how to make sentence *correctness,* sentence *clearness,* sentence *effectiveness,* and sentence *appropriateness* contribute to the correctness, clearness, effectiveness, and appropriateness of the longer units (paragraphs, themes, papers) that you write.

As a supplementary aid, the "Glossary of Sentence Errors" (Section 50) contains an alphabetical list of sentence errors, brief discussions, and cross references to more detailed discussion and suggestions.

# 31  *Sentence fragment and incompleteness of meaning*

### 31a  *Avoid using unjustifiable sentence fragments*
An unjustifiable sentence fragment is a word or group of words (1) which does not make sense to the reader or (2) which is not clear or effective because it is set apart from other words with which the reader expects it to be associated. The error is also

called the "period fault," since it can be considered an error in punctuation, but it is more commonly considered an error in sentence construction. (Review the correct uses of the period, Section **86**.)

Common kinds of unjustifiable sentence fragments are dependent clauses and phrases. (See "Phrases" and "Clauses," Sections **72, 73**.) Each kind is given discussion in Section **31b** and **c**. Unjustifiable sentence fragments can be eliminated by several methods:

⟶ 1. Attach each fragment to an independent statement or to a statement making sense, if the fragment naturally and logically belongs with that statement.

⟶ 2. Revise so that the fragment becomes included as part of a complete statement (compound subject, compound predicate, compound sentence, complex sentence, etc.) .

⟶ 3. Make each fragment complete by providing it with a subject and predicate so that it fulfills the grammatical definition of a sentence.

NOTE 1: Using a semicolon ("semicolon fault," Section **89d**) instead of a period does not correct the sentence-fragment error, since the semicolon, also, conventionally sets off complete statements.

NOTE 2: For justifiable sentence fragments, see Section **31g**.

### *31b Avoid setting off a dependent clause as a sentence*

Dependent clauses frequently mistaken for sentences are adverbial and adjective clauses. The adverbial clause—especially one beginning with *although, though, because, while*—may be wrongly set off when it logically should be at the beginning or end of an independent clause. The adjective clause may be wrongly set off when it logically should be at the end of an independent clause.

*Wrong*    I have spent the last four summers doing day labor. *Because the pay was good and I needed money for my college expenses.* (Adverbial clause)

The governor decided not to veto the bill. *Even though there were parts of it that he did not like.* (Adverbial clause)

> I was a student for four years at Oriole High School. *From which I was graduated in June, 1968.* (Adjective clause)
> I have talked with a businessman. *Who thinks that the prospects for the next 12 months are excellent.* (Adjective clause)

Correction of the dependent-clause sentence fragment usually involves no change in the wording. Changes in capitalization, from a capital to a small letter, and in punctuation, from a period to a comma or no mark (see Sections **88f, 88m**), are enough. Or the dependent clause may be made independent by omitting the subordinating conjunction from the adverbial clause or by changing the relative pronoun to a personal pronoun in the adjective clause.

*Correct*    I spent the last four summers doing day labor because the pay was good and I needed money for my college education.

The governor decided not to veto the bill. There were parts of it, however, that he did not like.

The governor decided not to veto the bill, even though there were parts of it he did not like.

I was a student for four years at Oriole High School, from which I was graduated in June, 1968.

I have talked with a businessman who thinks that the prospects for the next 12 months are excellent.

I have talked with a businessman. He thinks that . . .

## 31c   Avoid setting off a phrase as a sentence

The phrases that cause trouble as sentence fragments are usually the following: participial, infinitive, absolute, prepositional, prepositional-gerund, appositional, subject (noun with modifiers), and verb (as the second member of a compound predicate).

To correct such sentence fragments, (1) attach the phrase to or incorporate it in the sentence with which it belongs, or (2) make the phrase a sentence by adding subject and predicate, for completeness.

In the following illustrations, each has at least two parts: the first contains a sentence fragment with a label as to its kind; a corrected version follows, using one or both of the methods just suggested.

*Incorrect*    *Having worked in a garage for four summers.* John thinks
                he is an experienced mechanic. (Participial phrase)
*Correct*      Having worked in a garage for four summers, John thinks
                he is an experienced mechanic.

*Incorrect*    I studied for hours every night. *Preparing myself to pass
                the College Entrance Board examinations.* (Participial
                phrase)
*Correct*      I studied for hours every night, preparing to pass the Col-
                lege Entrance Board examinations.

*Incorrect*    Harry now has two goals in life. *To graduate from college
                and to establish himself in business.* (Infinitive phrase)
*Correct*      Harry now has two goals in life. He wishes to graduate
                from college and to establish himself in business.
                Harry now has two goals in life: to graduate from college
                and to establish himself in business.

*Incorrect*    *Winter having come early that year.* The mountain passes
                were soon blocked by snow. (Absolute phrase)
*Correct*      Winter having come early that year, the mountain passes
                were soon blocked by snow.
                Winter came early that year, and the mountain passes
                were soon blocked by snow.

*Incorrect*    *After a long hard day of classes and studying.* A student is
                ready to tumble into bed early. (Prepositional phrase)
*Correct*      After a long hard day of classes and studying, a student is
                ready to tumble into bed early.

*Incorrect*    Some people constantly discuss politics. *Without really
                knowing what they are talking about.* (Prepositional-
                gerund phrase)
*Correct*      Some people constantly discuss politics without really
                knowing what they are talking about.

*Incorrect*    My mother spent her girlhood on a farm near Wildwood.
                *A small town in southeastern Ohio.* (Appositional
                phrase)
*Correct*      My mother spent her girlhood on a farm near Wildwood,
                a small town in southeastern Ohio.

*Incorrect*    We were fascinated by the scene at timberline. *Especially
                the stunted, twisted trees.* (Appositional phrase)
*Correct*      We were fascinated by the scene at timberline, especially
                the stunted, twisted trees.

*Incorrect*    *One of my neighbors, who killed all the weeds in his lawn
                by spraying them with a weed killer.* (Subject phrase)

| | |
|---|---|
| *Correct* | One of my neighbors killed all the weeds in his lawn by spraying them with a weed killer. |
| | One of my neighbors, who killed all the weeds in his lawn by spraying them with a weed killer, now has the most beautiful lawn in town. |
| *Incorrect* | *Even the winters, which are very long and severe in that climate.* (Subject phrase) |
| *Correct* | Even the winters are very long and severe in that climate. |
| | Even the winters, which are very long and severe in that climate, cannot compare with the winters I remember as a boy. |
| *Incorrect* | That night the river overflowed its banks. *And flooded the lowlands.* (Verb phrase) |
| *Correct* | That night the river overflowed its banks and flooded the lowlands. |

Admittedly, sentence fragments are frequently used by skilled writers for stylistic purposes, such as giving color to a passage or adding stress where it is needed. For example:

Cats have so many facets to their character, so many expressions. From the pot-pussy face that is the epitome of self-satisfaction to the meditative which, sphinxlike, seems to conceal so many mysterious, age-old thoughts and memories. From the anxiously anticipative to the frankly replete; from the ingenuous to the wistful. From the sociable to the aloof; from the indifferent to the alert.

—ALAN C. JENKINS, *Introducing Cats*

Students frequently complain that their instructors mark all fragmentary sentences as incorrect, even those they deliberately write for stylistic effect. The truth is that most instructors wish their students to use fragments for such purposes, or other appropriate ones, only after they demonstrate their knowledge of sentence completeness.

**31d   *Do not start a statement with one construction
and then stop or shift to another, leaving one
or more sentence elements incomplete***

The sentence-fragment error includes two other varieties:

*1. An incomplete and unfinished construction.* Sometimes a writer begins a statement, changes his construction and direction, forgets where he is, keeps adding words while moving in a different direction, and then stops before he has given meaning to the words he started with. Such unfinished constructions result in the following:

*Wrong*    A high school friend of mine, who, because he ran out of funds, had to leave college at the beginning of his sophomore year and go to work in a local factory.
Our college band, not being accustomed to the new conductor and resenting his extremely critical manner.

Such unfinished constructions may be made complete by the addition of pertinent material expressed in proper grammatical elements:

*Right*    A high school friend of mine who, because he ran out of funds, had to leave college at the beginning of his sophomore year and go to work in a local factory, saved enough money in three years to return to college and finish his education.
Our college band, not being accustomed to the new conductor and resenting his extremely critical manner, soon lost its morale and its high standing.

2. *A paradoxically complete-and-incomplete construction.* Sometimes a writer does begin with an independent clause, but he adds an unfinished statement and forgets to include material to coordinate with his first independent statement.

*Not clear*    I thought I would have an easy time in college, but when I arrived on the campus and learned how many classes I would have, how little free time for study, and how keen the scholarly competition.

*Improved*    I thought I would have an easy time in college, but when I arrived on the campus and learned how many classes I would have, how little free time there would be for study, and how keen the scholarly competition was, I immediately changed my mind about college being mostly fun and little work.

### 31e  Do not use punctuation marks to replace words needed for clearness and effectiveness

Sometimes a careless writer lets a mark of punctuation, usually a comma, replace a needed word: (1) *that* in an indirect question or quotation, (2) *that* in introducing other noun clauses as objects, (3) *that* as part of *so . . . that*; (4) the relative pronouns *who, whom, which, that* in adjective clauses.

*Incomplete*    We asked, she should consider being our candidate for Prom Queen. (Comma incorrectly substituted for *that* in an indirect question)

John replied, he would return next week. (Comma incorrectly substituted for *that* in an indirect quotation)

Henry never realized, he would learn to write so easily. (Comma replaces, wrongly, *that* in introducing a noun clause as object of a verb)

The man, I wrote to was the Registrar. (Comma incorrectly substituted for the understood relative pronoun *that* or *whom*)

The last house, we lived in was just the right size for our family. (Comma incorrectly substituted for the understood relative pronoun *which*)

People in Fayville are so friendly, I could live here forever. (Comma incorrectly substituted for *that* in the expression *so . . . that*)

NOTE: Let common sense be your guide. Often ellipsis, either with or without punctuation, is effective. See pp. 217, 435–436.

### 31f Avoid a telegraphic style in formal and informal writing

Because every word telegraphed, cabled, or radioed costs money, a telegraphic style is used for such messages. By omitting subjects or main verbs or auxiliary verbs or adjectives or adverbs or conjunctions or prepositions or pronouns, senders try to make themselves understood with the least possible number of words and thus at lowest cost.

Such writing can be understood even when important words are omitted. Otherwise, many important telegrams would be misinterpreted. The following message serves its purpose:

Letter received. Leaving tomorrow noon. Reserve room Carter Hotel. Arrive early evening. Get theater tickets Saturday matinee, night.

Appropriate for telegrams, day letters, night letters, cablegrams, and radiograms, such a style is inappropriate and ineffective in formal or informal writing, even for friendly letters.

## 31g   Use justifiable sentence fragments for clear and effective writing

Commonly defined, a sentence consists of a subject and predicate and expresses a complete thought. Yet various kinds of statements express a complete thought without a stated or implied subject or predicate. They are frequently found in narrative writing, occasionally in descriptive writing, rarely in expository and argumentative writing.

1. Some nonsubject-and-nonpredicate words or word groups are sentence fragments only grammatically; otherwise, they are clear, effective statements, such as the following:

Interjections: *Hush! Ouch! Indeed! Ah! Oh! Oh, oh! Pshaw!*
Greetings: *Hello. Good morning. Good evening. Good night. Good-by.*
Expressive or exclamatory statements: *Fine! Sure! Fire! At last! Never, never, never! What a day! Never again! Oh, for another vacation!*
Transitional statements: *But to continue. Enough for the actual story and its characters. Now another advantage. One other important matter. Now for the opposite point of view. To summarize. Now in conclusion.*

2. Considered as sentence fragments but justifiable and effective are elliptical sentences. An elliptical sentence is a grammatically incomplete group, a part of a sentence without a subject or predicate or both, but the omitted parts are understood from the context, from what precedes or follows. Ellipsis is common in recording dialogue or giving answers to questions, or even in some of the exclamatory and transitional statements in (1) above: *What a day (that was)! Never again (will I do that)! Now (here is) another advantage.*

Context is frequently important, as in answers to questions or in giving details after an assertion, using words like *yes, no, never, always, of course,* or statements such as the following (combinations of conversation and questions-answers) :

"Where have you been?"
"In the library."
"Were you studying?"
"No."

"When did you leave?"
"At four o'clock."
"Why are you so late?"
"Because I was delayed in traffic."

Some authorities call the complete subject-predicate sentence a *full* sentence, and the word or phrase answering a question, interrupting, or the like, a *minor* sentence.

NOTE: Frequently, of course, the word or group of words standing as a complete statement has a subject and predicate. If the single word is a verb or a phrase consisting of a verb with object or modifiers, "you" is very probably the understood subject, as in commands and requests: *Come here* (cf. *You* come here). *Stop! Proceed* with caution. *Obey* traffic signs.

3. For certain kinds of writing—not sustained formal or informal prose—sentence fragments are peculiarly appropriate, as in descriptive notes on books in a bibliography or reading list:

Charles Major. *When Knighthood Was in Flower*. A romantic novel dealing with Renaissance England. Of interest to the older teen-age group. Especially valuable for its vivid life and swift movement.

Such justifiable sentence fragments are used in this book, as in "Glossary of Sentence Errors" (Section 50), "Glossary of Diction" (Section 70), and "Glossary of Grammatical Terms" (Section 85).

## EXERCISES

A. Correct any unjustifiable sentence fragments in the following:

1. Over the years, I have been the owner of no less than 25 cats. (Not all at the same time, of course!)
2. I hope to be able to own my own house. Not just any house but a house I design and build myself.
3. If a sad mistake or experience has made one blue. He should try to see the humor of his mistake.
4. As long as I live, I'll never forget the beautiful rolling hills of Germany. With huge castles surrounded by dense forest.

5. All things considered, that was a very interesting summer. So interesting that I plan on doing the same thing this coming summer.
6. This body of water was bigger than any I had ever seen before. Perhaps because it was the Atlantic Ocean.
7. The lives of the American Indians were filled with superstitious beliefs. The rain dance especially.
8. There are no logical reasons for many superstitions. At least, none that are obvious.
9. She was beautiful and intelligent. A rare combination in a woman.
10. Today I started a new life. A fresh clean life. Full of new adventures and of new opportunities in a different world. Here in college.
11. Mackinac Island, which rises out of the Straits of Mackinac between Lake Huron and Lake Michigan.
12. I must do much better than I have been doing. If I am going to achieve my many objectives in college life.
13. I should like to go back to New York State for a visit. To the country where the air is fresh, the waters are clear, and the people are friendly.
14. And so it goes, summer vacation after summer vacation. The mountains one year, the lake the next.
15. Carefully I listened to every word of advice that my father gave me. How always to keep a sharp eye on my luggage. When to ask for information from the driver and when not to. Different methods that could be used for passing the time.
16. A good student needs to take challenging courses. Courses where the student knows he will have to work for his grade.
17. Now that I have determined what some people remind me of. I wonder what I remind people of.
18. I hope to travel through most of Europe. And finally terminate my travels by visiting the countries to the south of us.
19. I have ended the semester learning a great deal about English. Even though my themes are still filled with many serious mistakes.
20. The most important thing about spring at college is that the sun is out most of the time. No more walking to class in the darkness of early morning.

B. Make complete the sense of the following by substituting or adding necessary words, by revision, or by rewriting.

1. I applied at Lakeside College, and the answer was negative. Filled up for the next three years. Other colleges the same way.

2. I get a thrill from model railroading because all things that appear in miniature amaze me. Railroading in particular because railroading is colorful in actual life.
3. I believe I was 11 or 12 years of age, and while I didn't know much better at the time.
4. Twin Cave, which is a huge cave and which has never been completely explored. It reveals many large roomlike areas cut from the rock.
5. Though dependent on the will of his uncle, Sir William Thornhill, a gentleman who, content with a little for himself, permitted his nephew to enjoy the rest.
6. It's not like going for miles to fish, and then after fishing all day and night, and still going home without any fish.
7. My dormitory, I was told, when, after what seemed like running through a maze, I set my eyes on what was to be my abode for the coming semester.
8. There are many people who are out to achieve a particular goal, and even though they do not come up to our individual moral standards.
9. While a good driver, one who obeys all traffic signs and signals, who drives courteously and carefully at all times, is demonstrating one of the important marks of a good citizen.
10. Superstitious beliefs are started by people who assume something which has happened to them as a result of another event, which had taken place prior to the time of whatever happened to them.
11. Without my high school reputation as a football player I would not have received an offer to attend college on a scholarship, and therefore never having the opportunity to continue my education.
12. In one letter, the letterhead had only the name and address of the company, while in another letter the name of the company, home address, addresses of branch offices, and officers of the company.
13. You soon learn, and after these simple instructions about borrowing books from the library.
14. Would appreciate an early reply. Anxiously awaiting to meet you then.
15. I have come to the conclusion that since literature takes up time that high school teachers could spend in teaching writing.

# 32 Comma splice

Like the sentence fragment, the comma splice may be considered an error in punctuation or an error in sentence construction. With either label, the unjustifiable comma splice is a serious error that causes confusion to the reader, since the writer does not show him where one sentence ends and another begins.

The comma splice, also called the "comma fault" or "illiterate comma," is not an ordinary misuse of the comma. Instead, it is the error of using a comma to join two sentences; literally, the comma "splices" or links the sentences. In grammatical terms, the comma splice is the error of using a comma between two independent clauses not joined by one of the pure or simple coordinating conjunctions, *and, but, or, nor, neither, yet.* (See Section 88d.) The reader usually expects a sharper break, i.e., stronger punctuation between such clauses.

## 32a Avoid unjustifiable comma splices

The unjustifiable comma splice, as defined above, appears in several specific forms:

*1. Two statements which have no grammatical relationship but which are related by content.*

Incorrect    A meeting of the Botany Club will be held on Friday evening, several important matters are to be discussed.
             Classes will begin on September 20, freshmen should be on the campus for orientation the preceding week.

*2. Two related statements, the second of which begins with a personal pronoun, a demonstrative pronoun, or a demonstrative adjective, whose antecedent is in the first.* Personal pronouns, demonstrative pronouns, and demonstrative adjectives, though they often refer to antecedents in other sentences, do not make grammatical connections between clauses; only relative pronouns perform that function.

Incorrect    Father's office is on the 35th floor, it overlooks the Hudson River.
             My parents cannot come for Homecoming, they have other plans.

>   The dean considered a few minutes and then shook his
>   head, he did not say a word.
>
>   Go south until you come to the corner of State and Madi-
>   son Streets, this is one of the busiest intersections in the
>   world.

3. *Two statements, the second of which begins with or con-tains a conjunctive adverb* (see list of conjunctive adverbs in Sections **84c** and **89b**). Despite the word *conjunctive,* such adverbs do not make the close grammatical connections between independent clauses that are made by the pure conjunctions. Conjunctive adverbs show only a logical relationship; hence, the comma is not a strong enough mark of punctuation to stand between the clauses.

| | |
|---|---|
| *Incorrect* | We had made a wrong turn near Northville, thus we found ourselves traveling miles out of our way. |
| | My roommate spent money faster than he anticipated, therefore he had to drop out of school at the end of the first semester. |
| | The spring vacation ended on Thursday morning, however, I did not return from the South until Sunday evening. |
| | The University imposes no penalties for absences, you are, however, expected to make up all work that you miss. |

The comma-splice error can be corrected in several ways:

⟶ 1. Use a period after the first statement and a capital at the beginning of the second. This method may be objectionable if short, choppy, jerky sentences result (see Section **46**). It is effective, however, if the ideas are not too closely related and if a series of short, choppy, jerky sentences is avoided.

| | |
|---|---|
| *Correct* | My parents cannot come for Homecoming. They have other plans. |
| | A meeting of the Botany Club will be held on Friday evening. Several important matters are to be discussed. |

⟶ 2. Use a semicolon between the statements (see Section **89a,b**). This method is preferable when a conjunctive adverb is used to make clear a close or fairly close relationship between the two statements.

*Correct*    My roommate spent money faster than he anticipated; therefore he had to drop out of school at the end of the first semester.

The University imposes no penalties for absences; you are, however, expected to make up all work that you miss.

⟶ 3. Insert a pure conjunction between statements or as a substitute for the conjunctive adverb, and retain the comma (see Section **88d**). If ideas are closely related, this is an effective method, for the pure conjunction makes the close relationship evident. Sometimes, of course, the needed pure conjunction is not appropriate.

*Correct*    Classes will begin on September 20, and freshmen should be on the campus for orientation the preceding week.

The spring vacation ended on Thursday morning, but I did not return from the South until Sunday evening.

⟶ 4. Subordinate one of the statements and retain the comma. This is usually the most effective method if the thought expressed is not radically changed by the subordination. In fact, the comma-splice error is often the result of an attempt to show a causal relationship without proper subordination. One of the statements can be reduced to a dependent clause or to a phrase.

Corrected by using dependent clauses

Although the University imposes no penalties for absences, you are expected to make up all work that you miss.

My parents cannot come for Homecoming, since they have other plans.

If I had not been able to borrow money to complete my first year, I should have had to leave at the end of the first semester.

Go south until you come to the corner of State and Madison Streets, where the intersection is one of the busiest in the world.

Corrected by using phrases

On Friday evening a meeting of the Botany Club will be held, in order to discuss several matters. (Adverbial phrase)

Father's office is on the 35th floor and overlooks the Hudson River. (Verb phrase)

Father's office, on the 35th floor, overlooks the Hudson River. (Adjective phrase)

Having taken a wrong turning near Northville, we found ourselves traveling miles out of our way. (Participial phrase)

Go south until you come to the corner of State and Madison Streets, one of the busiest intersections in the world. (Appositional phrase)

In correcting the comma splice, do not make a "frying pan" error, an error worse than the one already made. Omitting the comma does not correct the comma splice; it replaces it by the more serious error of fused or blended sentences (see Section 33) .

### 32b   *Use a justifiable comma splice when it is appropriate and effective*

The foregoing discussion has dealt with the unjustifiable comma splice. Although occasional examples may be found in print, most writers and editors are careful to avoid the error, using instead the punctuation suggested above.

Certain kinds of comma splice are appropriate and effective, but be sure they are justifiable (even so, some instructors and writers prefer the semicolon as punctuation) :

1. When the independent clauses are very short, with the subjects usually the same:

I came, I saw, I conquered. (Julius Caesar's famous assertion)
You do work hard, you should work even harder.
Mother obeys signs, she is a careful driver.
Don't apologize, it isn't necessary.

If a conjunctive adverb joins even such short independent clauses, use a semicolon.

You do work hard; however, you should work even harder.
Mother obeys signs; therefore, she is a careful driver.

2. When the independent clauses, neither one very long, express contrast or the first clause makes a negative statement, the second an affirmative one:

This is Henry, that is George.

*Biology* comes from two Greek words: *bios* means "life," *logos* means "study."

We are not spending the summer in Maine, we are spending it in Wisconsin.

Some students like mathematics, others do not.

Perhaps the best example of the justifiable comma splice is in asking a question: the first clause is affirmative, the second is negative:

You have a copy of the assignment, haven't you?

The weather looks very stormy, doesn't it?

You will vote for Mary for Campus Queen, won't you?

## EXERCISES

A. Correct any unjustifiable comma splices in the following sentences. Wherever it is possible, correct each by all the methods suggested in Section 32a. Arrange your corrected versions in order of most to least effective.

1. I have found most of the information which you requested, if you should desire any additional information, do not hesitate to write me.
2. This scene reminded me of a miniature scale model, the only clue to the contrary was the movement of traffic.
3. I left out many important facts about camp, the singing, discussion groups, and worship all played a large part in my camp experience.
4. One common error in themes is incorrect spelling, the other is the occasional use of faulty diction.
5. The risks associated with keeping money at home are many, one must guard against fire, flood, tornadoes, and thieves.
6. Good letters are rarely "dashed off," usually they are the result of careful planning and writing.
7. In high school it is the teacher's job to educate the student, in college it is up to the student to achieve his own education.
8. There is no doubt about it, Yellowstone National Park is well worth an extended visit.
9. Before you come to college, no one tells you what to expect, you have to find out the hard way.
10. People don't care if it is raining or snowing, they still want to watch a football game.

11. There is just one problem, there isn't enough parking space for all the people who come to shop.
12. These are real championship cars, many are used at this speedway only.
13. It seems only yesterday that I was a freshman, now I am a member of the senior class.
14. My teacher was no longer interesting, Latin became cut-and-dried material.
15. On the ground it was over 100 degrees F., in the plane it was a comfortable 65 degrees F.

B. Correct any unjustifiable comma splices in the following sentences, using the method (Section 32a) which seems most appropriate to you.

1. The majority of business letters are well organized and well written, however, there are some which contain very serious errors.
2. I am sure of one thing, however, Rome, Paris, and London would not seem any more exciting to me than New York City.
3. By taking a variety of courses, I saw which field of science I liked best, also I gave myself a background for some of the courses that would be required at college.
4. I had to work on Sunday to catch up, otherwise we would lose a number of customers' jobs.
5. Our ship was scheduled to leave that evening, thus we had an afternoon to walk around in the city.
6. I like to write very much, in fact, I sometimes just sit down and start writing about the day's events.
7. People could work in the steel mills with very little education, consequently many people were drawn to Gary by the mills.
8. Most students maintain that they have used English all their lives, moreover, they say, "Why study something we already know?"
9. We had a wonderful time, nevertheless, we were glad to return to our own home and town.
10. My Irish blood comes from my father, and my English from my mother, therefore I'm an Irish-Englishman or an English-Irishman.
11. I live in a private home, as a result, my associations with other students are more limited than those of students living in the dormitories.
12. Some might say it was a warped idea, nevertheless, it was a point of honor to him to become rich with no formal education.
13. You go straight ahead on Route 45 until you cross the state line, then you are almost at your destination.

14. Daydreaming is one of the most prominent symptoms of spring fever, hence, there are those who would not consider daydreaming a true activity.
15. The reserved books can be used only in the library, accordingly, they are available for use at all times.

## 33 Fused sentences

*Fused* sentences are two grammatically complete sentences which are joined or run together with *no* mark of punctuation between. The reader is confused because the writer has not indicated where one complete thought ends and another complete thought begins.

**33a  Do not write two sentences with no punctuation between them; use a terminal mark (period, question mark, exclamation point) or a semicolon**

Fused sentences are a serious grammatical error, an error in punctuation, and a violation of the principle of unity. The error is even more flagrant than the comma splice, for the writer of a comma splice shows that he senses the need for punctuation of some sort.

A sentence is a complete and meaningful statement and should always be followed by a full stop, that is, by a terminal mark of punctuation (see Sections **86, 87**).

*Incorrect*    That night the river overflowed its banks and spread over the lowlands thousands of people were left homeless by the time the waters receded.

Judged by grammatical form, this "sentence" contains two independent statements. Each may be written as a separate sentence; or, if the writer thinks that the statements are sufficiently related in thought, a semicolon may be used, and the result is a compound sentence.

*Correct*    That night the river overflowed its banks and spread over the lowlands. Thousands of people were left homeless by the time the waters receded.

> That night the river overflowed its banks and spread over the lowlands; thousands of people were left homeless by the time the waters receded.

### 33b   *Never correct fused sentences by placing a comma between them*

If you correct the fused-sentences error by using a comma, your error is the comma splice (see Section 32). The four methods, therefore, for the correction of the comma splice should be carefully studied for similar correction of fused sentences.

## EXERCISE

Copy the following sentences and use capital letters (see Section 97) and necessary punctuation marks:

1. I grew up on a small farm not far from town thus I have experienced both country and town life.
2. We opened the door of the haunted house and looked around the house was empty except for a couple of chairs covered with sheets.
3. We first lived in Massachusetts then my father's business made us move to the Midwest.
4. Some people don't worry about their country they worry only about themselves.
5. I did not see anything very funny in having a flat tire in fact I wanted to forget about it as soon as possible.
6. In Wisconsin there are many farms throughout the countryside most of these are dairy farms.
7. Some students tell their parents they must have a new car otherwise they will quit college.
8. "John" is a simple name for a boy probably it is the most common boys' name in existence.
9. The date and time of the interview are all right however I am not sure where the interview is to take place.
10. Knowing how to use a dictionary is no problem each dictionary has a section in the front of the book telling how to use it.

# 34 Unity (oneness)

Unity, defined in Section **9,** applies not only to the theme but also to the paragraph (Section **25**) and the sentence. Clearness requires complete meaning from every sentence, but sentence unity is more than one simple idea or use of one short simple sentence.

A unified sentence may refer to several people, places, objects, or ideas and may be fairly long. For example, this is a unified sentence: "When this class is over and I have turned in my theme, I am going home and eat an ample breakfast; for some reason, breakfast tastes especially good after I have finished writing a class theme." The sentence is long and refers to several things, but it is unified because it has a oneness of purpose and of content. The ideas are closely related and form a unit of thought.

Another sentence could be one-fourth as long, refer to only one person, and yet violate the principle of unity: "John was a good student, and he had a TV set in his room" or "Born and reared in Canada, Grandfather spent his old age in England." The ideas in each of these sentences are not related; the sentences lack unity.

Unity in the sentence, essential to clear writing, is violated by (1) introducing too many details and (2) combining unrelated ideas. (Also, see Section **36.**)

### 34a   Avoid rambling sentences that introduce too many details

*Wrong*   We accepted the invitation to have the State High School Golf Tournament at Moose Junction, a small town in Minnesota, which has only 5000 inhabitants, but which contains several supermarkets, a number of churches, two good hotels, a number of motels, being on the junction of one United States highway and two state roads, and, since 1956, a drive-in restaurant as well as a golf course owned by a wealthy man named Putt.

In revision, long rambling sentences should be shortened, unrelated materials or ideas omitted, and some evidence of transition (Section **42**) used between sentences.

At least approaching unity, because of an attempt to keep the golf tournament as the central or single idea, a revision of the sentence above might read:

*Revised*    We have accepted the invitation to have the State High School Golf Tournament at Moose Junction, Minnesota, because of the facilities it offers. It is easily accessible by railroad and by several highways, United States Route 39 and two state roads, 138 and 139, which intersect there. The city has two good hotels and several motels; in addition, quite a number of the city's 5000 inhabitants have agreed to open their homes to the high school students. Restaurants are adequate, including a new large drive-in near the golf course. Naturally, the deciding factor in choosing Moose Junction has been this golf course. One of the best, in every sense, in the Midwest, it is owned and maintained by a golf enthusiast and wealthy man named, appropriately, Mr. Putt.

### 34b   *Avoid placing unrelated ideas in the same sentence*

Unrelated ideas can occur not only in the same sentence but also in different sentences, in the same paragraph, or even in the same theme. When such ideas occur in the same sentence, unity can sometimes be attained by subordinating one idea to another or otherwise showing some evidence of relationship. If the ideas are not closely related, they might be placed in separate sentences; if no relationship is evident, one of the ideas should be omitted.

*Wrong*      All my brothers are married, and they are all college graduates.

*Improved*   All my brothers are college graduates, and, since graduation, they have all married happily.

John was a good student, and, since his grades were high, he felt justified in buying a TV set to use as recreation.

Grandfather was born and reared in Canada, but, after many years, he moved to England and spent his old age there.

### EXERCISES

Revise the following sentences to give them unity:

1. I enjoyed our Halloween party very much, but it was a cold night.
2. John is a very fine dancer and plays the clarinet well.

3. The farmer who is superstitious will always expect rain three days during the week when it rains on Monday, and pioneers and early Americans would always check the husk on the corn for thickness; if the husks were thick, they prepared for a long and cold winter.
4. My oldest brother, James, is 25 years old, and he is married to an English teacher.
5. The town of Aurora has a population of 7000, and no farmers live in the town.
6. One hundred years ago John E. Sherman was elected mayor of our city; however, the present mayor is Wendell G. Orson.
7. We feel that our fraternity is the best at State College, which was founded in 1899 by two brothers, George and Daniel Slate; they founded the fraternity, not the college, which was established by an act of the State Legislature in 1870, and the moving spirit there was Morton Dowhill, the Speaker of the Senate.
8. For our evening meal we have to wear a dress shirt, tie, jacket, and suitable trousers and shoes, but the food is really special: roast lamb, beefsteak, roast beef, and pork chops are some of the main dishes that we have.
9. As I grew older, my desire to play basketball grew also, and when I entered high school I was too small to play my first two years of school, being only five feet tall, so I had to sit on the bench, but later in high school I began to grow, and before I graduated my senior year I was playing center on the first team, for I had grown 13 inches in two years.
10. "If I had a million dollars, I would buy me a new car and a new suit and a new pair of shoes and go all around the world and see it all and when the car got something wrong I would not wait to get it fixed, I would buy me another new car and give the old one to some kids and keep going and if it was water I would buy me an airplane and just keep going." (Schoolboy's theme on "What I Would Do with a Million Dollars," *This Week,* July 3, 1949)

# 35  Mixed and illogical constructions

In addition to unjustifiable sentence fragments (Section **31a,b, c,d**), unjustifiable comma splices (Section **32a**), and fused sentences (Section **33**), other hindrances to clear writing are mixed and illogical constructions.

*Construction* is a somewhat vague word. It means the grouping of words with other words or word combinations: the *arrangement* and *connection* or *relation* of two or more words in the phrase, clause, or sentence. Poor or bad or faulty or awkward construction therefore means poor arrangement, bad arrangement, faulty arrangement, awkward arrangement of words; or poor connection, bad connection, faulty connection, or awkward connection between words.

In sentence formation a *mixed and illogical construction* is a grouping of words which (1) is contrary to reason; (2) does not make good sense; (3) violates some principle of regularity; (4) omits an important and necessary word or words that would give proper grammatical relationship within the sentence; or (5) adds a word or sentence element that has no grammatical function to fulfill. Sentence structure should be clear; if it is not, the reason is frequently the writer's ignorance of grammar or slovenly thinking or both.

Your reader gives attention to your writing, but he cannot be expected to supply omitted words, spend time untangling involved and mixed constructions, or correct mistakes in thinking. He may make the necessary corrections as he reads, but his attention is unwillingly attracted to the errors and away from the communication of important ideas.

### 35a    *Do not omit a necessary main verb or an auxiliary verb*

Both formal and informal usage sanctions omission of words in writing and speaking. Such sentences as "He made such a speech as only a politician can [make]" and "I play a better game of tennis than my roommate [does]" are complete and correct without the added *make* and *does*. The following sentences, however, involve more serious breaches of clearness and correctness; in the first are two clauses, in the second a compound predicate, but the auxiliary verb (Section **78**) or the main verb (Section **79**) is improperly understood to be correct:

| | |
|---|---|
| *Doubtful* | The lawn *was* mowed and the hedges neatly trimmed. |
| *Improved* | The lawn *was* mowed and the hedges *were* neatly trimmed. |
| *Doubtful* | I never *have* and probably never *will write* excellent themes. |
| *Improved* | I never *have written* and probably never *will write* excellent themes. |

*35b   Include all words needed for clear expression of meaning*

If a necessary article, pronoun, preposition, or conjunction is omitted, your meaning is not clear; worse, it may be misinterpreted.

| | |
|---|---|
| *Doubtful* | The president and chairman of the committee accepted my petition. (This sentence means that one man is both president and chairman.) |
| *Improved* | The president and *the* chairman of the committee both accepted my petition. |
| *Wrong* | My father's name is Martin and has been a lifelong resident of Highland Park. |
| *Clear* | My father's name is Martin, and *he* has been a lifelong resident of Highland Park. |
| *Doubtful* | Father has great interest and high regard for my work. |
| *Improved* | Father has great interest *in* and high regard for my work. |
| *Doubtful* | I am asking that statement be made clearer. |
| *Improved* | I am asking *that* that statement be made clearer. |

In addition to including necessary articles, pronouns, prepositions, and conjunctions, revise any statement not clear because other essential words are omitted.

| | |
|---|---|
| *Not clear* | As far as that, we students would not be in favor. |
| *Clear* | As far as that proposal is concerned, we students are not in favor of having tuition fees increased. |
| *Not clear* | My roommate wears the clothes my sister in Chicago wears. |
| *Improved* | My roommate wears clothes like those my sister in Chicago wears. |
| *Not clear* | Like all the rest of the Home Economics students, my first two years of study are already planned. |
| *Clear* | Like the curricula of the other Home Economics students, my curriculum for the first two years is already planned. |
| *Not clear* | It will be a pleasure to have your parents for dinner this evening. |
| *Clear* | It will be a pleasure to have your parents as our dinner guests this evening. |

### 35c   *Avoid mixed, confusing "blends"*

Sometimes certain "blends" creep into thinking and writing: words or phrases or sentences may be wrongly blended (for an example of a wrong blending of words, see *irregardless,* Section **70,** Item 74). In the sentence "He had no automobile in which to ride in," the blend contains *in which to ride* and *to ride in.* Similarly, blending *where (at* or *in which)* with *at which* results in a statement such as "Where do you live *at*"? or "The room where I live *in.* . . ." Such constructions are mainly errors in diction (see Sections **54, 62, 67e**); other constructions involving longer sentence-elements are as much a result of careless thinking as of grammatical ignorance.

    1. A confusing blend occurs when a noun followed by an adjective-clause modifier or a parenthetic adverbial clause becomes blended with an independent clause:

| | |
|---|---|
| *Wrong* | Anyone who can be really happy, most people would look upon him with envy. |
| *Clear* | Anyone who can be really happy is looked upon with envy by most people. |
| | Most people would envy anyone who can be really happy. |
| *Not clear* | An automobile, unless you take good care of it, you will soon have to have it repaired. |
| *Improved* | Your automobile will soon have to be repaired unless you give it proper care. |

*Unfinished construction and a blend of confused ideas*

| | |
|---|---|
| | To me this is truly a book that, after read, you will never be the same again. |
| *Improved* | To me this is truly a great book; I believe that, after you have read it, you will never be the same person again. |

    2. Another confusing blend is that in which the writer begins with an indirect question and blends the direct question into the statement:

| | |
|---|---|
| *Confused* | If I had to do it over again, sometimes I wonder would I come to this college or go to work. |
| *Improved* | If I had to do it over again, sometimes I wonder whether I would come to this college or go to work. |

| | |
|---|---|
| *Confused* | Mary asked her adviser hadn't she already obtained credit for History 12. |
| *Indirect* | Mary asked her adviser whether she had not already obtained credit for History 12. |
| *Direct* | Mary asked her adviser, "Haven't I already obtained credit for History 12?" |

3. Similarly, a blend may confuse a direct and indirect quotation:

| | |
|---|---|
| *Confused* | Henry frankly admitted "that he was not studying as he should study." |
| | Henry frankly admitted "that I am not studying as I should study." |
| *Improved* | Henry frankly admitted that he was not studying as he should study. |
| | Henry frankly admitted, "I am not studying as I should study." |

## 35d   Avoid a mixed or double comparison

A frequent example of the mixed and confused blend occurs when a writer tries to include two comparisons in the same statement: (1) the grammatical positive and comparative degree of an adjective or an adverb (first set of examples below) or (2) the use of the superlative degree to include both a singular and a plural (second set of examples below). Good use sanctions the double comparison in the same sentence, but, for clearness and effectiveness, it demands that the second come after the first has been completed. (For other omissions of necessary words in comparisons, see Section 35f.)

| | |
|---|---|
| *Wrong* | My brother is *as* tall, if not taller, *than* my father. |
| | My record is *as* good, if not better, *than* your record. |
| *Improved* | My brother is *as tall as,* if not *taller than,* my father. |
| *but awkward* | My record is *as good as,* if not *better than,* your record. |
| *Preferable* | My brother is *as tall as* my father, if not taller. |
| | My record is *as good as* yours, *if not better.* |
| *Wrong* | My father is *one of the tallest if not the tallest man* in town. |

> The Battle of Waterloo was *one of the greatest if not the greatest battle* in all history.

*Preferable*   My father is *one of the tallest men in town, if not the tallest.*

The Battle of Waterloo was *one of the greatest battles in all history, if not the greatest.*

## 35e   *Make clear whether an object or term being compared is or is not part of a class or group*

Another mixed and confusing blend involving comparison occurs when a member or object of a class or group is also treated as a unique member. Avoid including within the class or group the object or term being compared, if it is part of the class or group. The excluding word *other* is needed.

*Inaccurate*   Straziboski is older than any man on the football team.
*Clear*   Straziboski is older than any *other* man on the football team.

*Inaccurate*   Henry has a higher scholastic average than any student in the College of Arts.
*Clear*   Henry has a higher scholastic average than any *other* student in the College of Arts.

Also, a member or object of a class or group may illogically be excluded from a group or class to which it belongs. Do not use the word *other* when the superlative degree indicates that the object or term compared is included within the group or class.

*Inaccurate*   Straziboski is the oldest of all the *other* men on the football team.
*Clear*   Straziboski is the oldest of all the men on the football team.

*Inaccurate*   Henry has the highest scholastic average of all the *other* students in the College of Arts.
*Clear*   Henry has the highest scholastic average of all the students in the College of Arts.

## 35f   *Do not omit words necessary in a comparison*

When a comparison is begun or implied, use the words necessary to complete it and to make it clear; also, do not omit the standard of comparison. Sometimes two dissimilar objects or persons and objects are compared, as in the last two examples below.

| | |
|---|---|
| *Doubtful* | He is so sick. |
| *Improved* | He is so sick that he cannot attend class today. |
| | He is really sick. |
| *Doubtful* | Country life is so friendly and peaceful. |
| *Improved* | Country life is so friendly and peaceful that many people will not live anywhere except in the country. |
| *Doubtful* | Your speech has been the greatest success. |
| *Improved* | Your speech has been the greatest success of any given thus far. |
| | Your speech has been a great success. |
| *Doubtful* | Mathematics interested Henry more than Nora. |
| *Improved* | Mathematics interested Henry more than it did Nora. |
| | Mathematics interested Henry more than Nora did. |
| *Doubtful* | His hands are bigger than any man I know. |
| *Improved* | His hands are bigger than those of any other man I know. |
| *Doubtful* | Our American workers are paid more than any other country. |
| *Improved* | Our American workers are paid more than the workers of any other country. |

## 35g  Avoid confusing double negatives

A violation of clear phrasing is the unjustifiable double negative. Although rigid double negatives—two or more negative adjectives or adverbs—have been allowable in past centuries, they no longer are acceptable in formal and good informal English. Illiterate speech abounds with such expressions as "can't hardly," "can't scarcely," "haven't scarcely," "I didn't get no food," "I didn't see nobody," or "Nobody isn't going to tell me nothing"; but even a fairly careful writer or speaker may slip into using *not* with such "negative words" as *but, nor, only, hardly,* and *scarcely.*

| | |
|---|---|
| *Questionable* | I *did not have but* four hours' sleep last night. |
| | You *can't help but* admire the man's courage. (See Section **70**, Item 32.) |
| | Some students *have not scarcely* enough money to pay for their bare necessities. |

*The sentence*

|            |                                                                 |
|------------|-----------------------------------------------------------------|
| *Improved* | I had *but* four hours' sleep last night.                       |
|            | You *can't help* admiring the man's courage.                    |
|            | Some students *have scarcely enough* money to pay for their bare necessities. |

Allowable and occasionally effective, although some writers consider them weak, are certain double negatives expressing a weak positive: using *not* with an adjective or adverb having a negative prefix or suffix or with negative prepositions like *against, without.*

Dealing with uninteresting subjects is a *not uncommon* experience of writers and speakers.
A flashlight is a *not unnecessary* piece of equipment.
Our chances of winning are *not entirely hopeless.*
Simple statements may sometimes be *not without* importance.

Sentences may of course contain more than one negative when the sense justifies the use:

That I was *not* present in class today is *not* true.
I can*not* tell why I was *not* able to concentrate in that test.
You *wouldn't* have known that I was *not* present if you had *not* been present yourself.

## EXERCISES

A. Words necessary for correctness or clearness are omitted in the following; supply them.

1. An extensive search of the literature has been made, and the results compiled.
2. Portable typewriters are similar but smaller than other typewriters.
3. Two years ago I took and passed a life-saving course was offered at the "Y."
4. No famous people reside in my home town, and never have.
5. They were glad that their garage had not been painted as many of their neighbors had been.
6. His nationality is Austrian and is proud of having a doctor's degree from University of Vienna.
7. The pay is good, surroundings pleasant, and opportunities excellent to meet successful men and women.

8. I thought of leaving immediately but decided that action would be childish.
9. This is a very casual style which has and will not decline in popularity for some time.
10. I am enclosing a collection of letters which I think you will be interested.

B. Correct the mixed or illogical constructions in the following sentences:

1. It was understood there was the possibility changes might be made was discussed.
2. This dislike of English I feel was due to the teacher was old that I had and was slipping in her ways of teaching.
3. I said, is this the French class, and the girl said yes.
4. Salt is one of the superstitions that people take seriously.
5. To quote a phrase I read somewhere, "a person can choose his friends but not his relatives," sounds just a bit vicious.
6. There are many aspects to having a cabin, family gathering, fishing, avoiding work and parties, all of these amount to fun and relaxation.
7. John wondered is he one of those strange people who enjoy to watch the sun rise.
8. When someone breaks a mirror and exclaims that he will now have seven years of bad luck doesn't really believe it.
9. The development of the individual into an independent, self-respecting person can be furthered by these books, and through them, a better world.
10. For there are many opportunities for someone with a college education and can apply them to today's living.

C. Correct any errors in comparison in the following sentences:

1. Colorful Colorado is the highest and one of the most scenic states in the United States.
2. In her portrayal of characters, Jane Austen was just as successful and more so than many of our present-day novelists.
3. Over the years our basketball team has been one of the best.
4. I can handle cars better than Mother.
5. Many small cities and rural communities are plagued with as much or sometimes even more crime than the big city.
6. I then began to realize that women were just as safe if not safer drivers than men.

7. I only hope I am able to accomplish as much and more than I have planned.
8. Other factories produce the largest quantity of cheese than any other city in America.
9. I study my books more than most students.
10. Natural scenes which people take for granted are as beautiful, or more so, than anything that was ever put on canvas.

# 36   *Faulty coordination*

Clear and effective sentences are so constructed that the relative importance of their elements is fully apparent. Are these elements coordinate, of equal rank? Are some of them subordinate? In clear and effective sentences, appropriate coordination and subordination are observed.

The immature writer phrases his sentences as a child speaks: a series of independent clauses loosely held together by coordinating conjunctions. A child very naturally might say: "We went to the circus, and we saw the clowns and we saw lots of animals and we drank pink lemonade." Even a college student might write: "We bought a new TV and it came last Saturday and we like it, for it has good clear pictures, and we like the old Western movies." Instead, a careful writer expresses ideas in constructions which show their appropriate importance. He coordinates equal ideas and subordinates minor ideas so that the important statement may be more emphatic.

## 36a   *Avoid stringy, running-on sentences*

Avoid excessive coordination, because it is childish, monotonous, and ineffective, and by avoiding it you avoid inaccurate and illogical coordination. Obviously, a stringy, running-on sentence goes on and on, because it overworks the possibilities of the compound sentence. Avoid excessive use of short independent clauses and of coordinating conjunctions between independent clauses. Reduce predication: change an independent clause into a dependent clause, a dependent clause into a phrase, a phrase into a single word (see Section **43a**) .

*Immature*

There are many reasons for unhappy marriages, and one of them is the husband is the athletic type and he likes to hunt and fish, but his wife despises the outdoors and she tries to make her husband stay at home and play bridge or some other kind of home occupation, and this always ends with one of them getting mad and one of them may say something that he or she doesn't really mean, and then the fight is on, for neither one will compromise.

*Improved*

Many reasons exist for unhappy marriages. One may be that the husband is fond of the outdoors, liking to hunt and fish. His wife, however, despises the outdoors and tries to interest him in home pastimes, such as bridge. Before long, both husband and wife are angry and say things that they don't really mean. Then the fight is on, for neither one will compromise and try to understand the other's point of view.

### 36b Avoid "seesaw" sentences

Another form of faulty coordination is the use of "seesaw" sentences (named from the game for children and some adults, using a balanced plank). These are compound sentences with two independent clauses of approximately equal length, whether joined by conjunctions or not. Alone or used occasionally, such a balanced sentence is effective; a succession of sentences of this kind is monotonous and ineffective. Usually one of the clauses can be subordinated.

*Ineffective*    I did not find too much to do between Christmas and New Year's, but I managed to attend a few good movies during this time. New Year's Eve wasn't too exciting either, and there were only the same old things to do. The "old gang" was together, more or less, and we had a fairly good time. Most of my old friends who were not attending college seemed immature, but I guess they will improve with time. All in all, it was nice to go home, but I certainly enjoyed seeing the campus again.

### 36c Avoid the overuse of so as a coordinating conjunction

*So* as a word has many necessary uses—as adjective, adverb, pronoun, interjection, conjunction, and part of *so . . . as, so that, so . . . that.* Therefore, *so* may well be avoided as a conjunctive adverb (even though correctly used as such, with a semicolon preceding) or between independent clauses with only a comma or no punctuation before it (more or less like a pure conjunction). The major objection to *so* in such constructions is simply ineffective overuse. Another objection is that use of *so* alone as a conjunction frequently gives a juvenile effect. Still another is that the conjunction *so* commonly is inappropriate in formal use. In constructions like those below, *so* can be replaced by *accordingly, as a result, consequently, hence, thereby, therefore,* or *thus,* or predication may be reduced.

| | |
|---|---|
| *Ineffective* | He had to study, *so* he did not attend the game. |
| | The bridge was out on Highway 40, *so* we had to make a long detour on Route 28. |
| *Improved* | He had to study; therefore he did not attend the game. |
| | Having to study, he did not attend the game. |
| | Since the bridge was out on Highway 40, we had to make a long detour on Route 28. |

In correcting overuse of *so,* guard against a worse error, the "frying pan" error: using another conjunctive adverb with a comma before it and writing an unjustifiable comma splice (see Section **32**).

| | |
|---|---|
| *Wrong* | The bridge was out on Highway 40, therefore we had to make a long detour on Route 28. |

Sometimes *so* is misused when the writer means *so that* or *in order that* in dependent clauses of result or purpose.

| | |
|---|---|
| *Ineffective* | The rain fell in torrents *so* the game had to be cancelled. |
| | The roads were slippery *so* we had to drive very slowly. |
| | Short assignments are given *so* students can master them. |
| *Improved* | The rain fell in torrents *so that* the game had to be cancelled. |
| | The roads were *so* slippery *that* we had to drive very slowly. |
| | Short assignments are given *in order that* students can master them. |

**36d  Avoid false coordination: do not join a relative
clause to its principal clause by and, but, or or**

Remember that *coordinate* means "of equal rank." An independent clause, therefore, cannot be joined to a dependent clause by a coordinating conjunction. *And, but, or,* and other coordinating conjunctions connect only elements that are equal in rank.

The most frequent violation of this principle is the so-called "and which" construction. Do not use *and which, but which, and who, but who,* etc., unless a preceding "which clause" or "who clause" is coordinate with it.

*Wrong*    He at first showed much energy, *but which* soon vanished.

Tompson is a man of intelligence, *and who* is an industrious worker.

I do not trust Henry, *or whom* I should not like to have as a close friend.

This is a beautiful golf course, *and which* you will enjoy playing on during your college years.

The simplest method of correcting these sentences is to omit the conjunctions, but remember to apply the principle of punctuation regarding restrictive and nonrestrictive clauses (Section 88m).

*Revised*    He at first showed much energy, which soon vanished.

Tompson is a man of intelligence who is also an industrious worker.

I do not trust Henry, whom I should not like to have as a close friend.

This is a beautiful golf course on which you will enjoy playing during your college years.

Another method of correcting this error is the use of parallelism (Section 44), by adding a "who clause" or "which clause" to be appropriately coordinate.

*Revised*    I do not trust Henry, whom I have come to know well but whom I should not like to have for a close friend.

This is a beautiful golf course which is open only to students and on which you will enjoy playing during your college years.

Tompson is a man who is intelligent and who is an industrious worker.

Sometimes such revision is wordy and ineffective, as in the last revised example. Made more concise, the sentence might read:

A man of intelligence, Tompson is an industrious worker.
*or*
Tompson is intelligent and industrious.

## EXERCISES

A. Rewrite the following sentences in order to eliminate improper coordination:

1. Decisive action is to be taken at the meeting, and at which everyone is urged to be present.
2. I met my brother yesterday and who asked me how my first week of college had been.
3. I would like to teach in a small consolidated school, but I am also taking speech therapy as a minor.
4. We went on a tour of our library and it proved to be very interesting.
5. On Christmas afternoon we went to church, and where a beautiful Christmas program was presented.
6. My history teacher became ill for a short time but there was no substitute teacher to replace him and we did not have any history classes for a week.
7. The road out of the City of Destruction to the Celestial City is filled with temptations and misleading paths upon which one is likely to stumble, and if he is misled.
8. All the cadets standing in formation are an impressive sight and which will not be forgotten soon.
9. When I looked out the night the snowstorm ended, I saw a world that was truly beautiful, and the trees had ice all over them, and the light made them sparkle, and the snow on the ground was as white as white could be.
10. I read many books in high school and when I graduated and entered college there were goals I had to reach which entailed hard work but which pleased my parents and me because I had a rather extensive vocabulary and reading background, and this was a great satisfaction to me, for I was soon making high grades in my English and other liberal arts courses.

B. Rewrite the following sentences in order to eliminate the overuse of *so*. Use different methods.

1. I had only a minor part in the play, so I was through at the end of the first act.
2. Do people want the government to spend more money so they can pay higher taxes?
3. I like to bowl and play golf, so I plan to take advantage of the facilities here.
4. Vacations are not numerous so it is important to enjoy every one of them.
5. A summer's work should give me enough experience so I can get a permanent job.
6. My second reason for studying is so I can make good grades and thus have a good scholastic record.
7. There are many art courses offered here so I shall have a wide choice.
8. The melodies of the mountains are simple, so they are easily remembered.
9. Many of my friends were home from other colleges, so we had several enjoyable reunions.
10. It is seldom that such an insect is found, so great pains must be taken not to destroy it.

# 37 *Faulty subordination*

Like appropriate coordination, appropriate subordination contributes to clear and effective writing by showing the relationship of less important to more important ideas.

Careful, thoughtful writing contains much subordination. A good writer, knowing that not all his ideas should be given equal rank, judiciously places them in constructions corresponding to their importance. Thus he writes unified and effective sentences. His thoughts are clearly communicated to his readers, for they see what the relationship of the sentence elements actually is.

The careful writer, in avoiding excessive and faulty coordination (see Section 36), also avoids excessive and faulty subordination. Reducing predication (Section **43a**) requires thought; you must be certain that you know exactly the relationships of your ideas in order to make your reader aware of exactly the same relationships.

### 37a   *Avoid putting a coordinate idea in a subordinate form*

*Inaccurate*   My older brother is heavy and slow, *while my younger brother is lithe and active.*

*With his Bachelor of Arts degree from Atwater College,* Father also received his Master of Arts degree there.

Our football team won the league championship, *although our basketball team finished in last place.*

To make these sentences and others like them more effective, change the subordinating conjunction to a coordinating conjunction, or otherwise coordinate the ideas:

*More effective*   My older brother is heavy and slow, but my younger brother is lithe and active.

Father received both his Bachelor of Arts and his Master of Arts degrees at Atwater College.

Our football team won the League championship, but our basketball team finished in last place.

### 37b   *Avoid putting the main idea of a sentence in a subordinate construction or a subordinate idea in a main clause*

*Upside-down subordination* exists when an idea of less importance is put in an independent clause, and the important idea is put in a dependent clause or phrase. Such a sentence is correct and usually clear, but it is not so effective as a sentence using the principle of important ideas in independent clauses, less important ideas in dependent clauses. Careful consideration of content reveals that often the most dramatic incident and the effect, rather than the cause, are major ideas; preliminaries, such as time, place, and attendant circumstances, are minor and subordinate ideas. Also, even when proper subordination is used, putting the dependent clause and the independent clause in the form of a periodic sentence adds to effectiveness (Section **74c**) .

*Ineffective*   My friends and I were 12 years old when we decided to visit a "haunted" house.

I kept telephoning Mary every 10 minutes, though she refused to answer.

We started across an intersection, when another car came in from the right and hit us.

*Improved*    When my friends and I were 12 years old, we decided to visit a "haunted" house.

Though I kept telephoning Mary every 10 minutes, she refused to answer.

Just as we started across the intersection, another car came in from the right and hit us.

## 37c  Avoid excessive subordination

Sentences containing overlapping subordinate statements are not effective. In such series, each clause or phrase depends upon a preceding clause or phrase. Sentence elements should be linked, but they should not be built like an accordion, or, to vary the simile, like stairs, where each step is attached to the one just above.

*Ineffective*    These are inexpensive toys which have been made in Japan where there is cheap labor which depends upon American trade.

I have been in the student show which has affected my grades because it has taken a lot of my evening time, when I should have been in my room studying since my assignments have become longer and more difficult.

*Improved*    These are inexpensive toys which have been made in Japan. Labor is cheap there, and laborers' wages depend upon American trade.

My being in the student show has affected my grades because it has taken much of my evening time. Instead of rehearsing, I should have been in my room studying, since my assignments have become longer and more difficult.

## EXERCISES

Rewrite the following sentences, correcting the faulty subordination.

1. We were almost home before our car skidded into another car and caused a wreck.

2. As the lightning struck the house, Mother was talking on the telephone.
3. The following day I was driving down the highway at a reasonable speed, when suddenly a car whipped past me.
4. Whitefish Bay is eight miles north of Milwaukee, having a population of about 12,000 people.
5. Our town is a purely residential town having its own school district consisting of a high school and a grade school which total about 900 students.
6. In my senior year we reached the finals, where we won our semifinal, the final, and the State Championship.
7. After being here a week, I discovered that one works all day in classes which seem to be so placed that I must run from one end of the campus to the other before I can attend them.
8. During my freshman year I am living in a rooming house which is owned by an elderly lady whose father was a college professor for some 50 years at Marion, which is another college in the state supported by public funds.
9. It was so dark that I had to turn on a light to read the clock in the kitchen that is directly opposite a large window which is on the east side of the house that is hidden from the street light by a large oak tree.
10. Of course we cannot always help everyone, but what I am saying is that when people ask for help from someone who could within his own limitations be of great help, when he doesn't.

# 38 Illogical dependent clauses

Sentence clearness and emphasis require the use of dependent clauses. Proper subordination through the use of such clauses calls for careful thinking. Therefore, in order to avoid confusion and ineffectiveness due in part to grammatical incorrectness, use dependent clauses correctly and clearly.

All dependent clauses have the functions of separate parts of speech—noun, adjective, adverb. To use one of them for another is like misusing the single-word parts of speech. Specifically, common errors include the following: adverbial clause used for noun clause, adverbial clause used as a substitute for a noun, and a complete sentence used for a noun clause or a noun.

### 38a   Do not use an adverbial clause as a noun clause

When a noun clause is grammatically needed as the subject of a verb, the object of a verb, or a predicate nominative noun clause, do not use an adverbial clause in its place. *When, where, because* clauses are frequent offenders. The obvious correction: substitute a noun clause for the adverbial clause or give the adverbial clause a verb to modify.

| | |
|---|---|
| *Dubious* | *Because he had no money* was the reason Henry dropped out of school. |
| | I see *where the paper says that colder weather is coming.* |
| *Correct* | *That he had no money* was the reason Henry dropped out of school. |
| | Henry dropped out of school *because he had no money.* |
| | I see *that the paper says that colder weather is coming.* |

*The reason is because* . . . needs further discussion. The construction has a long history of usage behind it, and it is found in the writing and speaking of many people, literary and otherwise. Those who object do so because the expression is illogical, even though many other acceptable expressions in English are illogical—idioms, for example. "Because" means "for the reason that," "the cause being"; since we do not say "The cause is because . . ." why say "The reason is because . . ."? Logically, we should give, not the *cause for the reason,* but the reason or cause itself, phrased as a noun, noun phrase, or noun clause.

| | |
|---|---|
| *Illogical* | The reason for my absence was because I overslept. |
| | The reason the airplane crashed was because the weather was foggy. |
| *Logical* | The reason for my absence was that I overslept. (Noun clause) |
| | The reason for my absence was oversleeping. (Noun) |
| | The reason the airplane crashed was foggy weather. (Noun phrase) |
| | The reason the airplane crashed was that the weather was foggy. (Noun clause) |
| | The airplane crashed because it became lost in the foggy weather. (Adverbial clause properly used) |

**249**

NOTE:  The adverbial phrase, *because of,* should be used only adverbially and not refer to or modify a noun.

| | |
|---|---|
| *Illogical* | The reason for my absence was because of illness. |
| *Logical* | The reason for my absence was illness. (Noun) |
| | The airplane crashed because of foggy weather. (Adverbial phrase properly used) |

## 38b   Do not use an adverbial clause in place of a single noun or noun phrase

Similar to errors mentioned in Section **38a** is the use of adverbial clauses for single nouns or noun phrases. Again, *when, where, because* clauses are the chief offenders in this type of incorrect subordination, especially in explanations or definitions.

To correct, substitute a single noun or a noun with modifiers for the adverbial clause or change the construction to make the adverbial clause grammatically correct.

| | |
|---|---|
| *Dubious* | Plagiarism is *where* you take the work of another and pass it off as your own. |
| | Passive voice is *when* the subject does not act but is acted upon. |
| | *When* you graduate from college is the time to take life seriously. |
| | My low grade on the test was *because* I had not studied for it. |
| *Correct* | Plagiarism is taking another's work and passing it off as your own. |
| | Plagiarism occurs when you take the work of another and pass it off as your own. |
| | Passive voice is used when the subject does not act but is acted upon. |
| | When you graduate from college, you should take life seriously. |
| | My failure to study for the test caused my low grade. |

## 38c   Use a noun clause, not a sentence, as the subject or complement of is and was

A sentence rarely can be used effectively as a grammatical subject or complement. Make the sentence (independent clause) into a dependent clause by using the proper subordinating conjunction, usually *that,* or change the sentence into a correctly used adverbial clause or reduce the independent clause to a phrase.

| | |
|---|---|
| *Dubious* | I had overslept was the reason I missed class yesterday morning. |
| | I went to a small rural high school is the reason I was not well prepared for college. |
| | Mary's only fault is she has a bad temper. |
| *Correct* | The reason I was not well prepared for college was that I went to a small rural high school. |
| | I was not well prepared for college because I went to a small rural high school. |
| | Mary's only fault is that she has a bad temper. |
| | Mary has only one fault: a bad temper. |

A quoted sentence, however, may be used as a noun.

| | |
|---|---|
| *Correct* | "Fools rush in where angels fear to tread" is a well-known quotation from Alexander Pope's "An Essay on Criticism." |

## EXERCISES

A. Compose 12 original sentences, of which four each illustrate proper use of, respectively, noun clauses, adjective clauses, and adverbial clauses.

B. Rewrite the following sentences, correcting the misuse of dependent clauses:

1. Simply because a speed limit is posted does not mean that the maximum speed is always safe.
2. In the fall, when the leaves of the trees are changing colors is a scene of beauty one can never forget.
3. The ideal situation is where one is doing the work he likes to do.
4. One reason I am taking English composition is because I want to learn to write correctly and effectively.
5. When I am awakened by a trumpet at seven o'clock in the morning is when I get angry.
6. The reason the trip takes so long is not because of heavy traffic but because of so many traffic lights.
7. The only time some people use a dictionary is when they have trouble with spelling.

8. This dormitory is no place in which to spend the next eight months was my primary thought as I entered my assigned room.
9. If someone was hurt or even killed and a person knew it was his fault would be enough punishment for him.
10. How I came to hate rainy weather was after joining the Army and being stationed at Fort Lewis, Washington.

# 39   *Misplaced modifiers*

In highly inflected languages, nouns, adjectives, adverbs, and verbs have varied and identifying endings by which relationships of words are usually shown. The English language, however, is not highly inflected. Consequently, clearness often depends in part or solely on the position of words in a sentence.

You should correctly place related words together so that the reader sees their connection and is not misled. It is especially important to place each modifier close to the word it modifies.

**39a   *Place clearly such words as* only, not, even, scarcely, *etc.***

Words like *almost, even, hardly, just, merely, nearly, never, not, only, quite, scarcely, seldom, today, tomorrow,* as well as other words like the correlative conjunctions *both . . . and, neither . . . nor, either . . . or, not only . . . but also,* should be placed in a sentence so that they convey precisely the meaning you intend.

Consider the difference in meaning of the following:

For my college expenses, I have *almost* saved $1200.
For my college expenses, I have saved *almost* $1200.

My *first* teacher's name was Rosemary.
My teacher's *first* name was Rosemary.

Or consider how the position of *only* changes meaning in a sentence:

*Only* the instructor told me to write a theme of 300 words.
The *only* instructor told me to write a theme of 300 words.

The instructor *only* told me to write a theme of 300 words.
The instructor told *only* me to write a theme of 300 words.
The instructor told me *only* to write a theme of 300 words.
The instructor told me to write *only* a theme of 300 words.
The instructor told me to write a theme of *only* 300 words.
The instructor told me to write a theme of 300 words *only*.

Words like those given are usually associated with the word or phrase immediately preceding or following. Even when no confusion results, effectiveness is better served when each is placed in its logical position.

| | |
|---|---|
| *Less effective* | Henry *only* wanted to borrow a few dollars. |
| | I *only* had two days left to finish my packing. |
| *More effective* | Henry wanted to borrow *only* a few dollars. |
| | I had *only* two days left to finish my packing. |

Also, watch *don't think*. If a sentence is a thought expressed in words, how can you express one if you don't think?

| | |
|---|---|
| *Dubious* | I *don't think* I'll ever forget my first day on the campus. |
| *Clear* | I think I shall *never* forget my first day on the campus. |

### 39b  *Place clearly phrases and clauses*

The suggestions about clearly placing words (Section **39a**) apply also to phrases and clauses. In general, place phrases and clauses near or next to the words they modify if there is the slightest chance of confusion. A dangling modifier (Section **40a**) may sometimes be only a misplaced phrase. In the following, the writers obviously did not mean what their sentences say:

A few years ago the White House in Washington was closed for alterations to visitors.
I decorated our Christmas tree with our family.
We all put our presents under the tree, which we had wrapped up the night before.

Sometimes rephrasing is necessary:

A few years ago the White House in Washington was closed to visitors while alterations were being made.

I helped my family decorate our Christmas tree.
We all put our presents, which we had wrapped up the night before, under our Christmas tree.

### 39c   Avoid a "squinting modifier"

"Squinting," in one sense, means "looking in two directions at once." A modifier is *squinting* when it refers to either of two parts of a sentence: what has gone before or what has followed. The inevitable result is ambiguity; just which of two possible meanings did the writer want his reader to accept?

For clearness, move the modifier and include it with the material it qualifies. If the sentence is still awkward, rewrite it. Punctuation may also help (see Section 88k), but it is not a safe guide.

| | |
|---|---|
| *Ambiguous* | Most boys who have the name John *somewhere along the line* get a nickname. |
| | All the family sat still *momentarily* with a surprised look on their faces. |
| *Clear* | Most boys who have the name John get a nickname somewhere along the line. |
| | All the family momentarily sat still, with a surprised look on their faces. |
| | All the family sat still, with a surprised look, momentarily, on their faces. |

## EXERCISES

Revise the following sentences so as to remove any lack of clearness or effectiveness due to misplaced modifiers:

1. Each day I see a new building going up from my study window.
2. In this book the author tells of roving around Europe in an autobiographical manner.
3. Some courses in composition require you only to write frequently and to speak occasionally.
4. I don't think certain articles in our book of readings are interesting.
5. Each spring my father and I pull the machinery out of the shed that we will need for sowing oats.
6. In the poem the heroine relates the story of her marriage to one of her girl friends.

7. In some courses the student is more required to work and think than just to copy and memorize.
8. As we interpret your directions, whenever it is possible, we should keep to the superhighways.
9. I have never had a shot hurt as this shot did before.
10. There are some instructors that cannot really explain what they want their students to know in a clear manner.
11. She nearly laughs with each word she speaks.
12. Today I registered as a freshman, and it almost took the whole day.
13. I hope to work in a mentally and physically handicapped clinic.
14. If I spend half an hour on the courses I have the next day, the night before, I find that I can get a better grade.
15. Everyone at the ceremony was impressed by the 63-year-old baby's christening dress.

# 40 Dangling modifiers

Dangling modifiers, those which do not properly or clearly depend on the right words, are of two kinds: dangling verbal phrases and dangling elliptical clauses. Ambiguity and even ludicrousness frequently result from their use.

## 40a Avoid dangling verbal phrases at the beginning of a sentence or independent clause

Dangling verbal phrases consist of participial, prepositional-gerund, and infinitive phrases. Such a phrase dangles when (1) it has no substantive (i.e., noun or pronoun) to modify or (2) the substantive is the wrong one. Usually the phrase begins the sentence or the independent clause and should therefore logically modify the subject of the sentence or the clause. The most ludicrous examples are those in which a phrase expressing motion modifies a subject that is stationary or a phrase expressing fixity modifies a moving subject.

*Ludicrous*  Approaching the campus, the tower of University Hall appeared above the skyline. (Dangling participle)
Flying high above the clouds, the earth was completely invisible. (Dangling participle)

> After seeing Niagara Falls, other falls seem small by
> comparison. (Dangling prepositional-gerund phrase)

Not so serious but still to be avoided are less ludicrous and
incongruous modifiers.

*Correct and
clear*

> In preparing for a test it is advisable to review
> thoroughly. (Dangling prepositional-gerund phrase)
> Approaching the campus, we saw the tower of Univer-
> sity Hall above the skyline.
> As we approached the campus, the tower of University
> Hall appeared above the skyline. (*Better:* . . ., we
> saw the tower of . . .)
> Flying high above the clouds, the passengers were un-
> able to see the earth.
> Since the plane was high above the clouds, the earth
> was completely invisible to the passengers.
> After one has seen Niagara Falls, other falls seem small
> by comparison.
> In preparing for a test, a student should review
> thoroughly.
> When a student is preparing for a test, it is advisable
> to review thoroughly. (*Better:* When a student is
> preparing for a test, he should review thoroughly.)

In business letters, the dangling *enclosed you* phrase is common—does it mean that *you* are enclosed?

*Dangling*

> Enclosed you will find an order blank.
> Enclosed please find a check for $7.85.

*Improved*

> You will find an order blank enclosed.
> A check for $7.85 is enclosed.
> I am enclosing a check for $7.85.

The dangling infinitive phrase is less frequent and incongruous, because a writer usually has in mind an adverbial *in order to*
phrase. Many introductory infinitive phrases state or suggest purpose. Clearness and effectiveness are served when such phrases
depend upon the noun or pronoun indicating the one who has
the purpose in mind.

| | |
|---|---|
| *Questionable* | To succeed in life, ambition is necessary. |
| | To play golf well, a good set of clubs is needed. |
| *Improved* | To succeed in life, a man must have some ambition. |
| | To play golf well, you need a good set of clubs. |

Occasionally, even an introductory prepositional phrase is dangling:

| | |
|---|---|
| | After graduation from high school, my father asked about my future plans. |
| *Better* | After I graduated from high school, my father asked about my future plans. |
| | After graduation from high school, I was asked by my father about my future plans. |

Sometimes the dangling phrase is merely a misplaced modifier (see Section **39b**), as in the two incongruous examples below.

| | |
|---|---|
| *Incongruous* | Hanging from the very top of the tree, Grandfather saw a robin's nest. |
| | Buried several inches underground, our dog tried to locate the bone. |
| *Improved* | Grandfather saw a robin's nest hanging from the very top of the tree. |
| | Our dog tried to locate the bone buried several inches underground. |

Sentences containing dangling verbal phrases may be corrected in several ways: (1) expand the verbal phrase to a dependent clause; (2) supply the noun or pronoun which the phrase should modify; (3) place the phrase so near the proper substantive that no confusion results. Such corrections eliminate dangling modifiers, but some are awkward and inconsistent, and the sentence may need rephrasing. For examples, see the sentences labeled "improved" above.

### 40b Avoid dangling verbal phrases tacked on at the end of a sentence or independent clause

Participial phrases tacked on to the end of a statement with *thus*, *thereby*, and *therefore* are also dangling because they have no noun or pronoun to modify. Clearness is assured if these dangling modifiers are removed by (1) making the participle a member of a compound predicate or (2) rephrasing the sentence.

*Questionable*   I was ill for several weeks, thus causing me to fall behind in my work.

We lost the last game of the season, thereby preventing us from going to the Rose Bowl.

*Improved*   I was ill for several weeks and thus fell behind in my work.

We lost the last game of the season and were thereby prevented from going to the Rose Bowl.

My several weeks' illness caused me to fall behind in my work.

Our loss in the last game of the season prevented us from going to the Rose Bowl.

When a verbal phrase is used to specify a general action, it is not considered a dangling modifier:

*Approved*   Generally speaking, tuition fees should not be increased.

Such words or phrases as *considering, concerning, according to, owing to,* etc., are used prepositionally, not as verbals. Thus, "*Considering* everything, the proposal was fair" is a correct and clear sentence.

### 40c   *Avoid dangling elliptical clauses*

The *dangling* elliptical clause (see Section **73b** for discussion of elliptical clauses) is one in which the understood subject and predicate are not the same as those of the main clause. The usual offenders are clauses introduced by *before, after, while, when, though,* and *if.*

As from dangling verbal phrases, ambiguity and ludicrousness result from dangling elliptical clauses.

Before warmed up, you should never race a motor.
While studying last evening, the lights went out.
When six years old, my grandmother died.
Though failing the course, my instructor kept encouraging me.
If traveling in the tropics, light clothing should be worn.

Two ways of correcting dangling elliptical clauses are the following: (1) insert in the dependent clause the subject and verb or part of verb needed to make the sentence clear or (2) change the subject or subject-verb in the independent clause so that it, or they, would be clear logically if also expressed in the dependent clause.

*Clear*    Before warmed up, a motor should never be raced.
Before it is warmed up, you should never race a motor.
While studying last evening, I found myself suddenly in darkness; the lights had gone out.
When I was six years old, my grandmother died.
Though I was failing the course, my instructor kept encouraging me.
If traveling in the tropics, you should wear light clothing.

## EXERCISES

The following sentences contain dangling modifiers at the beginning or end or dangling elliptical clauses. Rewrite each sentence, correcting the error by using one or more of the methods suggested in Section 40a–c.

1. Looking out my window, many red lights from emergency vehicles could be seen.
2. After traveling farther, the signs began appearing more regularly.
3. The article is not written in technical language, thus making it easy for the layman to understand.
4. Being unmarried, all the girls in Junior High School loved the handsome young chemistry teacher.
5. Enclosed with this letter you will find your membership card.
6. If writing a letter by hand, a good fountain pen or ball-point pen should be used.
7. This report is filed with the Federal Aviation Agency, thereby completing the pilot's preparation for a trip.
8. After walking for 50 yards, the land gradually began to slope downward.
9. To enjoy poetry it should be read slowly and carefully.
10. At the age of two my father bought a small farm near this college town.
11. Upon checking into the hospital, a cute nurse of about 18 showed me to my room.

12. Going east, the main object of the trip will be visiting Maine.
13. Shortly after entering Germany, the inns and hotels became more attractive.
14. When boiled, Mother would shell and slice the eggs for the salad.
15. Many interesting topics are to be found browsing through the dictionary.
16. Hanging from the ceiling, you will see a beautiful, old-fashioned chandelier.
17. After a quick walk through the crowds, the New York Public Library offers a haven from the hustle-bustle of the street.
18. Coming toward the house, the white fence posts can be seen, no matter what the direction of approach.
19. As a college professor, I am sure you can give me advice about the electives I should take as a high school senior.
20. I have seen the sun come up over the beautiful mountain top many times, sitting around a nice warm fire with the odor of frying bacon drifting through the air.

# 41 *Split constructions*

Nothing is actually incorrect about separating or splitting closely related materials. From the point of view of the reader, the objection to splitting involves clearness and, even more, effectiveness.

Since English is not a highly inflected language and since many English words show little if any inflectional change, it is important to keep related elements together (Section 39). Writers sometimes unnecessarily separate closely related elements, and the result is awkwardness and ambiguity, not clearness and effectiveness.

Closely related parts in a sentence are verbs in a verb phrase, coordinate sentence elements, subject and predicate, verb and object, verb and complement, preposition and object, the two parts of an infinitive, and other word combinations logically belonging together.

## 41a *Do not needlessly separate the parts of a verb phrase*

When more than one verb word is involved, the normal verb phrase in English consists of the auxiliary verb and the main verb. Apply the tests of smoothness and logic, clearness and effectiveness in separating these verb forms.

Single adverbs splitting a verb phrase are usually effective and rarely awkward:

*Awkward*    We *shall see* never his like again.

*Effective*    We *shall* never *see* his like again.

When long phrases or clauses do the splitting, however, keep the parts of a verb phrase together.

*Awkward*    Many a none-too-brilliant student *has,* by persistent and conscientious study, *been* successful in achieving high grades.

*Improved*    By persistent and conscientious study, many a none-too-brilliant student *has been* successful in achieving high grades.

*Awkward*    He *is,* despite many objections from his parents, *going* to study music and painting.

*Improved*    He *is going* to study music and painting despite many objections from his parents.

Despite many objections from his parents, he *is going* to study music and painting.

### 41b   *Avoid a widely split infinitive*

In some verb constructions the infinitive is used without its accompanying sign *to*; in other verb constructions the sign of the infinitive *to* is necessary. When words, phrases, or even clauses come between *to* and the verb, the construction is called a *split infinitive.*

Split infinitives have been used by many reputable writers, but a study of these examples shows that in effective writing rarely is more than a single word, usually an adverb, used between *to* and the verb. In "He failed *to* entirely *pay* for it," *entirely* is properly and effectively placed next to the verb *pay,* which it modifies. And in certain expressions the split infinitive is necessary, as in the following: "In an emergency we may be forced *to* more than *double* our production."

Let clearness, naturalness, and effectiveness be the tests for split infinitives. The use of a phrase or a clause as a separating element is rarely clear or natural or effective.

| | |
|---|---|
| *Ineffective* | Our family physician telegraphed us *to* as soon as possible *come.* |
| *Improved* | Our family physician telegraphed us *to come* as soon as possible. |

**41c   *Avoid unnecessary and ineffective separation
of subject and predicate, verb and object,
verb and complement, preposition and object,
or other closely related sentence elements***

| | |
|---|---|
| *Awkward and ineffective* | My brother, as soon as he received a favorable reply to his application, left for New York for an interview. (Subject and predicate separated) |
| | Mary asked, even before my sentence was completed, the exact meaning of my statement. (Verb and object separated) |
| | His remark was, despite its seemingly apparent innocence, both impolite and unkind. (Verb and predicate adjectives separated) |
| | With, and no one hopes for any other kind, good weather, we should arrive early in the afternoon. (Preposition and object separated) |
| *Improved* | As soon as he received a favorable reply to his application, my brother left for New York for an interview. |
| | Even before my sentence was completed, Mary asked the exact meaning of my statement. |
| | Despite its seemingly apparent innocence, his remark was both impolite and unkind. |
| | With good weather, and no one hopes for any other kind, we should arrive early in the afternoon. |

On occasion, greater clearness may be achieved by separation, as suggested in "Misplaced Modifiers" (Section **39**), or both greater clearness and smoothness, as in this sentence, where verb and object are split in the improved version:

| | |
|---|---|
| *Vague* | In his remarks the psychologist discussed everyday matters and people whom you and I know *as simply as a child.* |
| *Improved* | In his remarks the psychologist discussed, *as simply as a child,* everyday matters and people whom you and I know. |

Such separation of closely related elements should be made for appropriate and specific purposes, never aimlessly. When it is effective, as in transposed and suspensive elements, do not hesitate to use it. (See Section **47d.**)

*41d Place coordinate sentence elements together*

When two coordinate phrases or two coordinate dependent clauses are used in a sentence, one should not come at the beginning and the other at the end. For effectiveness keep them together and indicate their relationship by the appropriate coordinating conjunction. (See also Section **44.**)

| | |
|---|---|
| *Ineffective* | *Although he was a good tennis player,* he was not able to make the varsity squad, *although he practiced daily.* |
| *Effective* | *Although he was a good tennis player* and *although he practiced daily,* he was not able to make the varsity squad. |
| *Ineffective* | *With fair weather,* we should have an enjoyable fishing trip, *with good luck.* |
| *Effective* | *With fair weather* and *good luck,* we should have an enjoyable fishing trip. |

**EXERCISES**

Point out and correct all faulty split constructions in the following sentences:

1. It, as I have found, seems sometimes an almost impossible task.
2. The way it looks now, during vacation I should have gotten everything I planned to do, done.
3. I would, since I worked for you three summers ago, like to use your name as a reference in my "job-hunting."
4. It is my fondest wish to go back to Washington to once again and with more time at my disposal view those memorable sights.
5. In fact, every day would find me out on the pier, which seemed to extend an endless distance into the ocean, fishing.

# 42   *Transition*

Individual sentences may be correct, clear, effective, appropriate and yet not be clear or effective when put together in a paragraph. If the order of sentences within a paragraph is logical, any lack of clearness probably is due to faulty *transition*. Remember that *transition* means passing from one place, state, or position to another, and that *evidence of transition* consists of linking or bridging devices.

Three kinds of transition apply to writing: between paragraphs (Section 11), within the sentence, and between sentences. When used within the sentence, transitional devices usually come between clauses; when used between sentences, they come near or at the beginning or end of the sentences they link. Not only must your thoughts progress logically; your reader also must readily grasp both them and their interrelations. Only thus can effective communication be achieved.

### 42a   *Make sentence transitions clear by using transitional words and phrases*

Transitional words and phrases are not needed within or between all sentences, and your best guide is consideration for your reader: have you made the relationship between ideas evident to him?

1. Between dependent and independent clauses evidence of relationship is expressed by (a) *subordinating conjunctions* (for a fairly complete list and the relationships they express, see Section **84e**) and (b) *relative pronouns* (see Section **71d2**).

2. Between independent clauses or between sentences, evidence of relationship is expressed by (a) *personal pronouns* (see Section **75a**); (b) *demonstrative pronouns* (see Section **71d3**); (c) *simple* or *pure conjunctions* (see Section **84a**); (d) *correlative conjunctions* (see Section **84b**); (e) *conjunctive* or *parenthetic adverbs* (see Section **84c**); (f) other pertinent *parenthetic phrases* (useful in showing transition between sentences as well as between paragraphs—see Section **11a1**).

In using these transitional words and phrases, remember that the beginnings and endings of sentences are emphatic positions. Pure conjunctions must, of course, come at the beginning of sentences or clauses, subordinate conjunctions and relative pronouns at the beginning of dependent clauses; conjunctive adverbs and parenthetic phrases may come at the beginning of independent clauses, but here and in sentences they add effectiveness by being placed as second or third words.

Special care should be taken when you move from your own writing to quoting or phrasing others' materials. Examples:

. . . As Abraham Lincoln said, in his "Address at Gettysburg," ". . . ." The result is that . . .

Certain lines from Shakespeare's *Julius Caesar* well summarize this philosophy:

In considering ideals over and beyond our vocational activities, let us remember the Bible verse concerning man's need to live by more than bread alone.

### 42b   Make sentence transitions clear by repetition of nouns and by use of pronouns

The most effective kind of repetition for sentence transitions is the use of pronouns referring to preceding nouns and pronouns. Synonyms are also effective. Occasionally, too, key or important words can be repeated in several sentences, but such repetition for sentence transition is not nearly so effective as it is for paragraph transition.

In the following sentences, from the first two paragraphs of Thomas Henry Huxley's "The Method of Scientific Investigation," the italicized words illustrate the various devices for sentence transition.

The method of scientific investigation is nothing but the expression of the necessary mode of working of the human mind. *It* is *simply* the *mode* at which all phenomena are reasoned about, rendered precise and exact. . . .

You will understand *this better, perhaps, if* I give *you* some familiar example. *You* have all heard it repeated, *I* dare say, that *men of science* work by means of *induction and deduction, and* that by the help of *these operations, they,* in a sort of sense, wring from nature certain *other* things which are called natural laws and causes, and that out of *these,* by some cunning skill of *their* own, *they* build up hypotheses and theories. *And* it is imagined by many that the operations of the common mind can be *by no means* compared with *these processes, and* that *they* have to be acquired by a sort of special apprenticeship to the craft. To hear *all these* large words *you* would think that the *mind* of *a man of science* must be constituted differently from *that* of *his* fellow men; *but if you* will not be frightened by terms, *you* will discover that *you* are quite wrong, *and* that *all these* terrible apparatus are being used by *yourselves* every day and every hour of *your* lives.

### 42c  *Avoid labored and artificial transitions in sentences*

The major purpose of transitions is to show relationship and the direction of relationship; a secondary but not unimportant aim is to make evident this relationship smoothly, skillfully, and unobtrusively.

In this example, transitions are needed between short choppy sentences and clauses:

Baseball is said to be the national game; I do not like it. If it is the national game, thousands must enjoy watching it, or playing it. I know people who do not ever attend a game; I know people who see as many as 50 games a year. I should not make a dogmatic statement about the appeal of the sport; I have never witnessed a game.

In a first revision, the student conspicuously inserted transitional words and phrases, here italicized, at the beginning of each sentence or independent clause, as follows:

Baseball is said to be the national game; *however,* I do not like it. *Yet* if it is the national game, thousands must enjoy watching it, or playing it. *To be sure,* I know people who do not ever attend a game; *on the other hand,* I know people who see as many as 50 games a year. *Perhaps* I should not make a dogmatic statement about the appeal of the sport; *you see,* I have never witnessed a game.

After considering Section **47**, "Position and Arrangement," and Section **48**, "Variety," and letting pronouns and repetition serve as part of the transitional devices, the student produced this further revision. Greater clearness and smoothness are gained with the italicized words:

*Although* baseball is said to be America's national game, I do not like *it*. *Yet* if *it* is the *national game,* hundreds must enjoy playing the *game* and thousands must enjoy watching *it*. I know people who see as many as 50 or 60 *games* a season and who drive many miles to see *them;* on the other hand, I know people who never attend a *game* and who wouldn't walk across the street to see *one. Perhaps* it is all a matter of *sporting* taste, *and perhaps* I should not make a dogmatic statement about the appeal of *baseball. You see,* I have never seen a *game, and* I prefer a *sport* that I can take part in, peacefully, quietly, badly perhaps, and without "fan"-fare. *I prefer* golf.

## EXERCISES

A. Copy one long or several short paragraphs of prose (without conversation) from your book of readings. Underline the various devices for transition between sentences and between clauses. Write a brief paragraph (approximately 100 words) commenting on the methods used.

B. Apply the directions in Exercise A to an article in a current magazine.

## 43 *Conciseness*

*Conciseness* literally means "expressing much in a few words; brief and to the point." Logically, therefore, conciseness is primarily a problem in diction, and as such it is discussed in Section **67.** There the discussion concerns words and word combinations in phrases, such as avoidance of superfluous words, unnecessary repetition, reduction of wordy phrases, circumlocutions and euphemisms, and overuse of modifiers. But conciseness is also a problem in writing sentences.

A sentence may be complete and unified and yet be ineffective because it is wordy. A sentence of 100 words may be concise, and one of 20 may be wordy. No sentence can be effective when it contains too many words or ideas—or too few.

In the clear and effective use of "how many words?" the golden mean of word number applies to parts of sentences, to sentences, to paragraphs, to themes. Its guiding suggestion: Do not use so many words that meaning is lost in a forest of verbiage and so few that meaning is obscured through brevity. The problem is one of effectiveness. Wordiness, like long-windedness in speech, is never effective.

In addition to the advice concerning conciseness in word use (Section **67**), two suggestions apply specifically to sentences.

### 43a   Reduce predication

At various places—in this *Handbook* and by your instructor—you are advised to *reduce predication*.

Reducing predication means reducing the number of words to make an assertion, cutting out all unnecessary words by making one word serve the purpose of two or three or more. For example, one synonym can replace several words without jeopardizing in any way the intended meaning. For clearness and effectiveness, a writer will

⟶ 1. Combine two short sentences into one (see also Section **46**):

*From*   I am a freshman in the School of Home Economics. I am specializing in Applied Design.

*To*   I am a freshman in the School of Home Economics, specializing in Applied Design.

⟶ 2. Reduce a compound sentence to a complex or simple sentence:

*From*   Henry H. Abbott has been a leader in campus activities and scholarship, and there is not a student who does not admire and respect him.

*To*   Henry H. Abbott, who has been a leader in campus activities and scholarship, is admired and respected by every other student.

⟶ 3. Reduce a complex sentence to a simple sentence:

*From*   Henry H. Abbott, who has been a leader in campus activities and scholarship, is admired and respected by every other student.

*To*   Henry H. Abbott, a leader in campus activities and scholarship, is admired and respected by every other student.

——→ 4. Reduce clauses to phrases (see preceding example also) :

*From*  . . . a haze which resembled the color of smoke.
*To*    . . . a haze like the color of smoke.

——→ 5. Reduce clauses and phrases to single words:

*From*  . . . waiting until I became frantic.
*To*    . . . waiting frantically.

*From*  . . . a haze like the color of smoke.
*To*    . . . a smoke-colored haze.

——→ 6. Reduce two or more words to one:

*From*  . . . a member of a fraternity.
*To*    . . . a fraternity member.

*From*  . . . an instructor in the Department of Mathematics.
*To*    . . . a mathematics instructor.

*From*  . . . are going to attend.
*To*    . . . will attend.

Study the following series of reductions. In the first statement are 19 words. In the last statement are seven words. Has the last omitted any essential information not included in the first?

1. In the distance we could see the tops of the Rocky Mountains. These mountain tops were covered with snow.
2. In the distance we could see the tops of the Rocky Mountains, which were covered with snow.
3. In the distance we could see the Rocky Mountains, which were covered with snow.
4. In the distance we could see the Rocky Mountains, covered with snow.
5. In the distance we could see the snow-covered Rocky Mountains.
6. In the distance we saw the snow-covered Rocky Mountains.
7. We saw the distant, snow-covered Rocky Mountains.

### 43b Avoid sentences containing unnecessary details

A sentence containing unnecessary details illustrates the fault of *prolixity*, i.e., a long-winded and tiresomely wordy sentence. Since it extends to tedious length, it is ineffective because its details obscure or weaken the point of the main idea.

Last summer the local junior golf tournament was won by my brother Harry with a set of golf clubs that he had purchased two years before from a friend of mine who had bought a new set and who sold the boy his old clubs at a bargain price.

"We want to thank you for your communication letting us know about your change of address, and we are pleased to tell you that we have made the necessary changes on the company records so that we shall send you all future mail at the correct address." (From a life insurance company letter)

Freed of unnecessary details, these sentences say:

Last summer my brother Harry won the local junior golf tournament with a second-hand set of clubs.

"Thank you for sending us your new address. We've noted the change on our mailing lists."

## EXERCISES

A. Look up in a good dictionary the following nouns: *brevity, circumlocution, curtness, diffuseness, periphrasis, pleonasm, prolixity, redundancy, sententiousness, succinctness, tautology, terseness, verbiage, verbosity.* Write expanded definitions of any five (see Sections 17c2a and 24b7).

B. Look up in a good dictionary the following adjectives: *compendious, concise, diffuse, laconic, pithy, prolix, redundant, succinct, summary, terse.* Write expanded definitions of any five (see Sections 17c2a and 24b7).

C. Study several of your recent themes. Can you make them more concise and effective by following the suggestions in Section 43a?

D. Make more concise the following:

1. I remember two things I did that first night of college. They were getting acquainted with my new roommate and watching TV in the dormitory lounge.
2. I waited for the signal which would indicate that the hunt had begun. I did not hear it, however. The dogs were all barking and the horses were stamping their feet. Between the barking of the dogs

and the stamping of the horses all other sounds and noises were drowned out.

3. There are two main highways leading into and going through Brookville. They are Highway 41, running south from Chicago to Florida, and Highway 28, running northeast and southwest.
4. When I arrived at the doctor's office, I noticed that he had a beautiful reception room. The room was furnished with modern furniture and with a warm-colored carpet on the floor and with soft, soothing colors on the walls.
5. Our city now has a new park that was opened not long ago. The land which it occupies was, not long ago, just a piece of swamp and wasteland which has since been drained, filled in, and leveled off.

# 44  Parallelism

*Parallel,* a word from mathematics, in its usual sense means two lines extending in the same direction and at the same distance apart at every point. Teachers of writing have adopted the words *parallelism* and *parallel* to mean "close resemblance, similarity"; that is, when two or more ideas in a sentence are related and serve a similar purpose, they are phrased in the same grammatical form.

When not overused, parallel construction is an excellent device for correctness, clearness, and effectiveness. It shows immediately what ideas are of equal importance; it helps to make sentences grammatically correct; and, appropriately used, it is one means of attaining or contributing to an emphatic, vigorous style.

The simplest form of parallelism is two or more words in a series. Using more complex forms, the writer can make two or more phrases parallel or two or more dependent clauses or two or more independent clauses or two or more sentences or even two or more paragraphs.

*Words*

Henry is *slow* but *thorough.*
The American colors are *red, white,* and *blue.*
My favorite boyhood activities were *hunting, fishing,* and *trapping.*

| | |
|---|---|
| *Phrases* | Both *at home* and *at school* Joe has his mind only on basketball. |
| | Every afternoon my grandfather is at the barber shop *telling yarns about his youth* or *hearing the yarns that his cronies tell.* |
| *Dependent clauses* | I was desperate *when I arrived late on the campus* and *when I found that no desirable rooms were available.* |
| *Independent clauses* | Julius Caesar's most famous statement was this: *"I came, I saw, I conquered."* |
| *Sentences* | Alfred Lord Tennyson was the British poet who wrote lyrics in his early life and dramas in his closing years. Robert Browning was the British poet who wrote dramas in his early career and other forms of poetry in his later life. |

As an effective test for true parallelism, draw lines under the parallel elements. Then draw a corresponding number of lines in parallel form and write the underlined words on them. Examples from the illustrations above:

Every afternoon my grandfather is at the barber shop
   telling yarns about his youth
   or
hearing the yarns that his cronies tell.

Julius Caesar's most famous statement was this:
   I came,
   I saw,
   I conquered.

### 44a   *Sentence elements that are coordinate in rank and meaning should be parallel in structure*

An infinitive phrase should be coordinate with an infinitive phrase, a prepositional phrase with a prepositional phrase, a participial phrase with a participial phrase, a dependent clause with a dependent clause, an independent clause with an independent clause. The principle applies to other kinds of phrases and to similar kinds of words.

| | |
|---|---|
| *Wrong* | He liked to row and playing tennis. |
| *Right* | He liked to row and to play tennis. |
| | *or* |
| | He liked rowing and playing tennis. |
| | |
| *Wrong* | Our Glee Club sings at many school functions, engagements in nearby towns, and concert tours. |
| *Right* | Our Glee Club sings at many school functions, has engagements in nearby towns, and makes other concert tours. |
| | |
| *Wrong* | An all-round student would like to make Phi Beta Kappa and that he might earn a varsity letter. |
| *Right* | An all-round student would like to make Phi Beta Kappa and to earn a varsity letter. |
| | *or* |
| | An all-round student has two ambitions: a Phi Beta Kappa key and a varsity letter. |

Observe how a parallelism diagram helps to distinguish faulty parallelism from true parallelism:

He liked   to row                          to row
        and                            and
        playing tennis.                to play tennis.

Our Glee Club sings at
   many school functions,
   engagements in nearby towns,        sings at many school functions,
   and                                 has engagements in nearby towns,
   concert tours.                       and
                                        makes other concert tours.

An all-round student would like
   to make Phi Beta Kappa                   to make Phi Beta Kappa
   and                                      and
   that he might earn a varsity letter.     to earn a varsity letter.

Absolute parallelism is not always required. In the following the form is not parallel, but the functions are. In the first example, parallel elements are adverbial; in the second, three nouns (two proper, and one common noun with modifier) are parallel.

The second speaker talked *slowly* and *with a slight stammer.*
I saw *John, Henry,* and *a man whom I did not know.*

NOTE: For clearness, parallelism is necessary in outlines: in the sentence outline all coordinate divisions should be sentences; in the topic outline all coordinate divisions should be the same kinds of words, phrases, or clauses. (See Section **6f2**.)

### 44b   Sentence elements following correlative conjunctions should be parallel in form

The four common pairs of correlative conjunctions, *both . . . and, either . . . or, neither . . . nor,* and *not only . . . but also* (see Section **84b**), coordinate and correlate similar ideas. Each member of the pair should be followed *immediately* by the same grammatical form, two similar words, two similar phrases, or two similar clauses.

| | |
|---|---|
| *Faulty* | I *neither* have the time *nor* the inclination to play basketball. |
| | *Either* you can cash your check at the bank *or* at the local bookstore. |
| | The committee requests that you be *either* seated before the beginning of the concert *or* that you wait outside until the conclusion of the first number. |
| *Improved* | I have *neither* the time *nor* the inclination to play basketball. |
| | You can cash your check *either* at the bank *or* at the local bookstore. |
| | The committee requests *either* that you be seated before the beginning of the concert *or* that you wait outside until the conclusion of the first number. |

Parallelism diagram:

I have neither the time
     nor     the inclination to play basketball.

You can cash your check either at the bank
                         or     at the local bookstore.

The committee requests either that you be seated before the beginning of the concert
                        or     that you wait outside until the conclusion of the first number.

### 44c   Avoid ineffective partial parallelism

In using the formula A, B, and C for a series of elements, make certain that the sentence elements are similar in idea and parallel in form. If they are not, a faulty and unemphatic series will result.

| | |
|---|---|
| *Undesirable* | The story is *vivid, interesting,* and *has a simple plot.* |
| *Improved* | The story is *vivid, interesting, simple in plot.* ⟨ |
| | *or* |
| | The story is *simple, interesting,* and *vivid.* |

| | |
|---|---|
| *Undesirable* | Uncle James has worked *in the steel mills, ordnance plant, a factory,* and *kept a filling station.* |
| *Improved* | Uncle James has worked in *the steel mills, an ordnance plant,* and *a factory;* he has also kept a filling station. |

Parallelism diagrams:

| | |
|---|---|
| *Showing error* | The story is vivid, |
| | interesting, |
| | and |
| | has a simple plot. |
| *Showing corrections* | Uncle James has worked in the steel mills, |
| | an ordnance plant, |
| | and |
| | a factory; |
| | he has also kept a filling station. |

## 44d   Avoid misleading parallelism

Use the same structural form only for sentence elements of equal value. Apparent parallelism misleads in two ways:

1. Certain ideas are arranged in parallel form, but they are neither parallel nor coordinate in content; little logical relationships exists in the ideas expressed. Example (second idea not related to first) :

My roommate's brother recently bought a new British sports model car imported directly from England and manufactured in one of the Midland counties of that country.

Example (third idea not parallel in thought with the first two ideas) :

The speaker pointed out that college graduates have more earning power, enjoy a higher social status, and do not care very much about intercollegiate athletics after they graduate.

2. A series of elements may appear to modify the same element when really not parallel. Two phrases or two clauses may begin with the same words, but they do not introduce parallel elements of ideas. Apply the parallelism diagram as a test.

*Dubious*      *For* your traveling convenience *for* a small fee, you can obtain an internationally valid credit card.

It is important *that* each of you bring along a prospective member *that* you can wholeheartedly recommend.

*Improved*    To help you travel conveniently, you can obtain, for a small fee, an internationally valid credit card.

It is important that each of you bring along a prospective member whom you can wholeheartedly recommend.

## EXERCISES

A. Make parallelism diagrams for all parallel elements in the following passages, each of which is from the work of a master of English prose:

1. The world will little note nor long remember what we say here, but it can never forget what they did here. It is for us, the living, rather, to be dedicated here to the unfinished work which they who fought here have thus far so nobly advanced. It is rather for us to be here dedicated to the great task remaining before us; that from these honored dead we take increased devotion to that cause for which they gave the last full measure of devotion; that we here highly resolve that these dead shall not have died in vain; that this nation, under God, shall have a new birth of freedom; and that government of the people, by the people, for the people, shall not perish from the earth.

—ABRAHAM LINCOLN, "Address at Gettysburg"

2. Studies serve for delight, for ornament, and for ability. Their chief use for delight, is in privateness and retiring; for ornament, is in discourse; and for ability, is in the judgment and disposition of business. For expert men can execute, and perhaps judge of particulars, one by one; but the general counsels, and the plots and marshalling of affairs, come best from those that are learned. To spend too much time in studies is sloth; to use them too much for ornament, is affectation; to make judgment wholly by their rules, is the humour of a scholar.

—FRANCIS BACON, "Of Studies"

B. Correct all errors in faulty parallelism in the following sentences. Except where correlative conjunctions are involved, (1) change the structure of the first element to agree with that of later ones and then (2) change the structure of later elements to agree with that of the first.

1. The morning was dark, cold, and there was a little snow in the air.
2. This could be the reason why I did not like my teacher and she not liking me.
3. Mr. Bennet was not only a failure as a husband, but as a father as well.
4. Mary is a cute 5 feet, 5 inches tall, auburn hair, blue eyes, and full of enthusiasm.
5. My father said that I could drive the car and to be careful because the tires were in bad shape.
6. In registering, the student often finds that the classes he wanted are either full or cannot be fitted into his time schedule.
7. There are girls in my dorm who got average grades in high school and getting above average grades now.
8. St. Francis intended to found a society of men desiring to return to the manners of the primitive church and who would profess absolute poverty.
9. Since it was Easter, and because of the many flowers in bloom, the explorer decided to give the area the name of Florida.
10. In careless driving, the driver not only risks the life of his own passengers, but also the lives of others.
11. Students use a dictionary for the following reasons: word meaning, spelling, pronunciation, and to find names of places and people.
12. He is neither honest nor can he be relied upon.
13. Some of the worries and responsibilities that go along with management are labor problems, maintaining efficient production, and above all to increase profits for the firm.
14. He not only works hard on his lessons but also on extracurricular projects.
15. Mr. Collins' reasons for marrying were as follows: (1) to set an example to his parishioners; (2) because it would make him happy; and (3) his having been advised to marry by a noble lady.

# 45   Consistency

*Consistency* in a sentence or in a series of sentences means that two or more elements agree and remain similar unless a good reason exists for shifting. To write appropriately and effectively, be consistent in tense, voice, mood, pronoun reference (number and person) , and diction.

*45a   Be consistent in the use of tense*  (see Section **80d**)

*45b   Be consistent in the use of subject and voice in a sentence*  (see Section **81c**)

*45c   Be consistent in the use of mood or mode*  (see Section **82d**)

*45d   Be consistent in the use of number*
Frequent errors in inconsistent use of number are shifts from singular nouns to plural nouns or plural nouns to singular or failure to make pronouns and antecedents agree in number (see Section **77**) .

*Faulty*     People in college should be mature, and, as such, *a student* should accept *their* responsibilities.
            If an intelligent *man* works hard, *they* will usually succeed.
*Correct*    People in college should be mature, and, as such, *students* should accept *their* responsibilities.
            If an intelligent *man* works hard, *he* will usually succeed.

For consistency in use of collective nouns with pronouns and predicates, see Section **77c**.

*45e   Be consistent in the use of the class or person of pronouns*
A shift in pronoun reference violates the general principle that pronouns and antecedents agree in person (see Section **77**) . The most frequent occurrence of the error is in shifting from the third person to the inappropriate second person *you*. (See also Section **14a**.)

*Faulty*     If *one* studies hard enough in high school, *you* will have no trouble with college subjects.

*Correct*    If *one* studies hard enough in high school, *he* will have no
trouble with college subjects.

### 45f  *Be consistent in your diction*

Keep in mind the general level and tone of your writing, the
kind of reader you are writing for, and the nature of your subject. For example, do not mix slang or colloquialisms with formal
literary language or with dignified informal writing, as in a
letter of application. On the other hand, in a friendly, chatty letter to your family or friends, don't use the longest and most
literary words you can find. (See Sections **53, 56, 57, 62, 63, 68.**)
Use appropriate diction and use it consistently.

## EXERCISES

Rewrite the following sentences, making them conform to principles of consistency.

1. Taking drugs to keep awake retards rather than quicken the mind.
2. Finally our destination was reached, and, as the bus door opened,
   all 20 of us eagerly climbed out.
3. After I had had several tranquilizing pills, three men came in with
   one of those beds to transport you to the operating room.
4. Offices of advertising agencies began at 23rd Street; the garment
   industry begins at 37th Street.
5. Today I began preparing to leave for college, and several tasks had
   to be performed in preparation for my leaving.
6. When I feel bitter, taking your spite out on a golf ball is better
   than taking it out on your friends.
7. He was a far different man when he returns than he was when he
   started.
8. When people have the same likes and dislikes, more fun can be had
   by all.
9. In high school or college, a student should not take easy courses if
   they want to get the best education possible. Besides, you learn
   more from the more difficult courses if you work at it.
10. When one enters Colorado from the east, he would think it to be
    another state of plains.
11. A student may spend too much time in activities, and before long
    college will become an obligation that has to be met by him.
12. The British middle class was conscious of their social positions and
    were constantly trying to improve it.

13. There is no sense in a person's buying a dictionary that does not meet your needs.
14. I must regulate myself with a strict schedule so that valuable time will not be lost.
15. If one were not fortunate to be born in the upper classes in ancient Rome, you did not have a life of much promise.

# 46   Choppy sentences and clauses

### 46a   Avoid writing a series of short, jerky sentences

An occasional short sentence is effective, but a series of short sentences conveys a sense of choppiness and jerkiness, violating unity, clearness, effectiveness, even appropriateness. Such a series is monotonous; it gives undue emphasis to relatively unimportant ideas. Give thought to the relationship of ideas and then coordinate or subordinate them properly in a longer, unified sentence (see Sections **36, 37**) .

*Faulty*      Mulberry is a small town in Clinton County. It is in the northwestern part of Indiana. It is located 10 miles west of Frankfort and 15 miles east of Lafayette on State Road 38. It has a population of about 1050. It is an incorporated town and is governed by a local town board. It boasts a city water works, a volunteer fire department, and a public library. It has its own newspaper, *The Reporter,* published weekly.

*Improved*    Mulberry, a small town in Clinton County in northwestern Indiana, is located 10 miles west of Frankfort and 15 miles east of Lafayette on State Road 38. With a population of about 1050, it is an incorporated town, governed by a local town board. It boasts a city water works, a volunteer fire department, a public library, and its own newspaper, *The Reporter,* which is published weekly.

### 46b   Avoid writing a series of sentences containing short, jerky independent clauses

You cannot eliminate a series of short, jerky sentences by combining them into compound sentences with independent clauses joined by pure conjunctions and conjunctive adverbs or separated by semicolons. Such a series of short clauses is also ineffective. As a writer mindful of your reader, you should apply to such choppy clauses the principles of coordination and subordination (see Sections **36, 37**) .

*Faulty*  Mt. Vesuvius is a volcano in southern Italy; it is not very far from Naples. Sometimes the volcano is active; sometimes it is not. During its more or less quiet periods, many people come to Naples to visit it. The visitor has several choices to ascend the sides of the volcano; then he can visit the base of the new but smaller cone. From Naples he can go by train; many people do. He can go by bus; many people do (the bus may be publicly operated or it may be part of a private tourist excursion) . Or he can take a taxi; this method is for the more affluent.

From the base of the huge volcano itself, there were, when Mother and I were there, two ways to reach the volcano cone: one was by cable car, the other was by car and foot. Mother and I chose the latter. The road was under construction; once we had to wait for a load of stone to be unloaded before we could pass.

We finally reached the end of the road. Here we hired a guide to take us to the cone. The path we followed was very narrow and steep; in fact, it was so steep that the guide put a belt over his shoulder, and Mother held on to it as we climbed.

From the cone, looking down the side of the mountain, we could see the black lava from the last eruption; it had destroyed many houses. The strange thing was that the people had rebuilt their houses on the lava. This kind of reasoning I cannot understand.

Mother was much too scared to enjoy the scenery from the cone, but I thoroughly enjoyed it, and she remembers the trip as a great experience.

—Student theme, "To the Top of Mt. Vesuvius"

*Improved*  Mt. Vesuvius is a volcano, sometimes active, sometimes not, in southern Italy, not very far from Naples. During its more or less quiet periods, many people come to Naples to visit it. Visitors have several choices to visit the base of the volcano. Some go by taxi, a method used by the more affluent; many go by public bus or on a private tourist bus; and many more go by train, the method Mother and I chose.

Of the two ways to reach the cone, one by cable car and the other by car and foot, Mother and I chose the latter. The road was under construction, and once we had to wait for a load of stone to be unloaded before we could pass. When we reached the end of the road, we hired a guide to take us to the cone. The path we followed was very narrow and steep, so steep, in fact, that the guide put a belt over his shoulder for Mother to hold to as we climbed.

From the cone, looking down the side of the mountain, we could see the black lava from the last eruption, which had destroyed many houses. The strange thing was that the people had rebuilt their houses on the lava, because of a process of reasoning that I could not understand.

Mother was much too scared to enjoy the scenery from the cone, but I thoroughly enjoyed it. We both remember the trip as a great experience.

## EXERCISES

A. Combine the following groups of sentences into complex, compound, or compound-complex sentences:

1. Not far from Rocky Mountain National Park is Mt. Evans. It is 14,260 feet high.
2. South of the plains region is the hill country of our state. This region is made up of rolling hills interlaced with deep valleys.
3. Next semester I plan to do some clerical work. This will be a way to earn some spending money. I feel it will make me budget my time.
4. Many magazines flood the literature market of today. These range from magazines about sports to magazines about electronics.
5. It was a cold, crisp, and windy Saturday afternoon. The ice was hard, clear, and snow-free. It was one of those rare winter days in northern Ohio. Conditions were perfect for ice-skating.

B. Rewrite the following paragraphs in order to eliminate the short, choppy, jerky sentences. Paragraph unity may also need attention.

1. There are certain things which those who get good grades usually have in common. They are good listeners. They are well-read. They

have a broad range of interests. They are energetic and ambitious. They are skillful at taking notes. They have good memories.

2. The house I shall describe is located on an 80-acre plot of land north of the city. The entire estate is surrounded by a high steel fence. There is only one entrance. It has two steel gates. They resemble the entrance to a cemetery. There is a long, narrow drive. It leads back to several large barns. A second fence surrounds the house. From this fence you can see the house and the lights from it. They seem to be blue. To get a closer view, one must climb the fence. This is not advised. There are Saint Bernards waiting on the other side.

3. The card catalog is very helpful. The card catalog is at the head of the stairs on the second floor. All the cards are white. They are 3 by 5 inches in size. The cards are arranged in alphabetical order. Important things to know are the author's name and the title of the book. Otherwise, a subject heading should be used to find these. Knowing these three things, one can use any card catalog efficiently. All the books are alphabetized in the card catalog. Each has a number in the upper left-hand corner. This number on the card corresponds to the same number on the spine of the book. Cards in the card catalog sometimes give a very brief idea of the content of the book. So the card catalog plays a very important part in the library. It is invaluable to the user.

# 47 Position and arrangement

In addition to applying the suggestions for emphatic diction (Section **64**), for correct, clear, and effective word arrangement (Sections **39–42** and **44**), and for proper coordination and subordination (Sections **36, 37**), give careful attention to the position and arrangement of words in sentences, since effectiveness can also be attained by arrangement for maximum impressiveness. Naturally, not all words or ideas in a sentence are of equal importance; consequently, place the elements of your thought so that relatively unimportant items will remain in the background and important ones will achieve prominence.

### 47a   Place strong and relatively important words and ideas at the beginning or end of a sentence

The conspicuous and emphatic parts of a sentence and of independent clauses are the beginning and end. Like other first and last impressions, they are remembered. Sentences should usually be built with the most important idea at the beginning or end, places where the attention of the reader is most keen. Remember, also, that transitional words and phrases, although seemingly colorless, are important and frequently deserve near-beginning positions (see Section 42) . On the other hand, prepositions, pure conjunctions, and many other parenthetical expressions are usually not pivotal or important words and usually should not begin a sentence.

| | |
|---|---|
| *Ineffective* | In effect, what you are saying will improve the morale of our campus. |
| | The operation was a long and delicate one. However, Mother will recover, the physician says. |
| | These are the dormitories which the women students live in. |
| | Mrs. Brown is the only person here whom we haven't spoken to. |
| *Improved* | What you are saying will improve, in effect, the morale of our campus. |
| | The operation was a long and delicate one; however, the physician says that Mother will recover. |
| | These are the dormitories in which the women students live. |
| | Mrs. Brown is the only person here to whom we haven't spoken. |

Placing prepositions at the end of sentences is not grammatically wrong, nor is there any question of clearness. The problem is solely one of effectiveness—a weak word in a strong, emphatic sentence position. Hence, the joking rule which violates its suggestion:

| | |
|---|---|
| | A preposition is a weak word to end a sentence with. |
| *Improved* | A preposition is a weak word with which to end a sentence. |

Remember, however, Sir Winston Churchill's famous reply to those who objected to his use of prepositions at the end of sentences:

This is the kind of thing up with which I don't intend to put.

A newspaper columnist once wrote to someone who had criticized his ending a sentence with a preposition; perhaps inadvertently, he also illustrated the weakness of such sentence endings:

What do you take me for? A chap who doesn't know how to make full use of all the easy variety the English language is capable of? Don't you know that ending a sentence with a preposition is an idiom many famous writers are very fond of? They realize it's a colloquialism a skillful writer can do a great deal with. Certainly it's a linguistic device you ought to read about.[1]

### 47b  Use periodic sentences to secure emphasis

For discussion of the effectiveness of periodic, loose, and balanced sentences, see Section 74c.

### 47c  Arrange ideas in the order of their importance so as to secure climax

Sentence climax means arranging a series of ideas in a sentence so that each succeeding idea has greater force than its predecessor. The idea implied or expressed by the phrase "last and most important" is a fair statement of the order of climax. Consider the following:

| | |
|---|---|
| *Unemphatic* | For months I looked forward to college with anxiety, fear, excitement, and interest. |
| *Improved* | For months I looked forward to college with interest, anxiety, excitement, and fear. |
| *Unemphatic* | Some of my teachers have been bad, some excellent, some indifferent, and some fair. |
| *Improved* | Some of my teachers have been bad, some indifferent, some fair, and some excellent. |

[1] *Word Study,* April, 1949.

*Unemphatic*     Children are often frightened by storms: the crashing of the thunder, the pouring of the rain, the vivid flashes of lightning, and the steady blowing of the wind.

*Improved*     Children are often frightened by storms: the steady blowing of the wind, the pouring of the rain, the vivid flashes of lightning, and the crashing of the thunder.

**47d  Use words out of their natural order, occasionally, as a method of emphasis**

The usual or normal English word order is subject–verb–object or complement, but other arrangements can be used to make the sentence effective. Three frequently used methods are the following:

1. *Inverted word order:* placing the verb or the object or complement before the subject (see Section **48b**) or placing the object before the verb, if not too awkward.

2. *Transposed word order:* placing adjectives after the subject, or, if usual there, placing them before; placing adverbs before the verb; varying the position of parenthetic words, phrases, and sometimes clauses; placing the adverbial clause before the independent clause.

*Normal*     The cold, wet, and weary mountain climbers descended to the base camp.

The dog, alone, was left to guard King Richard's banner.

Our star two-mile runner increased his lead over his opponents steadily, effortlessly, relentlessly.

On the other hand, extending our travels for an additional month in Europe might be too expensive for us.

Can Spring be far behind, if Winter comes?

*Transposed and effective*     The mountain climbers, cold, wet, and weary, descended to the base camp.

Alone, the dog was left to guard King Richard's banner.

Steadily, effortlessly, relentlessly, our star two-miler increased his lead over his opponents.

Extending our travels, on the other hand, for an additional month in Europe might be too expensive for us.

If Winter comes, can Spring be far behind?—Shelley

*3. Suspended or suspensive word order:* placing a phrase, dependent clause, or independent clause between two important elements and thus temporarily suspending complete meaning. (But see Section 41.)

| | |
|---|---|
| *Normal* | Your short story needs considerable revision, to be honest and frank. |
| | Our chances of victory are good, since we have practiced long and hard. |
| | My first Soap Box Derby race came on my 14th birthday. I remember it well. |
| *Suspensive and effective* | Your short story, to be honest and frank, needs considerable revision. |
| | Our chances of victory, since we have practiced long and hard, are good. |
| | My first Soap Box Derby race—how well I remember it—came on my 14th birthday. |

### 47e  Repeat important words to gain sentence emphasis

Faulty repetition should be avoided (see Section **67e,f**), but the effectiveness of many sentences can be increased by repetition of pivotal words. Thus the ideas are driven home. Notice, however, that effective repetition does not occur in one sentence but in a series of sentences.

Study the effect of repetition in the following:

*Give! Give money* when you see that women and children are hungry. *Give* sympathy when you can cheer a beaten man. *Give* time to study conditions in your own community. *Give* your whole self in an attempt to change and better the life of all humanity.

### EXERCISES

A. Study sentence beginnings in any five paragraphs in your book of readings or in a current magazine. How many begin with ineffective words or phrases? How can the sentences be improved?

B. Study sentence endings in any five paragraphs in your book of readings or in a current magazine. How many end with ineffective words or phrases? How can the sentences be improved?

C. Rewrite the following sentences, arranging the ideas in the order of climax:

1. As time went on, she began to love him, then to admire him, and then to like him very much.
2. My father gets and deserves the respect, love, and affection of every member of our family.
3. There have recently been some exciting developments in international, state, cosmic, national, and local affairs.
4. My young brother John now has these ambitions in life: to make a fortune, have a newspaper route, own a dog, get married, and graduate from high school.
5. The basic thing that is needed in the world is love: love of parents, love of God, love of all things good, love of country, love of mankind, love of animals, and love of flowers.

# 48 *Variety*

A series of sentences monotonous in structure is not effective. Your reader tires of a long succession of identical sentences, or nearly identical ones, just as he tires of sameness in anything. Such sentences have been called "ding-dong" sentences—the same structure in sentence after sentence—from the *ding* of a bell followed by the inevitable *dong*. Variety is more than the spice of writing; it is a quality that accurately reflects the mature or immature processes of a mind.

Monotony may be caused by a series of short, simple sentences (see Section 46) ; by a series of sentences in which the arrangement of parts is inevitably subject–verb–object or predicate complement (see Section 48b) ; by a series of compound "seesaw" sentences (Section 36b) ; by a series of sentences beginning with the same word or same kind of phrase or same kind of dependent clause (Section 48a) ; by a series of similarly constructed complex sentences; or by a series of sentences of approximately the same length (Section **48c**) .

Revise sentences to make sure that they have variety. Vary their length and, occasionally, their normal word order. Use declarative, imperative, interrogative, and exclamatory sentences (see Section **49b**) , and use periodic sentences as well as loose sentences (see Sections **49c** and **74c**) . Subordinate ideas and thus construct complex sentences (see Section **37**) to take the place of too many simple and compound sentences.

### 48a Do not begin successive sentences with the same word or phrase or dependent clause

Avoid, whenever possible, outworn beginnings such as *there is, there are, it, this, that, the, he, I,* and *we* or beginning a sentence with the same words that end the previous sentence (Section **67c, 69b**) .

*Awkward*       It was just the kind of trip our high school class had planned. It was just the time of year for the trip. It was the consummation of our four years of planning.

*Improved*      It was just the kind of trip our high school class had planned and just the right time of year for the trip, the consummation of our four years of planning.

*Awkward*       Electronics is a very large and difficult field. Electronics takes in all kinds of electrical behavior and equipment. Electronics was originally just a branch of the communications field but is now a field of its own. Electronics has to do with the conduction of electricity in gases and in certain solid materials.

*Improved*      Electronics, a large and difficult field, takes in all kinds of electrical behavior and equipment. Originally just a branch of the communications field but now a field of its own, it has to do with the conduction of electricity in gases and in certain solid materials.

Do not begin every sentence with a phrase and do not overuse the same kind of phrases (prepositional, participial, prepositional-gerund, absolute, adverbial) as a beginning. Note the monotony of the following:

Having considered going to college, I wrote to various colleges about admission. Receiving their catalogs, I gave them careful study. Deciding that engineering was my major field of interest, I applied for admission at Kansas Tech. Being accepted, I made plans to be on the campus by mid-September. Having carried out these plans, I am now here, writing this orientation theme.

Do not begin every sentence with a dependent clause (a *when, while, if, since, because* clause, etc.) . To begin with a series of dependent clauses is monotonous; to begin these clauses with the same subordinating conjunction is deadly.

Changing the phrases in the faulty example above to dependent clauses is merely changing the grammatical form of the monotony:

When I considered going to college, I wrote to various colleges about admission. After I received their catalogs, I gave them careful study. As soon as I had decided that engineering was my major field of interest, I applied for admission at Kansas Tech. After I was accepted, I made plans to be on the campus by mid-September. Since I have carried out these plans, I am now here, writing this orientation theme.

### 48b   *Do not place the subject at the beginning of every sentence*

The usual or normal English word order, as indicated in Section **47d,** is subject + verb + complement (direct object, object complement, predicate noun, predicate adjective) or subject with modifiers, verb with modifiers, complement with modifiers. The reader expects this usual word order; it is clear but it may not strike his attention.

Deviation from this order avoids monotony, does attract attention, and is emphatic. You can give variety to your sentences, to a series even of simple sentences, by using various beginnings.

⟶ 1. Certain adjective modifiers, usually placed after the subject, being placed before it, instead.

With cold hands and feet, wet clothing, and weary and aching muscles, the mountain climbers descended to the base camp.
Having attained his goal in business, Father is planning to retire.

⟶ 2. Apposition (rare).

A sadder and a wiser man, the Wedding Guest returned home.

⟶ 3. Adverbial word, words, or phrases.

Coldly and cheerlessly, the December evening set in.
During the years of his earnings, a wise man will provide for his future.

⟶ 4. Dependent adverbial clause (a common construction in English).

When a close contest ends, even the spectators are limp and exhausted.

⟶ 5. Correlative conjunctions.

Neither roses nor lilies will be in bloom in time for the flower show.

⟶ 6. Predicate (alone: rare) or phrase and predicate preceding subject.

Came that long-dreaded week of the semester: final examinations.
Over hill and dale roamed the Happy Wanderers.

⟶ 7. Direct object or indirect object preceding subject and verb.

If any, speak; for him have I offended.—SHAKESPEARE, *Julius Caesar*
John we elected captain of the swimming team.

⟶ 8. Predicate complement (usually adjective) preceding subject and verb.

John my name is.
Swift and fleeting are the days of our life.
Fortunate are those who can study with people about them.

⟶ 9. A phrase (forms: absolute, infinitive, participial, prepositional, prepositional-gerund). Examples, in the order given:

The floods having subsided, the people returned to their homes.
To achieve high grades in every course is any student's worthy ambition.
Having thoroughly toured the museum, we felt our time had been well spent.
In the dormitory of our fraternity 30 men have sleeping quarters.
After arriving on the campus, come first to the Welcome Desk in the Administration Building.

NOTE: Some of the foregoing suggestions for effective beginnings of sentences can also be used for effective endings, if they vary the usual word order of subject–verb–object or complement.

## 48c   *Vary the length of successive sentences*

Sentences vary in length from long and medium-long sentences to short sentences of one word or of a few words only. Monotony results when every sentence is approximately the same length. If the sentences are all short, they resemble the writing of a childish or immature person; at best, they give a choppy, jerky effect (Section **46**). The same number of words in a series of medium-long or long sentences is likewise undesirable. Vary the length of your sentences. Twelve to 20 words is a good average. For variety, use an occasional sentence of three or four words, one of 30 or 40. A judicious mixture makes for clearness, interest, emphasis, and effectiveness.

## 48d   *Vary the form of successive sentences*

Not every successive sentence should be simple, complex, compound, compound-complex, periodic, or loose. Sentences of the immature person are likely to be predominantly simple or compound, whereas the work of an effective writer will abound in variety, a judicious mixture of sentences with ideas effectively coordinated and subordinated (see Sections **36** and **37**).

## EXERCISES

A. Make a study of any five paragraphs in five articles in your book of readings or in a current magazine. Prepare a summary report for each five paragraphs, giving the following kinds of information:

1. Number of simple sentences.
   Number of complex sentences.

Number of compound sentences.
Number of compound-complex sentences.

2. Number of sentences.
Number of words in each sentence.
Average length of sentences.
Number of words in longest sentence.
Number of words in shortest sentence.

3. Number of sentences beginning with subject or subject and modifiers.
Number of sentences beginning with inverted order (adverbial phrase, predicate, object, etc.) .
Number of sentences beginning with phrases.
Number of sentences beginning with adverbial clauses.

4. Number of periodic sentences.
Number of loose sentences.

Write a paragraph of comment on each author's use of sentence variety.

B. Apply the methods of A to one of your recent themes. What are your conclusions?

C. Write two or three original sentences illustrating each of the beginnings listed and illustrated in Section **48b.**

D. Write five original sentences with effective endings varying the usual order of subject–verb–object or complement.

E. Rewrite the following paragraphs, improving and varying the sentence beginnings:

1. De Soto is a small town in eastern Indiana. It is approximately seven miles northeast of Muncie, Indiana. De Soto has a population of approximately 100. De Soto's business district consists of a filling station, an elevator, and a small store. De Soto is so close to Muncie that most buying is done there. De Soto is actually becoming a suburb of Muncie, since most of its population are employed in Muncie.

2. I use most of the different sections of my dictionary. I use the pronunciation symbols when I am trying to learn the correct pronunciation of a word. I use the definitions when I see or hear a word I do not know the meaning of. I find the dictionary is invaluable to me for the correct spelling of words. I turn to the abbreviations section when I see an abbreviation in a newspaper, magazine, or other periodicals. I turn to the section on populations to settle many arguments about the

size of different cities, states, and countries. I have seldom used the
section on foreign words and phrases.

3. Around the State Capitol, which is the largest in the country,
is built the city of Austin. Located on a rise of ground, the State Capitol overlooks the Colorado River. Stretching from the Capitol to the
river is Congress Boulevard. Situated along Congress Boulevard are the
large office buildings, department stores, and other business establishments. As the Capitol is the hub of Austin, so Congress Boulevard is the
hub of the Austin business district. Extending on either side of Congress Boulevard for a distance of 10 blocks are all types of businesses.
Once out of the business district, Austin's beautiful residential areas are
encountered. With tree-bordered streets, these are generally clean, well-
kept neighborhoods. Perched on the hills surrounding what is known as
"Old Austin" are large and beautiful modern homes. To the north of
the Capitol, the University of Texas can be seen.


# 49 *Appropriateness: types of sentences*

Appropriateness involves using the most suitable kinds of sentences to convey purpose and meaning clearly and effectively.
Sentences differ in grammatical classification, in meaning and
purpose, in word order and arrangement of ideas, and in length.
A thoughtful, judicious mixture of varying sentences contributes
to a clear and effective style.

But the mixture must be carefully planned; mere variety in
sentence structure is not sufficient to make a paragraph effective.
You should analyze your sentences and, if necessary, rephrase
them to insure not so much their variety as their suitability to
the subject of a given paragraph.

For example, John R. Tunis in a description of a tennis
match wished to convey an impression and tone of almost breathless excitement, of frenzied activity. He wrote these lean, trim,
terse sentences notable for their tonal quality, not for their varying structure:

The Saturday crowd kept coming. Soon all grandstand seats were
gone. A row of standees pushed in behind us. Boxes like ours were valu-

able as more persons lined up. Someone poked my brother in the ribs and offered us a dollar for our perch. One dollar! We gasped. Then we looked back to the street where we'd seen the matches of the first afternoon. The club had erected a high green curtain to shut off the view of the courts. We declined the offer.

Had the author continued to use such brief sentences in an extended series, they would have become both monotonous and inappropriate.

For a contrasting example, if a writer wished to create an atmosphere of mysteriousness, of wonder, of rapt discovery, of dawning awareness in a hushed setting, he would more appropriately construct a series of sentences that seem to swell and roll in a noticeable rhythm, as do these from Joseph Conrad's *Youth*:

And this is how I see the East. I have seen its secret places and have looked into its very soul; but now I see it always from a small boat, a high outline of mountains, blue and afar in the morning; like faint mist at noon; a jagged wall of purple at sunset. I have the feel of the oar in my hand, the vision of a scorching blue sea in my eyes. And I see a bay, a wide bay, smooth as glass and polished like ice, shimmering in the dark. A red light burns far off upon the gloom of the land and the night is soft and warm. We drag at the oars with aching arms, and suddenly a puff of wind, a puff faint and tepid and laden with strange odors of blossoms, of aromatic wood, comes out of the still night—the first sigh of the East on my face. That I can never forget. It was impalpable and enslaving, like a charm, like a whispered promise of mysterious delight.

In short, a group of sentences should be appropriate not only to the ideas being developed but also to the purpose they are intended to fulfill and the effect they are designed to have on readers.

### 49a  Use the appropriate kind of sentences according to grammatical classification

Sentences are classified grammatically as simple, compound, complex, and compound-complex (see Section **74a**) .

1. Are your ideas best expressed in two sentences?

2. Are your ideas best expressed in a simple sentence? With numerous phrases and word modifiers? With a minimum of modifiers?

3. Are your ideas best expressed in a compound sentence?

4. Are your ideas best expressed in a complex sentence?

5. Are your ideas best expressed in a compound-complex sentence?

### 49b   Use sentences appropriate for the expression of meaning and purpose

Declarative, imperative, interrogative, and exclamatory sentences (see Section **74b**) serve specific purposes.

1. Use declarative sentences for statements of fact or condition. They are appropriate for all kinds of narration, description, exposition, and argument.

2. Use imperative sentences for giving directions, giving advice, or addressing someone directly. When you are writing completely from the reader's point of view, and using, as in this sentence, the second person *you,* meaning specifically and directly *your* reader, use imperative sentences.

3. Use interrogative sentences when asking direct questions or rhetorical questions (asked, for effect, of one person or group, but without the expectation of direct answers). A paragraph of such questions can be monotonous, but one or two direct questions in a paragraph of declarative or imperative sentences can be appropriate and effective.

4. Use exclamatory sentences—such as "What a day!"—when they serve interest, emphasis, and effectiveness. Like a series of interrogative sentences, a series of exclamatory sentences is monotonous and ineffective, but an occasional exclamatory sentence, appropriately used, is an excellent means of achieving clearness, interest, and effectiveness.

### 49c   Use the appropriate kinds of sentences for clear and effective arrangement of ideas in sentences

Loose, periodic, and balanced sentences (Section **74c**) serve purposes of appropriate arrangement of ideas.

1. Use loose sentences when important statements or statements making sense come first, followed by less important statements or dependent sentence-elements.

2. Use periodic sentences, not too frequently, when you reserve or suspend the important ideas and independent sentence-element until near the end of the sentence.

3. Use a balanced sentence usually for contrast or comparison of important ideas.

Within the sentence, also, for clear and effective arrangement of ideas, consider the appropriateness of word order (Section 39), parallelism (Section 44), position and arrangement (Section 47), and variety (Section 48).

*49d   Use the most appropriate kinds of sentences*
*according to length*  (see Section 48c)

**EXERCISES**

A. In three paragraphs of an article in your book of readings or in a current magazine, analyze each sentence according to its appropriateness for both subject and reader. Apply the tests suggested above for appropriateness.

B. Apply the directions given in Exercise A to one of your recent themes.

C. Write a paragraph of moderate length. Follow these directions from the beginning to the final stage: first, use only short simple sentences; second, use longer simple sentences; third, change these longer simple sentences to compound sentences; fourth, change the compound sentences to complex sentences; fifth, change the complex sentences to compound-complex sentences; last, choose the most effective sentences and write the most effective final draft possible.

D. Compose five loose sentences of varied structure: fairly short simple sentence, fairly long simple sentence, compound sentence, complex sentence, compound-complex sentence. Rewrite these loose sentences and make them periodic ones.

# 50  Glossary of sentence errors

A survey of the following errors, alphabetically arranged, may aid in checking flaws in your writing and in referring you to more detailed discussion and suggestions for avoiding such errors.

1. "And which, but which, and who, but who."  Joining relative clauses to independent clauses by using a pure con-

junction; i.e., making dependent clauses coordinate with independent clauses—an impossibility. (Section **36d**)

2. Appropriateness, lack of. Failure to use, for clear and effective expression, the appropriate kinds of sentences according to grammatical classification (simple, compound, complex, compound-complex), kinds of meaning and purpose (declarative, imperative, interrogative, exclamatory), kinds of arrangement (loose, periodic, balanced), and length. (Section **49a,b,c,d**)

3. Arrangement. See *Position and arrangement,* Item 29.

4. Blended sentences. See *Fused sentences,* Item 19.

5. Blends, confusing. A mixing of the meaning of overlapping words or phrases or a blending of a direct and indirect question or a direct and indirect quotation. (Section **35c**)

6. Choppy sentences. See *Sentences, choppy,* Item 35.

7. Climax, faulty order of. Failure, in a series of ideas, to arrange the order so that the weakest is put first, next stronger next, and so on, with the strongest last. (Section **47c**)

8. Comma splice or comma fault or illiterate comma. Using a comma between two independent clauses not joined by a pure conjunction or, meaning almost the same, "splicing" two complete sentences with a comma if the second sentence does not begin with a pure conjunction. (Section **32**)

9. Comparisons, mixed, double. Using illogically the grammatical positive and comparative degree of adjectives or adverbs in one single statement or including a member in a group or class and yet as a single member or excluding a member from a group or class in which it belongs. (Section **35d,e,f**)

10. Conciseness, lack of. Using unnecessary or too many words to express ideas clearly, effectively, appropriately—through failure, chiefly, to reduce predication. (Section **43**)

11. Consistency, lack of. Unjustifiable shifting, in a sentence or sentences, of tense, voice, mood, number or the class or person of pronouns. (Section **45a,b,c,d,e**)

12. Constructions, mixed and illogical. Starting a sentence and shifting to a different construction; adding to already complete statements other statements incomplete and leading nowhere; using mixed and confusing "blends," mixed or

double or illogical comparisons, and double negatives. (Section 35a,b,c,d,e,f,g)

13. Coordination, false, inaccurate. Ineffective use of independent clauses in compound sentences: stringy running-on sentences, Item 38; using seesaw sentences, Item 32; joining relative clauses to independent clauses by using pure conjunctions, Item 1; and coordinating clauses with inexact conjunctions. (Section 84a)

14. Dangling elliptical clauses. A dependent clause with its subject and/or predicate omitted because understood from the subject and/or predicate of the independent clause. However, the omitted parts are not the same as those expressed in the independent clause—hence, a dangling elliptical clause. (Section 40c)

15. Dangling verbal phrases. An introductory participial, prepositional-gerund, or infinitive phrase which should modify the subject of the sentence; if the subject is not the noun or pronoun logically and clearly modified, the effect is ludicrous. (Section 40a) Sometimes a participial phrase is tacked on the end of a sentence with *thus, therefore,* or *thereby,* and it dangles without any noun to modify. (Section 40b)

16. Dependent clauses, illogical. The use of noun clauses or adverbial clauses to serve as grammatical parts of speech which they cannot correctly or effectively serve: that is, an adverbial clause used for a single noun, noun phrase, or noun clause; or use of a sentence, instead of a noun clause, to serve as subject of a verb or as predicate complement. (Section 38a,b,c)

17. Double negatives. Using two or more negative words—adverbs, adjectives, nouns—to express a single negative. (Section 35g)

18. Frying pan errors. From "out of the frying pan into the fire"; the correction of one error, like the "comma splice" or the "*so* fault," by making a worse error. (Sections 32a, 36c, 77f)

19. Fused sentences. Two sentences in succession with no mark of punctuation between and with no capital letter to indicate the beginning of the second sentence. (Section 33)

20. Illiterate comma. See *"Comma splice,"* Item 8.

21. Incompleteness of meaning. Grammatically complete sen-

tences which are incomplete or vague in meaning because of omission of needed main verbs, auxiliary verbs, articles, pronouns, prepositions, conjunctions, or words in comparisons; or because of substitution of punctuation marks for necessary words; or because of a telegraphic style. (Section **31d,e,f**)

22. Modifier, misplaced.   A word, phrase, or sometimes a dependent clause so placed in a sentence that it modifies words other than the one it should clearly modify. (Section **39a,b**)

23. Modifier, squinting.   A word, phrase, or sometimes a dependent clause used between two parts of a sentence, so that it could modify either, i.e., squinting or looking in two directions at once. (Section **39c**)

24. Negatives, double.   See *Double negatives,* Item 17.

25. Omission of necessary words.   See *Incompleteness of meaning,* Item 21.

26. Oneness, lack of.   See *Unity, lack of,* Item 47.

27. Parallelism, faulty.   Not using the same grammatical constructions for sentence elements coordinate in rank, such as coordinate words or phrases or clauses. Faulty parallelism frequently occurs after correlative conjunctions or in a series of several sentence elements when one or more are not parallel grammatically with the others. (Section **44a,b,c,d**)

28. Period fault.   See *Sentence fragment,* Item 34.

29. Position and arrangement, ineffective.   Failure to use the following: sentence beginnings and endings for important words and ideas (Section **47a**) ; occasional periodic sentences (Section **47b**) ; order of climax (Section **47c**) ; words out of natural order (Section **47d**) ; repetition of important words (Section **47e**) ; and active voice instead of passive voice (Section **81e**) .

30. Prolixity.   A sentence or sentences containing unnecessary words or unnecessary details. (Section **43b**) See also *Conciseness, lack of.*

31. Punctuation marks vs. words.   Omitting words like subordinating conjunctions and relative pronouns and replacing them by a punctuation mark, usually a comma. (Section **31e**)

32. Seesaw sentences.   An ineffective series of compound sentences, each containing two independent clauses of approximately the same length, whether joined or not by pure conjunctions or conjunctive adverbs. (Section **36b**)

33. Semicolon fault.   Use of a semicolon to separate a dependent clause or a phrase from the complete statement on which each depends for clear meaning. (Sections **31a, 89d**)
34. Sentence fragment, unjustifiable.   A word or group of words not conveying complete sense to the reader and usually not containing a subject and predicate. The error may consist of a dependent clause or one of several kinds of phrases: absolute, appositional, infinitive, participial, prepositional, prepositional-gerund, subject, verb. (Section **31a,b,c**)
35. Sentences, choppy.   A series of short, perhaps simple, sentences, the result being monotonous and jerky reading—analogous to riding a boat on short, choppy waves. (Section **46**)
36. Sentences, rambling.   Sentences having grammatical completeness but violating unity by containing too many details. (Section **34a**)
37. Sentences, running-on.   A form of rambling sentences (see Item 36), consisting usually of a series of short independent clauses separated by semicolons or joined by pure conjunctions or conjunctive adverbs. (Section **36a**)
38. Sentences, stringy.   A series of short independent clauses as if combined or knotted into a string. See *Sentences, rambling,* Item 36, and *Sentences, running-on,* Item 37.
39. Separation of parts, needless.   Unnecessary, unclear, or ineffective separation of the following: parts of a verb phrase; subject and predicate; verb and object; verb and complement; preposition and object; coordinate sentence elements; *to* and the infinitive verb. (Section **41a,b,c,d**)
40. "So" overused.   Monotonous, overfrequent, and therefore ineffective joining of two independent clauses by the conjunctive adverb *so*. (Section **36c**)
41. Split infinitive.   Separating widely and unnecessarily, by adverbs or adverbial phrases, the sign of the infinitive, *to,* and the infinitive verb. (Section **41b**)
42. Stair-step construction.   An independent clause followed by a series of dependent clauses or phrases, each dependent on the one just preceding—somewhat analogous to stairs, where each step is attached to the one just above. (Section **37c**)
43. Subordination, excessive.   Putting a coordinate idea in subordinate form, putting a subordinate idea in a main clause, or writing a series of dependent clauses and phrases with

each depending, respectively, on the material just preceding (*Stair-step construction,* Item 42) . (Section **37a,b,c**)

44. Tautology.   Sentences containing useless or unnecessary repetition of an idea or ideas. (Section **67a**) See also *Conciseness, lack of,* Item 10.

45. Telegraphic style.   A style omitting as many words as possible and yet conveying an understandable message. Not appropriate for formal and informal writing. (Section **31f**)

46. Transition, lack of, or faulty.   Failure to make evident, unobtrusively, the relationship—or bridges, crossings-over—between sentences or clauses by means of transitional words and phrases, use of pronouns, and repetition of key nouns. (Section **42a,b,c,d**)

47. Unity, lack of.   Inclusion of too many details or several unrelated and incongruous ideas in a sentence. (Section **34**)

48. Upside-down subordination.   A somewhat ineffective complex sentence in which the more important idea is in the dependent clause, the less important in the independent clause. (Section **37b**)

49. Variety, lack of.   An ineffective series of sentences monotonous in structure because of the following: similar beginnings of successive sentences; unvarying position of subject at beginning; same length of sentences; same form of sentences; overuse of short sentences; seesaw sentences. (Section **48a, b,c,d**)

50. Word order.   See *Modifier, misplaced,* Item 22, and *Position and arrangement, ineffective,* Item 29.

# THE
# WORD
## (SECTIONS 51-70)

Words are the units of composition, and the art of prose must begin with a close attention to their quality.

—HERBERT READ, *English Prose Style*

# THE
# WORD

THE word is the smallest unit of speech or writing which has meaning by itself. In length, it may vary from one letter (*a, I, T*) to many letters and syllables (e.g., *antidisestablishmentarianism*). Problems with words involve spelling and diction; each is important and difficult.

*Correct spelling* is mandatory in all printed materials; even errors caused only by faulty proofreading are inexcusable. Correct spelling should also be the aim in all longhand writing and typescript, since two or three misspelled words in an otherwise well-written paper are irritating and distracting. Misspelling is therefore looked upon by instructors, employers, business and professional associates, and friends as a serious fault.

*Diction* is the choice of a word or words or groups of words for the expression of ideas. As thus defined, diction applies to both writing and speaking, although "diction" has additional meaning when applied to speech, since it involves enunciation, voice control, and voice expression. From the Latin *dictio,* meaning "saying, word," the root *dict* adds meaning to words like *dictaphone, dictate, dictator, dictionary, dictograph,* and *dictum.*

Words are the most important medium for communicating thought from one person to another. Compare, for example, word use with other communication media like painting, sculpture, architecture, music, and dancing. Because many different ideas can be expressed in many different shades of meaning and emphasis, with many words to choose from, and because many errors in word choice need to be avoided, students frequently maintain that diction is the most difficult part of composition to master.

The following sections will help you improve your diction. Section **51** introduces you to your dictionary. Section **70**, "Glossary of Diction," with perhaps more discussion and illustration than your dictionary gives, contains a list of common errors in the use of specific words and phrases. The other sections, from **52** through **69**, deal with *appropriateness, correctness, clearness,* and *effectiveness:*

**APPROPRIATENESS IN THE USE OF WORDS**—Section **53**

**CORRECTNESS IN THE USE OF WORDS**

Spelling—Section **52**
Illiteracies—Section **54**
Improprieties—Section **55**
Slang—Section **56**

**CLEARNESS IN WORD CHOICE**

National diction—Section **57**
Foreign words and phrases—Section **58**
Contemporary diction—Section **59**
Neologisms—Section **60**
Technical words—Section **61**
Idiomatic English—Section **62**

**EFFECTIVENESS IN WORD CHOICE**

Exact and precise diction—Section **63**
Emphatic diction—Section **64**
Figurative language—Section **65**
Freshness—Section **66**
Conciseness—Section **67**
Gobbledygook and jargon—Section **68**
Euphony—Section **69**

Some of these sections simultaneously deal with appropriateness, correctness, clearness, and effectiveness. For example, incorrect idiomatic usage can be neither clear nor effective; figurative language is clear and effective, but mixed figures are incorrect, ineffective, and vague in meaning; exact and precise diction is not only clear but also effective and correct. The outline above, therefore, may be useful in keeping your attention focused on important principles.

# 51  Using the dictionary

To write and speak competently, you need as an indispensable guide a reliable dictionary. If you have not done so yet, make the acquaintance of your dictionary *now*. Better still, make it your friend. Best of all, make it your constant companion. To paraphrase the advice of Samuel Johnson, the great lexicographer, about learning to write well: "Give your days and nights to wise study of your dictionary."[1]

## 51a  Choose a reliable dictionary

An appeal to "*the* dictionary" as an authority is as illogical as saying, "Don't buy me a book; I already have one," or "It must be so; I saw it in print." Dictionaries may be good, mediocre, or bad. Some, like a pocket dictionary, are so small that they are virtually worthless except as a limited guide to spelling, to one simple meaning, and perhaps to pronunciation. Others, of fair size, may be so hastily and carelessly produced that they are unreliable. Even the name "Webster," no longer copyrighted, appears alike on both reliable and unreliable dictionaries.

Choose and *buy* a dictionary which you, your bookstore, and your instructors can trust to give satisfactory answers to these questions:

⟶ 1. Has this dictionary been recently published or recently revised?
⟶ 2. Is it kept up-to-date? (Look for the latest copyright date on the back of the title page.)
⟶ 3. What are the qualifications of those who compiled and edited it and of those who served as advisers or contributors?

---

[1] "Whoever wishes to attain an English style, familiar but not coarse, and elegant but not ostentatious, must give his days and nights to the volumes of Addison."—Samuel Johnson, "Addison," *Lives of the English Poets*, World's Classics Edition (London, New York, and Toronto: Oxford University Press, 1906), I, 466. (An example of Addison's writing is on pp. 26–27.)

——→ 4. What is the reputation of the company that publishes it?

——→ 5. Is it sufficiently large (approximately 100,000 or more entries)?

——→ 6. Does it contain adequate directions for its easy and effective use?

——→ 7. Is the information concerning words adequate and satisfactory, i.e., accurate and clear? (See Section 51c)

——→ 8. Is the other information in prefatory and supplementary pages useful and satisfactory? (See Section 51d)

Other desirable features or tests are attractive covers, clear type, printing on readable paper, convenience in handling, and favorable judgments of competent critics.

Five reliable and recommended desk dictionaries, with abbreviated titles in preceding parentheses, are:

(ACD)    *The American College Dictionary.* (New York: Random House)

(RHDC)   *The Random House Dictionary of the English Language.* College Edition. (New York: Random House)

(SCD)    *Funk & Wagnalls Standard College Dictionary.* Text Edition. (New York: Harcourt, Brace & World, Inc.)

(WNWD)   *Webster's New World Dictionary of the American Language.* College Edition. (Cleveland and New York: The World Publishing Company)

(W7NC)   *Webster's Seventh New Collegiate Dictionary.* (Springfield, Massachusetts: G. & C. Merriam Company)

These dictionaries are somewhat comparable in quality, size, and price. All have similar materials, yet each has one or more features—its "sales differential"—that one of or all the others do not possess, as a glance at the table of contents shows. But each should admirably serve the needs of most intelligent adults— both as undergraduates and graduates.

Excellent larger dictionaries, fairly expensive and fairly bulky, and containing much more information, are usually found for reference in libraries, study centers, classrooms, and offices:

*New Standard Dictionary of the English Language.* Unabridged. (New York: Funk & Wagnalls Company, Inc.)

*The Random House Dictionary of the English Language.* The Unabridged Edition. (New York: Random House)

*Webster's Third New International Dictionary of the English Language.*
   Unabridged. (Springfield, Massachusetts: G. & C. Merriam Company)

More for scholarly language and linguistic reference than for everyday use is the *Oxford English Dictionary,* or OED, reissued in a
corrected edition in 1933 in 12 volumes and a supplement (Oxford:
The Clarendon Press). The *Concise Oxford Dictionary* (COD) is based
on OED.

### 51b   Learn the general use of your dictionary

A reliable dictionary is a guide to use of English. It is an "authority" in the sense that it *records* and *interprets* English words
and phrases, according to literally thousands, perhaps millions,
of case-studies. The occasional use of a word in print—in advertisements, newspapers, magazines, even in well-considered books
by famous writers—or misuses and mispronunciations of words by
respected speakers or on radio and TV broadcasts do not make a
word, an expression, a pronunciation generally acceptable.

   Even entry in a reliable dictionary does not guarantee that
the word is in good use or that special meanings of the word are
appropriate in current English. Such words or meanings have
been recorded because they have been or are being frequently
used. Your dictionary, then, does not legislate, dictate, or pre-
scribe: it indicates what is *general* language practice, both acceptable and unacceptable. When you have specific or particular
problems about usage, apply in your own writing and speaking
the general information which the dictionary has recorded and
interpreted.

   In initiating and developing friendship with your dictionary,
turn first to the table of contents to see what kinds of information
and materials the editors have included. Examine the insides of
the front and back covers. At least skim the prefatory pages, as
well as any supplementary materials at the back. Next, read
carefully any tables or editorial sections—or included articles that
enable you to use the book more effectively.

### 51c   Master the variety of information given for word entries

To utilize your dictionary profitably, make the following pages
*must* reading:

ACD: inside front covers and p. xxviii, "Explanatory Notes," then pp. xix–xxvi.

RHDC: inside front covers and pp. xxii–xxxi, "A Guide to the Dictionary."

SCD: inside front covers and pp. xxii–xxvi, "The Plan of This Dictionary."

WNWD: inside front covers and pp. ix–xiv, "Guide to the Use of the Dictionary."

W7NC: inside front cover and pp. 7a–14a, "Explanatory Notes"; p. 15a, "Pronunciation Symbols," and pp. 16a–21a, "A Guide to Pronunciation."

Also, (1) be sure to find the page or pages giving time-saving abbreviations and their meanings: countries, languages, grammatical terms, usage labels, specialized fields, and the like, and (2) be sure to understand the typographical symbols used: the centered dot, accent marks, hyphens, parentheses, brackets, slanted lines or reversed virgules, and the like.

To help you visualize the wealth and variety of useful, valuable information, each of the recommended-desk-dictionary publishers has available a one- or two-page composite specimen well worth study, as a tangible guide to this wealth and variety.[2]

With these guides you should have little trouble mastering the variety of information given for each of the 100,000 or more word entries. Summarized, this information includes the following:

### 1. VOCABULARY ENTRY

The basic or "entry" word is emphasized by being in black type at the left margin. How is information about the word entry arranged: pronunciation, definitions, word-origin, synonyms? Run-on entries—the word with suffixes—may be in the same paragraph. Does the main alphabetical list include abbreviations, foreign words, names of people, names of places, and the like, or are these entered in separate sections?

### 2. SPELLING

In addition to one or a dominant form, the entry word, spelling includes any variant spellings, capitals for proper nouns and ad-

[2] ACD: in *Using the Dictionary: A Study Guide*; RHDC: in *A Student Guide to the Random House Dictionary of the English Language, College Edition*; SCD: inside back cover; WNWD: reverse side of paper jacket attached to cover; W7NC: *A New Outline for Dictionary Study*.

jectives, word combinations when written solid or hyphenated
or as two words, and any spelling change when a letter or letters
are dropped or added—as in plurals of nouns, the principal parts
of verbs, the present participle, the form for the third-person-
singular-present of verbs, and the comparative and superlative
degree of adjectives and adverbs.

**3.  SYLLABICATION**

In division of words into syllables, note the marks used, usually a
centered dot; does or when does an accent mark replace the dot?
Note hyphens in compound words. Use syllabic information to
help pronounce words—and so to aid in spelling—and to divide
words if division is needed at ends of lines.

**4.  PRONUNCIATION**

In pronunciation, with 26 letters of the alphabet, some 45 to 65
sounds, and 250 common spellings of sounds, you need all the
help your dictionary can give. Note the respelling-as-pronounced
form after the main entry. Refer as needed to the main pronunciation key and to its more frequently used items (usually inside
the cover or at the bottom of each right-hand page) . For foreign
sounds, your dictionary may have a separate key. For accent or
stress, learn which marks are used for primary stress, which for
secondary stress, and what dieresis (¨) means. Finally, note alternative pronunciations and any label about them.

**5.  PART(S) OF SPEECH (FUNCTIONAL USE
    OF WORDS) AND INFLECTED FORMS**

Every word in English is, in grammatical terms, a "part of
speech," and in some meanings or uses a word serves as two or
more parts of speech. The traditional grammatical terminology
is used by all five desk dictionaries (as well as by the larger dictionaries listed on pp. 307–308) . Information is also given about
the regular and irregular plurals of nouns, various regular and irregular verb changes, and the degrees of adjectives and adverbs.
    To give adequate information about the eight parts of
speech, your dictionary lists some 50 traditional grammatical
labels, sometimes spelled out, sometimes abbreviated and explained in the list of abbreviations. Such a list is a reminder that
some knowledge of traditional grammar and grammatical terms

is necessary for intelligent and effective use of the dictionary (see sections in this *Handbook* on "Grammar," especially Section **85**) .

### 6.  MEANINGS OR DEFINITIONS

Learn the following about the definitions: (a) their meanings of the same word as different parts of speech; (b) their main classifications, their subclassifications, and the method of so indicating; (c) their method or order of arrangement (by historical development, by frequency of occurrence, or by general to specialized meanings) ; (d) the method of entry for capitalized and small-letter words; and (e) the treatment of homographs and homophones.

For any given word, choose the meaning that fits your writing or reading purpose, since words may have one or more of the following meanings: historical meaning, traditional meaning, figurative meaning, or new meaning.

Hyphenated words and two or more words forming phrases which have idiomatic, specialized, or figurative meaning are explained in the regular alphabetical listing, either entered separately or put under the main word.

> **lock away,** to store or safeguard in a locked box, container, etc.
> **lock out,**  1. to shut out by or as by locking the door against. 2. to keep (workers) from a place of employment in an attempt to make them accept the employer's terms.
> **lock, stock, and barrel,** [Colloq.], completely.
> **lock up,**  1. to fasten the doors of (a house, etc.) by means of locks. 2. to enclose or store in a locked container.  3. to put in jail.
> **under lock and key,** locked up; safely put away.

From Webster's *New World Dictionary* of the American Language, College Edition, copyright 1966 by The World Publishing Company.

### 7.  LEVELS AND LABELS OF USAGE

Your dictionary enables you to judge the acceptability of a word by the absence or presence of a restrictive label, perhaps pertaining to the word in all its uses and meanings or perhaps to only some of these. Any word not accompanied by a restrictive label or explanatory comment is or should be appropriate in formal and informal English, and any word or phrase labeled "colloquial" or "informal" is generally acceptable in *all* informal speech and writing. (See Section **53.**) All other labels are guides to special appropriateness of word use.

Four classifications of restrictive labels are common:

a. *Geographical,* indicating a country or section of a country where the word is common: *Chiefly U.S., British, Scotch, New England, Southern, Southwest, Western U.S., dialect,* etc. It is not surprising that geographical labels are necessary, for English is the native language of nearly 300,000,000 people in various parts of the world, and it is a second language for one-third to one-half more.

b. *Time,* indicating that the word is no longer used, is disappearing from use, or is still used but has a quaint form or meaning: *obsolete, archaic.* (See Section 59.)

c. *Subject,* indicating that a specialized word or a specialized meaning belongs to a restricted department of knowledge like science, technology, trade, profession, sport, and the like.

d. *Cultural,* indicating whether the word or a special use is substandard or acceptable as informal or formal English: *illiterate, slang, dialect* (may be geographical also) , *colloquial, poetic, literary.* A foreign word or phrase not Anglicized will also bear its language label. (See Sections 53, 54–56, 58.)

NOTE: No Supreme Court in language exists to which final appeal can be made. Lexicographers can only use their best judgment in compiling and interpreting language data. Dictionaries may differ, therefore, in the labels they attach to certain words or certain meanings. For example, the same word in several dictionaries may have the label "obsolete," "archaic," "dialect," or even no qualifying label at all. Remember also that some dictionaries are more permissive than others, and hence differ, for their makers tell us it is often difficult to apply a label like "colloquial" or "informal" or one like "slang" to a word or phrase out of context.

For an example of the range of permissiveness applied to usage, consider the comments on *ain't* in W7NC and RHDC. The former states: "Though disapproved by many and more common in less educated speech, used orally in most parts of the U.S. by many educated speakers, especially in the phrase *ain't I.*" RHDC comments in a usage note following the main entry: "*ain't* is so traditionally and widely regarded as a nonstandard form that it should be shunned by all who prefer to avoid being considered illiterate. *Ain't* occurs occasionally in the informal speech of some educated users, especially in self-consciously folksy, humorous contexts (*Ain't it the truth! She ain't what she used to be!*), but it is completely unacceptable in formal writing and speech."

## 8.  ORIGIN

The origin of a word—linguistically speaking, its etymology—is usually one of two types: (a) whenever known, the ancestral or foreign languages from or through which the word attained its English form (Old English, Latin, Greek, German, and French have been heavy contributors, but some 150 other languages have had a part) or (b), less commonly, a narrative account of how the word was formed or received its meaning (see in your dictionary, for example, *derrick, burke, macadam, radar*).

Find in your dictionary the page or pages giving the language or word-origin abbreviations and symbols that are used and apply them to a random sampling of words. This information, usually entered between brackets, may come near the beginning or at the end of the vocabulary entry.

## 9.  SYNONYMS

Synonyms are words that in one or more of their definitions have the same or similar meanings. Frequently these approximate equivalents have differences in meaning that enable you to choose precise and emphatic words (see Sections **63, 64**). So necessary is this study that entire volumes have been compiled to aid speakers and writers: *Webster's Dictionary of Synonyms*; *Crabb's English Synonyms*; *Roget's International Thesaurus of English Words*; Richard Soule, *A Dictionary of English Synonyms and Synonymous Expressions*.

Your dictionary, at the end of many of its word-entries, includes a listing and frequently a brief discussion of synonyms, showing the differences in meaning of apparently similar words; it may indicate by a number which usage is part of synonymous meaning. Virtually every page offers one or more examples.

## 10.  ANTONYMS

Antonyms are pairs of words that have opposite or negative meanings: *man–woman, man–boy, man–beast, man–God, holy–unholy,* etc. These opposite meanings are not all-inclusive: a word may be an antonym of another only in a certain limited meaning. One antonym of *man* concerns sex; another, age; another, biology;

another, religion. Your dictionary suggests antonyms for many words.

**11. OTHER INFORMATION**

Other information as part of an entry or as separate entries in the main part of your dictionary includes abbreviations; biographical names; capitalized words and words spelled with both capitals and small letters; cross references to words listed elsewhere; examples of word use in phrases and sentences; foreign words and phrases (usually so labeled or given a special symbol) ; geographical names; homographs and homonyms (respectively, words spelled alike but having different meanings and words spelled differently but pronounced alike) ; meaning of idiomatic phrases; prefixes, suffixes, and other combining word-elements; and, for appropriate words, pictorial or graphic illustrations.

**51d Become familiar with additional miscellaneous information in your dictionary**

The wealth of information included under each vocabulary entry (see Section 51c) is supplemented in reliable dictionaries by other material in the front and back pages. Become familiar with it. In addition to a discussion of spelling (orthography) , pronunciation, usage levels, etc., sections may give guidance on punctuation, grammar, letter writing, proofreading, and rhyming; a list of American colleges and universities; and other useful and interesting information.

**51e Use your dictionary to improve and increase your vocabulary**

For greater effectiveness in writing, speaking, reading, and listening, you should constantly improve and enlarge your vocabulary. Knowledge of a foreign language, listening to good speakers in person or on radio and television, carefully reading the works of good writers, and giving attention to the meanings of prefixes, suffixes, and root words and to synonyms and antonyms are effective aids.

Building an adequate vocabulary is not the work of a week, month, or even year, but intelligent use of a dictionary will accomplish much for you in a comparatively short time. Three suggestions are as follows.

1. Learn the meaning of as many prefixes and suffixes as you can. When these are attached to a word, notice how either the meaning or the part of speech is changed. Of some 140 prefixes and some 115 suffixes, here are representative examples:

| Prefixes | | Suffixes | |
|---|---|---|---|
| *ante-* (before) | antedate<br>anteroom | *-ful* (characterized by<br>or as much as will<br>fill) | beautiful<br>spoonful |
| *anti-* (against,<br>opposite) | antisocial<br>antiwar | *-hood* (state, condi-<br>tion, character) | childhood<br>falsehood<br>likelihood |
| *hyper-* (beyond<br>the ordinary) | hypercritical<br>hypersensitive | *-less* (without) | faultless<br>hopeless |
| *il-, im-, in-, ir-*<br>(not) | illiterate<br>illogical<br>impossible<br>immature | *-ly* (like) | saintly<br>womanly |
| | inaccurate<br>indefinite<br>irreligious<br>irresponsible | *-meter* (measure) | speedometer<br>thermometer |
| | | *-polis* (city or resi-<br>dent of) | Indianapolis<br>metropolis |
| *poly-* (many) | polygon<br>polysyllable | | cosmopolitan |
| *post-* (after) | postseason<br>postwar | *-ship* (condition, char-<br>acter, skill) | friendship<br>statesmanship |
| | | *-some* (tendency) | loathsome<br>meddlesome |

| Other Common Prefixes[3] | | Other Common Suffixes[3] |
|---|---|---|
| *a-* | *neo-* | *-age* |
| *audio-* | *non-* | *-al* |
| *auto-* | *off-* | *-er* |
| *bi-* | *out-* | *-est* |
| *bio-* | *over-* | *-fold* |
| *co-* | *per-* | *-graph* |

[3] For the meaning of these prefixes and suffixes, see your dictionary. Also, an excellent discussion of prefixes, suffixes, and compound-word elements is given in Arthur G. Kennedy, *Current English* (Boston: Ginn and Company, © 1935), pp. 335–350.

| | | |
|---|---|---|
| *com-* | *peri-* | *-ine* |
| *cross-* | *pre-* | *-ish* |
| *de-* | *pro-* | *-ist* |
| *dis-* | *pseudo-* | *-ity* |
| *en-* | *re-* | *-let* |
| *ex-* | *semi-* | *-like* |
| *extra-* | *sub-* | *-logy* |
| *fore-* | *super-* | *-ment* |
| *inter-* | *syn-* | *-ness* |
| *intra-* | *tel-* | *-phone* |
| *micro-* | *trans-* | *-ward* |
| *mid-* | *un-* | *-ways* |
| *mis-* | *under-* | *-wise* |
| *multi-* | *up-* | *-y* |

For similar study: the combination of two root words (*absent-minded, air-conditioned, masterpiece, playbill, trademark*) and the combination of prefixes and suffixes (*autograph, biography, euphony, geology, homograph, perimeter, telephone*).

2. Either read with a dictionary at hand, examining words about which you need information, or make lists of unfamiliar words and look them up later.

3. List words you hear in lectures or conversations, study them in a dictionary, and add them to your active vocabulary by using them in your conversation and in your writing.

An effective step toward building an active vocabulary is checking your list of words periodically, perhaps once a week, for words which appear twice or oftener. These are likely to be met repeatedly; use them often and make them part of your speaking and writing vocabulary.

Following are 20 not uncommon words which any student, adopting this plan, can add to his vocabulary:

| | |
|---|---|
| 1. adversity | 11. meticulous |
| 2. arduous | 12. ostensible |
| 3. assiduously | 13. pedantic |
| 4. belligerent | 14. polemical |
| 5. efflorescence | 15. precocious |
| 6. exotic | 16. prolixity |
| 7. fortuitous | 17. recalcitrant |
| 8. heterogeneous | 18. sophistication |
| 9. inimical | 19. succinct |
| 10. loquacious | 20. versatility |

# EXERCISES

A. Write a 400-word paper to be read by or to the members of your English class, on one of these subjects:

An Introduction to My Dictionary
The Uses of a Dictionary
Good and Bad Features of My Dictionary
How To Use a Dictionary
Why Everyone Should Own a Desk Dictionary
How To Pronounce Words
Special Features of My Dictionary
The Dictionary as a Source for Synonyms and Antonyms
Supplementary Information Supplied by My Dictionary
Usage Labels as Illustrated in My Dictionary
A Précis of Pages —— to —— in the Preface of My Dictionary
What My Dictionary Says About Spelling (Punctuation, Letter Writing)
The Section on American Colleges and Universities in My Dictionary
What My Dictionary Says About the Names of Days of the Week
What My Dictionary Says About the Names of Months

B. Read carefully every word on *one* page of your dictionary. Write a 400-word paper telling some of the interesting items you have found.

C. What does your dictionary say about the letters of the alphabet? For example, write a paper on the information given for two or three of the following (include capitals and small letters) : *A, I, O, Q, S, V, X, Y.*

D. To become more familiar with the resources of your own dictionary, complete the exercises in the booklet prepared by its publisher (your instructor will very likely have a supply of such booklets for class use) :

*Using the Dictionary: A Study Guide,* for use with *The American College Dictionary.* (New York: Random House)

*A Student Guide to the Random House Dictionary of the English Language, College Edition.* (New York: Random House)

*A Dictionary Study Guide,* for use with *Funk & Wagnalls Standard College Dictionary.* Text Edition. (New York: Harcourt, Brace & World, Inc.)

*A Guide to Dictionary Study,* for use with *Webster's New World Dictionary of the American Language.* College Edition. (Cleveland and New York: The World Publishing Company)

*A New Outline for Dictionary Study,* for use with *Webster's Seventh New Collegiate Dictionary.* (Springfield, Massachusetts: G. & C. Merriam Company)

E. For a definite period of time (say, two to four months), follow the individual plan for vocabulary building suggested in Section **51e** 2, 3. Then write for yourself or your instructor a 400-word paper on the results.

# 52  *Spelling*

Spelling is not a problem in word choice, but it does concern word use and is an important part of word study. The one thing demanded of anyone who has had educational advantages is that he be able to spell. In your daily work or in social situations, you may not need to be able to add a column of figures. Few people will care. Not often will you be thought stupid if you don't know the dates of historical events—say, the Battle of Austerlitz. Your knowledge of economics can be nil. You may not know the difference between an oboe and an ibis, an atom and a molecule. But if you can't spell, you're in trouble. Rightly or wrongly, fairly or unfairly, misspelling is the most frequently accepted sign of illiteracy.

Why is this? You can argue that the ability to think clearly is far more important than spelling. So are clear expression of thoughts, an attractive personality, and demonstrated ability in one's job. The fact remains that incorrect spelling is heavily penalized in our society—so heavily that it keeps people from getting jobs they want or prevents them from moving up to better positions. Inability to spell gives people complexes just as much as unsureness about grammar or proper methods of dress and social behavior.

The main reason for this somewhat illogical reliance on spelling as an index of intelligence and literacy is that correct spelling is the one fixed and certain thing about our language. The overwhelming majority of English words are spelled in only one way; all other ways are wrong. The accepted system *is* accepted. It is the system in which our business communications, our magazines, our newspapers, and our books have been written for generations. This uniformity applies to no other aspect of our language.

Admittedly, the spelling of English words *is* difficult. For centuries many words have been spelled "without rhyme or reason," and through this method, or lack of it, their spelling became fixed. Very likely, in past centuries enough people misspelled certain words so that the misspelled forms came to be considered correct. In fact, the process is still going on.[4] But the possibilities are that only minor changes will be made in English spelling and that the spelling we have now will remain as it is or will change slowly. English-language spelling is, therefore, much like English-language grammar, which a linguistics scholar has called "as pigheaded and stubborn . . . as the human minds that evolved it—and as illogical."[5] Many words contain silent letters; many are not spelled as they sound; many which sound alike (homophones) are spelled differently; and spelling by analogy is not a safe guide.

The first step in correct spelling is to cultivate the *desire* to learn, really to want to become a competent speller. The second is to take the necessary *time* to learn. The third is to use all available *means* to learn. The chronically and consistently poor speller should obtain a special book which deals solely with spelling problems and which provides many spelling exercises. Numerous such books are for sale.[6]

Although most college students are not, by birth and constitution, chronic misspellers, many do have trouble with spelling.

---

[4] For example, *benefitted* and *benefitting* were considered misspelled until a few years ago; now they appear as alternate correct spellings.

[5] Harold Whitehall, "The English Language," *Webster's New World Dictionary*, p. xxii.

[6] Among such recent books are the following: Paul Richard Craven, *Sight and Sound: A Handbook of Spelling* (Belmont, Calif.: Dickenson Publishing Company); Patricia M. Fergus, *Spelling Improvement: A Program of Self-Instruction* (New York: McGraw-Hill); Falk S. Johnson, *A Spelling Guide and Workbook* (New York: Holt, Rinehart and Winston); Norman Lewis, *20 Days to Better Spelling* (New York: Harper & Row); Julia N. McCorkle, *Learning To Spell* (Boston: D. C. Heath); Joseph Mersand, *Spelling Your Way to Success* (Great Neck, N.Y.: Barron's Educational Series); Thomas Clark Pollock and William D. Baker, *The University Spelling Book* (Englewood Cliffs, N.J.: Prentice-Hall); Harry Shaw, *Spell It Right!* (New York: Barnes & Noble); Harry Shefter, *Six Minutes a Day to Perfect Spelling* (New York: Pocket Books); Genevieve Love Smith, *Spelling by Principles* (New York: Appleton-Century-Crofts).

The three steps—*desire, time,* and *means*—include the following:

——→ 1. Pronounce words correctly.
——→ 2. Watch for variations between spelling and pronunciation.
——→ 3. Mentally *see* words as well as hear them.
——→ 4. Use a dictionary to fix words in your memory.
——→ 5. Watch for unpronounced (i.e., silent) letters.
——→ 6. Use memory devices to help remember troublesome words.
——→ 7. Learn a few simple rules for spelling.
——→ 8. Write and proofread words carefully in order to avoid errors caused not by ignorance but by carelessness.
——→ 9. Be suspicious about the spelling-appearance of a word and take the small amount of time necessary to check its spelling in your dictionary.
——→ 10. List the words you misspell.

## 52a   *Pronounce words correctly*

You should recognize at once that pronunciation is not a safe guide to spelling. Aside from many fine distinctions in sound, English pronunciation has between 45 and 65 common sounds. Our 26 vowels and consonants must represent these sounds; to do so, the English language uses approximately 250 *spelling combinations!* For example, the simple sound of long *e* is represented, inconsistently, by 13 spellings: *ae* (*Caesar*), *ay* (*quay*), *e* (*evening*), *ea* (*read*), *ee* (*need*), *ei* (*receive*), *eo* (*people*), *ey* (*key*), *i* (*police*), *ie* (*piece*), *oe* (*amoeba*), *ui* (*suite*), and *y* (*melody*). Even worse, long *o* in English can be spelled in 27 ways![7]

Correct pronunciation may help, but mispronunciation is a definite hindrance. It is responsible for a large number of misspelled words, for it is difficult to spell correctly a mispronounced word. Could anyone spell *Egypt* if it were pronounced "eggpit"? Or *garage* pronounced "gararge"?

1. Do not add vowels or consonants in pronouncing such words as *athletics, disastrous, height, hindrance, remembrance,*

[7] On the other hand, the letters *ough* can be *pronounced* in many different ways. This sentence contains eight (there are still others): "A rough-coated, dough-faced ploughman thoughtfully strode, coughing and hiccoughing, through the streets of Scarborough." (In the United States, *plow* and *hiccup* are the preferred spellings for those two words.)

and *similar,* and you will not misspell them as "ath*a*letics" or "ath*e*letics," "disast*e*rous," "height*h*," "hind*e*rance," "rememberance," and "simil*i*ar."

2. Do not omit necessary consonants in pronouncing such words as *environment, enthusiasm, February, government, library.*

3. Do not omit syllables in pronouncing such words as *accidentally, convenience, criticism, interesting, laboratory, miniature, sophomore, temperament, valuable,* even though, when some of these are said fast, they sound like "int'resting," "lab'ratory," "soph'more."

4. Do not mispronounce the prefixes of words, such as "preform" for *perform,* "prehaps" for *perhaps,* "perfix" for *prefix,* "porposal" for *proposal.*

5. Carefully examine words that contain silent letters. In a number of English words, the following letters are often silent: *b (doubt, subtle, thumb); c (muscle, scene); ch (schism, yacht); d (handsome, Wednesday); e (bite, come;* see Section **52e**5); *g (gnat, sign); gh (bough, height); h (ghost, honest); k (knife, know); l (calm, would); n (hymn, solemn); p (raspberry, pneumonia); s (aisle, island, demesne); t (listen, mortgage); u (guess, rogue); w (answer, snow, write).*

6. Be suspicious of words containing lightly stressed or unstressed syllables. The technical name *schwa* (ə) is given to indicate the sound, a kind of "uh"; the vowel used may be any one of the six, *a, e, i, o, u, y: dollar, grammar; corner, model; nadir, peril; professor, sponsor; murmur, sulfur; martyr.* In such words, exaggerate the "trouble spots": *grammAr, sepArate, repEtition, mathEmatics, humOrous, existEnce, dEscribe.*

Cultivate the habit of spelling troublesome words aloud, syllable by syllable, writing them, and then spelling them aloud again in order to relate the sound to the spelling.

### 52b Actually see words as well as hear them

One method of improving spelling is to look at, or repeat, a word until you really *see* it. Correct pronunciation is helpful to an "ear-minded" person in spelling correctly, but to visualize words is also important. Frequently you say of a word you have written, "That doesn't look right." Many students constantly misspell words because they have never learned to observe a printed page; their errors in spelling come from an unwillingness or apparent inability to *see*. Look at the word alone or in its context, pronounce it, study it, write it, see it with your eyes shut, write it again, see whether it is correct, write it again, pronounce it. This method is particularly valuable when you are dealing with tricky words which for no apparent reason (1) may drop letters; (2) add or transpose letters; (3) change one or two letters for others; or (4) contain unpronounced letters. Examples: *curious* but *curiosity*; *explain* but *explanation*; *fire* but *fiery*; *maintain* but *maintenance*; *proceed* but *procedure*; *pronounce* but *pronunciation*; *repeat* but *repetition*.

The most frequent error in visualizing words is mistaking one for another similar to it or one pronounced like another but spelled differently (homophones). Observe these pairs or triplets:

*accept, except
*advice, advise
*affect, effect
altar, alter
an, and
angel, angle
are, our, or
ascent, assent
bare, bear
biding, bidding
breath, breathe
capital, capitol
*choose, chose
cite, sight, site
clothes, cloths
*coarse, course
complement,
  compliment
conscience, conscious
counsel, council,
  consul
dairy, diary
decent, descent
desert, dessert
device, devise
dew, do, due
dining, dinning
dual, duel

ever, every
fair, fare
formally, formerly
*forth, fourth
freshman, freshmen
*hear, here
hoping, hopping
human, humane
*its, it's (*never* its')
*knew, new
know, no
*later, latter
*lead, led
least, lest
lightening,
  lightning
*loose, lose
*lose, loss
medal, metal
of, off
on, one
passed, past
peace, piece
*personal, personnel
plain, plane
*precede, proceed
presence, presents

*principal,
  principle
*quiet, quite, quit
right, rite, write
road, rode
shone, shown
shudder, shutter
stationary,
  stationery
steal, steel
straight, strait
*than, then
*their, there,
  they're
therefor, therefore
*thorough, through
though, thought,
  through
threw, through
*to, too, two
*want, wont, won't
weak, week
*weather, whether
*were, where
whose, who's
woman, women
*your, you're

The words marked * are frequently misspelled in written work, although any student could probably spell such words correctly in a spelling test. Understand the meaning of each word and do not use one when you mean the other. (See Section **63**.)

## 52c  Use the dictionary to help in your spelling

When you are suspicious of the spelling of any word, check its spelling immediately in the dictionary. If you cannot find it, look up and down the column, since a silent letter may be causing the trouble: *aghast* will be there but not "agast." If the initial letters confuse you, ask someone for suggestions: you will not find *mnemonic* under *n,*[8] *philosophy* under *f, pneumonia* under *n, psychology* under *s*.

Knowledge of the etymology (origin, derivation) of a word also helps you to spell correctly. For example, if you know that *dormir* is the French word for *sleep* (from Latin *dormitorium*) you will not spell *dormitory* with an *a* for the *i*. Sometimes, too, spelling the simpler or root form of the word helps: *contribute, contribution,* not "contrabution"; *finite, definite, infinite,* not "definate," "infinate"; *please, pleasing, pleasant,* not "plesant"; *prepare, preparation,* not "preperation"; *relate, relative,* not "relitive"; *ridicule, ridiculous,* not "rediculous." But watch the tricky words that vary from their roots (Section **52b**) .

Similarly, a study of prefixes and suffixes—noting their meaning and spelling—enables you to spell correctly by grouping similar forms in a way that emphasizes their resemblance. See Section **51e** for lists of common prefixes and suffixes.

Further assistance in the use of your dictionary for spelling is available if your dictionary has among its supplementary aids an article on orthography or correct spelling. Read carefully any such article.

## 52d  Use memory devices to help you remember troublesome words

Some memory devices apply to groups of words, such as the common spelling rules (Section **52e**) and the rhyme for the *ei–ie*

---

[8] Look up *mnemonic*. It is an imposing but useful word for a memory device of the kind listed in the following sections. You have been using mnemonics most of your life. The term applies to a basic characteristic of the human mind.

words (Section **52e**1). Others apply to specific words, such as the root-word plan illustrated just above in Section **52c**. Other individual examples:

*I* am (is) always in *busIness.*
In *exisTENce* you find *TEN*; in *mainTENance* you need *TEN.*
*Grammar*—spell the first syllable, *gram,* and add its last three letters in reverse order, *mar.* Or: Bad *grammar* will *mar* your writing.
*Omitted, omitting,* and *omission* OMIT an extra *m.*
*Necessary*—pronounce *NEcessity* first.
*Possess, possesses, possessing, possession*—put in as many *s*'s as you can.
*PrincipLE* means a *ruLE,* a theory, a standard; otherwise, *principAL* is used (and the *principAL* of a school can be a *PAL*).
*SePARate* means to set *aPART.*

For similar troublesome words, each student should create his own memory devices.

## 52e    Learn a few simple rules for spelling

Numerous rules for spelling cover certain words and classes of words, but remember that the words came *first,* the rules *second.* These rules are generalized statements applicable to a fairly large number of words, but not all; consequently, every rule has its exceptions.

For the words ending in *able* or *ible, ant* or *ent, ance* or *ence, ise* or *ize* or *yze, tion* or *sion,* and for the addition of *s* or *es* to words ending in *o* (see Section **71c**4) no safe guide exists except memory or constant reference to the dictionary.

The eight rules that follow, with their corollaries, are easily learned; mastering them will eliminate many recurring errors. (See Section **52f**.)

⟶ 1. Words containing *ei* or *ie*

Write *i* before *e*
Except after *c,*
Or when sounded like *a*
As in *neighbor* and *weigh*
*Either, neither, leisure, seize*
Are exceptions; watch for these.

This rule or principle applies *only* when the pronunciation of *ei* or *ie* is a long *e*, as in *he*, or the *a* sound, as in *pale*: *believe, chief, deceive, field, niece, relieve, siege, yield, view, freight, reign, veil.*

A memory device for remembering whether the *e* or *i* comes after the *c* or *l* is the key word *Celia* (or *Alice* or *police* or *lice*). Another memory device: *ie* is the usual spelling when an *r* follows: *brigadier, cashier, cavalier, fierce, financier, frontier, pier.*

If the sound of *ei* or *ie* is other than long *e* or *a*, the principle does not apply: *conscience, conscientious, foreign, forfeit, height, omniscient, raciest, science, species, their, weird.* Nor does it apply, except coincidentally, to the *ie* in words which are applications of the *y* rule (see Section **52e2**).

⟶ 2. Final *y*

The final *y* rule, the most commonly illustrated spelling principle, is especially helpful, when words end in *y*, in forming the plurals of nouns; the third person singular present tense, past tense, and past participle of verbs; adjectives from nouns; nouns from adjectives; adverbs from adjectives; and the comparative and superlative degrees of adjectives and adverbs.

a. Words ending in *y* preceded by a consonant usually change *y* to *i* before any suffix except one beginning with *i* (such as *-ing, -ish, -ist*) or before the possessive sign *'s*:

activity, activities (*noun*)
library, libraries (*noun*)
carry, carries, carried, carrying (*verb*)
try, tries, tried, trying (*verb*)
study, studies, studied, studying (*noun, verb*)
beauty, beautiful (*noun* to *adjective*)
empty, emptiness (*adjective* to *noun*)
lucky, luckily (*adjective* to *adverb*)
easy, easier, easiest (*comparative, superlative*)

Proper-name exceptions: Proper names ending in *y*, especially family names, simply add *s* to form their plurals, regardless of whether a vowel or a consonant precedes the final *y*:

The *Murphys* and the *Kellys* are good friends of ours.
Portraits of the three *Marys* appear in some paintings.

Grandfather knew the two *Germanys* well: the one of pre-1939 and the one of post-1945.

Important common-word exceptions: one-syllable adjectives adding *ly* or *ness*: *shy, shyly, shyness; wry, wryly, wryness* (but *dryly, drily, slyly, slily* are commonly used) ; and a few polysyllables adding *ship, like, hood: ladyship, citylike, babyhood.* Note also *busyness* (state of being busy) .

b. Words ending in *y* preceded by a vowel do not change *y* to *i* before suffixes or other endings.

| | |
|---|---|
| day, days | annoy, annoyed, annoying |
| turkey, turkeys | array, arrayed, arraying |
| valley, valleys | obey, obeyed, obeying |

Important exceptions: *day, daily, lay, laid* (but *allay, allayed*) ; *pay, paid; say, said; slay, slain.* But in good use are *gayly, gaily, gayety, gaiety.* Note that nouns of two or more syllables ending in *-quy* regularly change *y* to *i* and add *es: colloquy, colloquies, soliloquy, soliloquies.*

$\longrightarrow$ 3.  Doubling final consonant

a. One-syllable words and words of more than one syllable accented on the last syllable, when ending in a single consonant (except *x* equal to *ks*) preceded by a single vowel, double the consonant before adding an ending which begins with a vowel.

This rule is valuable in forming the past tense, past participle, and present participle of many regular verbs and in forming the comparative and superlative degrees of adjectives. Common endings beginning with a vowel are the following: *-ed, -es, -ing, -er, -est, -able, -ible, -ance, -ence, -ish,* and *y.*

| | |
|---|---|
| acquit (*qu* equals *kw*) , acquitted, acquitting, acquittal | clan, clannish |
| admit, admitted, admitting, admittance | forget, forgettable, unforgettable |
| | man, mannish |
| drop, dropped, dropping | red, redder, reddish, redden |
| overlap, overlapped, overlapping | run, running, runner |
| plan, planned, planning | tax, taxes, taxable |
| refer, referred, referring | tin, tinny |

Important exceptions: *transferable, transference, gases, gaseous, humbugged, humbugging.*

b. If the accent is shifted to an *earlier* syllable when the ending is added, the final consonant is not doubled.

refer, referred, referring, *but* reference
prefer, preferred, preferring, *but* preference

Exception: *excellent, excellence.*

c. Derivatives from basic words that change pronunciation from a long vowel to a short vowel follow the doubling rule:

bite, biting, *but* bit, bitten
flame, inflame, inflamed, *but* flammable, inflammable
write, writing, *but* writ, written

d. Words ending in a final consonant preceded by two vowels do not double the final consonant:

appear, appeared, appearing, appearance
need, needed, needing, needy
train, trained, training, trainee

e. Words ending in *two* different consonants do not double the final consonant:

bend, bending (*not* "bendding")
insert, inserted, inserting (*not* "insertted," "insertting")
turn, turned, turning (*not* "turnned," "turnning")

f. Words not accented on the *final* syllable do not ordinarily double the final consonant:

happen, happened, happening
murmur, murmured, murmuring

A large group of words usually ending in *l*, not accented on the last syllable, violate the rule by having alternate spellings:

*marvel, marveled, marvelled, marveling, marvelling, marvelous, marvellous; tranquil, tranquilize, tranquillize, tranquility, tranquillity.*

⟶ 4. The "one-plus-one" rule

When the prefix of a word ends in the same letter with which the main part of the word begins, or when the main part of the word ends in the same letter with which the suffix begins, be sure that both letters are included. Otherwise, do not double the letters.

The same rule applies when two main words are combined, the first ending with the same letter with which the second begins: *roommate, bookkeeping, glowworm, bathhouse.*

In your study of spelling, note how words are spelled when word bases have prefixes like *dis-, il-, ir-, mis-, over-, un-,* and *under-* or suffixes like *-less, -ly, -ment, -ness,* and *-ship.*

| | | | |
|---|---|---|---|
| dissatisfied | unnoticed | overdo | meanness |
| illiterate | underrate | undecided | reckless |
| irresponsible | disappear | accidentally | severely |
| misspell | disappoint | soulless | greatness |
| overrun | incomplete | occasionally | contentment |

Exceptions: *eighteen,* not "eightteen"; *questionnaire.*

Words ending in *-ic* without an *al*-form add *ally*: *basic, basically; specific, specifically; terrific, terrifically.*

Naturally, three identical consonants or vowels are never written solidly together: *cliff-face,* not "cliffface"; *shell-like,* not "shelllike"; *still-life,* not "stilllife"; *cross-stitch,* not "crossstitch"; *yell-leading,* not "yellleading."

⟶ 5. Final silent (unpronounced) *e*

A final silent *e* is an *e* ending a word but not pronounced; its function is to make the other vowel of the syllable long; *rate* (but *rat*); *mete* (but *met*); *bite* (but *bit*); *note* (but *not*); *cute* (but *cut*).

a. Most words ending in silent *e* drop the *e* before a suffix beginning with a vowel but keep the *e* before a suffix beginning with a consonant.

| | |
|---|---|
| argue, arguing | amuse, amusement |
| arrive, arrival | bare, bareness |
| believe, believing | hope, hopeless |
| guide, guidance | safe, safety |
| ice, icy | sincere, sincerely |
| live, livable | tire, tiresome |
| true, truism | use, useful |

Exceptions: when final silent *e* is preceded by another vowel—except *e*—the final *e* is not retained before a suffix beginning with a consonant: *argue, argument*; *due, duly*; *true, truly*; *agree, agreement*.

NOTE: Some adjectives formed by adding *-able* to silent *e* words have alternate spellings: *likable, likeable*; *lovable, loveable*; *usable, useable*.

b. Words which end in *-ce* or *-ge* retain the *e* when *-able* and *-ous* are added, in order to prevent giving a hard sound (*k* or *ga*) to the *c* or *g*:

| | |
|---|---|
| marriage, marriageable | change, changeable |
| notice, noticeable | courage, courageous |
| service, serviceable | outrage, outrageous |

Compare the pronunciations of *cable* and *serviceable, gable* and *changeable*.

c. The few words ending in *ie* (pronounced like long *i*) in which the *e* is also silent, change *ie* to *y* before *ing*, perhaps to prevent two *i*'s from coming together.

| | |
|---|---|
| die, dying | hie, hying (*but also* hieing) |
| lie, lying | tie, tying (*but also* tieing) |
| vie, vying | |

d. The silent *e* is retained in the *-ing* forms of *dye, singe, swinge,* and *tinge* (*dyeing, singeing, swingeing, tingeing*) to distinguish these words from *dying, singing, swinging,* and *tinging*.

329

⟶ 6.  The inserted -*k*- rule

In the few words ending in *c* to which a suffix is added beginning with *e, i,* or *y*, the letter *k* is usually inserted before the suffix in order to prevent mispronunciation by retaining the hard sound of *c*. Note the different pronunciation, for example, between *picnicking* and *icing*.

| | |
|---|---|
| frolic, frolicked, frolicking | picnic, picnicked, picnicking |
| mimic, mimicked, mimicking | shellac, shellacked, shellacking |
| panic, panicky | traffic, trafficked, trafficking |

⟶ 7.  The -*ceed,* -*cede* rule

For words ending in a "seed" sound, memorize the three words spelled with a -*ceed* ending and the one ending in -*sede*; all other words in this group end in -*cede*:

exceed, proceed, succeed
supersede
accede, antecede, cede, concede, intercede, precede, recede, retrocede, secede

Memory devices:

*S* begins the first and last syllable of *supersede*.
To suc*ceed* as a safe driver, pro*ceed* carefully and do not ex*ceed* the sp*eed* limit.

⟶ 8.  -*s* and -*es* endings

When nouns and verbs end in an *s* sound (*ch, sh, j, s, x,* or *z*) and the plural of nouns or the third-person-singular of verbs requires an extra syllable to pronounce, -*es* is added. If no extra syllable is pronounced or if the word ends in silent *e,* only *s* is added. (See also Section **71c**1,2.)

| -*es* | -*s* |
|---|---|
| buzz, buzzes (*noun, verb*) | advice, advices (*noun*) |
| box, boxes (*noun, verb*) | argue, argues (*verb*) |
| church, churches (*noun*) | edge, edges (*noun, verb*) |
| filch, filches (*verb*) | noise, noises (*noun, verb*) |
| polish, polishes (*noun, verb*) | table, tables (*noun, verb*) |

### 52f  Use some easily applied method to memorize the spelling rules

Memorizing a simple key word or a common example of each rule can help you both to memorize the rule and to recite it from your example.

As illustration, make yourself sure of the spelling of the following words: *spot, spotted, spotting, spotter, spotty.* From these memorized words you can read off the rule. Note that to the word *spot* is added *-ed, -ing, -er, -y*—that is, suffixes beginning with a vowel. Notice that *spot* is a one-syllable word; that it ends in one consonant (*t*); that this consonant is preceded by one vowel (*o*); that when a suffix beginning with a vowel, like those listed, is added, the final *t* or consonant is doubled.

So, too, memorize *refer, referred, referring, referral, referrer, referent, referee, reference, referendum.* Note one important difference between *spot* and *refer*: the latter is a two-syllable word, with the accent on the last syllable. But it also has one final consonant (*r*) preceded by one vowel (*e*). To the word a suffix beginning with a vowel is added; hence, the final *r* is doubled in the four words following *refer*. What about the last four words with one *r*? Note that the accent has shifted from the last syllable of *refer* to the first syllable or another syllable in *reference, referee, referent, referendum.* When this shift of accent occurs, the doubling of the final consonant, here *r*, does not take place.

These two illustrations show a simple method of memorizing Rule 52e3. It can be applied to all the other rules.

### 52g  Use the proper punctuation mark for correct spelling

When they are necessary, use the apostrophe, as in contractions (Section 93b), and the hyphen, as in compound words (Section 92b): *don't, haven't, o'clock, self-propelled, brother-in-law, drive-in.*

### 52h  Do not carelessly misspell words

Many spelling errors are caused by carelessness, not ignorance. Studies of lists of misspelled words from themes reveal the following percentages concerning misspellings: failure to spell easy words by pronunciation and syllable, 6 percent; failure to apply spelling rules, 9 percent; tricky words (silent letters, exceptions to rules, words not spelled as pronounced, etc.) , 19 percent; sheer carelessness and failure to proofread, 66 percent. The careful student will proofread his written work once or twice solely for the purpose of finding misspelled words.

Remember that the simple, easy words, not the difficult ones, cause most trouble in careless misspelling.

Do not omit letters or carelessly transpose letters of words or write two words as one when they should be written separately. Examples:

| | |
|---|---|
| a lot, *not* "alot" | in fact, *not* "infact" |
| certain, *not* "certian" | in spite, *not* "inspite" |
| Christian, *not* "Christain" | research, *not* "reaserch" |
| doesn't, *not* "does'nt" | thoroughly, *not* "throughly" |
| first, *not* "frist" | wouldn't, *not* "would'nt," etc. |

### 52i   Keep a list of the words you most frequently misspell

Learning to spell correctly seems a difficult task because so many words must be mastered. But no one is expected to be able to spell all words, on demand, and only a comparatively few words are the most persistent troublemakers. Curiously enough, words like *Mississippi, Tennessee, literature,* and *extracurricular* are not frequently misspelled; rather, words like *too, all right, it's, its, there, their* most often are the offenders (see Section **52b,h**) .

Keep a list of words you misspell and study them, perhaps according to Section **52a,b,c,d,e**, until you learn their spelling. For *you* this is the most important and useful list. Other lists vary from 10 to 25 spelling demons (words most people always misspell) [9] up to about 1000 words labeled "most frequently misspelled."

The following list of 400 words is fairly representative. Your own list will contain words not given here, but see that none of the following remains on your list very long. Master the spelling of these words, trying to master five words a day. They are numbered and spaced for such study.

---

[9] Such as *apocryphal, battalion, catarrh, desiccate, diphtheria, ecstasy, erysipelas, exhilarated, heinous, idiosyncrasy, liquefy, maintenance, meringue, naphtha, pejorative, perseverance, psoriasis, rarefy, sacrilegious, scintillate, seize, siege, supersede, villain, weird.*

1. abbreviation
2. absence
3. academic
4. accelerate
5. accidentally

6. accommodation
7. accompanying
8. accumulation
9. accustomed
10. achievement

11. acknowledge
12. acquaintance
13. across
14. adequate
15. adjustment

16. admittance
17. advantageous
18. advertisement
19. advisable
20. alleged

21. allotted
22. almost
23. among
24. analysis
25. anniversary

26. announcement
27. answer
28. anxiety
29. apartment
30. apology

31. apparatus
32. apparently
33. appearance
34. argument
35. article

36. astronautical
37. athletics
38. attendance
39. audience
40. auxiliary

41. awkward
42. bachelor
43. balance
44. basically
45. becoming

46. beginning
47. believing
48. beneficial
49. boundary
50. brilliant

51. business
52. calendar
53. candidate
54. career
55. category

56. certain
57. challenge
58. changeable
59. characteristic
60. chosen

61. column
62. commercial
63. committee
64. communication
65. comparatively

66. comparison
67. competition
68. conceivable
69. conference
70. confidence

71. conscientious
72. consequently
73. consistent
74. contemporary
75. continually

76. contribution
77. controlling
78. convenience
79. correspondence
80. counsellor

81. countries
82. courageous
83. courteous
84. criticism
85. curiosity

86. dealt
87. deficient
88. definitely
89. democracy
90. description

91. desirability
92. despair
93. desperate
94. determination
95. dictionary

96. difference
97. difficulty
98. diminish
99. disappear
100. disappoint

101. disastrous
102. disease
103. dissatisfied
104. distribution
105. divine

106. division
107. dormitories
108. economical
109. efficient
110. eighteen

111. elaborate
112. eligible
113. eliminate
114. embarrass
115. encouragement

116. enthusiasm
117. entrance
118. environment
119. equally
120. equipped

121. erroneous
122. especially
123. exaggeration
124. excellent
125. exceptionally

126. excitement
127. exercise
128. exhausted
129. existence
130. experience

131. explanation
132. extraordinary
133. facilities
134. familiar
135. fascinating

136. February
137. fictitious
138. fiery
139. financially
140. flammable

141. foreign
142. forty
143. friendliness
144. fundamental
145. government

146. gradually
147. grammar
148. guidance
149. handicapped
150. handsome

151. height
152. hindrance
153. holiday
154. honorable
155. hospitality

156. humiliate
157. humorous
158. hundred
159. hungry
160. hurriedly

161. hypocrisy
162. illiterate
163. imaginary
164. immediately
165. incidentally

166. independence
167. indispensable
168. infinite
169. influential
170. inimitable

171. initiative
172. innocent
173. insistence
174. integration
175. intellectual

176. intelligence
177. interesting
178. interpretation
179. interruption
180. interview

181. intolerance
182. introduction
183. invitation
184. irrelevant
185. irresistible

186. jeopardize
187. kindliness
188. knowledge
189. laboratory
190. laboriously

191. language
192. legibility
193. legitimate
194. leisurely
195. liable

196. libraries
197. likelihood
198. literature
199. livelihood
200. loneliness

201. maintenance
202. manageable
203. manipulate
204. manufacturing
205. marriageable

206. mathematics
207. measurable
208. mechanical
209. merchandise
210. millionaire

211. miniature
212. miscellaneous
213. mischievous
214. misspelled
215. momentarily

216. monotonous
217. mysterious
218. nationalities
219. naturally
220. necessary

221. negative
222. negligent
223. neighborhood
224. neither
225. niece

226. nineteen
227. ninety
228. ninth
229. nonsense
230. noticeable

231. numerous
232. obedience
233. obstacle
234. occasionally
235. occupying

236. occurrence
237. official
238. omission
239. operation
240. opinion

241. opponent
242. opportunities
243. opposition
244. optimistic
245. ordinarily

246. original
247. outrageous
248. pamphlet
249. panicky
250. parallel

251. particularly
252. peaceable
253. peculiarities
254. penniless
255. perceive

256. performance
257. perhaps
258. permanent
259. permissible
260. perpetuate

261. perseverance
262. persistent
263. personnel
264. persuade
265. physician

266. planning
267. pleasant
268. plenteous
269. politician
270. portrayed

271. possession
272. possibility
273. potential
274. practically
275. preceding

276. predicate
277. predictable
278. predominant
279. preference
280. preferred

281. prejudice
282. preliminary
283. preparation
284. presumptuous
285. privilege

286. probably
287. procedure
288. process
289. professional
290. prominent

291. promotion
292. pronunciation
293. propaganda
294. quantity
295. questionable

296. questionnaire
297. realize
298. reasonable
299. receive
300. recognition

301. recollection
302. recommendation
303. recurrence
304. reference
305. referred

306. regrettable
307. relative
308. relieve
309. religious
310. remembrance

311. removable
312. repetition
313. representative
314. reputation
315. research

316. resolution
317. resistance
318. resources
319. respectfully
320. responsibility

321. ridiculous
322. righteous
323. roommate
324. sacrilegious
325. safety

326. satirical
327. satisfactorily
328. scarcity
329. schedule
330. scholarship

331. secondary
332. secretary
333. seize
334. selection
335. semester

336. separate
337. serviceable
338. severely
339. shining
340. significance

341. similar
342. sincerely
343. singular
344. sixtieth
345. solution

346. sophomore
347. specialization
348. specifically
349. specimen
350. speech

351. sponsor
352. stratosphere
353. strength
354. substantiate
355. substitute

356. subtle
357. sufficient
358. superfluous
359. supersede
360. surprise

361. suspicious
362. technical
363. technique
364. television
365. temperature

366. temporarily
367. testimony
368. thirtieth
369. thorough
370. tomorrow

371. tradition
372. transferred
373. transportation
374. truly
375. Tuesday

376. twelfth
377. unanimous
378. uncontrollable
379. undoubtedly
380. unforgettable

381. unfortunate
382. until
383. unusually
384. usefulness
385. valuable

386. versatile
387. visible
388. volume
389. voluntary
390. wealthiest

391. weariness
392. Wednesday
393. weird
394. welcome
395. welfare

396. wherever
397. wholly
398. wonderful
399. writing
400. written

## EXERCISES

A. Keep a list of the words which you misspell and study them, perhaps according to Section 52a,b,c,d,e, until you learn their correct spelling.

B. Copy the following. Leave under each enough space for writing 10 words. Fill in up to 10 words from a selected article or articles, each 10 words to illustrate the rules indicated.

1. *ei–ie* rule words (Section 52e1)
2. *ei–ie* nonrule words (Section 52e1)
3. *y*-rule—words changing final *y* to *i* (Section 52e2a)
4. *y*-rule—words retaining final *y* (Section 52e2b)
5. words doubling final consonant (Section 52e3a)
6. words not doubling final consonant (Section 52e3d,e,f)
7. words illustrating the "one-plus-one" rule (Section 52e4)
8. words dropping final silent *e* (Section 52e5a)
9. words retaining final silent *e* (Section 52e5b)
10. inserted -*k*- words (Section 52e6)
11. *-ceed, -cede* words (Section 52e7)
12. nouns adding *s* for plurals (Section 52e8)
13. nouns adding *es* for plurals (Section 52e8)
14. verbs adding *s* for third person singular (Section 52e8)
15. verbs adding *es* for third person singular (Section 52e8)

C. In the following, 50 words are incorrectly spelled. List these words on a separate sheet of paper and opposite each give the correct spelling. If a word is incorrectly spelled more than once, list it only once.

After I had been admitted to Atwood University and had completed my registeration, I was very much surprised to recieve a letter from my grandfather. Now, Grandfather was never very much of a man for writting letters, but approximatly every week or so his communications continued to arrive. I am sure that at times it was not convient for him to write (he as much as said so frequently), but he had the urge, so he said, to tell me of his own experiences at Atwood.

Grandfather early wrote about my making friends. He had made the aquaintance, he said, of many people during his first weeks at Atwood, from whom he chose a few intimates. These people he had met in the classroom, at some of the fraternities, in the Union, in resturants, and on the atheletic field. He treated every one in a courtious manner and never cracked jokes at their expense; so doing, he had learned, was a sure way to forfiet their respect.

One of Grandfather's closest associates was Bill Jones, whom he had met at one of the dormatories. Bill was a very tempermental person, but all in all he had a genius for getting along with people, and Grandfather benefited greatly from his comradship. About the middle of the first semester they became roomates.

From Bill Jones Grandfather learned much about the art of studying. Up to the time of their rooming togeather, Grandfather was much disatisfied with his scholastic record, and even though he tried to learn to study, he sometimes was so poorly prepared, usually in mathmatics and English, that he was almost too much embarassed to go to class. Bill made a begining of his work on Grandfather's scholarship by giving him simple explainations of his more difficult assignments, but he was more interested in teaching the methods and dicipline of study. Once Grandfather had mastered these, the maintainance of high marks became for him an easy task.

One of Bill's secrets was concentration; if you divide your attention, you get nowhere. Another was not postponing getting to work. Grandfather admitted, for example, that the night before his grammar test, he spent the evening playing pool at the Union. He had alloted two hours for his review, but the evening just seemed to dissappear, and when Grandfather got to his room, he was too tired to worry about his lack of knowlege, and went immediatly to bed. He was not much mistified when he failed the test, and he even thought of quiting school. But about that time he met Bill, and aquired valuble study habits. No longer was he an irresponsable student, handicaped by a lack of study method. Study was now his first neccessary task. When the next grammar test came, he was so good that he could spot an independant clause a paragraph away; and by the time of the punctuation test, he had mastered the comma, had good control of the semicoln, and was even using recklessly but correctly quite a number of appostrophes.

In high school Grandfather had been a notorously poor speller. The adolescent love notes that Grandfather wrote to the girl accross the aisle contained so many wrongly spelled words that the young lady broke off the correspondance. Love couldn't erradicate Grandfather's spelling disease, and after this disasterous adventure he swore that he would overcome his trouble; but he didn't. It was method, not love, that Grandfather needed, and Bill Jones supplied the answer. Grandfather still spelled a word wrong occassionally, but he became so persistent in his study of the words spelled by rule, the tricky words, and the words spelled according to sylable that when he took the spelling test for the first time, he had only one mispelled word.

I could go on and on telling of the referrences to college life made in Grandfather's letters, and of the many occurences of which he wrote.

But I don't want to be accused of wordyness, and, anyway, I've given you a general idea of the content of these letters.

Long before the end of the year I became conscious of the fact that Grandfather was trying to decieve me in a polite way; he was really giving me advice by means of his letters, but whenever I accused him of this fact, he swore to his innocense and vowed that his only object was to entertain me and, perhaps, keep me from becoming homesick. I never did quite beleive him.

# 53 *Reputable or standard diction (appropriateness)*

Reputable or Standard English is, in general, the English widely recognized as acceptable; it is used in various situations and on various occasions by those we consider social, professional, and educational leaders: writers, editors, publishers, ministers, lawyers, judges, school teachers, college professors, and the like. As Professor Charles C. Fries says, Standard English is "the practice of the socially accepted, those who are carrying on the important affairs of English-speaking people."[10]

Diction or word-choice should be *correct, clear,* and *effective.* It should conform to Standard English, but since no standards of diction can be absolute, perhaps the most worthwhile guide is *appropriateness* (according to time, place, occasion, circumstances). For example, language used in a discussion in your home or in the dormitory is not precisely the language used in a classroom or church discussion group. Words used casually but correctly with your roommate are hardly the words you would use in an interview with your dean or prospective employer. Following the principles of the process of communication, you, as writer or speaker, should adapt your language to your reader or listener, your subject, and the occasion.

For useful purposes, diction can be divided into three broad groups: formal standard, informal standard, and substandard.

[10] "Usage Levels and Dialect Distribution," *The American College Dictionary,* p. xxv. An interesting and useful general guide: Margaret Nicholson, *A Dictionary of American-English Usage* (New York: Oxford, 1957).

## 53a   *Use formal standard English when it is appropriate*

*Formal standard English* is used where and when dignity and seriousness are concerned: lectures and addresses, sermons, arguments and judgments in law courts, discussions and debates in legislative assemblies, legal and scientific writing, writing aimed at being permanent literature (belles-lettres), newspaper editorials, carefully edited serious books and magazines, minutes of meetings, and the like. As a student you use formal standard diction when you are on your "very best" language behavior, as in application and certain other business letters, serious friendly letters (like condolence letters), petitions, scientific and technical papers, research papers, theses, and some of your themes. Your guide: your dictionary may label a word or expression "formal," but any word or phrase with no label or condemnation should be appropriate in formal standard English.

*Examples*     John failed his final examination in mathematics.
              I shall (will) not return.
              May I introduce my fiancée?

## 53b   *Use informal standard English when it is appropriate*

*Informal standard English*—frequently termed "colloquial"[11]— is most commonly used when writers and speakers are—shall we say?—on their "good" or "moderately good" behavior. Such situations are others than those mentioned in Section **53a**: the language of normal everyday conversations, friendly and familiar, and the same friendly and familiar tone in much writing—most

---

[11] Three dictionaries have dropped the label "colloquial": one on the grounds that this label "is now so widely misunderstood by the public as to be no longer serviceable" (*Standard College Dictionary*, which uses instead the label "informal") and the other two on the theory that it is difficult, if not impossible, to use the label with words out of context (*Webster's Third New International Dictionary* and its derivative, *Webster's Seventh New Collegiate Dictionary*).

The words "colloquial" and "colloquialism" may therefore be passing out of use as language labels. As defined in the Third Edition of *The Harper Handbook of College Composition*, "A *colloquialism* is a word or phrase used in conversation and indispensable to an easy informal style of writing and speaking. . . . Remember two important statements about colloquialisms. First, a colloquialism is never a localism; that is, it is not a provincialism or regionalism. Second, no stigma attaches to any word labeled 'colloquial.' Such words are *not* vulgar, bad, incorrect, substandard, or illiterate" (pp. 406–407).

friendly letters, many business letters, letters home, notes and memoranda, familiar essays, and some of your themes. The language is more casual, more relaxed, less precise, less dignified and serious, but generally acceptable. Your guide: the label "colloquial" or "informal," or equivalent comment, in your dictionary. (See also Section 51c7, concluding NOTE.)

| | |
|---|---|
| *Examples* | John flunked his final math exam. |
| | I am (I'm) not coming back. |
| | This is my girl. |

NOTE: (1) "formal" and "informal" apply to both writing and speaking; (2) both kinds of language can be used by the same writer and speaker on different, appropriate occasions; (3) depending upon the occasion, degrees of formality and degrees of informality exist in language, as in dress, but sometimes no rigid border lines separate these degrees. "Informal," for example, is a broad term; its range is from language just above slang to language just below formal.

## 53c   Avoid substandard diction

*Substandard diction* is the written and spoken language of the uneducated, of the least educated, of those who have neither ability nor desire to speak and write formal and informal English, and of those who know better but do not care. Such substandard diction is further discussed in some of the sections that follow; it may consist of misspellings (Section 52), illiteracies (Section 54), improprieties or ungrammatical expressions (Section 55), excessive and unskillful use of slang (Section 56), dialect (Section 57), obsolete and archaic words (Section 59), unaccepted newly coined words (Section 60), and, in speaking, mispronunciations.

Only on rare occasions—purposes of humor or irreverence or irony or recording illiterate conversation or using improprieties or dialect or slang in fiction—is substandard diction appropriate. Many past and present examples do exist of excellent dialect and part-dialect short stories and novels by reputable writers. Equally effective examples exist of eloquent writing and speaking by poorly educated persons deeply sincere in what they said. But anyone with a high school education or beyond should not need substandard English to help him express his serious ideas. Dictionary entries and labels of substandard English, therefore, are more likely recorded for our guidance in reading than for our use in writing.

*Examples*  John sure goofed his math final.
I ain't a-comin' agin.
Wantcha ta meet my doll.

Further subdivisions of language could be made, but, as indicated, for practical purposes the foregoing three are sufficient. Naturally, these divisions are not completely exclusive. The following diagram makes graphic the three groups: standard formal, standard informal, and substandard or illiterate English.

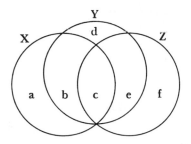

The three circles X, Y, Z represent the three sets of language habits.
  X—formal literary English, the words, the expressions, and the structures one finds in serious books.
  Y—colloquial English, the words, expressions, and the structures of the informal but polite conversation of cultivated people.
  Z—illiterate English, the words, the expressions, and the structures of the language of the uneducated.
  b, c, and e represent the overlappings of the three types of English.
  c—that which is common to all three: formal literary English, colloquial English, and illiterate English.
  b—that which is common to both formal literary English and colloquial English.
  e—that which is common to both colloquial English and illiterate English.
  a, d, and f represent those portions of each type of English that are peculiar to that particular set of language habits.

**EXERCISES**

Study consecutive or miscellaneous pages of your dictionary.

A. Collect from 25 to 50 examples or words or phrases labeled "informal" or "colloquial." Write a 400-word paper on "Informal English," based on your findings.

B. Collect from 25 to 50 examples of words or phrases labeled "substandard." Write a 400-word paper on "Substandard English," based on your findings.

# 54 Illiteracies

### 54 Understand the nature and use of illiterate words and phrases

*Illiteracies* are single words or groups of words forming part of substandard English (see Section 53c); they are, naturally, not acceptable in formal standard or informal standard English.

If illiteracies occur frequently enough in writing, they are recorded in dictionaries with a label like "illiterate" or "substandard" or "nonstandard" or "vulgarism" (the language of the uneducated).[12] Some are labeled "dialect" or "dialectal" when the words or phrases occur in small or traditionally nonstandard English areas, like a specified rural or mountainous region.

A word once popular and still used as a descriptive word for an illiteracy is "barbarism." It came from "barbarian," which came from the Greek word for "foreigner," literally and accurately used of foreigners not included in Greek civilization, no matter how high their own culture (such as Persian) might be. Hence, in the original meaning, a barbarian was simply one who did not belong. By analogy, a "barbarism" is linguistically a word or phrase not acceptably included in the language.

Common illiteracies are (1) mis-forming some of the pronouns (see Section 77g) and (2) words formed by adding -ed to past participles of verbs: *hisself, theirselves; borned, kepted,*

---

[12] Some dictionaries use for "illiteracy" only the terms "substandard" or "nonstandard."

*losted, mistakened.* Other common examples are: *acrossed, ain't, afeard, anywheres, boughten, brung, drownded, irregardless, nohow, nowheres, ourn, snuck* (past of *sneak*).

Characteristic of uneducated people and usually avoided by educated people, illiteracies can at times be used effectively in serious writing for the purposes that all substandard English serves (Section 53c).

## EXERCISES

A. Write a short paper summarizing what your dictionary tells you of these words applied to language: *barbarism, illiteracy, impropriety, solecism, vulgarism.* Use, if possible, dictionary examples of each.

B. From what is the word *vulgarism* derived? What is the difference between *vulgarism* and *vulgarity*?

C. Make a list of 25 illiteracies heard in the conversation of others or reported in books.

D. Below is a selection from a narrative which includes the speech of an uneducated person. From it compile a list of words that are illiterate and another list that includes words common to informal and formal "good" English.

"It's the onluckiest place ennywhar nigh about," said Nathan White, as he sat one afternoon upon the porch of his log-cabin, on the summit of Old Rocky-Top, and gazed up at the heights of the T'other Mounting across the narrow valley. "I hev hearn tell all my days ez how, ef ye go up thar on the T'other Mounting, suthin' will happen ter ye afore ye kin git away. An' I knows myself ez how—'t war ten year ago an' better—I went up thar, one Jan'ry day, a-lookin' fur my cow, ez hed strayed off through not hevin' enny calf ter our house; an' I fund the cow, but jes' tuk an' slipped on a icy rock, an' bruk my ankle-bone. 'T war sech a job a-gettin' off'n that thar T'other Mounting an' back over hyar, it hev l'arned me ter stay away from thar."

—CHARLES E. CRADDOCK, "Over on the T'other Mounting,"
*In the Tennessee Mountains*

# 55  *Improprieties*

Unlike illiteracies, *improprieties* are recognized English words
which are misused in function or meaning and therefore are examples also of substandard English (Section **53c**) . The word constituting an impropriety is acceptable; its misuse causes an error
in diction.

## 55a  Avoid improprieties in grammatical function

One classification of improprieties includes words acceptable as
one part of speech but unacceptable as another: nouns improperly substituted for verbs, verbs for nouns, adjectives for nouns,
adjectives for adverbs, prepositions for conjunctions; another
consists of misuses of principal parts of verbs.

A word identified as more than one part of speech may be so
used without question, but ordinarily do not make a given word
a new part of speech until this new function—linguistically
known as *functional shift* or *functional change*—is sanctioned by
good use and so recorded in a reliable dictionary. Unfortunately,
like the compounding of words, so many examples exist that not
all can be recorded, especially when words that are usually nouns
are being properly used as adjectives—*camp* rules, *college* customs,
*teacher* shortage, *study* hall, *life* span, *road* surface—or adjectives
as nouns (often with *the* and noun understood) —the *weak* and
the *weary*, to admire the *beautiful*, to ignore the *temporary* and
seek the *permanent*.

Here are some unjustifiable examples:

| | |
|---|---|
| *Verbs used as nouns* | *eats, an invite, a think, advise* |
| *Nouns used as verbs* | *birthing* an idea, *biographing*, to *host*, *ambi-tioned*, *heired* |
| *Verb forms* | *seen* for *saw*; *don't* for *doesn't*; *done* for *did*; *laying* for *lying*; *setting* for *sitting*; *hadn't ought*; *of* for *have* |
| *Adjectives used as adverbs* (see Section **83**) | |

## 55b  Avoid improprieties in meaning

A second classification of improprieties includes words like or
almost like other words and used inexactly or wrongly for them.
Such words include:

*1. Homophones:* two or more words that have the same pronunciation, but are different in spelling, in meaning, and in origin: *hour, our, are; pale, pail; sew, so, sow; bough, bow; row, roe.*

*2. Near-homophones:* two or more words almost but not quite pronounced or spelled alike: *later, latter; midst, mist; medal, metal.*

*3. Homographs:* two or more words that have the same spelling but are different in meaning, origin, and perhaps pronunciation: *air* (atmosphere) and *air* (melody); *bow* (to bend forward), *bow* (the forward end of a ship), *bow* (used to play a violin); *row* (a straight line), *row* (to propel a boat), and *row* (a noisy dispute).

In writing, bear in mind the lack of clarity caused through confusing homophones, near-homophones, and homographs. Homographs cannot cause misspelling, but they can cause ambiguity and confusion. If you are in doubt about the meaning or spelling of a word or two similar words, the usual advice about the dictionary applies.

More extensive lists: for spelling, see Section **52b,** and for exactness and precision, see Section **63a,b.**

## EXERCISES

A. Use correctly in sentences 10 of the pairs of words listed in Section **52b.**

B. Use correctly in sentences 10 of the pairs of words listed in Section **63a.**

C. In the Craddock paragraph in Exercise D, p. 344, make a list of the improprieties.

D. From the following paragraphs (from a first-person point-of-view short story) make two lists: one of illiteracies (Section **54**) and one of improprieties:

I got another barber that comes over from Carterville and helps me out Saturdays, but the rest of the time I can get along all right alone. You can see for yourself that this ain't no New York City and besides that, the most of the boys works all day and don't have no leisure time to drop in here and get themselves prettied up.

You're a newcomer, ain't you? I thought I hadn't seen you round before. I hope you like it good enough to stay. As I say, we ain't no

New York City or Chicago, but we have pretty good times. Not as good, though, since Jim Kendall got killed. When he was alive, him and Hod Meyers used to keep this town in an uproar. I bet they was more laughin' done here than any town its size in America.

—RING LARDNER, "Haircut"

E. Correct any improprieties in the following sentences:

1. During the first few days all the freshmen had to be originated.
2. Be a good listener and do not interpret the person who is talking.
3. A petty criminal is one who has been convicted of immorality many times.
4. I like a band that plays marital music; it makes me feel like marching.
5. We have practiced soil conversation on our farm for many years.
6. In Washington, don't miss seeing the impressive stature of Abraham Lincoln.
7. "Are you implicating," I said, "that I don't know what I'm talking about."
8. I was never able to interrupt poetry to the satisfaction of my teacher.
9. Our sociology teacher has no trouble getting us to precipitate in discussions.
10. To the great volume of Indiana history, our own community has attributed one of the most colorful chapters.

# 56  Slang

*Slang* is a label for words and phrases ranging from the lower ranks of acceptable colloquialisms or informal standard English (Section 53) down to the lowest levels of illiteracies (Section 54).

Characteristics of slang include flippant, eccentric, or exaggerated humor; forced, fantastic, or grotesque novelty; clipped or shortened forms—attempts, often successful, to be vivid, lively, vigorous, colorful. On the positive side, slang does express feeling, and, being lively, vigorous, colorful, often humorous, it provides short cuts in expression and, until it becomes trite (Section 66), it prevents artificiality in writing.

Slang expressions may appeal to popular fancy or to some segment of it (for example, college slang, military slang, baseball slang, music slang), and some slang words and expressions may for a time be used over a wide area, endure for a considerable time, and find their way into reliable dictionaries with the "slang" label attached. Eventually, some of these words and phrases may receive the respectable label "informal" or "colloquial" or be "promoted" to no label at all. Remember, however, that some dictionaries are more permissive than others and may differ in their labeling. Furthermore, so many examples of past and present slang exist that rather large dictionaries have been compiled that contain *only* slang expressions.[13]

## 56a   *Train yourself to recognize slang expressions*

Slang expressions appear as one of several forms:

1. Neologisms (newly coined words) which remain slang: *geezer, grandiferous, hornswoggle, moniker, simoleon.* Not all newly coined words, however, are slang. (See Section **60**.)

2. Words formed from others by abbreviating or by adding endings to change the part of speech: *legit, phony, prexy, psych out, snafu* (*s*ituation *n*ormal, *a*ll *f*ouled *u*p).

3. Words in otherwise acceptable use given extended meanings: *buck, chicken, creep, dish, square.*

4. Words formed by compounding or coalescing two or more words: *attaboy* (that's the boy), *egghead, sawbuck, screwball, whodunit, beatnik.*

5. Phrases made up of one or more newly coined words (neologisms) or one or more acceptable ones: *blow one's top, conk out, get in orbit, goof off, off one's rocker.*

## 56b   *Avoid slang in formal and informal standard writing*

Slang may occasionally serve the purposes of substandard English (see Section **53c**) but, although popular, it has little place in

13 For those interested in exploring slang words and phrases, see for American slang the following: Lester V. Berrey and Melvin van den Bark, *The American Thesaurus of Slang*, 2nd ed. (New York: Thomas Y. Crowell Company, 1953), and Harold Wentworth and Stuart B. Flexner, *Dictionary of American Slang* (New York: Thomas Y. Crowell Company, 1967). For British slang, see Eric Partridge, *A Dictionary of Slang and Unconventional English*, 5th ed. (New York: Macmillan, 1961).

standard formal writing and in most standard informal writing. Sound reasons exist for avoiding it:

1. Many slang words and phrases are understood by only a limited group or in a limited area, are unintelligible to many readers and listeners, and thus violate the principle of national use. (See Section **57**.)

2. Many slang words and phrases last for a brief time and then pass out of use, become unintelligible, and thus violate the principle of contemporary use. (See Section **59**.)

3. The use of slang expressions keeps a writer from searching for the exact word needed to express precise meaning. Many slang expressions are only rubber stamps; they do not express exactly or fully any critical judgment or intelligent description. To argue that such words convey precisely the intended meaning is to reveal poverty of vocabulary or careless thinking or laziness. A serious charge against slang is that it becomes a substitute for thinking.

4. Slang does not serve the primary purpose of writing: conveying a clear message from writer to reader. This objection to slang is evident from the brief discussion above.

5. Finally, slang is not appropriate in standard formal and most standard informal writing because it is not in keeping with the context. Once again, words should be appropriate to the reader, the writer, the occasion and the subject matter (Section **53**) .

## EXERCISES

A. Write a brief paper comparing and contrasting the meanings given by your dictionary for the following: *slang, argot, cant, dialect, jargon, lingo, shoptalk, vernacular.*

B. Collect at least 25 examples of slang words and phrases from your dictionary. What does each mean?

C. Collect at least 25 examples of slang words and phrases heard around the campus. From your list write a 400-word theme on the subject, "College Slang, 19———."

# 57   *National diction*

Television, radio, motion pictures, books, magazines, and news-papers—the media of mass communication—have helped to make American English *national*. That is, any writer or speaker can assume that he will be understood by any American reader or listener if he uses words and phrases common to all parts of our country and thus more or less immediately intelligible. Hence, a characteristic of correct, clear, and effective diction is that it should be in national and general use.

## 57a   *Use and understand appropriate nationalisms*

Broadly defined, an English *nationalism* is a word or phrase common in or limited to English used by one of the English-speaking nations. *Americanism* and *Briticism* refer to words or word meanings common, respectively, in the United States[14] and the British Isles; *Scotticism* is an idiom or mode of expression peculiar to the Scottish people; logically, other labels might be *Canadianisms, Australianisms, New-Zealandisms,* and *South-Africanisms.*

All dictionaries label many such expressions "U.S.," "Chiefly U.S.," "British," "Chiefly British," "Scottish," or the like, not perhaps so much to guide us in our writing—except when we write to someone in a non-American nation—as to help us understand them when we come across them in the writings of any writer writing in English anywhere in the world. Examples:

*Americanisms*    *calaboose* (prison, jail), *catchup* (tomato sauce), *levee* (an embankment), *stump* (travel to electioneer), *tote* (carry, or a load), *bellhop, caboose, gangster, gusher, haberdasher*

14 More comprehensively, a two-volume reference work, *A Dictionary of Americanisms on Historical Principles,* records only words of American origin and words with a distinctively American meaning, *American* here referring only to the United States. Also, a monumental and fascinating work that richly rewards browsing is H. L. Mencken's in three volumes: *The American Language: An Inquiry into the Development of English in the United States,* 4th ed., *Supplement I, Supplement II* (New York: Knopf, 1936, 1945, 1948).

| *Briticisms* | *accumulator* (storage battery), *croft* (small enclosed field), *barrister* or *solicitor* (lawyer), *petrol* (gasoline), *tube* (subway) |
| *Scotch dialect* | *auld* (old), *awee* (a little while), *bairn* (child), *bree* (broth), *canty* (cheerful) |

## 57b   Use localisms when they are appropriate

A *localism* is a word or phrase used and understood primarily in a particular section or region. It may therefore also be called a *regionalism* or a *provincialism* (apparently because, formerly, English used in London was "good English"; English used outside London in the "provinces" was not good English but "provincial").

The northeastern, southern, southwestern, and western areas[15] of the United States are especially rich in colorful localisms which add flavor to speech but which may not be immediately intelligible in other areas. For a resident of one of these areas, such expressions are difficult to detect, because as writer or speaker he accepts them as reputable and assumes that they are generally understood, since he himself has known and used them from childhood. Although words and combinations of words used locally may not be explained in print anywhere, dictionaries do label or define many words according to the geographical area where they are common. Examples:

| *Northeastern* | *down-Easter* (a native of New England, especially of Maine), *moosewood* (striped maple), *selectman* (a town official), *skunk cabbage, sugar maple* |
| *South* | *butternuts* (a kind of brown overalls), *corn pone* (corn bread), *granny* (a nurse), *hoecake* (a cake of Indian meal), *lightwood* (pitchy pine wood) |
| *Southwest* | *longhorn* (formerly a variety of cattle), *maverick* (an unbranded animal), *mesa* (flat-topped rocky hill with steeply sloping sides), *mesquite* (spiny tree or shrub), *mustang* (small, hardy, half-wild horse) |

15 For illustrating localisms and regionalisms, these major divisions will serve. Linguistic scholars, considering both word occurrence and pronunciation, make finer distinctions than the four areas mentioned: for example, the eastern part of the United States is divided into North, North Midland, West Midland, South Midland, and South, and for the entire United States the divisions are, broadly, New England, North, Midland, South, West, Southwest, Northwest.

| Western | *coulee* (narrow, steep-walled valley), *dogie, dogy* (motherless calf), *grubstake* (supplies or funds furnished a prospector), *rustler* (cattle thief), *sagebrush* (a flower of the aster family) |

Should localisms be used? The only satisfactory answer is appropriateness. If you live in an area or address people in an area where localisms are easily understood, they are appropriate in speaking and in informal writing. But in formal writing for such a geographical area and in formal and informal speaking and writing to be understandable in other sections, avoid localisms in the interests of clearness.

Localisms can also include *dialect*—written or spoken expression used in a limited geographical area or used by a certain social group in a limited area (like the Pennsylvania Dutch) or used by a certain social group on a more extensive geographical scale, like Scottish dialect.

### EXERCISES

A. Make a list of 10 to 25 localisms heard in your neighborhood or vicinity. Write a short paper on them to be read in class.

B. From time to time study consecutive or miscellaneous pages of your dictionary. Compile three lists of 25 to 50 words each, one of words in meaning or by label being "Regional American Words," one of words labeled "British" or "Chiefly British," and one of words labeled "Scottish" or "Chiefly Scottish." Using an appropriate title, write three 400-word papers, one based on each of the three lists.

## 58  Foreign words and phrases

For Americans a foreign word or phrase is one from a non-English language. Naturally, then, words and phrases that have come to us from other English-speaking countries—such as the British Isles, Canada, Australia, New Zealand, South Africa—are not foreign, although some may be uncommon in American (U.S.) English. Of course, one English ancestor—Anglo-Saxon or Old English—is a completely foreign language, and another ancestor—Middle

English—is partly foreign and rugged reading, so that to understand both Old English and Middle English some special training is necessary. Even some Scottish writing, like some of the poems of Robert Burns or Sir Walter Scott's recording of conversation, seems almost foreign.

Literally thousands of foreign words have come into our language from Greek, Latin, and French, and literally hundreds more from other languages. Depending upon your dictionary, you will find from 40 to 150 foreign-language abbreviations used for word origins and meanings.

Two things happen to these foreign words and phrases: (1) if they have been widely used or used over a long period, or both, they are Anglicized and become a part of our everyday language and are recorded in dictionaries like any common word; (2) if the conditions of (1) have not been met, the word or phrase remains foreign; as such, and if occasionally used, it is or should be indicated in dictionaries as foreign, partly as a guide for a writer to use italics if he uses the word or phrase in his writing (see Section **96**).

Anglicized examples: a priori, à la mode, blitz, chef, habitué, smorgasbord. Non-Anglicized examples: *Anno Domini, fait accompli, cause célèbre, ex libris, mañana, Weltschmerz.*

## 58 Use common sense in your use of foreign words and phrases

A good guide: if the word or phrase has been Anglicized or if no good English equivalent exists, use it. But why *merci beaucoup* for "thank you" or *Auf Wiedersehen* for "good-by"? Even "a" or "an" serves better than "per": "$5 an hour." Do not use such foreign expressions too frequently or merely to convince the reader of your erudition and affected dignity.

### EXERCISES

Study consecutive or miscellaneous pages of your dictionary.

A. Compile a list of 25 foreign words or phrases, with their meaning and language, that have not been Anglicized or become a part of current English.

B. Compile a list of 25 foreign words or phrases, with their meaning and origin, that have been Anglicized or become a part of current English.

# 59   Contemporary diction

## 59a   Use diction that is in present-day use

In addition to reputable and national diction (Sections **53a,b** and **57**), a third characteristic is needed for correct, clear, and effective diction: present-day use, that is, words intelligible to contemporary readers and hearers.

But sometimes characterizing phrases are broad; for example, *modern* English is the English used after 1475 or 1500, although linguists divide the last 500 years into two subdivisions, Early Modern English, 1475–1700, and Late Modern English, from 1700 on. Words are constantly going out of use or being less frequently used because language is constantly changing. New words and phrases in form and meaning take the place of the old (see Section **60**). Current dictionaries contain many new words and many new meanings of words that were unknown even 25 or 30 years ago; these same dictionaries indicate by label or absence of label which words are in acceptable present-day use (see Section **53**).

## 59b   Avoid words and expressions not in present-day use

Except for somewhat doubtful purposes of humor, guard against using expressions that may persist in your vocabulary because you have seen them in books or reprints of books written centuries ago. Out-of-date expressions—the actual words themselves which have disappeared from current English and, more commonly, certain meanings of words which in other meanings are frequently and acceptably used—are of three kinds: obsolete words, archaic words, and poetic words in prose. Note, in checking, that dictionaries do not always agree in their labeling or in using any label.

*1. Obsolete words.* An *obsolete* word is one that has completely passed out of use—either in its form or in one or more of its meanings. Because many examples exist, a dictionary may set an arbitrary date—say, 1755—and use the label "obsolete" for words not found in standard use after that date. Examples:

| | |
|---|---|
| *In form* | *egal, enwheel, lieve, mammer, ronyon* |
| *In meaning* | *curious, emboss, garb, nice, prevent* |

2. *Archaic words.* An *archaic* word is old-fashioned, a word common in earlier speaking and writing, but appearing only rarely (note: some dictionaries label certain words "rare") in modern writing, again some arbitrary date being set, like 1755. Such words may be retained in special contexts, such as legal and Biblical expressions. Like obsolete words, many so-called archaic words are archaic in only one or two meanings, in current use in others. Examples: *anon, and, cote, marry, y-clept.*

3. *Poetic words. Poetic diction* is the term used for words or word-meanings that have usually been (or still are, occasionally) used in poetry but not in prose. For almost two centuries, however, much poetic diction has consisted of imaginative *combinations* of words rather than of particular isolated words themselves.

"Poetic" words, sometimes so labeled in dictionaries, sometimes labeled "archaic," are usually archaic words found in poetry written in or designed to create the atmosphere of a somewhat remote past. Examples are certain contractions such as *'tis, 'twas;* the use of *-st, -est, -th, -eth* endings on present-tense verbs: *dost, would'st, doth, leadeth;* and words like *glebe, 'neath, oft, oftimes,* and *ope.*

Worth noting is that obsolete, archaic, and poetic words are so labeled in dictionaries primarily as helpful to present-day readers of older writers and writings or of present-day writings portraying faithfully the manners, customs, and language of a long-past era, as in histories, historical novels, and the like.

## EXERCISES

A. Study consecutive or miscellaneous pages of your dictionary. Compile three lists of 25 to 50 words each, one of "obsolete," one of "archaic," and one of "poetic" words. From your lists write three papers, entitled, respectively, "Obsolete Words," "Archaic Words," "Poetic Words."

B. Read several of the older English or Scottish popular ballads or Samuel Taylor Coleridge's "The Rime of the Ancient Mariner." Compile and explain a list of the archaic words.

# 60   *Neologisms*

### 60   *Use neologisms appropriately*

Language, like life and knowledge, is constantly changing. Just as words labeled obsolete and archaic disappear or appear less frequently, so too new words are constantly being added. If they fill a real need, they survive, are accepted, and become part of contemporary English; if they do not, they quietly disappear, and are seen and heard no more.

A neologism is a word newly coined to fill a need—a "make-a-word-for-it." Sometimes, of course, perhaps often, an established word is given a new meaning, and then the word is not technically a neologism, unless it is a newly coined homograph (same spelling, different origin). Given time to prove their worth and general acceptance, many neologisms find their way into reliable dictionaries.

Words are coined in various ways:

1. Needed words in the fields of sciences, technology, and business, to describe new inventions, discoveries, applications, and occupations: *astronautics, astrogate, automation, countdown, H-bomb, cyclotron, computerize, realtor, beautician.*

2. Adaptation of common words—often, by analogy, such as adding *-ize* to nouns to form verbs or adding a suffix like *-wise* to form adverbs: *vacationize, signaturize, bookwise, citywise, avoirduprose, cinemactress, millionheiress.*

3. Combinations of two or more common words, the so-called portmanteau words: *brunch* (*br*eakfast and l*unch*) ; *cheeseburger* (*cheese* and ham*burger*) ; *chortle* (*ch*uckle and sn*ort*) ; *motel* (*mo*tor and ho*tel*) ; *smog* (*sm*oke and f*og*) ; *transistor* (*trans*fer and re*sistor*) ; *witticism* (*witty* and criti*cism,* coined by John Dryden, British writer, in 1677!) .

4. The initial letters or syllables of common words: *loran* (*lo*ng *ra*nge *n*avigation) ; *radar* (*rad*io detecting *a*nd *r*anging) . Such a word is an "acronym."

5. Virtually or completely new formations: *gobbledygook* (Section 68) ; *bafflegab* (baffling gab) ; *blurb; heebie-jeebies; nylon.*

6. Words from a major change in our national way of living, like a depression or a war. From World War II: *bazooka, blitz, genocide, jeep, quisling.*

7. Registered trade names or trademarks (even though in dictionaries, the private property of their owners) and/or their derivatives: *Kodak, Dacron, Linotype, simonize, technicolor.*

Depending on the dictionary you own, newly coined words which appear there may have no label or be labeled "informal" or "colloquial" or "slang," with perhaps even a brief history of their origin or originator. If you use neologisms in your writing or speaking, be sure they are appropriate to content and reader, that is, easily understood by the people whom you are addressing.

**EXERCISES**

A. Read several issues of *Time* magazine and bring to class a representative list of 20 neologisms that appear there.

B. Read the latest articles of several newspaper columnists and make a list of any neologisms you find.

# 61  Technical words

Technical words have special meanings for people in particular fields, professions, arts, occupations, or recreations, such as sports.

To such words some 30 to 50 special subject labels are attached in dictionaries, from "Aeronautics" through "Zoology." Almost every page of your dictionary contains examples of words with these technical labels (see Section 51c7c). In the last 30 years, many new words and meanings have come from fields like chemistry, electronics, astronautics, nuclear physics, automation, medicine, and other sciences.

Thousands of technical words are not in general dictionaries, but the number included is sufficiently large for the general reader not to have to be baffled on seeing them in print. When technical words are widely used or extend their meanings, their subject labels may be dropped. Some examples (made popular by special fields) are *broadcast* (from radio), *telescope* (from astronomy), *weld* (from engineering), *chisel* (from carpentry), *diagnose* (from medicine), *daub* (from painting), *mold* (from sculpture), *starry* (from astronomy), *arch* (from architecture), *virtuoso* (from music and art).

### 61   *Use technical words and phrases appropriately*

A specialist writing for or speaking to other specialists uses many difficult technical terms. If he communicates with others in his general scientific field, he uses terms that are less difficult. If he addresses the nonspecialist, he should avoid all technical terms or use only those generally understood. These three approaches divide the style used into *technical, semitechnical,* and *nontechnical* or *popular.* For example, few of us could understand a technical treatment of a subject in the magazine *Electronics.* More of us could understand its treatment in *Scientific American.* All of us could understand it if it were adapted for one of the general magazines on the newsstands.

Therefore, in using technical words in any writing that you do, apply for the sake of clearness the advice given about jargon in Section **68b.**

**EXERCISE**

From time to time study consecutive or miscellaneous pages of your dictionary. Make a list of at least 50 technical words labeled as to field. Also, copy their meanings. Write a 400-word paper on "Some Technical Words, Their Meanings, and the Fields They Represent."

## 62   *Idiomatic English*

Idiomatic English, applied to diction, concerns words used mainly in combination with others. *Idiom* and *idiomatic* are from the Greek words *idioma* and *idiomatikos,* the key meaning of which is "peculiar, peculiarity." Because of this key meaning, for idiomatic expressions there are no laws or principles describing their formation (comparable, for example, to principles describing tense formation or uses of punctuation marks). Each idiomatic expression, a law to itself, may violate grammar or logic or both; yet it is an acceptable phrase, familiar, widely used, easily understandable—for the native-born.

Not only English but every language has its idioms, its peculiarities. French and German and Spanish idioms are difficult for us to understand and master, and many foreign expressions cannot be translated literally. In literal translation, the French say, "Here one speaks French" and "We have come from eating"; the English equivalents are, "French is spoken here" and "We have just eaten."

Likewise, idiomatic English is difficult not only for foreigners but also for all who do not read or carefully listen. For example, we may tell a foreign student not to say "many man," "many man is," "a students," "10 foot," and then we confuse him by saying, correctly, "many a man is," "a few students," and "a 10-foot pole." Or we have trouble explaining proper negative prefixes, like *indescribable* but not "undescribable" or *undesirable* but not "indesirable."

The many idiomatic expressions in English permit only a few generalized statements. One is that words combined may lose their literal meaning and indicate something only remotely suggested by any one word: *lay up, heavy hand, toe the line, bed of roses, get even with, dark horse, open house, read between the lines, black list.*

An adaptation of the foregoing statement is that the parts of the human body and words expressing activity have suggested many idioms: *fly in the face of, burn one's fingers, stand on one's own feet, keep one's eyes open, keep body and soul together, all thumbs, make believe, take to heart, do oneself well, ride it out, ride herd on,* etc.

A third generalization is that hundreds of idiomatic phrases contain adverbs or prepositions with other parts of speech. No "rule" guides their use; yet certain combinations are allowable and clear while others are not. Examples: *run down, run in, run off, run out, walk off, walkover, walk-up, get nowhere, get through, get off.*

## 62   *Use acceptable idiomatic English*

Two suggestions for your use of idiomatic English:

1. Use appropriate idiomatic expressions. They make writing and speech vigorous, imaginative, and effective. They are part of the essential material of which language is made: the widespread, everyday usage of cultivated people.

2. Verify through your dictionary the acceptance of the idioms you use. The most commonly used are recorded there, usually following the key word—noun, adjective, verb—to which has been added some other part of speech, usually a preposition or adverb. Some such combinations cannot be acceptably used, and such expressions are unidiomatic. Examples:

| *Unidiomatic* | *Idiomatic* |
|---|---|
| according with | according to |
| acquaint to | acquaint with |
| angry at (a person) | angry with |
| authority about | authority on |
| cannot help but (talk) | cannot help (talking) |
| conform in | conform to, with |
| in search for | in search of |
| prior than | prior to |
| responsible on | responsible for (to) |
| unequal for | unequal to |

Other prepositions and adverbs used with the same key words change the meaning, limit it, and make it more clear. Examples:

agree
- *to* a proposal
- *on* a plan
- *with* a person

contend
- *for* a principle
- *with* a person
- *against* an obstacle

differ
- *with* a person
- *from* something else
- *about* or *over* a question

impatient
- *for* something desired
- *with* someone else
- *of* restraint
- *at* someone's conduct

rewarded
- *for* something done
- *with* a gift
- *by* a person

wait
- *at* a place
- *for* a person
- *on* a customer

Dictionaries usually record the more common idiomatic phrases after the definitions of the word entries. For examples of such recording, see p. 311.

**EXERCISE**

Make the following sentences idiomatically acceptable by listing the prepositions which would properly fill in the blanks:

1. Jane is too careless —— her appearance.
2. John is now reconciled —— living on a small salary.
3. Please don't meddle —— affairs not your own.
4. That species is peculiar —— this vicinity.
5. You will find Mary —— home this afternoon.
6. Some people cannot bear to part —— a prized possession.
7. What do you infer —— that proposal?
8. Your mother is apprehensive —— your safety.
9. Are you really independent —— your father?
10. This letter means that he will accede —— your request.
11. Some students are unconcerned —— the consequences they will face.
12. In my opinion the study rooms are the most important asset —— the library.
13. Our citizens are conscious —— the fact that we have a great need for more industries.
14. The only difference —— them and other students is that they took all the easy courses they could.
15. For many years Mr. Brown has had the reputation —— being a very successful businessman.


# 63 *Exact and precise diction*

Exact and precise diction is essential for clearness and effectiveness. Since the primary purpose of writing is communication, it is important that words express exactly and precisely what you mean.


## 63a  *Use exact words*

Exact diction concerns exact word order, i.e., misplaced modifier (Section 39a), right word vs. wrong word, and double-meaning words and phrases.

| | |
|---|---|
| *Wrong-word examples* | John and Mary were a handsome couple as they walked down the *isle*. Later they spent their honeymoon on an *aisle* in the West Indies. |
| *Ambiguous examples* | If Joe doesn't study more, he will get exactly what he deserves; and if he studies harder, he will get exactly what he deserves. |
| | Those people certainly got an awful lot for their money [overheard at a real estate development]. |

*Exact* words are not misused for, or confused with, words alike or similar in sound and spelling—homonyms, homographs, homophones—nor are they closely enough like others to be improprieties in function or meaning (Sections **52b, 55b**). In addition to the homonyms and near-homonyms listed in Section **52b**, other trouble-causers with subtle or not-so-subtle differences in meaning are in the following list (those preceded by * are discussed in "Glossary of Diction" (Section **70**) :

| | |
|---|---|
| adverse, averse | *farther, further |
| *advise, inform | *fewer, less |
| allowed, aloud | *formally, formerly |
| *all ready, already | healthful, healthy |
| *all together, altogether | *if, whether |
| allude, elude | imply, infer |
| allusion, illusion | instance, instants |
| *almost, most | interest, intrigue (v.) |
| *amount, number | irrelevant, irreverent |
| *anxious, eager | *leave, let |
| *apt, liable, likely | lessen, lesson |
| believe, *feel | *lie, lay |
| *beside, besides | luxuriant, luxurious |
| climactic, climatic | moral, morale |
| confidently, confidentially | official, officious |
| continual, continuous | *party, person, individual |
| convince, persuade | practicable, practical |
| credible, creditable, credulous | *raise, rise |
| *disinterested, uninterested | *respectfully, respectively |
| expect, suspect | *sit, set |

### 63b    Use precise words
*Precise* words are exact words, but they are more. Any of several words may convey a general meaning (Section **64a**), but even if

you have a choice of several words approximating what you wish to say, each idea has a word or phrase which will express your meaning more precisely than all others. It is your obligation to find this word or phrase. In the search, a thesaurus is an excellent reference book to have available. Frequently, too, your choice is from several words with nearly identical meanings, and study of the synonyms listed for an expression in a dictionary or thesaurus enables you to choose a more precise term. For example, before allowing a word like *cheerful* or *cheery* to stand in one of your themes, find out whether one of the following adjectives will communicate your meaning more precisely: *blithe, gay, jocose, jocular, jocund, jolly, jovial, joyful, joyous, merry, sportive.*

Do not, however, let the use of synonyms lead you into a different kind of error-absurdity: two words may be synonymous in one meaning but not in another. Consider the following ludicrous uses of synonyms for, respectively, *steal, vision,* and *face:*

The moon is *pilfering* over the mountaintop.
In her beautiful new gown Mary was a *sight* at the wedding.
In the poem Lancelot says that the Lady of Shalott had a lovely *map.*

Exactness and preciseness in diction require you to think clearly and carefully. Sometimes the first word that comes to mind is the exact word or the most precise one that can be used; more often it is not. Exact and precise diction results only when the reader understands exactly and precisely what the writer intended to communicate.

## EXERCISES

A. Substitute better words for any weak ones in the following sentences:

1. It seems funny how Nature provides us with so much beauty.
2. A Thanksgiving dinner without a turkey is dreadful.
3. The weather in Arizona and California is simply terrific.
4. Our high school building is one of the prettiest in the state.
5. Most of the brands of portable typewriters on the market are fine.
6. I am anticipating my four years of college to be very interesting.
7. Our college now has one of the nicest gyms among colleges of our size.
8. I had a feeling that my freshman year was going to be just awful.

9. Trying, not winning, is the most important factor in the game of life.
10. Sir Walter Scott has a perfectly lovely view toward knights and ladies.

B. In the following sentences, the writers obviously did not say what they intended to say. What did they mean to say?

1. Dennis never struck me as a close friend.
2. I then stopped in across the street to learn how old Mrs. Jones is.
3. There in the street I found my eyes resting on top of the Empire State Building.
4. The dinner is to honor residents and interns who are leaving the hospital and their wives.—News item.
5. Henry and his brother would take stomach aches from the green apples.
6. It will be good to get away from bookies for two weeks at Christmas.
7. We are having my aunt and uncle for Christmas dinner, and I am sure we will enjoy them.
8. I think I shall never forget a talk by the Coke machine, before I left high school.
9. We next visited a furniture factory, where hundreds of antiques are manufactured every day.
10. With nothing to do on New Year's Eve, and feeling degraded, I went to a party given by my neighbors.

# 64   *Emphatic diction*

Emphatic words contribute to effective diction. Such words are exact and precise (Section **63**) and illustrate also the principles discussed in the next five major sections (**65, 66, 67, 68, 69**). Three additional suggestions for emphatic diction are treated here: specific vs. general words, concrete vs. abstract words, connotative vs. denotative words.

## 64a   *Prefer specific to general words*

Emphatic diction uses expressive nouns, adjectives, verbs, and adverbs. A *general* word names a broad concept: class names of nouns (*animal, clothing, devices, land, street*), conventional verbs (*go, move, say*), and vague adjectives and adverbs (*good, bad, gladly, fast*). Especially colorless diction results from overuse of the forms of *to be* (*am, is, are, was, were,* etc.).

A *specific* word names a narrow concept—*collie, leotard, pasture, flashlight, boulevard, totter, dash, shout, errorless, excruciating, mile-a-second, triumphantly*—and each of these could be further narrowed. A specific word is a vivid word, hence a clear word; an active, hence a lively, word; and a pleasant, hence an easy-to-look-at, word. Why is the second sentence following more effective?

There was a pleasant stream flowing down the mountain.
Serpentining Chestnut Creek felt its way noisily down Mount Greyrock
over smooth, greenish-white stones.

Other general words are so vague and indefinite that they only approximate an idea. With the aid of a thesaurus you can surely find specific words for any of the following ineffective words and phrases:

| | | | |
|---|---|---|---|
| aspect | field | manner | quality |
| case | fine | matter | question |
| character | great | nature | situation |
| condition | instance | nice | state |
| cute | interesting | personality | style |
| degree | item | persuasion | thing |
| element | job | phase | type |
| factor | lot | point | vital |
| feature | lovely | problem | way |

| | |
|---|---|
| *Vague and indefinite* | a fine day |
| | a great game |
| | a good job |
| | *thing* used for any idea or object, as "another thing to remember" |
| *Specific* | a memorable day |
| | a crucial (or championship-deciding) game |
| | a worthwhile achievement |
| | another argument to remember |

## *64b*   *Prefer concrete to abstract words*

An *abstract* word gives no clear picture; it is often a general word like some of those in the preceding section or like some of the following: *beauty, culture, efficiency, effectiveness, wealth.* A *concrete* word expresses something tangible, something usually perceivable by one or more of the senses—sight, sound, smell, taste, touch, something pleasant or unpleasant: *lilacs, crimson, drumbeats, rose-scented, lemony, jagged, incarnadined.* "He closed the door" pictures movement; "he slammed the door" gives picture and sound. *Weep* suggests sight and feeling; *sob* adds hearing and movement.

Excellent examples of concrete words are onomatopoeic words, i.e., "make-a-name-for-it" words or words which express or suggest sounds: *meow, bark, hoot, lowing, rustling, murmuring, thud, crash, pop, ripple, singsong.*

Specific and concrete nouns, therefore, colorful and dynamic adjectives and adverbs, verbs which tell of action (motion) or relate to the senses (emotion), specific and concrete phrases—all help make writing more forceful.

The following statement is perfectly true:

> Jonathan Swift, who as a writer kept a journal, composed essays on religion and politics, and wrote satires, said good words make a good style.

Instead, however, a writer put it this way:

> Jonathan Swift, whose writing experience carried him all the way from the baby-talk of his *Journal to Stella* through the fire and thunder of his essays on religion and politics to the satire of his *Gulliver's Travels,* said shrewdly that writing style is "proper words in proper places."                    —"On Writing Clearly," *The Royal Bank of Canada Monthly Letter,* July, 1957

## *64c*   *Understand the difference between denotative and connotative words*

If your purpose is writing exposition or argument (see Section 17c,d), you will use words that are as exact and specific as possible. Clearness is a basic guiding principle. Even in such writing, however, as well as in narration and description, search for words which suggest more than they say, which stimulate the imagination.

*Denotative* words express merely what the definitions of the words say; they are clear and are to be taken in their literal, explicit meaning for neither more nor less than they say: *house, woman, dog, city, New Orleans.*

*Connotative* words include implied, suggestive, or associated meanings. They stimulate the imagination and are emphatic: *home*—comfort, love, shelter, intimacy, privacy, etc.; *mother*—love, devotion, understanding, sacrifice, etc.; *dog*—affection, care, trouble, fun, love, loyalty, obedience, etc.; *New Orleans*—the Mississippi, the levees, the old French Quarter, Creole life, the Sugar Bowl, Mardi Gras, etc.

No guiding principle can be given for the choice and use of words rich in connotative meanings, except, perhaps, the guides of clearness and effectiveness. One simple caution is that you do not exaggerate unduly in your word choice; otherwise, you reduce effectiveness (Section **65c**).

Worthy of study is the 23rd Psalm (Holy Bible, King James Version). Note its use of specific, concrete, connotative words; the extended metaphor (Section **65a**); its use of few general, abstract, and denotative words; and its effective use of some archaic words (the translation was published in 1611):

The Lord is my shepherd; I shall not want.

He maketh me to lie down in green pastures; he leadeth me beside the still waters.

He restoreth my soul: he leadeth me in the paths of righteousness for his name's sake.

Yea, though I walk through the valley of the shadow of death, I will fear no evil; for thou art with me; thy rod and thy staff they comfort me.

Thou preparest a table before me in the presence of mine enemies; thou anointest my head with oil; my cup runneth over.

Surely goodness and mercy shall follow me all the days of my life; and I will dwell in the house of the Lord for ever.

## EXERCISES

Among others, eight well-known masters of English prose are quoted in this book: Joseph Addison (p. 26–27), Jonathan Swift (p. 27–28), Francis Bacon (pp. 81, 276), Charles Dickens (pp. 85–86, 179),

Henry David Thoreau (p. 169–170), Washington Irving (p. 180), Abraham Lincoln (p. 276), Joseph Conrad (p. 295). Choose five.

A. For each chosen, list five examples of specific words and five examples of general words (adjectives, adverbs, nouns, verbs). Section **64a.**

B. For each chosen, list five examples of concrete words and five examples of abstract words (adjectives, adverbs, nouns, verbs). Section **64b.**

C. Name several words which have the same general meaning as the word italicized but which are more exact and emphatic: (1) a *tall* building; (2) your *nice* child; (3) a *talkative* man; (4) a *kind* person; (5) a *loud* noise; (6) he *worked* hard; (7) she *walked* in; (8) a *leading* merchant; (9) I was *surprised*; (10) it's a *pleasant* room; (11) a *dislike* of war; (12) a *good* mind; (13) he *got* on the carousel; (14) he *ran* quickly; (15) a *small* animal; (16) the doorbell *sounded*; (17) a miserable *house*; (18) Dr. Jones is a *specialist*; (19) a *delightful* book; (20) an interesting *trip*.

# 65   *Figurative language*

## 65a   *Make occasional use of figurative language when it is appropriate*

Clear and effective language, in prose as well as in poetry, uses appropriate figures of speech. *Literal language* is language that means exactly what it says, in a matter-of-fact and plain-fact way. If you say, "Since it was raining very hard, I hurried up the hill and into my house," you literally tell what happened. *Figurative language* is language that suggests sense-impressions, exaggerated activity, images, imagination, pictures; i.e., it suggests "figures" to the mind. Although the words are exact, precise, concrete, and picturesque, the language is not literally true, but we find it clear and effective if the suggestion or association is appropriate. "Since it was raining like an April flood, I flew up the hill and into my house."

Found occasionally in prose are the following figures of

speech, which, like the parts of speech, occur in both speaking and writing:

1. *Simile,* a figure of comparison: an *expressed* comparison using the words *like* or *as*: "She sings like an angel." "In boxing he fights like a tiger." "The miniature plane flew as gracefully as a bird."

2. *Metaphor,* a figure of comparison: an *implied* comparison; the reader or listener uses his imagination to see the likeness: "She is an angel when she sings." "In the ring he is a tiger."

3. *Synecdoche,* a figure of association: use of a part or an individual for the whole class or group, or the reverse. Part for whole: "The Spanish Armada, which tried to invade England in 1588, consisted of 120 sail," i.e., ships. Whole for part: "Atwood defeated Dorchester U. in the championship game," i.e., the two universities did not play, but their football teams did.

4. *Metonymy,* a figure of association, somewhat like synecdoche; use of the name of one thing for that of another suggested by it. "My friends agree that Mother sets a good table," i.e., prepares good food.

5. *Personification:* giving nonhuman objects the characteristics of a human being: "The breezes whispered, and the trees sighed and moaned."

6. *Hyperbole* (note suggestion of *effectiveness* in the definition) : "exaggeration, or a statement exaggerated imaginatively, for effect; not to be taken literally." Some similes and metaphors express hyperbole: "An ancient man—as old as Methuselah, I'd say—tottered across the street." "The towering mountain peaks pierced the heavens." The hyperbole is effective in this review of a circus: "It is as impossible to give a complete evaluation of what went on as it would be for a fly perched on a wide screen to summarize a movie" (Dick Shepard, *The New York Times,* April 5, 1967) .

In general, figurative language, being imaginative and picturesque, adds clearness and effectiveness to writing. But do not consider figurative language as a mere ornament of style; do not use it too frequently; and remember that direct, simple statement is generally preferable to a series of figures, always preferable when the figures are elaborate, artificial, or trite. Many worn-out similes are trite phrases (Section **66**) : *brave as a lion, brown as a berry, busy as a bee, clear as crystal, cold as ice.*

## 65b   *Avoid the use of mixed and inappropriate figures of speech*

Mixed figures of speech are those in which the images suggested by the language cannot be clearly related. Similes or metaphors are especially likely to become mixed, through over-elaborateness, inconsistency, and incongruity. Examples of inappropriate or mixed figures:

When I graduate, I hope to become a well-oiled cog in the beehive of industry.

After the football season many a player who was a tidal wave on the football field has to put his nose to the grindstone and study.

We are going to have to look the problem in the eye with an open mind.

Some day we will make a start on cleaning the house of freedom, but we must hurry, for there are sharks in these waters.

When parents discipline their children sensibly, a child has attained a foothold by which he can police himself.

## 65c   *Avoid excessive exaggeration*

Hyperbole can be used effectively, but it can be misleading because of its inexactness and possible ludicrousness. "As a boy I used to die laughing at my grandfather's jokes." Ineffective words because they exaggerate too much with little clear meaning and because they are overused are such words as *amazing, awful, divine, exciting, ghastly, gorgeous, great, horrible, marvelous, out of this world, phenomenal, sensational, splendid, terrible, terrific, thrilling.* For example, a girl described a campus dance as "a complete disaster." On the other hand, perhaps the other extreme (*understatement*) was reached by a combat pilot bringing home his badly battered plane: he described his dangerous mission as "quite a ball."

## EXERCISES

A. Paraphrase into literal language the beautiful figurative language of the 23rd Psalm, King James Version of the Bible, p. 367.

B. Make a list of 25 to 50 effective figures of speech which you have found in your reading. Label each, if it is an example of one of the figures of speech defined in Section 65a.

C. Each sentence or group of sentences in the following contains a figure of speech from a published writer. On a separate sheet, number each item, and give the name of the figure of speech contained in it.

1. Her black hair surrounded her brow like a forest.—THOMAS HARDY
2. She was a phantom of delight
   When first she gleamed upon my sight;
   A lovely apparition, sent
   To be a moment's ornament.—WILLIAM WORDSWORTH
3. Can Honour's voice provoke the silent dust, or Flattery soothe the dull cold ear of earth?—THOMAS GRAY
4. At critical times in our history, the White House in Washington has announced special TV talks to the nation.—Newspaper item
5. There is the New York of the commuter—the city that is devoured by locusts each day and spat out each night.—E. B. WHITE
6. Bliss was it in that dawn to be alive,
   But to be young was very heaven!—WILLIAM WORDSWORTH
7. He can talk French as fast as a maid can eat blackberries.—THOMAS HARDY
8. Above me are the Alps, the palaces of Nature, whose vast walls have pinnacled in clouds their snowy scalps.—BYRON
9. The commuter is the queerest bird of all. The suburb he inhabits has no essential vitality of its own and is a mere roost where he comes at day's end to go to sleep.—E. B. WHITE
10. You shall not press down upon the brow of labor this crown of thorns; you shall not crucify mankind upon a cross of gold.—WILLIAM JENNINGS BRYAN

D. Point out any inconsistent figurative language in the following, and rewrite the sentences containing it.

1. The European laborer has both his calloused hands resting firmly on terra firma.
2. "We have straddled the fence with both ears to the ground at the same time too long," said the speaker.—News item
3. By learning to fly and by becoming a doctor, I can kill two birds with one stone.
4. Make hay while the sun shines, or you may find yourself out on a limb with your nose to the grindstone.
5. Don't be surprised, if you encounter difficulties on the highways and byways of life, to find many others in the same boat.

## 66 *Freshness*

Effectiveness is aided by freshness of diction; it is hindered by triteness. Trite or hackneyed expressions, or clichés, are words and phrases that have lost their force through overuse. The origins of the words *triteness, hackneyed,* and *cliché* are illuminating: "triteness" comes from the Latin word *tritus,* the past participle of *terere,* meaning "to rub, to wear out"; "hackneyed" is derived from the idea of a "hackney," or carriage let out for hire, devoted to common use, and thus worn out in service; "cliché" comes from the French word *clicher,* meaning "to stereotype, to cast from a mold, to use over and over."

Thus trite words and phrases are but rubber stamps or ineffective repetitions of thought and expression. They may be overworked quotations, overworked similes, overused proverbs, and/or outworn phrases from speech, literature, and newspapers. They save the writer the trouble of thinking exactly what he means, but their use results in stale and ineffective writing. Such words and phrases inevitably seem humorous; they are, indeed, regularly used for humor or irony by fiction writers and columnists. Used seriously, they are signs that the writer or speaker is naïve.

### 66  *Avoid trite language*

Familiarity with trite words and expressions is likely to cause them to occur to us more readily than others more effective. Look with suspicion, therefore, on each word or phrase that leaps to mind until you are sure that it is exact, fresh, and unhackneyed. Be on your guard against general nouns and adjectives (Section **64a**) and against adjectives of hyperbole (Section **65c**) and others like *fierce, grand, lovely, nice, wonderful.* Watch especially for overused similes. Remember, also, that words and phrases that do not seem trite to you may be clichés to any reader familiar with overworked expressions.

Literally thousands[16] of examples of trite words and phrases exist. A few illustrations are given:

[16] See Eric Partridge, *A Dictionary of Clichés,* 4th ed. (New York: Macmillan, 1950) .

*Overused similes*

| | |
|---|---|
| deaf as a post | light as a feather |
| fat as a pig | limp as a rag |
| flat as a pancake | red as a beet |
| fresh as a daisy | stubborn as a mule |
| hungry as a bear | tired as a dog |

*Overused proverbs and literary allusions*

best-laid plans
a fool and his money
fools rush in where angels fear to tread
give hostages to fortune
sadder but wiser
where ignorance is bliss

*Other trite phrases*

| | |
|---|---|
| a cold sweat | goes without saying |
| as a matter of fact | in this day and age |
| bright and early | interesting to note |
| easier said than done | last but not least |
| first and foremost | sigh of relief |

## EXERCISES

A. Compare and summarize the meanings given in your dictionary for *banal, cliché, commonplace, hackneyed, stereotyped, trite.*

B. Make a list of 20 trite expressions which you have used in recent themes or conversations, or which you have overheard.

C. Copy the following sentences and underline on your paper the trite expressions in each. Substitute more effective expressions for the ones you have underlined.

1. Along the line of government policies, my uncle opposes farm subsidies.
2. First and foremost, my ambition is to complete my four years here.
3. I think most parents do a wonderful job raising their children.
4. The accidents we saw on our trip last summer were very few and far between.
5. It seems to be the policy here to have no late afternoon classes.
6. Many New Year's Eve parties last until the wee small hours of the morning, when the participants wend their way homeward.
7. It is interesting to note that some British authors have adopted the American spelling of certain words.
8. All in all, the grade on my theme was bad enough, but the instructor's written comments added insult to injury.

9. As of now, some students get bored stiff and let activities play an important part in their lives; there is a dire need for some activities, but some should be conspicuous by their absence, and the student should strike a happy medium between studies and activities.
10. Last but not least, there are Grandfather's moods. Sometimes he gets as blue as indigo and says he is being cast off like an old shoe.


# 67   Conciseness

Diction, to be effective, must be economical. Writing should not be sketchy, nor should necessary words be omitted (see Section 35a,b), but wordiness weakens the force of expression.

In forceful writing, the ratio of ideas to words is high. In poetry, consisting of "words in their best possible use," "each word must carry 20 others upon its back," and prose can effectively approach poetry in this technique. Conciseness alone does not achieve effective writing, but it is difficult to write forcefully if two or three or more words are used to convey an idea that one could express. Effective examples of conciseness are Lincoln's Gettysburg Address (267 words) and, from the King James Version of the Bible, the Ten Commandments (75 words) and the Golden Rule (11 words).

Three types of wordiness applying particularly to sentence content and structure—wordy predication, use of unnecessary details (*prolixity*), and use of too many modifiers—are discussed in Section 43. Conciseness also applies to words and phrases as part of a sentence. Both general and specific suggestions to achieve this conciseness follow.

### 67a   *Avoid useless repetition of an idea already expressed*

Useless repetition of an idea in a different word, phrase, or clause is called *tautology* or *redundancy*. It is illustrated by the following:

*Wordy*          Father was anxious for my brothers' success in their chosen professions, eager that they succeed, and zealous that they achieve the self-satisfaction of being successes in life.

This absolutely new and novel innovation in our services will please our customers; it has just been introduced for the first time and will cause pleasure to many people.

*Improved*   Father was eager for my brothers' success in their chosen professions.

An innovation in our services will please our many customers.

Hugh Downs, an NBC broadcaster, stresses the lesson thus: "Avoid redundancy, since said repetitive redundancy subjects the hearer to many unnecessary repetitions of phrases repeated over and over again."[17]

Even with only two to four words, tautology may appear: one of the words expresses the idea, and the other word or words add nothing. Common examples are: using *again* or *back* with many verbs beginning with *re-* (*repeat again, return back*) ; adding an unnecessary *up* (see Section **70**, Item 141) ; and using intensifying adverbs or *more* or *most* with absolute-meaning adjectives or with adjectives and adverbs already ending in *-er, -est* (see Section **83g,h**) .

Other common examples are the following:

| | | |
|---|---|---|
| absolutely essential | entirely eliminated | old adage |
| audible to the ear | fellow classmates | personal friend |
| Christmas Eve evening | few (many) in number | round in form |
| combine together | final outcome | a short half-hour |
| complete monopoly | first beginnings | small in size |
| completely unanimous | four-cornered square | this afternoon at |
| consensus of opinion | important essentials | 3 P.M. |
| cooperate together | join together | this morning at |
| descend down | long length | 9 A.M. |
| each and every one | loquacious talker | visible to the eye |
| endorse on the back | necessary essential | |

**67b   Do not use two, three, or more words**
**where one or two will serve**

The moral of "few words for many" is in the following: To the simple question of whether rules should be observed, an adminis-

17 Quoted in *The William Feather Magazine,* June, 1966.

trator wrote: "The implementation of sanctions will inevitably eventuate in subsequent repercussions." What he meant was "Yes."

Frequent examples of wordiness and their improvement:

| *Reduce these* | *to these* |
|---|---|
| a certain length of time | a certain time |
| am, is, are going to | shall, will |
| as a result of | because |
| at the present time | now |
| before long | soon |
| by the time | when |
| due to the fact that | due to, since |
| during the time that | while |
| inasmuch as | since |
| in regard to | about |
| insofar as | because, since, as |
| in the event that | if |
| in this day and age | today |
| in view of the fact that | since |
| it is interesting to note that | (begin with word following *that*) |
| on condition that | if |
| one of the purposes (reasons) | one purpose (reason) |
| prior to | before |
| provided that | if |
| subsequent to | after |
| the length of 5 feet | 5 feet (or 5 feet long) |
| with the exception of | except |

**67c   Avoid beginning sentences or clauses with
there is, there are, there have been, *etc.***

Although an additional example of Section **67b**, the overuse of "there" beginnings merits special discussion. Usually, such a "there" beginning is superfluous, adding nothing. Occasionally, one may be justified, as in "there are four genders in English," and you will find them used by many writers. But each time you see such a beginning, ask yourself whether the writer could have used a more effective way of expressing his ideas. (See "Expletive," Item 47 in "Glossary of Grammatical Terms," Section **85**.)

| | |
|---|---|
| *Wordy* | *There were* four students nominated for class president. |
| | In the library *there are* many reference books to help you. |
| | In our little town *there* live 1300 people. |
| *Concise* | Four students were nominated for class president. |
| | The library has many reference books to help you. |
| | In our town live 1300 people. |

## 67d   Use direct words instead of circumlocutions and euphemisms

Special applications also of Section **67b** are *circumlocutions* and *euphemisms*. A *circumlocution* is, literally, a "roundabout way of speaking": *a person connected by consanguinity or affinity* for *relative*; *devouring element* or *veritable inferno* for *fire*; *devotion to fiscal responsibility* for *prompt payment*; *deliver an address* for *speak*; *food preparation center* for *kitchen*; *savory repast* or *delicious viands* for *meal*. *Euphemisms* are mild, inoffensive words or expressions for blunter, less pleasant, and perhaps more effective words: *last obsequies* for *funeral*; *pass away* for *die*; *perspire* for *sweat*; *prevaricate* for *lie*.

| | |
|---|---|
| *Wordy* | He has pursued his course of studies along the lines of mechanical engineering. |
| | Grandfather was called home and passed to the Great Beyond in 1967. |
| | Students who disobey regulations will be separated from the university. |
| *Concise* | He has studied mechanical engineering. |
| | Grandfather died in 1967. |
| | Students who disobey regulations will be expelled. |

## 67e   Do not use again a conjunction or preposition already used for its specific purpose

Faulty repetition results when a conjunction or a preposition (*that, in,* etc.) already used is repeated. Necessary grammatical relationship needs only the one word, not both.

| | |
|---|---|
| *Bad* | I hope *that* after I graduate *that* I will be able to go into business for myself. |
| | Don't think *that* because you have never had an accident *that* you can't easily have one. |

Characteristic of my cousin is the high degree of honesty *in* which he believes *in*.
*At* what place are you living *at* now?
The Reference Room, *in* which we went *through* quickly, seemed to be the most interesting.

**67f**  *Do not repeat a pronoun after a noun used as subject of a sentence; such a pronoun is superfluous.*  (See Section **77h**.)

**67g**  *Avoid objectionable repetition*
       *of identical words and phrases*

More of a problem perhaps, of euphony than of conciseness, objectional repetition of identical words and phrases is discussed in Section **69b**.


## EXERCISE

Apply principles of conciseness to the following sentences:

1. A statement like that is very unique.
2. These various lakes are connected together by man-made canals.
3. Dr. Hugh H. Brown, M.D., is our family physician.
4. Many a famous person has written an autobiography of his own life.
5. My tuition came to a total of $950 dollars.
6. Each and every step upward made us feel that we were real mountain climbers.
7. I hope that after I graduate that I will be able to go into business for myself.
8. For some students an average college day begins at 6:30 A.M. in the morning and usually ends about 11:30 P.M. that night.
9. In the modern department stores of today there will be seen many new novelties.
10. In this theme I will explain three vocations in which I am interested in.
11. A good poultry raiser can count on a yearly income of $20,000 a year.
12. Although there have been nine years that have passed since the accident, I remember it very vividly.
13. Good English, it has been reiterated very often, is important to each and every individual student.
14. I would like to thank you for offering me a position with your company.

15. In order to avoid repeated repetition, I usually try to find synonymous words of nearly the same meaning.
16. I will be applying to six department stores in Chicago, and I will
be applying for the executive-training programs.
17. Since I am not satisfied with my term paper so far, I am going to
make a fresh start; I am going to begin anew on my term paper by
starting from scratch.
18. In the summers we enjoy the rural life of the country, but in the
fall we are glad to return to the urban life of the city.
19. In short, the speaker concluded, and to put it briefly, concisely,
succinctly, and in as few words as possible, "Either you have talent
or you don't."
20. In my travels the place I remember most vividly is Great Smoky
Mountains National Park. Great Smoky Mountains National Park
is in eastern Tennessee and western North Carolina.

# 68  *Gobbledygook and jargon*

Two kinds of writing, among others, are guaranteed to kill clearness and effectiveness: *gobbledygook* and *jargon.*

### 68a  *Recognize and avoid the various forms of gobbledygook*

*Gobbledygook* (or "gobbledegook") is a word coined about 1940
by a Texas Congressman, Maury Maverick (1895–1954), to describe much official government writing. The word was modeled
either on *hobbledehoy* or the meaningless sounds of a turkey's
gobble—hence its central characteristic, *meaninglessness.* Other
characterizing adjectives are "unintelligible," "foggy," "obscure,"
"involved," "repetitious," "pedantic," "pompous," "impressively
ornate," "flowery," "extravagant."

Three objections to gobbledygook are the following:

1. Gobbledygook overuses polysyllabic words—words of three
or more syllables, often of Latin origin. A pertinent example, which occurs in various versions, is the following advice to
writers (followed by its simple meaning) :

In promulgating your esoteric cogitations and articulating your
superficial, sentimental, and psychological observations, beware of plati-

tudinous ponderosity. Let your conversational communications, extemporaneous decantations, and unpremeditated expatiations demonstrate a clarified conciseness, a compact comprehensibleness, sans coalescent conglomerations of precocious garrulity, jejune bafflement, asinine affectations, rhetorical rodomontade, and thrasonical bombast. In your calligraphic communications, let your verbal evaporations and expatiations have lucidity, intelligibility, and veracious vivacity. Sedulously shun all polysyllabic profundity, obnoxious jocosity, pompous propensities, pusillanimous vacuity, pestiferous profanity, ventriloquial verbosity, elaborate eloquence, and similar transgressions, observable or apparent.

In other words, in your speaking and writing, *say what you mean and don't use big words!*

More familiar examples of gobbledygook words are: *comestibles* for *food*; *emporium* for *store*; *inebriated* or *intoxicated* for *drunk*; *peregrinations* for *travel*; *pulchritudinous* for *beautiful*; *ratiocinate* for *think*; *underprivileged* for *poor*.

2. Gobbledygook may use too many shorter words that confuse or hide meaning. During World War II, Federal workers were told what to do in case of an air raid. As originally written:

Such preparations shall be made as will completely obscure all Federal and non-Federal buildings occupied by the Federal Government during an air raid for any period of time from visibility by reason of internal or external illumination. Such obscuration may be obtained either by black-out construction or by termination of the illumination.

As simplified by President Franklin D. Roosevelt:

Tell them that in buildings where they have to keep the work going to put something over the windows; and, in buildings where they can let the work stop for a while, turn out the lights.[18]

3. Gobbledygook may, often does, use an overabundance of circumlocutions (see Section **67d**).

To avoid gobbledygook and to write clearly and effectively, use the short word instead of the long, if it will serve as well.

[18] Both examples from John O'Hayre, *Gobbledygook Has Gotta Go* (Washington: U.S. Government Printing Office) , p. 39.

Short words are usually more understandable, more sincere, and less self-conscious than polysyllabic words. Someone gave good advice when he said, "Short words are words of might"—worthy of note because English has more monosyllabic words than any other major language except Chinese. Such advice does not exclude the use of polysyllabic words; it means that these should not be used if they cause writing to have the characteristics of gobbledygook mentioned above.

### 68b   Understand and use common sense in dealing with jargon

In some meanings, *jargon* (from Old French, "a chattering of birds") and gobbledygook are synonyms: unintelligible, meaningless, confused writing and speech. Some of the examples above are illustrations. In other meanings, jargon, like gobbledygook, uses mainly uncommon or unfamiliar words, often technical words (Section **61**), unintelligible to the average educated reader. Such jargon, naturally, is to be avoided or used with extreme care.

For example, you as a student may plan to specialize in an art, a science, or a profession. In writing about your field, for your English and other courses on the campus, and in later communications, let the reader or listener you address establish your vocabulary in treating technical subjects. In general, avoid jargon in its meaning of a writer's using in his nontechnical writing a language peculiar to or understood only by members of a certain profession, trade, science, sect, or other special group: legal jargon, medical jargon, pedagogic jargon, sports jargon, etc. Special vocabularies—often containing unacceptable slang and neologisms—also exist in many nonprofessional areas, such as truck-driving, TV broadcasting, and the like. Even thieves and the underworld have a jargon of their own. As student-writer, then, do not bring in unexplained jargon words or phrases from your other courses—biology, economics, education, psychology, sociology, or the like.

### EXERCISE

(1) What gobbledygook words and phrases are used in the following sentences? (2) Rewrite each sentence, using clear and effective English.

1. Ah, how invigorating to quaff the immaculate waters of a frigidized mountain spring!
2. Every morning I imbibe deep inhalations of uncontaminated ozone.
3. Our improved financial status has eliminated our former eleemosynary situation.
4. As a child, my great-grandmother perambulated six quotidian miles to a diminutive bucolic edifice of erudition.
5. Most amicable felicitations on your colossal proliferation of dissertations on the nidification of ornithological specimens.
6. Meeting a fair damsel whom he knew walking across the campus greensward, John extended an invitation for a savory repast at the University Dining Salon.
7. Some students resort to hyperbolic prevarication to explain their procrastinating propensities.
8. I would not asseverate that Joe is a chronic prevaricator; I would asseverate that he bears the responsibility for multitudinous terminological inactitudes.
9. It was veritably inexorable that final examinations would be reinstituted at this institution of learning; they will have an expediting amelioration on the semester's closing chronology; they will also instigate much clandestine cerebral activity.
10. As chronology relentlessly progresses toward the payment of fees, I realize that the elimination of my temporary liquidity deficiency is of pressing importance for the restoration of a permanently sound financial structure.

# 69  *Euphony*

*Euphony* means "pleasing sound." Its antonym is *cacophony,* "harsh, ugly sound." Say each word aloud several times, and notice that the words illustrate their definitions. Even in silent reading the sense conveyed is lessened, attention distracted, by disagreeable combinations of cacophonous words.

Effective writing, of course, symbolizes sounds that please the ear, not the eye. The *sense* of words is more important than their *sound,* but good prose contains words whose sound and sense are harmonious. Reading aloud is a good method of detecting euphonious and uneuphonious sounds in your writing and in that of others.

### 69a  Avoid awkward and harsh combinations of sounds

Euphonious prose rarely contains *rhyme,* overuse of *alliteration,* or frequent repetition of *unpleasant sounds.*

 *1. Rhyme:* similarity of sound of vowels and consonants: *sound, found; bubble, trouble.*

*Dubious* I am writing this letter to tell you my health is better.

 *2. Alliteration:* several successive or closely placed words beginning with the same sound, usually the same consonant.

*Effective* lean and lithe; misty mountains; ripples of rapture
*Overuse* As Bill brought his boat up on the beach, the balmy breezes blew over the bay.

 *3. Unpleasant sounds:* overuse of words containing *k, ck* sounds; hissing sound of *s;* nasal sounds of *m, n;* gutteral sound of *g.* Pleasant sounds are suggested, usually, by words containing, for example, letters like *l, r, z,* or the *z*-sound of *s.*

*Harsh* Gregory's a go-getter; backed against the wall and with bleak and black prospects, he'll get going and never get into the gutter.
*Pleasant* Roses are flinging their fragrant perfume through the air.

### 69b  Avoid overuse of the same or similar-sounding words

Overuse of the same or similar-sounding words distracts a hearer's attention and is likely to distract the reader. A twofold principle is involved here: both euphony and conciseness (Section **67g**). Unless a word or phrase is repeated for effectiveness or clarity, faulty repetition may be corrected by substituting equivalent expressions (synonyms or apposition), by the use of pronouns, by judicious omission, or by recasting the sentence.

 1. Overuse through repetition of the same words:

My coming to college was made possible by some money, which was made possible by a job I had last summer.

2. Overuse of *homographs*: words with the same spelling but of different origin and meaning.

The leader of the local lead corporation said that we would continue to lead in the production of lead.

3. Overuse of *homonyms*: words with the same pronunciation but different in origin, meaning, and often spelling.

The Student Tribunal meets every Thursday afternoon to mete out justice to student offenders.

4. Ending a sentence with a word or phrase and beginning the next sentence with the same word or phrase or nearly the same phrase.

*Dubious*    A good example of a historical novel is Charles Dickens' *A Tale of Two Cities*. *A Tale of Two Cities* is a story of the French Revolution.

*Improved*    A good example of a historical novel is Charles Dickens' *A Tale of Two Cities*. This is a story of . . .

A good example of a historical novel is Charles Dickens' *A Tale of Two Cities,* which is a story of . . .

NOTE: Repetition, however, even if faulty, is preferable to artificial and awkward avoidance of it.

*Artificial*    Some newspapers publish news; other organs of the press issue material that frequently has only an approximate degree of timeliness.

*Improved*    Some newspapers publish news; others publish material that has only an apparent timeliness.

## EXERCISES

A. Write a short paper in which you distinguish among *euphony, euphemism, euphuism*. Consult your dictionary if necessary.

B. Write 10 sentences that contain sounds not pleasing to the ear. Rewrite or revise your sentences, showing how they can be made euphonious.

C. In accordance with the principles of euphony, rewrite the following sentences:

1. Snow, you know, is nothing to be alarmed about, though.
2. The source of fun in college can be traced back to four main sources.
3. Any squat, squalling, squealing children, squinting, squirming, and screeching, should be squelched.
4. Mt. Evans claims to have the highest highway in the world with a highway leading to its high summit.
5. The most important tool to a student in school is the library.
6. Maps do no good when one is in the midst of towering buildings with millions of cars milling around.
7. Getting up tired, doctors say, is the worst way to start the day.
8. Our neighbor tells us that his niece is having a nice time on the beach at Nice, France, where the weather has been very nice this winter.
9. I had never ridden in an airplane until the summer of 1968. During the summer of 1968, I paid a short visit to an aunt and uncle of mine, and they planned for my ride.
10. In organizing this organization, we hoped to organize a group that would become prominent among campus organizations.

## 70 Glossary of diction

The following glossary, alphabetically arranged and numbered for easy reference, contains words and expressions often misused and/or confused. The list, not all-embracing, is a short-cut discussion of some of the more common problems of usage. If you want more detailed information or if you do not find listed the word or phrase you are seeking, consult your dictionary.

A few of these expressions, those labeled "illiteracies" (i.e., substandard or nonstandard), are to be avoided in both formal and informal English. Many other expressions are inappropriate only in formal English. Apply the advice of Section **53a,b** as you interpret the comments provided.

Worth remembering, too, is that usage is constantly changing; expressions now restricted in some way may later be standard.

Furthermore, because no dictionary or grammar is a final authority, some usages are disputed; nor do the reputable dictionaries always agree. But authorities on and users of present-day English as a growing and changing language are, compared to their predecessors, less conservative, less dogmatic, more liberal, more tolerant, and more permissive—i.e., in much currently acceptable language there are optional and allowable choices, and even replacements.

1. A, an.   See pp. 424–425.
2. Above.   Used as adverb, preposition, noun, and adjective. As an adjective it means "as written or discussed previously on the same or a preceding page."

   The *above* quotation also has a symbolic meaning.

3. Accept, except.   *Accept* means "to receive," "say yes to"; *except* as verb means "to exclude"; as preposition, "other than."

   He *accepted* the invitation.
   I agree to the conditions if I may *except* the fourth on the list.
   No one *except* me knew the answer.

4. Accidently.   An illiteracy (see Section 54). Use *accidentally*.
5. Ad.   Colloquial or informal for *advertisement*. In formal writing avoid such shortened forms as *ad, exam, lab, phone,* and *prof*.
6. Advise.   A verb overused ineffectively, especially in letters, for "inform," "tell." The noun form is spelled *advice*.
7. Affect, effect.   *Affect,* as verb, means to "influence" or "assume"; *effect,* as verb, means "to cause," "to bring about," and as noun means "result."

   A great teacher can *affect* his students.
   Though nervous, he *affected* nonchalance.
   This testimony *effected* a change in the verdict.
   What *effect* do high altitudes have on human beings?

8. Ain't.   A contraction of *am not,* considered illiterate or dialectal, and also wrongly used for *is not* (he *ain't* here) and

*are not* (they *ain't*). *Ain't* is cautioned against in standard English, except for humorous purposes (see Section **51c7**). Virtually every other contraction, although usually avoided in formal English, is in good use in informal English: *isn't, aren't* (but *not* "aren't I?"), *wasn't, weren't, haven't, hasn't* (but not "hain't"), *doesn't, don't* (see Item 43, below), *didn't, won't, shan't,* etc.

9. All, all of. The *of* is preferably (concisely) omitted before a noun but must be used before the appropriate pronouns: *all* the students, *all* the snow; *all of* it, us, you, them.

10. All ready, already. *All ready* (two words) means "completely ready" or "everything (or every one) is ready"; *already* means "previously," "by this time."

> After thorough training, I was *all ready* for my first solo flight.
> We are *all ready* for the tour of the museum.
> Hurry! It is *already* past noon.

11. All right, alright. *All right* is overworked to mean "satisfactory," "very well." *Alright* is not an acceptable word.

12. All the farther, all the faster. These and similar expressions are colloquial or dialectal when the meaning is "as far as," "as fast as," etc.

> This is *as far as* we are going. (Not "This is *all the farther* we are going.")
> Is this *as fast as* your car will go? (Not "Is this *all the faster* your car will go?")

13. All together, altogether. *All together* means "everybody (or everything) in one place"; *altogether* means "wholly, completely."

> My brothers and sisters were *all together* for the first time this year.
> The witness seemed *altogether* sure of his statements.

14. Almost, most. *Almost* is an adverb meaning "nearly"; *most* as pronoun or adjective means "the greater part or number." As adverb it is used in forming some superlative degrees of

adjectives and adverbs (see Section **83e**). But *most* is now used colloquially or informally for *almost*.

The work is *almost* finished.
*Most* people have to work for their living.
*Most* everyone was in favor of going skiing.

*All most* is an impropriety and *allmost* is an illiteracy.

15. Also, then.   Each word is frequently ineffective and improper when used as a conjunction to join words. (Section **84d**)

16. Alumnus (male graduate), alumna (female graduate), alumni (male or male and female graduates), alumnae (female graduates) of a high school, academy, college, university, seminary.   These four words from the Latin retain their Latin number and gender.

17. A.M. or A.M. (midnight to noon); P.M. or P.M. (noon to midnight).   Both are clear indicators of time. Do not add "in the morning," "in the afternoon," or "o'clock." (Section **67a**) Figures, not words, are conventionally used; omit 00 with on-the-hour figures.

We left here at 8 A.M. and arrived in Detroit at 3:45 P.M.

Make 12 o'clock time clear by saying 12 *noon* or 12 *midnight*.

18. Among, between.   Both are Anglo-Saxon words, the former literally meaning "in a crowd," the latter meaning "by two." *Among* shows the relation of more than two objects or persons; *between* refers to only two, or, in special uses, to more than two when each object or person is individually related to each of the others.

He distributed the prizes *among* the five winners.
He divided the prize *between* Jack and Joe.
This water-level route runs *between* New York, Albany, Cleveland, and Chicago.
The five candidates for Prom Queen were all so beautiful that it was difficult to choose *between* them.

19. Amount, number.   *Amount* is used with a unified mass; *number,* with separate units.

What is the *amount* of your cash?
I have a *number* of quarters and half-dollars.
The *amount* of space needed depends upon the *number* expected.

20. And etc.  Redundant. *Etc.* is the abbreviation for Latin *et cetera,* meaning "and so forth." Also see Item 50, below.

21. Anxious, eager.  In precise use, *anxious* implies "anxiety," "worry," "uneasiness"; *eager* means "keenly desirous," "wanting to," not "worried about." However, one acceptable definition of *anxious* is "earnestly desirous" or "eagerly wishing."

I am *anxious* about Father's health.
I am *eager* to hear all the news from home.

22. Anywheres, nowheres, somewheres.  Illiteracies or dialectal words. Omit the *s* from these words.

That morning I could not find my car keys *anywhere*.
When we were ready to leave, the kitten was *nowhere* to be seen.
*Somewhere* in the dormitory we must have a good violinist.

NOTE: *Anyplace, noplace, someplace*—each written as one word—are usually illiteracies, although some authorities give *anyplace* colloquial or informal status. The words should not substitute for *anywhere, nowhere, somewhere.* But as two words these expressions are acceptable:

I shall meet you at *any place* you name.
There is *no place* like home.
I have left my books at *some place* or another.

23. Apt, liable, likely.  *Apt* suggests "fitness," "tendency," "natural bent or inclination"; *liable* implies "openness or exposure to something burdensome or disadvantageous"; *likely* means "expected," "probable." *Apt* and *likely* are sometimes interchangeable but usually not in the meaning of "probability."

She is *apt* in mathematics.
If an accident is your fault you are *liable* for damages.
It is *likely* to rain. (Not "it is *apt* to rain" or "It is *liable* to rain.")

24. As. (1) Overused and sometimes vague as a conjunction for *since, because, when, while*:

*As* it was raining, we decided . . . (Use *since*.)

(2) misused as a substitute for *that* or *whether*:

I doubt *as* I can. (Use *that*.)

(3) *As . . . as, so . . . as.* Some writers and authorities prefer *as . . . as* in affirmative comparisons and *so . . . as* in negative ones:

I am *as* tall *as* my father.
I am not *so* tall *as* my older brother.

Examples by good writers exist, however, showing the two pairs used interchangeably, *as . . . as* in negative and *so . . . as* in affirmative comparisons.
25. As good as, if not better than, or similar words in a mixed comparison. (Section **35d**)
26. Awful, awfully, terrible, terribly, etc. Vague words, and the adverbs are also loose overworked intensives for overworked *very*, etc. (See *Very*, Item 142 below, and also Section **65c**.)
27. Awhile, a while. *Awhile* is an adverb; in *a while, while* is a noun.

Wait *awhile,* and I'll go with you.
I cannot go for *a while*.

28. Beside, besides. *Beside* is usually a preposition meaning "by the side of"; *besides* is a preposition meaning "except" or "in addition to," and, more commonly, an adverb meaning "moreover."

A willow is growing *beside* the brook.
*Besides* oversleeping, I have no excuse.
Who is going *besides* you and John?
I have studying to do; *besides,* I want to go to bed early.

29. Bunch. Colloquial or informal but overused word for "a group of people."

*Dubious*    A *bunch* of us study in the library every evening.
*Improved*   A *group* of us . . .

30. But, nevertheless. Repetitious when both are used, since each means a contrast.

The team played very well, *but* it can play better.
The outlook seemed hopeless; *nevertheless,* we kept trying.

31. Can, may.    (Section **78h**, Items 8 and 10)

32. Can but, cannot but, cannot help but.    *Can but* is acceptable and means "bound to," "no possible alternative." *Cannot but* is informal with the same meaning; although it is a double negative and so objected to by some, one authority says it has long "been established in formal literary usage." *Cannot help but* is an illogical double negative (*cannot help + but*) which has not been acceptable. Omit *but*. (Section **35g**)

We *can but* pray that the rumor is not true.
I *cannot but* wonder at your decision.
I *cannot help* writing you about this matter.

33. Can't hardly or scarcely.    An illogical double negative. Omit the contraction of *not*. (Section **35g**)

"I *can hardly* hear you," said Professor Jones.

34. Case.    Overused as a word having little specific meaning; similar words are *phase, factor, instance, nature, thing,* etc. (Section **64a**)

35. Center around.    An illogical phrase. Objects or persons surround the center, not vice versa. Use *center on* or *upon* or *concentrate.*

36. Contact, contacted.    Overworked terms coming from business. Possible replacements: *communicate, call, call upon, telephone, get in touch with.*

37. Cute.   Overworked colloquial or informal word for *attractive, pleasing, clever, lovely, pretty, dainty, shrewd, sharp,* etc.

38. Data.   Plural form of a naturalized Latin word, *datum,* "something known." When it means information (i.e., facts and figures), the use of *data* with a singular verb is widespread.

39. Date.   Used colloquially or informally for the "time" one has a social appointment or the "person," usually of the opposite sex, with whom the appointment is made.

> I have a *date* with John for the Junior Prom.
> Mary is John's *date* for the Junior Prom.

40. Different than, different to, different from.   *Different than* and *different to* are common British idioms but are considered in the United States as colloquial or informal by some authorities, improper and incorrect by others, although these idioms have long literary usage to support them. *Different than* followed by a clause is gaining widespread acceptance. *Different from* has no objectors to its formal and informal use.

> A small college is *different from* a large university.
> Transportation now is *different than* (*from what*) it was in Grandfather's youth.

41. Disinterested, uninterested.   *Disinterested* means "unbiased," "not influenced by personal reasons"; *uninterested* means "having no interest in," "not paying attention." Colloquially or informally, *disinterested* means *uninterested, indifferent.* See paragraph development illustrating "contrast" for further discussion of *disinterested* and *uninterested,* p. 173.

42. Disregardless.   See *Irregardless.*

43. Don't, done.   *Don't* is used incorrectly as a contraction in the third person singular, present tense. The correct form is *doesn't. Done* is incorrectly used as the past tense of *do.* Principal parts: *do–did–done.*

It *doesn't* (not *don't*) make any difference.
He *doesn't* (not *don't*) know any better.
We *did* (not *done*) our studying last evening.

44. Due to.   As compound prepositions, *due to* (from the adjective *due*), *owing to* (from the participle *owing*), and *caused by* (from the participle *caused*) are adjective phrases, in good use, *due to* meaning "scheduled" or "caused by":

The plane was *due to* arrive at noon.
The power failure was *due to* the storm.
Accidents *due to* careless driving can be avoided.

Adverbial meanings have been and are expressed by *because of, on account of.* In recent years *due to* has become a synonym for *because of*—objected to by some, labeled colloquial or informal by others, and completely accepted in good use by still others. Whatever you and your instructor decide, remember that, in many uses, *due to the fact that* is a wordy way of saying *since* or *because.*

45. Each . . . are.   An error in grammatical agreement. *Each,* if not followed by *one,* is a pronoun implying *one,* and any plural words used in modifying phrases do not change the number. (Section **76c**)

46. Each other, one another.   Reciprocal pronouns. (Section **71d8**)

47. Eager.   See *Anxious.*

48. Either, neither, either . . . or, neither . . . nor.   As pronouns in formal writing, *either* means "one of two"; *neither* means "not one of two." The statements about "each . . . are" (above) apply if "one" is understood.

*Either* (one) of you is a desirable candidate.
*Neither* (one) of the proposals was accepted.

However, although *either* and *neither* should have singular verbs, in informal use a plural verb is commonly used, and even in formal English, as one authority says, "Educated users of English do use these words sometimes with a plural."

As correlative conjunctions, *or* is used with *either, nor* with *neither.* (For grammatical agreement of subject and predicate, see Section 76g,h.) The use of *either . . . or, neither . . . nor,* coordinating more than two words, phrases, or clauses, is sanctioned by some dictionaries but not by others.

49. Enthuse.   Colloquial or informal. For formal writing, prefer "be enthusiastic," "become enthusiastic," "show enthusiasm."

50. Etc.   An abbreviation of the Latin phrase *et cetera,* "and so forth." Preferably, *etc.* should be avoided. Too often it is a confession that the writer can think of nothing further to add to a list; if he can, he might justify *etc.* See also *And etc.,* above.

51. Exam.   See *Ad.*

52. Except.   See *Accept.*

53. Farther, further.   Interchangeable, but many writers prefer *farther* to indicate "space," "a measurable distance," and *further* to indicate "greater in degree, quantity, or time," and also "moreover," "in addition to."

We decided to drive 30 miles *farther* before we camped.
Next week we shall discuss this matter *further.*

54. Feel.   Overused for *believe.* Precisely, *believe* suggests "think," "have convictions about"; *feel* suggests "feeling," "emotions," not "reason." However, one acceptable definition of *feel* is "think, believe, consider."

I *feel* cheerful when I read your letters, for I *believe* you have the right attitude toward life.

As a linking verb, *feel* is followed by an adjective, as *I feel bad* (not *badly*), *happy, angry, sure, sorry, warm,* etc.

55. Fellow, fella, feller.   *Fellow* is a word of many meanings, ranging from low to high, socially. Colloquial or informal for "individual," "person," "one," "man," "boy," "student." *Fella* and *feller* are slang, dialectal, or illiteracies.

56. Fewer, less.   Both imply a comparison with something larger in number or amount. *Fewer* applies only to number:

*Fewer* accidents occurred after STOP signs were put up.

*Less* is used in various ways: applied to material in bulk in reference to amount (*less* money in the bank); with abstractions (*less* courage); with attributes such as degree and value (a nickel is *less* than a quarter).

The *less* steel we have, the *fewer* automobiles we can manufacture. The *fewer* members our club has, the *less* our income will be.

57. Fine.  A much overused word in the general sense of approval. Find a more specific, concrete word. (Section **64a**)

58. Fix.  A word of many meanings. Colloquial or informal: as a verb, "to arrange matters," "to get revenge"; as a noun, for "predicament," "difficulty." Dialectal or colloquial: as a verb, "to prepare, get ready." Fill in these meanings:

I can *fix* a date for Saturday night.
A tough gangster always *fixes* his enemies.
With my car locked and the keys inside, I certainly was in a *fix*.
I was *fixing* to go home.
Mother *fixed* lunch as soon as we arrived.

59. Formally, formerly.  *Formally* means "in a formal or precisely proper manner"; *formerly* means "in the past."

60. Funny.  An overworked colloquial or informal word for "strange," "queer," "odd," "remarkable." Find a more precise word. (Section **64a**)

61. Get, got, gotten.  These words have numerous precise, informal, slang, and idiomatic meanings. See your dictionary. Examples:

I've *got* to (must, ought to) go home next week.
I'm sorry, but I don't quite *get* (understand) you.
When do we *get* in (arrive) at Seattle?

62. Good, well.  *Good* is an adjective: "to have a *good* time," "to give a *good* performance." *Well* functions as either adjective or adverb, but with different meanings: as adjective, "in good health," and as adverb, "ably."

Since my illness, I have felt *well* all summer.
The team played *well* during the first half.

As a synonym of "well," *good,* as adverb, is regarded by some authorities as substandard, by some as dialectal, by some as colloquial.

63. Grand, great.   Overused adjectives for *admirable, delightful, excellent, impressive, magnificent, splendid,* etc. Find more precise words. (Section **64a**)

64. Guy.   Slang or informal for *boy, man, fellow.*

65. Had.   An impropriety when used for *have* after auxiliary verbs in such expressions as *would had, could had, might had, should had,* etc.

66. Had better, had best.   Idiomatic phrases meaning "ought to," "would be wise to."

67. Help but.   See *Cannot help but.*

68. I, me.   The former is nominative case, the latter objective. Watch especially as predicate nominative and in a compound phrase after a verb or preposition. (Sections **75c,d**)

69. If, whether.   In some uses *if* and *whether* are interchangeable. In precise use, *if* introduces one condition only and *whether* includes alternate choices, usually with "or not" implied or expressed and usually after such verbs as *ask, doubt, know, learn, say, wonder, understand.*

*If* the weather turns extremely bad, the flight will be canceled.
I wonder *whether* the flight will be canceled.
We did not learn *whether* the class would meet tomorrow or not.

70. In, into.   After verbs indicating motion to a place, *into* is generally used:

When he walked *into* the room, he found the meeting in progress.

*In* is used to indicate location or motion within relatively narrow limits:

The stolen car had been parked *in* Brown's Parking Lot.
She paced up and down *in* the classroom for the whole period.

71. In back of. *Back of* is colloquial or informal for *behind*; the *in* is superfluous. *In the back of* and, curiously, *in front of* are proper in both formal and informal usage.

*In the back of* the building are seven windows.
The car is parked *in front of* the house.
Some people hide money *back of* a mirror. (Colloquial)
Some people hide money *behind* a mirror. (Formal)

72. Individual. See *Party, person.*

73. Inside of, off of, outside of. As prepositional phrases, the *of* is superfluous, although *inside of, off of* are used informally, especially when *inside of* means "within a time limit."

*Inside* the house the lights have been turned on.
The boy fell *off* his bicycle.
All business was completed *inside of* an hour.
You should have a passport to travel *outside* the United States and its possessions.

Note use of *outside* and *inside* as nouns:

The *outside* of our house needs a coat of paint.
We are getting new floor pads for the *inside* of our car.

74. Irregardless, disregardless. Both words are illiteracies, substandard. *Irregardless* was apparently formed from a confused blend of *irrespective* and *regardless,* and *disregardless* by adding another negative syllable to an already negative word. In good use are *disregard* (verb), meaning "pay no attention to," and *disregardful* and *regardless* (both adjectives), meaning "careless, unmindful, heedless, without regard."

75. Is when, is where. Misuse of adverbial clauses for noun clauses and, more important, inexact phrasing in definitions. (Section **38**)

76. Its, it's, its'. See Section **94i.**

77. Job. Frequently and inexactly used in the sense of achievement. The chief objection to the word is its overuse to cover many general and inexact meanings in praise or dispraise of virtually everything. Find a more specific, concrete word (see Section **64a**).

> *Dubious*      The coach has done a good *job* with his material.
> Hemingway did a splendid *job* in his short stories.
> My roommate is doing a fine *job* in chemistry.
> Sue certainly did a bad *job* as leading lady in the play.

78. Kid, kids.   As noun, *kid* is colloquial or informal for a child or young person; unacceptable when meaning college students, football players, one's adult friends, and the like. As verb, slang, when meaning "tease, make fun of, or deceive someone."

> *Unacceptable*      Those college All-Star *kids* sure played their hearts out against Green Bay.
> But Father, all the *kids* in my dorm are going.
> You're *kidding*; let's be serious and don't *kid* me any more.

79. Kind of a, sort of a, type of a.   The *a* is superfluous. Logically, the last word should indicate a class, not one thing.

> What *kind of* TV program is this?
> He is the *sort of* person you like to associate with.
> Only this *type of* flower is suitable for this *kind of* soil.

80. Kind of, sort of.   Colloquial or informal when used to mean "almost," "rather," "somewhat."

> The people streaming home at night look *kind of* tired.
> After a mediocre performance an actor is *sort of* disgusted with himself.

81. Lab.   See *Ad.*
82. Leave, let.   Each word has various meanings, but *leave* in the sense of "cause to remain" and "go away from" is often confused with *let* in the sense of "allow," "permit," "cause."

> If you *leave* a good student undisturbed, he can soon get his work done.
> *Let* me take your book back to the library.
> *Let* the thermostat be set at 72 degrees.

83. Less.   See *Fewer*.
84. Liable, likely.   See *Apt*.
85. Lie, lay.   See Section **71g.**
86. Like.   A word of many meanings and with uses as suffix, adjective, noun, adverb, preposition, transitive verb, intransitive verb, and conjunction. For *like* as conjunction, see Section **84f.**
87. Lots of, a lot of, whole lot.   Colloquial or informal for "many," "much," "great deal." The chief objection is overuse of the vague general word *lot*. Find a more specific, concrete way of saying what you mean. (Section **64a**)
88. Mad.   With a number of meanings such as "insane," "frantic," "frenzied," *mad* is colloquial or informal when used to mean "angry," "furious."
89. May, can.   See Section **78h,** Items 8 and 10.
90. Moral, morale.   *Moral*: relating to right vs. wrong in regard to character or conduct; teaching a lesson. *Morale*: referring to the state of mind of a group: confidence, courage, hope, etc.

John believes in high *moral* principles.
The *moral* of the play is: "Be tolerant."
As the tourney opened, the *morale* of our team was high.

91. Most.   See *Almost*.
92. Muchly.   An illiteracy. Substitute *much, very, greatly.*
93. Nice.   A word with various meanings, including "agreeable," "pleasant," "attractive," "pretty," "delightful." Its overuse indicates the need for more specific, concrete substitutes. (Section **64a**)
94. Nowheres.   See *Anywheres*.
95. Number.   See *Amount*.
96. Of.   An impropriety when used for *have* after auxiliary verbs. (See Section **78d**; see also Item 73, above.)
97. Off of.   See *Inside of*.
98. O, oh.   The former is usually part of a vocative, is always capitalized, and is rarely followed by a mark of punctuation:

O Richard! Come here, please.

*Oh* is an interjection, may be followed by a comma or an exclamation point, and is capitalized according to the usual rules.

Oh! What a pity!
But, oh, what trust we placed in him!

99. Outside of.  See *Inside of.*
100. Party, person, individual.  *Party* implies a group, and, except in legal and telephonic language, should not be used to refer to one person except colloquially or informally. *Individual* refers to a particular or single person. *Individual,* as an adjective, means "single," "separate," "particular"; it is therefore repetitious and unnecessary when used to modify *person,* as "individual person," or when "each" has been used, as "each individual member." As nouns, *individual* and *person* are synonyms.
101. Pass out.  Slang in the sense of "faint," "become completely unconscious."
102. Passed, past.  Past participles of the verb, *pass,* but not used interchangeably, in referring to time. *Passed* forms part of the active-voice predicate; *past* is used in the passive-voice predicate and as an adjective, in the meaning of "something ended."

Time has *passed* rapidly.
That time is *past.*
Some *past* events are well worth remembering.

103. Pep, peppy.  Slang or informal for *zest, vigor, energy, liveliness, vivacity,* etc., and corresponding adjectives, *zestful, vigorous, lively, energetic,* etc.
104. Phase.  See *Case.*
105. Phone.  See *Ad.*
106. Plenty.  As an adverb, colloquial or informal for "very," "fully."

The weather is *plenty* hot this summer.

107. Plus.  Not effective as a synonym for *and* or *with.*

| | |
|---|---|
| *Dubious* | My roommate and I, *plus* the two boys across the hall, have bought a new TV set. |
| *Improved* | The two boys across the hall, my roommate, *and* I have bought a new TV set. |

108. **Pretty.** Overused as an adverb meaning "rather," "moderately," "somewhat."

This is a *pretty* large assignment.
I did *pretty* well on the last test.

109. **Principal, principle.** *Principal* is a noun meaning "sum of money" or "a chief person" and an adjective meaning "chief" or "main." *Principle* is always a noun meaning "a doctrine," "a rule of conduct," "a governing rule or truth."

My older brother is now a high school *principal*.
My *principal* objection is the time needed.
Mr. Brown is a man of high *principle*.
What is the *principle* on which this machine works?

110. **Prof.** See *Ad*.

111. **Proven.** In good use as one of the two past participles (interchangeable) of *prove*. Principal parts: *prove–proved–proved* or *proven*.

112. **Provided, provided that, providing.** *Provided* and *providing* are in good use as conjunctions, with the meaning "if," "on condition," "in case," "it being understood." They are often followed by *that,* but *that* seems unnecessary.

*Provided* I am asked, I shall join your organization.
We are driving home next week, *provided* there is no snow on the roads.
I plan to pay my tuition next week, *providing* my father sends me the money.

113. **Quite a.** Colloquial or informal phrase meaning "more than a," or "to considerable extent or degree," as *quite* a few, *quite* a while, *quite* cold.

114. **Raise, rise.** See Section **71g.**

115. Real.  Usually considered colloquial or dialectal as an adverb meaning "very" or "really." More effective: "Are you *really* sure of what you say?"
116. Reason is because . . .  See Section **38a**.
117. Respectfully, respectively.  *Respectfully* means "in a respectful manner" and is the proper conventional closing for certain business letters; *respectively* means "severally," "each in the order given."

> Indianapolis, Springfield, and Madison are the capitals, *respectively,* of Indiana, Illinois, and Wisconsin.

118. Right along, right away, right off, right then, etc.  Colloquial or informal phrases. In formal writing, substitute *directly, immediately,* etc.
119. Seen, saw.  The principal parts of *see* are *see–saw–seen. Saw* is improperly used as a past participle; *seen* is improperly used as the past tense.

> *Right*    I *saw* him yesterday.
> We have *seen* the flower exhibit.

120. Shall, will.  Auxiliary verbs having various uses and meanings. See Sections **80b** and **78h4,5**.
121. Should, would.  Auxiliary verbs having various uses and meanings. See Section **78h6,7**.
122. Sit, set.  See Section **71g.**
123. So.  *So* has various uses as adverb, conjunction, pronoun, interjection, and in combinations like *so as, so that.* Two objectionable uses of *so,* on the basis of effectiveness, are: (1) overuse of *so* as a conjunction between independent clauses; see Section **36c**. (2) Overuse of *so* as an intensive—a general substitute for *extremely, indeed, very;* these, too, are overused and might often be omitted. (See *Very,* below.)

> *Dubious*   You were *so* careless on your last theme.
> Her formal dress is *so beautiful.*
> *Approved*   You were careless on . . .
> Her formal dress is beautiful.

124. So . . . as. See *As* (3) above.
125. Somewheres. See *Anywheres*.
126. Sort of a, Sort of. See *Kind of a, Kind of*.
127. Sure. Both adjective and adverb, but colloquial or informal in the latter use for *surely, certainly, indeed*.
128. Swell, super. Slang or colloquial words used to express general enthusiasm, such as "first rate, excellent, stylish, superfine, great." Other more effective words are available. (Section **64a**)
129. Terrible, terribly, terrific. See *Awful*.
130. That, this. As adverbs, used with some adjectives and adverbs of quantity and extent: *that much, this much, that far, this far*. Colloquial or dialectal with other adjectives and adverbs, as in the following:

I didn't realize you were *that* good.
The runner was *that* tired he could not finish the race.
How can any test be *this* difficult?

More effective:

I didn't realize you were as good as you say.
The runner was so tired he could not finish the race.
How can any test be as difficult as this one?

For *that* introducing restrictive relative clauses, see Section **88m-R1**.
131. Then. See *Also*.
132. These kind, those kind, these sort, those sort. *Kind* and *sort* are singular nouns, *these* and *those* are plural modifiers. Use *this kind, this sort, those kinds, those sorts*.
133. This. See *That*.
134. Thusly. An illiteracy for *thus*.
135. To, too, two. Correct usage here is mainly a matter of careful spelling. *To* is a preposition, "to the library," or the sign of the infinitive, "*to* study." *Too* is an adverb meaning "also" or "overabundance of," or "excessively": "I, *too*, am going, but John is *too* sick to go." *Two* is the number: "*two* girls," "the *two* of us."

136. Too.   Overused as an intensive or as a replacement for *very* and consequently ineffective. See *Very,* below.

137. Try and.   Widely used as colloquial or informal for *try to.*

138. Type.   Not acceptable as a substitute for *type of,* although such use is becoming common in business English and informal speech. But since we do not say "what kind car" or "what sort insect," why say "what type car" or "what type insect"? For comment on *Type of a,* see *Kind of a,* above.

139. Uninterested.   See *Disinterested.*

140. Unique.   See Section **83h.**

141. Up.   Redundant when used with verbs which already include the idea, as *rise up, stand up, end up,* etc. But *up* is needed in many idiomatic expressions, like *bring up, keep up, lay up, move up, sit up, tie up.*

142. Very.   (1) *Very,* like *so, surely, too, extremely,* having been overused, has lost much of its value as an intensive. Use these words sparingly; consider whether your meaning is not just as emphatic without them: "You are *very* positive about the matter." (2) *Very* is used informally to qualify participles in predicates; formal use adds adverbs like *much* or *greatly,* unless the participle seems more adjective than predicate-participle:

| | |
|---|---|
| *Informal* | The students were *very surprised* by the announcement. |
| | Mother was *very shaken* by the bad news. |
| *Formal* | The students were *very much surprised* by the announcement. |
| | Mother was *very greatly shaken* by the bad news. |
| | Dormitory counselors *are greatly discontented* with the attitude of a few trouble-makers. |

143. Well.   See *Good.*

144. Where at.   As two words, redundant for *where.* Avoid such statements as "He did not know *where* he was *at*" and "Where do you *stay at* in New York City?"

145. Whether.   See *If.*

146. While.   As conjunction, *while* means "during or at the same time that," "as long as"; it is colloquial or informal when used in the sense of "although" or "whereas."

*While* sick, some students kept attending classes.
You thought I was lying, *while* I was telling the truth.

147. Who, whom.   See Section **75i,** Note.
148. Will, would.   See *Shall, should.*
149. -wise.   A suffix added to nouns to form adverbs, in the general meaning of "with reference to." Now much overused, but sometimes used acceptably, compounds formed with *-wise* often add no further information: *edgewise, saleswise, moneywise,* etc., almost *ad infinitum.* Examples of acceptable words are *clockwise, sidewise.*
150. Worst kind, worst sort, worst way.   Slang when used for *very much, greatly, intensely.*

# GRAMMAR
## A Useful Review
### (SECTIONS 71-85)

True ease in writing comes from art, not chance,
As those move easiest who have learned to dance.
—ALEXANDER POPE, *An Essay on Criticism*

# GRAMMAR

A S a college student you are expected to use the language that others with your educational and social advantages do. Therefore, in carrying on your affairs, through language, both in college and in later life, you should have pride in knowing and being able to use words, forms of words, and word combinations appropriate to English as it is spoken and written by educated people—formal when needed, informal when appropriate.

Certain grammatical knowledge can help you to write *correctly*.[1] If you write *correctly*, grammar can help you write *clearly*; if you write *correctly* and *clearly*, grammar can help you write *effectively* and *appropriately*.

A practical reason, therefore, exists for studying grammar. Knowing many grammatical terms does not guarantee good writing—it is even possible, though unlikely, that a gifted person who did not know a single grammatical term could write competently. But most of us need guidance in writing and speaking, and we obtain that guidance most easily and efficiently through some grammatical vocabulary.

What, then, is grammar? *The American College Dictionary* gives this simple definition: "the features of a language (sounds, words, formation and arrangement of words, etc.) considered systematically as a whole, especially with reference to their mutual contrasts and relations." That is, grammar is notation and organization of usage.

Even more simply, grammar deals with words and their relationships to each other or one another; it is a descriptive statement of the way a language works. It includes a discussion of the forms of words, their use in phrases, clauses, and sentences, their tenses, cases, or other changes in form. It is the sci-

[1] For the definition of *correct, correctly, correctness* as used in this book, see footnote, p. 5.

entific record of a series of observed language phenomena, but, like many records, it is subject to constant fluctuations. A useful review concentrates on those words, their changes, and their relationships that assist in making writing and speaking correct, clear, effective, and appropriate. By mastering the useful principles of grammar, you make them serve you in your own writing and speaking.

Grammar is *descriptive*; its application is *prescriptive*. It is descriptive in that it records the actual and changing status of words and their relationships, descriptive in showing how words are said or written, not how they should be said or written. It is not properly considered as a list of rules, imposed by authorities, a rigid set of *do's, do not's, avoid's*. Yet there must be a certain amount of prescription if speaking and writing are to conform to principles generalized from description. For example, description shows that pronouns following prepositions are in the objective case. If your own usage is to conform to the description, you follow the prescription: *Use the objective case of pronouns following a preposition.*

A "Glossary of Grammatical Terms," alphabetically arranged, is given as Section 85, p. 537. Refer to this list for guidance, when necessary, as you study the following pages.

# 71  *Words*

A *word* is a letter or a combination of letters, a sound or a combination of sounds, forming a unit of thought capable of being used as an utterance.

## 71a  *Learn to identify each word as a part of speech*
Words are classified according to their use in larger units of thought—in phrases, clauses, and sentences. This functional classification results in *parts of speech*, a descriptive phrase applied to words used in speaking and writing. A part of speech, therefore,

is a word—sometimes a combination of words serving the purpose of one word—used to express a definite idea, such use becoming clear only in relation to surrounding words. Every word must be one of the eight parts of speech: *noun, pronoun, adjective, verb, adverb, preposition, conjunction, interjection.* Every word in your dictionary bears at least one such label.

NOTE: These grammatical names and many other grammatical terms used in this book are conventional and traditional; but they are the labels used, and considered valuable as being widely understandable, by every highly respected dictionary of the present time. For another approach to the subject, see Appendix C, pp. 675 ff.

Many words are used as only one part of speech, but since our language is constantly changing and since words also change in meaning, the function of words reflects such change. The same word, therefore, depending on use and meaning, may be two or more parts of speech. In fact, *functional change* or *shift* means that a word assumes a new function without a change in form, such as an adjective being used as a noun or a noun as an adjective. When general, these uses are recorded in dictionaries. For example, *iron* is a noun in *made of iron,* an adjective in *an iron bar,* and a verb in *to iron a shirt.* Even when not recorded in dictionaries, examples of functional change are numerous: *college, university,* and *campus,* theoretically only nouns, serve the functions of adjectives—since no adjective forms exist except the awkward *collegiate*—in phrases like *college* students, *college* athletics, *university* buildings, *university* courses, *campus* customs, *campus* activities.

Ordinarily, however, unless your dictionary permits, do not use nouns for verbs, nouns for adjectives, nouns for adverbs, adjectives for nouns, adjectives for adverbs or adverbs for adjectives, adjectives for verbs, verbs for nouns. (See Sections **55, 71f, 83.**) Notice, however, that often a slight change in a word, such as a different ending, can change a word from one part of speech to another: *arrive* (verb), *arrival* (noun). To determine what part of speech a given word is, see how the word is used in the sentence or clause or phrase of which it is a part.

## 71b  Distinguish carefully the purposes that words serve

Although words are classified according to one of the eight parts of speech, they can be classified also according to the purpose that they serve:

⟶ *Naming* words: nouns and pronouns
⟶ *Asserting* words: verbs and verbals
⟶ *Modifying* words: adjectives and adverbs
⟶ *Joining* words: prepositions and conjunctions
⟶ *Exclamatory* words: interjections

## NAMING WORDS: NOUNS AND PRONOUNS

A *noun* (from a Latin word, *nomen,* meaning "name") denotes or "names" a person, animal, place, or thing, a quality, state, idea, or action. Common nouns name or represent all members of a common group: *man, office, city, building, state.* Proper nouns name particular members of a group and are capitalized: *Mary, Mr. Ward, Benjamin Franklin, Chicago, Florida.* Some common nouns are concrete: *book, candy, hammer*—names of objects that can be perceived by the senses of hearing, sight, smell, taste, touch: *song, sweater, perfume, coffee, velvet.* Some are abstract nouns: *duty, honesty, intelligence, sadness*—names of abstractions that cannot be perceived by the senses. Some are collective nouns: *crew, family, assembly*—names used for groups considered as units.

Nouns belong to a very large class of words that have, usually, certain characteristics in common:

1. Nouns can be, and usually are, preceded by such words as *the, a, an, my, your, his, her, our, their, this, that, some, each.*

2. Nouns can be, and often are, accompanied by qualifying words (adjectives) which usually precede but sometimes follow.

3. Certain groups of nouns have typical endings—such as *-al, -tion, -ness, -ment, -ure*—which distinguish them from corresponding verbs (e.g., *arrive, arrival, determine, determination, argue, argument*) or from corresponding adjectives (e.g., *goodness, good*) .

4. Nouns are sometimes distinguished from identically spelled verbs by accent: *sub'ject, subject', proj'ect, project'.*

5. Nouns are marked by their occurrence in a certain set of positions, e.g., usually before the verb in some statements, after the verb in others, after prepositions, and after other nouns; that is, a noun may be the subject of a verb, direct or indirect object of a verb, objective complement, object of a preposition, in apposition.

6. Nouns are, or may be, marked by other characteristics: number, gender, case: *number*—singular (one) or plural (more than one) ; *gender*—masculine, feminine, neuter, common; *case* —a common form for both nominative and objective and a special form for the possessive (genitive) .

7. Nouns are distinguished from other words by adding certain endings to show possession and, usually, to show plural.

Memory devices for recognizing nouns: nouns can be preceded by one of the words mentioned in Item 1, above; nouns usually add *s* or *es* to form their plural; nouns usually add *'s* to form the singular possessive case.

For diagraming nouns, or pronouns, in a sentence as subject, object of verb, or object of preposition, see pp. 439–445.

### 71c   *Do not carelessly use the singular form of a noun for the plural or the plural form for the singular*

*Wrong*    For the college power plant many *ton* of coal are needed annually.

A good student has many favorable *characteristic*.

Becky Sharp is portrayed as a very scheming *women*.

More than 800 *freshman* assembled in the chapel.

Plurals of nouns are formed as follows:

1. Most nouns form the plural by adding *s* to the singular: *dog, dogs*; *student, students*; so do nouns ending in silent *e*: *college, colleges*; *face, faces*.

2. Nouns ending in a sibilant or *s* sound (*ch, sh, s, x, z*) add *es*: *church, churches*; *bush, bushes*; *glass, glasses*; *fox, foxes*; *buzz, buzzes*.

3. Nouns ending in *y* form their plural according to the *y* spelling rule. (See Section **52e2**.)

4. Nouns ending in *o* preceded by a vowel add *s*: *radio, radios*. Some nouns ending in *o* preceded by a consonant form

their plurals with *s*: *photo, photos*; *piano, pianos*; others with
*es*: *echo, echoes*; *potato, potatoes*; still others with *s* OR *es*:
*motto, mottos, mottoes*; *zero, zeros, zeroes*. No safe rule exists to
guide you.

5. Nouns ending in *f* are so variable that a dictionary should
be consulted: *chief, chiefs*; *loaf, loaves*. Nouns ending in *ff* add
*s*: *sheriff, sheriffs*. Most nouns ending in *fe* change *fe* to *ve* and
add *s*: *wife, wives*; *knife, knives*.

NOTE: Normal use, *leaf, leaves*; nickname of baseball and hockey
teams, Maple *Leafs*.

6. Some irregular plurals occur: change of vowel or vowels:
*man, men*; *mouse, mice*; peculiar ending added: *child, children*;
*ox, oxen*.

7. Many nouns—mainly categories of animals, birds, and fish
—have the same singular and plural, the so-called zero plural:
*deer, moose, sheep, grouse, salmon, trout*.

8. Compound nouns ordinarily form the plural by adding *s*
or *es* to the important word in the compound: *sons-in-law,
passers-by*. If the word elements are so closely related as to be
considered a single word, the end of the word is pluralized:
*handfuls*.

9. Certain nouns of foreign origin retain the plural of the
language from which they were borrowed: *alumnus, alumni*;
*beau, beaux*; *hypothesis, hypotheses*; *libretto, libretti*. Some have
two plurals, foreign and anglicized: *index, indices, indexes*;
*cherub, cherubim, cherubs*. Many borrowed words, however,
have gradually assumed plurals with *s* or *es*: *area, areas*; *campus,
campuses*.

When in doubt concerning the spelling or the specific form
of the singular or plural, consult your dictionary.

For plurals of figures, alphabetical letters, and words as
words, see Section 93c.

## 71d Distinguish carefully the different kinds and purposes of pronouns

A *pronoun* (*pro,* literally "for" or "instead of," plus *noun,*
"name") substitutes for or replaces a noun, a noun equivalent,
or sometimes another pronoun. Its purpose is, primarily, to

prevent overuse and repetition of the noun. Every pronoun, except indefinite pronouns, refers directly or by clear implication to a noun or another pronoun—called the *antecedent* of the pronoun—and it agrees with that antecedent in person, number, and gender: "Each *man* in favor will please raise *his* hand." "Does every *girl* here have *her* luncheon ticket?" (See Section **77.**)

Pronouns, used in all the grammatical functions of nouns (subjects of sentences or clauses, apposition, direct or indirect objects of verbs, etc.), are of eight kinds: (1) personal, (2) relative, (3) demonstrative, (4) interrogative, (5) reflexive, (6) intensive, (7) indefinite, and (8) reciprocal. Even so, pronouns belong to a small class of words—some 80 in all. Some of them, depending on their kind, are formally distinguished from nouns by having special possessive and objective forms and by not being accompanied, usually, by an article or other adjective.

1. *Personal* pronouns refer to an individual or individuals. Of all the kinds of pronouns, personal pronouns cause the most trouble; they have 30 case forms. Some of these include all genders, and some have special forms for masculine, feminine, or neuter.

Personal pronouns also bear the labels of first person, second person, third person: *First person pronouns* indicate the speaker or writer—as singular or as plural. *Second person pronouns* indicate the person or persons spoken to or written to, with the same forms for both singular and plural. Gender or sex is the same for all first and second person pronouns. *Third person pronouns* indicate the person or persons spoken or written about —and here sex or gender needs consideration: singular masculine, singular feminine, singular neuter, and plural for all genders. A table of these pronouns is given in Section **75a.**

2. A *relative* pronoun has a double duty: to relate or connect an adjective clause to the antecedent, a noun or a pronoun, and to serve as a substantive in the dependent clause. The same forms—*who, whose, whom, which, that*—serve for gender or number; their being singular or plural or having gender depends on their antecedents. The choice of a relative pronoun is also determined in part by its antecedent: *who, whose,* and *whom* are used to refer only to persons; *which* is used in reference to things (inanimate objects, animals) and may be used for a group of persons; *that* may refer to either things or persons.

The girl *who* won the Junior Prom beauty contest is now an airline hostess. (Singular)
The girls *who* served as the Queen's court are also airline hostesses. (Plural)
This company owns only one small ship, *which* is used for river traffic. (Singular)
A New York company owns seven large freighters, *which* ply between Europe and America. (Plural)
The man *that* I mean was named Mortimer Taylor. (Singular)
The men *that* I like have the same interests as I do. (Plural)

*That* and *which* have no changes in form (compare with *who, whose, whom*). The possessive case of the pronoun *which* is indicated by *of which* or *whose,* if no awkwardness results with the latter. A possessive, *of that,* is never used.

*Who, which,* and *that* are the most frequently used relative pronouns; *whoever, whomever, whichever,* and *whatever* are less frequently used relative pronouns; *whosoever, whichsoever,* and *whatsoever* have almost entirely gone out of current use.

3. A *demonstrative* pronoun points out, points to, calls attention to, identifies. It has different forms for number but not for gender or case. The most important demonstrative pronouns are *this* (singular), *that* (singular), *these* (plural), *those* (plural), *such* (singular or plural).

*This* is the book that I have recommended.
*That* is the record I have just bought.
*These* are your books; *those* on the desk are mine.
*Such* are the magazines that our teacher recommends.

These five words can also be used as adjectives: *this* and *that* modify only singular nouns, *these* and *those* only plural nouns, and *such* either singular or plural.

*This* magazine is interesting, *that* kind of book is dull.
*These* magazines are interesting, *those* kinds of books are dull.
*Such* a book and *such* magazines are worth reading.

4. An *interrogative* pronoun (*who, which, what,* occasionally *whoever, whichever, whatever*) introduces a question.

*Who* will read his book report on Wednesday?
*Which* is the best road to take to Louisville?

*What* do you think about extracurricular activities?
For *whom* are you writing this theme?
*Whoever* would think of playing such a trick?
*Whatever* could have caused such a rumor?

*Whose,* as possessive, can of course accompany a noun. *Which* and *what* are frequently used as adjectives also.

*Whose* notebook was left in the classroom?
*Which* book do you recommend as an exciting novel?
*What* road should I take to Louisville?

5. A *reflexive* pronoun is used for simple reference to the subject; it usually follows a verb or preposition and directs, refers, or *reflects* its action back to the subject. Composed of the personal pronoun forms with *self* or *selves,* the most frequently employed reflexive pronouns are *myself, yourself, himself, herself, itself, ourselves, yourselves, themselves* (and the indefinite *oneself*).

6. *Intensive* pronouns have the same forms as the reflexive pronouns, but they appear in an appositive position and are used to emphasize or *intensify* a noun or other pronoun. Use of commas depends on whether the apposition is considered close or parenthetical.

Yesterday my roommate hurt *himself* playing basketball. (Reflexive use)
He *himself* decided to go out for basketball. (Intensive use)
Some students consider *themselves* lucky to be here. (Reflexive use)
The seniors *themselves* chose the day for their commencement. (Intensive use)
Mary asked *herself* the question many times. (Reflexive use)
Sometimes she talked aloud to *herself*. (Reflexive use)
She *herself* finally reached a satisfactory decision. (Intensive use)

7. *Indefinite* pronouns are less exact in meaning than other pronouns. They are *pronouns* because they refer to antecedents; they are *indefinite* because the antecedents are not specifically named persons, places, or things. Among the more frequently used indefinite pronouns are the following: *another, any, any-*

*body, anyone* or *any one,*[2] *anything, all, each, everybody, everyone* or *every one,*[2] *everything, few, many, nobody, no one, nothing, one, oneself* (as indefinite reflexive), *several, some, somebody, someone.* Compound forms built upon the pronoun *one* or the element *body* have a possessive form ending *'s,* like *anyone's, everybody's, one's.* Indefinite pronouns involve grammatical problems of agreement which are discussed in Sections **76c** and **77a.**

8. A *reciprocal* pronoun indicates an interchange of action suggested by the verb. This interchange or cross relationship may be seen in the following sentences involving the only two reciprocal pronouns in English:

My roommate and I always confide in *each other.* (Two only)
The members of the party exploring the cave shouted to *one another.*
  (Three or more)

The two pronouns are, however, often interchanged in informal use. Possessive forms add *'s: each other's, one another's.*

## ASSERTING WORDS: VERBS AND VERBALS

### 71e   *Understand clearly the functions and uses of verbs*

A verb is a part of speech that asserts something, says something, expresses action or occurrence, expresses a state of being or existence. Like nouns, verbs belong to a large class of words that have, usually, certain characteristics in common: by the use of endings, auxiliary verbs, and/or changes in form, verbs serve the purposes listed below. Also, alone or with auxiliary verbs, a verb may make a positive statement, make a conditional statement or statement of probability, give a command, ask a question, make an exclamation.

---

2 *Anyone* and *any one,* as well as *everyone* and *every one,* are ordinarily interchangeable, but when followed by a preposition like *of, in, from,* the two-word form is used.

*Any one* in the class may volunteer.
*Every one* of you should attend.

Today *is* Friday, the 13th. (Positive statement)
If you *are* lucky, you *win* first prize. (Condition and positive statement)
*Plan* to attend Tuesday's meeting. (Command)
You *have* many students here, *haven't* you? (Question)
You *were* really the winner! (Exclamation)

In addition to helping express the verb functions mentioned above, auxiliary or helping verbs (Section **78**) add particular shades of meaning—usually of time (Section **80**), tone (Section **80**), voice (Section **81**), or mood (Section **82**) —to what is called the main verb (Section **79**). Such combinations are called *verb phrases.*

Next Friday *will be* Friday, the 13th. (Positive statement, and time or tone)
I *have written* 16 themes this semester. (Positive statement, and time or tone)
We *may have* to have another meeting this month. (Probability)
*Be prepared* to come to this meeting. (Command)
*Will* you please *let* us *know* your plans? (Question)
You *were* really *surprised!* (Exclamation)
I *do believe* in thorough proofreading. (Tone, emphatic)
This theme *was revised* four times. (Voice)
If you *had not been* late, you *would have seen* the thrilling touchdown run. (Mood)

Various uses of verbs—the main verb alone or auxiliary and main verb—are the following:

1. To express *time* (tense): present, past, future, present perfect, past perfect, future perfect. See Section **80** for discussion.

2. To express *tone*: simple, progressive, emphatic. See Section **80** for discussion.

3. To express *agreement with subject in number and person.* See Sections **76** and **80** for discussion.

4. To express *active* or *passive voice.* See Section **81** for discussion.

5. To express *mood* or *mode*: indicative, imperative, subjunctive. See Section **82** for discussion.

For diagraming verbs as predicates in a sentence, see pp. 439–445.

### 71f  *Distinguish between predicate verbs and verbals*

A *predicate verb* is a *verb* or *verb phrase* used in the predicate of a clause or a sentence where it makes a statement about the subject. The italicized verb or verb phrases in the examples in Section **71e** are predicate verbs. Nearly every clause or sentence contains them. Predicate verbs agree (are in concord) with their subjects in number and person (see Section **76**).

*Verbals* are *verb forms* that cannot serve as predicates; the verbals are *participles, gerunds,* and *infinitives.* Understanding the differences between predicate verbs and verbals helps to avoid a serious error in writing, the use of unjustifiable sentence fragments (see Section **31**). Ordinarily, for clearness and effectiveness verbals or verbal phrases should not stand alone. If a group of words contains a verbal and is designed for predication, it should include with the verbal the kind of verb or verb phrase which serves as the predicate of the clause or sentence.

A *participle* is a word which has the function of both verb and adjective. The *present participle* always ends in *-ing* (*speaking, singing*). The *past participle* has various forms (*spoken, sung, walked, sat*). The *perfect participle* consists of *having* or *having been* followed by the past participle (*having sung, having been asked*). (See Section **79**.) The participle as verb form can take an object and be modified by an adverb; the participle as adjective can be modified by an adverb and can itself modify a noun or pronoun.

*Coming* events cast their shadows before. (Adjective)
Expertly *driving* the car in traffic, Harry has no fear of cities. (As adjective, *driving* modifies *Harry*; as verb, it is modified by the adverb *expertly* and it takes a direct object, *car.*)
This brightly *polished* silver is beautiful. (As adjective, *polished* modifies *silver,* is modified by the adverb *brightly.*)

The *gerund* is a verbal noun usually ending in *-ing* (*speaking, singing*). Because the *-ing gerund* has the same spelling as the present participle, be careful to note the difference in use: the participle is a *verbal adjective,* the gerund is a *verbal noun.* The gerund as a verb form can take an object and be modified by an adverb; the gerund as noun can be modified by an adjective and can be the subject or object of a verb or the object of a preposition.

*Playing* tennis is good exercise. (Gerund is subject of sentence, but as verb form it takes a direct object, *tennis.*)

Some people enjoy *spending* money generously. (As noun, the gerund is object of the verb *enjoy;* as verb, it in turn has an object, *money,* and is modified by the adverb *generously.*)

Henry paid for his education by *planning* carefully. (As noun, the gerund is object of the preposition *by;* as verb, it is modified by the adverb *carefully.*)

Steady *running* won the race for Henry. (As noun, the gerund is subject and is modified by the adjective *steady.*)

A sad task is *writing* your friends bad news. (As noun, the gerund is a predicate nominative; as verb, it takes both an indirect object, *friends,* and a direct object, *news.*)

An *infinitive* is a word which has the function of a verb; as such, it is used alone or after most auxiliary verbs (Section **78h**) and forms part of the predicate. Preceded by *to,* called the "sign of the infinitive," the infinitive is still a verb or verb phrase, but as such, it does double duty: verb and noun, verb and adjective, verb and adverb. The *present infinitive* (*to speak, to sing*) is the first principal part of the verb (Section **79**) ; the *perfect infinitive* is formed with *to have* followed by the past participle (*to have spoken, to have sung*) .

I must *study* tonight. (Infinitive as verb and part of predicate.)

Will you please *reply* by return mail? (Infinitive as verb and part of predicate.)

*To work* intelligently is sometimes difficult. (Infinitive as noun is subject of sentence; as verb form it is modified by an adverb, *intelligently.*)

*To win* a scholarship means constant study. (Infinitive as noun is subject of sentence; as verb form it has a direct object, *scholarship.*)

The best time *to study* is early in the morning. (Infinitive serves as adjective.)

I came *to inquire* about your vacation. (Infinitive serves as adverb.)

For discussion of the infinitive and participle in the principal parts of verbs, see Section **79**.

**71g   Do not use a transitive verb for an intransitive verb
or an intransitive verb for a transitive verb**

Verbs are classified as either *transitive* or *intransitive*. *Transitive* literally means "passing over, crossing over, building a bridge across." A *transitive* verb is followed by a direct object which completes the meaning of the verb. In other words, a transitive verb is a bridge, a means of crossing over from subject to object. "The teacher *accepted* my excuse." An *intransitive* verb requires no direct object to complete its meaning, does no crossing over. The meaning ends with itself, but it may of course have word, phrase, or clause modifiers. "I *am going*; I *am going* very soon; in fact, I *am going* just as soon as I can."

Determining whether a verb is transitive or intransitive (the same verb frequently may be either and be so labeled in your dictionary) depends on meaning, on the idea the writer wishes to show.

I *obeyed* the traffic officer's instructions. (Transitive)
Father now *owns* three garages. (Transitive)
He gave me instructions; I *obeyed*. (Intransitive)
After his introduction, the speaker *paused*. (Intransitive)

For almost all practical purposes in writing, being able to distinguish transitive and intransitive verbs is useless information. If you must decide, try the following blank-filling memory device (for example, with *try*) :

Let's —— it. (A verb is transitive if it can be inserted in this blank.)
Let's ——. (A verb is intransitive if it can be inserted in this blank.)

Concerning three pairs of verbs, transitive-intransitive information is useful, but if you memorize these verbs, principal parts, and meanings, you can forget about the transitive-intransitive distinctions:

*Transitive*     *lay–laid–laid, laying*
*Intransitive*   *lie–lay–lain, lying*

Each word has many meanings, but they are related when *lay*, meaning "to place," also means "to cause to lie." Confusion arises because the word *lay* forms a principal part of each verb; therefore, notice especially the principal parts of each verb and do not confuse the past tense, past participle, and present participle of *lie* with the forms of *lay*.

Please *lay* the books on my desk. (From *lay*)
I *laid* some of them there yesterday. (From *lay*)
As I was *laying* them there, the telephone rang. (From *lay*)
When I am tired, I *lie* down for a while. (From *lie*)
Yesterday I *lay* down for a short time. (From *lie*)
As I was *lying* there, the telephone rang. (From *lie*)
After I had *lain* down an hour, the telephone rang again. (From *lie*)

| | |
|---|---|
| *Transitive* | *raise–raised–raised, raising* |
| *Intransitive* | *rise–rose–risen, rising* |

These verbs also have many meanings, but they are related when *raise* means "cause to rise." Keep in mind the principal parts and the present participle and note also that with neither of these verbs is *up* needed. (See *Up*, p. 404.)

*Raise* your right hand, please. (From *raise*)
The speaker *raised* the microphone six inches higher. (From *raise*)
Please *rise* when you recite. (From *rise*)
The elevator *rose* rapidly to the thirtieth floor. (From *rise*)
Because of heavy rains, the river has *risen* two feet since yesterday.
  (From *rise*)

| | |
|---|---|
| *Transitive* | *set–set–set, setting* |
| *Intransitive* | *sit–sat–sat, sitting* |

These verbs, likewise, have many meanings (*set* is even intransitive in one of them, like "The sun *sets*"), but they are related when *sit* means "to place oneself" and *set* means "cause to sit." In these meanings, using *set* for *sit* is dialectal and an impropriety.

Please *set* the large box in the closet. (From *set*)
Now I shall spend some time *setting* the small boxes on the top shelf.
  (From *set*)
Don't slouch; *sit* up! (From *sit*)

Yesterday I *sat* at my desk for four hours. (From *sit*)
My roommate is *sitting* at his desk now. (From *sit*)


## EXERCISE

Make a list of numbers from 1 to 15. Opposite each, write from the following sentences the correct forms of *lay–lie, raise–rise, set–sit* (see Section **71g**) :

1. Every day dictionaries are *laying lying* unused on the desks of students.
2. It does not do a car any good to *set sit* out in the open all winter.
3. It began getting dark in this old house, and my fears began to *raise rise* again.
4. Having delivered his ultimatum, the prosecuting attorney *sat set* down.
5. That first night on the campus, I *laid lay* on my bed wondering what the next day would bring.
6. Not allowed to have a car here at college, I dream of that little sports car *setting sitting* in the garage at home.
7. Each afternoon the campers were required to *lay lie* in their bunks for an hour to rest.
8. Why did the ghost of Hamlet's father *raise rise* from the grave?
9. I have really *sat set* down my thoughts about what I want, and this is the only answer I can reach.
10. After that first day of working I was so tired that I don't even remember *laying lying* down.
11. An elderly gentleman *setting sitting* next to me on the plane asked me where I was going.
12. With developments in medical science, man's life expectancy will *raise rise* by many years.
13. In front of me was a hen partridge *setting sitting* on her nest of eggs.
14. The air is brisk today, and the snow *lays lies* packed where it has fallen.
15. The walls of the cliff *raise rise* straight up from the bottom of the canyon.


## MODIFYING WORDS: ADJECTIVES AND ADVERBS

"Modify" means to describe or limit or particularize. Modifying words are adjectives and adverbs, as are adjective and adverbial phrases and adjective and adverbial clauses; they stand in a grammatically subordinate relationship to other words and phrases.

### 71h   For correct and exact meaning, understand the functions of adjectives

An *adjective* modifies a noun or pronoun by describing, limiting, particularizing, or in some other closely related way making meaning more nearly exact. It may indicate quality or quantity, identify, or set limits. Specifically, therefore, adjectives tell *what kind of, how many, which one*. Members of a large class of words, they are further distinguished by showing, with an ending (*-er* or *-est*) or an adverb (*more* or *most, less* or *least*), a comparison of two or more persons or things (see Section **83e**).

Adjectives are usually of three general types: *descriptive*: a *black* dress, a *smashed* thumb, a *round* object; *limiting*: the *sixth* period, her *former* home, *several* times; *particularizing*: an *easy* lesson, an *American* citizen, a *college* graduate. Another classification includes *common* adjectives and *proper* adjectives (from proper nouns), important only because proper adjectives begin with a capital letter: an *American* play; *Italian* olives.

Many adjectives have endings that ordinarily mark them as adjectives. The more important of these endings include:

| | |
|---|---|
| *-able* (*-ible*) | payable, desirable, likable, permissible |
| *-al* | cordial, promotional, optional, musical |
| *-ary* | elementary, visionary, contrary, secondary |
| *-en* | rotten, golden, wooden, molten |
| *-ful* | beautiful, faithful, hurtful, sinful |
| *-ic* | metric, carbonic, Byronic, artistic |
| *-ish* | mannish, selfish, Danish, dwarfish |
| *-ive* | permissive, constructive, excessive, decisive |
| *-less* | faithless, timeless, lawless, guileless |
| *-like* | childlike, dreamlike, homelike, lifelike |
| *-ous* | vigorous, nervous, marvelous, advantageous |
| *-some* | lonesome, tiresome, handsome, bothersome |
| *-y* | muddy, stony, funny, dreamy, seedy |

The words *a, an, the* are classed as adjectives because they always accompany a noun or, infrequently, a pronoun. They certainly have no descriptive power, but in a limited sense they limit. Compare

man    *a* man    *the* man
deer    *a* deer    *the* deer

*A* and *an* are *indefinite articles*; *the* is the *definite article*: *a* physician, *the* physician; *an* orange, *the* orange. The initial sound of the following word determines the choice of *a* or *an*: *a* is used before a word beginning with a consonant sound, even though the initial letter is a vowel; *an* is used before a word beginning with a vowel sound (including silent *h*).

*an* adult    *an* hour    *a* hero    *a* problem    *a* European visitor

An adjective may modify a noun by preceding it, as single adjectives or a series of single adjectives usually do:

A *merry* laugh greeted us.
*Red, green,* and *yellow* lights are traffic signals.

Certain adjectives or adjective combinations may either precede or follow the noun; others, like restrictive adjective phrases and clauses (see Section **88m**), must follow:

Our delegate *alone* will travel to Washington.
Food *enough* (or *Enough* food) has been provided for everyone.
The traffic lights, *red, green,* and *yellow,* were visible for blocks ahead.
The boy *in the brown suit* is my brother.
The girl *who is rising to speak* is the valedictorian.

Another position of adjectives in sentences is after certain verbs, the so-called linking verbs (Section **78**):

The corn is *green.*
The water felt *warm.*
The children have grown *taller.*

Such adjectives are related to the subject, the word they modify. For fuller discussion, see Sections **78a,b, 83c.**

Errors in the use of adjectives and adverbs are discussed in Sections **83a,b,c,d.**

### 71i   *For correct and exact meaning, understand the functions of adverbs*

An adverb modifies a verb, an adjective, or another adverb by describing, limiting, particularizing, or in some other closely related way making meaning more nearly exact. Adverbs—like adjectives, members of a large class of words—usually tell *how, how much, how often, when, where, why*; they typically express certain relationships such as attendant circumstances, cause, concession, condition, degree, exception, inference, manner, means, place, purpose, result, time. Also, like adjectives with endings *-er* or *-est* or the adverbs *more* or *most, less* or *least,* they show comparison of two or more persons or things (see Section **83e**).

A distant skylark sang *faintly.* (Adverb modifies verb *sang.*)

We heard it *only once.* (Adverb *once* modifies verb *heard*; adverb *only* modifies adverb *once.*)

*Then* the skylark sang *again.* (Both adverbs, *then* and *again,* modify verb *sang.*)

I do *not* see my hat *anywhere.* (Both adverbs, *not* and *anywhere,* modify verb *see.*)

We were *almost* ready to start. (Adverb modifies the adjective *ready.*)

Close the door *very slowly.* (Adverb *very* modifies the adverb *slowly,* which modifies the verb *close.*)

Some students, *however,* are planning to spend the vacation in Florida. (Adverb connects this statement to a preceding one.)

Adverbs have the following characteristics:

1. Adverbs are commonly distinguished from corresponding adjectives by the suffix *-ly*: *warm, warmly; angry, angrily*; but some words ending in *-ly* are adjectives (*manly, lonely, friendly*). (See Section **83d.**)

2. Certain adverbs are distinguished from corresponding nouns by the suffixes *-wise* and *-ways*: *lengthwise, sideways.*

3. Certain adverbs are distinguished from similarly spelled prepositions in not being connected to a following noun:

| | |
|---|---|
| *Adverb* | He came *up*. |
| *Preposition* | He came *up* the street. |

4. Like adjectives, but unlike nouns and verbs, adverbs may be preceded by words of the "very" group (intensifiers), such as *very, extremely, exceedingly, right*:

The *very beautifully* dressed girl is the class queen.
He went *right* by.

Adverbs modifying adjectives and other adverbs are usually placed just before the words they modify. Adverbs modifying verbs can be placed almost anywhere in the sentence, clearness and smoothness permitting.

Both adjectives and adverbs have changes in form to indicate three degrees of *comparison—positive, comparative, superlative: good, better, best; great, greater, greatest; slowly, more slowly, most slowly*. For discussion, illustration, and application, see Section **83e,f,g,h.**

Errors in the use of adjectives and adverbs are discussed in Section **83a,b,c,d.**

For diagraming adjectives and adverbs in a sentence, see pp. 439–447.

## JOINING WORDS: PREPOSITIONS AND CONJUNCTIONS

### 71j *Distinguish between the functions of prepositions and conjunctions*

A *preposition* (note its literal meaning: *pre,* "before," plus *position*) is a linking word used before a noun or pronoun to show its relationship to (that is, how it modifies) some other word in the sentence, usually a verb (*consist of*), noun (*need for*), or adjective (*proficient in*) ; members of a very small class of words, prepositions express varied relationships, as the list shows: time, space, exception, and the like. The following list contains most of the prepositions used in English:

| | | | |
|---|---|---|---|
| about | beside | in | since |
| above | besides | inside | through |
| across | between | into | throughout |
| after | beyond | like | till |
| against | but | near | to |
| along | by | notwithstanding | toward |
| alongside | concerning | of | under |
| amid | despite | off | underneath |
| among | down | on | until |
| around | during | onto | unto |
| at | ere | outside | up |
| before | except | over | upon |
| behind | excepting | per | with |
| below | for | regarding | within |
| beneath | from | save | without |

Each preposition of course precedes its object (see Section **75d**) —noun, pronoun, noun phrase, or noun clause. In some word combinations the preposition may, paradoxically, follow its object:

*In which house* do you live?
*Which house* do you live *in*?
The man *for whom* I am working . . .
The man *whom* I am working *for* . . .

Compound prepositions, consisting of two or more words, serve the purpose of a single one-word preposition. The most common are the following:

| | | |
|---|---|---|
| as for | for fear of | in view of |
| as to | for the sake of | on account of |
| aside from | in accordance with | owing to |
| because of | in addition to | pertaining to |
| by means of | in behalf of | regardless of |
| by reason of | in case of | with a view to |
| by way of | in company with | with reference to |
| contrary to | in favor of | with regard to |
| due to | in regard to | with respect to |
| exclusive of | in spite of | with the exception of |

For the use of certain prepositions to form idiomatic expressions, see p. 360.

A conjunction, a member also of a small class of words, is a linking word used to connect words or groups of words (phrases or clauses) in a sentence or even to connect sentences. Conjunctions and their use are discussed in some detail in Section **84**.

These seven kinds of words—nouns, pronouns, verbs, adjectives, adverbs, prepositions, and conjunctions—are the traditional and principal parts of speech, so classified on the basis of their meaning, form, or grammatical function.

## EXCLAMATORY WORDS: INTERJECTIONS

*71k   Use interjections for effectiveness and appropriateness*

The eighth part of speech, the *interjection,* is an exclamatory or parenthetic word which has little, if any, grammatical connection with the remainder of a sentence; in fact, it frequently serves alone as a sentence: *Whoops! Ouch! "Oh,* must you go?" "And here, *alas,* our good fortune ended."

The following list contains most of the interjections found in English:

| | | | | |
|---|---|---|---|---|
| ah | encore | hi | O | ugh |
| aha | eureka | hist | off | what |
| ahoy | good | ho | oh | whew |
| alas | good-by (e) | huh | ouch | whist |
| amen | gosh | humph | pooh | whoa |
| ay | halloo | hurrah | pshaw | whoopee |
| bah | heigh | hush | shoo | whoops |
| behold | hello | huzza | so | why |
| boo | hem | indeed | there | woe |
| botheration | here | lo | tush | wow |
| bravo | hey | mum | tut | zowie |

Occasional interjections are effective, but overuse gives the effect of a strained or immature style. For their punctuation, see Sections **87a** and **88n2**.

## EXERCISE

Copy the following sentences. Put one each on a page of paper, with one word only on a line, in column form, beginning at the extreme left margin. After each word write the part of speech that it is: noun, pronoun, adjective, verb, adverb, preposition, conjunction, interjection.

1. Many students attend football games every week during the season, although we notice that some work busily in the library even while the games are in progress.
2. A Canadian humorist and professor of economics once said that for a great university only three things are needed: a library, a body of interested students, and a scholarly faculty; what do you think of that statement?
3. Ah, if only more of our students would put their studies above their activities, this college would become a great center of learning; will you be the student who will first set the example?
4. Words are a vital part of our everyday life, but we seldom stop and think whether or not the form and meaning were the same throughout the centuries that have passed.
5. I had always been brought up with the idea that going to college was just the thing to do; indeed, my parents always expected that I would some day go to college, they planned for it, and they planted their ideas firmly in my mind.

# 72 *Phrases*

**72** *Identify phrases correctly, both for clearness and effectiveness in writing and to avoid unjustifiable sentence fragments*

A *phrase* is a group of two or more related words not containing a subject and a predicate. It serves usually as a single part of speech.

## PHRASES CLASSIFIED ACCORDING TO USE

A phrase usually fulfills the functions of a single noun, adjective, verb, or adverb. Phrases containing adjectives modifying nouns or containing adverbs modifying verbs are labeled according to their stronger words, that is, noun phrases or verb phrases.

Our city is proud of *its wide, well-paved, shady streets and boulevards.* (Noun phrase)
Many a river *runs swiftly and silently to the sea.* (Verb phrase)

A phrase can be used in a sentence as a noun is used, as subject, object, etc. It is called a *noun phrase.*

*Freshmen and sophomores* live in campus dormitories. (Noun phrase as subject)
*Playing on a major football team* was his special ambition. (Noun phrase as subject)

A phrase may modify a noun or pronoun; it may function, that is, as a single adjective functions. Such a phrase is called an *adjective* (or adjectival) *phrase.*

Our city is proud of *its wide, well-paved, shady* streets.
The farmers *in the West* (compare the *western* farmers) need rain.

A phrase may modify a verb, adjective, or adverb; it may function, that is, as a single adverb functions. Such a phrase is called an *adverb* (or adverbial) *phrase.*

Many a river runs *swiftly and silently to the sea.*
Our fullback fumbled *on the 2-yard line.*

Modifying phrases, both adjective and adverbial, are classified as *nonrestrictive* and *restrictive*; for definitions and for punctuation, see Section **88m-N** and **88m-R.**
A *verb phrase* consists of a group of words serving the function of a verb, such as an auxiliary verb with its main verb or a verb with its modifiers. A *verb phrase* is not the same as a *verbal phrase*: participial, gerundial, infinitive, defined below.

By June your first college year *will have been completed.*
Every student *should write correctly, clearly, effectively, and appropriately.*

## PHRASES CLASSIFIED ACCORDING TO FORM

Phrases may also be classified according to form; such phrases usually receive their name from their initial or more important word. Six common divisions are the following:

*Prepositional* (used as adjectives or adverbs, rarely as nouns) :

The house *on the corner* is the home of Mayor Williams. (Adjective)
The road winds *through the mountains* and down *into a valley.* (Adverb)
*Without saving* is to be without money when it is needed. (Noun)

*Participial*:

*Puffing like steam engines,* we reached the top of the tower.
*Being thoroughly tired,* we rested there an hour.
*Having completed my assignments,* I went to bed.

*Gerundial*:

*Winning first place in the speech contest* was his special ambition.
The audience enjoyed *his playing of the Viennese waltzes.*

*Prepositional-gerundial* (a phrase introduced by a preposition which is followed by the gerund as noun) :

*After graduating from college,* I plan to go to medical school.
We won *by having a superior line and a faster backfield.*

*Infinitive*:

*To win games* is the aim of every team.
He has worked hard *to achieve success.*

NOTE: Participial, gerundial, and infinitive phrases serve the same purpose that is served by single participles, gerunds, and infinitives (see Section 71f). Except for absolute phrases, these and prepositional phrases can also be classified according to use, since a phrase usually serves as a single part of speech.

*Absolute*:

*Night coming,* we ceased our work.
*My theme written,* I signed my name to it and turned it in.
John went to bed, *his work being finished.*
*The game (being) over,* we started a victory parade.

The *absolute phrase* or *absolute expression,* sometimes called *nominative absolute,* usually consists of a noun followed and modified by a participle or participial phrase, with participle expressed, occasionally understood. It is a phrase because it cannot stand alone as a sentence; absolute, because it modifies no single word in the sentence of which it is a part, although it has a close thought relationship to the sentence or some word or phrase in it. (See also Section 88p.)

## EXERCISES

A. From two or three pages of prose in your book of readings or in a current magazine, list at least 10 phrases that include all the following types: (1) prepositional, (2) participial, (3) gerundial, (4) prepositional-gerundial, (5) infinitive, (6) absolute.

B. After each phrase in the list you compiled according to Exercise A, indicate how the phrase was used: noun, adjective, adverb, or part of predicate.

# 73 Clauses

A clause is a group of words having a subject and predicate and forming part of a sentence. Clauses are of two kinds: *independent* (or *main* or *principal*) and *dependent* (or *subordinate*).

## 73a Identify independent clauses carefully for effectiveness in writing and for correctness of punctuation

An *independent clause* makes a complete grammatical statement and may stand alone; that is, it makes reasonable sense if the remainder of the sentence is omitted. It could stand as a sentence. Context, of course, is usually necessary for completely clear meaning.

> Although I should have studied last evening, *I watched several TV programs.* (Independent clause)
> I watched several TV programs. (Sentence)

More than one independent clause may be contained in a sentence:

> *My roommate studied,* but *I watched several TV programs.*

Even a one- or two-word imperative (see p. 447), with the understood subject *you,* can serve as an independent clause:

> Stop, look, and listen!
> Come early and stay late.

## 73b   Identify dependent clauses carefully, as a safeguard against writing unjustifiable sentence fragments and against incorrect punctuation

A *dependent clause,* or *subordinate clause,* is not capable of standing alone but depends on the remainder of the sentence for its meaning. Dependent clauses function as nouns, adjectives, or adverbs. Like an independent clause, a dependent clause contains a subject and predicate; it shows that it is dependent, usually, by the linking word that joins it to the independent clause.

### NOUN CLAUSES

In the following examples the dependent clause is used as a noun; each italicized clause functions exactly as would a single noun.

> *What you paid* was too much. (Noun clause used as subject; compare: The *price* was too much.)
> He promised *that he would give me the money.* (Noun clause used as object of verb *promised*; compare: promised *a gift of money.*)
> I am not aware of *what he has in mind.* (Noun clause used as the object of the preposition *of*; compare: I was not aware of *his thoughts.*)
> Your remark *that you hate college* surprises me. (Noun clause used as an *appositive*; see *Appositive,* in Glossary, Section 85; compare: Your remark, *hatred of college,* . . .)

His remarks usually were *whatever came to his mind first.* (Noun clause used as a *predicate complement*; see *Complement,* in Glossary, Section 85; compare: . . . were *his first thoughts.*)

**ADJECTIVE CLAUSES**

In the following, the dependent clause is used to modify a noun or pronoun; each italicized clause functions as would a single adjective.

The farmers *who live in the West* need rain. (Compare: The *western* farmers need rain.)

"We, *who are about to die,* salute you!" (Clause modifies pronoun *we*; compare: We, *dying* soon, salute you!)

The price *which he paid* was too much. (Clause modifies *price.*)

You are the very person *whom I wanted.* (Clause modifies *person.*)

He is a boy *I never admired.* (Clause modifies *boy*; *whom* after *boy* is understood.)

**ADVERBIAL CLAUSES**

Dependent clauses function as adverbs to modify a verb, an adjective, or an adverb, as in the following; each italicized clause functions as would a single adverb.

I shall pay the bill *when you send it.* (Clause modifies the verb *shall pay*; compare: I shall pay the bill *later.*)

You study more efficiently *than I do.* (Clause modifies the adverb *more efficiently.*)

As a residential town, West Liberty is more desirable *than East Liberty is.* (Clause modifies the adjective *more desirable.*)

For dependent clauses—usually adjective, sometimes adverbial—as *nonrestrictive* and *restrictive* and their punctuation, see Section **88m-N** and **88m-R.**

**ELLIPTICAL CLAUSES**

Ellipsis means the omission from a clause or sentence of a word or words, not needed because understood from other words or from context. An elliptical clause is a special kind of clause. It is occasionally an independent clause; usually it is a dependent clause with its subject and part of its predicate omitted, since these are clearly understood from the main clause. In the following examples, the words shown in brackets are often omitted in speaking and writing.

Some of the patriots carried guns, others [carried] swords, still others [carried] clubs and sticks.

He was 18 years of age; his brother [was] 12 [years of age].

Although [I was] ill, I insisted on attending class.

When [he is] in New York, John goes to the theater every night.

While [she was] sewing, Mother listened to the radio.

(For errors in the use of elliptical clauses, see Sections **40c** and **75h**.)

## EXERCISE

From two or three pages of prose in your book of readings or in a current magazine, list at least 10 clauses that include all the following types: (1) independent clause, (2) noun clause, (3) adjective clause, (4) adverbial clause.

# 74 *Sentences*

Constructively defined, a *written sentence*[3] is a word or group of words expressing a complete thought, that is, conveying understandable meaning from writer to reader. To explain further, as a conventional unit of writing:

1. It is a word or group of words that makes an independent statement, assertion, inquiry or question, request, command, wish, or exclamation.

---

[3] Some linguists define a *spoken sentence* differently:

"In English speech a spoken sentence generally ends with a drop in pitch, while level or rising pitches with an utterance signalize the presence of clausal or phrasal constructions."—*Standard College Dictionary*

"A grammatically self-contained speech unit . . . that in speaking is phonetically distinguished by various patterns of stress, pitch, and pauses."—*Webster's Seventh New Collegiate Dictionary*

"Linguistically, as much of a speaker's expression as he places between definite final pitches and pauses."—*Webster's New World Dictionary*

Or, as it is defined linguistically, using linguistic language and symbols: "A sentence is an utterance, either from silence to silence, or from / 2 ³ ′ ³ ∤ / or any falling clause terminal to silence, to / 2 ³ ′ ³ ∤ /, or to any falling clause terminal."—*Standard College Dictionary* (p. xviii)

2. It usually consists of a subject and predicate, although various kinds of statements express a complete thought without a stated or implied subject or predicate. (See Section **31g.**)

3. It begins with a capital letter. (See Section **97b.**)

4. It ends with a terminating mark of punctuation (usually period, question mark, or exclamation point—see Sections **86a, b,c, 87a,b**) .

Most statements giving complete meaning contain a *subject* and a *predicate*. The subject is the name of the person (persons) or thing (things) —noun, pronoun, noun phrase, noun clause— about which the verb makes a statement or assertion. The predicate is a verb or verb phrase which makes a statement about the subject: an assertion, an action, a condition, a state of being. The verb or verb phrase agrees with the subject in number and person. Obviously, subject and predicate have to be defined in terms of each other: a statement without a subject has no predicate; a statement without a predicate has no subject. It is worth remembering that in clear and effective writing, participles, infinitives, and gerunds cannot serve as predicates.

A *simple subject* is only the noun or pronoun or series of nouns or pronouns serving as subject; a *complete subject* is the simple subject with all its modifiers. A *simple predicate* is only the verb, verb phrase, or series of verbs serving as predicate; a *complete predicate* is the simple predicate with all its modifiers.

The green *house* is for sale. (Simple subject)
*The green house on the hill* is for sale. (Complete subject)
*The green house and two acres of land* are for sale. (Compound subject)
*What you say and what you do* are no concern of mine. (Compound subject)
All of us *shouted*. (Simple predicate)
All of us *shouted with pleasure because of our victory*. (Complete predicate)
I *wrote* the letter last night *and mailed* it this morning. (Compound predicate)

To reinforce your knowledge of grammar, you may find diagraming of value. This is a mechanical device by which you are aided in identifying words as parts of speech, in identifying phrases and clauses, and in indicating the uses or functions in a sentence of these words, phrases, or clauses. These purposes of diagraming are accomplished through the use of lines: horizontal lines, perpendicular lines, slanting lines, curved lines, and dotted lines.

But diagraming, although it seems like a game, is only a *means* to an end, not an *end* in itself; it is simply a device to help you identify and see the relationships between various parts of a sentence.

The parts of the sentence are put on lines in the positions indicated in the following skeleton diagram; the three important parts, subject, predicate, object (or object complement) are usually put on a horizontal line, and any modifiers are usually placed appropriately on lines underneath.

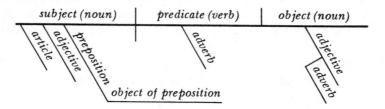

With actual words in the spaces, a diagramed sentence looks like this:

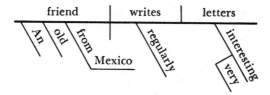

### 74a  *Understand the grammatical classification of sentences in order to obtain variety in your expression of the relationship of ideas*

Sentences are classified—according to the number of clauses they contain—as *simple, compound, complex,* or *compound-complex.*

A *simple sentence* contains only one subject and one predicate and expresses only one thought, although part of the thought can contain several related ideas. It could serve as an independent clause if other clauses were added to it. If the simple subject contains two or more nouns or pronouns or noun phrases or noun clauses joined by the proper conjunction, the descriptive term used is *compound subject.* If the simple predicate contains two or more verbs joined by the proper conjunction, the descriptive term used is *compound predicate.*

The simple sentence is excellent for the expression of one idea or two or more simple, uncomplicated ideas.

Our campus has paved roads. (Simple subject, simple predicate)
Oaks, maples, and elms line the campus roads. (Compound subject, simple predicate)
The speaker rose and bowed. (Simple subject, compound predicate)
My father and mother discuss and settle every important family matter. (Compound subject, compound predicate)
Alumni, faculty, and students attended the game, cheered the team, and celebrated the victory. (Compound subject, compound predicate)

In a sentence diagram, the simple predicate, the direct object, the object complement, the predicate noun (or pronoun), and the predicate adjective are written on the main long horizontal line. Subject and predicate are separated by a perpendicular line intersecting the horizontal line. The direct object is separated from the verb by a short perpendicular line extending up from the horizontal line. The object complement, the predicate

| Children | like | candy |
|---|---|---|
| *subject* | *predicate verb* | *object* |

| We | have elected | John \ | captain |
|---|---|---|---|
| *subject* | *predicate verb phrase* | *direct object* | *object complement* |

| This | is \ | he |
|---|---|---|
| *subject* | *predicate* <br> *(linking verb)* | *predicate pronoun* |

| Father | will be \ | glad |
|---|---|---|
| *subject* | *predicate* <br> *(linking verb)* | *predicate adjective* |

noun or pronoun, or the predicate adjective is set off by a short slanting line extending up to the left from the horizontal line. The following four diagrams illustrate the principles just stated and are examples also of how simple sentences are diagramed.

When conjunctions are used, dashes or dotted lines (usually perpendicular) are used to join, and the conjunction is written along or across such a line.

To diagram a simple sentence with a compound subject, compound predicate, and compound object:

Freshmen and sophomores read or write stories and essays.

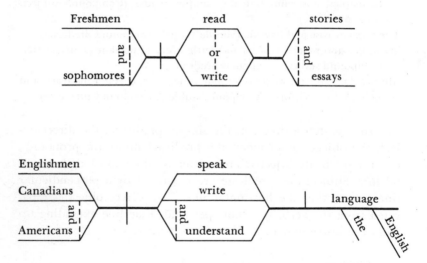

To diagram a sentence containing adjective and adverbial modifiers: Slanting lines below the horizontal line are used for adjective and adverbial modifiers; each adjective or adverb is on a separate line.

The old man slowly but carefully signed his name.

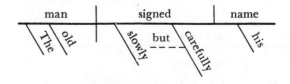

An adverb modifying an adjective or another adverb is written on an additional slanting line (or a stair-step line), thus:

The very old man walked extremely slowly.

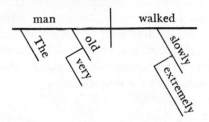

A *compound sentence* contains two or more independent clauses. Each clause of a compound sentence is grammatically capable of standing alone. The compound sentence is excellent for expressing two or more equally related parts of one main idea.

In Arizona the days are warm, but the nights are cool.
On our vacation Mother read, and I wrote letters.
Our team may not always win; nevertheless, it should try.
Some students learn quickly and easily, others prepare assignments in moderate time, and still others toil from dawn to midnight to get their work done.

To diagram a compound sentence:

I like movies, but John prefers radio dramas.

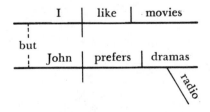

A *complex sentence* contains one independent clause and one or more dependent (subordinate) clauses. The complex sentence is excellent for expressing two ideas, one of which is not so important as the other.

Leonard is a student who puts his studies above his activities.
If the weather is fair, we shall go to the lake for the weekend.
Helen said that she had spent four hours writing her theme.

To diagram a complex sentence: Noun clauses usually occupy the position of subject or object; an adjective clause is linked with a vertical dotted line to the noun it modifies; an adverbial clause is linked with a vertical dotted line to the proper word it modifies in the independent clause. Any conjunction expressed is written across the dotted line.

Noun clause as subject:

What you say has convinced me.

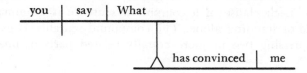

Noun clause as object:

John said that he had studied his lesson faithfully.

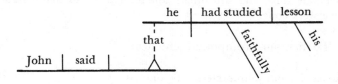

Adjective clauses:

Men who work diligently usually succeed.

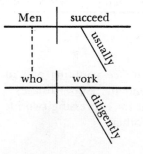

I met a friend whom I like.

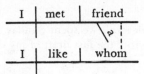

Adverbial clauses:

We won the game because we had the better team.

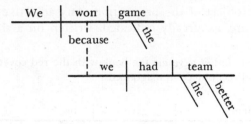

Mary is taller than her mother is.

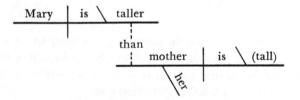

John drives faster than he should drive.

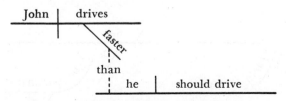

A *compound-complex sentence* contains two or more independent clauses and one or more dependent clauses. The compound-complex sentence is excellent for expressing two

443

equally related parts of one larger idea and one or more ideas not so important as either of the two main ideas.

Since the day was unpleasant, we spent Sunday indoors; John studied
    mathematics, and I wrote the first draft of my theme, which is due on
    Tuesday.

    Simple, compound, complex, and compound-complex sentences may and usually do contain various kinds of phrases. Diagraming phrases can be done as follows:

    Prepositional phrases are attached below the words they modify by a slanting line for the preposition and a horizontal line for the object of the preposition. Any adjectives modifying this object are, as already indicated, written on a slanting line.

A friend of my father gave me the book with the red cover. (Note how
    *me*—the indirect object—is diagramed.)

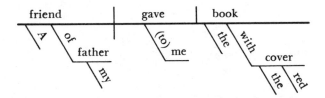

    Participial and infinitive phrases (as adjectives or adverbs) are attached to the words they modify by means of a line that curves into a horizontal line. Any objects, adjectives, or adverbs in these phrases are placed as indicated above.

The man wearing the brown hat is the man to be nominated for president.

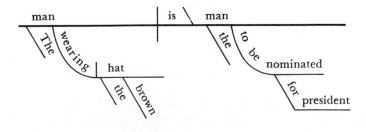

A gerund phrase or an infinitive phrase used as a noun is put on a horizontal line supported by a vertical line placed to indicate whether such phrase is the subject, object, predicate noun, etc. A noun clause or an infinitive "clause" (see Section **85,** Item 67) is similarly supported. Within these phrases or clauses, objects, adjectives, adverbs, and the like, are placed as indicated above.

Gerund phrase as subject of a verb:

Occasionally reading a good book is a worthy achievement.

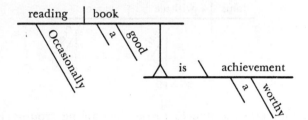

Infinitive phrase as predicate noun:

A precept worthy to be followed by everyone is freely to forgive your enemies.

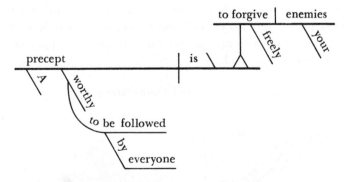

An infinitive "clause":

Henry asked me to lend him my dictionary.

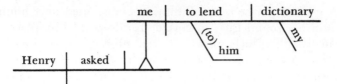

Sometimes a sentence may contain parts in inverted or transposed order; these parts must be put in the proper places in the diagram according to the directions already given.

Never again will John see so exciting a game.

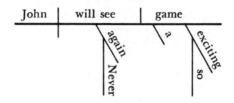

Certain other sentences cause diagraming trouble because we try to fit various constructions into a rigid pattern and order, like subject-verb-object, and often these constructions simply will not fit. Difficult to diagram are sentences containing what seem like independent units, i.e., material not directly modifying any word in the sentence. Such units are absolute phrases, nouns in direct address, the expletive *there,* interjections, and a few adverbs or adverb phrases which seem to modify the whole sentence.

Absolute phrases are placed on a vertically supported line but are enclosed in brackets:

The tire being repaired, we continued our journey.

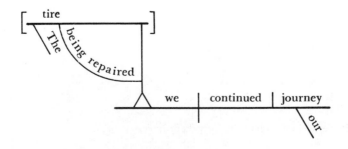

A noun in direct address or the expletive *there* may be placed on a line above the sentence diagram; its position is not important, but it could be placed above the words near which it is placed in the sentence. Another solution is to put the independent units in parentheses at the beginning of the sentence diagram.

John, there is a letter for you on the table.

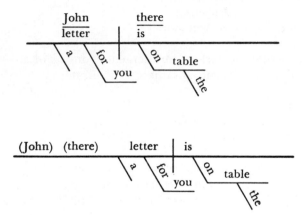

### 74b Understand the classification of sentences for the expression of meaning and purpose in clear and effective writing

Sentences are also classified according to *meaning* and *purpose,* that is, according to the kind of statement that each makes.

A *declarative sentence* makes an assertion or states a fact, a possibility, or a condition.

This dormitory houses 120 students.
It may rain before tomorrow.
If it rains tomorrow, we will have to change our plans.

An *imperative sentence* expresses a request, an entreaty, or a command.

Fill out the enclosed application blank and send it in immediately.
Please ask your friends to attend this important meeting.

Attend every class before and after the vacation period, or be prepared to suffer the consequences.

An *exclamatory sentence,* which may even consist of a word, a phrase, or a dependent clause, expresses strong feeling or surprise.

Ouch! Stop!
Attention, please! Danger ahead!
Oh, if only you had telephoned!
Thank goodness, you are here at last!

Frequently the exclamatory sentence consists of an exclamatory word + complement + subject + predicate:

How lovely these roses are!
What a brilliant student you have become!
What a busy day we have had!

An *interrogative sentence* asks a question, makes a direct inquiry. It can be written in several different ways:

1. By placing the subject after the auxiliary verb: *Are* you going? *Have* you bought any oranges? *Did* you study last night?

2. By using an interrogative pronoun or pronoun adjective: *Who* is it? *Which* is my book? *What* pages should we read?

3. By using an interrogative adverb: *How* are you? *When* did you arrive? *Where* have you traveled?

4. By adding an interrogative statement to a declarative sentence: You have many visitors here, *haven't you?* You did study, *didn't you?*

5. By a question mark after a declarative statement: *You're going home? You've been to the theater?*

**74c   *Understand the arrangement of ideas in
         sentences for effectiveness of expression***

Sentences are also classified—according to the *arrangement* of their content—as *periodic* or *loose* (a *balanced* sentence is a variety of either the periodic or the loose sentence) .

In a *periodic* sentence, the words are so arranged that the meaning is not completed until the end or near the end; that is, the independent clause, the main verb, the direct object, the complement, or some other completion word or group of words is placed at or very near the end of the sentence. Such a sentence provides suspense and variety; something is held back, and the reader continues in a state of expectation.

In a *loose* sentence, a full or moderate completeness of meaning is obtained long before the end; that is, in compound sentences and in complex sentences with the dependent clause following the independent clause, some complete meaning is possible before the end of the sentence.

Orientation for freshmen will begin Sunday; class schedules will be arranged on Wednesday; and regular classes will start Thursday. (Loose)

John liked football and hockey as spectator sports, but he preferred participation sports like golf and bowling. (Loose)

Please be on the campus by Sunday morning, unless you receive notice to the contrary. (Loose)

Unless you receive notice to the contrary, please be on the campus by Sunday morning. (Periodic)

Tired, muddy, and soaked thoroughly by the steady downpour, both football teams welcomed the ending-the-game whistle. (Periodic)

To students in despair about their prospects of success in college, words of encouragement from a teacher mean a great deal. (Periodic)

Achieving knowledge and skills to earn a comfortable living, making friendships that will be lifelong, and enjoying actively or passively some carefully selected activities—these are worthy aims for every college student. (Periodic)

Conversation and informal writing contain many more loose sentences than periodic, because a loose sentence is, probably, a more natural means of expression. Because of this predominance, an occasional periodic sentence is effective. Although it is also a natural form of expression, the periodic sentence is less common —hence its effectiveness; overuse, however, may become awkward, artificial, and monotonous.

A *balanced* sentence is so written that similar or opposing thoughts or ideas have similar grammatical phrasing. One part *balances* another: independent clause and independent clause, dependent clause and dependent clause, phrase and phrase (see "Parallelism," Section 44) ; most effective, however, is the use of independent clauses to make statements emphatic through comparisons and contrasts.

Spring is planting time; summer is growing time; autumn is harvest time.
In the morning I attend classes; in the afternoon I study; in the evening I work.
A wise man changes his mind, a fool never.
You can take a man out of the country; you can't take the "country" out of a man.

For further discussion of the sentence, see "The Sentence," Sections **31** through **49**.

## EXERCISES

A. From two or three pages of prose in your book of readings or in a current magazine, list under these headings up to five sentences each of the following types: (1) simple sentence, (2) compound sentence, (3) complex sentence, (4) compound-complex sentence.

B. After each of your sentences in Exercise A, write (P) if the sentence is periodic and (L) if the sentence is loose.

### DIAGRAMING EXERCISES

Diagram the following sentences:

1. Father has appointed Mary his secretary.
2. Books, magazines, and newspapers are available in the library.
3. Busy people receive and send many letters.
4. Some students are steady and persevering in their work.
5. For most of the afternoon we talked, watched TV, and played bridge.
6. Henry has worked faithfully to achieve his ambition.
7. To recognize one's errors is to take the first step toward improvement.
8. Father wrote that he would arrive on Friday.
9. I shall bring you the book when I go to the library tomorrow.
10. You must obey traffic rules, or some policeman may arrest you.
11. Mother, who is kind and generous, does sometimes lose her temper.
12. I am looking forward to your coming to the University in September.

13. I am telephoning what I have to say, and then I shall confirm it by letter.

14. You should remember that traffic regulations are devised and enforced for the safety of drivers, passengers, and pedestrians.

15. A day to be remembered will be the day when we are granted our diplomas and become alumni of this university.

# 75 Case

*Case* is a grammatical term referring to one of the forms that a noun or pronoun takes to indicate its relation to other words. The three cases in English—nominative or subjective, possessive or genitive, objective or accusative—appear in the singular and plural.

The *nominative* case of nouns and pronouns refers to grammatical subject or predicate complement. The *objective* case of nouns and pronouns refers to objects of prepositions and to direct and indirect objects of verbs. For the *possessive* case, see Section **75j–m.**

In English, case and case endings are less important grammatically than in other languages you may study, such as German, Spanish, Italian, Latin, or Greek. For example, English nouns have no distinguishing endings to show the difference between nominative and objective case; in German and Latin, nouns are declined to show endings for nominative, possessive, dative (indirect object), and objective (see Glossary, Section **85**). Also, Latin nouns have still another case, the ablative case, with appropriate endings. In German and Latin, also, adjectives are fully declined, but English adjectives in general take no endings.

The following principles for the use of the nominative and objective cases rarely apply to nouns but are a guide for the use of the pronoun forms (see Sections **71d** and **75a**). Most difficulty comes from case forms of the personal pronouns and the relative or interrogative pronoun *who*. Grammatical problems arise because these pronouns, unlike nouns, have different forms for the nominative and objective cases.

**75a   Learn the different forms of personal,
relative, and interrogative pronouns**

PERSONAL PRONOUNS

*Singular*

| NOMINATIVE | POSSESSIVE | OBJECTIVE |
|---|---|---|
| *1st person* I | my, mine | me |
| *2nd person* you | your, yours | you |
| *3rd person* | | |
| *masculine* he | his | him |
| *feminine* she | her, hers | her |
| *neuter* it | its | it |

*Plural*

| | | |
|---|---|---|
| *1st person* we | our, ours | us |
| *2nd person* you | your, yours | you |
| *3rd person* | | |
| *all genders* they | their, theirs | them |

When there are two possessive forms of the personal pronoun, the first one given in the list above is followed by the noun
it qualifies as a possessive adjective; the second is used alone, as
a possessive pronoun.

*My* book is on the desk; *yours* is on the shelf.
The book on the desk is *mine*.
*His* appointment is in the morning; *hers* is in the afternoon.

RELATIVE AND INTERROGATIVE PRONOUNS

*Singular and Plural*

| NOMINATIVE | POSSESSIVE | OBJECTIVE |
|---|---|---|
| who | whose | whom |

No change in form occurs in the use of *that* and *which*.

**75b   The subject of a sentence or a clause
is in the nominative case**

If the subject is a noun, forget about its case. Even an illiterate
American could not get its grammatical form wrong. If the
subject is a pronoun, used as the first or even the second member

of a compound subject, again only a poorly prepared college freshman would be confused.

My father and *I* (not *me*) have gone on many fishing trips.
*He* (not *himself*) has been a very desirable roommate.
As for my mother, Father and *she* (not *her*) have always encouraged me
to do my best.
*Who* (not *whom*) is speaking, please?

### 75c A predicate complement is in the nominative case (see "Complement," Section 85)

Predicate complement means a noun (no problem), a pronoun (nominative case, essentially), or a predicate adjective (not an adverb) used after a linking or copulative (coupling) verb (Section 78). Not nouns, but only pronouns have different forms for nominative and objective. After a coupling or copulative verb the nominative or subjective case of pronouns is used, not the objective case.

This is *he* (not *him*) speaking.
That is *she* (not *her*) there at the desk.
It was *they* (not *them*) who made the decision.

The foregoing principle usually applies to all the personal pronouns and usually to spoken English (except in dialogue) after "This . . . ." and "It . . . ." But there is controversy. Prescriptive grammarians apply the rule rigidly, but other authorities say that, although *it is I* is expected at the formal level, *it is me* is an acceptable informal idiom. The objective cases of the other pronouns, singular and plural, are found in informal speech and writing, but not so commonly. Perhaps all such formal and informal uses are rare, and both "it is I" and "it is me" are commonly replaced by "This is Jones" or a simple "Yes" to the question, "Is this Jones?" Or follow the advice of the editors of the Merriam-Webster dictionaries: "An educator is probably required to point out that no matter how acceptable 'It is me' can be proved to be, it probably should not be insisted upon if one knows that the hearer will make serious adverse judgments of an individual on account of it."—*Word Study*, April, 1966

*75d   The object of a verb or preposition is in the objective case*

The words *objective* case are used of nouns or pronouns as objects of prepositions or as direct or indirect objects of verbs. A *direct* object is a noun, pronoun, or noun clause following a preposition or following a transitive verb.

Your book is on the *table*. (Object of preposition)
I have written many *themes*. (Object of verb)
I am sending *what you have ordered*. (Object of verb)

A *simple* object is the noun or pronoun or noun clause alone. A *complete* object is a simple object together with its modifiers. A *compound* object consists of two or more nouns or pronouns or noun clauses.

As direct objects, again, nouns or *it* or *you* cause no trouble. Only the pronouns—*who* vs. *whom, I* vs. *me, she* vs. *her, he* vs. *him, we* vs. *us, they* vs. *them*—must be carefully observed.

Mary looked very innocent; no one blamed *her*.
Their winning first place was good news for *them*.
A committee of *us* students is assisting in the planning.

Pay special attention to the cases of pronouns used as the second member of a compound object.

About Mary? We are inviting both John and *her* to come. (Not John and *she*.)
This matter concerns only *him* and *me*. (Not *he* and *I*.)
I understand a special invitation to join is being sent to *you* and *me*. (Not *you* and *I*.)

When in doubt, reverse the order temporarily (see Section **77e**) ; scarcely anyone would say, "Give *I* and Bill the books" or "Give the books to *I* and Bill."

*75e   The indirect object of a verb is in the objective case*

An *indirect* object is a noun or pronoun preceding the direct object of the verb, before which the word *to* or *for* is understood. When such an object follows the direct object, the preposition *to* or *for* is used.

Give (to) *us* our daily bread.
Write (to) *me* a letter about your plans.
If you do (for) *him* a favor, he will never forget it.
Tell (to) *whom* my story? John? I should say not.

### 75f The subject, object, or objective complement of an infinitive is in the objective case

Infinitives are certain verb forms preceded by an expressed or implied *to*. As with the other principles in this section, pronouns, not nouns, cause trouble.

His friends helped *him* succeed. (*Him* is the subject of *succeed*.)
His friends caused *him* to succeed. (*Him* is the subject of *to succeed*.)
The class has named *me* to serve as treasurer. (*Me* is the subject of *to serve*.)
*Whom* did you take *her* to be? (I.e., did you take *her* to be *whom*?)
   (*Her* is the subject of *to be*; *whom* is an objective complement agreeing in case with *her*.)
Did you think *her* to be *me*? (*Her* is the subject of *to be,* and *me* is an objective complement after *to be*.)

   If the grammar in the five preceding examples seems unduly complicated, just pretend that the pronoun is the object of the verb preceding it and is modified by the infinitive. Your writing will turn out to be just as correct. If you write constructions like the foregoing and are puzzled about correcting them, revise and recast the sentence.

## NOMINATIVE AND OBJECTIVE CASES

### 75g An appositive should be in the same case as the noun or pronoun it explains or identifies

This principle, again, demands care in the use of the proper case forms of pronouns.

Two people, *she* and *I,* are the only candidates with a chance to win. (Nominative)
The dean gave friendly advice to both of us, James and *me*. (Objective)
Last evening the club pledged two additional men, my roommate and *me*. (Objective)

### 75h   *An elliptical clause of comparison, preceded by than or as, requires the case called for by the expanded construction*

If you supply the missing word or words in an elliptical clause (see pp. 435–436), you should have little trouble about the correct case form.

I am as strong as *he* (is). (Nominative)
You are much taller than *I* (am). (Nominative)
Mother does not drive a car as well as *I* (do). (Nominative)
I do not like her as much as (I like) *him*. (Objective)
I do not like her as much as *he* (likes her). (Nominative)
This TV program amused you much more than (it amused) *me*. (Objective)
This TV program amused you much more than *I* (amused you). (Nominative)

### 75i   Who *and* whoever *are used as subjects of verbs or as predicate pronouns;* whom *and* whomever *are used as objects of verbs and prepositions*

Many grammatical errors arise from misunderstanding the pronoun forms *who* or *whom* and *whoever* or *whomever*. This discussion supplements and expands that given above, Section **75a–h.**

1. The following sentences illustrate the proper use of *who* and *whoever,* nominative forms serving as subjects of the verbs in the dependent clauses:

I demand membership for *whoever* wishes it. (*Whoever* is the subject of the verb *wishes;* the whole dependent clause is the object of the preposition *for.*)
The question of *who* can ask for membership should not arise. (*Who* is the subject of *can ask;* the whole dependent clause is the object of the preposition *of.*)
This book tells *who* is *who* in America, and that one tells *who* was *who.* (Each *who* before *is* and *was* is the subject; each *who* after *is* and *was* is a predicate pronoun.)

In other words, subject of a verb takes precedence over object of a preposition or verb, when pronoun case forms are in question.

2. The following sentences illustrate the proper use of *whom* and *whomever,* objective forms serving as objects in the dependent clauses:

This is the same man *whom* I saw at Oak Bluffs last summer. (Direct object of *saw.*)
Ask *whomever* you desire. (Direct object of *desire;* the dependent clause is the object of *ask.*)
The letter began, "To *whom* it may concern." (Direct object of *concern;* the dependent clause is the object of the preposition *To.*)
Grandfather tells the same yarns to *whomever* he meets. (Direct object of *meets;* the dependent clause is the object of the preposition *to.*)

3. The nominative and objective cases are frequently confused because of intervening words. The case of a pronoun depends upon its use in the sentence and must not be influenced by words which come between the pronoun and other words determining its case.

He asked me *who* I thought would be chosen. (Check by omitting *I thought.*)
*Who* do you suppose drew up these plans? (Check by omitting *do you suppose.*)
I danced with the girl *whom* no one suspected we had chosen "Beauty Queen." (Check by omitting *no one suspected.*)

4. Whenever you are in doubt about *who* or *whom,* substitute *he* or *him* and see which makes sense:

*Who/whom* are you writing to? (to *who/whom* are you writing?)
*He/him* are you writing to? (to *he/him* are you writing?)
This is the kind of student *who/whom* we need.
. . . we need *who/whom.*
. . . we need *he/him.*

NOTE: Current-usage studies, although with some objection from some grammarians, indicate that *who* is replacing *whom* in some uses, partly because keeping them straight is difficult and partly because many people start a relative clause or an interrogative sentence with *who,* not knowing how it is going to end. In informal English many authorities agree that *who* may replace *whom* when it stands before a verb or preposition of which it is the object, but *whom* should be used when as object it directly follows the verb or preposition. Precise speakers and writers probably still observe the conventional distinctions of *who* vs. *whom*: *who* only as subject, *whom* only as object.

| | |
|---|---|
| *Informal* | *Who* are you visiting in New York? |
| | *Who* are you selling your typewriter to? |
| *Formal* | You said you were visiting *whom* in New York? |
| | To *whom* did you wish to speak? |
| | The people *whom* we met were on a tour similar to ours. |

## POSSESSIVE (GENITIVE) CASE

### 75j   Use the correct form of a particular noun in the possessive (genitive) case

Although it is sometimes called the *genitive* case, the usual word in English is *possessive*. (In other languages, such as German and Latin, the genitive case has various uses, including the expression of possession.) In English the possessive case serves three purposes: (1) to indicate ownership, the usual use of the case; (2) to indicate association with or to identify (see examples below); and (3) to indicate measurement of time or space (see Section **75m**).

Mother's purse contains an assortment of things. (Possession)

My father's profession differs from my grandfather's occupation. (Association)

Colonel Rufus M. Brown is in charge of our Reserve Officers' Training Corps. (Association)

Mark Twain's novels and Edgar Allan Poe's short stories are still enjoyed by millions of Americans. (Identification)

New York City's airports are among the busiest in the world. (Identification)

Misuse of nouns in the possessive case is usually due to carelessness. Many students write the plurals of nouns when such nouns should be in the possessive case, either singular or plural. Although it is a grammatical term, possessive case of nouns in English is formed by a punctuation mark, the apostrophe, according to the principles stated in Section **93a,b,c,d,e,f.**

**75k    Avoid awkwardness and incorrectness in the use
of the possessive case; use an *of* phrase instead**

For avoiding awkwardness in showing possession of inanimate objects, for avoiding other awkwardness and incorrectness, and for variety, the possessive case is expressed by an *of* phrase. Occasionally, and idiomatically, an inanimate object may be in the possessive case (see Section **75m**), but the use is usually awkward.

*Awkward possession of inanimate objects*
    The *trees'* leaves were turning green.
    The *wastebasket's* contents were on fire.
    We pledges waxed and polished the *dining room's* floor.
*Improved*
    The leaves *of the trees* were turning green.
    The contents *of the wastebasket* were on fire.
    We pledges waxed and polished the floor *of the dining room.*

Both awkward and incorrect is the use of a phrase containing "one of the," then a plural possessive, and then a singular noun. Rephrasing is needed.

*Awkward and incorrect*
    The waiter accidentally spilled coffee on *one of the girls' dress.*
    We held our after-graduation party at *one of the boys' home.*
*Correct*
    The waiter accidentally spilled coffee on the dress of *one of the girls.*
        (or: on *one girl's dress*)
    We held our after-graduation party at the home of *one of the boys.*
        (or: at *one boy's home*)
*Variety (either alternative is correct)*
    The home *of my parents* (or: my *parents'* home) is on Laurel Avenue.
    The report *of the committee* (or: the *committee's* report) is due next week.
    The extracurricular activities *of any student* (or: any *student's* extracurricular activities) should not interfere with his studies.

NOTE: An acceptable, although probably unnecessary, idiom is the *double possessive,* an *of* followed by a noun in the possessive case:

A classmate of my *sister's* spent the weekend with us.
We are reading two plays of *Shakespeare's*.

**75l** *A noun or pronoun linked immediately with a gerund should preferably be in the possessive case*

The possessive case with a gerund is usually clear, whereas the objective case with the gerund may not be.

*Awkward*    He resents *you* being more popular than he is.

Most of the members paid their dues without *me* asking them.

The teacher praised John for *him* taking careful lecture notes.

The other girls objected to *Mary* spreading such a rumor.

*Improved*    He resents *your* being more popular than he is.

Most of the members paid their dues without *my* asking them.

The teacher praised John for *his* taking careful lecture notes.

The other girls objected to *Mary's* spreading such a rumor.

When the possessive case with a gerund is awkward, as, for example, when other words come between the two, recast the sentence.

*Awkward*    No rules exist against *anyone's* in this class saying what he thinks.

*Improved*    No rules exist against any class *member's* saying what he thinks.

Do not confuse the possessive-with-gerund and noun-or-pronoun-with-participle constructions.

*Clear*    The class members heard their *teacher* asking for greater care in their written work.

The class members responded to their *teacher's* asking for greater care in their written work.

**75m** *Use the possessive case to express extent of time or space*

The principle stated in Section **75k** should not be followed explicitly if it produces awkwardness or violates good idiomatic usage. Although inanimate objects are rarely put in the possessive case, good English idiom prefers the possessive case for certain nouns of measure, time, and the like. It is not a question of ownership or possession; it is simply an effective expression of measure, extent of time, etc. The usual time nouns are *second, minute, moment, hour, day, week, month, semester, year, decade, century, winter, spring, summer, autumn, today, tomorrow, yesterday.* Instead of an awkward "of" phrase, the following expressions are preferable and desirable:

| | |
|---|---|
| a day's work | a dollar's worth |
| a moment's notice | a stone's throw |
| 10 minutes' walk | at his wit's end |
| three years' experience | the law's delay |
| a summer's work | tomorrow's weather report |
| two semesters' study | 4 inches' space |
| at arm's length | for charity's sake |

For some of these ideas, of course, hyphenated expressions are acceptable and sometimes preferable alternatives: *a 10-minute walk, a five-mile drive, a two-semester course, a 95-yard run* (vs. *a 95 yards' run*).

## EXERCISES

A. Write brief sentences in which you use "he and I" (1) as subject of independent clause, (2) as subject of dependent clause. and (3) in apposition. Write brief sentences in which you use "him and me" (1) as direct object of verb, (2) as indirect object of a verb, (3) as object of a preposition, and (4) in apposition.

B. Copy the following sentences, correcting all errors in the use of case. Specify each kind of error.

1. Everyone believes in some kind of superstition, even me.
2. A person such as me can study only so many hours without a break.
3. Robert Browning's marriage to Elizabeth Barrett was a wondrous love story that lifted both he and his wife to greater poetic activity.
4. Each night we have a contest among my roommates and myself to see who can finish his assignments first.
5. George grew up by showing off his knowledge even to those who knew far more than him.
6. Most sports fans belong in this category, especially us.

7. With defeat on the faces of we students, we sadly left the stadium and the Homecoming game.
8. There in my room stood a girl about the same height as me.
9. We, a few friends and me, were on our way to a picnic.
10. At the bus station, I saw another boy; I conjectured that he, like I, had been home for a short vacation.
11. We always find that many thousands of people are less fortunate than us.
12. Mother and Father were tired of walking and left Mary Anne and I to explore on our own.
13. I really can't describe a woman such as her; you would have to meet her to know her.
14. Our heroine finally came to understand that human nature, not her, had control over people's falling in love.
15. This vacation will be a good chance for all my friends and I to exchange college experiences.

C. Copy the following sentences, correcting all errors in the use of possessive case. Explain each kind of error.

1. Our doubts about us ever getting there began to grow.
2. The horn should also be used to warn unsuspecting pedestrians of the automobile's presence.
3. I don't mind you asking me a few questions.
4. I have had four years experience working in machine shops.
5. After 10 minutes deliberation, the judges' announced that they had reached a decision.
6. When I was very young, I recall my mother telling me about my ancestry.
7. Mr. Brown was a great teacher; hardly a day goes by without him being remembered.
8. I did not do as well as I expected to do in my last semesters 'courses.
9. If you have typhoid shots, there is less chance of you getting typhoid fever.
10. In the spring the canyon's trees again put forth their leaves.
11. After a half hour the pilot decided we had had our moneys worth and brought us back to land.
12. The manager of these large supermarkets salary may be between $25,000 and $50,000 a year.
13. The green in the leaves seems to bring out all of the dark brown or black of the tree's bark.
14. After three or four hours caroling, everyone heads for one of the members house, where a party is held.

15. My parents said that they are not going to pay for me going to college next semester if I don't pass all my courses this semester.

D. On a separate page, list the numbers 1 to 15. Opposite each number write the italicized word that precise writers and speakers would probably use in each case:

1. I would get into an argument with *whoever whomever* said anything about my driving habits.
2. In college I hope that I meet the person *who whom* I want to marry.
3. A few other campers had arrived *who whom* also needed to purchase supplies.
4. With the assistance of these people, *who whom* Jane later discovered were her cousins, she established a school for poor children.
5. We always kept a sharp lookout for old Mr. Jones, a man *who whom* we children seemed to fear.
6. What a surprise to have a roommate *who whom* you haven't seen for eight years!
7. I believe in God: at Thanksgiving this is *Who Whom* I give thanks to.
8. She went to live with Michael Henchard, the man *who whom* she at the time believed was her father.
9. Every student in college will have teachers *who whom* he likes and teachers *who whom* like him.
10. I had four older brothers and sisters *who whom* I had to obey.
11. We marched around the campus with shouts of *who whom* we wanted for our class president.
12. Our town has a doctor *who whom* we believe is a very clever surgeon.
13. Nothing on the envelope indicates *who whom* the letter is from.
14. My father always votes for the man *who whom* he thinks would do the best job regardless of party.
15. Next month's issue will answer these football questions: *Who whom* will our team beat? *Who whom* might it lose to? *Who'll whom'll* be the top 10 players?

# 76  *Agreement of subject and predicate*

Grammatical agreement means *unison* or *concord* or *harmony* of parts of a sentence. Thus when a subject agrees with its predicate, both the subject and the verb in the predicate are alike in having the same *person* (first, second, or third) and *number* (singular or plural).

### 76a   *A predicate normally agrees with its subject in person and number*

Few problems in agreement arise because English verbs (except *to be*—see p. 484) have the same form for singular and plural and for *all* persons except the third person singular present tense. Most nouns and verbs form their plurals in directly opposite ways. Except for special groups, nouns form their *plurals* by adding s or *es*: *desk, desks; glass, glasses; lady, ladies.* (See Section **71c.**) Most verbs add an s in the third person singular. Do not be misled by an s sound in the verb. Examine carefully the following forms, first, second, and third person singular, present tense:

| | | | | | |
|---|---|---|---|---|---|
| I do | go | ask | possess | exist | suppose |
| You do | go | ask | possess | exist | suppose |
| He does | goes | asks | possesses | exists | supposes |
| The man does | goes | asks | possesses | exists | supposes |

In the plural, with *we, you, they,* the *men,* etc., only one plural form is used: *do, go, ask, possess, exist, suppose,* etc.

*John is* my older brother. (Subject and predicate are singular.)
*My two younger brothers are named* Henry and Robert. (Subject and predicate are plural.)

   Errors in agreement that do occur are serious; they are usually subtle and idiomatic, and so the principle—that subjects and predicates agree in number—seems difficult to apply. Usually errors appear when a writer or speaker is confused about the number of the subject because of other words intervening before the verb, or when he uses a verb to agree not with the grammatical form of a subject but with its meaning—as is sometimes logical and acceptable. In short, you need to know what the subject is, whether it is singular or plural, and what its true meaning is.

Section **76a** states the general rule; to understand variations and to avoid serious errors, study the following sections.

**76b**  *A verb should agree with the subject, not with a noun*
*which intervenes between it and the subject, when such*
*noun is an appositive or the object in a phrase containing*
**together with, along with, as well as, in addition to,**
**except, but, no less than, after**  (But see Section **76d**)

I, the president, *am*  (not *is*)  the one to introduce the speaker.

The *architecture* of our college buildings *is*  (not *are*)  beautiful.

The *reason* for the sudden change in plans *was*  (not *were*)  not apparent.

*He,* together with John and David, *is*  (not *are*)  going.

*Mary,* as well as some members of her family, *was*  (not *were*)  determined to stay longer.

*Candidate* after candidate *tries*  (not *try*)  out for the leading role every spring.

**76c**  **Singular pronouns require singular verbs; the following**
**pronouns are singular: another, anybody, anyone, anything,**
**each, either, everybody, everyone, everything, many a**
**one, neither, nobody, no one, one, somebody, someone**

Each *has* his own spending money.

Someone *was making* unnecessary noise.

One of you *has made* a mistake.

No one *skates* better than Thomas.

**76d**  *Certain nouns or pronouns are considered singular*
*or plural according to the singular or plural*
*number of the key word in a modifying phrase*

Examples are *some, all, half, none*  (*no one* or *not any*) , *what,*
*which.*

*Some* of my *money has* been lost.
*Some* of our *students have* been awarded scholarships.
No food is left; *all* of *it has* been eaten.
No students are left on the campus; *all* of *them have* gone home for
  vacation.
*Half* of this *building is* to be completed by autumn.
*Half* of the *buildings* on our campus *are* of red-brick construction.
*Which* (one) of the rooms *is* reserved for the meeting?
*Which* (ones) of the rooms *are* reserved for students?

*None* (literally *no one,* but frequently meaning *not any*)
may be followed by either a singular or a plural verb. Studies of
the use of *none* show that it is as frequently followed by a
plural as by a singular verb, especially when the phrase modifying *none* contains a plural noun.

*None* (no one) of the students in our dormitory is a candidate for a
  class office.
*None* (not any) of our students have recently disobeyed any college
  regulations.

A tricky subject-predicate combination is one beginning
with *what,* a pronoun used in both the singular and plural.
When it is used in the sense of *that which,* it has a singular
predicate. When it is used in the sense of *those (persons) who* or
*those (things) which,* it has a plural predicate.

*What is* to come is not known.
*What are* known are the things that happened yesterday.

### 76e  *For nouns plural in form but singular in meaning use a singular verb*

The following are always used with singular verbs: *molasses,
news,* and *stamina;* a few others may be used with singular
verbs: *amends, headquarters, means, summons,* and *whereabouts.*
(For the use of *data,* see "Glossary of Diction," Section **70.**)
When in doubt about any particular word, especially those
words ending in *-ics* (*athletics, economics, mathematics, physics,*
etc.), turn for guidance to your dictionary, which also has a brief
discussion under the suffix *-ics.*

Good news *was* in yesterday's paper.
Politics *has* always been one of Father's major interests.

Subjects plural in form, which describe a quantity or number, require a singular verb when the subject is regarded as a unit.

Ten miles *is* too far to walk.
Five dollars *was* asked for the desk lamp.
Three-fourths of a bushel *does* not seem enough.

In mathematical expressions, either singular or plural form is allowed:

Four times three *is* (*are*) twelve.
Six and six *make* (*makes*) twelve.
Two from five *leaves* (*leave*) three.

### 76f Use a plural verb, ordinarily, with two or more nouns or pronouns joined by and

The house and the automobile *were* both painted green.
Behind the wall *stand* a house and a garage.
Both the secretary and the treasurer *have* agreed to be present.

When the two nouns or pronouns form a single thought or have a closely related meaning or mean one thing or one person, a singular verb is used.

My oldest pal and best friend *is* my roommate this year.
Last year the secretary and treasurer of our club *was* John Poe.
The sum and substance of the speaker's remarks *has* caused much comment.
My house and home *is* at 1707 Maryland Drive.

NOTE: Idiomatically, two or more singular nouns joined by *and,* but with the first noun preceded by *every* or *each,* take a singular verb:

Every man, woman, and child here *is* an expert swimmer.
Each boy and girl here *has* received polio shots.

**76g**   *Two or more singular subjects joined by* or *or* nor
*or two singular subjects joined by* either . . . or,
neither . . . nor *require a singular verb*

Father or Mother *is* to represent our family at the meeting.
Neither John nor Henry *makes* very high grades.
Either economics or history *is* the course I shall elect next semester.

**76h**   *When the parts of the subject differ in number or person
and are joined by* or, nor, either . . . or, neither . . .
nor, *the verb agrees with the nearer subject member*

A European history course or any English courses *are* not among the
courses that I like.
Neither the students nor the teacher *wants* to meet at 7 o'clock.
Either some of my classmates or I *am* willing to write the petition.
Either some of my classmates or Henry *is* willing to write the petition.
Either Henry or some of his classmates *are* willing to write the petition.

**76i**   *Relative pronouns referring to plural antecedents
require plural verbs; relative pronouns referring
to singular antecedents require singular verbs*

Each house has its own elected *officers, who conduct* the business of the
house.
Each house has its own *president, who conducts* the business of the
house.
Our city has three excellent *beaches, which attract* many of our residents each summer.
Our city has an excellent *beach, which attracts* many of our residents
each summer.
My dictionary concludes with some *pages that contain* a list of American universities.
My dictionary has *one page that contains* a guide to pronunciation.

　　1. A troublesome application of this principle concerns *one
of those who* or *one of those which.*

My English teacher was one of those high school *teachers who were*
always getting off the subject.

This is one of the most important *events that have* ever occurred to me.
I happen to be one of those *people who like* to travel.
I hope to get a ride from *one* of my friends *who is* driving to Philadelphia.

In sentences like these, check carefully to see which is the *true* antecedent of the relative pronoun. Sometimes putting the *of* phrase first will help:

Of the important sporting *events that take* place each year, the Indiana High School Basketball Tournament is one.
Of those *people who like* to travel, I happen to be one.

2. If *the only* or some similar qualifying words precede *one,* the relative pronoun and the verb are singular:

He is *the only one* of those present *who wants* to argue.
My English teacher was *the only one* of my high school teachers *who was* always getting off the subject.

3. Sometimes you can determine the antecedent by the proper use of *who* or *which*:

This is a *list* of students *which has* been prepared.
This is a list of *students who have* been invited.

## 76j  Forms of to be agree with the subject, not with the predicate noun or pronoun

In some constructions, between two nouns or pronouns comes some form of the verb *to be: am, is, are, was, were, have been, has been.* The noun or pronoun coming first is considered the subject.

The best part of the meal *is* the coffee and cookies.
Coffee and cookies *are* the best part of the meal.

**76k**   *After expressions using* there *and* here—*like* there is,
        there are, there was, there were, there has been, there
        have been, *and other verbs—the verb is singular or
        plural according to the number of the subject,
        which in these constructions follows the predicate*

There *seem* (not *seems*) to be one book and three magazines missing.
Fortunately, there *exist* (not *exists*) people who can help us.
There *have been* (not *has been*) many exciting games this fall.
At camp there *were* (not *was*) baseball, softball, tennis, and swimming.
Here *is* (not *are*) my reason for studying history and economics.
Here *are* (not *is*) the students who were elected class representatives.
Here *are* (not *is*) Brown, Smith, and Jones, our three highest in scholar-
    ship.

NOTE:   Two or more singulars joined by *and* make a plural subject (see Section **76f**) .

    The same principle applies when *there* or *here* is replaced
by other words and the subject still follows the predicate:

In front of our Administration Building *stands* (not *stand*) a towering
    oak.
In front of our Union Building *stand* (not *stands*) an elm, two maples,
    and an oak.

NOTE: Sentences or clauses beginning with *there is, there are,*
etc., can be correct, but such beginnings are often wordy, ineffective, and avoidable (Section **67c**) .

**76l**   *A collective noun takes a singular verb when the
        group is regarded as a unit, a plural verb when the
        individuals of the group are regarded separately*

A *collective noun* is the name of a group composed of individuals but considered as a unit. Common collective nouns are *army,
assembly, audience, clergy, committee, company, couple, crew,
crowd, family, flock, group, herd, jury, mob, multitude, orchestra,
pair, personnel, squad, team, union.* Most of these nouns also
have plural forms: *army, armies; assembly, assemblies; company,
companies; crowd, crowds; team, teams;* etc.

Without the *s,* they are considered singular and take a singular verb and singular pronouns when the collection of individuals is thought of as a unit, as a whole; they are considered plural and take a plural verb and plural pronouns when the members of the group are thought of as individuals, acting separately. (For collective nouns as antecedents of pronouns, see Section **77c.**)

Our crew [a unit] *is* going to compete this afternoon.
Our crew [members] *have* been on shore leave and *are* coming aboard in a few hours.
The team *has* elected Robbins captain.
The team *have* been unable to agree on a man for captain.
The family next door *is* named Brown.
The family *were* seated in armchairs on the lawn.

## EXERCISES

A. Make a list of numbers from 1 to 15. Opposite each, write the correct form of the verb from the italicized forms in the following sentences:

1. Homecoming weekend we freshmen had to sleep on the floor, for there *wasn't weren't* enough beds.
2. This dam, with the four or five other dams along the river, *form forms* part of the network of hydroelectric plants.
3. Neither one of my parents *know knows* much about mathematics.
4. The only other equipment you will need *are is* eating utensils, a flashlight, and a pocket knife.
5. My keeping New Year's resolutions *has have* always failed in past years.
6. Liking outdoor work is one of the reasons that *make makes* me want to go back to the farm.
7. Whenever either of us *has have* a problem, we talk it over until we reach a solution.
8. There *are is* in my family my mother, my father, my sister, and I.
9. I am one of the millions of people who *has have* been bitten by the golf bug.
10. Building model airplanes *require requires* a great deal of time and patience.
11. Each of the houses in this restored village *has have* antique furniture.

12. The location of the complimentary close and of the signature *seem seems* unusual in some business letters.
13. Neither the other students nor the instructor *was were* surprised when I came in late.
14. Charles Dickens' greatest achievement *is are* the novels that he wrote.
15. For breakfast there *was were* ham, fried potatoes, eggs, and toast.

B. Rewrite the following sentences, correcting the lack of agreement between subject and predicate:

1. Descriptive and narrative exposition have been used in this theme.
2. Row after row of beautiful hotels are visible across the lake.
3. The main character and hero of one of Dickens' famous novels are David Copperfield.
4. By 6 P.M. the cheering, the celebrating, and the shouting was over.
5. The subject matter of William Wordsworth's many sonnets are extremely varied.
6. All the alumni likes to see a beautiful girl chosen as Homecoming Queen.
7. In college I should say that, at the most, five outside activities is the limit.
8. Our local steel mill, along with several smaller industries, provide jobs for most of the people in our town.
9. The pleasures and enjoyment a wife gets out of life makes all of her efforts and hard work worthwhile.
10. Such training, with other desirable qualifications, are essential for a rewarding career.
11. If you can say that either of these beliefs apply to you, then you are superstitious.
12. The equipment that is found in most offices include filing cabinets, typewriters, and adding machines.
13. Her personality, both its good and bad points, make her a very unusual and unforgettable character.
14. My two aunts are concerning themselves with things that does not have anything to do with them.
15. The Department of Home Economics here at Atwood University is interested in the purchase of sewing machines and have several questions to ask.

# 77   Pronoun and antecedent

An *antecedent,* which literally means "going before," is the substantive (noun or pronoun) to which a pronoun refers or for which it is substituted. Sometimes, illogically but clearly, the antecedent follows the pronoun. (For discussion of pronouns, see Section **71d.**)

A pronoun agrees with its antecedent in gender, number, and person, but its use with other words determines its correct case. Since a pronoun (*pro-* means "for") is a word used instead of a noun or a group of words serving as a noun, such a noun or noun group—called the *antecedent*—must be unmistakably clear if your reader is not to be misled or confused.

The *woman* put on *her* hat. (Singular antecedent, feminine)
The *women* put on *their* hats. (Plural antecedent, feminine)
The *boy* misplaced *his* tickets. (Singular antecedent, masculine)
The *boys* misplaced *their* tickets. (Plural antecedent, masculine)
When *he* finally arrived, *Father* explained why he was late. (Pronoun precedes antecedent)

## 77a   Singular pronouns refer to singular antecedents (see also Section **76c**)

Has anyone here forgotten *his* dictionary?
The student was lucky to find the dictionary that *he* had lost.
In the new dormitory, each girl will have a room to *herself.*
Every person in favor will please raise *his* right hand.
Everybody is expected to do *his* share.

Since or when the sense of *everybody, anyone,* etc., is *many* or *all,* the plural personal pronoun referring to these indefinite pronouns is frequently found in both formal and informal English: "Everybody is expected to do *their* share of the work." Such use is preferable to the somewhat artificial and even awkward "Everybody is expected to do *his* or *her* share of the work." Notice, however, that a singular, not a plural verb form is used.

### 77b   *A pronoun agrees with the nearer of two antecedents*

Occasionally, two antecedents, different in gender or in number, are in a sentence. With two antecedents and only one pronoun, the pronoun referring to the antecedent nearer to it is used.

He loves anything and everybody *who* is connected with his work.
He loves anybody and anything *which* is connected with his work.
With artificial plants, neither the flower nor the leaves will ever lose
   *their* freshness.

### 77c   *A collective noun used as an antecedent takes either a singular or plural pronoun depending on whether the collective noun is considered as a unified group or a group of individuals acting separately* (see Section 76l)

The crowd of men took off *their* hats. (The *crowd* acted as individuals.)
The crowd shouted *its* approval. (The *crowd* acted as a unit.)

Be consistent in the use of collective nouns with singular or plural predicates and with singular or plural pronouns.

| | |
|---|---|
| *Inconsistent* | The class *was* unanimous in *their* choice of a president. |
| *Consistent* | The class *was* unanimous in *its* choice of a president. |
| *Inconsistent* | The team *were* unable to agree on whom *it* considered *their* most valuable player. |
| *Consistent* | The team *were* unable to agree on whom *they* considered *their* most valuable player. |
| | The team *was* almost immediately ready with *its* choice of *its* most valuable player—Harry Brown, the center. |

### 77d   *Do not confuse the relative pronouns* who, which, *and* that

*Who* usually refers only to persons; *which* usually refers only to inanimate objects or a group of persons; and *that* refers to persons or things.

| | |
|---|---|
| *Wrong* | The horse *who* stands there is a thoroughbred. |
| | The person *which* you mentioned is away from the city. |
| | The freshman class, *who* is the largest in our history, is also our best scholastically. |

(For the use of *that, which,* and *who* in restrictive and nonrestrictive adjective clauses, see Section **88m-R.**)

**77e  In the use of I in a compound subject or me in a compound object, politeness suggests that the I or me come last**

The same politeness applies to *we* in a compound subject and to *us* in a compound object.

| | |
|---|---|
| *Dubious* | *I* and my roommate are both studying engineering. |
| | Last spring the fraternity pledged *me* and six other boys. |
| | *We* and our neighbors have a community picnic each fall. |
| | Orientation meetings will be held in September for *us* and our parents. |
| *Preferable* | My roommate and *I* are both studying engineering. |
| | Last spring the fraternity pledged six other boys and *me.* |
| | Our neighbors and *we* have a community picnic each fall. |
| | Orientation meetings will be held in September for our parents and *us.* |

**77f  Do not use myself, himself, *etc., unless an intensive or reflexive idea is present*** (see Section **71d**)

| | |
|---|---|
| *Incorrect* | John and myself can carry it. |
| *Correct* | John and I can carry it. |
| *Incorrect* | This is a matter that concerns only you and myself. |
| | This is a matter that concerns only you and himself. |
| *Correct* | This is a matter that concerns only you and me. |
| | This is a matter that concerns only you and him. |

In correcting the error just discussed, do not make a "frying pan" error (a worse error than the original one) by using the wrong case of the personal pronoun.

| | |
|---|---|
| *Wrong* | John and me can carry it. |
| | This is a matter that concerns only you and I. |
| | This is a matter that concerns only you and he. |

## 77g   *Do not use illiterate forms for reflexive or intensive pronouns*

Such illiterate forms are *meself, mineself, youself, hisself, itsself, ourself* (see dictionary), *theyself, theyselves, theirself, theirselves, themself.*

The correct forms are the following: *myself, yourself, himself, itself, ourselves, yourselves, themselves* (see Section **71**d5,6).

NOTE: These directions refer to the compound (joined) forms. *Self* as noun can be modified by the possessive pronoun plus an adjective: *my real self, her true self, their own selves,* etc.

## 77h   *Avoid using a personal pronoun directly after a noun as subject and referring to it*

Reference of pronoun after noun is useless for both clearness and effectiveness. Avoid sentences like these:

My friends *they* expected me to go with them everywhere.
Father *he* thinks that sometimes I spend too much money.
Our high school English teacher *she* did more for us than she will ever realize.

## 77i   *Avoid reference of pronouns to nouns in the possessive case*

The use of pronouns referring to nouns in the possessive case is grammatically correct but usually ineffective, since nouns as subjects or objects stand out more clearly. One method of improvement is reversing the case: pronoun in possessive, noun in nominative or objective.

| | |
|---|---|
| *Dubious* | In my English professor's classroom, he uses many interesting audiovisual aids. |
| | Many valuable antiques are in my grandmother's home, and she is proud of them. |
| *Improved* | My English professor uses many interesting audiovisual aids in his classroom. |
| | Grandmother is proud of the many valuable antiques in her home. |

## 77j   *Avoid implied reference for a pronoun*

The relation of a pronoun to its antecedent must be clear and unmistakable, except for indefinite pronouns (Section **71d7**). The reference word should be placed close to its antecedent in order that no intervening words may cause confusion. A *relative* pronoun must be in the same sentence as its antecedent, but *personal* or *demonstrative* pronouns may be placed some distance away, frequently in other sentences, if there is no intervening noun or pronoun to cause confusion.

Implied reference occurs when the antecedent of a pronoun is not actually expressed but must be inferred from the context. One of the most common forms of implied reference is the use of the pronouns *it, this, that, which* to refer to an entire preceding statement rather than to some noun or pronoun in that statement.

You, as writer, must decide whether such words refer to an implied antecedent, whether such implied reference is clear, or whether the antecedent is contained, paradoxically, in a statement that follows. Frequent occurrence of implied reference is found in the work of many reputable writers, and when lack of clearness is avoided, the use may be effective.

Faults in implied reference of *it, which, this, that, these, those,* etc., may be corrected by (1) summing up the idea of the preceding statement in a noun acting as the antecedent; (2) rephrasing the sentence to eliminate the pronoun or to give it a clear and appropriate antecedent.

| | |
|---|---|
| *Doubtful* | Tuesday noon I became ill and *it* became steadily worse during the day. |
| *Improved* | Tuesday noon I became ill and felt steadily worse during the day. |
| *Doubtful* | On the first floor we saw where the fiction books are kept. *This* concluded our library tour. |
| *Improved* | When we saw where the fiction books are kept on the first floor, we concluded our library tour. |
| *Doubtful* | For a vacation we had everything from camping stoves to sleeping bags. *That* influenced our decision. |
| *Improved* | For a vacation we had everything from camping stoves to sleeping bags. That equipment influenced our decision. |

| | |
|---|---|
| *Doubtful* | I am a trifle lazy, *which* is made obvious by my constant procrastinating. |
| *Improved* | I am a trifle lazy, a fact which is made obvious by my constant procrastinating. |
| *Doubtful* | I mislaid your address, *which* was the reason why I did not write sooner. |
| *Improved* | I mislaid your address, a fact which kept me from writing sooner. |
| | I mislaid your address and therefore could not write to you until I found it. |
| *Acceptable* | I could also tell you of my experiences in Alaska, but *that* is another story. (Antecedent follows pronoun.) |

Confusion and ineffectiveness may also arise when *this, that, these, those,* and *such* are used as demonstrative adjectives.

| | |
|---|---|
| *Doubtful* | The dean's attitude gave me *that* sinking feeling. |
| *Improved* | The dean's attitude gave me a sinking feeling. |
| | The dean's attitude depressed me. |
| | The dean's attitude gave me that sinking feeling which accompanies frustration. |
| *Doubtful* | Every summer at Sunset Bay we meet *those* wonderful people. |
| *Improved* | Every summer at Sunset Bay we meet wonderful people. |
| | Every summer at Sunset Bay we meet those wonderful people who make the town what it is. |

Even the definite article *the* is sometimes misused as a kind of demonstrative adjective. This use is vague and ineffective; either avoid it or amplify it to clearness.

| | |
|---|---|
| *Vague* | These island people were evidently in *the* early stage of cultural development. |
| *Improved* | These island people were evidently in *an* early stage of cultural development. |
| *or* | |
| | These island people were evidently in *that* early stage of cultural development which precedes any use of complex machines and mechanisms. |

**77k   *Avoid the indefinite use of* you**

In some informal writing, an expression such as *"You* can see the importance of money" is permissible, even though *you* may refer to no particular person or group. In general, however, when using *you,* be sure that you mean the person or persons whom you are addressing. For example, the following is inappropriate in a paper designed for reading by an adult: "When you become a Boy Scout, *you* learn many useful things." (See Section **4b.**) If you wish to refer to a number of people in general and to no one in particular, use indefinite pronouns like *one* or *anyone* or a general noun like *person* or *student.*

| | |
|---|---|
| *Dubious* | In high school you should do more theme writing. |
| *Preferable* | In high school the student should do more theme writing. |
| | When a youngster becomes a Boy Scout, he learns many useful things. |

For the use of *you* as an appropriate or inappropriate theme beginning, see Section **8b6.**

**77l   *Avoid the indefinite use of* it**

*It* as a third person singular pronoun, neuter, should usually have an appropriate antecedent. Also, when *it* is used impersonally and acceptably *(it* seems, *it* is possible, *it* is raining, etc.) , do not use another *it* in the same sentence to refer to a definite antecedent.

| | |
|---|---|
| *Dubious* | In this magazine article *it* states that not all wars are victories for the victors. |
| *Better* | This magazine article states that not all wars are victories for the victors. |
| *Dubious* | Bar Harbor is a beautiful summer resort; we liked *it* very much and *it* is possible that we shall go there again. |
| *Better* | We liked Bar Harbor very much as a summer resort, and *it* is possible that we shall go there again. |
| *Dubious* | Our roof needs patching, and when *it* rains *it* leaks badly. |
| *Better* | Our roof needs patching, and *it* leaks badly in rainy weather. |

Also, more effective expressions can be used for the following:

| | |
|---|---|
| *Dubious* | I didn't think I'd make *it* to class this morning, but I made *it*. |
| | If you want to succeed, you will have to stick *it* out. |
| *Improved* | I didn't think I'd reach class this morning, but I did. |
| | If you want to succeed, you will have to stick to your aims. |

### 77m   Avoid the indefinite use of they

*They, their, theirs, them,* as plural forms of the third person personal pronoun, should have definite antecedents: plural nouns or other pronouns in the plural. Otherwise, do not use these pronouns.

| | |
|---|---|
| *Dubious* | *They* say Mexico is very popular among tourists. |
| *Better* | Many people are saying that Mexico is popular among tourists. |
| *Dubious* | For shopping in Chicago, we like *their* large department stores. |
| *Better* | For shopping, we like Chicago's large department stores. |
| *Dubious* | In my high school *they* had excellent courses in English and mathematics. |
| *Better* | My high school had excellent courses in English and mathematics. |

### 77n   Avoid double reference for a pronoun

Double reference sometimes occurs when two antecedents are possible for a single pronoun. The pronoun reference is therefore ambiguous; instead, the antecedent should be clear and definite.

Ambiguous reference can be corrected by (1) repeating the antecedent, (2) using a synonym for the antecedent, (3) changing the wording so that the antecedent of each pronoun is unmistakable.

| | |
|---|---|
| *Dubious* | When a salesman hands over an article to a customer, *he* is not always certain of its worth. |
| *Better* | A salesman is not always certain of the worth of an article when he hands it over to a customer. |

| | |
|---|---|
| *Dubious* | When Mother talked to Grandmother last evening, she (*who?*) said that everything was going well. |
| *Better* | Mother talked to Grandmother last evening and said . . . Last evening Mother talked to Grandmother, who said that . . . |

## EXERCISES

A. Correct all errors of disagreement between pronoun and antecedent.

1. The youth hostel is an inexpensive place to stay, and any young people traveling can use them.
2. If you desire any further information or references, I shall be glad to send it.
3. The hero of the novel was moody, and it became worse in the course of the narrative.
4. My reaction to the TV mystery program is quite favorable, for I enjoy most of them.
5. Edward was always attentive, which earned for him his instructor's respect.
6. I feel sorry for an only child because they have no chance to share experiences with their brothers and sisters.
7. If the student does not understand the directions, he should ask the teacher to explain it to him.
8. It is the mosquito who causes malaria and yellow fever.
9. A friend of mine borrows money and never pays it back; this really bothers me.
10. When we were in high school, we didn't make our own decisions without first talking it over with your parents, teachers, or friends.
11. Your surroundings should be pleasant, which will make your studying more enjoyable.
12. The library stacks may be the perfect place to study for some people, but I find it too quiet.
13. Each person has their own individual way of writing a business letter.
14. I do not know whether this has been the feelings of anyone before.
15. It is believed that if one carries a rabbit's foot, it will bring them good luck.
16. Where is the skilled craftsman of yesterday? Very few of them are left.

17. If students fail to take advantage of the library, he is losing a valuable helper.
18. I am sure that October, November, and December will always be as interesting to almost everyone as it is to me.
19. St. Francis spent part of his life caring for the lepers, which were isolated from their fellow men.
20. We hear rumors about different instructors. Some are that he gives terrible exams or that his lectures are boring or that he is unfair in his grading.

B. Correct all errors in pronoun use in the following sentences:

1. In New York City they have regular cruises around Manhattan Island.
2. I do not mind early-morning classes except for that long walk from the dormitory to the classroom.
3. My mother, my sister, and myself go downtown often for our dinner.
4. We began scouting around for a haunted house, but found them rather scarce.
5. My roommate is the kind of person that you like to live with.
6. Two years ago I and some of my friends went on a fishing trip in northern Wisconsin.
7. There is an advantage in living in a small town. One of these is that everyone knows everyone else.
8. If problems are taken care of immediately, you will have no future worries about it.
9. Now that I have decided to become a doctor, I believe it runs in the family.
10. As for quotation marks, I failed to use it properly to set off words from the remainder of the sentence.
11. Samuel Johnson was very good as a lexicographer; after taking eight years to complete it, it sold out two editions within a year.
12. The published themes are written by English students, which, incidentally, are mostly freshmen.
13. John would go out of his way to help someone in distress, someone who was feeling sorry for themselves.
14. Although I am looking forward to starting classes on Monday, I keep wondering what it will be like.
15. Not every pharmacist works in a drug store; in fact, most of them work in research or in the wholesale business.
16. Most of the college professors have received a doctor's degree in his particular field.

17. I have two brothers and two sisters which are all younger than myself.
18. If a person drives at high speed on an icy road, they may end up in a ditch.
19. Cars have safety belts now, and if this is buckled, you have a good chance of surviving a crash.
20. I never thought it was possible that I could get up in front of a group and say something that made sense, but I did it. I cannot really say that I enjoyed it, but it wasn't really as bad as I thought it was going to be.

# 78  Linking and auxiliary verbs

To write correctly, clearly, effectively, and appropriately, you need an adequate understanding of linking and auxiliary verbs. Such verbs, basic in many foreign languages, are also basic in English.

## LINKING VERBS

Most verbs assert action, but a few express a static condition or state of being. Most, not all, of these "inactive" verbs are *linking* (or *joining* or *copulative*) verbs. They serve the purpose of *coming between* or *coupling* or *linking* two substantives or a substantive and an adjective. The substantive following the linking verb is a *predicate noun* or *predicate pronoun* (never a direct object). Nouns cause no trouble; pronouns may present problems (see Section **75c**). An adjective following the linking verb is a *predicate adjective,* for it modifies the subject, not the predicate (see Section **83c**).

The most common linking verb is *to be,* in its various forms of number, person, tense, and mood (for table of these forms, see pp. 484–485; for the meaning of tense, see Section **80**; for the meaning of mood, see Section **82**). Other common linking verbs are *appear, become, feel, grow, look, prove, remain, seem, smell,*

# LINKING AND AUXILIARY VERBS

|  | TO BE<br>*be was been* |  | TO HAVE<br>*have had had* |  | TO DO<br>*do did done* |  |
|---|---|---|---|---|---|---|
| Principal parts | | | INDICATIVE MOOD | | | |
| Singular | Singular | Plural | Singular | Plural | Singular | Plural |

**Present tense**

| | | | | | | |
|---|---|---|---|---|---|---|
| 1st person | I am | we ⎫ | I have | we ⎫ | I do | we ⎫ |
| 2nd person | you are | you ⎬ are | you have ⎫ | you ⎬ have | you do | you ⎬ do |
| 3rd person | he is | they ⎭ | he has ⎬ | they ⎭ | he does | they ⎭ |
| | (she, it) | | (she, it) ⎭ | | (she, it) | |

**Past tense**

| | | | | | | |
|---|---|---|---|---|---|---|
| 1st person | I was | we ⎫ | I ⎫ | we ⎫ | I ⎫ | we ⎫ |
| 2nd person | you were | you ⎬ were | you ⎬ had | you ⎬ had | you ⎬ did | you ⎬ did |
| 3rd person | he was | they ⎭ | he ⎭ | they ⎭ | he ⎭ | they ⎭ |

**Future tense**

| | | | | | |
|---|---|---|---|---|---|
| 1st person | I shall be | we shall be | I shall have | we shall have | |
| 2nd person | you will be | you will be | you will have | you will have | |
| 3rd person | he will be | they will be | he will have | they will have | |

**Present perfect tense**

| | | | | | |
|---|---|---|---|---|---|
| 1st person | I have been | we ⎫ | | | |
| 2nd person | you have been | you ⎬ have been | | | |
| 3rd person | he has been | they ⎭ | | | |

**Past perfect tense**

| | | | |
|---|---|---|---|
| 1st person | I ⎫ | we ⎫ | |
| 3rd person | you ⎬ had been | you ⎬ had been | |
| 2nd person | he ⎭ | they ⎭ | |

NOTE: The future tense of *do* and the present perfect, past perfect, and future perfect tenses of *have* and *do* are rarely, if ever, used as *auxiliary* verb forms, nor are the verbal forms of *do* (*doing, done*) so used. As *main* verbs, they form these tenses as does any other main verb. See pp. 501–509.

## Future Perfect Tense

| | Singular | Plural |
|---|---|---|
| 1st person | I shall have been | we shall have been |
| 2nd person | you will have been | you will have been |
| 3rd person | he will have been | they will have been |

## SUBJUNCTIVE MOOD

### Present tense

| | Singular | Plural |
|---|---|---|
| 1st person | (if) I | (if) we |
| 2nd person | (if) you } be | (if) you } be |
| 3rd person | (if) he (she, it) | (if) they |

| | Singular | Plural |
|---|---|---|
| 1st person | (if) I | (if) we |
| 2nd person | (if) you } have | (if) you } have |
| 3rd person | (if) he (she, it) | (if) they |

| | Singular | Plural |
|---|---|---|
| 1st person | (if) I | (if) we |
| 2nd person | (if) you } do | (if) you } do |
| 3rd person | (if) he (she, it) | (if) they |

### Past tense

| | Singular | Plural |
|---|---|---|
| 1st person | (if) I | (if) we |
| 2nd person | (if) you } were | (if) you } were |
| 3rd person | (if) he | (if) they |

NOTE: The other tense forms, in the subjunctive mood, of *to be, to have, to do* are identical to the corresponding tense forms of the indicative mood.

### Verbals (*nonfinite verb forms*)

| | | |
|---|---|---|
| *Present infinitive* | to be | to have |
| *Perfect infinitive* | to have been | to have had |
| *Present participle* | being | having |
| *Past participle* | been | had |
| *Perfect participle* | having been | having had |
| *Present gerund* | being | having |
| *Perfect gerund* | having been | having had |

NOTE: Gerunds have the same form as participles, except that there is no past gerund.

*sound, stand, taste, turn.* Except for forms of *to be,* these other linking verbs are followed by adjectives—rarely, if ever, by pronouns or nouns as predicate substantives. When these verbs are followed by nouns or pronouns as direct objects, they are not linking verbs but imply or express action (see Section **78a,** below). They are linking verbs if you can substitute some form of *to be* for them, especially *is, are, was, were.* Of course, some verbs not expressing action, such as *endure, exist, lie, sit, wait,* are not considered linking verbs. In the following examples, the linking verbs are in italics; the words linked are in small capitals.

My NAME *is* JOHN.

THIS *is* my ROOMMATE.

MR. BROWN *was* my English INSTRUCTOR last semester.

My ROOMMATE *is* DARK-COMPLEXIONED.

MR. BROWN *will be* BUSY tomorrow.

The WEATHER *seems* (*is*) COLD today; tomorrow IT may *turn* (*grow, become, be*) COLDER.

The EXCITEMENT *became* (*seemed, grew, was*) GREATER as the game progressed.

These CLOUDS *appear* (*look, seem, are*) SALMON-COLORED.

## 78a   Do not confuse a linking verb with a verb expressing action

Distinguish carefully between the meanings of the same verb word when it asserts action of the subject in one meaning and does not assert action in another; in the latter sense only is it a linking verb, followed by an adjective, not by an adverb (see Section **83c**). Observe differences in the following:

The river *looks* muddy this morning. (Linking)

John *looked* steadily at the scene before him. (Action)

Oranges *taste* sweet. (Linking)

Mary carefully *tasted* the salad. (Action)

We do not *feel* bad about our defeat. (Linking)

In the dark John stumbled against the furniture and *felt* his way carefully across the room. (Action)

**78b** *Use correct grammatical agreement in a linking verb, the correct pronoun case after it, and, as predicate complement, an adjective, not an adverb*

For correct agreement, see Section **76**; for correct case, see Section **75**; for adjective-adverb use, see Section **83**. Remember that when the linking verb is specifically described, an adverb is used; when the subject is described, an adjective is used.

## AUXILIARY VERBS

**78c** *Use the correct form of the auxiliary verb with a main verb*

An auxiliary verb "helps out" a main verb; that is, it helps to form some of the tenses and the tone (see Section **80**), the mood (see Section **82**), the voice (see Section **81**) of the main verb and sometimes to express other precise ideas (see Section **78h**). It may have little meaning of its own, but it changes the meaning of the main verb, which contains the central or "key" meaning of the verb phrase. In the following sentences, the italicized form is an auxiliary verb, the boldface form is the main verb.

John *has* **gone** home.
The furniture *will be* **shipped** by express.
As we *were* **coming** home, we *were* **stopped** by a policeman.
I *did* **mail** your letters.

The most common auxiliary verbs are forms of *to be* (*am, is, are, was, were, been*), *to have* (*has, had*), and *to do* (*does, did*). A table showing the various forms of these as auxiliary verbs is given on pp. 484–485. Other common auxiliary verbs are *shall, should, will, would, may, might, can, could, must,* and *ought.* Less frequently used are *let, need, used,* and *dare* (see Section **78h**).

**78d** *Never use* of *as a substitute for the auxiliary* **have**

The error of *of* used for *have* is frequently made after *shall, will, should, would, may, might, could,* and *must.* Sound, not grammar, causes the error: a careless speaker might pronounce *have* (as infinitive) and *of* alike, and then he confuses them in his writing. Here careful speech helps in correct writing.

*Wrong*    You should *of* informed me sooner.
            It might *of* been much worse.
            Mother must *of* paid this bill, for she has a receipt.

### 78e  Use the correct form of the main verb with the auxiliary verb

Given the principal parts of the main verb (see Section **79**) and knowing the auxiliaries, you can form any desired tense, tone, mood, and voice, if such exist in good English usage. Present infinitive (with or without the sign *to*), past participle, and present participle ending in *-ing* are the parts of the main verb used with auxiliaries. (See Sections **71f** and **85,** and tables on pp. 502–503 and 514–515.)

### 78f  Distinguish between a verb form used as an auxiliary and a verb form used as a main verb

At least three specific verbs, dependent on purpose, may be either auxiliary verbs or main verbs. *To be* may be a linking and therefore main verb, or it may help to express the progressive tone or the passive voice; *to have,* the auxiliary in the perfect tenses, and *to do,* expressing emphasis in the present and past tenses, are also used as main verbs. Notice the differences in the following:

His name *was* John. (Main verb)
He *was* named John. (Auxiliary verb)
He *was* telephoning when I came. (Auxiliary verb)

I *have* no money. (Main verb)
I *have* lost my money. (Auxiliary verb)

She *does* her work well. (Main verb)
She *does* spend her money foolishly. (Auxiliary verb)

For the various meanings of *have* and *do* as main verbs, see your dictionary.

## 78g Do not use the same verb form to serve as both auxiliary verb and main verb

| *Incorrect* | His name *was* John and given him by his grandfather. |
|---|---|
| | She *does* her work well but spend money foolishly. |
| *Correct* | His name *was* John, and it *was* given him by his grandfather. |
| | She *does* her work well, but she *does* spend foolishly the money that she earns. |

## 78h Use the correct auxiliary verb

The meanings of the commonly used auxiliary verbs are in your dictionary. These verbs and their more common uses are as follows:

⟶ *1. to be—*

used in all tenses in forming the progressive tone and the passive voice. (See Sections **80b** and **81a.**)

used in the present and with an infinitive or present participle or past participle to indicate futurity, duty, possibility, purpose:

Professor Brown *is to* speak this evening. (Futurity)
You *are to* report here at 4 o'clock. (Duty)
They *were to* visit London yesterday. (Possibility)
I *am* looking for a better position. (Purpose)

⟶ *2. to have—*

used in the present perfect, past perfect, and future perfect tenses; also in the perfect infinitive and the perfect participle. (See Section **80b.**)

used with the infinitive to express necessity or obligation: "I *have* to leave now."

⟶ *3. to do—*

used to express emphasis (emphatic tone) in the present and past tenses. (See Section **80b.**)

used to avoid repetition of a verb or full verb expression: "John slept as soundly as I *did.*" "I shall go when you *do.*"

⟶   *4. shall—*

    used as the precise auxiliary for the first person, future and future perfect tenses (but see pp. 506–508) .

    used in the second and third persons to express command or determination: "You *shall* not borrow my clothes, and your friends *shall* not play that trick on me again."

⟶   *5. will—*

    used as the precise auxiliary for the second and third persons, future and future perfect tenses (but see pp. 506–508) .

    used in all three persons to express willingness, intention, or consent: "I *will* write to you tomorrow." "I *will* help you with your chemistry." "You *will* be a candidate?"

    used in the first person to indicate determination or resolution: "We *will* rush your order immediately."

⟶   *6. should—*

    used as a kind of "past" tense of *shall,* in the first person, but weaker in emphasis: "I *should* prefer not to come." "I *should* not judge him harshly."

    used frequently in a conditional meaning: "If I *should* decide, I shall let you know." "If John *should* call, tell him to leave a message."

    used in all three persons to express duty or propriety or necessity: "You *should* attend class regularly." "One *should* reply to letters promptly." "He *should* return library books or pay for them."

    used in all three persons to express expectation: "By dusk we *should* be halfway to St. Louis." "Mary *should* arrive home by noon if she left early this morning."

⟶   *7. would—*

    used as a kind of "past" tense of *will,* in the second and third persons, but less strong in meaning: "You *would* not recognize him."

NOTE: If the verb in the independent clause is in the past tense, use *would* to express futurity in the dependent clause; if the verb in the independent clause is in the present tense, use *will* in the dependent clause: "Henry *said* that he *would* go." "Henry *says* that he *will* go."

> used frequently in a conditional meaning, or after a conditional clause: "If you *would* consent, everyone would be happy." "If the weather were good, he *would* walk in the park."
>
> used to express determination: "He *would* do it, no matter how much we protested."
>
> used in all three persons to express repeated or habitual action: "Last summer I *would* read three books every week."
>
> used infrequently to express wish or desire: "*Would* that I had gone with you!"
>
> used in place of *will* to make a statement less blunt: "That action *would* be most discourteous."

⟶ 8. *may*—

> used to express permission or sanction: "*May* I borrow your book?" "You *may* have it until tomorrow." "If I *may* say so, the idea is absurd."
>
> used to express probability, a wish, or a prayer: "It *may* rain tomorrow." "*May* your college years be happy ones!" "*May* Thy Will be done!"

⟶ 9. *might*—

> used as a kind of "past" tense of *may* to express the same ideas of possibility or probability in a weaker manner: "You *might* find the address in the telephone directory."

⟶ 10. *can*—

> used to express ability or power or qualifications or the idea of "being able to": "I *can* come at 6 o'clock." "He *can* do anything that you *can*."

NOTE: *Can* is a synonym for *may* in colloquial and informal expression, both used in the sense of permission or sanction; formally, the distinction between *can* and *may* ("ability" vs. "permission") is illustrated in this sentence: "I doubt that you *can*, but you *may* try if you wish."

⟶ *11. could—*

> used as a kind of "past" tense of *can* to express the same ideas in a weaker manner: "John *could* not do all the assigned work."

⟶ *12. must—*

> used to express obligation or compulsion: "Every man *must* do his part." "You *must* have your report in by next week."
>
> used to express reasonable certainty: "John left for Louisville this morning, and he *must* be there by now." "It *must* be about ten o'clock."
>
> used to express conviction or certainty: "With these heavy rains, floods *must* follow."

⟶ *13. ought—*

> used to express duty, obligation, or probability, one of the few auxiliary verbs followed by the sign of the infinitive (*to*) with the main verb: "You *ought* to write letters to your friends more frequently." "Everyone *ought* to pay his bills promptly." "The New York plane *ought* to arrive soon."

NOTE: *Have* and *had* are never used before *ought* or *must*.

| | |
|---|---|
| *Wrong* | I *had ought* to start studying. |
| *Right* | I *ought to have started* studying an hour ago. |

⟶ *14. let—*

> used to express the ideas of "allowing" or "permitting," "suggesting," "ordering": "*Let* me think a minute." "*Let* me call you tomorrow." "*Let's* go to the movies." "*Let* the man have his money."

⟶ *15. need—*

> used to express necessity or obligation: "I *need* not tell you the reasons." "You *need* bring only your pen and theme paper."

NOTE: As auxiliary verb, third person singular form is also *need*: "He *need* not doubt my word."

⟶ *16. used—*

in the past tense only, *used* expresses custom or habitual action: "On my vacation I *used* to lie in the sun for hours." "It *used* to rain every day in the mountains."

⟶ *17. dare—*

used, usually with *say,* to express probability: "I *dare* say it will be a good game." "I *dare* say you're right."

## EXERCISES

A. Read one or two pages of prose in a current magazine or in your book of readings. Make a list—up to 20—of the linking verbs that you find. Include the materials linked.

B. From the same material read in Exercise A, make a list—up to 20—of the auxiliary verbs that you find. Include the main verbs that they help out.

## *79  Principal parts of verbs*

Knowing principal parts of verbs and using proper auxiliary verbs (see Section **78c–h**) when necessary, you can express both a great variety of meaning and precise shades of meaning. This variety is made possible through the proper use of tense (Section **80**) and of active and passive voice (Section **81**). Errors in tense and voice are often caused by insufficient knowledge of the principal parts of verbs.

In every language, verbs have principal parts, sometimes three, as in German, sometimes five, as in French, Spanish, and Italian. The English verb has three principal parts: *present tense* (present infinitive), *past tense,* and *past participle.* Example: *see, saw, seen.* An excellent way to recall the principal parts of a verb is to substitute those of any verb for the following:

I *see* today.                   I *work* today.
I *saw* yesterday.               I *worked* yesterday.
I *have seen* every day.         I *have worked* every day.

Almost a principal part and a necessary verb form is the present participle, formed by adding *ing* to the present infinitive form. This "fourth" part, if in any way irregular, is given in your dictionary. Examples: *seeing, working, doing, beginning, choosing, raising.* The present participial form has constant use both as part of the predicate and as adjective (see Section **71f**).

I am *working* every afternoon. (Part of predicate)
This restaurant does a *thriving* business. (Adjective use)

## 79a  Add the proper endings, d, ed, or t, to form the past tense and past participle of regular verbs

The past tense and past participle of *most* English verbs are formed by adding the endings *d, ed,* or *t* to the present infinitive: *move, moved, moved; walk, walked, walked; mean, meant, meant.* Any comparatively recent verb added to our language also forms its principal parts with these endings: *telegraph, telegraphed, telegraphed; telephone, telephoned, telephoned; radio, radioed, radioed.*

Verbs forming their principal parts by adding endings *d, ed,* or *t* are called *regular* verbs (or *weak* verbs, although among the many so-called *weak* verbs in English, numerous variations exist —see Footnote 4, below). Notice that past tense and past participle forms are alike. When in doubt, look up the verb in your dictionary. If no additional forms follow the main entry, the past tense and past participle are formed with the endings *d, ed,* or *t.* Otherwise, the past tense and past participle, and even the present participle, are given immediately after the verb.

## 79b  Do not carelessly omit the ending of a regular verb, d, ed, or t, in the past tense or past participle

Since regular verbs form past tense and past participle by adding the endings *d, ed,* or *t,* omitting these endings from these forms is a serious error in grammar. Common trouble-causers are *attack, ask, prejudice, suppose, use.*

*Wrong*  We are *suppose* to get our work in on time. (Use *supposed*)
Last week I *ask* for permission to miss one class. (Use *asked*)

These children *use* to swim every day; now they are completely *use* to the water. (Use *used*)
We should not be *prejudice* against those who don't agree
with us. (Use *prejudiced*)

### 79c   Use your dictionary to find the principal parts of irregular verbs

*Irregular verbs,* many of which are sometimes called *strong* verbs,
form their past tense and past participle by a vowel change
within the verb, as well as by the occasional addition of an ending: *arise, arose, arisen; bear, bore, born (e) ; begin, began, begun;
give, gave, given; throw, threw, thrown.*[4]

Principal parts of any irregular verb are given in your dictionary, your safest guide. Immediately after the entry word are
the past tense, past participle, and present participle; any alternate forms are given also.

### 79d   Check carefully to see that you are using correctly the principal parts of commonly used regular and irregular verbs

The following verbs, some regular, most of them irregular, are
especially troublesome. Study them carefully; put them into the
three expressions on p. 493; memorize them. If other regular or
irregular verbs cause you trouble, copy their principal parts from
your dictionary and memorize them also.

| | | |
|---|---|---|
| 1. arise | arose | arisen |
| 2. ask | asked | asked |
| 3. attack | attacked | attacked |
| 4. bear | bore | borne (born: given birth to) |

[4] For practical, useful, present-day purposes, the general distinction between regular verbs (Section **79a**) and irregular verbs (Section **79c**) will
serve. But through the centuries, from Anglo-Saxon times, 290 variations of
"irregular" weak verbs have been found: many now obsolete or existing in
older poetry; some in current use that change the root vowel or spelling of
the present infinitive for the alike past and past-participle forms: *bring,
brought, brought; keep, kept, kept; sell, sold, sold; teach, taught, taught*;
and some few verbs having the same form for all three principal parts, like
*cut, hit, hurt, cost, set.* The list of so-called strong verbs numbers 95. See
George O. Curme, *Parts of Speech and Accidence* (Boston: D. C. Heath,
1935) , irregular weak verbs, pp. 272–296, and strong verbs, pp. 306–319.

| 5. beat | beat | beaten |
|---|---|---|
| 6. become | became | become |
| 7. begin | began | begun |
| 8. bid (auction) | bid | bid |
| 9. bid (command) | bade, bid | bidden, bid |
| 10. blow | blew | blown |
| 11. break | broke | broken |
| 12. bring | brought | brought |
| 13. broadcast | broadcast, broadcasted | broadcast, broadcasted |
| 14. build | built | built |
| 15. burn | burned, burnt | burned, burnt |
| 16. burst | burst | burst |
| 17. buy | bought | bought |
| 18. cast | cast | cast |
| 19. catch | caught | caught |
| 20. choose | chose | chosen |
| 21. come | came | come |
| 22. cut | cut | cut |
| 23. deal | dealt | dealt |
| 24. do | did | done |
| 25. draw | drew | drawn |
| 26. dream | dreamed, dreamt | dreamed, dreamt |
| 27. dress | dressed, drest | dressed, drest |
| 28. drink | drank | drunk, drunken (see dictionary) |
| 29. drive | drove | driven |
| 30. dwell | dwelt, dwelled | dwelt, dwelled |
| 31. eat | ate | eaten |
| 32. fall | fell | fallen |
| 33. feel | felt | felt |
| 34. find | found | found |
| 35. flow | flowed | flowed |
| 36. fly | flew | flown |
| 37. fly (baseball) | flied | flied |
| 38. forbid | forbade, forbad | forbidden |
| 39. forget | forgot | forgotten, forgot |
| 40. freeze | froze | frozen |
| 41. get | got | got, gotten |
| 42. give | gave | given |
| 43. go | went | gone |
| 44. grow | grew | grown |
| 45. happen | happened | happened |

| 46. hear | heard | heard |
| 47. help | helped | helped |
| 48. hit | hit | hit |
| 49. hurt | hurt | hurt |
| 50. keep | kept | kept |
| 51. know | knew | known |
| 52. lay | laid | laid |
| 53. lead | led | led |
| 54. learn | learned, learnt | learned, learnt |
| 55. leave | left | left |
| 56. lend | lent | lent |
| 57. let | let | let |
| 58. lie (falsehood) | lied | lied |
| 59. lie (recline) | lay | lain |
| 60. loose | loosed | loosed |
| 61. lose | lost | lost |
| 62. make | made | made |
| 63. mean | meant | meant |
| 64. pass | passed | passed, past (see p. 400) |
| 65. prejudice | prejudiced | prejudiced |
| 66. prove | proved | proved, proven |
| 67. put | put | put |
| 68. raise | raised | raised |
| 69. read | read | read |
| 70. ride | rode | ridden |
| 71. rise | rose | risen |
| 72. run | ran | run |
| 73. see | saw | seen |
| 74. set | set | set |
| 75. shake | shook | shaken |
| 76. shine | shone | shone |
| 77. show | showed | shown, showed |
| 78. sing | sang | sung |
| 79. sink | sank | sunk |
| 80. sit | sat | sat |
| 81. smell | smelled, smelt | smelled, smelt |
| 82. speak | spoke | spoken |
| 83. spell | spelled, spelt | spelled, spelt |
| 84. spoil | spoiled, spoilt | spoiled, spoilt |
| 85. spring | sprang, sprung | sprung |
| 86. stand | stood | stood |
| 87. steal | stole | stolen |

| 88. strike | struck | struck, stricken |
|---|---|---|
| 89. strive | strove, strived | striven, strived |
| 90. suppose | supposed | supposed |
| 91. swim | swam | swum |
| 92. take | took | taken |
| 93. teach | taught | taught |
| 94. tell | told | told |
| 95. think | thought | thought |
| 96. throw | threw | thrown |
| 97. use | used | used |
| 98. wake | waked, woke | waked, woken |
| 99. work | worked, wrought | worked, wrought |
| 100. write | wrote | written |

## 79e   *Do not confuse an irregular with a regular verb*

For centuries, most strong and weak verbs in English have kept the principal parts that they now have. Only in a few isolated instances has a strong or irregular verb changed to weak or regular (*help, holp, holpen* to *help, helped, helped*) or a weak verb added an alternative strong-verb ending (*prove, proved, proved* or *proven*).

Confusion or carelessness may cause you to add regular-verb endings to irregular verbs or to treat an occasional regular verb like an irregular verb.

*Wrong*   I was *borned* on a small farm in Ohio. (Use *born*)

All my early years were *pasted* there, and these *pasted* years were the happiest I have lived. (Use *passed* . . . *past,* respectively)

Once I was *losted* in downtown Chicago. (Use *lost*)

In our drawing class we *drawed* plans for several new buildings. (Use *drew*)

The trouble with these shirts is that they have *shrinked* too much. (Use *shrunk*)

These are errors in verb forms; they can also be considered illiteracies—errors in diction or word choice (see Section 54).

## 79f   *Do not misuse the past tense for the past participle or the past participle for the past tense*

The confusion of the past tense with the past participle is a serious grammatical error. Avoid it by memorizing the principal parts of all verbs used or, when in doubt, by consulting a dictionary.

*Past tense wrongly used for past participle*
    We have *did* the best we could. (Use *done*)
    We skated yesterday; the lake had *froze* over at last. (Use *frozen*)
    Our second semester has already *began*. (Use *begun*)
*Past participle wrongly used for past tense*
    I *seen* my duty and I *done* it. (Use *saw . . . did*)
    That night our All-Girls' Chorus *sung* like angels. (Use *sang*)
    I *drunk* two cups of strong coffee to keep awake. (Use *drank*)

You may be helped by remembering that in predicates and other verb phrases, past tense forms are not preceded by auxiliary verbs and that past participle verb forms are preceded by auxiliary verbs.

*Right*    The Army is *to attack*; the city is *to be attacked*.
           Mother and Father *use* good English; I *am used* to hearing good English.
           Three Boy Scouts *swam* across the river today; three others *had swum* across it last week.

## EXERCISES

A. At the top of a page write "Regular Verbs" and divide the page into four columns labeled, respectively, Present, Past, Past Participle, Present Participle. From one or two pages of prose in your book of readings or in a current magazine make a list of main (regular) verbs, placing each form in the appropriate column. Then fill in the other principal parts of the verbs you list.

B. Repeat Exercise A, except that "Irregular Verbs" should be written at the top of the page, and your list should be composed of main (irregular) verbs.

C. Give the correct forms of the verbs that appear in parentheses in the following sentences:

1. During the evening we were many times (bite) by mosquitoes.
2. My teacher (lead) me into reading many good books.
3. For such simple questions every student should have (know) the answers.
4. It is not easy to remember how much money one has (give) to people who have (come) to the door.

5. Don't leave your books (lie) around; they may be (steal).
6. The horse should easily have (spring) over the barrier.
7. Children like to have pictures (hang) on the walls of their rooms.
8. His shirts had (shrink) to the point of being almost unwearable.
9. Some students never have (bear) their share of responsibilities.
10. You should not have (lend) him so much money.

D. Correct all errors in the use of regular verbs in the following sentences:

1. A teacher is suppose to present his material in an interesting way.
2. You might say that I am prejudice, since I have lived on a farm all my life.
3. I am finding it difficult to become accustom to some of the regulations.
4. I don't know what would have happen to me if I hadn't waken up.
5. My father has help many worried people find an answer to their problems.
6. In high school we were not use to such long assignments.
7. We couldn't have ask for any worse weather than we got.
8. When I finish basic work, I plan to enroll in some advance courses.
9. I do not always use the right words where I am suppose to use them.
10. It has been prove that handicapped people work as well as those not handicapped.

E. Correct all errors in the use of irregular verbs in the following sentences:

1. It is hard to study when one is wore out.
2. After dinner, songs were sang for about an hour.
3. I had never gave much thought to the matter before.
4. There are five reasons why I have chose to study agriculture.
5. In our home we have always drank tea or coffee for breakfast.
6. Whenever the pond is froze over, we go ice-skating.
7. I've never saw my father angry with any one of his children.
8. Having went through college yourself, you know what we are facing.
9. In college I have ran up against some pretty puzzling problems.
10. By that time certain facts had began to stand out in my mind.

# 80   *Tense and tone*

Tense indicates time of action or time of static condition expressed by a verb. Three divisions of time, *past, present,* and *future,* are shown by six tenses in English: *present tense, past tense, future tense, present perfect tense, past perfect tense, future perfect tense.*

Within some tenses, verbs also have certain "tones" which express precisely what the writer wishes to say: *simple tone, progressive* or *continuing tone,* and *emphatic tone.* (See Section 80b.)

English, unlike a highly inflected language such as German or Latin, has few distinctive tense *forms,* verbs with change of endings to indicate time. Instead, English tenses are revealed mainly through auxiliary verbs and only occasionally by a verb ending.

Students frequently have difficulty in using tenses, but such difficulty is caused by ignorance of the functions of the six tenses, by the writer's not thinking out carefully the *time* expressed in his ideas, and by his not spending the small amount of effort necessary to learn how in English the various tenses and tones are formed.

Study carefully the following comments on the meaning of time in each tense and on the formation of tenses and tones. Study also the table on pp. 502–503.

### 80a   *Use the correct tense to express precise time*

The first three tenses are *present tense, past tense,* and *future tense*—sometimes called primary tenses:

*1. Present tense* indicates that the action or condition is going on or exists *now.*

A careful driver *watches* the road constantly. (Simple)
Our team *is playing* in Philadelphia today. (Progressive)
Mary *does make* a nice appearance. (Emphatic)

*2. Past tense* indicates that an action or condition took place or existed at some definite time in the past—before *now.*

# TO SEE
## INDICATIVE MOOD, ACTIVE VOICE

Principal Parts:  see  saw  seen

|  | Singular | | Plural | |
|---|---|---|---|---|
|  | *Simple* | *Progressive* | *Simple* | *Progressive* |
| ***Present tense*** | | | | |
| 1st *person* | I see | am seeing | we ⎫ | are seeing |
| 2nd *person* | you see | are seeing | you ⎬ see |  |
| 3rd *person* | he sees (she, it) | is seeing | they ⎭ |  |
| ***Past tense*** | | | | |
| 1st *person* | I ⎫ | was seeing | we ⎫ | were seeing |
| 2nd *person* | you ⎬ saw | were seeing | you ⎬ saw |  |
| 3rd *person* | he ⎭ | was seeing | they ⎭ |  |
| ***Future tense*** | | | | |
| 1st *person* | I shall see | shall be seeing | we shall see | shall be seeing |
| 2nd *person* | you will see | will be seeing | you will see | will be seeing |
| 3rd *person* | he will see | will be seeing | they will see | will be seeing |
| ***Present perfect tense*** | | | | |
| 1st *person* | I have seen | have been seeing | we ⎫ | have been seeing |
| 2nd *person* | you have seen | have been seeing | you ⎬ have seen |  |
| 3rd *person* | he has seen | has been seeing | they ⎭ |  |

## Past perfect tense

| | | | |
|---|---|---|---|
| 1st person | I | } had seen | had been seeing |
| 2nd person | you | | |
| 3rd person | he | | |

| | | |
|---|---|---|
| we | } had seen | had been seeing |
| you | | |
| they | | |

## Future perfect tense

| | | |
|---|---|---|
| 1st person | I shall have seen | shall have been seeing |
| 2nd person | you will have seen | will have been seeing |
| 3rd person | he will have seen | will have been seeing |

| | | |
|---|---|---|
| 1st person | we shall have seen | shall have been seeing |
| 2nd person | you will have seen | will have been seeing |
| 3rd person | they will have seen | will have been seeing |

## Verbals (nonfinite verb forms)

| | Simple | Progressive |
|---|---|---|
| Present infinitive | to see | to be seeing |
| Perfect infinitive | to have seen | to have been seeing |
| Present participle | seeing | (none) |
| Past participle | seen | (none) |
| Perfect participle | having seen | having been seeing |
| Present gerund | seeing | (none) |
| Perfect gerund | having seen | having been seeing |

NOTE: Gerunds have the same form as participles, except that use of a past gerund is rare: "The battlefield was filled with the *injured* and the *slain*," i.e., really a form of ellipsis for "the injured and the slain soldiers."

As we *drove,* we *watched* the road constantly. (Simple)
Our team *was playing* in Cleveland yesterday. (Progressive)
Mary *did appreciate* the compliment. (Emphatic)

3. *Future tense* indicates that action will take place, or that a certain condition will exist, in the future—after the present, after *now.*

We *shall arrive* in Pittsburgh tomorrow. (Simple)
Our team *will be playing* in Pittsburgh on Tuesday. (Progressive)
The weather *will be* warmer by mid-July. (Simple)

The other three tenses—*present perfect, past perfect,* and *future perfect*—are called *secondary* or *compound* or *perfect* tenses. The key word is *perfect* or *perfected,* in the sense of *completed.* In these tenses—
The action or condition has begun.
The action or condition begins.
The action or condition has continued.
The action or condition continues.
The action or condition will continue.

   **and,** in addition,

The action or condition has just been completed.
The action or condition is being completed.
The action or condition will be completed by a certain
   stated or implied period.

4. *Present perfect tense* indicates that an action or condition was begun in the past and has just been completed or is still going on. The present perfect tense presupposes some relationship with the present.

You *have been* very ill. (Illness has just ended.)
The ice on the lake *has melted.* (The melting has just been completed.)
The class *has been writing* steadily for an hour. (The writing began an
   hour ago and is still going on.)

5. *Past perfect tense* indicates that an action or condition was begun at some point in the past and was completed at some point in the past, or has just been completed. It presupposes

some action or condition expressed in the past tense, to which it is related.

The roads were impassable because the snow *had fallen* so fast. (The falling of the snow *began* in the *past* and *ended* in the *past*.)

Henry worked in a drug store; he *had been* there a year when he resigned. (His work there *began* in the *past* and *ended* in the *past*.)

   6. *Future perfect tense* indicates that an action or condition began in the past or begins in the present and will be completed at some future time, stated or implied.

I *shall have spent* all my money by June. (Spending *began* in the *past*, *will be finished* by June.)

The snow *will have melted* before you arrive. (Melting of snow *has begun, is continuing,* and *will soon be completed*.)

One year from now my father *will have been working* for his present employer exactly 20 years. (Work *began 19 years ago, is continuing,* and *will be completed* in the future.)

## HOW TO FORM TENSES AND TONES

### 80b  Use the correct tense form and tone form to express precise meaning

In the *active* voice, tense and tone are formed according to the directions given below (for a discussion of *voice* and of the *passive* voice, see Section **81**) .

   Within certain tenses, verbs also have certain tones which express precisely what the writer wishes to say. These are the *simple* tone, the *progressive* or *continuing* tone, and the *emphatic* tone. For example, consider the differences in the following —all present tense:

I *study* my assignments every day. (Simple tone)
Right now I *am studying* my history assignment. (Progressive tone)
I *do study* each of my assignments two or three times. (Emphatic tone)

   The *simple* tone is a concise statement, a kind of snapshot picture or instantaneous action. The *progressive* tone indicates, in general, a kind of moving picture, a continuing action or state of being within a tense limit. The *emphatic* tone serves both to emphasize a statement and—by use of inverted order—commonly to ask a question.

SIMPLE TONE

**Present tense**

The present tense is the first principal part of the verb. All forms in the singular and plural are alike, *except* the third person singular, which varies from all the other forms by adding *s* or *es* or, if the verb ends in *y*, by applying the *y* rule (Section **52e2**).

| | | | | |
|---|---|---|---|---|
| I *go* | I *do* | I *come* | I *speak* | I *pass* |
| he *goes* | he *does* | she *comes* | she *speaks* | he *passes* |

**Past tense**

The past tense of the verb is the second principal part given in your dictionary (see *regular* and *irregular* verbs in Section **79a,c**). Except for *was* and *were,* all singular and plural forms are alike: *had, did, came, spoke, went.*

**Future tense**

The future tense, as *future* tense, is formed by the auxiliary verb *shall* in the first person and the auxiliary verb *will* in the second and third persons preceding the present infinitive without the sign *to*:

| | |
|---|---|
| I *shall* come. | We *shall* come. |
| You *will* come. | You *will* come. |
| He *will* come. | They *will* come. |

Careful writers and speakers still observe these distinctions between *shall* and *will* as auxiliaries in the future tense; but the distinction is breaking down in current use, partly because it does not seem important, partly because *will* suggests the idea of willingness, as in *I will speak* (i.e., *am willing to speak*) *before your group.* As auxiliary, *will,* in general usage, expresses futurity in all persons. But if *shall* and *will* are precisely used, in questions the form is used which will be expected in the answer:

"*Shall* you be in class Monday?"
"I certainly *shall.*"

"*Will* the others be there?"
"They *will*."

(For *shall* and *will* as auxiliary verbs with other meanings, see Section **78h4,5**.)

Even careful and precise speakers and writers, however, use other perfectly acceptable and idiomatic ways of expressing future time. These include the present tense accompanied by an adverb or adverbial phrase of time or expressions like "going to," "plan to," or "am (is, are) to." Expressions like the following express future time:

The new students arrive tomorrow.
I am taking my entrance examinations next week.
This Saturday the team leaves for University Park to play Penn State.
I am going to pay my tuition fees tomorrow.
We plan to attend the convention in Detroit in March.
My teacher is to give a major speech there.

### Present perfect tense

The present perfect tense (for meaning, see Section **80a4**) is formed by using the auxiliary verb *have* (*has*) with the past participle.

I *have* just *completed* writing my theme. (Simple)
We *have had* a wonderful summer in Europe. (Simple)
John *has been* studying for more than two hours. (Progressive)

### Past perfect tense

The past perfect tense (for meaning, see Section **80a5**) is formed by using the auxiliary verb *had* with the past participle.

By last June I *had finished* my first two years of college.
When I left, the judges *had* not yet *made* their decision.
Before I came to college, I *had read* many of Shakespeare's plays.

### Future perfect tense

The future perfect tense (for meaning, see Section **80a6**) is formed by using the future of the auxiliary verb *have* (*shall have, will have*) with the past participle.

I am completing my freshman year, and three years from now I *shall have graduated* from this university.

By July 5, 1976, this country *will have celebrated* the 200th anniversary of its independence.

## Verbals

For *verbals,* or nonfinite verb forms, the formation is as follows:

*Present infinitive,* usually without the sign *to,* is given as the first principal part of the verb: *to be, to do, to have, to see.*

*Perfect infinitive* of any verb is formed by using the present infinitive of the auxiliary verb, *to have,* followed by the past participle: *to have been, to have done, to have had, to have seen, to have come.*

*Present participle* is formed by adding *ing* to the present-infinitive form, equivalent in most verbs to the present-tense form: *being, doing, having, seeing, coming.* If the infinitive ends in silent *e,* the silent *e* spelling rule applies (Section **52e5**).

*Past participle* is the third principal part of any verb. When in doubt about its formation, see your dictionary.

*Perfect participle* is formed by using the present participle of the auxiliary verb, *having,* followed by the past participle: *having been, having done, having had, having seen, having come.*

### PROGRESSIVE TONE

The progressive tone forms in each tense are built by using the proper tense forms of the auxiliary verb *to be* (pp. 484–485) followed by the present participle of the main verb: *am coming, were coming, will be coming, have been coming, had been coming, will have been coming.* (See the table on pp. 502–503.)

### EMPHATIC TONE

The emphatic tone, used only in the present and past tenses, indicative mood, active voice, is formed by the auxiliary verb forms of *do* with the present infinitive of the main verb. The emphatic tone has two common uses: (1) to emphasize and (2) to ask a question: I *do* study. I *did* study. *Do* you plan to come? *Did* you know the answers?

| Present | | Past | |
| --- | --- | --- | --- |
| *Singular* | *Plural* | *Singular* | *Plural* |
| I do see | we do see | I did see | we did see |
| you do see | you do see | you did see | you did see |
| he does see | they do see | he did see | they did see |

With the foregoing information mastered, you should have little difficulty in using the correct tense and tone form for any given time of action or state of being.

## CONSISTENCY OF TENSE USE

When a verb is used alone in a sentence, the tense should express the precise time. When two or more verbs are used in a sentence, (1) two or more members of a compound predicate expressing the same time should have the same tense; (2) verbs in the clauses of a compound sentence should be clear and consistent in their tenses; (3) the tense of the verb in a dependent clause is determined by the tense of the verb in the main clause.

**80c** *Use the present tense to express a timeless or universal truth or, in a dependent clause, a general truth*

Iron, copper, and tin *are* metals.
The power of logical thinking *distinguishes* man from the animals.
In the Middle Ages some people did not believe that the earth *is* round.
In high school I learned that the speed of light *is* 186,000 miles a second.

**80d** *Be consistent in the use of tense*

Since *tense* means the time of the verb, do not shift unnecessarily from one tense to another. In an error frequent in amateur narrative and narrative exposition, the writer shifts from past to present or from present to past or back and forth between the two. Therefore, do not allow the tense of a verb to be attracted into the past when it should be present tense: "On our way home, we visited Gloucester, Massachusetts. The houses there were old and picturesque." Does the writer mean that the houses are no longer there?

*Inconsistent*    My nearest approach to death came last summer. I was walking slowly down a little-traveled country road when a car came suddenly over the rise in the road. It dashes wildly down the road, careening and twisting as if its driver is crazy. I think he is going to strike me, and I jump across the ditch and over the fence. Thus, I saved my life.

*Consistent*   My nearest approach to death came last summer. I was walking slowly down a little-traveled country road when a car came suddenly over the rise in the road. It *dashed* wildly down the road, careening and twisting as if its driver *were* crazy. I *thought* he *was* going to strike me, and I *jumped* across the ditch and over the fence. Thus, I saved my life.

## 80e   Do not misuse the past tense for the present perfect tense or the present perfect tense for the past tense

*Bad*   You received the check your father is to send?
The snow fell heavily since yesterday.  (It is still snowing.)
Mr. Brown has died a year ago.

*Improved*   You have received the check your father was to send?
The snow has fallen heavily since yesterday.
Mr. Brown died a year ago.

## 80f   Use the appropriate tense of participles

Using participial forms depends on the ideas you are expressing. Ordinarily, however, a present participle indicates action at the time expressed by the main verb (present or present perfect tense) ; a past or perfect participle indicates action previous to that of the time expressed by the main verb (past or past perfect tense) . Notice participles and main verbs in the following:

*Traveling* constantly from coast to coast, my parents *see* much of this country. (Participle in present tense, main verb in present tense)
*Traveling* from coast to coast, my parents *have seen* much of this country. (Participle in present tense, main verb in present perfect tense)
*Having traveled* from coast to coast, my parents *saw* much of this country. (Participle in present perfect tense, main verb in past tense)
*Making* a good academic record, Henry *expects* to get excellent letters of recommendation. (Participle in present tense, main verb in present tense)
*Having made* a good academic record, Henry *obtained* many excellent letters of recommendation. (Participle in present perfect tense, main verb in past tense)

## 80g   Use the appropriate tense of infinitives

Your use of one of the infinitive tenses—present infinitive or perfect infinitive—likewise depends on the ideas you are expressing.

Ordinarily the *present infinitive* expresses action occurring or state of being existing at the same time as the main verb or supposed to occur or exist at a time after the main verb.

Mr. Brown, I am happy *to meet* you.
I have been asked *to invite* you to our meeting.
Mr. Jones was reported *to be* a candidate for city treasurer.

The *perfect infinitive* ordinarily indicates action which has occurred or state of being which has existed before the time of the main verb:

Mr. Brown, I am happy *to have met* you.
Every member is pleased *to have listened* to you as our speaker.
Mr. Jones was reported *to have been* a candidate for city treasurer.

## 80h  Be consistent in the use of tense in dependent and independent clauses

Consistency demands the correct "sequence of tenses," i.e., order of events in time and proper expression of that order. Note these principles:

1. When the tense in the independent clause is the *present,* the *future,* the *present perfect,* or the *future perfect,* any tense may be used in the dependent clause which will adequately express the thought.

I always *tell* people that I *live* in Detroit.
Henry *tells* me that he *will visit* Niagara Falls.
Henry *will* also *tell* you that he *will visit* Niagara Falls.
John *tells* me that he *has seen* Niagara Falls.
I *have told* you that I *have* not *seen* Niagara Falls.
By June I *shall have finished* all the courses that *are required* for graduation.

2. When the tense in the independent clause is *past* or *past perfect,* a past tense or past perfect tense should be used in the dependent clause (except to express a timeless or universal truth or general truth, Section **80c**) .

John *told* me that he *saw* Niagara Falls yesterday.
John *told* Henry that he *had seen* Niagara Falls a year ago.

Our instructor *told* us yesterday that our themes *would be* (not *will be*) due tomorrow.

I *had told* John last week that we *had worked* too hard the week before.

3. For the use of tense in contrary-to-fact statements, see Section **82c.**

## EXERCISE

From two to three pages in your book of readings or in a current magazine, make a list of five examples of each of the following: (1) verb or verb phrase (part of predicate) ; (2) participle or participial phrase; (3) gerund or gerundial phrase; (4) infinitive or infinitive phrase. After each indicate within parentheses (1) what the tense is and (2) what the tone is.

# 81  *Voice* (*active and passive*)

*Voice* is the grammatical term indicating, by the use or form of the verb, whether the subject of the sentence or clause is acting or being acted upon. In the *active voice* of verbs expressing action, the subject (person or thing) is literally the actor, the doer —like a surgeon in an operation. In the *passive voice,* the subject does nothing, is literally passive or inactive, and is acted upon or has something done to it—like the patient in an operation.

John *wrote* a short story. (Active voice)
A short story *was written* by John. (Passive voice)
We *drive* our car several thousand miles a month. (Active voice)
Our car *is driven* (by us) several thousand miles a month. (Passive voice)

### 81a  *Use correct forms of the auxiliary and main verbs in forming the passive voice*

Like verbs in the active voice, verbs in the passive also have tense (time) and tone. To form the passive voice, use the auxiliary verb *to be* in its various forms and the past participle of the main verb. Study the forms of this auxiliary verb (table, pp. 484–485) and then study the table on pp. 514–515, noting how auxiliary forms are applied.

Note also that in tone the passive voice has all the forms in the simple tone; it has none in the emphatic tone; and it uses, commonly, in the progressive tone the present, past, and future tenses only. The compound tenses (present perfect, past perfect, future perfect) in the progressive can be formed, but they are cumbersome, awkward, and uneuphonious. The ideas in the perfect progressive tenses (*have been being seen, had been being seen, shall have been being seen*) are more easily and effectively expressed by the simple tone of these tenses (*have been seen, had been seen, shall have been seen*).

### 81b Do not use intransitive verb forms in a passive-voice construction

With a transitive verb (see pp. 421–422) a direct object receives the action of the verb; with an intransitive verb no such object is needed. Only transitive verbs, therefore, can be used in the passive voice. In this process, the direct object of the transitive verb is shifted in front of the verb and becomes the subject, and the subject of the transitive active verb becomes the expressed agent (preceded by the preposition *by*) or the implied agent.

John Brown writes novels. (Active voice, transitive verb)
Novels are written by John Brown. (Passive voice)

Our class has performed many experiments dealing with moisture condensation. (Active voice, transitive verb)
Many experiments dealing with moisture condensation have been performed. (Passive voice; "by our class," the agent, is implied.)

A passive-voice construction is sometimes used when an indirect object is made the "passive" subject in a rephrased sentence.

Father gave me some money. (Active voice)
Some money was given me by Father. (Passive voice; direct object has become subject.)
I was given some money by Father. (Passive voice; indirect object has become subject.)

# TO SEE

## INDICATIVE MOOD, PASSIVE VOICE

Principal Parts: see  saw  seen

|  | Singular | | Plural | |
|---|---|---|---|---|
|  | Simple | Progressive | Simple | Progressive |
| **Present tense** | | | | |
| 1st person | I am seen | am being seen | we ⎫ | |
| 2nd person | you are seen | are being seen | you ⎬ are seen | are being seen |
| 3rd person | he is seen | is being seen | they ⎭ | |
|  | (she, it) | | | |
| **Past tense** | | | | |
| 1st person | I was seen | was being seen | we ⎫ | |
| 2nd person | you were seen | were being seen | you ⎬ were seen | were being seen |
| 3rd person | he was seen | was being seen | they ⎭ | |
| **Future tense** | | | | |
| 1st person | I shall be seen | shall be being seen | we shall be seen | shall be being seen |
| 2nd person | you will be seen | will be being seen | you will be seen | will be being seen |
| 3rd person | he will be seen | will be being seen | they will be seen | will be being seen |
| **Present perfect tense** | | | | |
| 1st person | I have been seen | | we ⎫ | |
| 2nd person | you have been seen | | you ⎬ have been seen | |
| 3rd person | he has been seen | | they ⎭ | |

## Past perfect tense

| | | |
|---|---|---|
| 1st person | I | |
| 2nd person | you | } had been seen |
| 3rd person | he | |

| | | |
|---|---|---|
| | we | |
| | you | } had been seen |
| | they | |

## Future perfect tense

| | |
|---|---|
| 1st person | I shall have been seen |
| 2nd person | you will have been seen |
| 3rd person | he will have been seen |

| | |
|---|---|
| | we shall have been seen |
| | you will have been seen |
| | they will have been seen |

## Verbals (nonfinite verb forms)

| | *Simple* |
|---|---|
| *Present infinitive* | to be seen |
| *Perfect infinitive* | to have been seen |
| *Present participle* | being seen |
| *Past participle* | (none) |
| *Perfect participle* | having been seen |
| *Present gerund* | being seen |
| *Perfect gerund* | having been seen |

NOTE: Gerunds have the same form as participles.

His company granted John a month's vacation. (Active voice)
John was granted a month's vacation by his company. (Passive voice;
   indirect object has become subject.)
A month's vacation was granted John by his company. (Passive voice;
   direct object has become subject.)

Verbs with intransitive meaning are not used in the passive
voice.

| | |
|---|---|
| *Incorrect* | The river has been risen because of the recent rains. |
| *Correct* | The river has risen because of the recent rains. |
| *Incorrect* | The dog was sat on the chair. |
| *Correct* | The dog was made to sit on the chair. |
| *Incorrect* | Your letters have been lain on your desk. |
| *Correct* | Your letters have been laid on your desk. |

NOTE: Idiomatic usage permits an *apparent* passive construction
of a few intransitive verbs: "Jesus is risen"; "Mary is gone"; "I
am come to tell you the plans." Note, however, that the subject
of the active and "apparent passive" remains unchanged.

### 81c  Do not shift needlessly from active voice to passive voice

Clear, effective, appropriate use of voice is mainly a matter of
being consistent. Do not, therefore, shift needlessly from active
to passive voice or from passive to active, i.e., subject as actor or
as being acted upon, unless good reason exists for the shift. Not
only is such shifting annoying and troublesome to the reader,
but it causes a needless and ineffective shifting from one subject
to another in clauses and sentences.

| | |
|---|---|
| *Faulty* | You should follow a budget, and much money will be saved. |
| | When a person approaches the Great Smoky Mountains, a blue haze can be seen in the distance. |
| | Join the Navy and the world will be seen—through a porthole! |
| | I asked a question, but no reply was received. |
| *Improved* | You should follow a budget, and you will save much money. |
| | If you follow a budget, you will save much money. |

> When a person approaches the Great Smoky Mountains,
> he can see a blue haze in the distance.
> Join the Navy and see the world—through a porthole!
> I asked a question but received no reply.

### 81d  Use the passive voice in impersonal writing

Writing is impersonal when it avoids use of personal pronouns; it is completely impersonal when it avoids even the use of the indefinite pronouns like *one, someone, everybody* or nouns like a *person*, a *student*. In certain kinds of writing, as in recording laboratory experiments, giving conclusions, making recommendations, and the like, completely impersonal expression may be desirable and is achieved by using the passive voice. The agent or doer is usually not expressed, only implied.

> The experiment was performed in order to . . .
> The following facts were obtained. . . .
> The results were tabulated, and from them the following
> conclusions were reached. . . .
> On the basis of these conclusions, the following changes
> are recommended. . . .

### 81e  Avoid overfrequent use of the passive voice

Since a subject being acted upon is rarely as effective as a subject acting, the use of the passive voice often detracts from effectiveness in a sentence. Overuse of the passive voice can also result in wordiness, one aspect of gobbledygook (Section **68**). Active voice normally gives sentences greater force and strength. Therefore, make your themes live, move, or create an impression of movement, with the subjects of your sentences acting and not being passive or acted upon. To say "The motor was started" or "The way was lost" is not so effective as "I started the motor" or "We lost our way." Use verbs in the active voice whenever you want to express or imply action, mental or physical, unless your purpose in a sentence is to represent the subject as being acted upon. Even in sentences emphasizing inanimate things, choose carefully the appropriate voice: "The fluid runs through the tube at a constant rate" is preferable to "The fluid is run through . . . ." When you have chosen the grammatical voice you want, be consistent: shifting from active to passive distracts your reader.

| | |
|---|---|
| *Unemphatic* | A lecture *is scheduled to be given* by Professor Fowler on Wednesday. |
| | This essay *was read* by me four times before it *was understood.* |
| *Better* | Professor Fowler *will give* a lecture on Wednesday. |
| | I *read* this essay four times before I *understood* it. |

Occasionally, sentences do require a passive verb, especially when the agent is not expressed. Use the passive voice, therefore, whenever it is effectively appropriate, that is, when your purpose is to represent the subject of the sentence as acted upon and when you wish to emphasize the subject in the beginning position (Section 47a).

| | |
|---|---|
| *Effective* | A lecture on "Better Living at Less Cost" *will be given* on Wednesday by Professor Fowler. |
| | Our place of meeting *has been changed* from Room 414 to Room 24. |

As Sydney J. Harris wrote: "We have not passed that subtle line between childhood and adulthood until we move from the passive voice to the active voice—that is, until we have stopped saying, 'It got lost,' and say, 'I lost it.' "

## EXERCISES

A. From two or three or more pages in your book of readings or in a current magazine: (1) make a list, up to 20, of the verbs or verb phrases in the passive voice; (2) after each write the tense and tone that it illustrates.

B. Change all passive-verb forms in the following sentences to active voice:

1. Then a long trip was made by us to a room on the third floor, and a lecture on the library was given for about 25 minutes.
2. All the decorations were brought up from the basement, and the tree was begun to be decorated by our family.
3. My horse's wonderful disposition will always be remembered by me.
4. Any letters which will be written by me in the near future will probably be letters of inquiry and application.

5. The student was asked by the instructor to read the theme that had been written.
6. The roof was blown off by the storm, and the furniture was badly damaged by the rain.
7. When the question was asked by Mary, it was considered too difficult to be answered by the lecturer.
8. The vegetables are being cooked by the women, and the dessert is being bought by the men.
9. Being seen in public for the first time in weeks, John was asked by us how his illness had been overcome.
10. When your theme has been finished, your paper is to be folded and handed in.

# 82 Mood (mode)

*Mood,* literally, is a state or temper of mind; *mode,* literally, is a prevailing fashion or manner. In grammar, the *mood* or *mode* of a verb indicates the state of mind or the manner in which a statement is made: a fact, a request or command, a condition or probability. English commonly has three moods: *indicative, imperative,* and *subjunctive.* Other "states of mind" or "prevailing manners"—such as willingness, duty, propriety, necessity, expectation, permission, ability, obligation, compulsion, custom—are expressed by auxiliary verbs (see Section **78h**) .

### 82a   Use the indicative mood to express a fact or what seems to be a fact or to ask a question of fact

Verb forms in the indicative mood are the most frequently used verb forms in English. Outlines of the indicative mood of the auxiliary verbs *to be, to have, to do* and of the main verb *to see,* active and passive voice, are given in the tables on pp. 484–485, 502–503, and 514–515. Examples:

When *are* the term papers due? (Question of fact)
They *are* due on the second Friday in January. (Statement of fact)
Some medieval castles *have lasted* for centuries. (Statement of fact)

**82b   Use the imperative mood to express a command,
a polite request, a strong request, an order**

The imperative mood of the verb has only one form, the same form as the present infinitive without the sign *to*. It is both singular and plural. Examples: *come, do, be,* and three famous words from traffic, *stop, slow, yield.*

Forward, *march!* Company, *halt!* (Commands)
*Come* to the meeting and *bring* a friend with you. (Polite request)
This class will begin promptly at 8 A.M. *Be* here. (Strong request)
*Deliver* these flowers this afternoon. (Order)

**82c   Use the subjunctive mood to express (1) a condition
contrary to fact, (2) a supposition, (3) a highly
improbable condition, (4) doubt or uncertainty,
(5) necessity, (6) parliamentary motions, (7) a desire**

Distinctive subjunctive verb forms in current English have disappeared or are disappearing in favor of more commonly used indicative verb forms.

*Former use*    If it *be* possible, I shall come.
            A student, if he *write* well, will receive a high grade.
*Current use*   If it *is* possible, I shall come.
            A student, if he *writes* well, will receive a high grade.

The verb *to be* (both as linking and as auxiliary verb) has only two distinct subjunctive forms now in occasional use: the form *be* for all persons in singular and plural, present tense, and the form *were* for all persons in singular and plural, past tense. See "Subjunctive Mood," table on p. 485. The same table gives any currently used subjunctive forms of the verbs *have* and *do.*

For all other verb forms except *be,* and including *have* and *do,* the only subjunctive form different from the indicative in any tense is the third person singular present, which, by dropping the *s* ending, becomes exactly like the other forms:

| | | | |
|---|---|---|---|
| (if) I do | (if) I have | (if) I see | (if) I come |
| (if) you do | (if) you have | (if) you see | (if) you come |
| (if) he do | (if) he have | (if) he see | (if) he come |

Only rarely, however, can you find such main-verb subjunctive forms, third person singular, present tense, in current writing. Instead, both subjunctive and other nonindicative mood and nonimperative mood ideas are expressed by the use of auxiliary verbs: *should, would, can, could, may, might, must, ought, let, dare, need, used* (see Section **78h**).

| | |
|---|---|
| *Rare* | If she *come,* it will be a pleasure. |
| | If he *write* me, I shall reply. |
| *Common* | If she *can come,* it will be a pleasure. |
| | If he *should write* me, I shall reply. |

Our language still retains a number of subjunctive forms in sayings from times when this mood was more widely used: *Heaven forbid, Thy Kingdom come, if need be, he need not speak, suffice it to say, come what may, so be it,* etc. Also, careful speakers and writers employ the subjunctive mood to express the precise manner in which they make their statements, when the indicative mood would not serve effectively.

As indicated in the general principle introducing this section, current English uses subjunctive verb forms, especially of *to be* (*be* and *were*), to express:

1. A condition contrary to fact: something that is not true, that could not be true. A verb in the past tense or past perfect tense of the subjunctive mood is usually used in the dependent clause, and *should, would, could,* or *might* is usually used in the independent clause.

If you *were* I, you *would* do exactly the same thing.
If it *were* not so cold, we *could* go swimming.
If it *had* not *rained* yesterday, we *might* have seen two ball games.

Note that ordinarily *should, would, could,* or *might* do not appear in both the *if* clause and the independent clause.

| | |
|---|---|
| *Dubious* | If you *should* go to Chicago, you *would* see Lakeshore Drive. |
| | If John *would* reconsider, I *would* offer him the position. |
| *Better* | If you *should* go to Chicago, you *will* see Lakeshore Drive. |
| | If John reconsidered, I *would* offer him the position. |

But note also: when *should* replaces *if* in the dependent clause, use *would* or *will* in the independent clause:

*Should* you go to Chicago, you *would* (or *will*) see Lakeshore Drive.
*Should* John reconsider, I *would* (or *will*) offer him the position.

2. A supposition.

Suppose he *were* to ask you that question!
Let's assume that she *were* to be chosen campus queen.

3. A highly improbable condition, even though not completely contrary to fact.

He worked as if he *were* never going to have another chance.
If I *be* [*am*] too talkative at the meeting, please inform me at once.
If the program *be* [*is*] deadly dull, let's not complain.

The bracketed words *am* and *is,* indicative forms, are almost always used in current English.

4. Doubt or uncertainty.

He talks as if he *were* the only intelligent person in the group.
As though he *were* any smarter himself!

5. Necessity.

It is necessary that she *pass* this course in order to be initiated.
It is essential that Henry *appear* in person for the honor.
The dean of women insisted that Jane *come* to her office.
It is expected that every man *pay* his own way.

6. Parliamentary motions.

I move that the chairman *be authorized* to proceed.
The motion is that the remark of the last speaker *be expunged* from the record.
Resolved, that Henry *be made* an honorary member of this organization.
It is moved and seconded that he *pay* his dues in advance.

7.  A desire, wish, volition, recommendation.

She wishes that she *were* going to go along.
Our officers desire that you *be* rewarded.
"Thy Kingdom *come,* Thy Will *be done.*"
It is recommended that the class president *speak* at the reception and
*give* the address of welcome.

## 82d  Be consistent in the use of mood or mode, especially in parallel constructions

Be consistent in the use of the subjunctive mood or the indicative or the imperative, as in compound predicates and in two
or more parallel dependent clauses. Do not shift needlessly from
one to another or mix their use.

| | |
|---|---|
| *Inconsistent* | If I *were* in your position and *was* not prevented, I should certainly go. |
| | If it *does* not rain and if I *be* not called out of town, I shall attend the game. |
| | Last summer I *would* play golf every morning and *swam* every afternoon. |
| *Consistent* | If I *were* in your position and *were* not prevented, I should certainly go. |
| | If it *does* not rain and if I *am* not called out of town, I shall attend the game. |
| | Last summer I *would* play golf every morning and *would* swim every afternoon. |
| | Last summer I *played* golf every morning and *swam* every afternoon. |

## EXERCISES

A. From two, three, or more pages in your book of readings or in
a current magazine, make a list, up to 20, of the verbs or verb phrases
in the imperative mood and in the subjunctive mood (form) or expressing a subjunctive idea (use of appropriate auxiliary verbs, Section
78h) .

B. From the following sentences make a list containing the italicized forms that you prefer. If you choose the subjunctive form, state
which of the subdivisions under Section 82c you are following.

1. Assume, now, that she *was were* to be our official delegate.
2. If she *be is* chosen our delegate and *was were* sent to Chicago, would we be well represented?
3. To put this campaign over, it *be is* necessary that the class president *be is* here Tuesday to make final plans.
4. My only hope is that John *receive receives* full recognition for his work.
5. Heaven *grant grants* that he *be is* not seriously injured.
6. I strongly advocate that a vote of censure *be is* ordered.
7. Even though extreme measures for our safety *are be* taken, the consequences are dubious.
8. My, how he wished he *was were* a few inches taller.
9. It is imperative that there *is be* not the slightest delay.
10. It hardly seems possible that the doctor *is would be* willing to give that anesthetic to a baby.

# 83  *Adjectives and adverbs*

Ordinarily, determining when an adjective or adverb should be used is not difficult. An *adjective* modifies only a noun or pronoun; an *adverb* modifies only a verb, an adjective, another adverb, or, infrequently, the general idea of a sentence. The rule is simple, yet misuse of adjectives and adverbs is common. Two reasons for the confusion are discussed in Section **83c,d,** below. But, in general, if the word or phrase about which you are in doubt sensibly modifies a noun or pronoun, the chances are that it is an adjective. If it modifies or even loosely applies to the verb, it is an adverb. (For additional discussion, see Section **71h,i.**)

### 83a  *Do not use an adjective to modify a verb*

| | |
|---|---|
| *Wrong* | Our chemistry professor talks too *rapid*. |
| | Some people take themselves too *serious*. |
| | On every occasion my sister dresses *neat*. |
| *Correct* | Our chemistry professor talks too *rapidly*. |
| | Some people take themselves too *seriously*. |
| | On every occasion my sister dresses *neatly*. |

## 83b Do not use an adjective to modify another adjective or an adverb

*Wrong*　　The lecture was *dreadful* dull.
　　　　　This is a *strong* made piece of luggage.
*Correct*　The lecture was *dreadfully* dull.
　　　　　This is a *strongly* made piece of luggage.

## 83c After such verbs as be (am, is, are, was, were, etc.), appear, become, feel, grow, look, prove, remain, seem, smell, sound, stand, taste, turn, *the modifier should be an adjective if it refers to the subject, an adverb if it describes or defines the verb*

As discussed more fully in Section **78**, when these are linking or coupling verbs: the adjective is used after them, since it modifies the subject noun or pronoun; when these same verbs express action, the adverb is used; and after certain other verbs the adjective or adverb is used, depending on the meaning of the verb.

*Correct*　The cake tastes *good*. (Adjective)
　　　　　The girl looked *beautiful*. (Adjective)
　　　　　He looks *careful*. (Adjective, i.e., a person who is careful)
　　　　　After my illness, I feel *strong* again. (Adjective)
　　　　　The weather has turned *cold*. (Adjective)

　　　　　She looked at him *angrily*. (Adverb)
　　　　　He looks *carefully* at the merging traffic. (Adverb)
　　　　　The lecturer felt *strongly* about the interruptions; finally, he turned *coldly* toward his hecklers. (Adverbs)

The first five italicized modifiers are adjectives because they refer to the *subjects* of the sentences. The last four are adverbs because they modify *verbs*. (See Section **78a,b.**)

## 83d Be accurate in the use of words that may be either adjectives or adverbs and in the use of adjectives that end in ly

Another source of adjective-adverb confusion arises because the form of a word does not always reveal whether it is an adjective or adverb. Some adjectives and adverbs have identical forms (for example, *far, fast, little, less, least, much, more, most, well*) , but these naturally cause no trouble.

A number of adverbs have two forms, which may differ in meaning; the first form is exactly like the adjective and the second has *ly* added: examples are *cheap, cheaply; direct, directly; late, lately; loud, loudly; quick, quickly; slow, slowly.* Most words ending in *ly* are adverbs, but some are not: words like *deadly, goodly, holy, sickly, weakly,* are adjectives, and *ly* also is an adjective suffix meaning "like": *earthly, friendly, heavenly, homely, manly, motherly, saintly, timely, womanly.*

Consult your dictionary when in doubt; it tells which words are adjectives only, which are adverbs only, which may be either, and what their labels are—colloquial, informal, or, if unlabeled, proper in any use.

A sprinter is a runner who runs *fast.* (Adverb)
A sprinter is a *fast* runner. (Adjective)
Grandfather was a *kindly* (adjective) person; he treated *kindly* (adverb) everyone that he met.

### 83e   *Use the correct forms of adjectives and adverbs to indicate the three degrees of comparison*

Grammatically, comparison is the change in form of an *adjective* or *adverb* to indicate greater or smaller degrees of quantity, quality, or manner. The change is indicated by three methods: (1) by the use of different words, a somewhat uncommon method; (2) by adding endings *er, est* to one-syllable words and some of two syllables; (3) by using adverbial modifiers, *more, most* (upward comparison) , and *less, least* (downward comparison) , with words of two or more syllables when awkwardness results from adding the *er, est* endings. The three degrees of comparison are *positive, comparative, superlative.* Examples:

| *Positive* | *Comparative* | *Superlative* |
|---|---|---|
| good  (well) | better | best |
| little | less | least |
| bad | worse | worst |
| many | more | most |
| small | smaller | smallest |
| wisely | more wisely | most wisely |
| beautiful | less beautiful | least beautiful |

*Positive degree,* the first or simple form of an adjective or adverb, shows no comparison, no relationship; *comparative degree* shows relationship between or compares two persons, objects, or ideas; *superlative degree* shows relationship among or compares three or more.

Smith is a *tall* (*competent*) man. (Adjective, positive degree)

Smith is a *taller* (*more competent*) man than I am. (Adjective, comparative degree)

Smith is the *tallest* (*most competent*) man in our group. (Adjective, superlative degree)

The Wabash River flows *fast* (*violently*) during the rainy season. (Adverb, positive degree)

The Wabash River flows *faster* (*more violently*) in spring than in fall. (Adverb, comparative degree)

All months considered, the Wabash River flows *fastest* (*most violently*) in April, *least violently* in the winter months. (Adverb, superlative degree)

### 83f   Use the comparative degree for comparison between two things, the superlative degree for more than two

In incorrect and sometimes in informal usage we hear such statements as "In the Army-Navy series, Navy's team has been the best," or in a boxing match "May the best man win." In such statements, only two, not three or more, are being compared. Accurate speakers and writers would use *better* in such sentences.

Let us vote for the *better* of the two candidates. (Only two are concerned.)

Let us vote for the *best* of these five candidates. (More than two are concerned.)

In informal or colloquial English the superlative qualifying adverb *most* is sometimes used when no particular comparison is intended: "You are *most* generous." In such meaning, *most* is an intensive or a substitute for *very*: "You are very generous."

(For unjustifiable omissions in comparisons, see Section 35f; for mixed and illogical comparisons, see Section 35d,e.)

### 83g   *Avoid the trap of the double comparative or double superlative*

When comparative and superlative forms of adjectives and adverbs are formed by adding *er* and *est* endings, the adverbs *more* and *most* should never be used, even though such a model as Shakespeare slipped with "This was the *most unkindest* cut of all" (*Julius Caesar,* III:ii). Such expressions are not permissible even in informal usage.

*Wrong*      This test was much *more longer* than the one last month.
Our high school senior queen was the *most prettiest* of any we had chosen during my four years of high school.

### 83h   *Do not compare adjectives and adverbs that are in meaning logically incapable of comparison*

When their meaning is absolute, adjectives and adverbs are logically incapable of comparison, that is, of being used in the comparative or superlative degrees. What they say is said once and for all, nor should they have qualifying adverbs unless these mean "approaching absoluteness." For example, *unique* means "having no like or equal"; consequently, *very unique* and *quite unique* are illogical expressions. Other similar absolute words are *absolute, accurate, excellent, fatal, final, horizontal, impossible, parallel, perfect, perpendicular, round, square.*

More nearly accurate writing (not *"more* accurate") uses certain qualifying adverbs that do mean "approaching absoluteness," *nearly impossible,* not *completely impossible* or *more impossible; almost fatal,* not *completely fatal; almost square* or *more nearly square,* not *squarer; the most nearly round,* not *the roundest.*

### EXERCISES

A. Rewrite the following sentences, correcting all errors in the misuse of adjectives and adverbs:

1. Bears bothered us some as we camped in the park.
2. My most favorite hobbies are golf and bowling.
3. At times my roommate feels both sadly and badly about his past record in college.
4. Themes are not graded as strict in high school as they are in college.

5. I can now see my problems clearer than I did last year at this time.
6. The harvest tells whether a farmer will be able to live comfortable or not.
7. My ankle hurt so bad the next day that I couldn't walk.
8. A student should make out a study schedule and should follow it reasonable close.
9. Once correct pronunciation is achieved, one can spell some words easier.
10. In a small college there is likely to be a more friendlier atmosphere than in a large university.
11. Here I am trying to succeed in three major fields—scholastically, athletically, and socially.
12. It soon became apparent that I was not going to do good on the test.
13. Since I am the youngest of two children, I really know what I am talking about.
14. Some activities help to draw a group of students closer together.
15. On icy roads some drivers turn corners too sharp and they apply the brakes too sudden.

B. From each of the following sentences, list the italicized form that is correct:

1. Under a poor teacher the student is not able to learn very *rapid rapidly*.
2. If you treat some people *rude rudely,* they will be *rude rudely* to you too.
3. Many auto drivers wonder why other drivers do not drive *careful carefully*.
4. At the fairs in the past we have done very *good well* with our cattle and sheep.
5. Everyone takes a written test and a driving test; the actual driving test is the *worse worst* of the two.
6. Mother's health has improved *some somewhat* since you last saw her.
7. It is *remarkable remarkably* to see operations in this college function so *smooth smoothly*.
8. In rainy weather your brakes are not as *efficient efficiently* as on dry roads.
9. It takes more than money to make a person *real really* happy, but some money *certain certainly* helps.
10. I am glad to say that I am doing *excellent excellently* in all of my subjects.

# 84 *Conjunctions*

A *conjunction,* as a part of speech, is a word, sometimes several words with the force or meaning of one word, used to *join* or *link* or *connect* or *relate*. It has no other function than to couple two or more elements: words, phrases, clauses, and, occasionally, sentences.

You must know the various kinds of conjunctions in order to write clearly, effectively, and appropriately. Especially useful is this knowledge for punctuation (see Sections **88d,e,f, 89a,b,c**) and for transition between sentences and paragraphs (see Sections **42** and **11**). Conjunctions are divided into two main groups: (1) coordinating and (2) subordinating. Depending on your meaning, you may coordinate ideas in one of several ways or you may subordinate one idea to another.

A *coordinating conjunction* joins words, phrases, clauses, or sentences of equal rank, that is, elements not dependent on one another grammatically, although they may be in meaning—coordinate literally means of equal rank. Three kinds of conjunctions are classified as coordinating.

*1. Pure* or *simple conjunctions—and, but, or, nor, neither, yet*. Some instructors add *for* and *so,* and others add *while* (i.e., *but meanwhile*) and *whereas* (i.e., *but*). In common uses, these do one or more of the following: they, or most of them, join two or more words, two or more phrases, two or more clauses, or even sentences of equal rank (see Section **84a**).

Our University colors are blue *and* white. (Words joined)
John was not on the golf course *but* at the baseball game. (Phrases joined)
Since the weather is warm *and* since the snow is melting, we have given up our plans for skiing. (Dependent clauses joined)
Our plans were carefully made, *but* they did not work out. (Independent clauses joined)

*2. Correlative conjunctions—*words used in pairs and serving to emphasize the relationship between two ideas: words, phrases, dependent clauses, independent clauses. Most frequently used of these pairs are *both . . . and, either . . . or, neither*

. . . *nor,* and *not only* . . . *but also.* Sometimes other pairs are listed, but careful study reveals that they do not coordinate, but subordinate. For example, *whether* . . . *or* really means that two "whether" statements are joined by *or,* even though the second *whether* is understood: "Your English instructor doesn't care *whether* you attend *or* (*whether* you) don't attend the football games." (See also Section **84b.**)

*Both* Father *and* Mother hold degrees from Columbia University. (Nouns correlated)
The lilies of the field neither toil nor spin. (Verbs correlated)
You should observe good principles of writing, *not only* when you write formally, *but also* when you write informally. (Dependent clauses correlated)
In the library *either* you must be quiet *or* you must leave. (Independent clauses correlated)

3. *Conjunctive adverbs*—ordinarily, adverbs used parenthetically in a sentence but frequently used to relate two independent clauses or two sentences: words or phrases like *however, thus, besides, still, then, in fact, for example* (see Sections **84d** and **89b**) .

A student should learn how to use the library; *otherwise,* its resources will do him little good.

A *subordinating conjunction* serves only one purpose: to relate a noun clause or an adverbial clause to its independent clause (the adjective clause is related to its noun or pronoun by a relative pronoun) . Examples: *if, since, because, as, while, so that, although, unless, before.* (See also Section **84e.**)

Dues were increased *because* there was no money in the treasury. (Adverbial clause joined by *because*)
Henry said *that* he was thrilled by *what* he saw. (Noun clauses introduced by *that* and *what*)

Conjunctions, particularly when they join clauses, must be chosen with care, for they should always show clear and appropriate relationships of ideas. Often, a careless writer will use *and* where the relationship of clauses needs to be more clearly expressed, probably by use of subordination. (Section **84a.**)

The following suggestions deal both with the right or appropriate conjunction as a matter of diction and with the right or appropriate conjunction to indicate proper relationship of ideas.

### 84a    Distinguish among the purposes served by simple coordinating conjunctions

Purposes served by the simple coordinating conjunctions are the following:

1. Addition, along the same line or in the same direction of thought: *and.*
2. Affirmative alternation: *or.*
3. Contrast: *but, yet.*
4. Negative alternation: *nor, neither.*
5. Reason, result, purpose, cause: *for* (?) , *so.*

When independent clauses or dependent clauses or phrases are genuinely coordinated, respectively, with other independent clauses or dependent clauses or phrases, use the exact coordinating conjunction that relates them. Do not use *and* if *but* is the exact word, *or* for *but,* and the like.

*Inaccurate*    I wanted to study architecture, *and* my father wanted me to become a lawyer. (Use *but*)
We had a long detour, *but* we should have been here an hour ago. (Use *or*)
I had hoped you would go, *or* you did. (Use *and*)

### 84b    Use correlative conjunctions to correlate only two ideas

Purposes served by the correlative conjunctions are the following:

1. Addition, along the same line or in the same direction of thought: *both . . . and, not only . . . but also.*
2. Affirmative alternation: *either . . . or.*
3. Contrast: *not only . . . but also.*
4. Negative alternation: *neither . . . nor.*

Since by definition correlative conjunctions are used in pairs, their clear and logical use is to relate two ideas, not more than two. Each member of the pair is followed by the same grammatical construction. (For parallel structure, see Section **44b.**)

*Dubious*      *Both* my father, my mother, *and* my oldest sister are graduates of Northern University.

*Neither* rain, snow, hail, ice, *nor* tornado could have kept me from our high school Junior Prom.

At this early date it looks as if *either* Mary, Sue, Helen, *or* Sharon will win the Campus Queen contest.

NOTE: *Neither . . . nor* go together, not *neither . . . or.*

*Illogical*     Williamsport is *neither* the biggest *or* the most beautiful city in the state.

NOTE: As indicated in the "Glossary of Diction," Item 48, p. 393–394, the use of *either . . . or, neither . . . nor* to coordinate more than two words, phrases, or clauses is sanctioned by some dictionaries but not by others. Logic and clearness suggest that they relate two only.

## 84c   Distinguish among the purposes served by conjunctive adverbs

Purposes served by the conjunctive adverbs are the following:

1. Addition, along the same line or in the same direction of thought: *again, also, besides, furthermore, in addition, indeed, likewise, moreover, naturally, similarly, thereby, too.*
2. Affirmative alternation: *anyhow, moreover, still.*
3. Negative alternation: *however, instead, nevertheless, on the contrary, otherwise.*
4. Comparison: *in fact, in like manner, indeed, likewise, moreover, thus.*
5. Contrast: *anyhow, conversely, fortunately, however, instead, nevertheless, notwithstanding, on the other hand, still, yet.*
6. Example: *for example, in fact, indeed, namely.*
7. Place: *here, there.*

8. Reason, result, purpose, cause, summary: *accordingly, as a result, consequently, hence, so, surely, thereby, therefore, thus, truly.*
9. Time: *afterward, finally, henceforth, last, later, meanwhile, next, now, second, soon, temporarily, thereafter.*

NOTE: As illustrated above, two- or three-word phrases often serve the purpose and meaning of conjunctive adverbs.

### 84d   *Avoid using conjunctive adverbs to join words or phrases or dependent clauses*   (see Section **89b,d**)

The adverbs that can also serve as conjunctions relate only two independent clauses or two sentences.

| | |
|---|---|
| *Dubious* | Mother's favorite colors are blue and yellow, *also* pink. |
| | I worked on my theme for two hours, *then* revised it, and went to bed. |
| | At last reports the Channel swimmer had swum for 12 hours, *still* was going strong. |

In such sentences a pure coordinating conjunction should be used before the adverb, which becomes weakly parenthetical, or a second independent clause can sometimes be used.

| | |
|---|---|
| *Improved* | Mother's favorite colors are blue and yellow, and *also* pink. |
| | I worked on my theme for two hours; then I revised it and went to bed. |
| | At last reports the Channel swimmer had swum for 12 hours and was still going strong. |

### 84e   *Use the proper subordinating conjunction to express subordinate relationships*

Purposes served by the subordinating conjunctions are as follows:

1. Addition, along the same line or in the same direction of thought: *whereby, whereupon.*
2. Affirmative alternation: *else, whereas, whether.*
3. Comparison: *as, as . . . as, so . . . as, than.*
4. Concession: *although, even if, insofar as, in spite of the fact that, notwithstanding the fact that, though, unless, while.*

5. Condition: *although, as if, as though, except that, if, lest, once, provided, providing, though, unless.*
6. Contrast: *although, whereas.*
7. Manner: *as, as if, as though.*
8. Negative alternation: *except that, only, whereas.*
9. Place: *whence, where, wherever, whither.*
10. Reason, result, purpose, cause: *as, because, for, for the reason that, inasmuch as, in order that, lest, since, so that, that, such that, that, whereas, why.*
11. Time: *after, as, as long as, as often as, as soon as, before, once, since, till, until, when, whenever, while.*

*Faulty diction*      *Being as how* I was small, I did not make the football team. (Use *because*)

I do not know *as how I* could trust such a person. (Use *that*)

Father wrote me *how that* he had gone fishing. (Use *that*)

I read *where* Joe had broken another track record. (Use *that*)

Expenses became so unbearable *until* I sold my car. (Use *that*)

He did not get the telegram before he left *whereas* it was delivered late. (Use *because*)

## 84f  Be sparing in the use of like *as a subordinating conjunction*

In recent years *like* (for *as* or *as if*) has been increasingly used as a subordinating conjunction and has reached the status of having some dictionaries give it a "colloquial" label as a subordinating conjunction. Perhaps the chief objection to *like* in this meaning is not its use but its overuse (as with *so,* see Section **36c**) .

My face felt *like* it had been baked in a kiln for a week.
College teachers don't keep after you to do an assignment *like* the teachers do in high school.
Some people try to live *like* they were millionaires.
I felt *like* I had been tied to the bottom of the lake.
I was not named after my father *like* many sons are.

Overuse of *like* makes readers wish that writers would use an occasional *as, as if, though, as though,* for the sake of effective variety. However, do not become so word-conscious of *like* that you avoid it as a necessary preposition. In the following sentences, *like* should replace *as*:

I hope there are more instructors *as* my third example, and not any examples *as* the first two I have described.
Let us now discuss a spectator's sport *as* football and a participant's sport *as* bowling.

## EXERCISES

Correct all the errors in the use of conjunctions in the following sentences:

1. My neighbor had an unpleasant disposition, yet I did not like him.
2. On the library cards are numbers, also the title and author of the book.
3. My mother's ancestry is English, while my father is of German descent.
4. A mirror is made by man, therefore cannot hold any magical powers.
5. This novel may have been good in your opinion, and it was not good in mine.
6. Being that I am only a freshman, I have not needed to choose a specific major yet.
7. My parents are the best parents in the world; I may sound prejudiced, but I hope that I do.
8. Whereas clans were prominent in Scotland in the seventeenth century, not every Scotsman belonged to a clan.
9. My English teacher was a benevolent sort of person, but she would always help us in any way possible.
10. Although I am next in line in our family as far as age goes, but I'd rather introduce you to my younger brother.
11. Our college has admitted a very large number of new students, and no additional instructors have been hired.
12. In college it doesn't matter to my teachers whether I study, where in high school the teachers were always after me to get my work done.
13. We drove around the campus for a while, then returned to the motel for the night.
14. I was so sleepy when I finished studying until I just tumbled into bed.
15. I went to my room early that evening, but I had much work to do.

# 85 Glossary of grammatical terms

Many writers have partially forgotten definitions of most grammatical terms and entirely forgotten some others. Some can well be forgotten. A knowledge of others is necessary if you wish to phrase your ideas correctly, clearly, effectively, and appropriately.

The following list is primarily a reference list. Every important and useful grammatical term is here. Some rather unusual words or phrases, like *accusative, functional word,* and the like, will be defined, but for most you will be referred to other specific pages and sections for a fairly detailed definition or discussion as these terms apply to your writing. This list may well be referred to also as a guide when you study the sections on punctuation (**86–100**) and the sentence (**31–50**).

1. Absolute phrase or absolute expression, sometimes called nominative absolute. See p. 433.
2. Abstract noun. See p. 441.
3. Accusative. A *case* name meaning the same as the *objective* (which see). The word is rare in English but common in the study of some foreign languages like German and Latin.
4. Active voice. See p. 512.
5. Adjective. See Section **71h** for definition and Section **83** for discussion of right and wrong use of adjectives.
6. Adjective clause. See Sections **73b** and **88m**.
7. Adverb. See Section **71i** for definition and Section **83** for discussion of right and wrong use of adverbs.
8. Adverbial clause. See Section **73b.**
9. Agreement. Correspondence or sameness in number, gender, and person—between subject and predicate and between pronoun and antecedent. For fuller discussion, see Section **76** for subject-predicate agreement and Section **77** for pronoun-antecedent agreement.
10. Antecedent. See Section **77.**
11. Appositive. A substantive, usually a noun, added to or following another substantive to identify or explain it. The appositive signifies the same thing, and the second substantive is said to be in *apposition.* See p. 574.

One important product, *rubber,* this country had to import. (*Rubber* is in apposition with *product.*)

More hardy than wheat are these grains—*rye, oats,* and *barley.* (*Rye, oats,* and *barley* are in apposition with *grains.*)

An appositive, if a pronoun or pronouns, agrees with its substantive in number and case (see Section **75g**); it is set off by commas if its relationship is loose (nonrestrictive) and is used without punctuation if the relationship is close (restrictive).   See Section **88q.**

12. Articles.   See Section **71h.**
13. Auxiliary.   See Section **78c–h.**
14. Balanced sentence.   See Sections **74c** and **44.**
15. Case.   See Section **75.**
16. Clause.   See Section **73.**
17. Collective noun.   See p. 411 and Section **76l.**
18. Common noun.   See p. 411.
19. Comparative degree.   See Section **83e,f.**
20. Comparison.   See Section **83e.**
21. Complement.   A word or expression used to *complete* the idea indicated or implied by a verb. A *predicate complement* (sometimes called *subjective complement*) may be a noun, a pronoun, or an adjective that follows a linking verb and describes or identifies the subject of the linking verb (see pp. 453, 483, 486–487).

This book is *a novel.*
The leaves of this tree are *red.*

An *object* (*objective*) *complement* may be a noun or adjective that follows the direct object of a verb and completes the necessary meaning:

We are painting our house *gray.*
Our neighbors named their baby *Maryann.*
His teammates elected Schmidt *captain.*

Note that the verb is transitive (see Section **71g**) in a sentence or clause containing an object complement.

22. Complex sentence.   See pp. 441–443.
23. Compound object.   See Section **75d.**
24. Compound predicate.   See Section **74a.**
25. Compound sentence.   See p. 441.
26. Compound subject.   See Section **74a.**
27. Compound-complex sentence.   See pp. 443–444.
28. Concord.   In grammar, *concord* is a term meaning the same as *agreement.* See Section **76.**
29. Concrete noun.   See p. 411.
30. Conjugation.   The inflectional changes in the form or uses of a verb to show tense, mood, voice, number, and person. See these terms in this reference list for specific guidance and see also Sections **79, 80, 81, 82.**
31. Conjunction.   See Section **84.**
32. Conjunctive adverb.   See p. 531 and Sections **84c,d.**
33. Construction.   See pp. 231–232.
34. Coordinating conjunction.   See Section **84.**
35. Copula.   See p. 483.
36. Correctness.   *Correctness, correct, correctly* are used throughout this book not in an absolute sense but in the meaning permitted by every reliably standard dictionary: "in accordance with an acknowledged or accepted standard; according to recognized usage."
37. Correlative conjunctions. See pp. 530–531 and Sections **84b** and **44b.**
38. Declarative sentence.   See Section **74b.**
39. Declension (noun) and Decline (verb).   *Declension:* the inflectional changes in the form or use of a noun or pronoun to indicate case, number, and person. *To decline* means to give these grammatical changes. Examples:

|  | SINGULAR |  |  | PLURAL |  |  |
|---|---|---|---|---|---|---|
| *Nominative* | man | I | who | men | we | who |
| *Possessive* | man's | my, mine | whose | men's | our, ours | whose |
| *Objective* | man | me | whom | men | us | whom |

40. Demonstrative pronoun.   See Section **71d3.**
41. Dependent clause (or subordinate clause).   See Section **73b.**

42. Diagraming.   A mechanical method—by using horizontal, perpendicular, and slanting lines—of learning the parts of a sentence and their relationships. See pp. 437–447.

43. Direct address.   The noun or pronoun showing to whom speech is addressed (also called the *vocative*) :

> *Mother,* where are you?
> When we finish rolling the court, *Fred,* we'll still have time for two sets of tennis.
> Tell me, *sir,* where the Administration Building is.

44. Direct quotation.   See Section **94a.**

45. Double possessive.   See pp. 459–460.

46. Ellipsis, elliptical clause, elliptical sentence.   *Ellipsis* means the omission of a word or words from a clause or sentence; the word or words are not needed because they are understood from other words or from context. *Elliptical clause,* see pp. 435–436. *Elliptical sentence,* see pp. 217–218.

47. Emphatic verb form.   See pp. 501, 505–509.

48. Exclamatory sentence.   See Section **74b.**

49. Expletive.   Frequently when a writer is at a loss about beginning a sentence or independent clause, he resorts to an *expletive*—a word or words not needed for the sense but used merely to fill out a sentence or clause, with the subject following the predicate. The more common expletive is *there*; less common are *here* and *it*. The most common expletive phrases are *there is, there are, there was, there were, there has been, there have been, there will be* (for *Agreement* in using expletives, see Section **76k**) . Usually *there is* no weaker or more ineffective way to begin a sentence; occasionally, however, expletives are desirable or even necessary, but as a general principle they should be avoided whenever *there is* a better, more effective way of beginning a statement. (See Section **67c.**) Compare for effectiveness the following:

> There once stood a castle on this hill.
> A castle once stood on this hill.
> On this hill once stood a castle.

> There are three students sharing this room.
> Three students share this room.

50. Finite verb.   A verb form or verb phrase that serves as a predicate; it has number and person. Opposed to the finite verb is the nonfinite verb form, which cannot serve as a predicate; nonfinite forms are participles, gerunds, and infinitives. See Section **71e,f.**

51. Function word.   A word used to indicate a function of or relationship between other words. Conjunctions or prepositions, for example, are function words.

52. Functional change or shift.   See p. 410.

53. Future perfect tense.   See Section **80a6,b.**

54. Future tense.   See Section **80a3,b.**

55. Gender.   The classification of nouns or pronouns according to sex. The four genders are masculine, feminine, neuter, and common (either masculine or feminine) : *boy, girl, it, individual.* In modern English nearly all traces of grammatical gender, as these are indicated by endings, have disappeared: *poetess* is a disappearing word, though *actress* is still in good use. Gender, when indicated, is clear from the meaning of the noun or pronoun: *actor, actress, he, she, it.*

56. Genitive.   See Section **75j.**

57. Gerund, gerundial phrase, and prepositional-gerundial phrase.   For discussion of *Gerund,* see Section **71f.** For *gerundial phrase* and *prepositional-gerundial phrase,* see Section **72.**

58. Grammar.   The science dealing with words and their relationships to one another—in other words, notation and organization of usage. *Grammar,* a descriptive statement of the way language works, includes a discussion of the forms of words, their use in phrases, clauses, and sentences, their tenses, cases, or other changes in form according to their relationships with one another. See pp. 408–409. Also, Sections **71** through **84** are a useful review and guide. (Also, see *Rhetoric* below, Item 126.)

59. Imperative and imperative sentence.   For *imperative,* see p. 520. For *imperative sentence,* see Section **74b.**

60. Impersonal construction.   A method of phrasing in which neither personal pronoun nor a person as noun is stated as the actor. The passive voice is used, or words like *it* or *there.*

I have three reasons for my choice. (Personal)
Three reasons were given for this choice. (Impersonal)

We must consider three proposals. (Personal)
It is necessary to consider three proposals. (Impersonal)
   *or, less wordy,*
Three proposals must be considered.

61. Indefinite pronoun.   See Section **71d7**.
62. Independent clause.   See Section **73a**.
63. Indicative.   See p. 519.
64. Indirect object.   See Section **75e**.
65. Indirect question.   See Section **87c**.
66. Indirect quotation.   See Section **94i**.
67. Infinitive, infinitive phrase, and infinitive "clause."   For *infinitive,* see Section **71f**. An *infinitive phrase* is one introduced by an infinitive: *to study mathematics, to succeed in life.* An *infinitive "clause,"* sometimes so called, is a construction which is part of the predicate and in which a noun or pronoun in the objective case is followed by an infinitive or an infinitive phrase; the noun or pronoun is called its "subject" (Section **75f**) :

Mary invited *me* to attend the concert.
The Dean advised *us to take courses in foreign languages.*

68. Inflection.   A change in the form of a word to show a change in use or meaning. *Comparison* (see Section **83e**) is the inflection of adjectives and adverbs; *declension* (see Item 39, above) is the inflection of nouns and pronouns; and *conjugation* (see Item 30, above) is the inflection of verbs.
69. Intensive pronoun.   See Section **71d6**.
70. Interjection.   See Section **71k**.
71. Interrogative adverb.   An adverb used in asking a question: *where, when, how, why, and,* less commonly, *whence, whither.*

*Where* is University Hall? *When* was it built? *How* large is it?
*Why* is it called University Hall?

72. Interrogative pronoun.   See Sections **71d4** and **75a**.
73. Interrogative sentence.   See Section **74b**.

74. Intransitive verb.   See Section **71g.**
75. Irregular verbs.   See Section **79c.**
76. Linking verb.   See pp. 483–487.
77. Loose sentence.   See Section **74c.**
78. Mode.   See Section **82.**
79. Modify.   See Section **71h.**
80. Mood.   See Section **82.**
81. Nominative.   See Section **75.**
82. Nominative absolute.   See p. 433.
83. Nonfinite verb.   A verb form which cannot serve as predicate, since it shows neither person nor grammatical number. Nonfinite verb forms—the verbals—are gerunds, participles, infinitives (see Section **71f**; see also *Finite verb,* Item 50, above).
84. Nonrestrictive.   See Section **88m-N.**
85. Noun.   See Section **71a,b,c.**
86. Noun clause.   See Section **73b.**
87. Number.   The change in the form of a noun, pronoun, or verb to show whether one (*singular* number) or more than one (*plural* number) is indicated. The formation of the plural of *nouns* is discussed in Section **71c**; the few *pronouns* that have plural forms are listed in Section **75a.**

    Plurals of *verbs* are relatively simple. Main verbs have the same form for singular and plural except in the third person singular, present tense, which ends in *s* (*sees, moves, thinks,* etc.) or occasionally *es* (*goes*).

    Of the verb *to be,* in the present tense, *am* (1st person) and *is* (3rd person) are singular, *are* is 2nd person singular and 1st, 2nd, 3rd person plural; in the past tense, *was* is 1st and 3rd person singular, *were* is 2nd person singular and 1st, 2nd, 3rd person plural.

    Of the verb *to have, has* is the 3rd person singular, present tense form. Of the verb *to do, does* is the 3rd person singular, present tense form.

    Use your dictionary when you are in doubt about the singular or plural form of a noun, pronoun, or verb. (See also the tables on pp. 484–485, 502–503, and 514–515.)
88. Object.   See Section **75d.**
89. Object complement.   See *Complement,* Item 21, above.
90. Objective.   See Sections **75d,e.**

91. Participle and participial phrase.   For *participle,* see Sections 71f, 79. For *participial phrase,* see Section 72.

92. Parts of speech.   The classifications to one of which every word must belong: *noun, pronoun, adjective, verb, adverb, preposition, conjunction, interjection.* See each of these terms in Section 71.

93. Passive voice.   See pp. 512–518.

94. Past participle.   See Section 79.

95. Past perfect tense.   See Section 80a5,b.

96. Past tense.   See Sections 79 and 80a2,b.

97. Perfect infinitive.   See pp. 420 and 508.

98. Perfect participle.   See pp. 419 and 508.

99. Periodic sentence.   See Section 74c.

100. Person.   The change in the form of a pronoun or verb—sometimes, merely a change in use as with verbs—to indicate whether the "person" used is the person speaking (*first person*) the person spoken to (*second person*), or the person or thing spoken about (*third person*) : *I* read, *you* read, *he* reads, *she* reads, *we* read, *you* read, *they* read, *it* plays.

101. Personal pronoun.   See *Person,* above, and also Sections 71d1, 75a.

102. Phrase.   See Section 72.

103. Plural.   A classification of nouns, pronouns, subjects, and predicates, to indicate two or more units or members. See Section 71c. Note that a subject with two or more singulars joined by *and* becomes plural. See Section 76f. Also, see *Number,* Item 87, above.

104. Positive degree.   See Section 83e.

105. Possessive.   See Section 75j,k,l,m.

106. Predicate.   See pp. 436–439.

107. Predicate adjective.   See pp. 483, 487, 525.

108. Predicate complement, also called subjective complement. See Section 75c and pp. 483, 487.

109. Predicate noun or pronoun.   See pp. 453, 483, 487.

110. Preposition, prepositional phrase, and preposition-gerundial phrase.   For *preposition,* see Section 71j. For *prepositional phrase,* see Section 72.

111. Present participle.   See pp. 419, 494, 508.

112. Present perfect tense.   See Section 80a4,b.

113. Present tense.   See Section 80a1,b.

114. Principal parts.  See Section **79.**
115. Progressive verb form.  See pp. 501, 505, 509 and the table on pp. 502–503.
116. Pronoun.  See Section **71d.**
117. Proper noun.  See p. 411 and Section **97d,e.**
118. Pure conjunction.  See p. 530, and Sections **84a, 88d.**
119. Quotation.  Words written or said by someone. For definitions of and differences in punctuation between a direct and an indirect quotation, see Section **94a,b,c,d,i,j.**
120. Reciprocal pronoun.  See Section **71d8.**
121. Reference.  A word used with pronouns and their antecedents to indicate the relationship between them. The pronoun *refers* to or *points* to the antecedent; the antecedent is *indicated* or *referred* to by the pronoun. See Section **77.**
122. Reflexive pronoun.  See Section **75d5.**
123. Regular verbs.  See Section **79a.**
124. Relative pronouns.  See Sections **71d2, 75a.**
125. Restrictive.  See Section **88m-R.**
126. Rhetoric and rhetorical.  Among other meanings, *rhetoric,* as applied to high school and college writing and speaking, is the art or science of using the English language effectively, in prose or verse. *Rhetoric* includes items like literal diction, imaginative diction (such as figures of speech), sentence structures, and rhythms. The purpose of such rhetorical writing and speaking is to please, to persuade, to influence, such purposes coming from the ancient Greek word for "orator" *(rhetor)*. Popular since the days of an ancient Greek, Aristotle (384–322 B.C.), who wrote a book on the subject, the words *rhetoric* (noun) and *rhetorical* (adjective) are at some times used less widely, at other times more widely. We are again in the latter phase. *Rhetoric,* as applied to writing, includes clearness, effectiveness, appropriateness, even correctness, and this *Handbook* has in its various editions, including this one, preferred those specific words as simpler, more familiar, more understandable, more meaningful to today's college student. On the other hand, those who use *rhetoric,* as in *rhetoric* of the word or sentence or paragraph or theme, prefer it as a summarizing word for correct, clear, effective, and appropriate words, sentences, paragraphs, and themes.

127. Sentence.   See pp. 208–210 and Sections **74** and **31**.

128. Sentence fragment.   For discussion of justifiable and un-justifiable sentence fragments, see Section **31a,g**.

129. Sequence of tenses.   When independent and dependent clauses occur in a sentence, the tense or time relationship in these clauses should be clearly stated. Hence, sequence of tenses: the clear order of time in verb forms. For fuller dis-cussion, see Section **80h**.

130. Sign of the infinitive.   The word *to* accompanying the in-finitive form of the verb: *to* go, *to* see, *to* arrive. "I plan *to* go." "I hope *to* arrive next week." In certain expressions, especially with certain auxiliary verbs, the *to* is not used: "He can *go*." "I do *see*."

131. Simple sentence.   See pp. 438–441.

132. Simple verb form.   See pp. 501, 505–509, and the table on pp. 502–503.

133. Singular.   The number classification of nouns, pronouns, subjects, and predicates to indicate *one*: *boy, student, woman, I, he, she, it, is, has, was, goes, writes*. See *Number*, Item 87 above.

134. Strong verbs.   See Section **79c**.

135. Subject.   See pp. 436–440.

136. Subjective complement.   The same as *Predicate comple-ment*. See Section **75c** and p. 487.

137. Subjunctive.   See pp. 520–523.

138. Subordinate clause.   Another name for *Dependent clause*. See Section **73b**.

139. Subordinating conjunction.   See pp. 531–532 and Section **84e**.

140. Substantive.   An inclusive term for noun, pronoun, verbal noun (gerund, infinitive), or a phrase or a clause used like a noun. The practical value of the word *substantive* is that it saves repeating all the words which are included in this definition. The following italicized words are examples of substantives:

My *dog* is three years old.
*They* will arrive tomorrow; in fact, *everyone* is arriving tomorrow.
Your *coming* is looked forward to.
*To improve* myself is my *aim*.

*From Chicago to San Francisco* is a long *distance*.
*What you say* is no *concern* of *mine*.
Do *you* know *that he was here yesterday?*

141. Superlative degree.    See Section **83e,f.**
142. Syntax.    For all practical purposes, not a very useful word, as can be seen from the definition in any reliably standard dictionary. *Syntax* means the way in which words arc arranged and interrelated in sentences or parts of sentences. The words *grammar* and *grammatical* serve all usual purposes.
143. Tense.    See pp. 501–512.
144. Tone.    A word used in this *Handbook* to distinguish a characteristic of tenses of verbs, indicating within any one tense or time limit *emphasis* or *progress* or just plain *simple* time. See pp. 501, 508.
145. Transitive verb.    See Section **71g.**
146. Verb.    See Section **71e,f,g.**
147. Verb phrase.    See pp. 431–432. Distinguish between a *verb phrase* and a *verbal phrase* (participle, gerund, infinitive). See Sections **71f, 72.**
148. Verbals.    See Sections **71f, 80b.**
149. Voice.    See Section **81.**
150. Weak verbs.    See Section **79a.**

# PUNCTUATION AND MECHANICS
## (SECTIONS 86-100)

In his *Rules for Compositors and Readers,* Horace Hart recounts a story of Sheridan, who, called upon to apologize to a fellow Member of Parliament, said, "Mr. Speaker I said the honourable member was a liar it is true and I am sorry for it," and added that the honourable member could put the punctuation marks where he pleased. The story has a moral that every reader, writer, and printer will interpret for himself.

—G. H. VALLINS, *The Pattern of English*

# PUNCTUATION
# AND MECHANICS

**P**UNCTUATION is a system or method by which, through certain marks, the meaning of written or printed communication is made clear.

*Mechanics,* a somewhat vague word, here simply means the conventional or proper use of capitals and small letters, italics (underlining), abbreviations, and numbers in either figures or words.

Proper punctuation, an indispensable aid to correct, clear, effective, appropriate writing, developed originally because without it written language could not indicate certain qualities of speech, in which a pause or a rising inflection, for example, conveys meaning. These and other qualities of speech are reproduced in writing by certain marks of punctuation. Similarly, relationship between parts in a sentence is revealed by word order, but since modern English is not a highly inflected language, word order is flexible. In written English, therefore, various marks of punctuation suggest and indicate grouping, relationship, position, and kind of expression needed to convey meaning clearly.

The United States Government Printing Office *Style Manual* (1967) tells us: "The general principles governing the use of punctuation are (1) that if it does not clarify the text it should be omitted, and (2) that in the choice and placing of punctuation marks the sole aim should be to bring out more clearly the author's thought. Punctuation should aid in reading and prevent misreading."

With only a few words—even one word—punctuation marks change meaning. Note the differences conveyed in the following:

| | | |
|---|---|---|
| See! | What a pity. | I'm not shouting. |
| See? | What a pity! | I'm not shouting! |
| | What? a pity? | I'm not shouting? |

What do you think? I'm giving you four tickets to the concert.

What! Do you think I'm giving you four tickets to the concert?

Henry Browne firmly believes my roommate is the best athlete on our
campus.
Henry Browne, firmly believes my roommate, is the best athlete on our
campus.

Punctuation is thus an organic part of writing; it is neither
mechanical nor arbitrary. Usage does vary with individual writers, but fundamental principles remain the same. These fundamental principles, or descriptive "rules"—call them conventions,
if you wish!—are drawn from thousands of examples of punctuation as applied in writing and printing by authors, printers,
editors, and others whose knowledge and practice are respected.
When enough examples of one use of a certain punctuation
mark occur, we state this use as a general principle or rule, beginning it thus: "Use the . . . ." or *"Always* use the . . . ." When
most of the examples agree: "The mark is *usually* used . . .";
when not enough examples are found to make a generalization:
"The mark is *occasionally used* . . . ." Correct punctuation permits individuality only to the extent that communication of
ideas from writer to reader is aided, not impeded.

The most important marks of punctuation are:

| | | | |
|---|---|---|---|
| . | Period | — | Dash |
| ? | Question mark | - | Hyphen |
| ! | Exclamation point | ' | Apostrophe |
| , | Comma | " " | Double quotation marks |
| ; | Semicolon | ' ' | Single quotation marks |
| : | Colon | ( ) | Parentheses |

Less commonly used marks of punctuation are:

| | | | |
|---|---|---|---|
| [ ] | Brackets | *** | Asterisks |
| . . . | Ellipsis periods | ∧ | Caret |

A few marks used mainly for pronunciation or spelling are
listed in Section **95g,h.**

**THE FOUR PURPOSES OF PUNCTUATION**
Ordinarily you will apply a principle or specific "rule" of punctuation to a specific instance or sentence element. You must determine what you have that needs punctuation (see "Glossary

of Applied Punctuation," Section **100**) and then use the appropriate mark or marks. You may be helped in such application by remembering that punctuation serves *four general purposes*:

⟶ 1. To *end* or *terminate* a statement—use period, question mark, or exclamation point. (See Sections **86a, 87a,b.**)
⟶ 2. To *introduce*—use comma, colon, or dash. (See Sections **88a–c, 90a–c, 91a.**)
⟶ 3. To *separate* parts of a sentence or word—use comma, semicolon, colon, dash, hyphen, or apostrophe. (See Sections **88d–l, 89a–c, 90d,f, 91b–d, 92b,c, 93f.**)
⟶ 4. To *enclose* parts of a sentence or a whole section—use commas, dashes, quotation marks, single quotation marks, parentheses, brackets. *Enclosure marks are used in pairs, except when the capital letter at the beginning of a sentence takes the place of the first or when a terminating mark at the end takes the place of the second.* (See Sections **88m–t, 91e, 94a–h, 95a,b,d.**)

Different marks indicating these four principal purposes of punctuation are, obviously, not necessarily interchangeable. The comma and the dash, for example, can serve three of the purposes, but you must choose the appropriate mark that will best produce clearness and effectiveness.

Also, a progression in the strength of the punctuation marks indicates strength of ideas. For example: Very weak parenthetic material—no commas; weak—commas; strong—dashes; strongest — (possibly) parentheses. Very weak separation—no comma; normal separation—comma; stronger separation—semicolon; strongest (between sentences) —period, question mark, or exclamation point.

A more specific approach to punctuation is a study of each punctuation mark and its uses. Many of the principles make use of grammatical terms; if in doubt about their meaning, study their definitions in Section **85.** If you know what kinds of words, phrases, clauses, or sentences you have but are in doubt about the punctuation marks to use, consult the "Glossary of Applied Punctuation," Section **100.**

# 86  *The period*

The period (.) is usually a mark of termination, although it has a special use after abbreviations and, in series, a special use to indicate separation or omission.

**86a**   *Use a period at the end of a declarative sentence, a mildly imperative sentence (a command or a polite request), and an indirect question* (see Section **87c**)

When autumn comes, birds begin flying south. (Declarative)
Grandfather spends his winter vacations in Florida; Father spends his in Maine. (Declarative)
Drive carefully and avoid accidents. (Imperative)
Write all your business letters on business stationery. (Imperative)
Mr. Johnson asked when I could report for work. (Indirect question)
Tell me what he said. (Indirect question)

**86b**   *Do not punctuate sentence fragments as complete units of thought unless they obviously qualify as complete expressions*

For full discussion of the justifiable and unjustifiable sentence fragment ("period fault"), see Section **31**.

**86c**   *Use a period after a standard abbreviation and after initials*

Mr. and Mrs. James R. Brown live on Maple Street.
Henry H. Smith, M.D. (b. 1900; d. 1950)
Sept. 15; lbs.; n.b.; q.v.; A.M.; P.M.; i.e.; Ave.

(See Section **98c** for exceptions.)

If a declarative sentence ends with an abbreviation, one period only is used. If the sentence is interrogative or exclamatory, a question mark or exclamation point follows the abbreviation period. Inside the sentence, the abbreviation period is followed by any punctuation that would normally have been used.

**86d**   *Use periods properly in an outline*

See Section **6e**4 for instructions and Section **6b–d** for illustrations.

**86e   Use a period before a decimal, to separate dollars and cents, and to precede cents written alone**

4.25 percent        $5.75        $0.52

**86f   Use three spaced periods to indicate an intentional omission from a sentence or quotation**

Such periods, called ellipsis periods or suspension periods, are especially helpful when only part of a sentence or line of poetry is quoted. Thus:

. . . a man's reach should exceed his grasp,
Or what's a heaven for?
                —BROWNING, "Andrea del Sarto"

In the spring a young man's fancy . . .
            —TENNYSON, "Locksley Hall" ·

When ellipsis periods follow a complete sentence, the end-of-sentence period is also used.

The game was filled with dramatic moments. . . . No one will ever forget the long, spine-tingling, game-winning shot in the last second, just as the gun fired.

1. A question mark or exclamation point may follow ellipsis periods.
2. Do not use ellipsis periods as a substitute for the dash. See Section **91f**.
3. Do not use ellipsis periods purely as a stylistic device. Students occasionally use them to indicate that much more could be said. Generally, they have nothing in mind worth saying.
4. Asterisks (***), three in number, serve the same purpose as ellipsis periods, but they are used principally to indicate omissions of whole paragraphs or long passages.

**86g   Use no period at the end of a title or after a centered or side subhead in the body of a manuscript**

**86h   Use no period after a quotation mark that is preceded by a period**

*Wrong*        He said, "Stop at the next corner.".
*Right*        He said, "Stop at the next corner."

# 87 *The exclamation point and question mark*

The exclamation point (!) and the question mark (?), like the period, are usually marks of termination. (For typing the exclamation point, see Section 1c6.)

### 87a *Use the exclamation point to terminate a forceful interjection or to express surprise, emphasis, strong emotion, or command (i.e., a vigorously imperative sentence)*

Such statements may be single words or phrases or dependent clauses or sentences:

On guard!
Ouch! That hurt!
Oh, what a remark to make!
Help! Help! Fire!
What wonderful news!
Come at once!
Here's to Smithson, the College Man of the Year!

An exclamation point may also be used, but *not* overused, after phrases or sentences to express irony or humor. The internal exclamation mark for this purpose is put in parentheses.

You're a fine friend!
She said that she might possibly condescend (!) to write.

Do not overuse the exclamation point. The emotion must be strong, the surprise genuine, the command emphatic to call for this punctuation. Too frequent use of the exclamation point weakens its effectiveness. After mild interjections, use a comma (see *oh* in third example, above) and after mild exclamations and commands, use a period.

Be on time, please.

### 87b *Use a question mark at the end of every direct question*

For various ways of asking questions in English, i.e., of stating ideas in interrogative sentences, see Section **74b**.

Do you really know?
You really do know?
Why are you so eager to go?
Where is the Administration Building?
Which student left his dictionary in the classroom?
You're going home next week, aren't you?

NOTE 1: When a sentence asking a question ends with a direct quotation also asking a question, only one question mark is used—the one within the quotation. If the direct quotation is an exclamation, the question mark is omitted.

Who said, "What is Man?"
Was it the sergeant who shouted, "All lights out!"

NOTE 2: Some writers prefer to use a period instead of a question mark at the end of a polite request expressed as a question:

Will you please sign and return the enclosed card to the Registrar.

### 87c   Do not use a question mark after an indirect question

An indirect question is a question repeated in different words by the same speaker or by another person. The usual mark is a period (Section **86a**).

| | |
|---|---|
| *Wrong* | I asked whether I had heard the announcement correctly? |
| *Right* | I asked whether I had heard the announcement correctly. |
| *Wrong* | John wondered when we would be ready to go? |
| *Right* | John wondered when we would be ready to go. |

### 87d   Use question marks to indicate a series of queries in the same sentence

Will you be there? or your brother? or your parents?
Who will be there from your house? You? Your brother? Your parents?
*also*   Will you be there—or your brother—or your parents?
    Will you be there, or your brother, or your parents?

Notice (1) the different possibilities of capitalization and (2) the use of question marks within a sentence. Also, when a question is asked within a sentence—is it a rare occurrence?—dashes or commas are used, as in any noninterrogative statements like apposition or series:

The following publications are available: *What Should Our Schools Accomplish?, How Can We Organize Better Schools?,* and *How Can Citizens Help Their Schools?*
A good news story should answer the following: *who?, what?, when?, where?, how?,* and *why?*

Note further that, as in the sentences above, a period is not used with a terminating interrogative statement.

**87e    Use a question mark, enclosed in parentheses, to express doubt, uncertainty, or lack of available information**

Atwater College has a basketball player said to be 8 (?) feet tall.
The University of Socomber was founded in 1370 (?) .
Shakespeare was born on April 23 (?) , 1564.

Do not overuse the question mark for doubt or uncertainty. If you cannot find the exact information, use the question mark, but do not use it as an excuse for not *trying* to find such information.

**87f    Do not use a question mark in parentheses to indicate an ironical or humorous meaning**

*Undesirable*    The ambitious candidate boasted in a modest (?) way and never raised his voice above a gentle (?) roar.

## EXERCISES   (SECTIONS 86, 87)

A. Circle all the periods, question marks, and exclamation points on a page in your book of readings or in a current magazine. Account for the use of each mark by careful reference to one of the principles cited in Sections 86, 87.

B. Use the period, exclamation point, and question mark correctly in the following sentences, or if any of these marks are misused, make the necessary corrections.

1. Two planes leave for Rome every day, one at 9:15 A M and one at 7:35 P M

2. By now you have learned the value of a good dictionary, haven't you.
3. I thought I would not get homesick. How wrong I was.
4. Dr Smith is the best dentist in town; we and our neighbors, Mr and Mrs Thompson, have gone to him for years.
5. It is amazing how many good intentions—or should I say resolutions—I have.
6. There in the hallway was my brother, home from overseas. What a pleasant surprise.
7. They are wondering why they are not making more money, or why they did not get an advancement?
8. What is an education good for if you do not have friends.
9. Oh. Oh. Have I forgotten to proofread again.
10. One may ask why something happened to him after a black cat crossed his path?

# 88   *The comma*

The comma (,) serves the purpose of introducing, separating, or, with another comma, enclosing. Because it has varied and distinct uses and is the most frequently seen mark of punctuation, it is the most troublesome of all the punctuation marks; also, in many situations a choice is offered of use or nonuse. Always used within the sentence, the comma differs from terminal marks (period, question mark, exclamation point) in degree. It shows a brief pause, less separation than a full stop.

Note also that the comma, the semicolon, and the period form a series having relatively increasing strength. The *comma* is the weakest mark of the three, for it separates short groups within the sentence and indicates comparatively close connection. The *semicolon* is used between longer and more important groups within the sentence, or between those which have a comparatively less close relation in thought. The *period* is the strongest mark of the three: it points out the most important division of thought, the sentence; it also indicates separation of thought into independent units.

Obviously, the following "rules" for comma use are *for reference only*. Some of the more common uses every student should know, but no student is expected to rise and recite any rule on demand.

NOTE: Mastery of the comma depends on the individual. Some instructors in reading themes prefer to give students a specific reference discussing and illustrating comma use, the plan followed in this *Handbook*. Other instructors find satisfactory the assigning and use of six broad principles dealing with commas. These are as follows (with some parenthetic references to more detailed sections) :

⟶ 88/1  *Use a comma to separate long independent clauses of compound sentences* (Section **88d**)

⟶ 88/2  *Use a comma to set off long introductory subordinate elements, usually adverbial or participial* (Section **88f,g**)

⟶ 88/3  *Use commas to set off parenthetical word groups, including nonrestrictive elements, whether words, phrases, or clauses* (Section **88m,n,o,p,q,r,s,t**)

⟶ 88/4  *Use commas to divide elements in series* (Section **88h,i,j**)

⟶ 88/5  *Use commas in the conventional uses of setting off or enclosing dates, initials, numbers, letter salutations, etc.* (Section **88b,c,q,r,s,t**)

⟶ 88/6  *Use commas for clearness, that is, to prevent misreading* (Section **88k**)

## COMMAS TO INTRODUCE

*88a  Use a comma to introduce a word, a phrase, or, occasionally, a clause*

My aim in this course is easily stated, a high grade.
Only one other possibility remains, to travel by air.

I had an important decision to make, whether I should drop out of
school or borrow the money and continue.

The principle of the introducing comma applies also to
asking a mental question or expressing a thought or musing
aloud:

I wondered, should I tell Father the whole story?
I thought, you're in real trouble now.
Our next problem is, where do we go from here?

For a comparison of the introducing comma, as a less emphatic mark, with the colon and dash, see also Sections **90a,
91a.**

**88b**   *Use a comma to introduce, or separate, a short
quotation, especially in writing dialogue*

Henry said, "I'll never do that again."

1. If the "he said" or its equivalent follows, the quotation,
it is separated from it by a comma, provided a question mark or
exclamation point is not demanded.

"I'll never do that again," said Henry.

2. If the "he said" or its equivalent is inserted between the
parts of a quotation, it is enclosed by commas—provided one part
is dependent  (otherwise, see Section **94a**) :

"I'll never do that again," said Henry, "unless I lose my temper."

3. When the quotation being introduced is long or formal,
the colon replaces the comma (see Section **90d**) .
4. Make a careful distinction between quotations which are
really quotations of speaking or writing and quoted material
which is the subject or object of a verb or material stressed by
quotation marks such as titles, slang, and special word use. As
examples of such special uses, observe the following:

The usual remark is "May the better man win."

"Make haste slowly" is the motto that came to my mind.

If the "he said" comes between parts of a quotation, it is enclosed by commas.

"Itty-bitty" is not the exact phrase to use for "very small."

**88c** *Use a comma after the salutation to introduce a friendly letter* (see Section **90e**, also) *and after the complimentary close to introduce the signature of a friendly or business letter*

Dear John,    Dear Mary,    Dear Father,    Dear Mr. Nicholson,
Sincerely yours,    Cordially,    Very truly yours,

## COMMAS TO SEPARATE

**88d** *Use a comma to separate independent clauses joined by one of the pure or simple coordinating conjunctions:* **and, but, nor, or, neither, yet**

To this list, *for* (see Section **88e** for discussion of *for*) and *so* are sometimes added. *So* is a short word and as conjunction its meaning is *therefore* or *thus*; it assuredly coordinates, but the chief objection to it is its constant overuse (see Section **36c**).

I have not seen John recently, nor has anyone else seen him.

Commas are important marks of punctuation, and you will do well to master their use.

I tried to show him the error of his argument, but he would not be convinced.

"Consider the lilies of the field, how they grow; they toil not, neither do they spin."—Matthew vi:28

The dean had no specific objections, yet he would not approve our proposal.

The principle stated in Section **88d** is one of the most frequently used and illustrated in English writing. This frequency accounts for considerable flexibility in application, as follows:

1. If the independent clauses are short, the comma may be omitted before the pure conjunction, provided no misreading results (see Section **88k**). How short is short? If the independent

clauses consist of only subject and predicate, or of three or four words each, then they are obviously short and the comma may be omitted, except perhaps before *neither* and *yet*. Examples:

The rains came and the rivers rose.
I made a motion but no one heard me.
In the final judging, Mary did not win nor did Jane.
We ate bacon and the Joneses ate eggs. (Misleading)
We ate bacon, and the Joneses ate eggs. (Clear)

2. Fairly long clauses are sometimes written without a comma between them if their connection is particularly close. The comma, for example, is frequently omitted before the pure conjunction when the subjects of both clauses are the same (same noun or noun and pronoun) .

I read for an hour or two and then I studied.
Henry read the assignment over hurriedly and then he began a more careful rereading of it.

When the subject of the second clause is omitted, the sentence has merely a compound predicate and does not contain a comma before the conjunction, unless the members are unusually long. Use of a compound sentence or a simple sentence with a compound predicate depends on a writer's view of which is more effective for a particular purpose.

Bill came into the house and called excitedly to his mother.
The last person spoke clearly and made a favorable impression on the audience.

3. Use commas between short clauses to which you wish to give special emphasis.

You must pay promptly, or you will be penalized.
I did not expect to win, but I did.

NOTE: For punctuation of long independent clauses separated by a pure conjunction, see Section **89c**.

## 88e   Use a comma before the conjunction for

The word *for* is used either as a conjunction or as a preposition. A comma before it is a fairly sure sign that the word is a conjunction, no comma that it is a preposition. Of course, a prepositional phrase beginning with *for* and used parenthetically is enclosed by commas.

| | |
|---|---|
| *Conjunction* | I went home early last evening, *for* my parents did not wish to be alone. |
| | We cannot pay a bill as large as this, *for* we do not have the money in our treasury. |
| *Preposition* | I went home early last evening *for the purpose* of getting a good night's sleep. |
| | My high school, *for that matter,* has always had excellent teachers in English and mathematics. |
| | One convincing argument, *for example,* concerns our pocketbook. |

Because of its smallness, *for* is frequently listed with the other pure coordinating conjunctions (Section **88d**), even though its meaning is *because, as, since.* If you apply Section **88e,** the grammatical classification of *for* is of little importance.

## 88f   Use a comma to separate an introductory adverbial clause from the independent clause

When you have finished the examination, sign your name and turn in your paper.
Before John started on his trip, he made a careful plan of his itinerary.
If I arrive first, I'll wait for you in the library.

This principle applies only to adverbial clauses. An introductory noun clause is not set off by a comma; an adjective clause follows, not precedes, the noun or pronoun that it modifies.

What you say is true.
That your theme was turned in late is unfortunate.

Many introductory adverbial clauses are simply transposed elements. Inserted in their natural order, they may or may not have commas, depending upon meaning. Inserted elsewhere, they are enclosed by commas.

After you arrive on the campus, various meetings will be held to help orient you.

Various meetings, after you arrive on the campus, will be held to help orient you.

Various meetings will be held to help orient you after you arrive on the campus.

When the adverbial clause follows the independent clause:
1. Omit the comma if the adverbial clause is necessary to complete (i.e., if it restricts) the meaning of the sentence.

The accident occurred as I turned into Tenth Street.
John works because he has no other way to live.

2. Use a comma if the clauses are fairly long, or if a slight pause is desired; omit it if the clauses are short.

I'm quite willing to be a delegate to the convention, although there are others more capable than I.
I'll go, if I have to go.
I'll go if I have to go.

### 88g   Use a comma to set off an introductory modifying phrase containing a verb form

Not universally applied, this principle is so commonly illustrated that it is still recommended for the student-writer. The introductory phrase may be participial or prepositional, adjective or adverb. If an adjective phrase, it is very likely nonrestrictive (see Section **88m-R**) .

Half-concealed in the bushes, the dog watched us go by.
In order to play chess well, you must be mentally alert.
By studying slowly and carefully, John mastered the subject.
Because of his hidden fear of water, he refused to go swimming.

1. Neither an introductory gerund phrase nor an introductory infinitive phrase used as subject is a modifying phrase; therefore, neither one is set off by a comma unless for other

reasons. Frequently even a short modifying infinitive phrase is not set off.

Playing on a championship basketball team is a thrilling experience. (Gerund phrase as subject)

Playing on a championship basketball team, according to my roommate, is a thrilling experience. (Gerund phrase as subject, followed by parenthetic element)

To be a successful fisherman is not easy. (Infinitive phrase as subject)

To be a successful fisherman I use only the best equipment. (Introductory modifying infinitive phrase)

2. An introductory modifying phrase without a verb form, unless it is fairly long or fairly strongly parenthetic (see Section **88n**), is usually not set off by a comma.

Without fail I'll be there.

Because of lack of money some students have to drop out of school.

After careful consideration of the matter for a week or 10 days, we decided that the trip was too long to justify the expense.

NOTE: Many phrases containing verb forms do not come at the beginning of sentences, and usually they may be considered as some kind of parenthetic element, such as absolute phrases (Section **88p**) or nonrestrictive phrases (Section **88m-N**).

## 88h Use commas to separate words, phrases, or clauses in a series

1. One kind of series is represented by A, B, and C—three or more words, phrases, or clauses, with an appropriate pure conjunction joining the last two members.

I have brought my textbook, my notebook, and some theme paper with me.

You will find Tom around somewhere: in the living room, in the basement, or out in the garden.

He whispered, he muttered, but finally he shouted.

Some writers omit the comma before the conjunction: A, B and C. Since the use of this comma before the conjunction frequently results in greater clearness, however, present practice favors it (it is recommended, among others, by the United States Government Printing Office *Style Manual,* the University of Chicago's *A Manual of Style,* and the Modern Language Association *Style Sheet*) .

2. Another kind of series is represented by A, B, C—three or more words, phrases, or clauses, with no conjunctions. Commas are used after each member except *after* the last, unless the clauses are all independent (see Sections **89a, 32a**) .

This store sells newspapers, magazines, books on Sundays.
Joe believes in good sportsmanship on the football field, on the basketball court, in the swimming pool, on the golf course.

3. When a conjunction is used to join each pair, do not use commas separating members of a series, unless emphasis is desired.

I have read nothing by Swift or Milton or Wordsworth.
Billy says he is going to have ice cream and cake and pie and chocolate pudding for his dessert.
At times I have no energy, or enthusiasm, or skill. (Emphasis)

**88i**   *Use a comma to separate two or more adjectives when they modify, equally and coordinately, the same noun*

I bought an old, dilapidated chair and a new, ugly, badly faded rug.
Our Administration Building is surmounted by a tall, stately, ivy-covered tower.

When the adjectives are not coordinate, commas are omitted:

A thin steel cable is attached to the moss-covered old oaken bucket.
Even smaller European cities have especially beautiful public gardens.
To me Colonel Smith is the supreme example of a fine old Southern gentleman.
Mary always wore a broad pale green ribbon around her long golden hair.

Notice that a comma is never used to separate the last adjective from the noun.
Sometimes there may be doubt, as in "an old, dilapidated chair" above; then you must use your judgment in deciding, for,

admittedly, it is sometimes difficult to determine whether the adjectives are coordinate or not. Several tests, although not infallible, may help. One way of testing is to insert the coordinate conjunction *and* between the adjectives; if the *and* fits naturally, use a comma when it is omitted, otherwise not. Another test: if the position of the adjectives can be reversed, the adjectives are coordinate. Another test: does the first adjective modify the combined idea of the second adjective and the noun? If so, the adjectives are not coordinate. Also, if one of the adjectives describes shape or material or color, the adjectives are probably not coordinate.

### 88j Use a comma to separate contrasted coordinate elements

1. Such contrasted elements may be words or phrases:

Psychology begins with a *p*, not an *s*.
Your misspelling is due to carelessness, not to ignorance.
This garden spray is effective, yet safe.

2. Two clauses may contrast, especially when the two contain comparative adjectives or adverbs, or when the first is an independent declarative statement and the second an independent interrogative statement, a common way of asking a question (see Section **32b2**).

The higher we climbed, the more rarefied the atmosphere became.
The more tired the team became, the better it played.
The less haste some people make, the more progress they achieve.
You did telephone, didn't you?
We should have longer vacations at Thanksgiving, shouldn't we?
You believe I was justified, don't you?

### 88k Use a comma to separate words or other sentence elements that might be misread

*Misleading*   The day after a salesman called with the same product.
Outside the house needs a coat of paint; inside the walls need replastering.
Instead of a hundred thousands came.
In 1967 842 freshmen appeared on our campus.
Last week John was in bed with a cold and his older sister took care of him.

*Improved*        The day after, a salesman called with the same product.
                  Outside, the house needs a coat of paint; inside, the
                  walls need replastering.
                  Instead of a hundred, thousands came.
                  In 1967, 842 freshmen appeared on our campus.
                  Last week John was in bed with a cold, and his older
                  sister took care of him.

Constructions in which commas are needed to prevent misreading are usually questionable or faulty. If possible, rephrase such sentences to eliminate awkwardness and to increase clearness.

Instead of the hundred people expected, thousands came.
Last week, when John was in bed with a cold, his older sister took
   care of him.

**88I**  *Use the comma to separate thousands, millions,*
         *etc. (i.e., in numbers of four or more digits*
         *except numbers indicating years, telephone*
         *numbers, house numbers, and zip codes)*

In the fall of 1968 our freshman class numbered exactly 1,968 students.
In this contest 5,612 entries have been received.
If you telephone 534-1452, you will learn that the population of our
   city is now 312,456.
The government deficit may reach $5,565,000,000 this year.
The Blacks have moved to 8634 Avondale Avenue, Des Moines, Iowa
   50319. (NOTE: no comma before zip code)

NOTE: The comma is often omitted in *four*-digit numbers that do not belong to one of the exceptions listed ("1968 students," "5612 entries"). It is always used in numbers (not among the exceptions) from 10,000 up.

## COMMAS TO ENCLOSE

Commas are used in pairs—except at the beginning or end of a sentence—to enclose the following: nonrestrictive clauses and phrases, other parenthetical words, phrases, and clauses; other inserted sentence elements; absolute phrases; words or phrases in apposition; nouns or pronouns in direct address; places, dates, initials, degrees, or titles. For these elements, at the beginning of a sentence the capital replaces the first comma; at the end a terminating mark replaces the second comma.

**88m-N**    *Use commas to enclose* nonrestrictive
             *clauses and phrases*

**88m-R**    *Do not use commas to enclose*
             restrictive *clauses and phrases*

Clauses and phrases—usually adjectival, sometimes adverbial—are *nonrestrictive* when (1) they do *not* limit or restrict the word or words modified; (2) they *describe* (one meaning of an adjective) or add further information; (3) they could be omitted without affecting the clearness of the sentence; (4) they modify proper nouns or common nouns already limited by other modifiers.

Clauses and phrases—usually adjectival, sometimes adverbial—are *restrictive* when (1) they limit (another meaning of an adjective) or identify the word or words modified; (2) they could not be omitted without changing the meaning of the sentence or confusing it or making it nonsense; (3) they answer the questions *who?* or *which one?* about the word or words modified.

Proper identification of adjective phrases and clauses is necessary in order to punctuate them clearly according to **88m-N** and **88m-R,** above. Observe what the clauses, sometimes using identical wording, do in the following:

Indianapolis, *which is the capital of Indiana,* has a population of 492,000. (Nonrestrictive or nonlimiting clause; *Indianapolis,* as proper noun, is already identified)

The city *which is the capital of Indiana* has a population of 492,000. (Restrictive or limiting clause; *city* needs identification)

Chapter 10, *which tells of the rescue,* is especially well written. (Nonrestrictive or nonlimiting clause)

The chapter *which tells of the rescue* is especially well written. (Restrictive or limiting clause; omit it, and the sentence is not clear)

Students who are noisy and talkative should not be allowed in the Library. (Restrictive or limiting clause; omit it, and the statement is nonsense)

Further assistance in identifying restrictive and nonrestrictive statements:

*1. Clauses.* The relative pronouns, *who, whom, which, where, when,* may introduce either restrictive or nonrestrictive clauses (look at the noun modified). If these pronouns are omitted, i.e., understood, or if the relative pronoun used is *that,* the clause is restrictive. The test for adverbial clauses: if needed for clear meaning, they are restrictive (see Section **88f1**).

Arthur Johnson, *whom my brother met in Chicago,* has traveled widely. (Nonrestrictive or nonlimiting clause)

The man *my brother met in Chicago* has traveled widely. (Restrictive or limiting clause)

The car *that won the race* was Italian-built. (Restrictive or limiting clause)

*2. Phrases.* When an adjective phrase, not a series of adjectives, precedes its modifier, it is usually nonrestrictive; when it immediately follows, it may be restrictive or nonrestrictive (look at the noun modified) ; when it follows a few words farther on, with no sacrifice of clearness, it is usually nonrestrictive.

*Living very simply and economically,* Father and Mother have saved enough money to put me through college. (Nonrestrictive)

The book *lying there on my study desk* has had hard use. (Restrictive)

*Encyclopaedia Britannica,* Volume II, *lying there on my study desk,* has had hard use. (Nonrestrictive)

Some high school seniors think only of college entrance, *fully realizing that the next four years will be important for them.* (Nonrestrictive)

NOTE 1: Context sometimes determines whether a clause or phrase is restrictive or nonrestrictive. If the word or words are already identified by a phrase or clause, an additional modifier is likely to be nonrestrictive.

The man *who services our lawn mower every spring* is a genius. (Restrictive)

In Lewisville we found a little shop full of all kinds of mechanical gadgets and kept by a short, stout, middle-aged man. We have no doubt that the man, *who services our lawn mower every spring,* is a genius. (Nonrestrictive)

The man *sitting in front of me on the plane* was going to Los Angeles. (Restrictive)
The man in the Scotch tweed suit and wearing a brown straw hat, *sitting in front of me on the plane,* was going to Los Angeles. (Nonrestrictive)

NOTE 2: Two or more proper names with the same spelling may need identification; if so, their modifiers are nonrestrictive clauses or phrases.

The John Jones *who is our postman* is not the John Jones *who lives on University Avenue.* (Restrictive)
The Springfield *which is in Illinois* is a long way from the Springfield *which is in Massachusetts.* (Restrictive)

Occasionally, proper names in apposition are restrictive and, unlike other appositional phrases, are not set off by commas. See Section **88ql**.

NOTE 3. Avoid the error of double restrictions:

This is *my* new overcoat *that I bought last week.* (Both italicized elements are restrictive; one only should restrict.)
This is the new overcoat *that I bought last week.* (or:)
This is *my* new overcoat, which I bought last week. (*My* restricts; the clause is now nonrestrictive.)

### 88n   Use commas to enclose parenthetical words, phrases, or clauses

A fairly adequate test of a parenthetical expression is this: it may be omitted without materially affecting the meaning of the sentence or, frequently, though not always, its position in the sentence may be shifted without any change in meaning. Such parenthetical expressions often serve the purpose of transition (see Section **11a**).

*However,* we do not disagree too much.
We do not, *however,* disagree too much.
We do not disagree too much, *however.*
We must, *on the other hand,* discuss every aspect of the problem.
I should like, *if you will allow me,* to offer a substitute plan.

Parenthetic elements vary in intensity, and you show by punctuation their relative strength.

1. Many words and phrases are so weak that they require no punctuation.

I *also* believe in progress.
*In fact* I am inclined to agree.

2. Other words, like *oh, well, yes, no, too, namely, that is, etc., i.e., e.g.,* when used parenthetically, are enclosed by commas.

*Oh,* what a game!
*Oh, yes,* I agree completely.
*Well,* that was the remark that closed the discussion.
Then, *too,* other problems need consideration.
Am I going? *No,* I believe not.
Dictionaries, paper, pencils, pens, erasers, *etc.,* are used in the Writing Laboratory.

The letter combinations *i.e.* (Latin, *id est,* "that is") and *e.g.* (Latin, *exempli gratia,* "for example") are parenthetical elements always followed by a comma and preceded by a comma or a semicolon (see Section **89a**) .

Please report to Room 217, *i.e.,* the Writing Laboratory.
Your work has been satisfactory; *i.e.,* it has been accurate and it has been turned in promptly.
Certain universities, *e.g.,* the University of Illinois, Southern Illinois University, and Northern Illinois University, are primarily state-supported.

3. Some phrases and dependent clauses have enough parenthetic strength to require commas.

Consider, *for example,* the benefits of extracurricular activities.
Those activities, *as I said,* may require considerable time.

NOTE: Some short prepositional phrases are usually considered parenthetic and are set off by a comma at beginning or end, or enclosed by commas in the middle of the sentence. Such phrases include *for example, for instance, as a matter of fact, on the other hand, in the next place,* etc.

4. Independent clauses—as well as some phrases and dependent clauses used emphatically—are so strong, parenthetically, that the enclosure marks should be dashes or parentheses. (See Sections **91e, 95a.**)

There is no reason—*no good reason, that is*—for spending so much money now.

The lovely little town of Kickapoo Falls—*I was born there, you know*—hasn't changed much since I was a boy.

My father has been a physician (*he received his training at the University of Louisville*) in Kickapoo Falls for 30 years.

## 880 *Use commas to enclose inserted sentence elements*

Inserted sentence elements—emphatic, suspending, or transposed expressions—are somewhat similar to parenthetical words, phrases, and clauses. *Emphatic* expressions are set off because the writer thus indicates that he wants to stress them. *Suspending* expressions interrupt or retard the movement of the sentence, holding important information until near the end of the sentence. *Transposed* expressions, like *I believe, I think, it seems to me, I suppose, you see,* and, frequently, adjectives following their nouns, are out of their normal order and require punctuation not used in normal word order. Such inserted expressions are frequently more essential to the thought of the sentence than purely parenthetical material, but they are nonrestrictive or informative in function.

| | |
|---|---|
| *Emphatic insertion* | The speaker did make that statement, *as you will see if you read more carefully,* and I am certain that he meant exactly what he said. |
| *Suspending* | The play was especially good, *not only because it was convincingly acted,* but also because it was well plotted, with a double-surprise ending. |
| | Another secret for successful study, *and not many students know this,* is the preparation and use of a study schedule. |

| | |
|---|---|
| *Transposed* | Action, *I believe,* should be postponed. |
| | A conflict in dates, *it seems,* will cause a change in plans. |
| | A maple tree, *tall and well shaped,* stood in front of the house. |
| *Not transposed* | *I believe* (that) action should be postponed. |
| | *It seems* (that) a conflict in dates will cause a change in plans. |
| | A *tall and well-shaped* maple tree stood in front of the house. |

## 88p   Use commas to enclose absolute phrases

For definition and illustration of the *absolute phrase,* see p. 433. Note in the following that the phrase can come at the beginning, within the sentence, or at the end.

*The game (being) over,* the crowd soon scattered.
*The task having been finished,* we started on our return trip.
I went to the first desk, *my application (held) in hand,* and asked for Mr. Hall.
We needed a fourth member for our bridge club, *Mary Ellen having moved to another town.*

An absolute phrase should not be punctuated as a sentence (see Section *31c*).

## 88q   Use commas to enclose words in apposition

A word in apposition is a noun or pronoun (word or phrase) identifying in different words a preceding noun or pronoun. (See Section **85.**) Usually the appositional word or phrase is explanatory and therefore nonrestrictive (Section **88m-N**).

My father, *a physician,* has just retired from active practice.
This is Mr. Simpson, *our newly elected president.*
My task, *to compose a short story,* seemed hopeless.

1. Sometimes the appositional word or phrase limits or restricts (Section **88m-R**). Omit the commas when the appositive is restrictive or part of a proper name or closely related to the preceding word. The appositional word that restricts is usually a proper noun after a more general one. Also, a fairly safe con-

vention is to omit commas if apposition consists of one word only.

The poet Keats wrote distinctive sonnets.
We have recently seen an excellent performance of the play *Julius Caesar.*
Richard the Lion-Hearted was a famous English king.
My brother James is a senior in high school.

2. Omit the commas, usually, when the appositive is a noun clause.

The fact that I was ill caused my absence.

3. Frequently, words in apposition are introduced by *namely, for example, for instance, i.e., e.g.,* etc. These words and phrases are enclosed by commas, as parenthetical expressions. If these and the apposition are fairly strong—that is, long and emphatic—dashes should enclose them. (See Section **91e1.**)

Two of the candidates, *namely,* John Smith and William Arnold, are my friends.
Any difficult subject, *for example,* chemistry, needs careful study.
The various seasonal sports—*for example,* football in the fall, basketball in the winter, and baseball in the summer—attract millions of spectators.

4. When *such as* introduces an appositive word or phrase, it is preceded by a comma and has no punctuation following—*never* a comma or colon.

*Wrong*  Some of our cities, *such as,* New York, Chicago, and San Francisco, are thriving centers of commerce.
Some of our cities, *such as:* New York, Chicago, and San Francisco, are thriving centers of commerce.
*Right*  Some of our cities, *such as* New York, Chicago, and San Francisco, are thriving centers of commerce.

#### 88r Use commas to enclose nouns or pronouns or a noun phrase in direct address (*vocatives*)

*Mr. Brown,* will you speak next?
I am proud, *Father,* of what you have accomplished.

We are assembled, *ladies and gentlemen,* to discuss an important problem.

Will you please, *sir,* speak more distinctly?

Your class will not meet today, *George.*

**88s   Use commas to enclose places and dates explaining
preceding places and dates within a sentence**

Henry left on June 20, *1968,* to go to Cincinnati, *Ohio,* for an interview. (But note: Henry left on June 20th to go to . . .)

He told us to forward his mail to him at 5107 Madison Road, Cincinnati, Ohio 45202. (NOTE:  no comma precedes the zip code)

1. The second comma must be used when the state follows town or city and when the year follows both month and day. When only month and year are used, the use of commas around the year is optional: use two or do not use any.

In October, *1968,* he was transferred to Albany, *N.Y.*
   *or*
In October *1968* he was transferred to Albany, *N.Y.*

2. Note the choice of punctuation in the date line of a letter:

February 23, 1968
14 June 1968

**88t   Use commas to enclose initials, degrees,
titles, and the abbreviations of senior
and junior following a person's name**

Abbett, H. M., Abner, T. W., and Adams, R. B., head the list of names.

James Norman, M.D., and C. B. Hale, D.D., are the featured speakers on the program.

The son of William McAdams, Sr., is listed as William McAdams, Jr., on our records.

## UNNECESSARY COMMAS

**88u   Use no unnecessary commas; i.e., use commas
only where needed and justifiable**

Notice overuse of commas in the following: 19 words with 17 commas.

Moreover, Jones, who, as, indeed, you, probably, know, is, of course, Welsh, is, perhaps, coming, too, but, unfortunately, alone. (Source unknown)

Modern punctuation usage omits many commas that were formerly used; therefore, be able to account for each comma in your writing. In general, avoid using the comma needlessly to separate closely related sentence elements. Some of the more common misuses or overuses of the comma are discussed in the following series of "do not use" statements.

1. Do not use a comma to separate a subject from its predicate, a verb from its object or complement, or a preposition from its object. Noun phrases and clauses also act as subjects, objects, or complements of verbs and should not be separated by commas without logical reason.

*Wrong*    What you say, is true. (Noun clause as subject)
To do satisfactory work, is my aim. (Infinitive phrase as subject)
We asked, to hear the motion reread. (Infinitive phrase as object)
The reason is, that I have been ill. (Noun clause as predicate nominative)
I found, that college was not so hard after all. (Noun clause as object)
The coach believes, that the team will play a good game. (Noun clause as object)
No one should plan a long trip without, extensive and careful preparation. (Preposition and object separated)

2. Do not use a comma before the indirect part of a quotation. Frequently, the indirect quotation is a noun clause used as the object of the verb.

*Wrong*    The letter informed me, that I should report for an interview.
John told me emphatically, to come as early as I could.
The speaker asserted, that he stood squarely for progress.

3. Do not use a comma to set off quoted words which are not direct quotations but which use quotation marks to call attention to the words. For examples, see Section 88b4.

4. Do not use a comma indiscriminately to replace an omitted word. For examples, see Section **31e.**

5. Do not use a comma, ordinarily, to separate two words or two phrases joined by a pure coordinating conjunction or correlative conjunctions. (For contrasting elements, see Section **88j**; for independent clauses, see Section **88d.**)

*Wrong*    He has dignity, and integrity.
            The leader has strength of body, and firmness of purpose.

6. Do not use a comma indiscriminately after a pure or simple conjunction. But the use of other parenthetical or inserted elements may justify a comma after the conjunction.

*Wrong*    But, I shall never make that mistake again.
            We are leaving early, and, I shall expect to receive your
                check before I go.
*Right*      But, as a lesson learned from experience, I shall never make
            that mistake again.
            We are leaving early, and, to save trouble all around, I shall
                expect to receive your check before I go.

7. Do not use a comma before the first or after the last member of a series.

*Wrong*    Avoid a mixture of, red, yellow, green, blue, and brown
            paints.
            We went swimming in a cool, clear, smooth-flowing, river.

8. Do not use a comma to separate a *so . . . that* clause in a sentence.

*Wrong*    The game was so hard fought, that our players were com-
            pletely exhausted.
            I was so cold, that I thought I would never get warm again.

9. *Never* use a comma at the beginning of a line. It may be logical to place it before the word set off, separated, or enclosed, but American printing practice is that the comma is *always* placed at the end of the preceding line.

10. Do not use a comma after a dash or before the first of a pair of parentheses (see Section **95e**). For rare uses of commas after question marks, and, similarly, exclamation points, see Section **87d**.

11. Do not overuse commas; sometimes they come at reasonable places in the sentence, but not one may be necessary. (See Section **88n**.)

| | |
|---|---|
| *Unneeded commas* | After the game, my brother and I went home, by the long route, because we wanted, at all costs, to avoid the highway traffic. |
| *Omitted commas* | After the game my brother and I went home by the long route because we wanted at all costs to avoid the highway traffic. |

### 88v   *Avoid the comma splice*

For definition and discussion of this error and methods of correcting it, see Section **32**.

### EXERCISES

A. Choose a page from your book of readings or from a current magazine. Underline or circle every comma. Give a reason for each comma, or each pair of commas, according to the principles stated in Section **88**. Do not be surprised if a few of the commas are unconventionally used, unnecessary, or incorrectly placed.

B. In the following sentences commas are omitted. Where should they be properly used? For what reasons? (Sections **88a–k**.)

1. Should you take the wrong road you may never find the right road again.
2. You may choose easy courses and get high grades or you may choose difficult courses and really learn something.
3. When one gets there he has the feeling of having conquered the mountains for he can see for miles around.
4. Through a careful examination of ourselves our ability and the requirements for safe driving everyone can live in a safer world.
5. We have not made our decision yet nor can I tell you how soon we shall make it.
6. If everybody would ask himself what he has to be thankful for I know many of us would be surprised.

7. Once the plane takes off the stewardess is always there to help you.
8. By working hard for three months I received my first increase in pay.
9. Florida is visited all the year round but the busy season starts in December and lasts through March.
10. After wandering through the woods all afternoon I found enough mushrooms for our supper.
11. To demonstrate what I mean by a mean trick I'll relate an experience that happened to me.
12. The atmosphere of Holland Michigan is of the old world and all the charm of old Holland can be found there.
13. As reckless drivers we are always one jump ahead of the safety experts for we can think of other ways to kill ourselves.
14. A person susceptible to colds should avoid exposure to cold wet or snowy weather.
15. Many times when the snow falls and the wind blows the lane to our house is drifted with the snow.
16. Little brothers come in assorted sizes shapes and colors.
17. In the play the king had a long curly black beard.
18. You have been in college three months now haven't you?
19. The longer I watched the ice show the more I thought I would like to be a great skater too.
20. I unloaded my clothes and my parents left immediately for home.

C. Where are commas needed in the following sentences? Give your reasons. (Sections **88m–t.**)

1. Some people in traveling from Chicago Illinois to New Orleans Louisiana do the trip in easy driving stages.
2. Anyone that runs a stop sign or a red light in our town is liable to a fine of $18.75.
3. Mary being the oldest child thinks she can rule the smaller boys.
4. I have always believed that every person no matter what his age is should not quit learning.
5. Dr. Herbert Brook who is our family physician has had a great influence on my choice of career.
6. Ladies and gentlemen as we enter this next room note the large portrait on the right.
7. We did not know where the different classrooms were this being our first day on the campus.
8. Some students use a combination yawn one which indicates both tiredness and boredom.

9. This comment which appeared in all the advertisements was enough to make every youngster eager to see the program.
10. From September to Christmas we the students of this college are theoretically confined to the campus for the purpose of study.
11. The time being 8 P.M. the curtain rose and the play began.
12. It takes only 20 minutes to drive to the campus that is under normal conditions.
13. Freshmen who put activities above studies will very likely never become sophomores.
14. Off Marseilles France lies the island bastion Château d'If part of the setting of Dumas' *The Count of Monte Cristo.*
15. *Caroline* which is French and *Carolina* which is Italian are both diminutives from the medieval Latin name *Carola.*
16. My parents and I or I should say my father decided that we would drive to Mammoth Cave Kentucky.
17. The bird dog namely the pointer is the aristocrat of hunting dogs.
18. This is how according to tradition the idea of the Christmas tree and Yule log originated.
19. At any time of the year spring summer fall or winter there is always a tinge of beauty in the woods.
20. The old expression "Practice makes perfect" applies very well to the idea of writing effectively.

D. Commas in the following sentences are misused (see Section **88u**) . Why?

1. It is plain to see, that in our family it is an advantage to have at least two cars.
2. In the United States the most notable days in May are Mother's Day, and Memorial Day.
3. I believe, these courses demand too much of my time.
4. No doubt the pleasant weather, that usually accompanies July, is considered in vacation plans.
5. You expressed a desire to know, what type of business letters we expect to write in the future.
6. Clear communication, is very important everywhere you go.
7. The last and most important part of registration is, payment of fees.
8. In our state there is a place called, "New Salem State Park."
9. Some of the college students of today, have very poor study habits.
10. Oftentimes a question will arise in the form of, "Why are superstitions used?"

# 89   *The semicolon*

The semicolon (;) is a mark of separation only, a stronger mark than the comma, signifying a greater break or a longer pause between sentence elements. It is not, however, so strong as terminal marks of punctuation; its use indicates that two or more statements are not closely enough related to justify commas but are too closely related to justify being put in separate sentences. In all its uses, it separates coordinate elements.

**89a   *Use the semicolon to separate independent clauses not joined by a pure or simple conjunction, such as* and, but, or, nor, neither, yet (see Section 88d)**

Except for conjunctive adverbs (Section **89b**), this principle is that the semicolon is used between two independent clauses with *no* conjunction between them.

I am certain you will like this dress; it will suit you perfectly.
Please close the windows; the room is too cold.
You have only 10 more minutes; please stop writing and revise what
   you have written.

**89b   *Use the semicolon to separate coordinate independent clauses joined by a conjunctive adverb or a phrase which serves as a conjunctive adverb*: accordingly, also, anyhow, as a result, besides, consequently, finally, for example, furthermore, hence, henceforth, however, in addition, in fact, indeed, instead, likewise, meanwhile, moreover, namely, nevertheless, notwithstanding, otherwise, similarly, so, still, surely, then, therefore, thus, yet, *and similar equivalents of words and phrases* (see also Section 84c)**

I tried for two hours to solve the problem; *then* I gave up and worked
   on my English assignment.
This road has many sharp curves; *however,* a careful driver will have
   no difficulty.
Mr. Greene is a busy man; *in fact,* he seems busier than he really is.

To apply correctly and effectively the foregoing principle, keep in mind the following explanatory statements.

1. The semicolon is used immediately before the conjunctive adverb when the conjunctive adverb comes *between* the two independent clauses. If the conjunctive adverb is shifted to a position within the second clause, the semicolon separates the two clauses (see Section **89a**), and the adverb, depending upon its parenthetic strength, is or is not enclosed by commas (Section **88n**).

I tried for two hours to solve the problem; I *then* gave up and worked on my English assignment.
This road has many sharp curves; a careful driver, *however,* will have no difficulty.
Mr. Greene is a busy man; he seems busier, *in fact,* than he really is.

2. When the conjunctive adverb comes between the clauses, should there be a comma after it? In the absence of an unvarying principle, use as a guide the weakness or strength of the word or phrase, parenthetically, in relation to the second clause. If it is weak, omit the comma; if it is strong, use a comma; if it is mildly strong (like *therefore,* for example), use or omit, depending upon your desire to indicate a pause. Another guide: a comma follows a long conjunctive adverb or phrase (*nevertheless, in fact, for example,* etc.), but rarely follows a shorter one (*thus, hence, then,* etc.).

I have trained myself to read rapidly and carefully; *thus* I save myself many hours a week.
I did not favor spending the money; *nevertheless,* I did not vote against the proposal.
This climate is subject to sudden weather changes; *therefore* (or *therefore,*) you should bring a variety of clothing.

3. Distinguish between conjunctive adverb and simple conjunction. A conjunctive adverb is both conjunction and adverb; as such it has an adverbial function which no simple conjunction possesses. Furthermore, it is used only between independent clauses, or sentences, whereas a simple conjunction may join words, phrases, dependent clauses, independent clauses, or even sentences. (See Section **84**.)
4. Distinguish between a conjunctive adverb placed between independent clauses and a subordinating conjunction (*al-*

*though, because, since, whereas, inasmuch as*) introducing a dependent clause coming between the two independent clauses. The subordinating conjunction is preceded by a semicolon in such uses only when no pure coordinating conjunction joins the independent clauses (see Section **89a,d**) .

I shall attend the lecture this evening, *although I can ill afford the time.* (Dependent clause follows independent clause)
I shall attend the lecture this evening; *although I can ill afford the time,* I believe that I shall learn something of profit. (Two independent clauses separated, second being introduced by a dependent clause)

I am having trouble with English and chemistry, *because my high school training in these subjects was inadequate.* (Dependent clause follows independent clause)
I am having trouble with English and chemistry; *because my high school training was inadequate,* I have been assigned to noncredit sections in these subjects. (Two independent clauses separated, second being introduced by a dependent clause)

To eliminate any possibility of confusion or misunderstanding, two sentences might be preferable.

### 89c   Use the semicolon to separate independent clauses joined by a pure conjunction if the clauses are long or contain much internal punctuation

Long independent clauses—but be sure they are long—which contain complicated internal punctuation (a sprinkling of three, four, five, or more commas) should have a semicolon before the pure conjunction. In applying this principle, do not overuse the semicolon. The longer a sentence becomes, and the more involved its punctuation, the less likely it is to be clear. One, two, or even three commas in a sentence are scarcely enough to justify a semicolon before a pure conjunction, especially if the commas, or most of them, occur in the second clause.

Grandfather has been a steady, industrious worker all his life, and now his income from stocks, bonds, and other investments enables him to live comfortably.

Success in college, so some maintain, requires intelligence, industry, and honesty; but others, fewer in number, assert that only personality is important.

Whenever clearness might not otherwise be attained, use semicolons also to separate long phrases or long dependent clauses or a series of words.

The nominations for class president include the following: Adams, J. B., of New Richmond, member of Skull and Bones; Davis, H. M., of Belleville, formerly secretary of the Camera Club; and Wilson, M. L., of Newtown, captain of the football team.

Four good poems to read are the following: narrative, "The Prisoner of Chillon," by Lord Byron; descriptive-reflective, "Elegy Written in a Country Churchyard," by Thomas Gray; satirical, "To a Louse," by Robert Burns; and lyric, "To a Skylark," by Percy Bysshe Shelley.

### 89d   Do not use the semicolon to set off a phrase or a dependent clause

Ordinarily, the semicolon serves the same purpose as the period: to indicate the end of one complete thought and the beginning of another; it is this break in thought that your reader expects when he sees a semicolon. *One fairly safe guide is this: no period, no semicolon.* Setting off dependent clauses or phrases with semicolons leads to the same confusion, in your reader's mind, that is caused by the *unjustifiable sentence fragment* (see Sections 31 and 89b4) ; therefore, do not use the semicolon between unequal grammatical elements, i.e., between one complete grammatical element and one incomplete (but see Section **89c**) . Such an error is named "semicolon fault."

Frequent misuses of semicolons concern dependent clauses and participial or absolute phrases:

Inasmuch as Joe has a fiery temper; we have to be careful what we say to him. (Dependent clause)

The next meeting of the club has been postponed two weeks; because the members are on an inspection trip to Detroit. (Dependent clause)

I received an A on the test; although I was hoping for no more than a B. (Dependent clause)

If I were you; I should ask for a recount of the ballots. (Dependent clause)

Being careful to observe all traffic regulations; I am considered a good
    driver. (Participial phrase)
The excitement of our mock political campaign having died down; we
    once again turned our attention to our studies and the approaching
    final examinations. (Absolute phrase)

To correct semicolon errors like these, use no punctuation
or use the comma for the semicolon.

### 89e  *Do not use a semicolon for a colon*
###      *as a mark of introduction*

*Wrong*    My purpose is simple; to succeed in life.
           Yesterday the bookstores sold me the following; textbooks,
              theme paper, drawing instruments, and laboratory equip-
              ment.
           (In business letters) Dear Sir; Dear Mr. Woods; Gentlemen;

To correct semicolon errors like the foregoing, substitute
colons for the semicolons.

### 89f  *Do not use the semicolon for the dash as a*
###      *summarizing mark*  (see also Section **91d**)

*Wrong*    Class plays, debates, a newspaper, and the yearbook; these
           were the major nonathletic activities in our high school.
           Mathematics, chemistry, English; these give me more trouble
           than any other subjects.
*Right*     Class plays, debates, a newspaper, and the yearbook—these
           were the major nonathletic activities in our high school.
           Mathematics, chemistry, English—these give me more trouble
           than any other subjects.

## EXERCISES

A. The following sentences contain conjunctive adverbs or conjunctive adverb phrases. Where should semicolons and commas go?

1. We arrived in New York late at night thus we could not see much
   of the "big city."

2. A dress designer usually makes $7,000 to $8,000 a year however a famous dress designer can name his own price.
3. At first everyone laughed at the idea then someone said "Why not?"
4. The fog was so thick that our boat barely reached shore indeed I know of two boats that didn't.
5. The use of English refers generally to writing and speaking however my dictionary also gives information about the origin and history of words.
6. A conscience does not have a law to guide it in fact it has no guide other than one possibly developed within itself.
7. We do not plan to go on a tour therefore we can choose the places we wish to visit.
8. At home there were plenty of parties otherwise the holiday season would have been rather dull.
9. I have to choose one of four languages as a result I am seriously considering Russian, German, French, and Spanish.
10. Some people are not afraid of anything at least they do not act as if they were.
11. Our star miler has a very sore leg consequently he will not run in Saturday's race.
12. Herb Alpert and his Tijuana Brass were doing a show on the campus no tickets were left however when I went to buy mine.
13. He said the quotation was from Shakespeare nevertheless I was certain it was from the Bible.
14. My ambition then was to become a major-league baseball player henceforth I practiced baseball by day and dreamed baseball by night.
15. Now I am many miles from my parents I am therefore totally on my own.

B. How are semicolons misused in the following sentences?

1. We had heard that ghosts played in the cemetery nearby; and that they could be seen as cars drove along.
2. In the article, "How Ships Are Built"; I learned something about the superstitions that exist around shipyards.
3. "It won't work, I'm too old;" he said.
4. Although many people say that they do not believe Friday, the 13th, is unlucky; they are still extra cautious on that day.
5. The student cannot come to class with the attitude; "Well, here I am. Teach me."
6. But whatever the case, most of his "ideas" have come true; quite a prediction for a sixteenth-century author.

7. I succeeded in learning a little Portuguese; at least enough so that I could speak to the maid.
8. The sixth letter is strictly a form letter (even without salutation); although the letterhead and different-colored inks attract the reader's attention.
9. Sadness can come after a series of little disappointments; which at the time do not seem important.
10. It is a difference that is easy to see; yet hard to explain.
11. This assignment was a little odd; because, I was responsible for the safety of campers who were older than I.
12. It's a dreary, cold winter day; and it looks as if the racing black clouds will blanket the city with snow.
13. Finally to complete our overall picture of Mexico; we saw the churches.
14. If you like warm weather, like to travel, and have money; you would like to spend a winter in Florida.
15. An invalid's life requires not only the constant attention of the physician; but also the complete cooperation of his family.

# 90   The colon

The colon (:) is usually a mark of introduction, sometimes a mark of separation. Unlike the semicolon, which is used to separate coordinate sentence elements, the colon is primarily a mark for introducing lists, series, and quotations.

## 90a   Use the colon to introduce a word, phrase, or, occasionally, dependent clause when emphasis is desired

For a comparison of the colon, as a more emphatic mark, with the comma in such uses, see Section **88a**.

My aim in this course is easily stated: a high grade.
Only one other possibility remains: to travel by air.
This is our next problem: where do we go from here?
I am positive of one appeal which you cannot overlook: money.
These two things he loved: an honest man and a beautiful woman.

**90b** *Use the colon after an introductory statement
which clearly shows that something is to
follow: an enumeration, tabulation, list, etc.*

Three reasons have been given for his success: integrity, industry, and
a good personality.
Everything will be arranged: the paper provided, the test pencils
sharpened, the chairs placed.
For a few days' trip you will need the following: a change of clothes,
a few toilet articles, and a supply of money.

A brief pause comes between the introduction with its colon
and what happens; if clearness demands it, the best indication
of this pause is the use of words such as *the following* or *as follows,* as in the last illustration above.

Use the colon instead of the comma as an introductory mark
(Section **88a**) when other commas follow.

In high school I studied one foreign language, Spanish.
In high school I studied three foreign languages: German, French, and
Spanish.

**90c** *Use a colon to introduce a clause that
summarizes or gives an example of or
carries on the thought of a preceding clause*

Only skillful and infrequent use of the colon for this purpose is
effective. Its overuse is ineffective and misleading, because the
reader expects the conventional mark between such clauses to
be the semicolon, not an introducing but a separating mark.

The purpose of reading is not alone recreation: it is also information.
Many a man succeeds through sheer attention to industry: Benjamin
Franklin was such a man.
I went to the fair for two reasons: first, I wanted to visit the various
4-H exhibits, and, second, I wanted to see about a job for the summer.

**90d**   *Use the colon to separate the introductory*
*words from a quotation which follows, if*
*the quotation is formal, long, or paragraphed*
*separately*  (see also Sections **88b** and **94a**)

General Robert E. Lee once said: "*Duty* is the sublimest word in the
English language; no man should do more, nor should any man be
expected to do less."

The mayor arose, wiped his spectacles, cleared his throat, and said: "It
seems inevitable that we should have differences of opinion about this
important community problem."

The most important suggestions were made by William Furniss, who
spoke as follows: ". . ." (one or more paragraphs of the speech)

**90e**   *Use the colon after the salutation of a business letter*

The usual practice is to place a colon after the salutation of a
formal or business letter and a comma after the salutation of an
informal, friendly letter (Section **88c**) .

| | | |
|---|---|---|
| Dear Sir: | Dear Mr. Morris: | My dear Mrs. Burns: |
| Gentlemen: | Ladies: | To Whom It May Concern: |

**90f**   *Use the colon to separate the title of a book*
*from the subtitle, hour and minute figures*
*in writing time, the scene from the act of a*
*play, the chapter from a verse in the Bible*

Carl Sandburg is the author of *Abraham Lincoln: The Prairie Years.*
By my watch it is exactly 10:25 A.M.
The passage quoted occurs in Shakespeare's *Macbeth,* III:ii.
John iii:16 is my best-loved Bible verse.

In the last two examples and similar uses, the Modern Language Association *Style Sheet* suggests the following for documentation (Section **20g**) : period instead of colon, with no spacing; no comma after the title; no italics for the books of the
Bible; and small Roman numerals for play scenes and Bible
chapters: *Macbeth* III.ii; I Chron. xxv.8; Luke xiv.5.

**90g  *Do not use the colon when no punctuation is needed***
The colon is misused:

1. To separate prepositions from their objects or verbs from objects or complements.

*Wrong*    I am fond of: books, newspapers, and magazines. (Omit colon)

I like to read: novels, detective stories, and biographies. (Omit colon)

The three Ohio cities visited were: Toledo, Cleveland, and Dayton. (Omit colon)

2. In appositional phrases introduced by *such as.*

*Wrong*    In our community we enjoy a number of individual-participant sports, such as: tennis, shuffleboard, and bowling. (Use comma before as, and neither comma nor colon after it, or insert the words, *the following,* and keep the colon.)

3. In appositional phrases when the sentence continues after the apposition.

*Wrong*    I want these people: my father, my mother, and my grandparents, to be proud of me.
*Right*    I want these people—my father, my mother, and my grandparents—to be proud of me.

**90h  *Do not use the colon for the dash as a summarizing mark*  (see Section 91d)**
The colon looks ahead; the summarizing dash tells the reader what has preceded.

*Wrong*    Class plays, debates, a newspaper, and the yearbook: these were the major nonathletic activities in our high school.
Mathematics, chemistry, English: these gave me more trouble than any other subjects.

To correct sentences like these, replace the colon by the dash.

## EXERCISE

Some of the following sentences need colons and some already have them correctly or incorrectly used. Check each sentence carefully and make each one correct in its use of the colon.

1. Two main items a pilot looks for when checking the weather visibility and the direction and velocity of the winds.
2. Someone has said: "True achievement is measured by how much better off the world is for our having lived in it."
3. Some fields of study in civil engineering are: airport planning, architecture, bridge building, city planning, and road construction.
4. All of my jobs had one thing in common they showed me the varied reactions of many people.
5. Basically, the role Mr. Bennet assumes as both father and husband may be summed up in one word: failure.
6. Don't get me wrong I am not going to leave my future to Fate.
7. Another winter scene that I like to see is this a group of trees covered with snow, and a path winding down a hill.
8. Information is supplied concerning colleges such as: accreditation, control, date of founding, and location.
9. I have taught my dog a few simple tricks like: shaking hands, sitting up, rolling over, and lying down.
10. Now the thought struck me what am I doing here?
11. My dictionary has several pages of symbols on: astronomy, biology, chemistry, and mathematics.
12. At Derbytown there was everything that a boy could imagine activities from horseback riding to swimming.
13. Among favorite winter sports at some northern colleges are: iceskating, sledding, and tobogganing.
14. Three types of students: the mamas' boys, the boisterous types, and the shy, lonesome ones will be among those coming to college this September.
15. Practically all of the European family names were derived in one or more of the following ways (1) place of birth, (2) occupation, (3) ancestral names, and (4) a descriptive nickname.

# 91  *The dash*

The dash (—) serves the purpose of introduction, termination, separation, or, with another dash, enclosure.

The dash is a mark of punctuation most characteristically used to denote a sudden break or shift in thought. Although a stronger mark, it is approximately equivalent to a comma: both may be used in pairs or alone and between expressions of either coordinate or unequal rank. Logically, some other mark can usually be substituted for the dash, but its occasional use provides emphasis or surprise. (For those who type, see Section 1c6.)

**91a  *Use the dash to introduce a word, a phrase, or,  
occasionally, a clause when emphasis is desired***

For some of these purposes the comma or the colon is used. Compare the following illustrations with those in Sections **88a** and **90a.**

My aim in this course is easily stated—a high grade.
There is only one other possibility—to travel by air.
Our next problem is—where do we go from here?
Many a man needs only one thing for complete success and happiness
  —love.

**91b  *Use the dash to indicate an interruption,  
an unfinished statement, or an unfinished  
word (usually in dialogue), or to give the  
effect of stammering, sobbing, or halting***

George began, "May I ask—" but the Judge snapped, "No!"
"I hardly know how to express—" and then the speaker blushed, and
  sat down.
When John Smith comes in—oh, here you are now, John.
"I can't spell the word 'erysip—' "
M—m—m—Mary.   "Oh—oh—oh!"   "Y—y—yes."

Omit the period when such a statement terminates with a dash.

NOTE: Sometimes a *double* dash (four hyphens when typing) is used at the end of an unfinished statement (not within a line).

## 91c   Use the dash to indicate a break, shift, or turn in thought

Here is a fuller explanation—but perhaps your class will not be interested.
Do we—can we—dare we propose such action to the trustees?
He is the most despicable—but I should not say any more.

## 91d   Use a dash to separate a final clause summarizing a series of ideas that precede it

The usual summarizing words are *these, those, such.*

Mathematics, chemistry, English—these give me more trouble than any other subjects.
The meek, the kind, the gentle, the pure in heart—such are of the Kingdom of Heaven.
Food to eat, a place to sleep, a pleasant occupation, a congenial companion—what more can anyone ask from life?

No other marks of punctuation, such as the comma, semicolon, or colon, are used with the dash in this summarizing use; the semicolon or colon cannot be used in place of the summarizing dash (see Sections **89f, 90h**).

## 91e   Use dashes to enclose sharply distinguished parenthetical matter in order to secure emphasis, suspense, or clearness

We are in favor—completely in favor, we repeat—of the proposal.
I was surprised—in fact, pleasantly astonished—to hear of your splendid record.
My advice—if you will pardon my impertinence—is that you apologize to your friend.
My father is not afraid—he is a surgeon, you know—of performing the most delicate operation.

The following are special applications of the foregoing principle:
1. Long appositional phrases are likely to be enclosed by dashes.

Three candidates for public office—Wilson of New York, Matthews of Illinois, and Adams of Colorado—are in favor of larger old-age pensions.

For commas with shorter appositional phrases, see Section 88q.

2. When the parenthetical material set off by dashes requires an exclamation point or question mark, such punctuation precedes the second dash:

If I should fail this course—heaven forbid!—I shall have to attend summer school.

Better training in his field—or was it merely a desire to get away from home?—led John to choose an eastern university.

### 91f Use the dash to indicate the omission of words or letters (other than contractions)

Sergeant Y— was an excellent soldier.

NOTE: Sometimes a double dash is used to indicate the omission of a whole word or words—as in some exercises in this book.

The assignment for Friday is a theme entitled "How Not To ——." Each student should choose a specific topic.

### 91g Use the dash sparingly

Overuse of the dash is inadvisable. It is legitimately used in the instances cited in this section, but other marks of punctuation have their functions, too, and are usually more commonly used. Frequent use of the dash detracts from its effectiveness.

### 91h Never use the dash as a substitute for the period

Except for the use of the dash to mark unfinished statements or interrupted dialogue (Section 91b), the dash is never used for the period at the end of a sentence.

## EXERCISES

A. Encircle all the dashes on two pages of a textbook, your book of readings, or a magazine. Account for the use of each.

B. Where should dashes be placed in the following sentences? Why?

1. "She stands . . . with beauty in her heart and bounty in her hands" that is how one city is described in a song about it.
2. Very soon it is a matter of only a few weeks now I shall be a United States citizen.
3. The Plains of Abraham, the beautiful St. Lawrence River, and the Citadel these are among the places to be seen in Quebec.
4. The old gentleman had given to Michael a hungry, beaten child adequate food, clothing, and shelter.
5. This area, like most, is very hilly you might even say mountainous and covered with much tall timber and brush.
6. Instead of getting up at 4 A.M. and studying as I did this morning I will sleep until the last possible moment during vacation.
7. After walking for miles at least it seemed that way to me I realized that the scenery did not look familiar.
8. My twin brother and I have always been very close a fact which has helped us many times and we give moral and physical support to each other.
9. Kings and presidents, private soldiers, and famous musicians all of these have paraded up and down Washington's Pennsylvania Avenue.
10. Although marriage plans are not in the immediate future, any girl and I'm no different thinks about these plans often.
11. Finally you can be sure it took the judges quite a while my speech was declared the best given.
12. "I remember when" what a wealth of memories these words bring!
13. Just how far I shall go with the idea of building a new hi-fi set well, I'll have to wait and see.
14. This one character I can't remember his name caused all kinds of trouble to the Primrose family.
15. The numerous herds of deer, antelope, buffalo, and other wild animals what has happened to them?

# 92 *The hyphen*

The hyphen (-) is a mark of separation used only between parts of a word. Paradoxically, its most frequent use is unification, bringing together two or more separate words into a compound word which serves the purpose of a single part of speech. The hyphen, therefore, is more a mark of spelling than of punctuation, to indicate that two or more words or two or more parts of one word belong together.

No longer is the hyphen used—as it once was in older dictionaries—to indicate division of words into syllables. That purpose is now served by the dot: re·sist, ad·vo·cate, ir·re·sis·ti·ble (see Section 51c3). Hyphens used between syllables are an integral part of the word.

**92a** *Use your dictionary to determine whether certain*
*word combinations are written as two words,*
*as one word written solid, or as a compound*
*word with a hyphen between parts*

⟶ 1. Do not write as one word two or more words that should be completely separated.

⟶ 2. Do not write as two separate words any two words which should be written solid.

⟶ 3. Do not write as two or more words any word combinations which should be hyphenated. (See expanded discussion, Section **92b,** below.)

The use of a hyphen in joining compound words (two or more words used as a unit) varies greatly. No rules cover all combinations, which are so numerous that many such are not in your dictionary. Fortunately, many are, and when in doubt, consult it as your guide in hyphenating and compounding. If the compound word you seek is not there, apply the principles given below. As a further guide, however, the 1967 United States Government Printing Office *Style Manual* (pp. 82–130) lists some 21,000 words and indicates how they are written or printed: as one word, as two words, or as hyphenated words.

The general principle of word joining derives from usage, and word forms are constantly undergoing modification. When two or more words first become associated with a single meaning, they are written separately; as they grow to be more of a unit in common thought and writing, they are hyphenated; finally, they are written together as one word, with sometimes the second or hyphenated stage being by-passed. This evolution is seen in the following, the third word in each series now being the accepted form: *base ball, base-ball, baseball; basket ball, basket-ball, basketball; rail road, rail-road, railroad; week end, week-end, weekend.*

Many common expressions as nouns are still in the first stage: *mother tongue, boy friend, Girl Scout, girl friend, high school.* Consider also *post office,* but *postman, postmark, postmaster, postmistress.*

NOTE: If in your dictionary the words are not hyphenated or written as one word, and if Section **92b** does not apply, your safe practice is to use a space between the words.

## 92b    Use a hyphen to separate the parts of many compound words

Many compounds are always written solid, many are written with a hyphen, and many are written either with a hyphen or as two words, depending upon meaning (examples are given below). Note the difference in these:

After three years of service, Joe was a hardened, *battle-scarred* veteran.
The *battle scarred* the bodies and souls of all who took part.

The *above-mentioned* principles are frequently illustrated in writing.
The poem *above, mentioned* several times by the speaker, has been one of my favorites.

In the quarrel between Ellen and Sue, Jean served as a *go-between.*
In a field goal, the ball must *go between* the goal posts and over the crossbar.

Some politicians follow a *middle-of-the-road* course.
A careful driver will never drive down the *middle of the road.*

Hyphens are generally used:

1. Between two or more words modifying a substantive and used as a single adjective, especially when placed before the substantive. These combinations may consist of

a. an adjective or noun united with a present or past participle: *able-bodied, absent-minded, battle-scarred, bell-shaped, sad-looking, soft-spoken, wind-blown.*

b. two adjectives, or an adjective and a noun, or a noun and an adjective: *light-blue, Latin-American, ocean-green, midnight-black.*

NOTE: Use no hyphen with adjective-plus-noun as object: "We live in a *one-story* house." "Our house has only *one story.*"

c. a prefix or combining form attached to a capitalized word: *non-Christian, pre-Roman, pro-British, trans-Canadian, un-American.*

NOTE: Prefixes and suffixes attached to common words usually become part of the word, written solid; dictionaries often have long lists of these—see, for example, combining syllables like *non, over, un, under* in your dictionary.

d. an adverb and a present or past participle (unless the adverb ends in *ly*) : *above-mentioned, ever-rising, fast-moving, slow-witted, easily accomplished, swiftly moving.*

2. Between words of a compound noun:

a. three or more words: *mother-in-law, jack-of-all-trades.*
b. compounds having an adverb or a preposition as the second element: *go-between, looker-on, leveling-off.*
c. compounds having *fellow, father, mother, brother, sister, daughter,* or a similar word as the first element: *fellow-citizen, brother-classmates, sister-nations.*

3. Between compound words when, usually, *all, self, ex, half,* or *quarter* is the first element: *all-important, ex-president, half-asleep, half-truth, quarter-share, self-control, self-respect* (but, after frequent use, *selfsame, halfback,* and *quarterback*) . See Section **92a.**

4. Between a single capital letter joined to a noun or participle: *A-flat, H-bomb, S-curve, T-shaped, U-turn.*

5. Between elements of an improvised compound, usually adjectives: *know-it-all, make-believe, never-to-be-forgotten, never-say-die, seven-year-old.*

6. Between the parts of compound numerals if written out (from twenty-one to ninety-nine) : *forty-three, sixty-seven, eighty-two.*

7. Between the numerator and denominator of a fraction if written out: *two-thirds, four-fifths, one-thousandth* (but omitted when the hyphen already appears in either numerator or denominator: *twenty-four thirty-fifths; three ten-thousandths*) .

8. Between a numbered figure and its unit of measurement: *a 5-yard gain, 40-hour week, 10-day trip, 16-foot board.*

9. To avoid, usually, doubling a vowel or tripling a consonant: *anti-inflation, pre-existent, re-enact, semi-independent, shell-like, yell-leader.*

10. To prevent mispronunciation: *co-op, re-cover* vs. *recover, re-creation* vs. *recreation, re-treat* vs. *retreat.*

11. As a "suspensive hyphen" in pairs or more, when the first or second part of a compound word is used only once:

In literature, an elephantine style is *heavy-handed* or *-footed* writing.
Your next theme is to be a *400-* to *600-word* theme.
For our Homecoming display we brought some *8-, 10-,* and *16-foot* boards.

**92c    *Use a hyphen to indicate the division
of a word broken at the end of a line***

The rambling old house, it is true, would have looked con-
    siderably better if it had been freshly painted.

Occasionally, at the end of a longhand or typewritten line, a long word must be divided. Avoid such division if you possibly can, and do not divide the word if it is the last one on the page or the final word of a last full line of a paragraph. When division is necessary, follow these directions.

1. Place the hyphen at the end of the first line, *never at the beginning of the second.*

2. Never divide a monosyllable. Five- to eight-letter one-syllable words like *breathed, ground, quenched, strength, thought,*

and *through* cannot be divided. Write the entire monosyllable on the first line; if this is not possible, carry the whole word over to the next line.

3. Divide words of more than one syllable between syllables, but avoid dividing one-letter syllables from the remainder of the word, as well as any unpronounced *ed* in one- or several-syllable pronunciations. Undesirable: *a·bout*; *i·talics*; *man·y*; *ask·ed*; *dress·ed*; *attack·ed*. Also do not divide words with only five or fewer letters. Undesirable: *al·so, el·bow, in·to, on·ly, op·en*.

4. Do not divide the contracted part of a word from the main word. Undesirable: *would·n't, does·n't, they·'re*.

5. Do not divide the parts of a numeral stated in figures. Wrong: Our new dormitory will cost $3,435,·800.

6. When in doubt about correct syllabication, consult your dictionary in order to divide words properly. Several simple suggestions, however, apply to many words:

Prefixes and suffixes can be divided from the main words if they are separate syllables (but see 3, just above) : *pre·dominate, glad·ness*.

Compound words are divided between their main parts: *son·in·law*.

Two consonants are usually divided unless the consonants are part of one syllable: *win·dow, run·ning, pass·ing*.

NOTE: If you have material you plan to have printed, and if any line ends with a hyphen that separates parts of a compound word, write "hyph" or "stet" next to it; otherwise, the printer, in setting type, might make the compound a single word.

### 92d   *Use the hyphen to connect certain combinations of words, figures, letters, and letters and figures*

The years 1955-1969 have seen expanded enrollments in schools and colleges.

John Kline used to fly a DC-8 on the New York-Dallas run.

Monday-Friday classes will have one meeting more next week than Tuesday-Thursday classes.

Please study pages 3-14 for tomorrow's assignment.

The speech was carried live on a **CBS-NBC-ABC** hookup.

## 92e   Do not use a hyphen in place of a
## dash or a dash in place of a hyphen

In longhand, make the hyphen and the dash distinct. In typing, a dash consists of two hyphens.

## EXERCISES

A. Circle all the hyphens on one page of your book of readings, another textbook, or a magazine. Give the reason for each.

B. Copy the following words in a list, and make a list of the same words without the hyphens. What is the difference in meaning when the same word is hyphenated or written solid? *re-treat, re-creation, re-view, re-claim, re-dress, re-lay, re-search, re-turn, re-cover, re-act, re-collect, re-pose, re-tire, re-count, re-sign, re-prove, re-sound, re-solve, re-sort, re-cite.*

C. Indicate where hyphens should be inserted in the following sentences:

1. Most business letters are written on 8½ by 11 inch stationery.
2. On many of our trips we make use of the state owned and government owned parks.
3. My registration here as a freshman was a true once in a lifetime experience.
4. On the basketball floor Tim, with his 6 foot, 8 inch frame, was able easily to reach over his smaller opponents' heads.
5. After an hour or so of study, one would take a five or nine minute break.
6. Thirty five to forty five dollars a week is good income for a 12 year old boy.
7. I have learned that a tailor made suit is cheaper to buy than a ready to wear type.
8. I followed Father to the kitchen where, huddled over in one corner, was a little black faced, long legged, brown eyed boxer puppy.
9. If I were a freshman again, I would try to make a better than average grade on every test, quiz, or recitation.
10. Easter has long been celebrated as a coming of spring festival.
11. On county roads one should drive at a 40 mile per hour speed.
12. The community sponsored activities in my home town are of high quality.
13. Too many of us take what I call an on the spur of the moment action.

14. These model airplane kits have step by step instructions for putting the planes together.
15. "Amidst the general hum of mirth and conversation that ensued, there was a little man with a puffy Say nothing to me or I'll contradict you sort of countenance. . . ."—Charles Dickens, *The Pickwick Papers*

# 93  *The apostrophe*

The apostrophe (') as a mark of separation is used to indicate the possessive case of nouns and of indefinite pronouns (*another, everybody, no one,* etc.). It is also used to mark omissions in contracted words and numerals and to indicate the plurals of letters and numbers. Since the apostrophe is used only as part of a word, its use—like that of the hyphen—is as much a matter of spelling as of punctuation.

**93a  *Use an apostrophe and* s *or an apostrophe alone or* s *and an apostrophe to form the possessive case of nouns***

Applied, this general principle has five subprinciples:

1. A singular or plural noun not ending in *s* adds an apostrophe and *s*.

The *policeman's* car was waiting at the door.
Our fire department is ready for service at a *moment's* notice.
Mr. *Smith's* office is on the third floor.
A large department store sells *men's, women's,* and *children's* clothing.

NOTE: Words, usually of one syllable, ending in an *sh, ch, x,* and *z* add apostrophe and *s*.

The Reverend *Dr. Bush's* sermon on Sunday will be on "The *Church's* One Foundation."
Many languages contain translations of Karl *Marx's* works.
Carl *Schurz's* contributions to American life were noteworthy.

2. A plural noun, common or proper, ending in *s*, adds an apostrophe alone.

Some *students'* attitude toward activities is not quite the same as their *professors'* attitude.

During my three *months'* vacation, I worked in a store selling *boys'* clothing.

The *Smiths'* tour of Northern Europe began on June 15.

3.  A singular noun ending in *s* adds an apostrophe alone.

The principle applies usually to proper names, to which an added *s* is unnecessary, although some writers prefer it and perhaps pronounce an extra syllable, *es*. (Some writers add *s* to proper names of one syllable, an apostrophe alone to others.) Most common nouns ending their singular in *s* are the names of nonhuman objects and form their possessive with an *of* phrase. In words of more than one syllable ending in *s, x,* or *z,* add the apostrophe only.

*Keats'* (*Keats's*) sonnets are among my favorites, and they are included in Professor *Jones'* (*Jones's*) anthology.

Our *boss'* (*boss's*) working habits set us all a good example.

On the cover *of my atlas* (not the *atlas'* cover) was a drawing of the world.

Every student of Greek knows *Aristophanes'* comedies and *Sophocles'* tragedies.

Most students are eager to enroll in Professor *Wilcox'* English classes.

Grandfather buys all his clothing at *Kleinschmitz'* clothing store in Cleveland.

Some nouns, common and proper, usually of more than one syllable, ending in double *ss* or having an *s*-sound ending add only the apostrophe, mainly for euphony:

"For *goodness'* sake" was one of the *Duchess'* favorite expressions.

On New Year's Eve we all sing "Auld Lang Syne" for old *acquaintance'* sake, not for *conscience'* sake.

  *but*

Horace's and Eustace's names are somewhat uncommon.

4.  Compound nouns add apostrophe and *s* to the element nearer or nearest the object possessed.

John borrowed his *brother-in-law's* car.

Charge these goods to *John Brown, Jr.,'s* account.

Father left the restaurant wearing *somebody else's* hat.

5. In group or joint possession (two or more), add the apostrophe and *s* to the last member of the group, unless 3, above, applies.

I always use *Mason, Smith, and Brown's* sporting equipment.
Prescriptions are the main business of *Johnson and Stover's* drug store,
   but they are only a minor part of *Brown and Jones'* drug store.

NOTE: Indicate individual possession by using the possessive case of each element of the series.

I am interested in the *Army's* and *Navy's* recruiting campaign.
My sister is a baby-sitter for *Mrs. Brown's* and *Mrs. Wilson's* children.

### 93b Use an apostrophe to indicate that letters or figures have been omitted

Father was a member of the class of *'48*; I'm a member of the class
   of *'73*.
I myself never met a body *comin'* through the rye.

Contractions, usually pronouns or nouns combined with certain verbs, or the word *not* with certain verbs, provide common examples of this principle: *he's, it's, isn't, aren't, wasn't, weren't, hasn't, don't, doesn't, won't,* etc.

*John's* in New York now; Joe is coming next week.
When *you're* careful, you *shouldn't* have any trouble in catching your
   serious errors in writing.
Come now; you *don't* have to say, *"What's o'clock?"* *That's* a stilted
   way of saying *"What's* the time?"

NOTE: Observe that the apostrophe *replaces* the omitted letter:
*didn't,* not *did'nt*; *haven't,* not *have'nt*; etc.

### 93c Use an apostrophe and s to indicate the plurals of figures, alphabetical letters, and words considered as words

I have trouble making legible *8's*.
Uncrossed *t's* look like *l's*; undotted *i's* are read as *e's*.
Don't overuse *and's, but's,* and *for's* in your writing.
My uncle spent the first half of the *1950's* in uniform.

NOTE: An apostrophe is used in forming the plural of some abbreviation initials:

Three *G.I.'s* in my uncle's battalion were *Ph.D.'s* from an eastern university.

Where the omission of the apostrophe causes no difficulty in reading, many writers, editors, and printers omit the apostrophe in the foregoing uses, including plurals of words:

My uncle spent the first half of the *1950s* in uniform.
Three *G.I.s* in my uncle's battalion were *Ph.D.s* from an eastern university.
Many airlines have used many Boeing *707s* in the past.
Your writing contains too many *ands, ifs, buts,* and *whereases.*

**93d   *Do not use the apostrophe in forming
the plural of nouns or the third person
singular, present tense, of verbs***

*Wrong*     The *Smith's* are playing bridge with us tonight.
             There have been more *boys'* than *girls'* among our freshman
             *student's* the past few *year's.*
             Wet heavy snow *make's* winter driving difficult.
*Right*     The *Smiths* are playing bridge with us tonight.
             There have been more *boys* than *girls* among our freshman
             *students* the past few *years.*
             Wet heavy snow *makes* winter driving difficult.

**93e   *Do not use the apostrophe to form the possessive
case of the personal and relative pronouns***

| *Wrong* | | *Right* | |
|---|---|---|---|
| | our's | | ours |
| | ours' | | ours |
| | your's | | yours |
| | yours' | | yours |
| | his' | | his |
| | her's | | hers |
| | hers' | | hers |
| | it's | | its |
| | their's | | theirs |
| | theirs' | | theirs |
| | who's | | whose |

NOTE: *Never* use the apostrophe with the possessive *its*—one of the most common errors in student writing. *Its* is the possessive form of *it*; *it's* is the contraction for *it is* or *it has*; *its'* is an illiteracy nonexistent in correct writing.

When a dog wags *its* tail, that's a sign *it's* happy.

## 93f  Use the apostrophe and s to form the possessive case of indefinite pronouns

The possessive case of indefinite pronouns is illustrated as follows:

| | |
|---|---|
| anybody's | another's |
| everybody's | either's |
| no one's | neither's |
| one's | neither one's |
| someone's | other's (plural, others') |

You must have your father or mother sign this application; *either one's* (or *either's*) signature is satisfactory.
*Everybody's* business is usually *nobody's* business.

## EXERCISES

A. Circle all the apostrophes on a page of selected prose and give the reason for each.

B. Where are apostrophes needed in the following sentences? Why?

1. You will find the visitors apartments in the east wing of the dormitory.
2. Its a pleasant feeling to know that someone thinks youre brilliant.
3. After I receive my bachelors degree, I hope to continue on and obtain a masters degree.
4. By 12 oclock midnight I have all my next days studying done.
5. Stores in large cities feature by mail a personal shoppers service.
6. To me theres nothing as beautiful as new-fallen snow.
7. Our various families reunion last August was a great success.
8. Recently I finished reading Nathaniel Hawthornes *The Marble Faun.*
9. Now lets look at some possible solutions to some of todays problems.
10. Alaska has always been built up in peoples minds as a state where everythings big.
11. For vacation I have been dreaming of 12 hours sleep each night.

12. Eight of the worlds leading automobile racers had serious accidents last year.
13. Your work load in your field of study here will be somewhat heavier than the average college students.
14. One should always be tolerant of and respect others rights and opinions.
15. As a secretary a girl can get a position working in a physicians or dentists office.

   C. Apostrophes are misused in the following sentences. Make necessary corrections and explain each.

1. Many people are building new home's and spending money on luxury's like television.
2. The Norman Conquest, by reason of it's being French, brought the French language to England.
3. Every year thousands' of people swim in this lake.
4. If our neighbor is not working at his place, he is loafing at our's.
5. My English teacher did'nt want anyone in her class who would'nt work.
6. Walking in wet weather make's ones' feet cold and damp.
7. Various European country's scenery is simply breath-taking.
8. The mens' and womens' residence halls even have a childrens' playroom for visiting parents and friends.
9. Many of our postage stamps have prominent peoples' pictures printed on them.
10. This magazine-index volume includes the five year's materials from 1960 to 1965.

# 94 *Quotation marks*

Quotation marks, double (". . .") and single ('. . .'), are marks of enclosure for words, phrases, clauses, sentences, and paragraphs. By definition, *quotation* is repeating what someone has said or written, but the marks themselves have several specialized uses.

NOTE: Although some books, magazines, and newspapers use either single quotation marks or no quotation marks where, according to American convention, double ones would be used, neither of these practices is any criterion. The following principles explain conventional uses.

**94a** *Use quotation marks to enclose every complete direct quotation and each part of an interrupted direct quotation*

A direct quotation is the exact words of the person quoted, the original speaker or writer.

John asked, "What time shall I come?"
"Dinner will be served at seven," replied Mary.

Abraham Lincoln closed his Gettysburg Address as follows: ". . . and that government of the people, by the people, for the people, shall not perish from the earth."

"Father," I said, "may I have the car this evening?"
"And why," said Father, "do you need the car this evening?"

"I find your conduct reprehensible." He paused, and then continued, "However, we shall overlook it this time."

The *he said* or *said he* part, or its equivalent, inserted within a quotation is never preceded by the terminating period; instead it is preceded by a comma, unless a question mark or exclamation point is required. It is followed by a comma unless a stronger mark, period or semicolon, is demanded by the grammatical elements. The test: What mark would be used if the *he said* were omitted? Use that mark after the inserted part indicating the speaker.

Joe Smith is a friend of mine, but I haven't seen him for five years.
"Joe Smith is a friend of mine," I said, "but I haven't seen him for five years."

We have no vacancy now; however, we will keep your name on file.
"We have no vacancy now," the employment director said; "however, we will keep your name on file."

I bought my hat at Johnson's Stores. It was on sale.
"I bought my hat at Johnson's Stores," Henry told us. "It was on sale."

For further discussion of conventions in direct quotations: commas, see Section **88b**; colons, Section **90d**; capitals, Section **97b**.

*94b   In dialogue, use a separate paragraph for every
change of speaker, with quotation marks
enclosing each speech*  (see Section **29a**)

*94c   If a direct quotation extends for several
paragraphs, use quotation marks at the
beginning of each paragraph but at
the end of only the last paragraph*

NOTE: Often for such long quotations—50 words or more—quotation marks are omitted. Instead, the left and right margins may be wider and, if typewritten, material is single-spaced and, if printed, set in smaller type.

*94d   In formal writing or in good informal writing
use quotation marks to enclose words that
suggest a widely different level of usage*

If a word is appropriate, no quotation marks should be used as a form of apology. If it is not appropriate, the expression can usually be altered. In some instances, however, you may wish to shift to an expression having a specific, limited usage or usage label in order to communicate meaning realistically or emphatically (or you may be discussing such expressions as uses of words) . Such expressions may be illiteracies, slang, difficult technical words, or common words with a technical meaning (see Sections **54, 55, 56, 61**) .

The Mayor of our town, in my opinion, is a "stuffed shirt."
The policeman "lit into" me as if I had committed a major crime; when he finished, I "lit out" in a hurry.
Charlie told me facetiously that he had been "borned" in St. Louis.
When a critic of poetry speaks of "license," he may have in mind "poetic license."

But do not rely on this use of quotation marks as an excuse for inexact choice of words. Find the word that means exactly what you wish to say (see Section **63**) . Also, do not sprinkle your writing with quotation marks around words or expressions; enclose only those that would puzzle or mislead your reader. Words labeled *colloquial* or *informal* in your dictionary are not enclosed in quotation marks.

When words or expressions are enclosed in quotation marks in accordance with Section **94d,** commas are *not* used around them unless required for other reasons. Note examples above and see Section **88b.**

**94e**   *Use quotation marks to enclose chapter*
       *titles and the titles of articles, lectures,*
       *short stories, short poems, songs, and*
       *the like, when used in a body of prose*

When both chapter title and book title are mentioned, or titles of article and magazine, the book and magazine names should be indicated by italics (see Section **96a**).

For such information consult the chapter, "Private Preparatory Schools,"
   in the *American Educational Directory.*
Some humorous theatrical experiences are discussed in Jean Kerr's article, "What Happens Out of Town," in an issue of *Harper's Magazine.*

If there is no chance of confusion, quotation marks may be used instead of italics to indicate the names of ships, trains, airplanes, and the like, but the use of italics is preferred (see Section **96a**).

"The City of Los Angeles" leaves the Union Station at 9 o'clock.
We have booked passage to England on the liner "United States."

**94f**   *Use single quotation marks to enclose*
       *a quotation within a quotation*

"Tell me," Father asked Mother after the wedding, "whether the bride
   said, 'I promise to obey.' "
Our instructor said, "When you say, 'I'll turn in my theme tomorrow,'
   I expect it to be turned in tomorrow, not next week."

On the very rare occasions when it is necessary to punctuate a quotation within a quotation within a quotation, the order is double marks, single marks, double marks:

The speaker said: "I shall quote from a letter of a Civil War veteran:
   'When I was on sentry duty in Washington, a tall gaunt man stopped
   one day and said, "Good morning, soldier. How goes it?" It was Abraham Lincoln who thus greeted me.' "

### 94g   Use quotation marks always in pairs

Since quotation marks are marks of enclosure, they are used in pairs. They come at both beginning and end of the quotation.

*Wrong*     "I like football better than baseball, he said, and I like tennis better than either."

*Right*     "I like football better than baseball," he said, "and I like tennis better than either."

NOTE: One exception—a quotation covering two or more paragraphs (see Section **94c**) .

### 94h   Place quotation marks correctly with reference to other marks

1. The comma and the period come *inside* the quotation marks. This principle applies even when only the last word or alphabetical letter before the comma or the period is enclosed.

"I need your help now," she said. "I need it more than ever."

Some praised the performance as "excellent," and others thought it only "fair."

Items marked "A," "B," and "C" were inadvertently listed in this order: "A," "C," and "B."

NOTE: A frequent British practice is to put comma and period outside quotation marks, but we are dealing with *American* conventions.

2. A question mark, exclamation point, or dash comes *outside* the quotation marks unless it is part of the quotation.

Did she say, "I have enough money"?

She asked, "Have I enough money?"

"Have I enough money?" she asked.

What is meant by "dog eat dog"?

Our play was obviously a "bust"!

"The play was a 'bust'!" our coach exclaimed.

For use of question mark when both the nonquoted and the quoted elements are questions, see Section **87b**, Note.

3. Semicolon and colon come *outside* the quotation marks, although an occasional variation may be found.

Read E. B. White's "Walden"; it is, I think, his best essay.
Look up the following in "A Glossary of Famous People": Theodore
  Roosevelt, Woodrow Wilson, Dwight D. Eisenhower.

NOTE: With sentence-closing quotation marks, only one other punctuation mark is used, even though the usual rules call for another mark:

Three question-asking words are "What?" and "When?" and "Where?"
Someone sneezed just as our leader whispered "Quiet!"

### 94i  Do not put quotation marks around an indirect quotation

In an indirect quotation, a writer or speaker puts into his own words the words of someone else or, at a later time, his own words.

| | |
|---|---|
| *Wrong* | The employment manager said that "I should report for work on Monday." |
| *Right (indirect)* | The employment manager said that I should report for work on Monday. |
| *Right (direct)* | The employment manager said, "Report for work on Monday." |
| *Right (indirect)* | I replied that I should be happy to attend the dinner. |
| *Right (direct)* | I replied, "I shall be happy to attend the dinner." |

Note that the following can be either direct or indirect quotations:

| | |
|---|---|
| *Direct* | He answered, "Yes." |
| | To a question of that kind I shall have to say, "No." |
| *Indirect* | He answered yes. |
| | To a question of that kind I shall have to say no. |

### 94j  Do not confuse in one sentence a direct and an indirect quotation or a direct and indirect question  (see Section 35c2,3)

### 94k  Do not enclose in quotation marks
### the title at the beginning of a theme

The only exception to this principle is the use of a quotation *as* the theme title.

| | |
|---|---|
| *Usual title* | The Dangers of Too Little Learning |
| *Quotation as title* | "A Little Learning Is a Dangerous Thing" |

## EXERCISES

A. Study several pages of a short story or novel using dialogue. Examine the use of quotation marks and their position with other marks of punctuation. Discuss any uses which are not in accord with principles given in Section 94.

B. Write a short paper to illustrate the use of quotation marks and paragraphing (see Section 29a) on the subject, "A Dialogue Between —— and ——."

C. In the following sentences, make quotation marks, capitals, and commas conform to commonly accepted principles:

1. After I had completed my driver's training, Father said, "that I could apply for a beginner's license".
2. The old saying, 'the more the merrier—' well, it isn't necessarily true.
3. The area might be called "a sportsmen's paradise, for the woods are teeming with game.
4. At the end of the last class before vacation, our instructor said he would like to say one more thing: have a merry Christmas.
5. Here are words of wisdom for the ambitious, hard-working young person, "there is always tomorrow".
6. My dictionary defines *preface* as "something written as introductory or preliminary material to a book.
7. Our community recently honored my mother by naming her, "the typical American housewife;" naturally her family is very proud of her.
8. What makes the automobile so deadly is the 'nut' behind the wheel.
9. "Well, son, the justice drawled, $18.75."
10. It would be so easy to sleep through those early 8 o'clock classes is a favorite thought of most students.
11. You have asked me, "Why read"?
12. Can this really be happening to me? I said to myself.

13. The home of 600 happy people and a few soreheads—this the sign that the traveler sees as he enters my town.
14. I have read Keats' The Eve of St. Agnes and I think I have never read a more beautiful poem.
15. After you leave college and obtain a job the adviser told Henry you will find that coming in late and not appearing once or twice a week will have serious consequences.

# 95 Parentheses, brackets, and less frequently used marks

Parentheses ( ), sometimes called "curves," and brackets [ ] are marks of enclosure. The former find occasional use. The latter are infrequently used; in fact, they are not included on the regular keyboard of standard typewriters.

## 95a  Use parentheses to enclose parenthetical material which is remotely connected with the context

Many young Europeans (surely American students are just as intelligent) can speak several languages beside their own.
If anyone has not bought his ticket yet (reservations began a week ago), a few choice seats are still left.

To justify parentheses, be sure that your material is strongly parenthetic, i.e., usually long phrases, perhaps dependent clauses, or independent clauses—not words or most phrases or most dependent clauses. In such constructions the parenthetic material merely amplifies the thought. Thus many writers prefer dashes to parentheses (see Section **91e**). These marks may frequently be used interchangeably, although parentheses are more commonly used when the strong parenthetic material is more remotely related to the main statement.

NOTE: A question mark, exclamation point, and/or quotation marks may be used, if needed, within parentheses.

Some of our co-eds roller-skate (how ridiculous!) to class.
Effective figurative language (for example, Wordsworth's "trailing clouds of glory") helps to make a poem great.

## 95b    *Use parentheses to enclose amplifying references, directions, and numbering figures*

Study carefully the assignment on credits. (See Chapter V.)
Gulliver among the Lilliputians (see Book I) had some exciting experiences.
Shakespeare was born on April 23 (?) , 1564.
I am studying medicine for three reasons: (1) I like the subject; (2) my father and grandfather are doctors; and (3) our town needs additional doctors.

NOTE: The second ) of the pair ( ) also could be used alone with the numbers in the last example above.

## 95c    *Do not use parentheses to cancel parts of your writing. Erase or draw lines through the words you wish to delete*

## 95d    *Use brackets to enclose your comment inserted or interpolated in a quoted passage*

For all practical purposes, this is the only use of brackets, but on rare occasions they appear inside parenthesis marks to set off strong parenthetic material within strong parenthetic material.

"On the first float rode the Queen of the Tournament [Miss Emily Miller], her attendants, and two boys dressed as pages."
"In April of that year [1942] Johnson took out his first patent."
"Milton portrays Satan as a fallen angle [sic] of tremendous size."

NOTE: Do not confuse brackets and parentheses. Brackets are used to set off inserted matter in someone else's writing, i.e., your addition to *quoted* material, such as corrections, comments, or explanations; parentheses are used to enclose your own parenthetic material, according to Section **95a.**

## 95e    *Use other marks appropriately with parentheses and brackets*

Since parenthetic and bracketed materials go with what has preceded, no punctuation precedes the first mark; any needed punctuation follows the closing parenthesis mark or bracket. See second example under Section **95a** and first example under Section **95d**.

## LESS FREQUENTLY USED MARKS

Ellipsis periods and brackets are among the less frequently used marks of punctuation. Asterisks (Section **86f4**) and the marks discussed just below are not strictly punctuation marks, but symbols serving a purpose in writing. Except for the caret, this purpose concerns a mechanical method of indicating pronunciation.

### 95f  *Use a* caret (ʌ) *to insert an omitted expression or letter*

Place the caret below the line at the place of omission and write the inserted expression or letter directly above or in the margin.

### 95g  *Use a* dieresis (¨) *to show that the second of two vowels is pronounced in the following syllable*

With such words as *zoology, cooperation,* and *coordination,* present tendency is not to use this sign. It is useful, however, in words like *preëxistent, reënforce,* and *naïve,* in order to prevent momentary confusion or mispronunciation. A hyphen may also be used to indicate this separation of doubled vowels in words like *pre-existent* and *re-enforce*. Consult your dictionary for guidance.

### 95h  *Use an* accent or other mark, *usually with words of foreign origin, where the spelling requires it*

Acute accent (′) : *passé, cliché, fiancé, fiancée*
Grave accent (`) : *à la mode, frère*
Circumflex (^) : *hôtel de ville, tête-à-tête, raison d'être*
Cedilla (ç) : *façade, français, garçon*
Tilde (˜) : *cañon, mañana, piña, señor*
Umlaut (¨) : *schön*
Slash or diagonal or virgule ( / ) : to indicate "both or one of two," *and/or;* "one of two," *straggler/deserter;* "per," *miles/hour*

Again, let your dictionary be your guide.

## EXERCISE

Copy the following sentences, inserting parentheses or brackets where they belong.

1. With the arrival of the relatives one never knows how many confusion reigns.
2. Sometime in April, 1564 the exact day is not known William Shakespeare was born in Stratford-on-Avon, England.
3. There are two major divisions of Christmas presents: a those of a monetary value, and b those which money cannot buy.
4. Several essays by Ralph Waldo Emerson you do remember him? have been widely quoted.
5. My grandfather Jones Grankie as my sister and I always called him when we were children is a well-known dentist.
6. The first three years of my life 1950–1953 were spent in Germany my father was stationed there.
7. My first orchid, even though my boy friend did not have to pay for it his parents owned the greenhouse had great meaning for me.
8. The magazine article began: "People these days are to sic busy to care about anyone but themselves."
9. "*Plain Sense* was published early in the nineteenth century 1826 by a New York printer."
10. Totalitarianism see Chapter 10 was eagerly discussed.

# 96  Italics (underlining)

Words italicized in print, i.e., slanting letters, are underlined once, when you type or write in longhand. Quotation marks may also be used to set off such words, but since these marks have various other uses (see Section **94**), underlining is preferable.

**96a** *Use italics (underlining) to indicate titles of*
*magazines, newspapers, pamphlets, books,*
*long poems, plays, motion pictures,*
*musical comedies, operas, works of art,*
*and the names of ships, trains, and airplanes*

I came from California to New York on two streamlined trains, *City of Denver* and *City of Philadelphia,* and sailed for Naples on the Italian liner, *Cristoforo Colombo.* In the ship's library I read copies of *Newsweek* and *The New York Times,* and on deck I read Thomas Hardy's novel *The Return of the Native.* While reading, I occasionally paused to think of the many planes crossing overhead, and I was reminded of Charles Lindbergh's first transatlantic flight in his now-famous *Spirit of St. Louis.* Every night, on shipboard, some famous movie was shown, like a revival, *It Happened One Night,* or a contemporary one, *The Sound of Music.* For variety I visited the ship's Art Salon and listened to complete recordings of operas like Rossini's *The Barber of Seville,* or I pleasantly studied excellent copies of famous art masterpieces, like Leonardo's *Mona Lisa* and Raphael's *Madonna of the Chair.*

1. When you use the title of an article or story and the magazine in which it appears, in order to distinguish them use quotation marks to enclose the former and italicize the latter; apply the same principle to the chapter title of a book and the book. But do not italicize the title of your theme used in the position of the title. Note that titles of articles and short stories are not italicized in their position as titles.

Be sure to read Wilbur Carter's article, "Non-Military Uses of Atomic Energy," in *Harper's Magazine.*
Your parents will enjoy reading Chapter 17, "How to Stretch Dollars," in Allen Brown's book, *The Quest for Security.*

2. Include the definite or indefinite article if it forms part of the title: *The Merchant of Venice* (not *Merchant of Venice*) ; *A Fable for Critics* (not *Fable for Critics*) .
3. Do not add an article to a title if none appears in the original work: Shakespeare's *Twelfth Night* (not *The Twelfth Night*) .

4. Italicize the name of the city and the definite article if it is included in the title of a newspaper: *The New York Times; Chicago Tribune.* (Some instructors and style manuals suggest not italicizing the name of the city or the definite article in the title of a newspaper.)

5. According to convention, the Bible and the names of the books of the Bible are not italicized or enclosed in quotation marks: Matthew 14:12 (Matthew xiv:12).

### 96b    Use italics (underlining) to indicate foreign words or phrases

Foreign words that have not been naturalized in English should either be italicized or enclosed in quotation marks. Your dictionary will tell you whether foreign words and phrases are naturalized, i.e., are in good English use or still considered distinctly foreign.

This painting has about it a certain *je ne sais quoi* quality.
The foreign student in America must work out a *modus vivendi.*
On our campus we still find an occasional student suffering from *Weltschmerz.*

### 96c    Use italics (underlining) to refer to a word, letter, or number spoken of as such

Your undotted *i*'s look exactly like *e*'s.
You have written *6* every time that you meant to write *9.*
I stupidly wrote *Rode 39* when I had meant to write *Road 39.*
The four most frequently misused pairs of words in English are the following: *to* and *too, it's* and *its, their* and *there,* and *your* and *you're.*

NOTE: If it is more convenient, quotation marks may be just as clearly used in such examples as italics:

An "em" is a term frequently used in printing.

### 96d    Use italics (underlining) to emphasize a word, a phrase, or a statement

*Always* sign your name to a letter.
Never, *under any conditions,* keep poisonous substances in your medicine cabinet.

Used sparingly, italics for emphasis are effective. Overused, they become monotonous and ineffective.

**EXERCISE**

Recopy the following sentences, underlining the words that should be italicized. What are your reasons?

1. Many travelers regret the passing of the great transatlantic liners like the Queen Mary and the Queen Elizabeth.
2. Looking up the name Jane, we find it equivalent to Joan, and Joan is equivalent to Joanna, which is the feminine of John.
3. The British differ in their spelling of some words: they use more -our and -re endings instead of -or and -er.
4. I like to read and re-read famous works such as Mark Twain's Huckleberry Finn and William Shakespeare's Julius Caesar.
5. When the reader specifically is meant, the pronouns you, your, and yours are recommended.
6. The Chicago Tribune is the leading newspaper in the Midwest; The New York Times and The Christian Science Monitor are leaders in the East.
7. Our music director adds spice by the way he pronounces words, such as da-reem' for dream and ka-rye' for cry.
8. Monitor comes from the Latin word monere, which means to warn; the word monitor has been used (capitalized thus, Monitor) as the name of a ship.
9. Everyone who likes to travel should read magazines like Travel, Holiday, and The National Geographic Magazine.
10. Some people say au revoir and some say auf Wiedersehen; I'll stick with the plain, old-fashioned American good-by.

# 97 *Capitals*

The applications of capitalization are so numerous that rules or principles cannot be given to apply to every possible example. Stylebooks of various publishing firms usually contain from 20 to 40 pages dealing with capitals and lists of examples,[1] but for

[1] As a specific guide, the 1967 United States Government Printing Office *Style Manual* (pp. 33–59) lists some 3,500 words in its "Guide to Capitalization" based on the rules of capitalization.

the student-writer a few underlying principles may be helpful—
for reference, not for memorization.

**97a    *Capitalize each important word in titles
of themes, articles, pamphlets, books,
plays, motion pictures, poems, magazines,
newspapers, musical compositions, songs, etc.***

Capitalize, in accordance with this principle, the first and each
important word in titles, including infinitive sign, but with titles
do not capitalize articles, prepositions, or conjunctions, unless
these two last consist of five or more letters (a curious convention
that is quite generally observed) .

| | |
|---|---|
| Autumn Days on the Farm | Brown's *Other Worlds than Ours* |
| A Tour Through the UN Building | Gray's *Elegy Written in a Country* |
| Steps Toward Faster Reading | *Churchyard* |
| The Stars Pass By | Sheridan's *The School for Scandal* |
| History as a Literary Art | *The Saturday Evening Post* |
| How To Study Under Difficulties | Steinbeck's *The Grapes of Wrath* |
| *but* A Trip to Mammoth Cave | Listen and Learn Italian |

NOTE 1: Both common nouns in a hyphenated compound are
capitalized when capitals are needed, as in titles: Tennyson's
poem, "The Lotos-Eaters."

NOTE 2: The Library of Congress now advocates capitalizing
only the first word and any proper nouns or adjectives in a title.
Until such practice is more widely adopted, you are advised to
use the principle stated above.

**97b    *Capitalize the first word of the following:
(1) a sentence; (2) an expression serving
as a sentence; (3) a quoted sentence;
(4) divisions and subdivisions of outlines***

The rule of capitalizing the first word of every sentence is illustrated on
    every printed page.
Will you attend the meeting tonight, please?
Our instructor said, "Don't miss seeing that movie."

For capitalization in outlines, see Section **6b,c.**

NOTE: A complete statement, but not a quotation, within a sentence may begin with a capital if the writer so desires:

Our problem was, *Could* (or *could*) most of the students afford the trip?

When only part of a direct quotation is included within a sentence, it is usually not begun with a capital letter.

The press secretary, after a talk with Dr. Snyder, said that the President was "fine," and added that the doctor "just didn't want to take any chances with the flu."

## 97c Capitalize the first word of every line of poetry

We look before and after,
  And pine for what is not:
Our sincerest laughter
  With some pain is fraught;
Our sweetest songs are those that tell of saddest thought.
  —SHELLEY, "To a Skylark"

The foregoing illustrates traditional poetry. Some modern poetry is written without capital letters. If and when you quote poetry, use the capitalization employed in the poem.

## 97d Capitalize proper nouns

These include:

1. Names of people and titles used with or for specific persons: William Shakespeare, the President, Senator William E. Borah, Elizabeth II, the Treasurer, the General, Mr. Chairman, Father, Mother, the Bishop.

2. Capitalize academic-degree abbreviations used with or without a proper name:

Many colleges and universities offer the A.B. and A.M. degrees.
John S. White, M.D., and Professor Harry Bird, Ph.D., will debate the problem Tuesday evening.

3. Names of countries, states, regions, localities, other geographic areas, and the like: United States, England, Pennsylvania, the Old World, the Far East, the Midwest, the Rocky Mountains,

the Sahara Desert, the Mississippi River, Lake Michigan, the Badlands, the North Pole (see Section **97e**) .

4. Names of streets: Michigan Boulevard, Fifth Avenue, Ross Street, Hillside Drive, Old Mill Road (see Section **97e**) .

5. Names of the Deity and personal pronouns referring to Him: God, Heavenly Father, Son of God, Jesus Christ, Savior (Saviour) , His, Him, Thy, Thine. Also, capitalize Satan and words specifically denoting Satan: Father of Lies, the Devil.

6. Names for the Bible, the books of the Bible, and other sacred writings: Bible, the Scriptures, Book of Genesis, The Acts of the Apostles, Revelations, Koran.

7. Names of religions, religious groups, and religious documents: Protestantism, Roman Catholicism, Presbyterian, Jesuit, Unitarian, Apostles' Creed, the Dead Sea Scrolls.

8. Names of the days and the months (but *not* the seasons —see Section **97h3**) : Monday, Tuesday, etc.; January, February, etc.

9. Names of schools, colleges, universities: Hill School, Morton Grade School, Horace Mann High School, Kentucky Military Institute, Wabash College, Cornell University, University of Illinois (see Section **97e**) .

10. Names of historic events, eras, and holidays: Revolutionary War, Christian Era, Middle Ages, Renaissance, the Fourth of July, Labor Day, Thanksgiving, New Year's Eve.

11. Names of official governmental bodies and documents: the City Council, State Senate, Congress, United Nations, the Constitution, Federal Reserve Board, Magna Carta.

12. Names of races, organizations, and members of each: Indian, Malay, Negro, League of Women Voters, American Academy of Sciences, National League, New York Yankees, Big Ten Conference, Ivy League, an Elk, a Shriner, a Socialist.

13. Vivid personifications: Fate, Star of Fortune, Destiny, the power of Nature, the paths of Glory, the chronicles of Time.

14. Trade names: Bon Ami, Jello, Magnavox, Palmolive, Ry-Krisp, Wheaties.

15. All names similar or comparable to those in the foregoing 14 groups.

NOTE: If the second member of a hyphenated compound is a proper noun or proper adjective, it is capitalized: Latin-American, pre-Raphaelite, un-American, non-European.

### 97e Capitalize a common noun or adjective when it is a part of or helps to make a proper name

Missouri River, Rocky Mountains, Wall Street, Lexington Avenue, Blackstone Theatre, Washington High School, Swarthmore College, New York University, Roosevelt Dam, Yosemite National Park, Lake Erie, U. S. Highway 40, Route 33, Room 117, Chapter 26.

Common nouns and adjectives used alone are not capitalized: avenue, bay, building, college, county, dam, high school, island, lake, library, mountain, ocean, park, river, sea, strait, street, theater, university, professions, and the like.

He is not a professor.
This is Professor Smith.

My father is a dean in a college.
My father is Dean Williams of Seneca University.

These students attend the local high school.
John is a graduate of Rocktown High School.

The street in front of our house needs paving.
Three houses on Forest Street are vacant.

I have explored many of the rivers in our country.
The Brenta River is a well-known river in northern Italy, just outside Venice.

The mountains in eastern Tennessee are known as the Great Smokies.
The Great Smoky Mountains are well worth a visit.

NOTE: Interjections, except *O,* are common words, and within a sentence are not capitalized.

Sail on, O Ship of State.
On that day, alas, our high school days came to an end.

### 97f Capitalize words derived from proper nouns

Shakespearean (Shakespearian), American, Episcopalian, Biblical, Scriptural, Italian, Pennsylvanian, British.

Note two important specific applications and a list of exceptions.

1. The word *English* is always capitalized in reference to language and literature as well as its geographical application.

2. The first personal pronoun "I" is always capitalized. None of the other pronouns are capitalized unless they begin a sentence or a direct quotation or refer to the Deity (see Section 97d5).

3. Some proper nouns and derivatives of proper nouns (the number approaches 200) have been used in specific meanings so frequently that they are considered common and are not capitalized. When in doubt, consult your dictionary. A fair sampling of such a list includes:

| | | |
|---|---|---|
| braille | herculean | turkish towel |
| brussels sprouts | india ink | utopian |
| frankfurter | pasteurized | venetian blind |
| french dressing | roman type | vienna bread |
| french fried potatoes | swiss cheese | watt |

### 97g   Avoid careless writing of capitals

Do not carelessly write small letters so large that they resemble capitals. You disconcert and confuse your reader by this carelessness.

### 97h   Avoid unnecessary use of capitals

1. Do not capitalize names of points of the compass unless they refer to a specific section.

*Correct*   My home is in the East.
Texas is the largest state in the Southwest.
John lives west of the Allegheny Mountains.
I should like to live in the southern part of California,' or somewhere in the West.
Walk two blocks west; then turn north.

2. Do not capitalize earth, sun, moon except when they are used in association with other astronomical bodies that are capitalized:

Mercury and Venus are farther from the Sun than are the Earth, Mars, and Jupiter.

The sun is bright today, the moon will be full tonight, and the earth is filled with pleasant sounds and fragrant perfumes.

3. Do not capitalize the names of the seasons: spring, summer, autumn, fall, winter. Of course, if any season is personified, use a capital.

4. Do not capitalize nouns of kinship unless they are used as a substitute for a proper name. When preceded by an article or a possessive, they are common nouns.

*Correct*    My father is a dean.
At Seneca College, Father (i.e., Mr. Smith) is Dean of Men.
My sister thinks I am quiet, but Grandma and Mother say that I talk too much.
Every autumn my cousin Harry and I go hunting.
Every autumn Cousin Harry and I go hunting.

5. Do not capitalize a noun or adjective if the reference is to any one of a class of persons or things rather than a specific person or thing. For example, do not capitalize names of professions or occupations.

*Wrong*    My roommate is studying Engineering and expects to become a Teacher; I hope to become either a Doctor or a Dentist.

In capitalizing names of classes or college class members as members, follow the principle of consistency. One suggestion is that you do not capitalize the noun or adjective indicating college class members but that you do capitalize the name of a specific class.

Four of us are sharing a double room; Joe is a freshman, I am a sophomore, Bill is a junior, and Mike is a senior. On the floor below us every resident is a member of the Senior class and on the floor above us everyone is a member of the Freshman class.

6. Do not capitalize names of general college subjects unless they are proper names, but capitalize titles of specific courses:

Next year I shall have courses in history, Spanish, and journalism, and although I do not like science courses, I shall be required to take Mathematics 2 and Biology 12.

7. Do not capitalize unimportant words in titles (Section **97a**) or the first word of part of a direct quotation (Section **97b**) or common nouns and adjectives not part of or helping to make a proper name (Section **97e**).

NOTE: Do not be misled by current practices of some magazines and book publishers: using small letters for every word in titles.

*Undesirable*   "lincoln land in illinois"
*a book of readings for english and american literature*

## EXERCISES

A. Circle all the capitals on a page of prose selected from a textbook or magazine. Give the reason for each capital.

B. Copy the following sentences, making the misuse or nonuse of capitals conform to the principles stated in Section **97**.

1. Our english teacher often told us, "you can't judge a book by its cover."
2. Numerous examples can be cited from the bible and other Books about god and the greatness of his works.
3. The names of some of our States and many of our Cities have an indian origin.
4. I am registered as a Freshman in the college of home economics here at lakeside university.
5. She blurted out, "how about thursday or friday?" to which he replied, "fine!"
6. My freshman courses consist of plant science 140, english composition 101, chemistry 111 and 112, zoology 161, speech 114, and some Electives.
7. The mississippi river is the most famous river in American History; the kankakee river is not so well known.
8. The climate is mild in rome, italy; the coldest months are december, january, and february.
9. In little things Happiness is sometimes found, like an a on an english theme.
10. Every summer aunt laura and aunt ida come to visit us.
11. My main interests deal with the subjects of Chemistry, Guns, Airplanes, Rockets, and the Planet Earth.
12. Some english teachers hunt for Topic Sentences and Transitional Sentences the way a hunter hunts for game.

13. To reach chatsworth you must take u. s. highway 52 to junction 24, and then turn left on state route 24.
14. During his term of service my Father was sent to teach in several colleges in the east and in the south.
15. The poet shelley ends his famous poem, "ode to the west wind," with these words: "o wind, if winter comes, can spring be far behind?"

# 98 *Abbreviations*

### 98a  *Use only acceptable abbreviations in both formal and informal writing*

In all writing intended for information and convenience of a reader, avoid abbreviations that would be puzzling or unusual to him; write out words and expressions in full, unless condensation seems necessary or the spelled-out words are unconventional, like *Mister* and *Missus* (*Mistress*). Conventional abbreviations are illustrated by the following: *Mr., Mrs., Dr., Jr.*

In the following examples, exaggerated for illustration, puzzling and unusual abbreviations occur:

*Incorrect*     A new sec. is to be elected to replace the sec.-treas. who has resigned.

Many a chem. prof. grades too severely; many a lit. prof. grades too easily.

Meet me in the Cent. Station Wed. P.M.

Chicago, Ill., lies n.e. of the Miss. R.

1. Themes and other college written work are or should be formal writing or good idiomatic informal writing. Usually, use abbreviations only in footnotes and bibliographies of term and research papers. Specifically and as a general rule, *avoid in continuous prose the following abbreviations*:

a. Names of states, rivers, mountains, etc.: Ala., Pa., Ill. R., Appalach. Mtns.

b. Parts of geographic names: Ft. Wayne for Fort Wayne, N. Dakota for North Dakota, Pt. Arthur for Port Arthur. (*Saint*, however, is abbreviated before a place name: St. Louis, St. Bonaventure.)

c. Christian names: Jos. for Joseph, Benj. for Benjamin, Thos. for Thomas.

d. Names of months and days: Jan., Feb., Sun., Mon.

e. Most titles: Prof., Gen., Lieut., Pres.

f. Names of school and college subjects: chem., math., ed., P.E.

g. Words denoting length, time, weight, or capacity: in., ft., yd., sec., min., hr., mo., yr., oz., lb., qt., gal., pk., bu., bbl.

NOTE: Words of measurement and numerous other words are abbreviated in tables, footnotes, and bibliographies.

h. Miscellaneous words: st. for *street,* ave. for *avenue,* blvd. for *boulevard,* dr. for *drive,* pl. for *place,* r. for *river,* mt. for *mountain*; a.m. and p.m. (as substitutes for *morning* and *afternoon*: "this a.m. and p.m.") .

i. Symbols for words: & or + for *and*; % for *percent*; @ for *at*; © for *copyright* or *copyrighted*; × for *times* or *by* (3 × 54 or 8½ × 11) ; = for *equal (s)* ; # for *number* before a figure (#13) and *pounds* after a figure (15#) ; and the like. (For $ before a figure, like $5, see Section **99c7**.)

2. Certain abbreviations are permissible and should be used instead of the full word. These are usually conventional titles used before names of people and the letters after names indicating identification or educational degrees: Mr., Mrs., Dr., Ph.D., LL.D., D.D., Esq., Jr., Sr. Note that Rev. and Hon.—even when spelled out—are used with full names, not with the last name alone.

Mr. William Brown; Mrs. John Smith; Messrs. William Brown and John Smith; Dr. Albert Jones; Hon. James E. Mason; Rev. Gordon Graham (but note: *The Honorable* James E. Mason, *The Reverend* Gordon Graham, but *never* Rev. Graham) .

William Brown, A.B., A.M.; John Smith, Ph.D., LL.D.; Rev. Gordon Graham, D.D.
William Allen, Sr., and William Allen, Jr., were elected delegates.

Harry Jones, M.D., and his brother, Henry Jones, D.D.S., share an office.

Other necessary abbreviations include the following: a.m. and p.m. or A.M. and P.M., with numbers (7 a.m., 8:25 a.m., 2:10 p.m.) ; F. (for Fahrenheit) ; C. (for Centigrade), B.C. (before Christ) ; A.D. (Anno Domini, i.e., in the year of the Lord), etc., i.e., e.g., cf., and viz.

NOTE: B.C. follows the year, A.D. precedes it: 73 B.C., A.D. 1960.

## 98b   Do not use contractions in formal writing

A contraction is a form of abbreviation: a word written with an apostrophe to indicate the omission of a letter. Usually considered as proper in speech and in informal writing, such contractions as *aren't, isn't, can't, couldn't, don't, doesn't, hasn't, haven't, shan't, shouldn't, wasn't, weren't, won't, wouldn't, mustn't* are out of place in formal writing. (See Section 53.)

In reporting dialogue or conversation, however, use contractions correctly to convey the exact words of the speaker. Do not avoid contractions and other colloquialisms to the extent of making reports of conversation seem artificial and forced.

## 98c   Use a period after abbreviations, with few exceptions

The few exceptions are:

1. Contractions such as *don't, won't, isn't, haven't,* etc.
2. The ordinal numbers when written *1st, 2nd, 35th,* etc.
3. Shortened forms like *ad, phone, exam, lab* (see Section 70) .
4. Nicknames such as Bill, Joe, Al, Peg, Liz, etc.
5. A few specialized abbreviations, including broadcasting companies and stations: percent or per cent (avoid %) , TV, ABC, NBC, CBS, WEND, WBBM, WILL, KDAD, etc.
6. Letters for certain associations, unions, and government divisions and agencies: CARE, NASA, NSF, PHA, UNESCO, CIO, HEW, FBI, etc.

For some abbreviations, especially those in 6 above, the use or omission of periods is optional; for others, periods are required. As one dictionary says, variation in such use of periods is widespread, as well as in typeface and capitalization. When in doubt, follow the punctuation given in your dictionary.

## EXERCISE

Correct all errors in the use of abbreviations in the following sentences:

1. I have 8 o'clock classes every Mon., Wed., and Fri. a.m.
2. The prep schools in England are often called pub. schools.
3. Our home ec courses are not as easy as some non-ec students think.
4. My brother Thomas is 21 yrs. old, is 6′ 2″ tall, and weighs approximately 180#; by comparison, my brother John is only 5 ft. 5 in. tall and weighs 112 lbs.
5. At Morgan Park Mil. Acad. I had an excellent teacher who was a capt. in the U.S.M. Corps; he has since become a lt.-col.
6. When I finish my college chem and lab courses, I would like to go on to grad. school.
7. Henry has recently been awarded a scholarship to Col. Univ. in N.Y.C., N.Y.
8. The parade down Penn. Ave. was something to behold; I should like to be in Wash., D.C., and see another.
9. The assignments in our English comp. book deal with all phases of comp. and with some suggestions for lit. reading.
10. The three lines of the letter heading were: 222 Indep. Blvd., Phila., Pa., Feb. 15, '69.

# 99 *Numbers*

### 99a *Be consistent in your use of words*
### *or figures for numbers (numerals)*

Writing words for numbers or using figures for words, in sustained prose writing, is a matter of convention and custom. For most themes and other college writing, either of two principles serves; with an occasional variation, the two agree:

1. When a number can be expressed in one word or two words, write it out; otherwise, use figures: two, twenty-two, two hundred, 101, 749, 2,412, etc.

*or*

2. Use words for the numbers between one and ninety-nine; use figures for numbers above ninety-nine: 100, 200, 314, etc.

Some variations from the foregoing occur, as in the following suggestions (**99b,c,d**), which are not for memorization but for reference only. The United States Government Printing Office *Style Manual* (1967) and the stylebooks for printed news media, for example, state that as a general rule, within a sentence the numbers from one through nine should be spelled out and that the numbers 10 and up should be expressed in figures. (For the use of commas with four or more figures, see Section **881**.)

**99b   *Use words to represent numbers in special uses***

1. Indefinite expressions or round numbers.

> This theater will seat several thousand persons.
> Right now I am wishing for a million dollars.
> We have a hundred cows and six hundred chickens on our farm.
> The mid-fifties will probably be known as the atomic fifties.
> *but*
> The 1950s will probably be known as the atomic decade.

2. One number or related numbers at the beginning of a sentence.

> Three of our class officers are from the College of Engineering.
> Twenty to thirty students will be absent on an inspection trip to Detroit.

Use common sense in applying this principle:

| | |
|---|---|
| *Undesirable* | Three thousand two hundred and thirty-nine students are enrolled as freshmen this year. |
| | 3,239 students are enrolled as freshmen this year. |
| *Desirable* | A total of 3,239 freshmen . . . |
| | Enrolled as freshmen this year are 3,239 students. |

3. Numbers preceding a compound modifier containing a figure.

> To line this wall we need twelve ½-inch pieces of plywood.
> Our tent is supported by two 8-foot poles.

4. Fractions standing alone or followed by *of a* or *of an.*

> Be sure that the plywood is one-half inch thick.
> I live about one-fourth of a mile from the campus.

5. Numbers used with serious and dignified subjects.

> Pennsylvania is proud to be listed among the Thirteen Original Colonies.
> This bill was given serious consideration in the Seventy-eighth Congress.

NOTE: A spelled-out number is not repeated in figures in parentheses, except in legal documents.

> *Undesirable*    I enclose my check for ten dollars ($10) .
> Thirty (30) claims were made for damages.

## 99c  *Use figures to represent numbers in special uses*
1. Dates, including the day or the day and the year.

> Please return the blank by June 1.
> My parents were married on June 28, 1948.
> I worked on a farm from July 1 to September 1, 1968.

The proper date line for a letter is:

February 1, 1969
  *or*
1 February 1969 (no comma)
not figures like 2/1/69, except on the second page of business letters

2. House, room, area code, telephone, and zip code numbers.

> I live at 1607 Ravinia Road, Columbus, Ohio 43216; my telephone number is (614) 534-6061.
> Send your request to 33 Hubbard Street, Des Moines, Iowa 50318.
> Tomorrow this class will meet in Room 6, University Hall.
> We are staying at the Greenbriar Hotel, Room 712.
> My campus mailbox is Number 4.

3. Highway or comparable numbers.

> Take U. S. Highway 40 into Columbus and turn north on Route 33.
> Our best TV reception comes in over Channel 6.
> Trains for Chicago leave on Track 3.
> Flight 808, New York to Paris, leaves Kennedy Airport each night;
> use Gate 7 to the plane.

4. Measurements: age; degrees of temperature, longitude, latitude; distance; size; weight; containers; etc.

> Father is 42 years old, Mother is 39, and my baby sister is 6.
> The temperature has varied from 2 to 8 degrees below 0.
> The white lines on a football field are 5 yards apart.
> Standard stationery is 8½-by-11 inches in size.
> ¾-inch pipe      1-inch margin      5-foot pole
> 7 bushels          5 acres              2 gallons
> The parcel-post package weighed 6 pounds, 9 ounces.
> Everyone knows that 2 pints make a quart and 4 quarts make a gallon.

5. Time.

> 8 A.M. (*not* 8:00 A.M.)      12 M. (noon)      3:25 P.M.      half past 3
> 10 o'clock (*not* 10 o'clock A.M., or 10 A.M. in the morning)
> 8 years, 4 months, 27 days
> 6 days      3 minutes      2 months      9-hour day      5-day week
> I completed my assignment in 3 hours, 9 minutes, and 35 seconds.

NOTE: Omit 00 from even-hour time expressions. (See also Item 17, Section **70**.)

6. Percentage, proportion, and other mathematical expressions.

> 10 percent      one-half of 1 percent      4¼ percent bonds
> Many students waste 15 to 20 percent of their time just fooling around.
> To obtain the answer, multiply by 3 and divide by 6.
> The proportion of women to men on our campus is 1 to 4.

7.  Money.

> $4.55     $0.60     60 cents     $6 per bushel   (not $6.00)
>   35 cents apiece

NOTE:  Omit 00 in even-dollar expressions.

8.  Unit modifiers.

> 8-hour day     5-day week     10-foot pole     12-hour trip
>   20th-century progress

9.  Chapter, page, and footnote numbers.

> Chapter 12     See p. 144     pp. 312–315     See footnote 3 on p. 7

Sometimes chapters and preliminary pages of a book are numbered with Roman numerals (see Section **99e,** below), but some books now number preliminary pages 1a, 2a, 3a, 4a, etc.

## 99d   *Use figure-and-letter combinations appropriately*

Occasionally, a writer needs to use figures with letters, especially in expressing the ordinal numbers: 1st for first, 2nd or 2d for second; 3rd or 3d for third; fourth through twentieth, 4th, 9th 12th, 18th, 20th; others as they apply, 21st, 33rd, or 33d, 99th, etc.

Such combinations are appropriately used as follows: in tables; sometimes in numbering ideas in a paragraph or a succession of paragraphs; sometimes in dates, but not when the year follows immediately; and usually in expressing a numbered street from 10th on.

Your May 15th letter (or your letter of May 15th) has been received.
Your letter of May 15, 1968, has been received.
121 North First Avenue
Corner of Fifth Avenue and 10th Street
49 East 33rd Street     South 199th Street
After June 1st my address will no longer be 12 West Second Street; it
    will be 833 East 24th Street.
The 20th century is vastly different from the ninth century.
My sixth birthday and Grandfather's 60th occurred in 1957.

Notice, 1st, that no period follows the figure-with-letter combinations and, 2nd, that the principles about figures versus words (Sections **99b,c**) apply usually to figure-with-letter combinations.

### 99e  Use Roman numerals correctly

Until the tenth century, our numbers were Roman letters used as numerals. Our present figures came from the Arabs and are called Arabic numerals. Although these Arabic numbers are generally preferable, Roman numerals still find occasional use in current writing, as in preparing outlines (Section **6**), numbering the preliminary pages of a book (but see last paragraph in Section **99c9**), occasionally marking the date for a year, and frequently indicating acts and scenes of plays, volume numbers of magazines and books, and chapter numbers of books.

Large-capital Roman numerals are used after book (Book VI), volume (Volume or Vol. VII), part (Part II), act (Act III), unit or individual in a series (Charles XII, Elizabeth II), and sometimes for a year. Small-letter numerals, or sometimes small capitals, may be used for numbering preliminary pages, play scenes, tables and plates in printed or graphic materials, and sometimes Bible chapters.

Prince Hal and Falstaff first appear in Act I, Scene ii, of Shakespeare's *Henry IV*, Part I.

George I, George II, and George III reigned in the eighteenth century, George V and George VI in the twentieth.

The article "Grecian Architecture" is in Volume XII of the *Universal Encyclopedia*.

This imposing building bears the date when it was dedicated—MDCCCLXXIV.

The preliminary pages in this *Handbook* are numbered from i through xiv.

The table below shows how Roman numerals are formed: "a repeated letter repeats its value; a letter placed after one of greater value adds to it; a letter placed before one of greater value subtracts from it; a dashline over a letter denotes multiplied by 1,000." (From United States Government Printing Office *Style Manual*, 1967 Edition, from which the table is also taken.)

## ROMAN NUMERALS

| | | | |
|---|---|---|---|
| I | 1 | LXX | 70 |
| II | 2 | LXXV | 75 |
| III | 3 | LXXIX | 79 |
| IV | 4 | LXXX | 80 |
| V | 5 | LXXXV | 85 |
| VI | 6 | LXXXIX | 89 |
| VII | 7 | XC | 90 |
| VIII | 8 | XCV | 95 |
| IX | 9 | XCIX | 99 |
| X | 10 | C | 100 |
| XV | 15 | CL | 150 |
| XIX | 19 | CC | 200 |
| XX | 20 | CCC | 300 |
| XXV | 25 | CD | 400 |
| XXIX | 29 | D | 500 |
| XXX | 30 | DC | 600 |
| XXXV | 35 | DCC | 700 |
| XXXIX | 39 | DCCC | 800 |
| XL | 40 | CM | 900 |
| XLV | 45 | M | 1,000 |
| XLIX | 49 | MD | 1,500 |
| L | 50 | MM | 2,000 |
| LV | 55 | MMM | 3,000 |
| LIX | 59 | MMMM or $M\bar{V}$ | 4,000 |
| LX | 60 | $\bar{V}$ | 5,000 |
| LXV | 65 | $\bar{M}$ | 1,000,000 |
| LXIX | 69 | | |

### *Dates*

| | | | |
|---|---|---|---|
| MDC | 1600 | MCMXX | 1920 |
| MDCC | 1700 | MCMXXX | 1930 |
| MDCCC | 1800 | MCMXL | 1940 |
| MCM or MDCCCC | 1900 | MCML | 1950 |
| MCMX | 1910 | MCMLX | 1960 |

## EXERCISE

Correct any unconventional uses of figures and spelled-out numbers in the following sentences:

1. The greatest attraction of Niagara Falls is the one-hundred-and-sixty-five-foot drop where two hundred thousand cubic feet of water fall every second.
2. 750 dollars a month is not unusual as a starting salary for a highly trained college graduate.

3. In England there are one hundred and twenty-six churches dedicated to St. George.
4. I am taking English one hundred and one and mathematics one hundred and sixty-one; I am a 1st-semester freshman.
5. My brother stands five feet four inches tall and weighs one hundred and thirty-nine pounds.
6. Will you please come to dinner at our hall at six forty-five p.m. on Wednesday, March twenty-third?
7. To be admitted you must be in the upper 3rd and preferably the upper 4th of your graduating class.
8. I was born on April twelfth in Portland, Missouri, in the year nineteen hundred and fifty-one; we now live at twelve hundred and one Seventy-ninth Street, and my telephone number is three-seven-two-one-one-six-five.
9. My home town can be reached by U. S. Highway Fifty-two or State Roads Twenty-five, Twenty-six, and Forty-three.
10. I went to the Bursar's Office on the 1st floor of the Administration Building and paid the fees of ninety-two dollars and fifty cents.

## 100 Glossary of applied punctuation

In applying to your writing the general and specific punctuation principles reviewed in the preceding pages, answer the following questions when you have a problem about punctuation:

⟶ 1. Exactly what is here that requires punctuation? That is, what kinds of sentences? What kinds of elements within sentences? What kinds of relations between elements?

⟶ 2. What purpose do I want my punctuation to serve? Termination? Introduction? Separation? Enclosure? Correctness? Clearness? Effectiveness?

⟶ 3. What punctuation mark or marks will best accomplish that purpose?

When you have answered the first question—"Exactly what is here that requires punctuation?"—use the following to answer the second and third questions. Figures and letters in parentheses refer to sections providing detailed discussion and illustration.

1. Abbreviations.  Use a period after a standard abbreviation. (**86c**)
2. Absolute phrase (nominative absolute) .  Use commas. (**88p**)
3. Act–scene.  Separate by a colon. (**90f**)
4. Adjectives.  Two or more adjectives modifying, coordinately, the same noun, separate by commas. See also *Series,* below. (**88i**)
5. Adjective clauses and adjective phrases.  See *Clauses, dependent,* below, and see *Phrases,* below.
6. Adverbial clauses.  See *Clauses, dependent,* below.
7. Although.  Never preceded by a semicolon, unless other conditions warrant. See *Conjunctions, subordinating,* below.
8. Apposition.  Use commas. For long or emphatic appositional phrases, use dashes. (**88q, 91e**)
9. Because.  Never preceded by a semicolon, unless other conditions warrant. See *Conjunctions, subordinating,* below.
10. Break or shift in thought.  Use a dash. (**91c**)
11. Cancellation.  Do not use parentheses to cancel. Erase or draw a line through the material. (**95c**)
12. Chapter titles.  In a body of prose, enclose in quotation marks. As the heading of a chapter, use no punctuation. (**94e**)
13. Clauses.
    Independent clauses.    (1) Joined by pure coordinating conjunction, use a comma. If the clauses are long with complicated internal punctuation, use a semicolon. (**88d, 89c**) (2) Not joined by any conjunction, use a semicolon. (**89a**) (3) Joined by a conjunctive adverb, use a semicolon. (**89b**) (4) Used parenthetically, enclose in dashes or parentheses. (**91e, 95a**) (5) Between contrasting independent clauses, use a comma. (**88j**)
    Dependent clause.    (1) Adverbial clause preceding independent clause, use a comma. (**88f**) (2) Adverbial clause following independent clause: if restrictive, use no punctuation; otherwise, use commas if adverbial clause is nonrestrictive or fairly long. (**88f**) (3) Adjective clause: if nonrestrictive, use commas; if restrictive, omit punctuation. (**88m**) (4) Noun clauses: used as subject or object or complement, no punc-

tuation. (**88u**) (5) Dependent contrasting clauses, use a comma. (**88j**)

14. Complex sentence. See *Clauses, dependent,* above.
15. Compound predicate. With two members only, usually no commas; with three or more, commas. See *Series,* below.
16. Compound sentence. See *Clauses, independent,* above.
17. Compound words. Separate the parts by a hyphen or hyphens. (**92a,b**)
18. Conjunctions, coordinating. (1) Pure conjunctions joining independent clauses, use a comma before, but not after. (**88d**) (2) Pure conjunctions joining two words or two phrases, no punctuation; joining three or more, commas. (**88h**) (3) Conjunctive adverb (see *Conjunctive adverb,* below). (4) Correlative conjunctions: apply same principle as for pure conjunctions. (**88d,h**)
19. Conjunctions, subordinating. Never place a comma or a semicolon after, unless for other reasons; place a comma before if the clause is adverbial, is nonrestrictive, and follows the independent clause. (**88f,u, 89b**)
20. Conjunctive adverb. Use a semicolon before when placed between two independent clauses. Use a comma or no mark after, depending on parenthetic strength. (**89b**)
21. Contractions. Use an apostrophe. (**93b**)
22. Contrasted coordinate elements. Use a comma. (**88j**)
23. Coordinate adjectives. See *Adjectives,* above.
24. Correlative conjunctions. See *Conjunctions, coordinating,* above.
25. Dates or places. Enclose in commas when they explain preceding dates or places. (**88s**)
26. Decimal. Use a period preceding. (**86e**)
27. Declarative sentence. See *Sentence,* below.
28. Dependent clause. See *Clauses,* above.
29. Dialogue. Use quotation marks and commas. (**88b, 94a,b,c**)
30. Diction. Provincialisms, slang expressions, misnomers, and unusual technical terms, use quotation marks. (**94d**)
31. Direct address (Vocative). Use commas. (**88r**)
32. Dollars and cents. Use a period between. (**86e**)
33. Doubt or uncertainty. Use a question mark in parentheses. (**87e**)

34. Ellipsis.   See *Omission of words,* below.
35. Emphasis.   Italicize. **(96d)** Also see *Surprise,* below.
36. Exclamatory sentence.   See *Sentence,* below.
37. Figures.   Four or more figures, use a comma in front of each three numbers. **(88l)** For omitted figures, use apostrophe. **(93b)** To connect combinations of figures, use hyphen. **(92d)**
38. For.   As a conjunction, use a comma preceding. As a preposition, use no punctuation. **(88e)**
39. For example, for instance, namely, etc.   Used parenthetically, enclose in commas, unless they are followed by an independent clause; then use a colon or semicolon before, a comma after. **(88n,q)**
40. Fractions.   Use a hyphen between the numerator and the denominator. **(92b)**
41. Hour–minute.   Separate by a colon. **(90f)**
42. Imperative sentence.   See *Sentence,* below.
43. Independent clauses.   See *Clauses,* above.
44. Indirect question.   Use a period, not a question mark. **(86a, 87c)**
    Indirect quotation.   Use neither commas nor quotation marks. **(88u, 94j)**
45. Initials.   Use period after each when they precede proper name. **(86c)** Use periods and commas when they follow. **(88t)**
46. Inserted material.   (1) Inserted sentence elements, use comma or commas. **(88o)** (2) Omitted material inserted later, indicate by a caret (ʌ) . **(95f)**
47. Interjections.   Mild, use a comma; strong or fairly strong, use an exclamation point! **(87a, 88n)**
48. Interpolated material.   Use brackets. **(95d)**
49. Interrogative sentence.   See *Sentence,* below.
50. Interruption in dialogue.   Use a dash. **(91b)**
51. Introduction.   Before a word, phrase, or clause being introduced, use a comma, colon, or dash. **(88a, 90a,b, 91a)**
52. Irony.   Occasionally, indicate by an exclamation point within parentheses. **(87a)**
53. Misreading.   Between words and elements that may be misread, use a comma, or recast. **(88k)**

54. Namely. See *For example,* above.
55. Names of ships, trains, airplanes. Use quotation marks or italics. (**94e, 96a**)
56. Nominative absolute. See *Absolute phrase,* above.
57. Nonrestrictive clause. See *Clauses, dependent,* above.
    Nonrestrictive phrase. See *Phrases,* below.
58. Noun clause. See *Clauses, dependent,* above.
59. Numbers. See *Figures,* above.
60. Numerals. Use a hyphen between the parts if they are written out (from twenty-one through ninety-nine). (**92b**)
61. Object. Use no comma between a verb and its object or a preposition and its object (except for additional reasons) (**88u**)
62. Oh, O. *Oh,* a mild interjection, use a comma following; as a strong interjection, use an exclamation point. (**87a, 88n**) *O* (spelled thus), before a vocative, is followed by no punctuation. (**88n**)
63. Omission of letters and figures. In a contraction of words or dates, use an apostrophe. (**93b**) For other omitted letters from a word, use a dash. (**91f**)
64. Omission of words. Use ellipsis periods or asterisks. (**86f**)
65. Outline symbols. Use a period after each. (**86d**)
66. Parenthetic words, phrases, clauses. Weak, no punctuation; fairly to moderately strong, use commas; strong, use dashes or parentheses. (**88n, 91e, 95a**)
67. Phrases. (1) An introductory modifying phrase containing a verb form, use a comma; not containing a verb form, use no punctuation, unless fairly long or fairly strongly parenthetic—then use a comma. (**88g**) (2) Nonrestrictive phrases, use commas; restrictive phrases, use no punctuation. (**88m**)
68. Places. See *Dates or places,* above.
69. Plurals. Formed by adding *s, es,* or change in form. *Never* use an apostrophe, except to form the plurals of words as words, of letters, and of figures. (**93c,d**)
70. Possessive case. Use the apostrophe in forming the possessive case of nouns and indefinite pronouns. Do *not* use the apostrophe in forming the possessive case of other classes of pronouns. (**93a,e,f**)
71. Predicate. See *Compound predicate,* above.

72. Preposition and object.   Use no comma or colon between. **(88u, 90g)**

73. Provincialisms.   See *Diction,* above.

74. Pure conjunctions.   See *Conjunctions, coordinating,* above.

75. Queries, series of.   Use question marks. **(87d)**

76. Question.   After a direct question, use a question mark; after an indirect question, use a period. **(87b,c)**

77. Quotation.   (1) Enclose a direct quotation in quotation marks; use no quotation marks with an indirect quotation. **(94a,b,c,i)**   (2) A short direct quotation is set off by a comma; an indirect quotation is not set off by a comma. **(88b)**   (3) A long formal quotation is introduced by a colon. **(90d)**

Quotation extending over one paragraph.   Use quotation marks at the beginning of each paragraph, but at the end of only the last paragraph. **(94c)**

Quotation marks with other marks of punctuation.   **(94h)**

Quotation within a quotation.   Use single quotation marks. **(94f)**

78. References and directions.   When these amplify, enclose in parentheses. **(95b)**

79. Restrictive clause.   See *Clauses, dependent,* above.

Restrictive phrase.   See *Phrases,* above.

80. Salutation.   In a business letter, use a colon after; in a friendly letter, use a comma. **(88c, 90e)**

81. Sentence.   (1) After a declarative sentence, use a period. **(86a)**   (2) After a mildly imperative sentence, use a period; if it is vigorous, an exclamation point. **(86a, 87a)**   (3) After an interrogative sentence, use a question mark. **(87b)**   (4) After an exclamatory sentence, use an exclamation point. **(87a)**

82. Series.   Three or more words or phrases or clauses, separate by commas, including one before but not after the conjunction. **(88h)** When the conjunction joins each two members of the series, except independent clauses, use no punctuation. **(88h)** See *Clauses,* above.

83. Slang.   See *Diction,* above.

84. Stammering, sobbing, halting.   Use dash. **(91b)**

85. Subheads.   Use no period following. **(86g)**

86. Subject–predicate.   Use no comma to separate, unless parenthetic elements requiring commas intervene. (**88u,n**)
87. Subordinating conjunctions.   See *Conjunctions, subordinating,* above.
88. Such as.   Use a comma or no punctuation preceding; use no punctuation following. (**88q, 90g**)
89. Summarizing final clause.   Use a dash preceding. (**91d**)
90. Surprise, emphasis, strong emotion.   Use an exclamation point. (**87a**)
91. Suspended elements.   Use commas, usually. (**88o**)
92. Technical words.   See *Diction,* above.
93. Title–subtitle.   Separate by a colon. (**90f**)
94. Titles.   (1) Titles of books, long poems, pamphlets, magazines, newspapers, motion pictures, use italics, or, less preferably, quotation marks. (**94e, 96a**)  (2) Titles of magazine articles, short stories, and short poems, use quotation marks. (**94e**)  (3) Titles at the beginning of a theme or paper or chapter, use neither quotation marks around nor a period following. (**94k, 86g**)  (4) Titles (personal) and initials following a name, use comma preceding. (**88t**)
95. Transposed elements.   Use commas, usually. (**88o**)
96. Unfinished statement or word. Use a dash. (**91b**)
97. Verb–object and verb–complement.   Use no comma or colon to separate. (**88u, 90g**)
98. Vocative.   See *Direct address,* above.
99. Word division.   Use a hyphen at the end of the line, between syllables, when the word is continued on the next line. Never use a hyphen at the beginning of a line. (**92c**)
100. Zip code numbers.   Use no comma before or within and use no period after. (**88l,s**)

# APPENDIXES

# WRITING BUSINESS LETTERS (APPENDIX A)

THE letter is a widely used form of written communication. During your college years you probably will write many more letters than formal themes, and after graduation you will find it necessary to write even more letters than in college. So widely used a form of writing deserves attention; from the standpoint of utility only, training in no other form is so important, for the ability to write a good letter indicates much more than is commonly realized. Important businessmen and firms waste little time, for example, on applications written in slipshod style; friends frequently drift away when they receive hastily written scrawls instead of sincere, attractive letters. Often our business and social contacts are affected by ignorance of proper forms and conventions.

This universally used, important, and highly personal form of communication called a letter is, in a sense, a theme governed by the same rules and principles as other kinds. It should be *correct, clear, effective,* and *appropriate.* A good letter is rarely dashed off; instead, it is the result of careful planning, writing, and rewriting.

The two main kinds of letters are business letters and informal, friendly letters. Since the former are more "of the head" and the latter more "of the heart," only business letters are discussed in this Appendix. Forming a great part of American writing, business letters are largely utilitarian: they convey information by clear exposition. They thus illustrate admirably the process of communication: *you, the writer,* sending some specific question or information, *the subject,* to some specifically named person or company, *the reader.*

A writer of business letters is primarily concerned with *presentation* and *content,* or, respectively, arrangement and expression of material and subject matter included. Later in college you may take one or more courses in general business correspondence. Since, however, fewer than one-fifth of our colleges and universities offer even one such basic course, and since only a small number of students take advantage of it when offered, the following material introduces you to some general principles for use now or later in business correspondence.

# 1 *Presentation*

A good business letter creates a pleasing impression the moment it is taken from its envelope. Quality of paper, neatness of typing or writing, and arrangement of letter parts are almost as important to total effect as content is. Correctness and attractiveness in *form* reflect a courteous attitude toward the reader.

## STATIONERY

Use good-quality, white *unruled* paper, of standard size, 8½ by 11 inches, even for longhand letters. Do not use colored or unusual-sized sheets, or fraternity, club, or hotel stationery.

## TYPING

Type your letters, if possible, with a fresh black ribbon to insure legibility; have no strike-overs or visible erasures. (For typing conventions, see Section 1c.) Lacking a typewriter, write legible longhand with black or blue-black ink.

## FORM

Good business letters are arranged in a form that has now become so standardized that it is easy to follow. It consists of six parts:

1. The heading
2. The inside address
3. The greeting or salutation

4. The body
5. The complimentary close
6. The signature

Each part has certain set forms that must not be ignored or altered if your letter is to be conventional, attractive, and easy to read. Study the letters on pages 659 and 661, not only for observing the position of the parts but also for illustration of correct use and balanced arrangement of these conventionalized forms.

**The heading.** The heading contains the sender's full address —street, city, state, zip code number—and the date of writing. It is usually placed in the upper right-hand part of the sheet (but see p. 661), an inch or more below the top edge (see "Margins," pp. 654–655), and it ends flush with the right margin. It is single-spaced. Avoid abbreviations and using *st, nd, rd,* or *d* after the day. On stationery with a letterhead, only the date is added, ending flush with the right margin or centered directly beneath the letterhead. Use no punctuation at ends of lines except periods after conventional abbreviations; this system, now very widely used, is called "open punctuation."

**The inside address.** The name and address of the person or company written to should appear from two to four spaces below the heading and flush with the left margin. It is single-spaced. Again, avoid all but conventional abbreviations, and, in harmony with the heading, use no punctuation at ends of lines except periods after conventional abbreviations.

Some title should always precede the name of the person addressed: *Mr., Mrs., Miss.* A business title rarely precedes the name, but a person of professional standing may be addressed as *Dr., The Reverend, President, Dean, Professor, General,* etc.

NOTE: For proper titles of the following—a widow or divorced woman; armed services, diplomatic, government, legal, academic, religious (Catholic, Jewish, Protestant) personnel; and nobility in England, France, Germany, Italy, and Spain, complete information is given in some of the reputable dictionaries.[1]

---

[1] For example, *The Random House Dictionary of the English Language,* pp. 1903–1905; *Webster's Third New International Dictionary,* pp. 51a–54a; *Webster's Seventh New Collegiate Dictionary,* pp. 1173–1176; *Webster's New World Dictionary,* pp. 1717–1719.

If only the last name of the person written to is known, or his position in a firm, the letter is directed to the firm, with *Attention: Mr.* —— or *Attention: Director of Personnel* added. The attention line usually appears two spaces below the inside address and two above the greeting; it has no effect on the greeting itself, which is always determined from the first line of the inside address.

**The greeting or salutation.** The greeting or salutation is placed two spaces below the inside address and flush with the left-hand margin. It is usually punctuated with a colon only, never a comma, semicolon, dash, or colon and dash. The following forms of salutation, arranged in order of increasing formality, are correct. The one chosen should be in harmony with the first line of the inside address and the general tone of your letter. However, for most business correspondence, the *first* form listed in each group is preferable. Notice that "dear" is capitalized only when it is the first word.

| *To a man* | *To a woman* |
| --- | --- |
| Dear Dr. Bard: | Dear Mrs. Lord: |
| My dear Dr. Bard: | My dear Mrs. Lord: |
| Dear Sir: | Dear Madam: |
| *To a firm of men* | *To a group or firm of women* |
| Gentlemen: | Ladies: |

NOTE 1: The more personal form using the name of the person addressed is preferred to the more formal *Dear Sir* or *Dear Madam*. However, *Dear Sir* and *Dear Madam* are commonly used for addressing officials. (*Dear Sirs,* as greeting for a firm of men, is no longer used.)
NOTE 2: For people with the special titles mentioned in "The Inside Address," above, the dictionaries listed give the appropriate greeting or salutation to fit the title.

**The body.** The body of the letter contains the message and begins two spaces below the greeting. Most business letters are single-spaced, although a short message may be double-spaced for attractive arrangement on a large page. Single-spaced letters require two spaces between each paragraph. Paragraphs may be in block form (if the heading and inside address correspond in form) or indented. They may be indented, for clearness and effectiveness, even when the block system is used in other parts. If double spacing is used in the body of the letter, paragraphs are more clearly separated by indentation. On the typewriter, indentation may be five or 10 spaces; some letter-writers indent one space beyond the length of the greeting line.

Worth noting is that *paragraphs* in business letters are shorter than in most other kinds of prose; they usually vary in length from two to six lines. Longer paragraphs are rare; not infrequently one-line paragraphs are used. Such paragraphing enables the reader to get the message of each paragraph, and of the letter, easily, quickly, clearly, and effectively.

Messages too long for one page are continued on a second page, never on the back of a sheet. However, the second page must contain at least two lines, preferably more, in addition to the complimentary close and signature. A paragraph may be continued from one page to another, but at least two lines of the paragraph should appear on the page on which it begins or ends. Each additional page should carry a top line containing some sort of identification, such as addressee's initials or name, page number, and date: H. M. Brown—September 12, 1968—Page 2.

**The complimentary close.** The close is usually placed at the middle or slightly to the right of the middle of the page, two spaces below the last line of the body of the letter. Only the first word is capitalized. Punctuation is usually a comma. Correct forms, arranged in order of increasing formality and used to harmonize with the formality or semi-informality of the greeting, are as follows:

| | |
|---|---|
| Cordially, | Very sincerely yours, |
| Yours cordially, | Yours very sincerely, |
| Cordially yours, | Yours very truly, |
| Yours sincerely, | Very truly yours, |
| Sincerely yours, | Yours truly, |

*Respectfully yours* (never "Respectively yours") is commonly used in letters to public officials, to clergy and others in religious orders, and to those ranking above the writer in academic circles, like a college dean or president.

The close is independent of the last paragraph of the letter and is not linked to it by a participial phrase such as *Thanking you in advance, I remain,* or *Hoping for an early reply, I am.* Clever or original forms such as *Enthusiastically yours, Apologetically yours, Yours for lower taxes, Yours for a cheery Homecoming* are to be avoided (though they may sometimes be used in personal letters) .

**The signature.** The signature is placed directly below the complimentary close. If the signature (name) is typewritten, at least four spaces are needed for the insertion of the handwritten signature. Unless a letter is mimeographed or is plainly a circular letter, it should always have, in ink, a legible handwritten signature.

An unmarried woman places the title *Miss* in parentheses before her name; if *Miss* is included in the typewritten signature, it is not needed in the written signature:

(Miss) Elizabeth West

A married woman should sign her own full name, followed by her married name:

Anne Morris Shelton
(Mrs. Paul R. Shelton)

A man places no title before his written or typed name, such as academic degrees and courtesy or professional titles, *Mr., Dr., Rev.,* etc.; but the writer's business title is often given after, *General Manager, Superintendent, Vice President,* etc. Letter convention opposes putting an address under the signature; its proper place is in the heading.

## MARGINS

Balanced layout of the letter on the page is determined by the length of the message. The entire letter, including heading, inside address, complimentary close, and signature, should have the appearance of a rectangle, with top and bottom margins slightly wider than those at the sides. Side margins are at least an inch wide, and particular care must be taken to maintain as even a right margin as possible. Short business letters should be approximately centered, with wide margins.

For firms using window envelopes, requiring the inside address to be in the same position on every letter, long or short, the *standard line form* has been developed. The inside address begins a certain number of lines from the top edge. The first line of the body begins two spaces below the salutation; margins are smaller and uniform, about an inch, on each letter; and the typed lines cross the page, whether the letter is long or short.

## FULL BLOCK AND MODIFIED BLOCK FORMS

Arrangement of the lines of the heading and of the inside address may follow the *full block* or the *modified block* system, although the latter is more popular. In both, the second and third lines of the heading and of the inside address, respectively, begin directly underneath the beginning of the first line. In the full block form, all the parts of the letter, including the heading, complimentary close, and signature, begin at the left-hand margin. In the modified block form, the heading, complimentary close, and signature are in their conventional places, on the right side of the letter. See examples on pp. 659, 661.

## THE ENVELOPE

The envelope carries the sender's name and return address in the upper left-hand corner and the addressee's name slightly below center and to the right. The full address should be used, in harmony with the inside address on the letter, although double spacing of a three-line address on an envelope is helpful to the Post Office Department, which prefers indented lines as well as the placing of the state on a separate line, followed by the zip code number, preferably on the same line.

Conventional folding of the letter depends on the size of the envelope. When the large No. 10 (9½ by 4⅛) envelope is used, fold the lower third of the sheet over the message, fold the upper part down to within a half inch of the creased edge, and put the upper folded edge in the envelope first.

For the smaller No. 6¾ (6½ by 3⅝) envelope, fold the lower part of the letter page over the message to within approximately one-half inch of the top of the page. Next, fold from the right slightly more than one third, then from the left, leaving the left flap edge slightly short of the right folded edge. Insert the left folded edge in the envelope first.

The reason for these folds is obvious—courtesy to the reader. If he opens your letter in the conventional way, the letter comes out of the envelope half-unfolding itself, top edge and written face up, ready to be read. (The conventional way of opening for a right-handed person is as follows: the envelope is held in the left hand, with the address side face down, and the envelope flap at the top; the envelope is slit along the top long edge, and the letter is withdrawn by the right hand.)

Of course, for the window-frame envelope, the letter is folded so that the inside address fits the "window" and thus becomes also the outside address.

# 2  Content

In addition to adhering to general principles of effective writing, business letters should be clear, concise, complete, and courteous, four important C-words in letter writing. Since the object of a business letter is to convey information by precise exposition, and since you hope to secure the reader's attention, you should carefully plan every letter and its phrasing.

## OPENING SENTENCE

Open the letter with a statement of its subject or its purpose, a courteous request, a direct question, a simple direct important statement, or several of these in combination. Avoid rubber-stamp and abbreviated expressions like those listed under "Language" (below). Include briefly in the opening sentences or paragraph any pertinent background information which will clarify your message. Make the purpose of your letter evident, and arrange your thoughts in logical, easy-to-follow units. Separate ideas require separate paragraphs and should be developed according to the principles discussed in Sections **23, 24.**

## CLOSING SENTENCE

Your letter should close strongly and effectively. As indicated above under "The Complimentary Close," avoid weak participial or prepositional phrases. Make your last group of words a complete sentence: an invitation, a direct question, a courteous request, a restatement of the subject of the letter, or a significant and important statement.

## LANGUAGE

Remember your reader: avoid using too formal English, but at the other extreme avoid using trite, outworn, "business" expressions, sometimes referred to as "letter killers." The following is a representative list of such expressions:

| | |
|---|---|
| according to my records | in receipt of |
| am pleased to advise | meets your approval |
| as per | past favors |
| as soon as possible | permit us |
| at an early date | recent date |
| at this writing | regret to advise |
| at your earliest convenience | take the liberty of |
| attached hereto | thank you in advance |
| beg to acknowledge (state, advise, etc.) | under separate cover |
| | valued wishes |
| contents noted | we trust |
| enclosed herewith | wish to advise (state, inform) |
| enclosed please find | would advise (state, inform) |
| has come to hand | you may rest assured |

Use instead an informal and soundly idiomatic style. Colloquialisms are permissible, but avoid slang or a telegraphic style. Effective business letters use the same courteous and friendly language that is used in a business conversation over the telephone.

## TYPES OF BUSINESS LETTERS

The numerous kinds of business letters are classified according to their content or message. The most common types are:

1. Order letters and acknowledgments of orders
2. Letters asking or granting adjustments
3. Sales letters
4. Inquiries and replies; also, other letters of information
5. Credit letters (designed to encourage buying now and paying later)
6. Collection letters (designed to encourage paying, *now*)
7. Letters of application
8. Letters of introduction or recommendation

The four types you are likely to use, now and later, are represented below. For more detailed discussion of all various types of letters used in the transaction of business, you are referred to recent books which you will find listed in the card catalog of your library under "Business Letters" or "Letter-Writing —Business."

**Order letters.** Make your order letter—if you do not have a printed order blank available—brief, clear, and exact. Single-item order letters may concern tickets for the theater or a sports event, hotel reservations, a magazine subscription, a book, and the like. In multiple-item order letters, give a full description of the goods you wish to buy, including quantity, size, color, price, and any other available identifying data, such as catalog number and trade name. List separately, to facilitate reading, two or more items ordered in the same letter. Always specify methods of shipment and payment, and remember to mention any special information, such as delivery of the order by a certain date.

In the lower left-hand corner, several spaces under the last line of the body, write "Encl." (i.e., enclosure) if something is to be sent with the letter (check, sample, etc.). Whenever this is done, it serves to remind you, or whoever folds the letter, to be sure that the enclosure mentioned in the body of the letter is actually there; it is also a further indication, to the reader, of the enclosure.

The content of an order letter for one item follows—sent to the Box Office, St. James Theater, Chicago:

For the matinee performance on Saturday, November 23, 1968, please send me six tickets for "The Lonely Way" at $6.60 each, $39.60 total.

If tickets at this price are not available, please substitute those in the next-lower price range.

A money order for $39.60 and a stamped, addressed envelope are enclosed.

An order letter for five items follows:

612 East Maple Road
Lafayette, Indiana 47905
February 10, 1969

Cincinnati Film Supply Company
412 West Main Street
Cincinnati, Ohio 45202

Gentlemen:

From your February catalog, please send me by parcel post the following 2"-x-2" color slides:

| Cat. No. | No. of Sets | Name | Unit Price | Total |
|---|---|---|---|---|
| CK 159 | 1 | California Highways | $2.20 | $2.20 |
| CK 312 | 2 | California Beaches | 3.30 | 6.60 |
| PK 168 | 1 | Yosemite National Park | 2.75 | 2.75 |
| PK 169 | 1 | Yellowstone National Park | 2.75 | 2.75 |
| TK 98 | 3 | 1969 Tournament of Roses | 3.30 | 9.90 |
| | | | | 24.20 |
| | | Estimated parcel post charge | | .50 |
| | | Total .............................. | | 24.70 |

My check for $24.70 is enclosed.

Very truly yours,

*Edward J. Ryan, Jr.*

Edward J. Ryan, Jr.

Encl.

**Letters asking adjustment.** The letter asking adjustment—sometimes called a claim, or complaint, letter—is written not to accuse, blame, or threaten but to point out an error, such as shipment of wrong goods, damaged goods, failure to ship goods, an overcharge in a bill, and the like. Clarity is essential, brevity is desirable, and courtesy is diplomatic. Present the facts fairly; identify the unsatisfactory article or service, explain how it is unsatisfactory, and suggest or give the reader an opportunity to suggest adjustment. The letter that the reader writes to you is the adjustment letter.

If you have to write an angry letter, by all means write it, but lay it aside for a day; then destroy it, and write the kind of letter you would like to receive if your position were that of the reader.

Usually your adjustment-asking letter will consist of two to four paragraphs containing (1) a specific explanation of what is wrong, (2) the course of action you desire the reader to take, (3) sometimes, the inconvenience resulting to the writer, and (4) sometimes, the reader's gain by his making prompt adjustment. Circumstances determine the order in which these paragraphs come.

An example of a letter asking adjustment is on p. 661.

**Inquiries.** Most inquiry letters are written to obtain information about the products or services of a business firm. Some may be written to an individual for information concerning a subject on which he is an authority. Always make your request understandable; avoid vague and general questions and supply any information the reader needs in order to answer your questions definitely.

Routine requests for catalogs, price lists, or other prepared data may be limited to a one-sentence letter clearly identifying the desired material. If your letter is phrased as a question (*Will you please send me . . . ?*), punctuate it as a question.

Nonroutine inquiries require more detailed letters. For example, a letter asking about an organization's policies must explain the use to which the information will be put. A request stemming from a personal problem must give a clear explanation of the problem and an indication of the type of help needed.

The general plan for the inquiry letter, usually from two to four paragraphs long, is as follows: (1) reason for the inquiry,

612 East Maple Road
Lafayette, Indiana 47905
February 16, 1969

Cincinnati Film Supply Company
412 West Main Street
Cincinnati, Ohio  45202

Attention:  Adjustment Manager

Gentlemen:

My February 10 order, which arrived today,
contained three sets of the 1968 Tournament of
Roses instead of the three sets of the 1969
Tournament of Roses.

I am therefore returning by parcel post these
three sets, to be replaced by the 1969 sets ordered.

Very truly yours,

*Edward J. Ryan, Jr.*

Edward J. Ryan, Jr.

---

(2) the inquiry, (3) expression of appreciation (*never* a "thank
you in advance"). Sometimes material may be included to show
the reader how he will benefit by replying. When the inquiry
includes several questions, these are more effective when numbered and paragraphed separately.

If the person or firm addressed will eventually profit, no postage should be enclosed. Otherwise, apply this principle: When you ask for that which is of benefit only or primarily to you, enclose a stamped envelope addressed to yourself.

The following is the content of a letter of inquiry addressed to the Secretary-Treasurer, Institute of Electrical and Electronics Engineers, New York:

As a student in the College of Electrical Engineering at Athens University, I am interested in eventually obtaining full membership in the Institute of Electrical and Electronics Engineers.

I shall appreciate your answers to the following questions:
(1) Can an undergraduate student of electrical engineering obtain a junior membership in the I.E.E.E.? If so,
(2) What is the cost of such membership?
(3) Is such junior membership transferable to full membership when the student graduates from college?
(4) Does the junior membership fee include a year's subscription to the official magazine, *I.E.E.E. Spectrum?*

**Letters of application.** An effective letter of application stresses, throughout, the applicant's desire and ability to be of benefit to the prospective employer. Always emphasize what you, the applicant with your qualifications, can do for the employer, not what the latter can do for you. The letter must be courteous, straightforward, and sincere in tone, offering services without pleading or demanding.

Open your letter by applying for a specific position and indicating how you learned of the opening: from a teacher, another friend, an agency, a "Help Wanted" advertisement. If your application is unsolicited, give your special reason for applying. Present your qualifications—education, experience, interest, and aptitude—and emphasize those particularly useful to the employer. Devote a brief paragraph to personal information: age, health, and any other pertinent details. Include two or three references, listing them separately, either in the body of the letter or immediately after the close, with full names, titles, and addresses. Close your letter by requesting an interview at the employer's convenience. If you are in the same city, indicate where you may be reached by telephone.

NOTE: Always secure permission from the persons whom you wish to suggest as references and remember that it is courteous to write letters thanking them for their help.

The most effective letter of application is twofold: the *letter itself* and an *Information Record,* carefully prepared first. The latter gives in classified form all the applicant's assets bearing on the position (see example, below). The accompanying letter (example also, below) itself is fairly brief: direct application with, usually, source of information; a paragraph or two stressing pertinent points in the Information Record or additional information, without repeating material in the record; and a closing paragraph requesting an interview, with pertinent details, like time, place, and the like.

The content of the two-part letter of application is illustrated in the following:

The *letter* itself, sent by Richard M. Taylor, a junior at the University of Central Illinois at Concord, Illinois, to Mr. James R. Kirby, Director, Izaak Walton Boys' Camp, Mennedota, Michigan 49859, and dated November 15, 1968:

Mr. Frank McLane, Y.M.C.A. Director of Boys' Work here, has told me that you will be employing counselors at your camp this coming summer. Please consider me an applicant for one of the positions.

Enclosed is an Information Record, giving my qualifications for the position. The University courses I have listed are my favorites, and in those that I have already completed my grades have all been As.

My high school and college experiences, my special assets, and even many of my hobbies all point, so my University counselor tells me, to a future in which I should make working with boys my life's career. Nothing gives me greater satisfaction than to help develop a boy's character and to see his capabilities grow and broaden.

I should like to help boys at your camp in this way, and I feel confident that, with your advice and supervision, I can achieve my own and the boys' aims as well.

May I have an interview? I shall be home for the Thanksgiving vacation November 22 to 25, and for the Christmas vacation December 20 to January 3. During those vacation days, I can come to Mennedota at your convenience.

The *information record*:

INFORMATION RECORD
concerning
*RICHARD M. TAYLOR*

PERSONAL INFORMATION

*Age:* 20                               *Home Address:* 116 Main Street, Audubon,
*Height:* 6 feet, 2 inches          Michigan 49738
*Weight:* 180 pounds            *College Address:* 912 Stanford Street, Con-
*Health:* Excellent                  cord, Illinois 62526

EDUCATION

*High School:*    Audubon High School, Audubon, Michigan
                        Graduated, June, 1966
*College:*         University of Central Illinois, Concord, Illinois
                        Degree: Bachelor of Science, expected June, 1970
                        Major: Recreational Management
                        Minor: Physical Education
                        Scholarship standing: upper fourth of class
                        Courses bearing on summer's work, already completed:
                              Speech 212—Informal Speaking
                              Speech 214—Debating
                              Speech 321—Group Discussion
                              Psychology 120—Introduction to Psychology
                              Psychology 334—Psychology of Adolescence
                              Education 262—Summer Work Experience
                              Education 304—Principles of Teaching
                        Courses planned for second semester:
                              Psychology 345—Psychology of Leadership
                              Education 360—Methods of Teaching Vocational Sub-
                              jects
                              Physical Education 325—Principles and Types of Rec-
                              reational Leadership

EXPERIENCE

Assistant Boy Scout Leader—last two years of high school and first two
   years of college
Assisting (this college year, three afternoons a week) the Boys' Director of the local Y.M.C.A. Assignment: supervising swimming and
   basketball
Lifeguard, past two summers, Municipal Swimming Pool, Columbia
   Memorial Park, Audubon, Michigan

SPECIAL ASSETS

Played basketball and baseball all through high school; play golf for fun

Active in Boy Scout work since age of 8

Excellent swimmer since early boyhood; holder of the Red Cross First Aid and Life-Saving certificates

Member, Alpha Gamma Mu, a college service fraternity which concerns itself with helping young people

Experience (from foregoing) in getting along well with young people

Genuine interest in and liking for young people

REFERENCES (by permission, for education, experience, and character)

Professor Harold J. Creek, Department of Education, University of Central Illinois, Concord, Illinois 62526

Mr. Frank McLane, Director, Boys' Work, Y.M.C.A., Concord, Illinois 62526

Mr. Thomas R. Masters, Superintendent, Columbia Memorial Park, Audubon, Michigan 49738

Dr. Thomas J. Bloom, Pastor, First Methodist Church, Audubon, Michigan 49738

As a final suggestion, remember that all your letters—both business and friendly—are an unfailing reflection and representation of yourself. What you say and how you say it, the paper and ink you use, even the way in which you address the envelope and affix the stamp reflect your personality, just as do your diction, smiles, and gestures.

# THE ENGLISH LANGUAGE (APPENDIX B)

MOST of us do not realize that every word we speak or write (aside from newly coined phrases and slang) is a part of our language heritage, much of which goes back beyond the dawn of recorded history. We blithely take for granted a good deal that comes to us without effort on our part, including the language we glibly use with little or no thought of our linguistic inheritance. Perhaps this is as it should be, but even the simplest English words have a history, one that is occasionally fascinating and always worth more consideration than we think we can afford.

## The origins of English

The English we speak and write is descended from that spoken and written by immigrants from England, Scotland, and Ireland who settled in this country in the seventeenth century. Their language, in turn, had come, many centuries before, from dialects of ancient Germanic tribes. Precisely where and how these ancestral dialects themselves originated is somewhat shrouded in obscurity, but linguistic scholars have made some important discoveries and set forth some shrewd assumptions and guesses. It is true that scholars can only speculate about man's beginning languages, but the majority of linguistic sleuths agree that language, as such, came into existence at least a half million years ago and that only after the "invention" of language was man able to begin in earnest his slow development in what we call human culture. Scholars do not know exactly how many separate languages have existed in the past and exist now; estimates range from 2000 to 5000. Philologists do know, however, that the oldest writing now in existence is some six thousand years old.

The most remote roots of the language we now call English were probably in a tongue known as "Indo-Hittite," a speech that was flourishing in eastern Europe on plains north of the Black Sea some three or four thousand years before the Christian Era began. The ancient Hittites completed a move into Asia Minor about 2500 B.C.; another migration proceeded to Persia (Iran) and northern India. The languages of these migrants are now referred to as "Indo-Iranian." What dialects were left are called "Indo-European," a family of languages characterized by heavy inflection, grammatical number, and gender. For purposes of comparison, this family (a figure of speech, not an exact term) included basic vocabularies which had many correspondences in sound and meaning. Little is actually known about this almost prehistoric family of tongues, but the literature of those who had migrated was preserved in Sanskrit, a language that provided scholars with their first clues as to what "Indo-European" really was. In short, "Indo-European" is not the exact ancestor of English, but it does obliquely provide forms close to those of an ancestral original tongue. "Indo-European" was the first language family established (that is, reconstructed) by students of comparative linguistics and by philologists. This language family included several politically, militarily, and culturally important tongues, among them the Hellenic (Grecian) branch; an Italic branch from which grew Latin and, by descent, the "Romance" family of French, Spanish, Italian, Portuguese, etc.; Celtic, whose speakers pushed on to the Atlantic Ocean and planted a language the remnants of which are still found in modern Irish, Welsh, and the Gaelic of the Scottish Highlands; the Balto-Slavic group; and Germanic.

The Germanic branch of the Indo-European language system is the one to which English belongs. The original home of the *Germani* (as they were called in Latin and by predecessor Celts) was in northern Germany, along the shores of the Baltic Sea. From there, Germani migrated in several directions. For about one thousand years before the time of Christ, our linguistic ancestors were semisavages roaming through the forests and plains of northern Europe. These tribes, consisting of Angles,

Saxons, and Jutes, spoke several related and mutually intelligible dialects. Largely nomadic, these tribes conversed with one another but also with traders and soldiers of the then-powerful Roman Empire whom they occasionally encountered. In fact, from Roman traders and soldiers they appropriated words and thus began a process of borrowing which has continued to the present day.

## OLD ENGLISH

These Angles, Saxons, and Jutes began to cross the North Sea in the fifth and sixth centuries A.D., entering what is now Great Britain from their homes in Denmark and along the coast of northwest Germany. Specifically, the Saxons came from Holstein, a district in Germany; the Jutes came from Jutland, a peninsula comprising a portion of Denmark; the Angles came from Schleswig (a state of northwest Germany), taking their name from an "angle" of land between Schleswig and a neighboring province. The name of the Angles, both in Latin and in Germanic, was "Angli," which in Old English became "Engle." After about A.D. 1000, "Engla-land" (land of the Angles or English) was used as a name by all Germanic settlers in Britain. The word "Englisc" was applied to the closely related Germanic dialects then spoken. Thus, from the very beginning, English has consisted of a variety of dialects. We know little about the arrival of the Anglo-Saxons in England, but we do know that, after the year 600, many of them were at least partially converted to Christianity and that borrowing of words from Latin was accelerated.

The stock of words in Old English (or as it is sometimes called, Anglo-Saxon) was larger than one might expect from relatively primitive and largely nomadic tribes. Scholars have estimated, from writings which have been preserved, that Old English had a total vocabulary, or "word-hoard," to use the picturesque phrase of Anglo-Saxons, of nearly 50,000 words. The Old English vocabulary differed from counterparts in Modern English, but many words are easily recognizable: *fugol* (fowl); *weorc* (work); *heofon* (heaven); and *stān* (stone), for example.

In Old English, a noun *gelīca,* an adjective *gelīc,* a verb *līcian,* and an adverb and preposition *gelīce* are the predecessors of Modern English *like.* This comparison clearly suggests certain similarities but also points up differences in meanings, as well as the fact that words in Old English are often heavily inflected. Even so, our word *like* functions in sentences precisely as did its Old English forerunners: "I never saw his *like*" (noun); "as *like* as two brothers" (adjective); "you will *like* this" (verb); "*like* as not" (adverb); "run *like* a deer" (preposition).

Despite certain resemblances, however, Old English now seems as foreign to the speaker of Modern English as do Latin and German. Here, for example, is the Lord's Prayer in the dialect of King Alfred's time (849–899):

Fæder ūre þū þe eart on heofonum, sī þīn nama gehalgod.
Father our thou that art on heavens, be thy name hallowed.

Tōbecume þīn rīce. Gewurþe þīn willa on eorþan swā swā on
Come thy kingdom. Be done thy will on earth just as on

heofonum. Ūrne gedæghwāmlīcan hlāf syle ūs tō dæg. And forgyf
heavens. Our daily bread give us to-day. And forgive

ūs ūre gyltas, swā swā wē forgyfaþ ūrum gyltendum. And ne
us our guilts, just as we forgive those guilty to us. And do not

gelǣd þū ūs on costnunge, ac ālȳs ūs of yfele. Sōþlīce.
lead thou us into temptation, but unloose us from evil. Verily.

Numerous comments on this passage could be made, but these may be especially helpful:

1. The character þ, called a "thorn," has the sound of modern *th.*
2. Despite differences in spelling (and thus in pronunciation) several of the words are recognizable: *Fæder, nama, willa, forgyf,* etc.
3. Some of the words are inflected (changed) in ways no longer customary. *Heofonum,* for example, is a plural noun in the dative case for which we simply say "heaven."
4. Old English contained some words borrowed from Latin, but "native" words were often used in preference to borrowings. For example, *costnunge* was a native word which, of course, has been replaced by a borrowing from Latin, "temptation."

## MIDDLE ENGLISH

The period known as Old English continued up until the latter part of the eleventh century. At that time occurred an event which profoundly changed the course and fortunes of the English language, the Norman Conquest. Originally from Scandinavia, Normans had settled in northern France in the tenth century, had adopted the French language, and had acquired at least a veneer of French civilization. When the Norman French became masters of England after the Battle of Hastings in 1066, their language was used by the nobility, in courts of law, and in what might be termed polite society. The "common people" continued to use English, but their speech fell slowly to the level of what has been termed "peasants' patois." Without real standing, prestige, and guidance, English became more and more simplified and underwent revolutionary changes in grammatical structure, largely as the result of lost inflections and overall simplification.

In vocabulary, English appropriated many words from the new masters of the land, who spoke French almost exclusively. Before the end of the period called Middle English, that is, about 1475, many thousands of words had been taken into virtually every area of the English vocabulary, notably those segments dealing with law, religion, clothing, food, finance, and social rank and class. In addition to words appropriated directly from French, many others came into English from Latin via French adaptations of Latin terms. It has been estimated that almost half of the words used by Geoffrey Chaucer (1340–1400) were derived from Old French and Anglo-French.

Middle English is closer to Modern English than it is to Anglo-Saxon, but it still seems somewhat "foreign" to most present-day students. Here, for example, is the Lord's Prayer as it appeared in the first translation into English ever made of the entire Bible; the work is that of the fourteenth-century reformer John Wycliffe:

Oure fadir that art in heuenes, halwid be thi name; thi kyngdom cumme to; be thi wille don as in heuen and in erthe; 3if to vs this day ouer breed oure other substaunce; and for3eue to vs oure dettis as we for3eue to oure dettours; and leede vs nat in to temptacioun, but delyuere vs fro yuel. Amen.

And here is the Lord's Prayer as it appeared in the Authorized, or King James, Version of 1611. The passage consists of verses 9–13 of the sixth chapter of the book of Matthew:

9. After this manner therefore pray ye: Our Father which art in heaven, Hallowed be thy name.
10. Thy kingdom come. Thy will be done in earth, as it is in heaven.
11. Give us this day our daily bread.
12. And forgive us our debts, as we forgive our debtors.
13. And lead us not into temptation, but deliver us from evil: For thine is the kingdom, and the power, and the glory, for ever. Amen.

From this version, one can see that by 1611, English closely approximated contemporary speech. True, we would say "who is" rather than "which art," and might be inclined to leave out the phrase entirely in the interests of conciseness, but no real difficulties are presented by individual words or their order in sentences.

## MODERN ENGLISH

Perhaps the two real highlights in the growth and development of English have been its tendency toward simplification and its eagerness to borrow words and phrases from other languages.

As has been noted, Old English now seems a foreign language not solely because of vocabulary differences but because it was highly inflected and had a complex system of conjugations and declensions. For example, nouns included more than a score of different plural forms, but of these only a few have survived: *foot, feet*; *man, men*; *mouse, mice*; *child, children,* etc. Adjectives in Old English had many variations, all of which have been shed over the centuries except in a few demonstratives such as *this-these, that-those.* Several influences (especially the introduction of Scandinavian prepositions and pronouns like *until, same, they, them,* etc.) hastened the loss of inflections and enabled English to make a linguistic gain in directness and clarity.

After the Norman Conquest, the language became even more simplified. Several arbitrary genders were shuffled into "natural" gender; further inflectional endings were obscured and eventually were discarded. During the final years of the Middle English period, from about 1300 on, major changes in grammatical structure resulted in word order and intonation becoming primary devices for revealing and providing sentence meaning, just as they are today. The long history of the English language is primarily one of almost constant, steadily accelerating simplification.

The vocabulary of present-day English is estimated to be about half Germanic (English and Scandinavian) and half Romance (Latin and French). Such an estimate is quite rough, but it suggests that freedom in borrowing has immensely increased the richness of the English language over an extended period. This taking in of loan words, which began as we have noted even before Anglo-Saxon times in England, has increased in every succeeding century. It has been said that English has "a chronic case of linguistic indigestion." Scholars generally agree that the range and richness of the language compensate fully for whatever indigestion has been caused.

In such a brief and admittedly inadequate sketch as this, it is impossible even to list a representative sampling of the many thousands of borrowed words in English. But the sentences that follow may cause some surprise and may lead to a study of the origins and derivations which every good dictionary contains.

For one example, few modern speakers and writers of English are aware that such commonly used words as these came wholly from Scandinavian sources: *anger, awkward, bank, bull, call, crook, drown, egg, happy, kid, knife, leg, scare, skin, take,* and *ugly.* From French we have an almost uncountable number of words, including such simple ones as *city, justice, liberty, peer, residence,* and *village.* Every one of the seven liberal arts constituting a medieval course of study was Greek in origin: *grammar, logic,* and *rhetoric* (the trivium) and *arithmetic, geometry, astronomy,* and *music* (the quadrivium). Also Greek in origin are, for example, words dealing with theatrical performances, such as *comedy, drama, catastrophe, climax, scene,* and *theater* itself. Scores of prefixes and suffixes have aided in providing thousands of terms in biology, medicine, chemistry, physics, engineering, and other sciences. The earliest loan source of all, Latin, has contributed tens of thousands of words, among them, for example, *executor, item, index, memorandum, simile,* and *memento*. Long the language of scholarship and of the church, for many centuries Latin has opened her reservoirs for the coinage of new words and new word combinations.

Beginning about 1475, the year in which William Caxton printed his first book in English, the discovery of new lands brought additional thousands of words into the English language. From such hitherto remote regions as India, China, Africa, and North America came words to enrich the language. No part of the known world failed to contribute: Australian bushmen, for example, provided items such as *kangaroo* and *boomerang*; Malaysia contributed words like *bamboo, amuck, gingham,* and *gong*; our North American Indians offered *moccasin, moose, tomahawk, squaw, wampum, persimmon, papoose,* and many others.

The English language is a linguistic grab bag, but one with enormous range and flexibility. A polyglot language, English does not now exist in a "pure" state nor has it ever done so. Edmund Spenser, the sixteenth-century English poet, once piously and patriotically referred to Chaucer's language as "a well of English undefyled," but on this occasion Spenser was writing nonsense. The language has been made strong by its contacts with other languages, by its widespread use around the world, and by its never-ceasing borrowings here, there, and everywhere. Our language is indeed not "pure," but it is used and understood by vast numbers of people throughout the world. The willingness of the language and its users—some 300,000,000 of them—to adopt a useful term from any language and a persistent trend toward simplification and ease in structure have caused English to become a truly cosmopolitan language. If an international language is ever decided upon—a hardly likely occurrence—English has a better chance than any other language to play the role.

# LINGUISTICS
# (APPENDIX C)

LINGUISTICS is a term derived from the Latin word *lingua*, meaning "tongue," "language." The very origin of the word implies that linguistics and those who practice it, *linguists*, are more concerned with language as *speech* and its sounds than with *writing* and its meanings; a prime assumption of linguists is that language is basically a matter of speech.

The science of language known as linguistics is a branch of anthropology, that body of knowledge and speculation which concerns itself with the origins, physical and cultural development, and social customs and beliefs of mankind. (The word *anthropology*, which means "the science of man and his works," is made up of *anthro-*, a learned borrowing from Greek meaning "human," and *-logy*, a combining form used in the names of bodies of knowledge, as, for example, psychology and theology. The relationship of linguistics to anthropology is suggested by the commonly held belief that language ability is the dominant characteristic of human beings.) English linguistics involves examination of the structure and development of the English language—a study of how those who speak and write English actually form sentences and of the effects that making sentences have on their creators.

Linguistics involves technical and sophisticated areas such as *etymology* (the study of historical linguistic change, especially as applied to individual words, and an account of the history of a particular word) ; *morphology* (the patterns of word formation in a particular language, including inflection, derivation, and composition) ; *phonetics* (the science or study of speech sounds and their production, transmission, and reception, their analysis, classification, and transcription) ; *semantics* (the study of linguistic development through classifying and examining changes in word meaning and form) ; and *syntax* (a study of the rules for forming grammatical sentences in a language, the arrangement of words and phrases to show their relationships) .

Involved and intricate as this brief explanation is, still further detail is needed to define linguistics fully, because this highly technical field also involves items such as *juncture* (a distinctive sound feature marking the phonological boundary of a word, phrase, clause, or sentence) ; *phoneme* (a class or set of closely related sounds considered as a single sound) ; and *pitch* (the degree of height or depth of a tone or of sound, voice signals that indicate emphasis and that, for example, distinguish statements from questions) .

It is understandable that, in freshman English, a branch of anthropology can rarely be expected to receive the rigorous study it requires for adequate appreciation and application. The direct relationship of freshman composition and the science of linguistics becomes even more tenuous when the latter is logically seen to be a division of still other sciences than anthropology. Linguistics is linked with physiology and physics in its concern with the production, transmission, and reception of speech sounds. It is connected with psychology in its relation to the origin and meaningfulness of speech forms. And it is even linked with the humanities to the extent that linguistics is concerned with the expression of human thought in language. In short, linguistics is a deliberate, conscious, purposeful activity of the whole mind and its means of communication. Faced by a formidable body of technical material such as linguistics comprises, most students of writing—including those in freshman English—hastily retreat to a study of whatever minimum "grammar" is needed for the relatively successful completion of given assignments.

And yet backing away from linguistics is not an entirely sensible procedure because some understanding of linguistics, that "new look at grammar," as it has been called, can be both interesting and rewarding. A study of language can be worthwhile, despite the fact that no substantial body of evidence exists to prove that an organized and deliberately acquired knowledge of the structure of English makes a speaker or writer perform better than he otherwise would.

Language is basically an unconscious process. All of our lives we have automatically been using words and relating them to each other without conscious thought or care or even knowing what structures were involved. Without considerable knowledge of "grammar" we would never have been able to string together even the simple utterances and short sentences of late infancy and early childhood. And yet the ordinary user of English is no more able to state the "rules" of his language than he is to formulate the principles that enable him to recognize and describe a physical object and to determine its size, appearance, and distance from him.

Linguists, however, have tried to present in explicit, precise form just those facts about language that all of its speakers and writers know intuitively. They also have attempted to account for a native speaker's ability to understand virtually any sentence of his language and to produce sentences of his own which are immediately understandable to others.

That is, linguists have learned to work inductively, to distinguish speech characteristics from those of writing, to avoid making most value judgments about what is "right" or "wrong," "correct" or "incorrect," and to reject definitions and concepts which seem to them vague, circular, and confusing. They have sought to find out how people actually do speak and write and, secondarily, to mention only those judgments of how people *should* speak and write which seem to possess well-reasoned justification.

The development of a scientific description of language, derived partly from objective rather than subjective methods, has produced several linguistic approaches. The two best-known and thus far most widely accepted are called *structural linguistics* and *transformational grammar*. The first may be said to describe what a given language system is; the second explains how a given language system is formed.

# Structural linguistics

The term *structural linguistics* is something of a misnomer because all linguistics is necessarily concerned with structure (form, system) and because anyone who devotes himself to a study of language is to some degree a linguist. But structural linguistics, or *structural grammar,* or *structural analysis,* is a common designation for the kind of linguistic study that began with anthropologists in the United States about the turn of the century, flourished during the 1940s, and has since somewhat changed its focus and direction.

Language, say structural grammarians, is first of all a structure, a system, an involved set of patterns. Any such system, or set of patterns, they logically claim, can be explained systematically; that is, a series of patterns in spoken language can be isolated and described. Structural linguists claim that older, or "traditional," grammar, the kind primarily but not exclusively presented in *The Harper Handbook,* has explained only bits and pieces of the English language and has dealt inadequately with the ways in which words are formed and the methods by which they are selected and ordered in phrases, clauses, and sentences.

Second, structural grammarians insist that in describing a language one must actually set forth its *forms* and not merely label them. They object to traditional definitions of grammatical classes ("A noun denotes or names a person, place, or thing, a quality, idea or action"). Such definitions, according to the tenets of structural grammar, are logically indefensible and useless in practice. Structural grammarians contend that all such "semantic" or "notional" definitions are inadequate and that only linguistic forms can be made the subjects of precise statements.

All words, and combinations of words, give signals, each of which has a function. In structural grammar, emphasis is first placed on the *form* of the signals (system) and secondarily on meaning. To a structuralist, words and their functions are classified by formal and structural means (changes in the form of a word, the different ways it can be used in a sentence), with no particular regard for the meanings involved. That is, in structural grammar, "the cat's whiskers" and "the dat's whiskers" would receive equal attention because of the form and function of *cat* and *dat,* even though the latter is meaningless.

## FORM CLASSES

Using the principle that words having the same characteristics of inflection and the same positions in sentences should be grouped together, structuralists have come to recognize four *form classes* of words which correspond approximately to the parts of speech traditionally known as nouns, verbs, adjectives, and adverbs. The class to which a given word belongs may be identified by trying it out in test frames typical of the noun, verb, adjective, and adverb forms:

| | |
|---|---|
| *Noun* | He was selecting _____ (s) . |
| *Adjective* | This appears _____. |
| *Adverb* | She did it _____. |
| *Verb* | They will _____ (it) . |

## STRUCTURE WORDS

All other words—a few hundred as compared to many thousands of form-class words—are called *function* or *structure* words and consist mainly of pronouns, prepositions, and conjunctions. Their purpose is to supply information about the relationships of parts of a sentence made up of form classes of words. Being function words (*a, about, as, by, everyone, unless,* and *what* are samples) they have little meaning by themselves, but they do provide clues to the structure of a sentence; they supply a framework into which "form class" words can be dropped:

The _____ should _____ although a _____ seems _____.

In this sentence, the blanks can be filled by thousands of different words and word combinations, yet structurally the sentence remains the same.

The *bus* should *run* although a *breakdown* seems *imminent.*
The *soldiers* should *attack* although a *counteroffensive* seems *likely.*

## STRUCTURES AND FUNCTIONS

Combinations of form-class words and function words produce various kinds of structures: noun, verb, and modifier structures. Although noun and verb structures are named after the form-class words that generally are found in them, it is as *structures* —composed of single words or groups of words—that they are used like nouns or like verbs. All substantives—nouns, pronouns, verbal nouns, or phrases and clauses used like nouns— are noun structures. In the sentence, "Travel is broadening," the single word *travel* is a noun structure. In the sentence, "Most people believe that travel is broadening," *most people* and *that travel is broadening* are both noun structures.

Verb structures consist of words of the verb form class, together with such function words as linking verbs:

Children *squabble.*
Nobody *has been squabbling.*

Sometimes a structure word may be the entire verb structure:

We *are* squabblers.

Modifier structures are words from adjective or adverb form classes or groups of words used as adjectives and adverbs:

*My* sister is coming *too.*
He left *my* father *at a loss for words.*
People *who like seafood* are *often* gourmets.

## PATTERNS

Structural linguists normally classify sentences according to the structures they contain and the arrangement of these structures. Several different kinds of *patterns* result from such classification:

*Noun-verb (subject-verb)*
    Children play.
*Noun-verb-nonessential modifier (subject-modified verb)*
    Children play roughly.
    Children play in groups.

*Noun-verb-essential modifier (subject-verb-predicate adjective)*
    Children are noisy.
    This book seems heavy.
*Noun-verb-noun (subject-verb-subjective complement)*
    Pat and Mike are cousins.
    They are teachers.
    Borrowing without permission amounts to theft.
*Noun-verb-noun (noun-verb-object)*
    She cooked supper.
    Boys require heroes.

From such basic patterns, more complicated sentences may be evolved by using structures within structures, that is, by expanding through insertion of modifiers or through substitution of more complex structures for simple ones.

## PARTS OF PATTERNS

Structural grammar has provided an objective test for breaking a sentence into the structures it contains, so that the grammatical relationship of words may be revealed. Because a sentence may hold structures which themselves are parts of larger structures, the test assumes that any sentence, simple or compound or complex, consists mainly of two parts having a clear grammatical relationship to each other and that these parts also have parts in relation, and so on, until the sentence is broken down to its individual words. Here is a complex sentence:

The guitarist who plays at our dances won the contest.

Division of the sentence into two main parts would result in a cut between the words *dances* and *won,* thus showing the grammatical relationship of actor to action. This relationship may be made even clearer by substituting a single word on each side of the divisional cut:

The guitarist who plays at our dances / won the contest.
          He             did.

This test may be applied to breakdowns into smaller and smaller parts of the two main structures:

The guitarist / who plays at our dances // won / the contest.

Here, the clause *who plays at our dances* works as a modifier structure related to *the guitarist*; the verb *won* is complemented by the noun structure, *the contest*.

In further dividing the structures noted above, one may use the same rule of direct grammatical relationship:

The / guitarist (Modifier and noun structure)
who / plays at our dances (Subject and predicate of subordinate clause)
won / the contest (Verb and noun structure)
the / contest (Modifier and noun structure)

The prepositional phrase *at our dances* in the subordinate clause may also be divided:

at / our dances (Subordinator and noun structure)

In summary, structural linguistics attempts (1) to classify most words by their formal characteristics and their positions in sentences, not by semantic definitions; (2) to show that words appear in sentences as structures; (3) to reveal that a structure functions as a unit and that one structure can, and often does, contain another.

# *Transformational grammar*

Another school of linguists gradually became as dissatisfied with what they considered the deficiencies of structural grammar as they had been with the shortcomings of traditional grammar. In 1957, Professor Noam Chomsky of the Massachusetts Institute of Technology published *Syntactic Structures,* a work that raised many questions about language and language learning that Chomsky felt no previous "school of grammar" had successfully answered. His contention, eagerly embraced by the group that became his followers, is that when one learns a language he learns a sentence-making mechanism. This doctrine, which has become known as *transformational grammar,* or *generative grammar,* or *transformational generative grammar,* differs markedly from its predecessors—in some respects more widely from structural grammar than from traditional. It should be noted, however, that the new term has been widely misused: to Chomsky and most of his disciples, the term *generative* reflects a view of the purpose and function of a study of grammar; *transformation* refers to a device for indicating certain relationships between structures in a grammar. Although the terms are freely interchanged and combined, they are not entirely synonymous.

Whereas traditional grammar explains the way a language works and structural grammar sets forth a language system, *transformational* grammar explains the *processes* by which sentences are formed. Much as sewing instructions can tell us what a dress is by giving directions for making one, transformational grammar attempts to provide an understanding of English sentence construction through step-by-step directions. Transformational grammar begins by assuming that a few basic sentence patterns, similar to the patterns for structural grammar, may be called *kernel sentences.* These, when combined or added to or altered according to set rules, become *transformed sentences* or *transforms* and, again through single steps, are made into "pronounceable" English sentences.

## KERNEL SENTENCES

Beginning with kernel sentences, the first forming rule in transformational grammar reads like this:

S → NP + VP

The S stands for sentence, NP stands for noun phrase, and VP stands for verb phrase. The arrow (an arrow is used in every transformational grammar rule) indicates that the part of the formula on the right of the arrow is a fuller description of the part on the left. Thus S → NP + VP means "Sentence should be a noun phrase plus a verb phrase" and is an instruction to rewrite S as NP + VP.

The second rule, also written as a formula with an arrow, then explains what NP should be; it is devised so that the first instruction may be carried out.

NP → (D) + N

Here NP must be rewritten as a D (determiner, modifier) plus N, terms which themselves need covering rules:

D → *a, the*
N → *toy, cat, shovel, child,* etc.

NP, therefore, can be rewritten as *a* or *the* plus *toy* or *cat* or any other noun. Or, because D is surrounded by parentheses which indicate that D may, but need not, be present, NP may be rewritten in three ways:

*the shovel* (D: *the*)
*a child* (D: *a*)
*mathematics* (D: not used)

The preceding rules tell us how to make half the rewrite for S. For the other half, verb phrase, more rules are given:

VP → verb + NP
verb → *used, dug, walked, scolded,* etc.

With the elements of NP already known, the instructions for rewriting S are complete. Following the successive steps set forth, a kernel sentence can be formed, as illustrated below:

*Sentence*

| | |
|---|---|
| NP | VP |
| (D) N | VP |
| *the* N | VP |
| *the child* | VP |
| *the child* | verb (NP) |
| *the child* | *used* (NP) |
| *the child* | *used* (D) N |
| *the child* | *used a* N |
| *The child* | *used a shovel.* |

Omitting the use of NP in parentheses will result in another kind of sentence:

*Sentence*

| | |
|---|---|
| NP | VP |
| (D) N | VP |
| *the* N | VP |
| *the child* | VP |
| *the child* | verb (NP) |
| *The child* | *dug.* |

Many sentences may be produced from these simple rules, although many more rules are needed for certain refinements.

## TRANSFORMED SENTENCES

Kernel sentences are made by single-step rules; another set of rules exists for combining, adding to, and switching around the elements of kernel sentences in order to produce new, or "transformed," sentences. These rules, stated in formulas, cover such transformations as the kernel sentence "It is there" into "Is it there?"; "Where is it?"; "It is there, isn't it?"; "What is there?" The rules also cover the combining of kernel sentences to produce such sentences as "The greedy boy ate the corn." Because an adjective standing before the noun it modifies is considered as a predicate adjective from one kernel sentence incorporated into another kernel sentence, this sentence is a combination of two kernels:

The boy ate the corn.  
The boy was greedy. } The greedy boy ate the corn.

Likewise, rules cover substituting a *who* or *that* for the subject of one kernel sentence and then combining the results to effect a more complex sentence:

The cook was fired.  
The cook ruined the roast. } The cook who ruined the roast was fired.

Rules exist for such transforms as passives, emphatic sentences, other kinds of questions, and more complex forms. Here, for example, are some transforms derived from "Martha sent the package to Chicago":

1. The package was sent to Chicago by Martha.
2. What was sent to Chicago by Martha?
3. What did Martha send to Chicago?
4. Did Martha send the package to Chicago?
5. Where did Martha send the package?
6. Chicago is where Martha sent the package.
7. Martha did send the package to Chicago, didn't she?
8. Who sent the package to Chicago?

## PRONUNCIATION

The third major set of rules in transformational grammar applies to changing the results of transformations into pronounceable (sense-making) English sentences. Adequately presenting these rules demands so much space that their importance in the transformational approach to linguistics must be largely obscured here. However, this third set of rules accounts for many complexities in English sentences and would, for example, produce such results as this:

*The* + *skier* + *have* + present + *be* + -en + *compete* + -ing + *in* + *the* + *Olympics.*

New elements in this formula are the indication of tense, *present,* which must be part of VP in a rewrite, and the -*en* and -*ing* endings, which may be added and switched around. Accordingly, after all transformations have been made, final rules apply to make the sentence pronounceable. Such rules would read:

| | |
|---|---|
| *have* + present | *has* |
| *be* + -en | *been* |
| *compete* + -ing | *competing* |

Using these rules, the sentence would become: *The skier has been competing in the Olympics.*

# *Summary*

A thorough, coherent account of modern linguistics cannot be provided in space necessarily as short as this Appendix. But even if additional space were available, any account of the state of modern linguistics would lack adequacy and finality because most modern linguists differ among themselves and because new "schools" of linguistic study continue to crop up. Perhaps some years from now, a course in college composition can be more securely based on modern linguistics than is possible today, provided such a course is desired or needed. Until then, we must "make do" with the presently available applications of recent findings in linguistics. Many of these have been helpful in removing some of the admitted illogicalities and inconsistencies of a traditional grammar which, despite its deficiencies, has nevertheless worked remarkably well for many millions of people for several centuries.

This sound and helpful comment by Noam Chomsky on the present state of linguistic study and its potentialities comes from his *Cartesian Linguistics* (New York, 1966) :

Modern linguistics has provided a great deal of new information concerning a wide range and variety of languages. It has sought, with much success, to achieve significantly higher standards of clarity and reliability than those reached in earlier studies of language. At the same time, there has been a continuing interest in theoretical questions that has led to significant clarification of the foundations of linguistics. These advances make it possible to formulate, in a fairly precise way, the fundamental question of how experience and maturational processes interrelate within the framework of innate limiting conditions to yield the linguistic competence exhibited by a normal speaker of a language. It does not seem unrealistic, therefore, to hope that research of the sort that can be undertaken at present may lead to a plausible and informative account of the mental abilities that underlie the achievement of normal linguistic competence, abilities that may be as individual and species-specific as that of a bird to learn a particular class of songs, of a beaver to build dams, or of a bee to integrate its own actions into the intricate social activity of the hive.

# INDEX

# Index

Radio and television, as source of ideas, 29

*Raise, rise,* 422

Rambling sentences, 229–230, 301

*Random House Dictionary of the English Language,* 307, 309, 309 n., 317

Read, Herbert, quoted, 303

Readers, consideration for and study of, 11–12, 14–15, 22–23, 41, 86–89, 137

*Reader's Companion to World Literature,* quoted, 176, 198

*Reader's Digest,* quoted, 99

*Readers' Guide to Periodical Literature,* use illustrated, 125–126

Reading, as source for ideas, 29; note taking, 140–143

*Real,* 402

*Reason is because,* 249–250

Reasons, paragraph development by, 168, 175–176

Reciprocal pronouns, 414, 417

Recommendations, paragraphing for, 198–200; subjunctive, 523

Recopying, 10, 12, 91

Reduced predication, 268–269

Redundancy, 374–375

Reference books, 116–124; biography, 119; clichés, 372 n.; drama and theater, 120; general, 116–117; history, 120–121; language, 121, 307–308; literature, 122–123; research paper, 135 n.–136 n.; science, 124; slang, 348 n.; spelling, 319 n.; thinking, 65 n.

Reference of pronouns, 473–481, 545; double, 480–481; indefinite, 479–480

References, parentheses and, 616

Reflexive pronouns, 414, 416; misused, 475–476

Regionalisms, 351

Regular verbs, 494

Relative clause, coordination with principal clause, 243–244
 *See also* Adjective clause

Relative pronouns, 414–415, 452; implied reference, 477; number, 468–

469; misuse, 474; possessive case, 452, 606; with verbs, 468–469

Request, imperative mode, 520

Repetition, as transition, 61–62; 265–266; conjunctions, 377–378; effective, 85, 178–179, 287; emphasis, 287; faulty, 374–378; identical words and phrases, 378; ineffective, 178–179, 289–290, 374–378, 383–384; preposition, 377–378; pronouns, 378; same or similar words, 383–384; theme beginning, 44; useless, 374–378, 476

Research, defined, 133–134

Research paper, 96, 133–155; bibliography, 139–140, 149–151, 155; books on, 135 n.–136 n.; choosing and analyzing subject, 136–139; controlled, 134–135; documentation, 145–151; footnotes, 145–149; investigation, 139–140; library research paper, 134–151; note taking, 140–143; outline, 143–144; revision, 144–145; sample pages, 151–155; subjects, general and specific, 137–139; writing, 144

*Respectfully, respectively,* 402

Restrictive modifiers, clauses and phrases, 569–571; double restriction, 571

Reviewing, *see* Book reviewing

Revision, for clear thinking, 73–75; examples, 178, 203–205, 229–230, 241, 266–267, 280–282, 289; paragraphs, 202–205; research paper, 144–145; themes, 12–13, 90–93

Rhetoric, rhetorical, 2 n., 545

Rhetorical questions, 296

Rhyme, 383

*Right along, right away, right off, right then,* etc., 402

*Rise, raise,* 422

Robinson, Francis P., quoted, 199–200

Robinson, James Harvey, quoted, 46, 170

Roman numerals, form, 637–638; in outline form, 36–39; table of, 637–638

69 70 71   7 6 5 4 3 2 1

# Theme Record (with Number of Serious Errors)

Figures and letters in parentheses refer to *Handbook* sections.

| | 1 | 2 | 3 | 4 | 5 | 6 | 7 | 8 | 9 | 10 | 11 | 12 | 13 | 14 | 15 | 16 |
|---|---|---|---|---|---|---|---|---|---|---|---|---|---|---|---|---|
| NUMBER OF THEME | | | | | | | | | | | | | | | | |
| GRADE ON THEME | | | | | | | | | | | | | | | | |
| Adjective and adverb (83) | | | | | | | | | | | | | | | | |
| Capitals, abbreviations, italics (97, 98, 96) | | | | | | | | | | | | | | | | |
| Comma splice (32) | | | | | | | | | | | | | | | | |
| Comma misuse (88) | | | | | | | | | | | | | | | | |
| Coordination, subordination, parallelism (36, 37, 38, 44) | | | | | | | | | | | | | | | | |
| Dangling modifiers (40) | | | | | | | | | | | | | | | | |
| Diction (53–70) | | | | | | | | | | | | | | | | |
| Fused sentences (33) | | | | | | | | | | | | | | | | |
| Paragraphing (21–30) | | | | | | | | | | | | | | | | |
| Possessive case (75j–m, 93a–f) | | | | | | | | | | | | | | | | |
| Pronouns, nominative and objective case (75) | | | | | | | | | | | | | | | | |
| Pronouns, antecedents—agreement, reference (77) | | | | | | | | | | | | | | | | |
| Punctuation marks other than commas and semicolons, (86, 87, 90–95) | | | | | | | | | | | | | | | | |
| Semicolon misuse (89) | | | | | | | | | | | | | | | | |
| Sentence fragment and incompleteness of meaning (31) | | | | | | | | | | | | | | | | |
| Spelling (52) | | | | | | | | | | | | | | | | |
| Subject, predicate—agreement in number (76) | | | | | | | | | | | | | | | | |
| Variety in sentences (46, 47, 48) | | | | | | | | | | | | | | | | |
| Verb forms—mood, tense, etc. (78–82) | | | | | | | | | | | | | | | | |

Make a copy of this chart for additional theme records.

# Symbols Used in Indicating Errors in Writing

Figures and letters in parentheses refer to *Handbook* sections.

**aa**  adjective-adverb confusion (83)
**ab**  use of abbreviations (98)
**agr**  agreement of subject and predicate in number (76)
**amb**  ambiguous word or meaning (63)
**ant**  antecedent not clear (77)
**awk**  awkward phrasing (53, 64, 69)
**ba**  beginning abrupt (8b)
**c**  careless
**c to r**  not clear to reader
**ca**  wrong case (75)
**cap**  use a capital (97)
**cl**  lacking in clearness (12, 63)
**comb**  combine two or more simple sentences in a complex or compound-complex sentence (46)
**comp**  faulty comparison (83e–h)
**con**  consistency (14, 45)
**cont**  content vague and general (24)
**coord**  faulty coordination (36)
**cs**  comma splice (32)
**cst**  awkward or faulty construction (35, 36, 37, 38, 41)
**d**  faulty diction (70)
**da**  inappropriate diction (53)
**dcol**  colloquialism (53b)
**dcon**  concise diction needed (67)
**de**  exact diction needed (63)
**dem**  emphatic diction needed (64)
**deu**  euphony (69)
**dg**  gobbledygook (68)

**dil**  illiteracy (54)
**dim**  impropriety (55)
**dj**  jargon (68)
**dl**  localism (57b)
**dm**  dangling modifier (40)
**dmf**  mixed figure (65)
**dp**  precise diction needed (63)
**dr**  useless repetition (67)
**dsl**  slang (56)
**dtc**  technical word (61)
**dtr**  triteness (66)
**dw**  word wrongly divided (92c)
**e**  poor emphasis (64)
**ea**  ending abrupt, incomplete (8c)
**ef**  effectiveness of word or sentence construction (44, 47, 63, 64)
**ff**  following rules or pages
**fig**  use of figures, words (99)
**fn**  footnote form and punctuation (20g)
**fp**  "frying pan" error (32a, 36c, 77f)
**fs**  fused sentences (33)
**fw**  use figures for words (99)
**gl**  see Glossary (Sentence, 50; Diction, 70; Grammar, 85; Punctuation, 100)
**gr**  grammatical error (75, 76, 77, 79, 83)
**h**  excessive hyperbole, exaggeration (65e)
**id**  wrong idiom, unidiomatic (62)
**il**  illegible handwriting (1b)
**imp**  important
**ir**  irrelevant
**it**  italics (96)
**l**  illogical in thought (13c)
**lc**  lower-case letter, no capital (97)
**m**  wrong mood (82)
**mf**  questionable manuscript form (1)
**mm**  misplaced modifier (39)
**mod**  use of *a, an* (71h); adjective vs. adverb (83)
**n**  wrong number (71c, 76)